Bibliographies of
Twelve Victorian Authors

Bibliographies

of

Twelve Victorian Authors

Compiled by

THEODORE G. EHRSAM

and

ROBERT H. DEILY

under the direction of

ROBERT M. SMITH

1968

OCTAGON BOOKS, INC.

New York

Originally published by The H. W. Wilson Company in 1936

Reprinted 1968
by special arrangement with Theodore G. Ehrsam

OCTAGON BOOKS, INC.
175 FIFTH AVENUE
NEW YORK, N. Y. 10010

LIBRARY OF CONGRESS CATALOG CARD NUMBER: 68-16773

Printed in U.S.A. by
NOBLE OFFSET PRINTERS, INC.
NEW YORK 3, N. Y.

Preface

These twelve bibliographies of Victorian authors, compiled from more than two hundred sources, comprise bibliographical, biographical, and critical articles, pamphlets, essays, and books in English and in foreign languages employing the Latin alphabet. Unpublished masters' essays and doctoral dissertations have been included because, tho many of them may not be original contributions, they reveal what studies of these authors have already been made. Articles in daily newspapers, bare references to authors, or a few casual sentences about them in texts or other books, have not been included. The biographical and critical sections otherwise are as inclusive as we have been able to make them, and we trust will provide all that the student, the scholar, the book collector, the librarian, and the general reader will require. The lists are complete up to July 1934 in all the sources used, tho many items of later date have been added as the book was going thru the press.

For every entry we have striven to supply full information: for books and pamphlets we have given place of publication, publisher, and date of publication, in addition to the number of pages and the reviews of the item; for articles in periodicals we have listed the volume of the periodical, exact and inclusive pagination, month, and year; for all items we have endeavored to enter the exact title.

Finally, these twelve bibliographies are not merely compilations of previous lists; the majority of articles have been examined. Only in this way was it possible for the large number of reviews to be listed as such under their proper subject titles. As a final check, each volume of each major literary periodical has been examined for reviews and special articles.

We wish to express our thanks to the many libraries and librarians consulted in gathering our materials: in particular to the Library of Congress; to Harvard, Yale, Columbia, Princeton, and Lehigh Universities; and especially to the New York Public Library, where the main research was carried on. We are also grateful to Mr. H. S. Leach and Miss Mary E. Wheatley of the Lehigh University Library for suggestions, and to Professor P. M. Palmer for aid with the foreign references. To Miss Wanda J. Budd we are greatly indebted for her indefatigable labor in checking and compilation; and to The H. W. Wilson Company, our publishers, for constant encouragement and expert advice.

T. G. E.
R. H. D.
R. M. S.

TABLE OF CONTENTS

LIST OF PUBLICATIONS ABBREVIATED

Acad—Academy. London

Adel—Adelphi. London

Am J Philol—American Journal of Philogy. Baltimore

Am M—American Magazine. New York

Am R—American Review. New York; Formerly: Bookman. New York

And R—Andover Review. Boston; New York

Anglia—Anglia. Zeitschrift für Englische Philologie. Halle

Ann Pol et Litt—Les Annales Politiques et Littéraires. Paris

Appleton J—Appleton's Journal. New York

Appleton M—Appleton's Magazine. Philadelphia; New York

Archiv—Archiv für das Studium der neueren Sprachen und Literaturen. Brunswick

Art J—Art Journal. London

Ath—Athenaeum. London

Atlan—Atlantic Monthly. Boston

Bei Anglia—Beiblatt zur Anglia. Mitteilungen aus dem gesammten Gebiete der englischen Sprache und Litteratur. Halle

Blackw—Blackwood's Magazine. Edinburgh; London

Book B—Book Buyer. New York

Bookm (Lond)—Bookman. London

Bookm (NY)—Bookman. New York

Bookn—Book News Monthly. Philadelphia

Books—New York Herald Tribune Books. New York

Bost R—Boston Review. Boston

Boston Transcript—Boston Evening Transcript. Boston

Brit Acad Proc—British Academy . . . Proceedings. London

Brit Q—British Quarterly Review. London

C H E L—Cambridge History of English Literature

Cath World—Catholic World. New York

Cent—Century Illustrated Monthly Magazine. New York

Chamb J—Chambers's Journal. Edinburgh; London

Church Q R—Church Quarterly Review. London

Colburn—Colburn's New Monthly Magazine. London

Contemp—Contemporary Review. London

Cornhill—Cornhill Magazine. London

Cur Lit—Current Literature. New York

Dict N B—Dictionary of National Biography

Ecl M—Eclectic Magazine of Foreign Literature. Boston; New York

Edin R—Edinburgh Review. Edinburgh; London

Educa—Education, a Monthly Magazine. Boston

Engl Stud—Englische Studien. Leipzig

Engl Illus—English Illustrated Magazine. New York

Engl J—English Journal. Chicago

Engl R—English Review. London

Every Sat—Every Saturday. Boston

Fortn—Fortnightly Review. London

Fraser—Fraser's Magazine. London

Gent M—Gentleman's Magazine. London

Harper M—Harper's Monthly Magazine. New York

Harper W—Harper's Weekly. New York

Harv Mo—Harvard Monthly

Hibbert J—Hibbert Journal . . . London; Boston

Ind—Independent. New York

Int J Ethics—International Journal of Ethics. Philadelphia; Chicago

J Débats—Journal des Débats. Paris

J Ed—Journal of Education. Boston

J Engl & Germ Philol—Journal of English and Germanic Philology. Urbana, Illinois

Life & L—Life and Letters. London

Lippinc—Lippincott's Monthly Magazine. Philadelphia

Lit—Literature. London

Lit & Philos Soc—Literary and Philosophical Society of Liverpool. Proceedings. Liverpool

Lit Digest—Literary Digest. New York

Lit W—Literary World. Boston

Literatur—Literaturblatt für Germanische und Romanische Philologie. Heilbronn; Leipzig

Liv Age—Living Age. Boston

Lond Merc—London Mercury. London

Lond Q R—London Quarterly Review. London

Macmil—Macmillan's Magazine. London

Mag Art—Magazine of Art. London; New York

Manch Q—Manchester Quarterly. Manchester, England

Mercure Fr—Mercure de France. Paris

Meth R—Methodist Review. New York

Mod H R A—Modern Humanities Research Association. Bulletin. Cambridge, England

Mod Lang N—Modern Language Notes. Baltimore, Maryland

Mod Lang R—Modern Language Review. Cambridge, England

Mod Philol—Modern Philology. Chicago

Nat-Ath—Nation and The Athenaeum. London

Nat R—National Review. London

New Adel—New Adelphi. London

New Ecl—New Eclectic. Baltimore, Maryland

New Repub—New Republic. New York

New Statesm—New Statesman. London

New Statesm & Nation—New Statesman and Nation. London

N Y Times—New York Times Book Review. New York

19th Cent—Nineteenth Century and After. London

No Am—North American Review. Boston; New York

No Brit—North British Review. Edinburgh; London; New York

Notes & Q—Notes and Queries. London

Nuova Antol—Nuova Antologia di Lettere, Scienze ed Arti. Florence; Rome

Out—Outlook. New York

P M L A—Modern Language Association of America. Publications

Philol Q—Philological Quarterly. Iowa City, Iowa

Preuss Jahrb—Preussische Jahrbücher. Berlin

Pub W—Publishers' Weekly. New York

Quar R—Quarterly Review. London

Queen's Q—Queen's Quarterly. Kingston, Canada

Rev E S—Review of English Studies

R of Rs (Lond)—Review of Reviews. London

R of Rs (NY)—Review of Reviews and World's Work. New York

Revue A A—Revue Anglo-Américaine. Paris

R Litt Comp—Revue de Littérature Comparée. Paris

Revue de P—Revue de Paris. Paris

R Deux Mondes—Revue des Deux Mondes. Paris

Revue Germ—Revue Germanique, Allegmagne-Angleterre . . . Paris

R Pol et Litt—Revue Politique et Littéraire; Revue Bleue. Paris

Roy Soc Lit—Royal Society of Literature of the United Kingdom. Transactions. London

St J—St. James's Magazine. London

St P—St. Pauls Magazine. London

Sat R—Saturday Review of Politics, Literature, Science, and Art. London

Sat R Lit—Saturday Review of Literature. New York

Sch & Soc—School and Society. New York

Scrib M—Scribner's Magazine. New York

Sewanee R—Sewanee Review. Sewanee, Tennessee

So Atlan Q—South Atlantic Quarterly. Durham, North Carolina

So Biv—Southern Bivouac. Louisville, Kentucky

So M—Southern Magazine. Baltimore, Maryland

Spec—Spectator. London

Stud Philol—Studies in Philology. Chapel Hill, North Carolina

Sun M—Sunday Magazine. London

Temple—Temple Bar. London; New York

Theatre Arts Mo—Theatre Arts Monthly. New York

T L S—Times Literary Supplement. London

Tinsley's—Tinsley's Magazine. London

Unitar—Unitarian Review. Boston

Va Q R—Virginia Quarterly Review. Charlottesville, Virginia

W E R—Week-End Review . . . London

Westm—Westminster Review. London

Yale R—Yale Review. New Haven, Connecticut

ZFEU—Zeitschrift für Französischen und Englischen Unterricht. Berlin

Z V L—Zeitschrift für Vergleichende Litteraturgeschichte. Berlin

GENERAL ABBREVIATIONS

bibl	bibliography	ns	new series
diss	dissertation or doctoral thesis	p	page; pages
ed	edited; edition; editor	pref	preface
ff	typed pages or leaves	pseud	pseudonym
introd	introduction	rev	reviewed; revised
ms	manuscript	ser	series
nd	no date	transl	translated; translator
no	number	univ	university
np	no place	vol	volume

Directions for Use

I. The Chronological Outlines for handy reference contain in each case only the major works. The First Editions of these works will be found under the author's name in the main section III. For privately printed issues and minor works not reviewed, and for other than First Editions, the reader should consult the special bibliographies listed in Section II.

II. The Bibliographical Sections include in alphabetical order "point" bibliographies, important sales catalogs, books with appended bibliographies, and reading and reference lists.

III. The Biographical and Critical Sections are also arranged alphabetically. Signed articles are arranged alphabetically by author; unsigned articles are arranged alphabetically by title; unsigned, untitled articles are listed alphabetically by a title (enclosed in brackets) devised by the compilers.

Reviews, however, in accordance with standard practice, are listed in parentheses under the subject title of the book reviewed. No logical arrangement of these whether alphabetical or chronological, by authors, by dates, or by periodicals, has been attempted, since no arrangement can be carried out consistently, and any one of them turns out to be a disservice to many readers. Before a reader concludes that an article is missing, he should be sure that it is not listed as a *review* in its proper place among the review sections.

The two lists of an author's major works, one by date in I. *Chronological Outlines,* and one alphabetically by title under author's name in III. *Biographical and Critical Material,* enable the user to locate particular works if he knows either date of publication or title desired.

Matthew Arnold

Matthew Arnold

I. Chronological Outline

1822. Born December 24, Laleham.

1840. Alaric at Rome.

1843. Cromwell.

1849. The Strayed Reveller.

1852. Empedocles on Etna.

1853. Poems.

1855. Poems. Second Series.

1858. Merope.

1859. England and the Italian Question.

1861. Popular Education in France.

1861. On Translating Homer.

1862. On Translating Homer. Last Words.

1864. A French Eton.

1865. Essays in Criticism.

1867. On the Study of Celtic Literature.

1867. New Poems.

1868. Schools and Universities on the Continent.

1869. Culture and Anarchy.

1870. St. Paul and Protestantism.

1871. Friendship's Garland.

1873. Literature and Dogma.

1875. God and the Bible.

1877. Last Essays on Church and Religion.

1879. Mixed Essays.

1882. Irish Essays.

1885. Discourses in America.

1886. Special Report on Elementary Education Abroad.

1888. Died April 15, Liverpool.

1888. Essays in Criticism. Second Series.

1888. Civilization in the United States.

1889. Reports on Elementary Schools.

1891. On Home Rule for Ireland.

Matthew Arnold

II. Bibliographical Material

[Brown, G. A.]
Matthew Arnold. C H E L vol XIII p537-40

Carter, John, and Pollard, Graham
Arnold. *In* An enquiry into the nature of certain nineteenth century pamphlets. London, Constable, 1934. p159-64

Dawson, William Harbutt
Bibliography of Matthew Arnold's works. *In* Matthew Arnold and his relation to the thought of our time. New York, Putnam, 1904. p439-43

Dole, Nathan Haskell
Bibliography of Matthew Arnold's poetry. *In* The poetical works of Matthew Arnold. New York, Crowell [c1897] pxxiii-xxvii

Gates, Lewis Edwards
Bibliography. *In* Selections from the prose writings of Arnold. New York, Holt, 1898. pxc-xci

A list of Matthew Arnold's writings. Lit W 12:215 Je 18 '81

Matthew Arnold [a bibliography of his writings and of reviews of his works] Bulletin of the Boston Public Library 6:84-7 Ja '84

Matthew Arnold's earliest poem. Lit W 19:174-5 My 26 '88

Motter, Thomas Hubbard Vail
Check list of Matthew Arnold's letters. Stud Philol 31:600-5 O '34

Page, Curtis Hidden
Arnold; list of references. *In* British poets of the nineteenth century, ed. by C. H. Page; new ed. by Stith Thompson. New York, Sanborn, 1929. p725-6

Prideaux, William Francis
The bibliography of Matthew Arnold. [Refers to Smart] Notes & Q 8th ser 1:313-14 Ap 16 '92

Sells, Iris Esther
Bibliography. *In* Matthew Arnold and France. Cambridge, England, Univ. press, 1935. p[273]-276

Shorter, Clement K.
My bookshelves: Matthew Arnold. Bookm (Lond) 16:123-5 Ag '99

Slater, J. H.
Early editions: a bibliographical survey of the works of some popular modern authors. London, Kegan Paul, Trench, Trübner, 1894
(Rev by T. J. Wise in Bookm (Lond) 6:49-50 My '94)

Smart, Thomas B.
The bibliography of Matthew Arnold. London, Davy, 1892. [v]-x, 90p
(The most adequate bibliography of Arnold. Critical material concerning Arnold is also included, arranged chronologically)
(Rev in Nation (NY) 55:449-50 D 15 '92; Literary World (Lond) ns 45:106 Ja 29 '92)

Woods, George Benjamin
[Bibliography.] *In* Poetry of the Victorian period. New York, Scott, Foresman [c1930] p994-8

Matthew Arnold

III. Biographical and Critical Material

Abernethy, Julian W.
A lesson in style from Matthew Arnold's letters. Educa 16:583-8 Je '96

Ackermann, A. S. E.
Matthew Arnold: his death. Notes & Q 150:226 Mr 27 '26

Adams, Dorothy E.
Arnold's poetry in relation to Wordsworth. Masters essay, Univ. of Colorado, 1917. 44ff

Adams, James Truslow
Sweetness and light—sixty years after. Atlan 144:629-37 N '29; *same in* The tempo of modern life. New York, Boni, 1931. p148-68

Adams, William Davenport
The poetry of criticism: Mr. Matthew Arnold. Gent M ns 14:467-80 Ap '75

Adamson, C. S.
Matthew Arnold's letters. Acad 48:525 D 14 '95

Adamson, John William
English education, 1760-1902. Cambridge, University press, 1930. passim

Aikat, Amūlyachandra
see Amūlya-Chandra Aikat

Alexander, William (Bishop of Derry)
Matthew Arnold and his poetry. St J ns 8:29-38, 181-4, 236-42 O-D '71 [Reprinted from his "Afternoon Lectures"]
Matthew Arnold's poetry. *In* Afternoon lectures on English literature. London, Bell & Daldy, 1867. 4th ser p199-228

Alsop, J. W.
Mr. Matthew Arnold as critic and poet. [Read before the Liverpool philomatic society Ja 30 '78] Liverpool, 1879. 29p

America's impressions of Matthew Arnold. And R 1:84-8 Ja '84

Amūlya-Chandra Aikat
On the poetry of Matthew Arnold, Robert Browning and Rabindranath Tagore. Calcutta, Univ. of Calcutta, 1921. 346p

Amy, Ernest F.
Religious influences upon Clough and Arnold as seen in their poetry. Masters essay, Wesleyan univ. 1911

Anarchy better than culture: Matthew Arnold's repentance. [A mock retractation of the views expressed in "Culture and Anarchy"] Sat R 119:399-400 Ap 17 '15

Anderson, Melville B.
Arnold and his work. Dial 9:5-7 My '88

Andrews, William P.
Matthew Arnold; poem. Cent 36:417 Jl '88

Angell, J. W.
Matthew Arnold's indebtedness to Renan's "Essais de morale et de critique." R Litt Comp 14:714-33 O '34

Anscombe, Alfred
Matthew Arnold on modern hurry. Notes & Q 11th ser 4:37 Jl 8 '11

Appleton, Charles Edward
A plea for metaphysic. *In* Dr. Appleton, his life and literary relics, ed. by John A. Appleton and A. H. Sayce. London, Trübner, 1881. p160-243; *same in* Contemp 28:923-47 N '76 *and* Contemp 29:44-69 D '76

Appleyard, W. A.
Matthew Arnold: criticism of life. Nat R 16:659-66 Ja '91

[Appreciation] R of Rs (Lond) 67:24-7 Ja '23

Archer, Richard Lawrence
Secondary education in the nineteenth century. Cambridge, University press, 1921. p184-9

Armstrong, Richard Acland
Makers of the 19th century. London, Unwin, 1901
Matthew Arnold. *In* Faith and doubt in the century's poets. New York, Whittaker, 1898. p91-113
Matthew Arnold. *In* Latter-day teachers; six lectures. London, Kegan Paul, 1881. p27-54

Arnold, (Sir) Edwin
To Matthew Arnold; poem. Pall Mall Gazette Ap 15 '88

Arnold, Matthew
The bishop and the philosopher. Macmil 7:241-56 Ja '63
(Rev in Westm 79:265-72 Ap '63)
Civilization in the United States
(Rev in Our Day 1:493-9 Je '88; Lit W 19:168-9 My 26 '88)
A comment on Christmas
(Rev in Spec 58:447-8 Ap 4 '85)
Culture and anarchy. London, Smith, Elder, 1869. lx,272p
(Rev in Contemp 11:150-1 My '69; New Englander 29:182-5 Ja '70; Brit Q 52:170-99, 386-419 Jl, O '70; B. Taylor in Putnam's Magazine ns 3:491 Ap '69; G. E. Percy in Hours at Home 7:20-8 My '68; H. Hartshone in Lippinc 1:645-7 Je '68; Nation (NY) 9:411 N 11

'69; Ath 1:271-2 F 20 '69; Sat R 27:318-19 Mr 6 '69; Spec 42:295-6 Mr 6 '69; Quar R 137:389-415 O '74; R. St. J. Tyrwhitt in Contemp 13:362-80 Mr '70; No Brit 50:190-225 Mr '69; *same.* Liv Age 102:67-86 Jl 10 '69; W. Kirkus in Fortn 11:371-3 Mr '69; Lond Q R 33:209-20 O '69; Edin R 129:486-503 Ap '69; T L S Ap 21 '32 p286; E. J. Scovell in New Statesm 3:846 Je 25 '32; Notes & Q 162:126 F 13 '32; J. A. Falconer in English Studies 14:228-9 D '32)

Discourses in America. London, Macmillan, 1885. xiv,207p
(Rev in Nation (NY) 41:98-9 Jl 30, '85; [J. Jacobs in] Ath 1:817-18 Je 27 '85; W. Lewin in Acad 28:35 Jl 18 '85; Sat R 60:119-20 Jl 25 '85; A. H. Japp in Brit Q 83:20-31 Ja '86)

Empedocles on Etna, and other poems. London, Fellowes, 1852. viii,236p [signed "A"]
(Rev by A. Dudley in R Deux Mondes 70:1136-68 S 15 '54; Edin R 168:337-73 O '88; Ath 1:412 Ap 2 '53; Westm 61:146-59 Ja '54; No Am 77:12-24 Jl '53; Literary World (NY) 13:309-12 D 10 '53; Leader 4:41-3, 1146-7, 1169-71 Ja 8, N 26, D 3 '53; No Brit 19:209-18 My '53)

England and the Italian question. London, Longman, Green, Longmans, and Roberts, 1859. 45p
(Rev in Dublin University Magazine 54:470-4 O '59)

Essays in criticism [first series] London, Macmillan, 1865. xx,302p
(Rev by H. James, jr. in No Am 101:206-13 Jl '65; Spec 38:214-15 F 25 '65; No Brit 42:158-82 Mr '65; *same.* Ecl M ns 2:67-82 Jl '65; E. W. Gurney in Nation (NY) 1:24-5 Jl 6 '65; T. F. Wedmore in New Monthly Magazine 133:478-83 Ap '65; Atlan 16:255-6 Ag '65; New Englander 24:600 Jl '65; H. T. Tuckerman in Hours at Home 2:5-10 N '65; National Quarterly Review 11:401-5 S '65; Boston Review 5:511-13 S '65; American Presbyterian & Theological Review ns 3:644 O '65; Christian Examiner 79:433-4 N '65; Ath 1:615-16 My 6 '65; Sat R 19:235-6 F 25 '65; Victoria Magazine 4:469 Mr '65; Month 3:107-10 Jl '65; Brit Q 42:243-69 O '65; Contemp 10:317 F '69; Edin R 129:486-503 Ap '69; L. Etienne in R Deux Mondes p744-67 Ap 1 '66; Quar R 167:398-426 O '88)

Essays in criticism, second series. London, Macmillan, 1888. x,331p
(Rev by G. A. Simcox in Acad 34:345-6 D 1 '88; M. B. Anderson in Dial 9:284-7 Mr '89; Sat R 66:589-90 N 17 '88; D. C. Tovey in Reviews and essays. . . London, Bell, 1897. p[71]-87 [reprinted from Guardian]; Ath 1:273-6 Mr 2 '89)

Essays in criticism, third series. Boston, Ball, 1910
(Rev in Nation (NY) 91:371 O 20 '10; American Library Assn. Booklist 7:136

D '10; C. R. Knapp in Classical Weekly 4:145-6, 153-4 Mr 11, 18 '11)

A French Eton; or, Middle class education and the state. London, Macmillan, 1864. 122p
(Rev in Ath 2:137-8 Jl 30 '64; Cornhill 10:410-26 O '64; Macmil 10:175-6 Je '64; Critic (NY) 21:261-2 N 12 '92)

The French play in London. 19th Cent 6:228-43 Ag '79; *also in* Irish essays, and others. London, Smith, Elder, 1882
(Rev in Nation (NY) 29:143 Ag 28 '79)

Friendship's garland. London, Smith, Elder, 1871. xvi,172p
(Rev in Blackw 109:458-60 Ap '71; Spec 44:616 My 20 '71; noted in Ath 1:271 Mr 4 '71)

God and the Bible, a review of objections to "Literature and Dogma." London, Smith, Elder, 1875. lii,394p
(Rev in New Englander 35:403-4 Ap '76; Nation (NY) 22:86 F 3 '76; Ath 2:781-2 D 11 '75; A. Réville in Acad 8:618-19 D 18 '75; Spec 49:407-9 Mr 25 '76; Ath 2:769 D 13 '84)

Higher schools and universities in Germany. London, Macmillan, 1874. lxxxviii,270p
(Rev in Nation (NY) 18:414-15 Je 25 '74; Ath 1:459 Ap 4 '74; Sat R 37:599-600 My 9 '74)

Introduction. *In* Ward, Thomas Humphry, ed. The English poets. . . London, Macmillan, 1880
(Rev in Nation (NY) 30:439-40 Je 10 '80; International Review 9:472-5 O '80; J. C. Shairp in Acad 19:112-13 F 12 '81; Quar R 153:431-63 Ap '82)

Irish essays, and others. London, Smith, Elder, 1882. xvi,308p
(Rev in Critic (NY) 2:126 My 6 '82; Dial 3:10 My '82; Lit W 13:141-2 My 6 '82; Ath 1:339-40 Mr 18 '82; M. Stokes in Acad 21:242-3 Ap 8 '82; Sat R 53:333-4 Mr 18 '82)

Last essays on church and religion. London, Smith Elder, 1877. xxxiv,228p
(Rev by E. Dowden in Acad 11:430-1 My 19 '77; Nation (NY) 25:30 Jl 12 '77; Ath 1:439 Ap 7 '77; Contemp 29:953-5 Ap '77; International Review 4:558-9 Jl '77; Sat R 43:490-1 Ap 21 '77; Brit Q 66:39-51 Jl '77)

Lectures delivered before the University of Oxford
(Rev in Westm ns 24:469-82 O '63)

Letters from Matthew Arnold to John Churton Collins. London, Printed for private circulation, 1910. 10p (20 copies only)
[Concerned with education at the universities]

Letters of Matthew Arnold, 1848-1888, collected and arranged by G. W. E. Russell. London, Macmillan, 1895. 2 vols
(Rev by D. F. Hannigan in Westm 145:40-2 Ja '96; H. W. Mabie in Book

Arnold, Matthew—*Continued*

Reviews 3:217-20 D '95; E. Dowden in Sat R 80:757-8 D 7 '95; Spec 75:719-20 N 23 '95; Out 52:897 N 30 '95; Critic (NY) 27:360-1 N 30 '95; G. E. Woodberry in Bookm (NY) 2:508-10 F '96; Lit W 27:53 F 22 '96; Guardian 51:129-30 Ja 22 '96; Ath 2:745-6 N 30 '95; H. Walker in Acad 48:537-9 D 21 '95; H. W. Paul in Forum 20:616-30 Ja '96; M. Reed in New World 5:262-72 Je '96; Dial 19:376-8 D 16 '95; C. A. L. Morse in Cath World 63:486-96 Jl '96; A. Austin in Nat R 26:471-83 D '95; *same.* Liv Age 208:46-55 Ja 4 '96; *same.* Ecl M 126:223-31 F '96; Nation (NY) 61:451-2, 466-7 D 19, 26 '95; Sewanee R 4:181-8 F '96; A. W. Colton in Citizen (Phila) 2:173-5 Jl '96; T. H. Warren in Quar R 202:221-49 Ja '05; J. Morley in 19th Cent 38:1041-55 D '95; Hengesbach in Neue Philologische Rundschau no 25 '00; H. S. Krans in Out 78:679-82 N 12 '04; Liv Age 207:771-81 D 28 '95; Ath 2:745-6 N 30 '95)

The letters of Matthew Arnold to Arthur Hugh Clough, ed. with an introductory study by Howard Foster Lowry. London, Oxford univ. press, 1932. xi,191p (Rev by J. W. Dodds in Va Q R 9:453-6 Jl '33; Archiv 164:138-9 S '33; America 49:67 Ap 22 '33; D. Bush in Bookm (NY) 76:178 F '33; J. Zeitlin in Books My 21 '33 p14; M. D. Zabel in Commonweal 17:640-1 Ap 5 '33; H. Kingsmill in Engl R 56:227-30 F '33; L. Trilling in Nation (NY) 136:211 F 22 '33; New Repub 74:139 Mr 15 '33; J. Eglinton in New Statesm & Nation 5:226 F 25 '33; L. Bonnerot in Revue A A 10:532-3 '33; K. Young in Sat R Lit 9:539 Ap 15 '33; W. S. Knickerbocker in Sewanee R 41:152-74 Ap-Je '33; D. Cecil in Spec 150:48 Ja 13 '33; T L S Ja 12 '33 p13-14; S. Chew in Yale R 22:835-8 '33)

Literature and dogma; an essay towards a better apprehension of the Bible. London, Smith, Elder, 1873. xxxvi,388p (Rev by T. S. Perry in No Am 117:240-7 Jl '73; H. W. Preston in Atlan 32:108-12 Jl '73; Nation (NY) 17:131-2 Ag 21 '73; Lippinc 12:126-8 Je '73; Penn Monthly 4:577-83 Ag '73; E. E. Hale in Old and New 8:497-501 O '73; Scribner's Monthly 6:755-6 Ag '73; Galaxy 16:428-30 S '73; Overland Monthly 11:185-8 Ag '73; N. Porter in Christian Union 7:501-2 Je 25 '73; Christian Union 8:61-2 Jl 23 '73; New Englander 32:590-2 Jl '73; Methodist Quarterly Review 55:507-9 Jl '73; Baptist Quarterly 7:377-8 Jl '73; J. C. Parsons in Religious Magazine and Monthly Review 50:160-70 Ag '73; American Church Review 25:534-67 O '73; Universalist Quarterly 30:386 Jl '73; Ind 25:714 Je 5 '73; C. A. Aiken in Presbyterian Quarterly & Princeton Review ns 3:86-100 Ja '74; A. T. Bledsoe

in Southern Review ns 14:245-73 Ap '74; J. M. Sturtevant in New Englander 34:92-122 Ja '75; National Quarterly Review 35:55-82 Jl '77; F. W. Newman in Fraser ns 8:114-34 Jl '73; E. Simcox in Fortn ns 13:543-4 Ap '73; Ath 1:239-40 F 22 '73; Blackw 113:678-92 Je '73; *same.* Liv Age 118:39-50 Jl 5 '73; *same.* Ecl M ns 18:212-23 Ag '73; *same.* Lutheran Quarterly 3:537-61 O '73; Westm 99:262-3 Ap '73; Christian Observer 72:575-88 Ag '73; Dublin Review ns 20:357-80 Ap '73; Lond Q R 40:399-431 Jl '73; Spec 46:242-4, 278-9 F 22, Mr 1 '73; J. L. Davies in Contemp 21:842-66 My '73; Spec 44:825-7 Jl 8 '71; *same.* Liv Age 110:529-33 Ag 26 '71; A. Réville in Acad 4:327-30 S 1 '73; C. Palfrey in Old & New 8:746-51 Ja '74; Theological Review 10:377-405 Jl '73; Congregationalist 2:338-46 Je '73; Ath 2:495 O 20 '83; Sat R 35:284-6 Mr 1 '73; Quar R 137:389-415 O '74; Westm ns 45:309-23 Ap 1 '74; Lobstein in Theologische Litteraturzeitung '03 p605)

Matthew Arnold's notebooks, with a preface by the Hon. Mrs. Wodehouse. . New York, Macmillan, 1902. viii, 137p (Rev in Ath 1:136-7 Ja 31 '03; Spec 90:534-5 Ap 4 '03; noted in T L S D 12 '02 p369-70)

Merope. A tragedy. London, Longman, Green, Longmans, and Roberts, 1858. lii,138p (Rev by W. C. Roscoe in Nat R 6:259-79 Ap '58; Christian Remembrancer 55:39-45 Ja '68; Fraser 57:691-701 Je '58; Ath 1:13 Ja 2 '58; Sat R 5:19-20 Ja 2 '58; Dublin University Review 51:331-44 Mr '58; *same.* Ecl M 44:59-71 My '58; New Quarterly Review no 21:123-35 My '58; National Magazine (Lond) 3:375 '58; Edin R 168:337-73 O '88)

Mixed essays. London, Smith, Elder, 1879. xii,347p (Rev by W. C. Brownell in Nation (NY) 29:276-7 O 23 '79; International Review 6:695-9 Je '79; Ath 1:303-4 Mr 8 '79; M. Pattison in Acad 15:425-6 My 17 '79; Blackw 126:89-100 Jl '79; Rose-Belford's Canadian Monthly and National Review 2:740-2 Je '79; Sat R 47:535-6 Ap 26 '79; Contemp 34:190-1 Ap '79; Quar R 148:292-5 Jl '79)

New poems. London, Macmillan, 1867. viii,244p (Rev in Nation (NY) 5:228-9 S 19 '67; I. G. Ascher in St J 21:375-82 F '68; Ath 2:265-6 Ag 31 '67; Spec 40:1003-5 S 7 '67; A. C. Swinburne in Fortn 8:414-45 O '67; Victoria Magazine 11:374-83 Ag '68; Ecl M 69:631-4 N '67; Hours at Home 5:569 O '67; Sat R 24:319-20 S 7 '67; Chamb J 4th ser 4:682-4 O 26 '67; Quar R 126:353-6 Ap '69; Edin R 168:337-73 O '88)

On the study of Celtic literature. London, Smith, Elder, 1867. xx,181p
(Rev in Christian Examiner ns 5:378 My '68; Ath 2:45-6 Jl 13 '67; Spec 40:696-8 Je 22 '67; H. S. Fagan in Contemp 6:257-61 O '67; Nation (NY) 2:627 My 18 '66; R. Giffen in Fortn 8:124-6 Jl '67; Pall Mall Gazette no 346:3-4 Mr 19 '66; Edin R 129:486-503 Ap '69; M. E. Henry-Ruffin in Cath World 58:884-90 Mr '94; J. Vendryes in Revue Celtique 31:214 '11)

On translating Homer. London, Longman, Green, Longmans, and Roberts, 1861. iv,104p
(Rev by C. C. Felton in No Am 94:108-25 Ja '62; Ath 1:430 Mr 30 '61; Sat R 12:95-6 Jl 27 '61; Christian Examiner 74:337-55 My '63; Fraser 63:703-14 Je '61; Blackie in Macmil 4:268-80 Ag '61; Ath 2:77 Jl 15 '05; Edin R 129:486-503 Ap '69; Atlan 14:136 Jl '64; L. Etienne in R Deux Mondes Ap '66 p744-67; Quar R 167:398-426 O '88; Ath 1:628 My 10 '62)

On translating Homer. Last words. London, Longman, Green, Longmans, and Roberts, 1862. vi,69p
(Rev in Westm 77:150-68 Ja '62; No Brit 36:345-80 My '62; Fraser 65:769-84 Je '62; Ath 1:628 My 10 '62)

Passages from the prose writings of Matthew Arnold. London, Smith, Elder, 1880
(Rev in Spec 53:969-70 Jl 31 '80)

Poems [issued at various dates: 1853, 1855, etc.]
(Rev by A. Poplar in Dublin University Magazine 43:737-40 Je '54; Ath 1:304-5 Mr 11 '54; Albion 15:405 Ag 23 '56; Boston Review 5:510-11 S '65; Christian Examiner 61:477 N '56; Blackw 75:305-13 Mr '54; Edin R 104:358-60 O '56; Spec 42:733-5 Je 19 '69; Spec 50:889-91 Jl 14 '77; Sat R 44:393-4 S 29 '77; Christian Remembrancer ns 27:310-33 Ap '54; Brit Q 55:169-85 Ap '72; *same.* Liv Age 113:482-99 My 25 '72; Church Q R 6:117-39 Ap '78; National Quarterly Review 40:488-91 Ap '80; Putnam's Monthly 3:452 Ap '54; Eclectic Review ns 9:276-84 Mr '55; Ath 2:271 Ag 28 '69; Brit Q 66:256-7 O '77; Fraser 49:140-9 F '54; G. E. Woodberry in Nation (NY) 27:274-5 O 31 '78; Putnam's Monthly 6:235-8 S '55; No Brit 21:493-504 Ag '54; Scribner's Monthly 17:448 Ja '79; Prospective Review 10:99-115 F '54; Leader 4:1146 N 26 '53; Fraser 49:140-9 F '54; Dublin University Magazine 51:331-44 Mr '58; *same.* Ecl M 44:59-71 My '58; Westm 61:146-59 Ja '54; Putnam's Monthly 8:658 D '56; No Am 96:126-48 Ja '63; New Quarterly Review 3:36-44 Ja '54; Dublin University Magazine 45:190-203 F '55; Lond Q R 33:512-14 Ja '70; Contemp 31:443-4 Ja '78; Ath

2:229-30 Ag 22 '85; J. Skelton [Shirley] in Fraser 80:667-9 N '69; Froude in Westm 61:77-84 Ja '54; W. M. Payne in Dial 4:221-2 Ja '84; Liv Age 102:259-63 Jl 31 '69; Quar R 126:353-6 Ap '69; Liv Age 166:503-6 Ag 22 '85; Edin R 168:337-73 O '88)

Poetical works
(Rev in Literary World (Lond) ns 42:426-7 N 21 '90; L. Johnson in Acad 39:31-2 Ja 10 '91; Quar R 167:398-426 O '88; Quar R 202:221-49 Ja '05)

Popular education of France with notices of that of Holland and Switzerland. London, Longman, Green, Longmans, and Roberts, 1861. lii,294p
(Rev in No Am 93:581-2 O '61; Ath 2:15-16 Jl 6 '61; Edin R 114:1-38 Jl '61)

Porro unum est necessarium
(Rev in Brit Q 69:62-70 Ja '79)

Reports on elementary schools, 1852-1882, ed. by Sir Francis Sandford. London, Macmillan, 1889. xv,302p
(Rev by P. A. Barnett in Acad 35:369-70 Je 1 '89; Ath 2:159 Ag 3 '89)

St. Paul and Protestantism. . . London, Smith, Elder, 1870. xl,176p
(Rev in Ath 1:669-70 My 21 '70; Christian Observer 70:353-64 My '71; Fortn ns 7:752 Je '70; Lond Q R 34:455-78 Jl '70; H. Lawrenny in Acad 1:282-3 Ag 13 '70; Edin R 133:399-425 Ap '71; Spec 43:642-4 My 21 '70; Quar R 130:432-62 Ap '71; Quar R 137:389-415 O '74; R. H. Hutton in Contemp 14:329-41 Je '70)

The scholar gypsy
(Rev in Studio 51:254 '11)

Schools and universities on the continent. London, Macmillan, 1868. xxviii,311p
(Rev in Lippinc 2:228-30 Ag '68; Ath 1:490-1 Ap 4 '68; Spec 41:497-9 Ap 25 '68; Contemp 9:145-9 S '68; F. W. Farrer in Fortn 9:709-11 Je '68; W. Bagehot in Fortn 9:639-47 Je 1 '68; Quar R 125:473-90 O '68)

Selected poems
(Rev in Yale Literary Messenger 43:303-8 Ap 18 '78; Nation (NY) 27:274-5 O 31 '78; Harper M 58:149 D '78; Scribner's Monthly 17:448 Ja '79; Atlan 43:410-13 Mr '79; National Quarterly Review 40:488-91 Ap '80; Dial 2:87 Ag '81; Ath 2:46 Jl 13 '78; Brit Q 68:288 O '78)

Selections from prose works
(Rev in Nation (NY) 66:225 Mr 24 '98; J. St. Loe Strachey in Spec 133:96-7 Jl 19 '24; Brit Q 72:256 O '80)

Special report on certain points connected with elementary education in Germany, Switzerland, and France. London, Privy Council, Commission on Education, 1886. 27p
(Rev in Lond Q R 67:256-82 Ja '87)

Arnold, Matthew—*Continued*
The strayed reveller, and other poems.
London, Fellowes, 1849. viii,128p
[signed "A"]
(Rev in Ath 2:982-3 S 20 '49; Blackw
66:340-6 S '49; Gent M ns 23:283-4 S
'49; Westm 61:146-59 Ja '54; No Am
77:12-24 Jl '53; Literary World (NY)
13:309-12 D 10 '53; Fraser 39:570-86
My '49; W. M. Rossetti in Germ no
2:84-96 F '50; English Review 13:211-13
Mr '50; Edin R 168:337-73 O '88)

Unpublished letters of Matthew Arnold.
Ed. by Arnold Whitridge. New Haven,
Yale Univ. press, 1924. 70p
(Rev in T L S Ja 17 '24 p36)

Works
(Rev in Lit W 14:452 D 15 '83; Brit
Q 42:243-69 O 2 '65; Edin R 129:486-
503 Ap '69; A. Whitridge in Sat R Lit
1:45 Ag 16 '24)

Arnold, Matthew (ed)
A Bible-reading for schools. The great
prophecy of Israel's restoration. Arranged and ed. with notes. . . London, Macmillan, 1872. xxxviii,65p
(Rev by T. K. Cheyne in Acad 9:163
F 19 '76; Westm 99:113-14 Ja '73; Acad
3:211 Je 1 '72; Ath 1:808-9 Je 29 '72;
S. Colvin in Fortn 18:240-1 Ag '72)

Isaiah of Jerusalem in the Authorized
English Version with an introd. corrections, and notes. . . London, Macmillan, 1883. iv,144p
(Rev by T. K. Cheyne in Acad 24:410-
11 D 22 '83)

Letters, speeches, and tracts on Irish
affairs. By Edmund Burke. Collected
and arranged. . . London, Macmillan,
1881. xiv,439p
(Rev by E. J. Payne in Acad 20:22
Jl 9 '81; Brit Q 74:459-60 O '81; Nation (NY) 1:568 N 2 '65)

Poems of Wordsworth, chosen and ed.
. . . London, Macmillan, 1879. xxxii,
325p
(Rev in Sat R 49:19-20 Ja 3 '80; Nation (NY) 29:59 Jl 24 '79; Dial 2:87
Ag '81; Critic (NY) 1:202-3 Jl 30 '81;
Ath 2:393-4 S 27 '79; Spec 52:1609-10
D 20 '79; J. A. Symonds in Fortn ns
26:686-701 N '79; W. Knight in Modern Review 1:235-8 Ja '80; Quar R
154:53-82 Jl '82)

Poetry of Byron, chosen and arranged
. . . London, Macmillan, 1881. xxxvi,276p
(Rev in Dial 2:87 Ag '81; Critic (NY)
1:202-3 Jl 30 '81; Ath 1:839-40 Je 25
'81; C. Monkhouse in Acad 20:131-2
Ag 20 '81; W. H. White in Contemp
40:179-85 Ag '81; Brit Q 74:471-2 O '81;
Quar R 154:53-82 Jl '82)

The six chief lives from Johnson's "Lives
of the Poets" with Macaulay's "Life
of Johnson." Ed. with a preface. . .
London, Macmillan, 1878. xxviii,466p
(Rev in Atlan 43:413 Mr '79; Ath 2:
393-4 S 28 '78; Spec 51:1306-7 O 19

'78; Sat R 46:434-5 O 5 '78; Brit Q
69:199-200 Ja '79; International Review
6:107 Ja '79)

[Arnold and Clough] Nation (N Y) 2:
372 Mr 22 '66

Arnold and Emerson. Unitar 21:172-3 F '84

[Arnold as inspector of schools] Educa
7:131 O '86

[Arnold on American newspapers] Book
B ns 5:133-4 My '88

Arnold on Emerson. Critic (N Y) 1:13-14
Ja 12 '84

Atwood, Olive
Our English visitor. Oberlin Review
11:100-1 Ja 19 '84

Auslander, Joseph and Frank Ernest Hill
The winged horse. Garden City, N.Y.
Doubleday, Doran, 1930. p366-71

Austin, Alfred
Matthew Arnold. *In* Poetry of the period.
London, Bentley, 1870. p118-55
Mr. Matthew Arnold. Temple 27:35-45,
175 Ag-S '69

Bagehot, Walter
Matthew Arnold on the London university. Fortn 9:639-47 Je 1 '68

Bailey-Kempling, W.
Matthew Arnold's "Horatian Echo."
Notes & Q 10th ser 3:6 Ja 7 '05

Barbour, Pearlalee
The influence of Wordsworth on the
poetry of Matthew Arnold. Masters
essay, Univ. of Oklahoma, 1932. 70ff

Barkley, C. W.
"The Forsaken Merman." Notes & Q
4th ser 3:116 Ja 30 '69

Barnard, Cyril C.
Byron. A criticism of Matthew Arnold's
essay. Engl Stud 65:211-16 '31

Barnett, Henry Green
Poetic criticism in Matthew Arnold.
Masters essay, Columbia univ. 1927

Barry, William
Catholics and modern literature. Dublin
Review 3d ser 14:45-64 Jl '85

Bartlett, R. E.
Matthew Arnold. Spec 61:574 Ap 28 '88

Bates, Katharine Lee
Matthew Arnold; poem. Lit W 14:415
D 1 '83

Bateson, Frederick W.
English poetry and the English language. Oxford, Clarendon press, 1934.
p105-7

Bayne, Peter
Mr. Arnold and Mr. Swinburne. Contemp 6:337-56 S-D '67; New Ecl 1:144-
64 F '68; *same.* Every Sat 4:753-61 D 14
'67

Bayne, Thomas
Matthew Arnold. St J 40:59-71 Ja '77

Matthew Arnold on nineteenth century eloquence. Notes & Q 11th ser 2:376 N 5 '10

Thackeray and Matthew Arnold. Notes & Q 8th ser 1:491 Je 18 '92

Beach, Leonard Brothwell
Arnold and Browning in their relation to Greek tragedy. Masters essay, Yale univ. 1930

Beatty, H. M.
Matthew Arnold's letters. T L S Ap 20 '22 p260

Beede, Margaret A.
The Hebraic of Matthew Arnold. Masters essay, Univ. of North Dakota, 1922. 53ff

Beers, Henry A.
Matthew Arnold in America. Cent 27: 155-7 N '83

Belben, Edward Philip
The three most famous prefaces. Notes & Q 9th ser 4:54-5 Jl 15 '99

Bell, C. C.
"The Scholar gipsy." T L S S 27 '23 p636
ibid O 11 '23 p670

Bendz, Ernst Paulus
The influence of Pater and Matthew Arnold in the prose writings of Oscar Wilde. Gothenburg, Wettergren & Kerver, 1914. 114p
(Rev in Acad 86:493 Ap 18 '14)

Benee, Maud Miriam Victoria
Wordsworth and Arnold. A comparison which seeks to discover the extent of the influence exerted by William Wordsworth upon Matthew Arnold. Masters essay, Univ. of Manitoba, 1927. 144ff

Benn, Alfred William
Reconstruction and reaction. In The history of English rationalism in the nineteenth century. London, Longmans, Green, 1906. vol. II p302-20

Bennett, S. Rowe
Spencer-Harrison-Arnold. An eclectic essay. Contemp 48:200-9 Ag '85

Bensley, Edward
Matthew Arnold's poems. Notes & Q 11th ser 7:397 My 17 '13

Benson, Arthur Christopher
Matthew Arnold. In The leaves of the tree. . . New York, Putnam, 1911. p388-423; same. No Am 194:136-52 Jl '11

Benson, M. Eloise
"In Memoriam," "Adonais," and Thyrsis" in relation to the thought of their time. Masters essay, State Univ. of Iowa, 1929. 75ff

Benton, Joel
Matthew Arnold. Appleton J 15:341-2 Mr 11 '76

Matthew Arnold's criticism of America. Christian Union 37:521-2 Ap 26 '88

The poetry of Matthew Arnold. Manhattan 2:524-30 D '83

Berenson, Bernhard
How Matthew Arnold impressed me. Harv Mo 5:53-6 N '87

Bernkopf, Charlotte Sophie
Goethe's influence on Matthew Arnold. Masters essay, Columbia univ. 1916

Bevington, Merle M.
The political and economic views of Matthew Arnold. Masters essay, Columbia univ. 1927

Bickley, Francis Lawrance
Matthew Arnold and his poetry. (Poetry and life series, no 6) London, Harrap, 1911. 118p
(Rev in Ath 2:266 S 2 '11)

Bigelow, John
Matthew Arnold and Franklin. Cent 36: 477 Jl '88

Binns, William
Matthew Arnold as a religious teacher. Theological Review 15:88-116 Ja '78

Birrell, Augustine
Matthew Arnold. Scrib M 4:537-45 N '88

Matthew Arnold. In Collected essays. London, Stock, 1902. vol II p125-54

Matthew Arnold. In Res judicatae; papers and essays. New York, Scribner, 1908. p181-223

Birss, John Howard
Whitman on Arnold; an uncollected comment. Mod Lang N 47:316-17 My '32

Blackshaw, Randall
Mr. Arnold's want of tact. Critic (NY) 5:31-2 Jl 19 '84

Blair, Elizabeth
Matthew Arnold as a poet. Vassar Journal of Undergraduate Studies 8:77-94 My '34

Blunden, Edmund [Charles]
Matthew Arnold. In Massingham, H. J. and Massingham, H. eds. The great Victorians. London, Nicholson and Watson [1932] p1-16

Nature in English literature. (Hogarth lectures no 9) London, Hogarth press, 1929. p104-5

Blunders of authors. Notes & Q 7th ser 7:392 My 18 '89

Boas, F. S.
Some poems of Matthew Arnold. Roy Soc Lit 2d ser vol XXIX p95-113 '09

Boase, Frederic
Arnold, Matthew. In Modern English biography. Truro, Netherton & Worth, 1908. vol IV p171-2

Boatman, Bertha Williams
Influences contributory to the poetry of Matthew Arnold. Masters essay, State Univ. of Iowa, 1927. 69ff

Bodkin, Maud
Poetry and dream. In Archetypal patterns in poetry. . . London, Oxford univ. press, 1934. p65-7

Bonnerot, Louis
La jeunesse de Matthew Arnold. Revue A A 7:520-37 Ag '30

Bookman, Rebecca
Matthew Arnold and education. Masters essay, New York Univ. 1931. 49ff

Bouchier, Jonathan
"Sweetness and light." Notes & Q 4th ser 10:293 O 12 '72

Thackeray and Matthew Arnold. Notes & Q 8th ser 2:51 Jl 16 '92

Bourdillon, Francis William
To Matthew Arnold in America; poem. *In* Sursum corda. London, Unwin, 1893. p33-4

Bouton, Archibald L.
Introduction. *In* Matthew Arnold, prose and poetry. New York, Scribner [c1927] pv-xxxiv

Bowker, R. R.
London as a literary center. Harper M 76:828-9 My '88

Boyd, A. J.
Arnold and the grand style. New York, Oxford University press, 1934. 12p

Boyer, Clarence Valentine
Self-expression and happiness. . . Int J Ethics 33:263-90 Ap '23

Bradfield, Thomas
Ethical tendency of Matthew Arnold's poetry. Westm 142:650-65 D '94; *same.* Ecl M 124:310-19 Mr '95

Bradley, Andrew Cecil
Arnold's "Signal elm." T L S N 23 '17 p569

Shelley and Arnold's critique of his poetry. *In* A miscellany. London, Macmillan, 1929. p139-62

Bradley, Cornelius Beach
The English essay: its development and some of its perfected types. Univ. of California Chronicle 1:385-407 '88

Breslar, M. L. R.
Arnold of Rugby. Notes & Q 9th ser 7:76-7 Ja 26 '01

Brinton, Mary Rice
Matthew Arnold. Masters essay, Univ. of Arizona, 1921. 112ff

Brock, Arthur Clutton. *See* Clutton-Brock, Arthur

Brooke, Stopford Augustus
Matthew Arnold. *In* Four Victorian poets. New York, Putnam, 1908. p56-144
(Rev in T L S My 21 '08 p161-2)

A poet of fifty years ago. Hibbert J 1:62-82 O '02

Brooksbank, B.
Matthew Arnold's "Negative." Speaker 20:17 Jl 8 '99

Brown, E. K.
The critic as Xenophobe. . . Sewanee R 38:301-9 Jl-S '30

The French reputation of Matthew Arnold. *In* Wallace, Malcolm W. ed. Studies in English, by members of University College, Toronto. [Toronto] Univ. of Toronto press, 1931. p224-54

Matthew Arnold and the Elizabethans. Univ. of Toronto Quarterly 1:333-51 '32

Brown, James Buchan [pseud]
see Selkirk, J. B.

Brown, Leonard
Arnold's succession: 1850-1914. Sewanee R 42:158-79 Ap '34

Brown, Stephen J. M.
The Homeric simile after Homer. Thought 4:584-98 Mr '30

Browne, Francis F.
Matthew Arnold; poem. Dial 9:5 My '88

Brownell, William Crary
Matthew Arnold. Scrib M 30:105-20 Jl '01

Matthew Arnold. *In* Victorian prose masters. . . New York, Scribner, 1909. p149-202
(Rev in Nation (NY) 74:17 Ja 2 '02)

Browning, Oscar
Arnold and Arnoldism. Academy (Boston) 6:14-18 F '91

Bryan, J. Ingram
The philosophy of English literature. Tokyo, Maruzen [1930] p221-2

Bulloch, J. M.
[Arnold's descent from an English king, Edward I] Book B 23:38-9 Ag '01

Bunbury, H. S.
An amateur evangelist. Pioneer no 10:48-50 Ap '87

By the waters of Babylon. Pioneer ns no 1:20-7 Ja '88

Burgum, Edwin Berry
The humanism of Matthew Arnold. Symposium 2:85-112 '31

Burns, Mary
The twentieth century estimate of Matthew Arnold as a critic of literature. Masters essay, Univ. of Kansas, 1931. 153ff

Burroughs, John
Arnold on Emerson and Carlyle. Cent ns 5:925-32 Ap '84

Arnold's view of Emerson and Carlyle. *In* Indoor studies. Boston, Houghton, Mifflin, 1889. p128-61

Matthew Arnold's criticism. *In* Indoor studies. Boston, Houghton, Mifflin, 1889. p79-127; same. Cent ns 14:185-94 Je '88

On the re-reading of books. Cent 55:149-50 N '97

Spiritual insight of Matthew Arnold. *In* The light of day. . . Boston, Houghton, Mifflin, 1900. p212-18

Burwell, Mary Anna
A study of Matthew Arnold's Tristram and Iseult. Masters essay, Univ. of Nebraska, 1929. 169ff

Bush, Douglas
The varied hues of pessimism. Dalhousie Review 9:271-81 O '29

Butler, A. G.
The three friends: story of Rugby in the forties. London, Frowde, 1900. 134p
(Rev in Nation (NY) 72:92 Ja 31 '01)

Byles, C. E.
Matthew Arnold and Christianity. New Century Review 6:222-30 '99

Matthew Arnold on modern hurry. Notes & Q 11th ser 3:488 Je 24 '11; ibid 4:37 Jl 8 '11

Cadman, Samuel Parkes
Matthew Arnold. *In* Charles Darwin and other English thinkers, with reference to their religious and ethical value. A series of lectures delivered before the Brooklyn Institute of Arts and Sciences during the autumn of 1910. Boston, Pilgrim Press [c1911] p209-69 bibl p276-7

Campbell, Reginald John
Thomas Arnold. (Great English Churchman ser) ed. by Sidney Dark. London, Macmillan, 1927. xiv, 242p
(Rev by C. L. Wells in Sewanee R 37:123-4 Ja '29; T L S Je 28 '27 p477)

Caricature. Acad 56:686-7 Je 24 '99

Carlisle, H.
A comment on "A comment on Christmas." Contemp 49:178-93 F '86

Carman, Bliss
Corydon: an elegy. Universal Review 5:425-37 N '89

Carr, Christopher [pseud]
see Benson, Arthur Christopher

Carter, John and Pollard, Graham
Matthew Arnold. *In* An enquiry into the nature of certain nineteenth century pamphlets. London, Constable, 1934. p159-64

Cazamian, Louis
A history of English literature. . . by Emile Legouis and Louis Cazamian. New York, Macmillan, 1929. p1147-51, 1224-7

Cazamian, Madeleine
Le roman et les idées en angleterre; l'influence de la science (1860-1890) (Publications de la faculté des lettres de l'université de Strasbourg. fascicule 15) Strasbourg, Librairie Istra, 1923. p22-31, 260-1

Centenary of Matthew Arnold. Boston Transcript Ja 6 '23 Book section

Chambers, (Sir) Edmund Kerchever
Matthew Arnold. . . (British Academy. London. Warton lecture on English poetry. [no 23] 1932) London, H. Milford [1932] 25p
(Rev in T L S Ap 21 '32 p286)

Chang, Hsin-Hai
Matthew Arnold and the humanistic view of life. Thesis, Harvard univ. 1922. Typed ms 499ff

Chapman, Edward Mortimer
The doubters and the mystics. *In* English literature in account with religion. Boston, Houghton, Mifflin, 1910. p431-41

Charpentier, John
La poésie Britannique et Baudelaire. Mercure Fr 147:319-20 Ap-My '21

Charteris, (Sir) Evan [Edward]
The life and letters of Sir Edmund Gosse. London, Heinemann [1931]

[Chauncey Depew on Arnold]
Book B ns 2:45 Mr '85

Chauvet, Paul
Matthew Arnold. *In* Sept essais de littérature anglaise. [A. E. Poe; J. Thomson; B. V.; O. Wilde; M. Arnold; Tennyson; E. B. Browning] Paris, Figuière, 1931. p114-50
(Rev in New Statesm 2:412 O 3 '31)

Cheney, John Vance
Matthew Arnold. *In* The golden guess. . . . Boston, Lee and Shepard, 1892. p75-119

Chesterton, Gilbert Keith
Introduction. *In* Essays literary and critical by Matthew Arnold. (Everyman's library) London, Dent [1906] pix-xiv; same. *In* G.K.C. as M.C., selected and ed. by J. P. de Fonseka. London, Methuen [1929] p19-28

Matthew Arnold. Bookm (NY) 16:116-20 O '02

The Victorian compromise. *In* The Victorian age in literature. New York, Henry Holt [1913] p73-9

Child, Margaret Sykes
A statistical investigation of the "Artistic Temperament" and its application to a group of nineteenth century English artists. Masters essay, Vassar College, 1923. 105p

Chilton, Eleanor Carroll and Agar, Herbert
The garment of praise. . . Garden City, N.Y. Doubleday, Doran, 1929. p261-83

Chislett, William, jr.
The classical influence in English literature in the nineteenth century. Boston, Stratford Co. 1918. p12-13

Christman, Lewis H.
Matthew Arnold as an ethical teacher. Meth R 105:885-93 N '22

Chubb, Edwin Watts
Literary recollections of Max Mueller. *In* Stories of authors, British and American. New York, Macmillan, 1926. p156-61

Clapp, Edwin Roosa
English literary criticism, 1830-1890. . . Harvard univ. . . summaries of theses. . . . Cambridge, Mass. 1931. p215-18 Diss. Harvard

Clark, Clarence Carroll
Matthew Arnold and his masters. Doctor's essay, Yale univ. 1903

Clark, Frank L.
On certain imitations or reminiscences of Homer in Matthew Arnold's "Sohrab and Rustum." Classical Weekly 17:3-7 O 1 '23

Clark, J. S.
Matthew Arnold. *In* A study of English prose writers. New York, Scribner, 1898. p507-23

Clodd, Edward
Matthew Arnold's poetry. Gent M ns 36:344-59 Ap '86

Clough, Arthur Hugh
Review of some poems by Alexander Smith and Matthew Arnold. *In* The poems and prose remains of Arthur Hugh Clough . . . ed. by his wife. London, Macmillan, 1869. vol. I p359-83 [From No Am 77:1-30 Jl '53]

[Clough-Arnold memorial] Acad 63:51 Jl 12 '02

Clutton-Brock, Arthur
Matthew Arnold. *In* Essays on literature and life. London, Methuen [1926] p124-36

Coan, Titus Munson
Matthew Arnold's critical writings. Manhattan 2:515-24 D '83

Coates, Florence Earl
Matthew Arnold. Cent ns 25:931-7 Ap '94

Matthew Arnold. . . Lippinc 84:670-4 D '09

Coblentz, H. E.
The blank verse of "Sohrab and Rustum." Poet Lore 7:497-505 '95

Coblentz, Stanton A.
The literary revolution. New York, Frank-Maurice, 1927. p115-17

Cochrane, Robert
Matthew Arnold. *In* The treasury of modern biography. Edinburgh, Nimmo, Hay, and Mitchell, 1892. p507

Coleridge, [Lord] Stephen
Famous Victorians I have known. London, 1928

Matthew Arnold. New Review 1:111-24, 217-32 Jl, Ag '89; *same.* Liv Age 182: 771-83 S 28 '89

Matthew Arnold. *In* The glory of English prose. New York, Putnam, 1922. p201-5

Collins, John Churton
Introduction. *In* Matthew Arnold's Merope . . . Oxford, Clarendon press, 1906. p1-23

Matthew Arnold. *In* The posthumous essays of J. C. Collins, ed. by L. C. Collins. London, Dent, 1912. p171-98

Colter, Mary Culbertson
A comparison between Arnold and Gray as elegiac poets. Masters essay, Columbia univ. 1903

Cone, Helen Gray
After reading Arnold's "Sohrab and Rustum." Critic (NY) 3:534 D 29 '83

Matthew Arnold; poem. Critic (NY) 13: 290 D 8 '88

Conklin, Judith Cecelia
Matthew Arnold as a literary critic. Masters essay, Columbia univ. 1915

Connolly, Terrence L.
Matthew Arnold: critic. Thought 9:193-205 '34

Conway, Moncure D.
The English lakes and their genii. Harper M 62:161-77 Ja '81

Cook, (Sir) Edward
The second thoughts of poets. *In* Literary recreations. London, Macmillan, 1919. p294-302

Cooke, George Willis
Matthew Arnold. Unitar 21:120-9 F '84

Cooper, Lane
Matthew Arnold's essay on Wordsworth. Bookm (NY) 69:479-84 Jl '29

Cotterill, H. B.
The dying life of a poet. T L S Ap 20 '22 p260-1

Courtney, (Mrs) Janet E.
Matthew Arnold. *In* Freethinkers of the nineteenth century. London, Chapman & Hall, 1920. p65-96

Covell, Albert Henry
Matthew Arnold as a critic. Hull prize essay, Univ. of Rochester, 1912. 12ff

The Craik and Arnold memorials. Lit W 19:184 Je 9 '88

Crane, William G.
Significance of Matthew Arnold's critical theory. Masters essay, State Univ. of Iowa, 1920. 79ff

Crawley, Richard
Horse and foot; or, Pilgrims to Parnassus. London, Hotten, 1868. p21-7 [Satire on Arnold]

Critics and criticism. Lit W 13:58 F 25 '82

Crooker, Joseph Henry
Matthew Arnold. New England Magazine ns 9:632-9 Ja '94

Crozier, John Beattie
My inner life . . . New York, Longmans, Green, 1898. p521-8

Cruse, Amy
Thyrsis: Culture and anarchy. *In* English literature through the ages. Beowulf to Stevenson. New York, Stokes [1914] p556-64

Culture and democracy. T L S Ag 21 '24 p505-6

Cunliffe, John W.
Mid-Victorian poets. *In* Leaders of the Victorian revolution. New York, Appleton-Century [c1934] p155, 228-34

Custer, Donald M.
Educational plan of Matthew Arnold. Masters essay, Univ. of Colorado, 1934. 54ff

Dale, Dorothy F.
A comment and questionnaire on "Selections from Matthew Arnold's poetry," edited by Houghton. London, Pitman, 1927. 32p

Dale, R. W.
Matthew Arnold and the nonconformists. Contemp 14:540-71 Jl '70

Dallas, E. S.
The gay science. London, Chapman and Hall, 1866. vol I p65-8

Davey, H.
Matthew Arnold on Beethoven. Notes & Q 12th ser 4:84-5 Mr '18

Davies, Frank J. J.
Matthew Arnold. T L S Mr 9 '33 p167
Matthew Arnold and education. Doctor's essay, Yale univ. 1934

Davies, Hilda I.
America and Matthew Arnold; contemporary American periodical criticism of Arnold. Masters essay, Columbia university, 1933. 151ff

Davies, John Llewelyn
Mr. Matthew Arnold's new religion of the Bible. Contemp 21:842-66 My '73

Davis, B. E. C.
Shakespeare's popularity. T L S Je 28 '17 p309

Dawson, William Harbutt
Matthew Arnold and his relation to the thought of our time. New York, Putnam, 1904. viii, 450p bibl p439-43 (Rev in Nation (NY) 78:318-19 Ap 21 '04; Ath 1:589-90 My 7 '04; Contemp 85:905 Je '04; Arena 31:658-60 Je '04; E. J. Rich in Dial 37:200-3 O 1 '04; H. S. Krans in Out 78:679-82 N 12 '04; A. S. Henry in Bookn 22:953-6 My '04; T. H. Warren in Quar R 202:221-49 Ja '05; H. W. Boynton in Atlan 93: 708 My '04; Literary World (Lond) ns 69:583-4 Je 17 '04; N. P. Gilman in Lit W 35:101 Ap '04)

Dawson, William James
Matthew Arnold. Great Thoughts ns 3:57-60 Jl 27 '89

Matthew Arnold. *In* The makers of English poetry. New York, Revell [c1906] p333-46

Matthew Arnold. *In* The makers of modern English. . . New York, Whittaker, 1890. p328-40

The death of Matthew Arnold. Ind 40: 490 Ap 19 '88

Death of Mr. Matthew Arnold. Liv Age 177:436-41 My 19 '88; Spec 61:538 Ap 21 '88; *same.* Liv Age 177:433-6 My 19 '88; Critic (NY) 12:193-4 Ap 21 '88

Deininger, M. Kathyrn
Matthew Arnold in relation to his age. Masters essay, Syracuse Univ. 1930. 64ff

DeMille, George E.
Stuart P. Sherman: the Illinois Arnold. Sewanee R 35:78-93 Ja '27

Derham, Milo G.
Borrowings from Homer in "Sohrab and Rustum." Colorado Univ. Studies 7: 73-90 D '09

Derry, William and Raphoe
Matthew Arnold; poem. Spec 61:575 Ap 28 '88; *same.* Liv Age 177:514 Je 2 '88

Dewey, John
Matthew Arnold and Robert Browning. *In* Characters and events; popular essays in social and political philosophy, ed. by Joseph Ratner. . . New York, Holt [c1929] vol I p3-17

Dilla, Geradine P.
The principal tones of Arnold's poetry. Poet Lore 32:279-87 '21

Dixon, James Main
Matthew Arnold. [Modern poets and Christian teaching, vol II] New York, Eaton and Mains [1906] 165p

Dixon, William Macneile
Arnold. *In* English poetry from Blake to Browning. London, Methuen, 1894. p193

English epic and heroic poetry. London, Dent, 1912. p278-80, 322-4

The poetry of Matthew Arnold. *In* In the republic of letters. London, Nutt, 1898

Dodwell, H. Herbert
Matthew Arnold as a critic. Macmil 91:417-27 Ap '05

Matthew Arnold as a social reformer. Macmil ns 1:53-65 N '05

Doggett, Carita
Matthew Arnold, the critical disciple of Charles Augustin Sainte-Beuve. Masters essay, Columbia univ. 1916

Dole, Nathan Haskell
Biographical introduction. *In* Matthew Arnold's poetical works. New York, Crowell [c1897] pix-xxii

Doorn, Willem van
Theory and practice of English narrative verse since 1833. Amsterdam [1932?] p93-101

Dowden, Edward
Matthew Arnold. *In* Chambers's cyclopaedia of English literature. Philadephia, Lippincott, 1903. vol III p591-600

Matthew Arnold as a poet. Atalanta 2: 809-13 S '89

Victorian literature. *In* Transcripts and studies. London, Kegan Paul, Trench, Trübner, 1896. 2d ed p207-11; *same.* Fortn 47:857-8 Je '87

Downes, Carl Sawyer
Arnold's poetry in its relations to romanticism. Thesis, Harvard univ. 1912. vi, 420ff Typed ms

Drinkwater, John
Some letters from Matthew Arnold to Robert Browning. Cornhill ns 55:654-64 D '23

Drinkwater, John—*Continued*
Victorian poetry. (People's library) London, Hodder & Stoughton, 1923 p86-90, 96-100

Duff, Mountstuart Elphinstone Grant
Matthew Arnold, 1822-1888. *In* Out of the past. New York, Dutton, 1903. vol II p68-111

Matthew Arnold's writings. Murray's Magazine 7:289-308 Mr '90

The plant allusions in the poems of Matthew Arnold. Nature Notes 1:81-4, 104-7 Je, Jl '90

[Duff on Arnold] Lit W 21:40 F 1 '90

Dunn, Henry
Facts, not fairy-tales. Brief notes on Mr. Matthew Arnold's Literature and dogma. London, Simpkin, Marshall, 1873. 87p

Dunn, Waldo Hilary
Arnold and the conduct of life. *In* Lectures on three eminent Victorians; delivered. . . [at] Janet Jacks Balch auditorium, Scripps college, April and May 1932 (Papers no 4) Scripps college, Claremont, Calif. 1932. p53-75

The **dying** life of a poet. T L S Ap 13 '22 p233-4

Eastern art and western critics. Edin R 212:450-1 O '10

Edgar, Pelham
Matthew Arnold as a writer of prose. Dalhousie Review 1:247-62 Jl '21

Matthew Arnold as poet. Royal Society of Canada. Transactions Section 2 3d ser 8:309-20 '14

Elias, Otto
Matthew Arnolds politische grundanschauungen. (Palaestra, 175) Leipzig, Mayer and Müller, 1931. v, 152p bibl p[149]-52 Diss. Berlin

Eliot, Thomas Stearns
Arnold and Pater. Bookm (NY) 72:1-7 S '30

Francis Herbert Bradley. *In* For Lancelot Andrewes. London, Faber and Gwyer [1928] p70-81

Matthew Arnold. *In* The use of poetry and the use of criticism. Cambridge, Mass. Harvard univ. press, 1933. p95-112

The second-order mind. Dial 69:586-9 D '20

Ellerton, F. G.
"The scholar gipsy." T L S S 20 '23 p620

Elliott, George Roy
The Arnoldian lyric melancholy. P M L A 38:929-32 D '23

The Arnoldian lyric melancholy. *In* The cycle of modern poetry. A series of essays towards clearing our present poetic dilemma. Princeton, Univ. press, 1929. p58-63

Elliott, Henry
Matthew Arnold as theatrical critic. Theatre (Lond) 30:70-5 Ag 1 '97

Ellis, Francis G.
Notes on Matthew Arnold's "Sohrab and Rustum," "The Scholar-gipsy," and "Thyrsis." (Normal Tutorial Ser) London, Normal Press, 1925. 40p

Elton, Oliver
Alfred Tennyson and Matthew Arnold. London, Arnold, 1924. 96p

Earlier critics; and Matthew Arnold. *In* A survey of English literature, 1830-1880. London, Arnold, 1920. vol I p254-78

England [note on Arnold] Nation (NY) 2:271 Mr 1 '66

Erigena quoted by Matthew Arnold. Notes & Q 12th ser 10:252 Ap 1 '22; Notes & Q 12th ser 11:159 Ag 19 '22

Ewing, Lucie Elizabeth Lee
Matthew Arnold. *In* George Frederick Watts, Sandra Botticelli, Matthew Arnold. New York, Grafton press [c1904] p51-64

Fanshawe, Reginald
Corydon, an elegy in memory of Matthew Arnold and Oxford. London, Frowde, 1906. viii, 113p

Farrar, Frederick William
Matthew Arnold. *In* Men I have known. New York, Crowell [c1897] p73-92

Fehr, Bernhard
Die englische literatur des neunzehnten und zwanzigsten jahrhunderts. Wildpark-Potsdam, 1928. p173-5, 183-5

Field, Michael
The rest of immortals; poem. Contemp 53:882-4 Je '88

Fife, M. B.
The late Matthew Arnold; poet and critic. Sun 2:88-91 Mr '89

Fishback, William Pinckney
Recollections of Lord Coleridge. . . Indianapolis, Bowen-Merrill, 1895. p117-33 (Lord Coleridge on Matthew Arnold. From the London Times of N 2 '91)

Fisher, Charles
Matthew Arnold as seen through his letters. Gent M 283:492-501 N '97; *same.* Liv Age 215:870-6 D 18 '97

A triad of elegies. Temple 108:388-96 Jl '96

Fisher, George Park
The theological ideas of Matthew Arnold. *In* The nature and method of revelation. New York, Scribner, 1890. p243-58

Fisher, P. J.
Matthew Arnold as poet. Holborn Review 65:41-56 Ja '23

Fitch, (Sir) Joshua Girling
Thomas and Matthew Arnold, and their influence on English education. (Great educators) New York, Scribner, 1897. iii-ix, 277p
(Rev in Acad 52:517-18 D 11 '97; Critic (NY) 31:186-7 O 2 '97; Church Q R 47:466-76 Ja '99; *same*. Liv Age 221: 99-106 Ap 8 '99; Lit W 29:133 Ap 30 '98; Spec 79:559-60 O 23 '97; W. M. Payne in Dial 24:113-16 F 16 '98)

Fleming, Dorothea Brown
A survey of the reviews of the literary criticisms of Matthew Arnold from 1853 until 1869. Masters essay, New York Univ. 1933. 60ff

Flexner, Abraham
Matthew Arnold's poetry from an ethical stand-point. Int J Ethics 5:206-18 Ja '95

Foerster, Norman
Matthew Arnold and American letters to-day. Sewanee R 30:298-306 Jl '22

Foley, John L.
What is permanent in Arnold's criticism. Masters essay, Columbia univ. 1920

Foreign authors in America. Bookm (NY) 13:377 Je '01

Forman, Harry Buxton
Matthew Arnold. *In* Our living poets. . . London, Tinsley, 1871. p309-32; *same*. Tinsley 3:146-55 S '68

"The **forsaken** merman." Nation (NY) 86: 28-9 Ja 9 '08

Francis, Averic Standish
"Sweetness and light." Unitar 26:345-57 O '86

A **French** critic. T L S Ja 1 '25 p9

Fry, J. F.
Matthew Arnold. Notes & Q 9th ser 4: 315 O 14 '99

Fry, James B.
Grant and Arnold. "An estimate." No Am 144:349-57 Ap '87
Mr. Matthew Arnold on America. No Am 146:515-19 My '88

Frye, Prosser Hall
Matthew Arnold. *In* Visions and chimeras. Boston, Jones, 1929. p62-77

Fuller, Edward
Arnold, Newman, and Rossetti. Critic (NY) 45:273-6 S '04

Furrer, Paul
Der einfluss Sainte-Beuve's auf die kritik Matthew Arnolds. Wetzikon, Aktienbuchdruckerei, 1920. 57p Diss. Zürich. bibl p57-[58]

Galton, Arthur Howard
Matthew Arnold: an essay on criticism. Century Guild Hobby Horse no 11:83-108 Je '88
Matthew Arnold; poem. Century Guild Hobby Horse no 14:70 Ap '89
Mr. Matthew Arnold. *In* Urbana scripta: studies of five living poets, and other essays. London, Stock, 1885. p77-107

The poetical works of Matthew Arnold. A note upon literature considered as a fine art. . . Century Guild Hobby Horse no 23:93-108 Jl '91

Some letters of Matthew Arnold. Century Guild Hobby Horse no 18:47-55 Ap '90

Two essays upon Matthew Arnold, with some of his letters to the author. London, Matthews, 1897. 122p
(Rev in Lit 2:173 F 12 '98; T. H. Warren in Quar R 202:221-49 Ja '05; Sat R 84:719-20 D 18 '97; Literary World (Lond) ns 57:246-7 Mr 18 '98)

Garlinger, St. Helene
The forsaken merman: a symphonic poem. Masters essay, Univ. of Southern California, 1930. 44ff

Garnett, Richard
Matthew Arnold. *In* Essays of an ex-librarian. New York, Dodd, Mead, 1901. p283-99
(Rev by H. W. Boynton in Atlan 89:850 Je '02)
Matthew Arnold. *In* Dict N B vol XXII p70-5

Garrod, Heathcote William
Matthew Arnold as critic. *In* Poetry and the criticism of life. Cambridge, Mass. Harvard univ. press, 1931. p67-84
The poetry of Matthew Arnold. *In* Poetry and the criticism of life. (The Charles Eliot Norton lectures for 1929-1930) Cambridge, Mass. Harvard univ. press, 1931. p23-66
The theology of Matthew Arnold. Liv Age 264:349-56 F 5 '10; *same*. Oxford and Cambridge Review no 6:17-31 Lent '09

Gatch, Louise
Tristram, Launcelot, and the Holy Grail, as treated by Tennyson, Arnold, Morris, and Swinburne. Masters essay, Univ. of California, 1911. 130ff

Gates, Lewis Edwards
Introduction. *In* Selections from the prose writings of Matthew Arnold. . . New York, Holt, 1898. p ix-lxxxix
Matthew Arnold. *In* Three studies in literature. . . New York, Macmillan, 1899. p124-211
[Poetry and prose of Arnold] Critic (NY) 36:268-72 Mr '00
The return to conventional life. *In* Studies and appreciations. New York, Macmillan, 1900. p44-54

Genius and versatility. Macmil 49:87-94 D '83

Gerould, Gordon Hall
Matthew Arnold's complete works. Bookm (NY) 59:460-2 Je '24

Gibson, Alice Schieffelin
Matthew Arnold's studies in French and German education. Masters essay, Columbia univ. 1902

Gilbert, Ralph Valentine
Matthew Arnold. *In* English writers. Philadelphia, Penn Publishing co. 1913. p141-5

Gladstone, W. E.
Bishop Butler and his censors. IV. Mr. Matthew Arnold. 19th Cent 38:1056-74 D '95

Godkin, E. L.
American opinion on the Irish question. 19th Cent 22:285-92 Ag '87

Goldmark, (Mrs) Ruth Ingersoll
The Hellenism of Matthew Arnold. *In* Studies in the influence of the classics on English literature. (Columbia univ. studies in English and comparative literature [no 26]) New York, Columbia univ. press, 1918. p83-106

Gone astray [signed "N. H."] Nation (NY) 3:136-7 Ag 16 '66

Good, Harry Gehman
Matthew Arnold after many years. School and Society 16:701-6 D 23 '22

Goodale, Ralph Hinsdale
Pessimism in English poetry and fiction, 1847-1900. *In* Abstracts of theses. . . Humanistic series Volume VI. . . Univ. of Chicago. Chicago, 1927. p347-51 Diss. Chicago

Goodrich, N. L.
Matthew Arnold's and Tennyson's exhibition of the thought of their age. Kent prize essay, Amherst college, 1901. Typed ms. in Amherst college library 53ff

Gosse, (Sir) Edmund
The literature of the Victorian era. Engl Illus 17:490-1 Jl '97

Matthew Arnold. *In* More books on the table. New York, Scribner, 1923. p379-87

Matthew Arnold and Swinburne. [Letters] T L S Ag 12 '20 p517

Mr. Matthew Arnold's earliest publication. Ath 1:533-4 Ap 28 '88

Gould, Elizabeth P.
Literature and dogma. Critic (NY) 3:431 O 27 '83

Gowen, Herbert Henry
Jottings. Mod Lang N 37:183 Mr '22

Grant-Duff, Mountstuart, E.
see Duff, Mountstuart E. G.

Grappe, Georges
Matthew Arnold. *In* Essai sur la poésie anglaise au xix° siècle. Paris, Sansot, 1906. p68-70

Graves, Alfred Perceval
Celtic nature poetry. *In* Royal Society of Literature of the United Kingdom. Essays by divers hands, being the Transactions of. Ed. by Lawrence Binyon. London, Milford, 1928. ns vol VIII p81-105

Gray, Stedman Haile
A study of Matthew Arnold on the side of religious emotion. Masters essay, Univ. of California, 1908. 87ff

[Grebanier, Mrs. Frances (Vinciguerra)]
Frances Winwar [pseud]
Poor splendid wings. Boston, Little Brown, 1933. xii, 413p bibl p393-404

Green, A. E.
The educational theories of Matthew Arnold. Masters essay, Univ. of Southern California, 1930. 53ff

Green, Alice Helen
The poet and his age; the poetry of Matthew Arnold as representative of the main movement of the Victorian mind. Masters essay, Columbia univ. 1929

Greenblatt, Milton
A history and comparative study of the Tristram story in English literature (as treated by Malory, Arnold, Tennyson and Swinburne). Masters essay, Columbia univ. 1931

Gregg, Paul Lawrence
Matthew Arnold's criticism of American society compared with that of twentieth-century American novelists. Masters essay, St. Louis Univ. 1934. 87ff

Grierson, Francis
The blunders of Matthew Arnold. Westm 157:300-6 Mr '02

Grierson, Herbert John Clifford
Lord Byron: Arnold and Swinburne. [Warton lecture on English poetry no 11 1920] London, Milford [1921] 31p

Lord Byron: Arnold and Swinburne. *In* The background of English literature. . . New York, Holt, 1926. p68-114

Griffin, Martin J.
Another view of Matthew Arnold's poems. Rose-Belford's Canadian Monthly and National Review 1:546-52 N '78

Griffiths, Janet
The influence of Sainte-Beuve on the critical works of Matthew Arnold. Masters essay, Northwestern Univ. 1932. 70ff

Griswold, Hattie Tyng
Mathew Arnold. *In* Personal sketches of recent authors. Chicago, McClurg, 1898. p78-95

Guerry, W. A.
Matthew Arnold and the Bible. *In* Matthew Arnold and the spirit of the age, ed. by G. White. New York, Putnam, 1898. p51-61

Gummere, Richard Mott
Matthew Arnold. Quar R 241:142-55 Ja '24

Gunsaulus, Frank W.
Matthew Arnold. *In* The higher ministries of recent English poetry. New York, Revell [c 1907] p53-106

Gurney, Ephraim Whitman
Matthew Arnold's essays. "Essays in criticism by Matthew Arnold." np[18-?] Typed ms in Harvard college Library. 17ff

Gutbier, Elisabeth
Psychologisch-ästhetische studien zu Tristandichtungen der neueren englischen literatur. Erlangen, Döres, 1932. 95p Diss. Erlangen

Guthrie, William Norman
Matthew Arnold. *In* Modern poet prophets. . . Cincinnati, Clarke, 1897. p123-45

Obermann and Matthew Arnold. Sewanee R 2:33-55 N '93

"Obermann" of Senancour and Matthew Arnold. . . *In* Modern poet prophets. . . Cincinnati, Clarke, 1897. p61-89

Hadley, Minnie E.
Matthew Arnold: a man of letters. Educa 23:47-9 S '02

Hall, F. H.
Arnold's "Signal elm." T L S N 16 '17 p556

Hall, Fred J.
"The scholar gipsy." T L S S 27 '23 p636 [See Ellerton, F. G.; Bell, C. C.]

Hall, Walter Phelps
The three Arnolds and their Bible. *In* Essays in intellectual history, dedicated to James Harvey Robinson. New York, Harper, 1929. p71-88

Halperin, Maurice
La passion restreinte le "Tristram and Iseult" de Matthew Arnold. *In* Le roman de Tristan et Iseut dans la littérature anglo-américaine au XIXᵉ et au XXᵉ siècles. Paris, Jouve, 1931. Diss. Paris. p20-30

Hamilton, Walter
Parodies of the works of English and American authors. . . London, Reeves and Turner, 1885. vol II p236-8

Handy, Sydney Speiden
Educational theories of Matthew Arnold. Masters essay, Columbia univ. 1919

Harding, Edward
Arnold's place in literature. Critic (NY) 12:201-2 Ap 28 '88

Matthew Arnold: paralipomena. Critic (NY) 13:161-2 O 6 '88

Harper, George McLean
Matthew Arnold and the zeitgeist. Va Q R 2:415-31 Jl '26. *Also in* Spirit of delight. London, Benn, 1928. p92-116 (Rev in T L S Ja 3 '28 p9)

Harris, Alan
Matthew Arnold: the unknown years. 19th Cent 113:498-509 Ap '33

Harris, Ambia Harris
Matthew Arnold's visit to America in 1883. Masters essay, Columbia univ. 1924

Harris, Frank
Contemporary portraits. New York, Brentano [c 1920] 1st ser p240-56; *same.* Acad 80:106-7 Ja 28 '11

Harrison, Frederic
Culture: a dialogue. *In* The choice of books. . . New York, Macmillan, 1888. p97-118; *same.* Fortn 8:603-14 N '67

Matthew Arnold. 19th Cent 39:433-49 Mr '96; *same.* Liv Age 209:362-72 My 9 '96

Matthew Arnold. *In* Tennyson, Ruskin, Mill. . . New York, Macmillan, 1900. p104-25
(Rev in Nation (NY) 70:483-4 Je 21 '00; R. Garnett in Bookm (Lond) 17:149 F '00)

Hart, Ella Bond
The critical essays of Matthew Arnold. Masters essay, Indiana Univ. 1912

Hart, Nina
The educational theories of Matthew Arnold. Masters essay, Columbia univ. 1906

Harvey, Charles H.
Matthew Arnold; a critic of the Victorian period. . . London, Clarke [1931] 256p (Rev in T L S Ja 14 '32 p24)

Matthew Arnold and his recent critics. Westm 159:421-8 Ap '03

Hayakawa, Samuel Ichiyé
The literary criticism of Matthew Arnold. Masters essay, McGill Univ. 1928. 132ff

Haynes, Edmund Sidney Pollock
Oxford and Cambridge; a study in types: Matthew Arnold and Leslie Stephen. Putnam 1:187-91 N '06

Hearn, Lafcadio
Matthew Arnold. *In* A history of English literature, in a series of lectures. Tokyo, Hokuseido press, 1927. vol II p697-9, 841-9

Matthew Arnold as poet. *In* Appreciations of poetry. . . New York, Dodd, Mead, 1916. p298-333

Pessimists. *In* Interpretations of literature. . . New York, Dodd, Mead, 1915. vol I p341-6

Hecker, I. T.
Two prophets of this age. [Emerson and Arnold] Cath World 47:684-93 Ag '88

Hellman, George S.
American and English poets. Dial 29:297-8 N 1 '00

Henderson, J. Scot
What Mr. Arnold's analysis involves. Spec 46:337-8 Mr 15 '73

Henley, William Ernest
Matthew Arnold. *In* Views and reviews. London, Nutt, 1890. p83-91

Hennessy, W. G.
Matthew Arnold as poet-philosopher. Masters essay, Boston Univ. 1924

Herford, Charles Harry
Matthew Arnold as a prophet. Liv Age 316:353-5 F 10 '23; *same.* Manchester Guardian D 23 '22

Hewlett, Henry G.
The poems of Mr. Matthew Arnold. Contemp 24:539-67 S '74

Higginson, T. W.
An American temperament. Ind 40:513 Ap 26 '88
Emerson and Arnold. Woman's Journal 14:1 D 15 '83

Hille, Hermann
Die kulturgedanken Matthew Arnolds und ihre verwirklichung in der pädagogik. Halle-Saale, Jung, 1928. 86p bibl p[81]-6 Thesis, Halle-Wittenberg

Hinchman, Walter S. and Gummere, Francis B.
Matthew Arnold. *In* Lives of great English writers from Chaucer to Browning. Boston, Houghton Mifflin, 1908. p461-71

Hinckley, Henry Barrett
Some of Arnold's qualities as a critic. Dial 24:68-9 F 1 '98

Hobohm, J.
Matthew Arnold als naturschilderer. . . Halle, 1913. 93p bibl p95 Diss. Freiburg

Hodges, Jesse Wilson
Matthew Arnold as a religious teacher. Masters essay, Univ. of Texas, 1920. 101ff

Hodgkins, Louise Manning
Arnold. *In* A guide to the study of nineteenth century authors. Boston, Heath, 1898. p96-101

Hodgson, Geraldine E.
Criticism at a venture. London, Macdonald [1919] p59-60

Hofmann, Dorothy Ethel
The religion of Matthew Arnold. Masters essay, Boston Univ. 1932

Houghton, Louise Seymour
Matthew Arnold and orthodoxy. New World 6:629-38 D '97

Houghton, Ralph Edward Cunliffe
The influence of the classics on the poetry of Matthew Arnold. . . Oxford, Blackwell, 1923. 3-[39]p (Noted in T L S O 18 '23 p693)
Letter of Matthew Arnold. T L S My 19 '32 p368

Houston, Percy Hazen
Matthew Arnold. *In* Main currents of English literature. New York, Crofts, 1934. new ed. completely rev. p337-44, 385-8
The modernism of Arnold. Sewanee R 35:187-97 Ap-Je '27

Hoyt, Arthur S.
Matthew Arnold, the poet of the questioning spirit. *In* The spiritual message of modern English poetry. New York, Macmillan, 1924. p163-82

Hsin-Hai, Chang. *See* Chang, Hsin-Hai

Hudson, William Henry
Matthew Arnold. *In* Studies in interpretation. . . New York, Putnam, 1896. p153-221

Hunt, Everett L.
Matthew Arnold: the critic as rhetorician. Quarterly Journal of Speech 20:483-507 '34

Hunt, Theodore W.
Matthew Arnold as an English writer. New Princeton Review 6:355-69 N '88
Matthew Arnold's English style. *In* Studies in literature and style. New York, Armstrong, 1891. p217-45
The poetry of Matthew Arnold. Meth R 14:757-68 '98
The poetry of Matthew Arnold. *In* English literary miscellany. Oberlin, Ohio, Bibliotheca Sacra co. 1914. ser II p215-35

Hunt, Wray W.
Matthew Arnold. Spec 70:452 Ap 8 '93

Hutton, Richard Holt
Brief literary criticisms. Selected from the "Spectator" and ed. by his niece, Elizabeth M. Roscoe. (Eversley ser) London, Macmillan, 1906. 428p
Mr. Arnold's sublimated Bible [and] Matthew Arnold as critic. *In* Criticism on contemporary thought and thinkers. London, Macmillan, 1894. vol I p214-20, 221-6
The poetry of Matthew Arnold. *In* Essays in literary criticism. Philadelphia, Coates [pref 1876] p301-55
The two great Oxford thinkers, Cardinal Newman and Matthew Arnold. *In* Essays on some of the modern guides of English thought in matters of faith. London, Macmillan, 1887. p99-144; *same.* Contemp 49:327-54, 513-34 Mr, Ap '86; *same.* Liv Age 169:95-111, 259-72 Ap 10, My 1 '86; *same.* Ecl M 106:739-53 Je '86

Hyde, A. B.
Matthew Arnold. Meth R 75:867-77 N '93

Ingram, Florence L.
Matthew Arnold, the educator. Educa 44:197-207 D '23

Innes, Arthur Donald
Seers and singers: a study of five English poets. London, Innes, 1893. xiii,222p (Rev in Literary World (Lond) ns 48:315 O 27 '93; Speaker 8:443 O 21 '93)

An **intellectual** angel. Spec 39:125-6 F 3 '66

Inwright, Hulda May
Some theories of higher education in Arnold, Mill, and Newman. Masters essay, Columbia univ. 1918

Is Matthew Arnold's poetry consoling? Spec 69:94-5 Jl 16 '92

Jack, Adolphus Alfred
Arnold. . . *In* Poetry and prose. . . New York, Dutton, 1912. p177-200

Jacobs, Joseph
Matthew Arnold. *In* George Eliot, Matthew Arnold, Browning, Newman; essays and reviews from the "Athenaeum." London, Nutt, 1891. p75-94
(Rev in Lit W 22:269-70 Ag 15 '91)
Matthew Arnold. *In* Literary studies. London, Nutt, 1895. 2d ed p77-94

James, Henry
Matthew Arnold. Engl Illus 1:241-6 Ja '84
Matthew Arnold's essays. *In* Views and reviews. . . Boston, Ball, 1908. p81-97

Japp, Alexander Hay
Matthew Arnold as lecturer and stylist. British & Foreign Evangelical Review 35:269-85 Ap '86

Jarratt, F.
Matthew Arnold on pigeons. Notes & Q 10th ser 10:198 S 5 '08

Joel, Karl
Die überwindung des 19. jahrhunderts im denken der gegenwart. Kantstudien 32:475-518 '27

Johnson, Lionel Pigot
Laleham; poem. Century Guild Hobby Horse no 18:56-7 Ap '90
Matthew Arnold. *In* Post liminium. . . New York, Kennerley, 1912. p288-98
[Poetry of Arnold] Acad 39:31-2 Ja 10 '91

Johnson, W. H.
The "passing" of Matthew Arnold. Dial 27:351-3 N 16 '99

Johnson, W. Knox
[Parallel to Quinet's "Church of Brou"] Ath 1:499 Ap 18 '03

Jones, William Lewis
Matthew Arnold. *In* C H E L vol XIII p95-114

Jottings on Arnold. Acad 60:555-6 Je 29 '01

Kaar, Margaret
Intuitive perception in the philosophy of Matthew Arnold and William James. Masters essay, Univ. of Utah, 1934. 57ff

Kane, Vincent Joseph
The political and economic opinions of Matthew Arnold. Masters essay, Columbia univ. 1930

Katscher, Leopold
Der dichter des "Empedokles auf dem Aetna." Nord und Süd 118:353-64 S '06

Keary, C. F.
Shakespeare's popularity. T L S Je 7 '17 p273

Keating, J. F.
Mr. Arnold as a teacher. Spec 49:1475 N 25 '76

Keeney, Joseph
A study of Matthew Arnold's conception of poetry. Diss. Univ. of California, 1932. xxii,260ff

Kellner, Leon
Die englische literatur der neuesten zeit. Leipzig, Tauchnitz, 1921. p225-30

Die englische literatur im zeitalter der königin Viktoria. Leipzig, Tauchnitz, 1909. p377-84

Kelman, John
Carlyle and Arnold. *In* Prophets of yesterday and their message for to-day. Cambridge, Mass. Harvard univ. press, 1924. p38-71
(Rev in Harvard Graduates' Magazine 32:696-7 Je '24)
Matthew Arnold. *In* Prophets of yesterday and their message for to-day. Cambridge, Mass. Harvard univ. press, 1924. p103-36

Kelso, Alexander P.
Matthew Arnold on continental life and literature. Oxford, Blackwell, 1914. [i-iii] 52p
(Rev in Spec 112:488-9 Mr 21 '14)

Kennedy, Walter
Mr. Arnold's want of tact. Critic (NY) 5:19 Jl 12 '84

Kent, Armine T.
A note on the poems of Matthew Arnold. Time (London) 2d ser 5:1-13 Ja '87

Keogh, Andrew
Letters of Matthew Arnold. Yale Univ. Library Gazette 6:14 '32

Ker, William Paton
Matthew Arnold. *In* The art of poetry... Oxford, Clarendon press, 1923. p139-60

Kerlin, Robert Thomas
Matthew Arnold: "A healing and reconciling influence"? Arena 32:362-91 O '04

King, Wilfrid
Matthew Arnold as a poet. Shanghai, Kelly and Walsh, 1934. 57p

Kingsley, Maud Elma
Outline studies of literature. Sohrab and Rustum [study no 46] Boston, Palmer, 1930. 32p

Kingsmill, Hugh [pseud]
see Lunn, Hugh Kingsmill

Knickerbocker, William Skinkle
Arnoldism. *In* Creative Oxford. . . Syracuse, New York, Univ. press [1925] p77-93
Culture factors in the early life of Matthew Arnold. Masters essay, Columbia univ. 1918
Matthew Arnold. *In* Creative Oxford. . . Syracuse, New York, Univ. press [1925] p128-49
Matthew Arnold at Oxford: the natural history of a father and son. Sewanee R 35:399-418 O-D '27
Matthew Arnold's theory of poetry. Sewanee R 33:440-50 O '25
Semaphore; Arnold and Clough. Sewanee R 41:152-74 Ap '33

Knight, G. T.
The theology of Matthew Arnold. Universalist Quarterly 47:339-54 Jl '90

Knight, William [Angus]
Matthew Arnold. *In* Retrospects. London, Smith, Elder, 1904. ser I p193-204

Knight, William—*Continued*
Personality and the infinite. Contemp 28:785-812 O '76

Koszul, André
Une lettre inédite de Matthew Arnold. R Litt Comp 3:652-4 O-D '23

Kronenberger, Louis
Re-reading Matthew Arnold. Sat R Lit 11:105-6 S 15 '34

Kuhns, Oscar
Matthew Arnold and Rossetti. *In* Dante and the English poets from Chaucer to Tennyson. New York, Holt, 1904. p198-202

Kynnersley, E. M. Sneyd
Arnold and the monitorial system. T L S O 4 '23 p652

Lang, Andrew
At the sign of the ship. Longman's Magazine 12:217-22 Je '88
Matthew Arnold. Cent 1:849-64 Ap '82
[Note on Arnold's letters] Cosmopolitan 20:673 Ap '96

Lassen, Margarete
Matthew Arnolds verhältnis zu den deutschen und zur deutschen literatur. Diss. Freiburg i. B. 1923. 101p

Laureates and poets. Nation (NY) 62: 26-7 Ja 9 '96

Lawrence, E. P.
An apostle's progress: Matthew Arnold in America. Philol Q 10:62-79 Ja '31

Lazarus, Emma
Critic and poet. Critic (NY) 4:4 Ja 5 '84
Critic and poet; poem. Critic (NY) ns 1:198 Ap 26 '84

Leach, Henry Goddard
The forsaken merman. *In* Essays in memory of Barrett Wendell, by his assistants. Cambridge, Mass. Harvard univ. press, 1926. p273-82

Leaves from a note-book. Of a discourse in Westminster Abbey. Macmil 65:152-7 D '91

LeGallienne, Richard
Matthew Arnold escapes the guillotine. Literary Digest International Book Review 2:439-40, 492-4 My '24
Matthew Arnold; poem. Acad 33:273 Ap 21 '88; *same.* Liv Age 177:514 Je 2 '88

Legard, A. G.
Matthew Arnold. The man and his work. Cornhill 47:252-6 S '19

Leiper, H. S.
Matthew Arnold's theory of culture. Kent prize, Amherst college, 1913. Typed ms in Amherst college library. 37ff

Leo, Brother
Matthew Arnold, poet and essayist. Cath World 116:320-30 D '22

Leonard, Chilson Hathway
Matthew Arnold. Sat R Lit 7:978 Jl 18 '31

Matthew Arnold in America. Doctor's essay, Yale univ. 1932
Two notes on Arnold. Mod Lang N 46: 119 F '31

Lerch, Charles H.
The spiritual side of Matthew Arnold. Reformed Church Review 4th ser 10: 74-84 Ja '06

Levy, Hermann
Matthew Arnold und das volkscharakterologische erkenntnis. Zeitschrift für völkerpsychologie und soziologie 5:303-25 S '29

Lewin, Walter
[Arnold on Emerson] Acad 26:101-2 Ag 16 '84

Lewis, Edward Dewart
The position of Matthew Arnold's theology in the development of theological thought in England. Masters essay, Univ. of Washington, 1924. 84ff

Lewis, Mannie R.
The leading influences of Arnold's poetry. Masters essay, Columbia univ. 1916

Lewisohn, Ludwig
A study of Matthew Arnold. Sewanee R 9:442-56 O '01; Sewanee R 10:143-59, 302-19 Ap-Jl '02

Link, Seymour G.
Arnold and America. Masters essay, New York Univ. 1930. 146ff

The **literary** pages of the "Spectator." Spec 141:646 N 3 '28

Littell, Philip
Matthew Arnold. *In* Books and things. New York, Harcourt, Brace and Howe, 1919. p180-6; *also in* New Repub 1:26 Ja 2 '15

Little, Edith Ann
Conflicting influences in Matthew Arnold's poetry. Masters essay, Univ. of Nebraska, 1932. 173ff

Lockwood, Ferris
Matthew Arnold's landscapes. No Am 147:473-4 O '88

Lovett, Robert Morss
Matthew Arnold today. Forum 71:666-9 My '24

Lucas, Frank Laurence
Arnold. *In* Eight Victorian poets. Cambridge, England, Univ. press, 1930. p39-54
(Rev in T L S N 13 '30 p936)

Lund, Thomas William May
Matthew Arnold. The message and meaning of a life. Liverpool, E. Howell, 1888. 28p

[Lunn, Hugh Kingsmill]
Matthew Arnold, by Hugh Kingsmill [pseud] New York, MacVeagh, Dial press, 1928. vi, 317p
(Rev in T L S D 13 '28 p978; New Statesm (Literary supplement) 32:v-vi N 3 '28; H. F. Lowry in Sat R Lit 5:368 N 17 '28; S. Strahan in Common-

weal 9:408 F 6 '29; author's note in
T L S Ja 3 '29 p12; R. E. Roberts
in Bookm (Lond) 75:182-3 D '28; W. A.
Gerhardi in Fortn 131:347-54 Mr '29)

Lyall (Sir) Alfred
Studies in literature and history. London, Murray, 1915. p57-66

Lynd, Robert
Keats. The Matthew Arnold view. *In* Old and new masters. London, Unwin, 1919. p64-9

Lyttleton, Arthur Temple
The poetry of doubt. Arnold and Clough. *In* Modern poets of faith, doubt, and other essays. London, Murray, 1904. p73-105

Mabie, Hamilton W.
Matthew Arnold. Christian Union 28: 358-9 N 1 '83

Macarthur, Henry
Matthew Arnold. *In* Realism and romance, and other essays. Edinburgh, Hunter, 1897. p139-64

McCall, Samuel
English views of America. International Review 13:426-36 N '82

McCallum, James Dow
The apostle of culture meets America. New England Quarterly 2:357-81 Jl '29

McCormick, Mary Ellen
Arnold and Clough: a comparative study of religious thought. Masters essay, Cornell Univ. 1929. 57ff

McDonough, John B.
The classical element in the poetry and literary criticism of Matthew Arnold. Masters essay, New York Univ. 1933. 48ff

McGill, Anna Blanche
The Arnolds. Book B 22:373-80, 459-66 Je, Jl '01

McInnis, M. A.
Arnold's theory of culture. Masters essay, Boston Univ. 1926

Mackie, Alexander
Nature knowledge in modern poetry, being chapters on Tennyson, Wordsworth, Matthew Arnold, and Lowell as exponents of nature-study. . . London, Longmans, Green, 1906. 140p

McLaughlin, Leo
The nature poetry of Matthew Arnold. Masters essay, Columbia univ. 1903

Magnus, Laurie
Introduction. *In* Dramas and prize poems. (Muses library) London, Routledge, 1906. pi-xxxii

Introduction. *In* Poems (prior to 1864) (Muses library) London, Routledge [1906] pi-xxviii

Tübingen. A footnote. Cornhill 73:735-8 D '32

Maischhofer, Alfons
Matthew Arnold als kritiker der französischen literatur. Diss. Freiburg i. B. 1922. 102p

Malleson, J. P.
Matthew Arnold and "Anglo-Saxon contagion." Notes Q 12th ser 5:38 F '19

The most eloquent voice of the nineteenth century. Spec 121:456 O 26 '18

Mallock, William Hurrell
The new republic. London, Chatto & Windus, 1877. vol I p94-7
[Parody of Arnold's metres]

Marshall, Edward
Robert Browning and the parodists. Notes & Q 7th ser 10:274 O 4 '90

Martin, Lorraince Marie
A comparison of the nature poetry of Wordsworth and Arnold. Masters essay, Univ. of California, 1922. 131ff

Marvin, Mary Benham
Matthew Arnold's poems as a criticism of the life of his time. Masters essay, Columbia univ. 1930

Matthew Arnold. Acad 68:191-2 Mr 4 '05; Beilage zu allgemeinen Zeitung '96; Bookn 25:417-20 F '07; Ecl M 86:760-1 Je '76; Ecl M 110:816-22 Je '88; Every Sat 12:351-5 Mr 30 '72; Journal of Education My 1 '88 p225-6, 241-2; Lit W 14:366 N 3 '83; Lit W 19:136 Ap 28 '88; Liv Age 177:433-6 My 19 '88; Liv Age 255:305-10 N 2 '07; Nation (NY) 46: 315-16 Ap 19 '88; Spec 61:538-40 Ap 21 '88; T L S D 21 '22 p849-50; T. P's Weekly 20:624 N 8 '12; University Magazine 1:14-32 Ja '78; Harper W 27:675 O 27 '83; Speaker 2:320-2 S 20 '90; Parodies 2:236-8 O '85; Parodies 6:200-2 Jl '89; Cent 23:849-64 Ap '82

Matthew Arnold. *In* Celebrities of the century. London, Cassell, 1887. p62-3

Matthew Arnold. *In* The Library of literary criticism of English and American authors. . . ed. by Charles Wells Moulton. . . Buffalo, New York, Moulton publishing company, 1904-05 vol VII p627-49

Matthew Arnold. *In* Men of the time: a dictionary of contemporaries. . . London, Routledge, 1879. 10th ed p44-5

Matthew Arnold. *In* Proceedings of the American academy of arts and sciences. Boston, Univ. press, Wilson, 1888. ns vol XV p349-53

Matthew Arnold [and his biographers] Acad 68:191-2 Mr 4 '05

Matthew Arnold and his critics. Acad 63: 476 N 1 '02

Matthew Arnold and insularity. Edin R 200:131-51 Jl '04; *same*. Ecl M 143:599-613 N '04; Liv Age 242:769-83 S 24 '04

Matthew Arnold and the theatre. T L S Ag 15 '02 p245-6

Matthew Arnold as a critic. Scottish Art Review 1:22-4 Je '88

Matthew Arnold as critic. Spec 61:1670-1 D 1 '88; Westm 80:469

Matthew Arnold as a lecturer. Christian Union 28:384-5 N 8 '83

Matthew Arnold as a poet. Yale Literary Messenger 43:303-8 Ap '78

Matthew Arnold; December 24, 1822-December 24, 1922. Nation (NY) 115:708 D 27 '22

Matthew Arnold, 1822-1888. Bookn 24:863-4 Ag '06

Matthew Arnold: his death. Notes & Q 150:268-9 Ap 10 '26

Matthew Arnold in the United States. Spec 56:1342-3 O 20 '83; *same.* Ecl M 101:845-7 D '83

The Matthew Arnold myth. Lit W 15:132-3 Ap 19 '84

Matthew Arnold. Obituary notice, Tuesday, April 17, 1888. *In* Eminent persons. Biographies reprinted from *The Times.* London, Macmillan, 1893. vol IV p87-96

[Matthew Arnold on culture and anarchy] Quar R 174:338-41 Ap '92

Matthew Arnold on free schools. Critic (NY) 9:116-17 S 4 '86

Matthew Arnold on nineteenth-century eloquence. Notes & Q 11th ser 2:438 N 26 '10

Matthew Arnold, poet and essayist. Brit Q 42:243-69 O 2 '65

Matthew Arnold: proving a negative. Notes & Q 12th ser 5:83 Mr '19

Matthew Arnold: reference. Notes & Q 12th ser 10:119 F 11 '22

Matthew Arnold [six parodies] Parodies 2:236-8 O '85 (from The World Ag 20 '79 p16-17 and S 24 '79 p16)

Matthew Arnold: "Thyestean banquet." Notes & Q 156:316 My 4 '29

Matthew Arnold twenty years after. Nation (NY) 86:416-17 My 7 '08

Matthew Arnold vs. Thomas Carlyle. Spec 41:788-90 Jl 4 '68; *same.* Liv Age 98:629-32 S 5 '68

Matthew Arnold [with a caricature by W. J. Welch] Once a Week 10:320-3 O 12 '72

Matthew Arnold [with portrait] Every Sat 9:798, 808 D 10 '70

Matthew Arnold's Alpine poetry. Canadian Alpine Journal 2 no 2:178-82 '10

Matthew Arnold's charm. Spec 75:814-15 D 7 '95

Matthew Arnold's "Church of Brou." Notes & Q 10th ser 6:196 S 8 '06

Matthew Arnold's debt to the Jews. Lit Digest 76:33 Ja 20 '23

Matthew Arnold's faith. Lit W 14:415 D 1 '83

Matthew Arnold's influence. American (Philadelphia) 7:37-8 O 27 '83

Matthew Arnold's last criticism. And R 9:512-18 My '88

Matthew Arnold's new Christian catechism. Spec 58:447-8 Ap 4 '85

Matthew Arnold's "Note-Book." Christian Century 40:7-8 Ja 4 '23

Matthew Arnold's poetry. Sat R 81:270-2 Mr 14 '96; Temple 84:106-11 S '88

Matthew Arnold's popularity. Spec 70:382-3 Mr 25 '93

Matthew Arnold's prose style. Dial 1:266 Ap '81

Matthew Arnold's reading. Out 91:144-5 Ja 23 '09

Matthew Arnold's visit. Lit W 14:446 D 15 '83

Matthew Arnold's writings. Torch 1:135-9 Je '88

Matthews, (James) Brander
Introduction. *In* Letters of an old playgoer. (Publications of the dramatic museum of Columbia University) New York, 1919. 54p

Introductory note [to Arnold's essay on George Sand and Balzac] Lamp 26:464-5 Jl '03

Matthew Arnold and the drama. Bookm (NY) 44:1-8 S '16

Matthew Arnold and the theatre. *In* The principles of playmaking. . . New York, Scribner, 1919. p265-85

Meissner, Paul
Pessimistische strömungen im englischen geistesleben des 19. jahrhunderts. Engl Stud 64:443 '29

Mendacious personal gossip. Nation (NY) 38:404-5 My 8 '84

Meredith, G. E.
Source of Arnold's power. Church Review 52:65-70 Jl '88

Merivale, Herman
Matthew Arnold; poem. Spec 61:543 Ap 21 '88; *same.* Liv Age 177:386 My 19 '88

Merriam, George S.
Some aspects of Matthew Arnold's poetry. Scribner's Monthly 18:281-90 Je '79

Mihills, Mildred
Studies in the poetry of Matthew Arnold. Masters essay, Univ. of Texas, 1915. 167ff

Mikell, H. J.
Arnold's character as revealed in his criticism. *In* Matthew Arnold and the spirit of the age, ed. by G. White. New York, Putnam, 1898. p93-103

Milford, H. S.
"The Scholar-gypsy." T L S O 4 '23 p652

Miller, Dickinson Sergeant
Matthew Arnold on the occasion of his centenary. New Repub 33:113-16 D 27 '22

Matthew Arnold on the "powers" of life. Int J Ethics 16:352-8 Ap '06

Minto, W.
Matthew Arnold's meliorism. Art Review 1:53-8 F '90

Mr. Arnold and the Cambridge dignitaries. Spec 46:276 Mr 1 '73

Mr. **Arnold** and the literary class. Critic (NY) 1:113 Mr 8 '84

Mr. **Arnold** as a moral and religious teacher. Spec 49:1402-3 N 11 '76

Mr. **Arnold** on America. American (Philadelphia) 7:198-9 Ja 5 '84

Mr. **Arnold** on American civilization. Ind 40:491-2 Ap 19 '88

Mr. **Arnold** on God. Spec 44:825-7 Jl 8 '71

Mr. **Arnold** on lucidity. Sat R 54:464-5 O 7 '82

Mr. **Arnold** on the enemies of culture. Spec 40:746-8 Jl 6 '67

Mr. **Arnold** on the middle classes. Sat R 21:161-3 F 10 '66

Mr. **Arnold** on the state. Spec 41:5-7 Ja 4 '68

Mr. **Arnold's** discomfort. Nation (NY) 46: 294-5 Ap 12 '88

Mr. **Arnold's** health in America. Critic (NY) 12:259 My 26 '88

Mr. **Arnold's** right to criticise. Critic (NY) 12:194 Ap 21 '88

Mr. **Arnold's** sublimated Bible. Spec 47: 1256-8 O 10 '74

Mr. **Arnold's** visit. Lit W 14:446 D 15 '83

Mr. **Matthew Arnold.** Ath 1:500-1 Ap 21 '88; Ecl M 73:551-9 N '69; Great Thoughts 9:95-9 F 25 '88; Pall Mall Gazette Ap 16 '88 p1, 8-9; Sat R 65:459-60 Ap 21 '88; Temple 28:35-48 D '69; Vanity Fair 6:154-5 N 11 '71

Mr. **Matthew Arnold** and the dissenters. Congregationalist 2:427-34 Jl '73

Mr. **Matthew Arnold** in Philadelphia. Lit W 15:14 Ja 12 '84

Mr. **Matthew Arnold** on culture. Sat R 24: 78-9 Jl 20 '67

Mr. **Matthew Arnold** on equality. Spec 51: 276-7 Mr 2 '78

Mr. **Matthew Arnold** on poetry and religion. Spec 53:649-51 My 22 '80

Mr. **Matthew Arnold** on the aristocratic creed. Spec 35:1438-9 D 27 '62

Mr. **Matthew Arnold** on the modern element in literature. Spec 42:222-3 F 20 '69

Mr. **Matthew Arnold** on the Pauline theology. A criticism. London, Nisbet, 1870. 8p [Reprinted from Edinburgh Daily Review]

Mr. **Matthew Arnold** on the situation. Sat R 63:10 Ja 1 '87

Mr. **Matthew Arnold's** new discovery. Spec 55:1281-2 O 7 '82

Mr. **Matthew Arnold's** retirement. Spec 59: 1519-20 N 18 '86; *same.* Liv Age 171: 758-60 D 18 '86

Mr. **Matthew Arnold's** visit. Nation (NY) 37:366-7 N 1 '83

Modern culture. Quar R 137:389-415 O '74

The **modern** poetry of doubt. Spec 43: 166-7 F 5 '70; *same.* New Eclectic Magazine 6:490-4 Ap '70

Moffatt, James
Matthew Arnold. Homiletic Review 85: 11-14 Ja '23

Moggridge, M. W.
Idyllic poetry. Macmil 38:108-9 Je '78

Monroe, Harriet
Matthew Arnold. *In* Poets and their art. New York, Macmillan, 1926. p175-8

Matthew Arnold's centenary. Poetry 21: 206-10 Ja '23

Montague, Charles Edward
Matthew Arnold. Lond Merc 19:278-84 Ja '29

Montgomery, Lois Elizabeth
Matthew Arnold and the Christian churches. Masters essay, Cornell Univ. 1920. 124ff

Moore, Charles Leonard
Arnold and Lowell. Dial 45:157-9 S 16 '08

The future of poetry. Forum 14:768-77 F '93

Moore, John Robert
The mood of pessimism in nature poetry; Bowles, Coleridge, and Arnold. Sewanee R 30:454-61 O '22

Moore, T. Sturge
A literary causerie; new ideas for old. Acad 70:286 Mr 24 '06

Matthew Arnold. Bookm (Lond) 63:136-9 D '22

Matthew Arnold's centenary. T L S D 28 '22 p873

More, Paul Elmer
Criticism. *In* Shelburne essays. New York, Putnam, 1910. 7th ser p213-44

Moreno, H. W. B.
"Sohrab and Rustum". . . dramatised by H. W. B. Moreno [Matthew Arnold's poem slightly abridged and adapted] Calcutta, Moreno, 1919. 13p

Morgan, Anna May
Matthew Arnold's use of figures of speech in Sohrab and Rustum and other poems. Masters essay, Louisiana State Univ. 1933. 57ff

Morley, Christopher Darlington
Matthew Arnold and exodontia. *In* The powder of sympathy. Garden City, New York, Doubleday, Page, 1923. p99-108

Morley, John
Recollections. New York, Macmillan, 1917. vol I p125-32

Morse, James Herbert
Matthew Arnold. Critic (NY) 3:437-8 N 3 '83

Morton, Edward Payson
The technique of English non-dramatic blank verse. Chicago, Donnelley, 1910. p118-19 Diss. Univ. of Chicago

"The **most** eloquent voice of our century." Notes & Q 11th ser 11:230 Mr 20 '15; Notes & Q 12th ser 12:414 My 26 '33

Mott, Lewis Freeman
Renan and Matthew Arnold. Mod Lang N 33:65-73 F '18

Motter, T. H. Vail
A new Arnold letter and an old Swinburne quarrel. T L S Ag 31 '33 p576

Moulton, Charles Wells, ed.
Matthew Arnold. *In* The library of literary criticism of English and American authors. New York, Malkan, 1910. vol VII p627-49

Mowbray, Jay Paul [pseud]
see Wheeler, Andrew Carpenter

Moynihan, Florence
Arnold the humanist. Cath World 116: 330-7 D '22

Murray, Gilbert
Poesis and mimesis. *In* Tradition and progress. Boston, Houghton Mifflin, 1922. p110-12

Murray, Ward Baxter
The influence of Epictetus and Marcus Aurelius upon the poetry of Matthew Arnold. Masters essay, Univ. of Utah, 1934. 100ff

Murry, John Middleton
Matthew Arnold, the poet. *In* Discoveries: essays in literary criticism. London, Collins, 1924. p201-12

Mustard, Wilfred Pirt
Homeric echoes in Matthew Arnold's "Balder dead." *In* Studies in honor of Basil L. Gildersleeve. Baltimore, Johns Hopkins press, 1902. p19-28

Myers, Frederick W. H.
Matthew Arnold. Fortn 49:719-28 My '88; *same.* Liv Age 177:545-50 Je 2 '88; *same.* Ecl M, 111:55-61 Jl '88

Nadal, Ehrman Syme
Matthew Arnold. Critic (NY) 2:135-6 My 20 '82

Matthew Arnold's poetry. Dark Blue 1: 711-16 Ag '71

Mr. Matthew Arnold. *In* Essays at home and elsewhere. London, Macmillan, 1882. p122-54

Nencioni, Enrico
Necrologia. Nuova Antol 99:345 My '88

Saggi critici di letteratura inglese. Firenze, 1897. p358-60

Nevinson, Henry Woodd
Sweetness and light. *In* Books and personalities. London, Lane, 1905. p41-8

Newbolt, Henry
Introduction. *In* Poems of Matthew Arnold. . . London, Nelson [1923] p i-xiv

Newman, Francis W.
Homeric translation in theory and practice. A reply to Matthew Arnold, Esq. London, Williams & Norgate, 1861. 104p

Newman, Louis I. and Richard B. Morris
The Jewish interests of Matthew Arnold. American Hebrew 112:185, 189, 191 D 22 '22

Newman and Matthew Arnold. T L S Mr 31 '21 p211

Newsam, W. C.
Matthew Arnold. Popular Poets of the Period no 8:225-8 Mr '89

[Nichols, John]
Merope. *In* Undergraduate papers. Oxford, 1858. p166-79

Nicolson, Marjorie
The real Scholar gipsy. Yale R ns 18: 347-63 D '28

Nitchie, Elizabeth
Vergil and the English poets. New York, Columbia univ. press, 1919. p216-17 Diss. Columbia univ.

Noble, Mildred J.
Science in the work of Matthew Arnold. Masters essay, Mt. Holyoke college, 1924. Typed ms. 85ff bibl 4ff

Nordby, Conrad Hjalmar
The influence of Old Norse literature upon English literature. (Columbia univ. Germanic studies vol I no III) New York, Columbia univ. press, 1901. p30-2

Norgate, G. Le Grys
Some aspects of Matthew Arnold. Temple 109:540-6 D '96

[Norton, Charles Eliot]
Matthew Arnold. *In* American Academy of Arts and Sciences. Proceedings. New series XV, whole series XX 111: 349-53 '88 [The same separated: Boston, Wilson, 1888. 5p]

Norton, Grace
Arnold's "Church of Brou." Nation (NY) 88:136-7 F 11 '09

[Note on Arnold] Nation (NY) 4:389 My 16 '67

[Note on Arnold's ancestry] Notes & Q 9th ser 7:77 Ja 26 '01

Noyes, Atherton
Matthew Arnold's poetry—an appreciation. (Colorado College publications. Language series) Colorado Springs, Colo. 1916. vol II p275-98

Numbers, imagination, and good government. Cent 58:161-2 My '99

Oakeshott, B. N.
Matthew Arnold as a political and social critic. Westm 149:161-76 F '98

Obituary. Acad 33:273 Ap 21 '88; Nation (NY) 46:315-16 Ap 19 '88; Notes & Q 7th ser 5:346-7 My 5 '88, correction p397 My 19 '88; Spec 61:538-40 Ap 21 '88

O'Brien, Edward J.
Introduction. *In* Essays in criticism third series by Matthew Arnold. Boston, Ball, 1910. p5-32

Oliphant, Margaret
Matthew Arnold, 1822-88. *In* The Victorian age of English literature. New York, Tait [c 1892] vol II p430-6, 570-5

Olivero, Federico
Thyrsis di Matthew Arnold. *In* Nuovi saggi di letteratura inglese. nd p269-73

Omond, T. S.
Arnold and Homer. *In* Essays and studies by members of the English association. Oxford, Clarendon press, 1912. vol III p71-91

On classic ground. Macmil 53:28-36 N '85

Orr, A.
Browning's relations to Matthew Arnold. Ath 2:129 Jl 25 '91

Orrick, James Bentley
Hebraism and Hellenism. [Speech by Matthew Arnold at the Anniversary Banquet of the Royal Academy, May 1, 1875] New Adelphi ns 2:50-6 S '28

Matthew Arnold and America. Lond Merc 20:389-97 Ag '29

Matthew Arnold and Goethe. (Publications of the English Goethe society ns vol IV) London, Moring, 1928. 54p (Rev by F. Bruns in Mod Lang N 43: 570 D '28; T L S Mr 15 '28 p182)

Our English visitor. Oberlin Review 11: 103-4 Ja 19 '84

Our great elegiac poet. Spec 67:638-9 N 7 '91

Packard, Louis R.
Lord Derby and Professor Arnold on Homer. New Englander 25:47-64 Ja '66

Pagan and medieval religious sentiment. Truth 33:10 Ap '29

Palfrey, Cazneau
Matthew Arnold and Israel. Old and New 8:746-51 D '73

Parker, George Lawrence
Matthew Arnold to the preacher. Homiletic Review 79:177-80 Mr '20

Parrott, Thomas Marc
The poetry of Matthew Arnold. *In* Studies of a booklover. New York, Pott, 1904. p1-55

The poetry of Matthew Arnold: a study. Princeton Univ. Bulletin 14:123-47 Je '03

Paton, Lucy Allen
A bit of art from Matthew Arnold. Poet Lore 8:134-9 Mr '96

Patton, William W.
Culture as a substitute for Christianity. New Englander 40:773-91 N '81

Paul, Herbert Woodfield
Matthew Arnold. (English men of letters) New York, Macmillan, 1902. viii, 188p
(Rev in Acad 63:197-8 Ag 23 '02; Ath 2:273-4 Ag 30 '02; Atlan 90:706-8 N '02; W. C. Brownell in Book B 25:318-20 N '02; A. S Henry in Bookn 21:53-5 O '02; W. M. Payne in Dial 33:157 S 16 '02; Ecl M 139:621-6 N '02 M. Todhunter in Engl Stud 33:138-42 '04; W. P. Trent in Forum 34:310-20 O '02; E. Wharton in Lamp 26:51-4 F '03; Liv Age 234:755-60 S 20 '02;

Nation (NY) 75:212 S 11 '02; Out 72: 852-3 D 6 '02; T. H. Warren in Quar R 202:221-49 Ja '05; Sat R 94: 395-6 S 27 '02; T L S Ag 8 '02 p233-4; Public Opinion (NY) 33:282 Ag 28 '02; Literary World (Lond) ns 66:172 S 12 '02; A. T. Quiller-Couch in Speaker ns 7:47-8 O 11 '02)

Matthew Arnold's letters. *In* Men and letters. London, Lane, 1901. p27-47

Payne, William Morton
Matthew Arnold. *In* The greater English poets of the nineteenth century. New York, Holt, 1907. p251-83

Peaslee, Arthur N.
Matthew Arnold on Emerson. Spec 110: 99 Ja 18 '13

Peck, Harvey Whitefield
Matthew Arnold as a poet. Arena 33: 155-61 F '05

Pellew, George
Matthew Arnold [a sonnet] *In* The poems of George Pellew. Ed. with an introduction by W. D. Howells. Boston, Clarke [c1892] p5; *same.* Lit W 24:72 Mr 11 '93

The **pets** of the poets. Spec 100:327 F 29 '08

Pfleiderer, Otto
The development of theology in Germany since Kant and its progress in Great Britain since 1825. London, Swan Sonnenschein, 1890. p330-3, 390-1

Phillips, E. M.
English friendships of Sainte Beuve. Mod H R A 1:17-25 Ap '27

Phillips, T. M.
Nature in modern English poetry. Manch Q 37:270-1 O '18

Pinchbeck, W. H.
Matthew Arnold, Shelley, Keats, and the yew. Notes & Q 10th ser 12:336 O 23 '09

A **plea** for the uncultivated. Nation (NY) 5:215 S 12 '67

The **poet** of elegy. Spec 58:937-8 Jl 18 '85; *same.* Liv Age 166:503-6 Ag 22 '85

Poetic charm. Spec 61:962-3 Jl 14 '88

The **poetic** place of Matthew Arnold. Spec 51:918-19 Jl 20 '78

Poetry and the intuition of immortality. T L S S 14 '16 p433-4

The **poetry** of doubt—Arnold and Clough. Church Q R 6:117-39 Ap '78; *same.* Liv Age 137:410-21 My 18 '78

The **poetry** of Matthew Arnold. Scottish Church 5:138-47 Jl '87

Poisblaud, Georges
La réligion fondée sur le vérifiable, d'après Matthew Arnold. Genève, Froreisen, 1910. 79p Thesis (Theol) Geneva

Pollard, A. F.
Matthew Arnold. *In* Dict N B vol XXII [supp] p71-6

Pond, J. B.
Matthew Arnold. *In* Eccentricities of genius. London, Chatto and Windus, 1901. p323-5

The **popularity** of Matthew Arnold. Spec 76:800-1 Je 6 '96

[**Portraits** of Arnold] *In* Warner, C. D. ed. Library of the world's best literature... Memorial ed. New York, Hill [c 1902] vol II ff p844; Appleton J 3:48 Ja 8 '70; Bookm (Lond) 78:cover and 109 My '30; Engl Illus 1:202 Ja 84; Sat R Lit 1:45 Ag 16 '24; Scrib 4:[536] N '88; University Magazine 1:facing 14 Ja '78; Bookm (NY) 16:116 O '02; Literary Digest International Book Review 2:439 My '24; Vanity Fair 6:154 N 11 '71; Bookm (NY) 5:99 Ap '97; Bookm (NY) 13:370 Je '01; Bookm (NY) 19:545 Ag '04; Universal Review 5:facing 425 N '89; Cent 23:802 Ap '82; Harper M 76:824 My '88; Engl Illus 17:489 Jl '97

Potter, Robert Anderson
Matthew Arnold's interpretations of Christianity in the light of modern thought and need. Masters essay, Vanderbilt Univ. 1932. 148ff

Powell, A. Fryer
Sainte-Beuve and Matthew Arnold. . . An unpublished letter. French Quarterly 3:151-5 '21

Powers, Horatio Nelson
Matthew Arnold. Dial 4:121-3 O '83
Memorial verses; poem. Lit W 19:152 My 12 '88

Powys, John Cowper
Matthew Arnold. *In* Visions and revisions. . . New York, Shaw, 1915. p153-65

Preston, Harriet Waters
Matthew Arnold as a poet. Atlan 53:641-50 My '84

Prideaux, W. F.
Matthew Arnold. Notes & Q 9th ser 4: 249-50 S 23 '99

Provincialism in theology. Spec 45:654-6 My 25 '72

Pughe, Francis Heveningham
Matthew Arnold as critic of his age and social reformer. Engl Stud 32:52-69, 200-17 '03

Quesnel, L.
Un moraliste anglais. Bibliothèque Universelle et Revue Suisse 32:309-34 '86

Quiller-Couch, (Sir) Arthur Thomas
Introduction. *In* The poems of Matthew Arnold, 1840-1867. London, Milford, 1913. pi-xxvii

Matthew Arnold. *In* Studies in literature. Cambridge, Univ. press, 1920. vol I p231-45

Raichlén, Mabel
The spiritual unrest in the early poetry of Matthew Arnold. Masters essay, Columbia univ. 1909

Raleigh, (Sir) Walter Alexander
Matthew Arnold. *In* Some authors. . . Oxford, Clarendon press, 1923. p300-10

Randolph, Henry F.
Pessimism and recent Victorian poetry. New Princeton Review 6:221-8 S '88

Rawnsley, H. D.
On reading the letters of Matthew Arnold; poem. Acad 49:58 Ja 18 '96

Rawnsley, Willingham Franklin
Matthew Arnold. *In* Introduction to the poets. London, Routledge, 1912. p203-10

Read, Minnie
Theories of poetry of Arnold's time and theories of the present time. Masters essay, Univ. of Oklahoma, 1921. 86ff

Reed, Myrom W.
A review of Matthew Arnold's "Literature and dogma." Milwaukee, Wisconsin, Des Forges, Lawrence, 1874. 3-24p

Renan's influence upon Arnold. Sat R 82:398-9 O 10 '96

Rendall, Vernon
Wild flowers in literature. London, Scholartis press, 1934

Rensselaer, M. G. van
Mr. Arnold and American art. Cent 36: 314-16 Je '88

Renwanz, Johannes
Matthew Arnold und Deutschland. Greifswald, Abel, 1927. 103p Diss. Greifswald

Repplier, Agnes
Some aspects of pessimism. Atlan 60: 756-66 D '87

A **representative** triad. Scribner's Monthly 7:470-4 F '74

Reputations reconsidered. IV. Matthew Arnold. Acad 53:77-8 Ja 15 '98

Reuschel, Karl
Matthew Arnolds "The Forsaken Merman" und sein deutsches vorbild. Germanisch-Romanische Monatsschrift 12:49-50 '24

Rhys, Ernest
Introduction. *In* On the study of Celtic literature, and other essays. (Everyman's Library) London, Dent [1910] pi-xvi

Matthew Arnold. *In* Lyric poetry. London, Dent, 1913. p353-5

Rice, Richard
Arnold and Joubert. Reader 6:712-18 N '05

Riveallan, A.
Matthew Arnold en Bretagne. Bulletin de l'Association France-grande-bretagne N '28

Robbins, Reginald Chauncey
Matthew Arnold. *In* Poems of personality. Cambridge, Riverside press, 1908. p154-8

Robbins, William
Matthew Arnold as a social and religious reformer, and his influence as reflected mainly in periodical literature. Masters essay, Univ. of British Columbia, 1934. 130ff

Robert Burns. Blackw 160:184-8 Ag '96

Robertson, Edward Stanley
"Sweetness and light." Spec 114:265 F 20 '15

Robertson, John George
Matthew Arnold and Goethe. London, Moring, 1928

Robertson, John Mackinnon
De mortuis. Matthew Arnold. *In* Criticisms. London, Bonner, 1903. vol II p186-97

Matthew Arnold. *In* Modern humanists reconsidered. London, Watts, 1927. p105-32
(Rev in T L S Ag 4 '27 p527)

Matthew Arnold. *In* Modern humanists; sociological studies of Carlyle, Mill, Emerson, Arnold, Ruskin, and Spencer, with an epilogue on social reconstruction. . . [Social science series 35] London, Sonnenschein, 1891. p137-83

Roe, Frederic William
Introduction. *In* Essays and poems of Arnold. New York, Harcourt, Brace [c 1928] pix-xxxvi

Roget, F. F.
Modern poets: Matthew Arnold. Ladder 1:78-83 F '91

Rohrer, Esther Jane
The aesthetic principles of Matthew Arnold. Masters essay, Univ. of Washington, 1930. 57ff

Roman Catholic education and Mr. Arnold. Spec 51:850 Jl 6 '78

Roman Catholic poets [with summary] Temple Bar 27:170-86; 28:33-48 S, D '69

Romer, V. L.
Matthew Arnold and some French poets. 19th Cent 99:869-80 Je '26

Roscoe, W. O.
The classical school of English poetry, Matthew Arnold. *In* Poems and essays. London, Chapman, 1860. vol II p38-80

Russell, E. R.
[Paper on Matthew Arnold] Read before the Literary and philosophical society of Liverpool.
(Rev in Spec 61:962-3 Jl 14 '88)

Russell, George William Erskine
Disregarded prophet [Matthew Arnold] *In* Politics and personalities. . . New York, Scribner, 1917. p318-24

A group of poets. . . *In* Portraits of the seventies. New York, Scribner, 1916. p293-7

Matthew Arnold. (Literary lives) New York, Scribner, 1904. xv, 265p
(Rev in Acad 66:298 Mr 19 '04; Ath 1: 496-7 Ap 16 '04; A. S. Henry in Bookn 22:953-6 My '04; Contemp 85:

904-5 Je '04; Cur Lit 37:433-6 N '04; E. J. Rich in Dial 37:200-3 O 1 '04; P. Aronstein in Engl Stud 35:322-5 '05; T L S Mr 25 '04 p94; H. W. Boynton in Atlan 93:707-8 My '04; Literary World (Lond) ns 69:266 Mr 18 '04; G. K. Chesterton in Bookm (Lond) 26: 17-18 Ap '04; N. P. Gilman in Lit W 35:101 Ap '04; H. D. Davray in Mercure Fr 50:549-50 My '04)

Matthew Arnold. *In* Selected essays on literary subjects. London, Dent, 1914. p49-67

Matthew Arnold. *In* Sketches and snapshots. London, Smith, Elder, 1910. p72-85

Matthew Arnold. Time (London) ns 7: 657-64 Je '88

Matthew Arnold; a memorial sketch. London, Printed for the subscribers to the Arnold Memorial Fund, 1889. 16p

Rutherford, Mildred
Matthew Arnold. *In* English authors. Atlanta, Ga. Franklin printing and publishing co. 1906. p571-5

Rylance, Joseph Hine
A tribute to Matthew Arnold. Two lectures delivered in St. Mark's Church, New York. . . [New York, K. Tompkins, 188-?] 6-36p

Sadler, (Sir) Michael Ernest
Matthew Arnold. 19th Cent 93:199-207, 366-77 F-Mr '23

Sagert, Louis A.
Matthew Arnold's early verse as an expression of doubt. Masters essay, Univ. of Iowa, 1931. 55ff

Saintsbury, George Edward Bateman
A history of English prosody from the twelfth century to the present day. London, Macmillan, 1910. vol III p248-58, 421-2

A history of nineteenth century literature. London, Macmillan, 1931. p281-7, 385-8

English criticism, 1860-1900. *In* History of criticism. Edinburgh, Blackwood, 1900-04. vol III p515-37

Matthew Arnold. (Modern English writers) Edinburgh, Blackwood, 1899. vi, 232p
(Rev in Acad 57:329-30 S 30 '99; R. Garnett in Bookm (Lond) 16:102 Jl '99; Lit 4:648-9 Je 24 '99; T. H. Warren in Quar R 202:221-49 Ja '05; Spec 83:156-7 Jl 29 '99; Nation (NY) 69:396-7 N 23 '99)

Matthew Arnold. *In* Corrected impressions; essays on Victorian writers. . . New York, Dodd, Mead, 1895. p138-56

Matthew Arnold. *In* Craik, Henry, ed. English prose. . . New York, Macmillan, 1907. vol V p699-704

Modern English prose. Fortn ns 19:253-4 F '76

Saleman, William
The Arnolds as educators. Educa 5: 425-9 Mr '85

Schelling, Felix E.
The English lyric. Boston, Houghton, Mifflin, 1913. p219-28

Schirmer, W. F.
Der englische roman der neuesten zeit. Kultur und Sprache '23

Schonberger, E. D.
Matthew Arnold—the apostle of light. Quarterly Journal Univ. North Dakota 15:27-34 N '24

Schrag, Arnold
Matthew Arnold, poet and critic. Basel, Reinhardt, 1904. bibl Diss. Basel, 1894

Scott, Ernest
Matthew Arnold and education. *In* Men and thought in modern history. Melbourne, Macmillan, 1920. p289-300

Scott, Margaret
A French critic. T L S Ja 1 '25 p9

Scott, W.
Matthew Arnold on nineteenth century eloquence. Notes & Q 11th ser 2:318 O 15 '10

Scott-James, R. A.
Introduction. *In* The poems of Matthew Arnold, 1840 to 1866. (Everyman's library) London, Dent [1908] pi-xv

Scudder, Vida Dutton
Arnold as an abiding force. Dial 27:481-2 D 16 '99

Arthur Hugh Clough. *In* The life of the spirit in the modern English poets. Boston, Houghton, Mifflin, 1899. p265-8

Matthew Arnold. *In* The life of the spirit in the modern English poets. Boston, Houghton, Mifflin, 1899. p247-64

The poetry of Matthew Arnold. And R 10:232-49 S '88

What to do according to Arnold. *In* Social ideals in English letters. new ed. Boston, Houghton, Mifflin, 1923. p233-42

Sedgewick, G. G.
Wordsworth, Arnold, and Professor Lane Cooper. Dalhousie Review 10:57-66 Ap '30

Selborne, Earl of
Disestablishment in Wales. Nat R 11: 300-8 My '88

[Selkirk, J. B.] Brown, James Buchan [pseud]
Modern creeds and modern poetry. *In* Ethics and aesthetics of modern poetry. London, Smith, Elder, 1878. p27-61

Sells, Iris Esther
Matthew Arnold and France. Cambridge, England, Univ. press, 1935. [v]-xv,282p bibl p[273]-276

Sessions, Frederick
Two pioneer educationists: Thomas and Matthew Arnold. *In* Literary celebrities of the English lake-district. London, Stock, 1905. p213-21

Shafer, Robert
Matthew Arnold. *In* Christianity and naturalism. . . New Haven, Yale univ. press, 1926. 2d ser p156-97

Shairp, John Campbell
Balliol scholars. 1840-1843. A remembrance; poem. *In* Glen Desseray and other poems, ed. by F. T. Palgrave. London, Macmillan, 1888. p209-20; *same.* Macmil 27:376-82 Mr '73

The literary theory of culture. *In* Culture and religion in some of their relations. Edinburgh, Edmonston & Douglas, 1870. p49-72

Sharp, Amy
Matthew Arnold. *In* Victorian poets. London, Methuen, 1891. p137-56 (Rev in Westm 137:110-11 '92; Speaker 4:206-7 Ag 15 '91)

Sharp, William
Introduction. *In* The strayed reveller, Empedocles on Etna, and other poems, by Matthew Arnold. London, Scott publishing co. [n. d.] pxi-xxxiv

On Matthew Arnold. *In* Papers critical and reminiscent... New York, Duffield, 1912. p1-17

Sheehan, P. A.
The poetry of Matthew Arnold. *In* Early essays and lectures. London, Longmans, Green, 1912. p150-64

The **Shelley** society. Sat R 61:354 Mr 13 '86

Shepard, William [pseud]
see Walsh, William Shepard

Sherman, Stuart Pratt
H. G. Wells and the Victorians. Nation (NY) 100:558-61 My 20 '15

Matthew Arnold: a summary. *In* Shaping men and women. . . ed. by J. Zeitlin. New York, Smith, 1932. p265-77

Matthew Arnold, how to know him. . . Indianapolis, Bobbs-Merrill [c 1917] 326p (Rev by I. Babbitt in Nation (NY) 105: 117-21 Ag 2 '17; M. C. Otto in Dial 62: 516-17 Je 14 '17)

Shindler, Robert
Tennyson, Arnold and Clough. *In* On certain aspects of recent English literature (Neuphilologische Vorträge und Abhandlung II) Leipzig, Teubner, 1902. p28-37

Shirley [pseud]
see Skelton, J.

Shorey, Paul
Matthew Arnold and Franklin. Nation (NY) 46:486 Je 14 '88

Shorter, Clement K.
My bookshelves: Matthew Arnold. Bookm (Lond) 16:123-5 Ag '99

Victorian literature. New York, Dodd, Mead, 1897. p17-21

Sibbald, William A.
Matthew Arnold as a popular poet. Macmil 89:385-400 Mr '04; *same*. Ecl M 142: 742-57 Je '04; *same*. Liv Age 241:83-98 Ap 9 '04

Sidgwick, Henry
The prophet of culture. Macmil 16:271-80 Ag '67; *same*. Ecl M 69:490-8 O '67; *also in* Miscellaneous essays and addresses. New York, Macmillan, 1904. p40-58

Sieveking, A. Forbes
Matthew Arnold's French quotation. Notes & Q 11th ser 4:149 Ag 19 '11

Sillard, Peter A.
Matthew Arnold intime. Atlan 95:264-9 F '05

Sinzheimer, L.
[Social writings of Arnold] Ethische Kultur 4:289, 297 '12

[Skelton, J.] Shirley [pseud]
The poetry of the year. Fraser 80:667-9 N '69

William Morris and Matthew Arnold. Fraser 79:230-44 F '69

[Sketch of Arnold] Homiletic Review 79: 173-4 Mr '20

Smalley, George W.
Matthew Arnold. *In* London letters. . . New York, Harper, 1891. vol I p289-302

Smith, Arnold
Matthew Arnold. *In* The main tendencies of Victorian poetry. . . London, Simpkin, Marshall, Hamilton, Kent, 1907. p116-34

Smith, Charles Forster
Matthew Arnold. Sewanee-R 7:189-220 Ap '99

Smith, Goldwin
Falkland and the Puritans. Contemp 29: 925-43 Ap '77

Smith, Sophie
Notes to Matthew Arnold's "Friendship's Garland." Masters essay, Columbia univ. 1934

Soleman, William
The Arnolds as educationalists. Educa 5: 425-9 Mr '85

Some aspects of Matthew Arnold's poetry. Scribner's Monthly 18:281-9 Je '79

Some poets of the Victorian era. IX Matthew Arnold. Acad 79:271-2, 295 S 17-24 '10

Some remarks on Mr. Matthew Arnold. Cath World 37:577-89 Ag '83

Sonnenschein, Adolf
On Mr. Matthew Arnold's "Special Report on Elementary Education on the Continent, 1886." *In* Educational codes of foreign countries. . . London, Swan Sonnenschein, 1889. 2d ed p3-14

Spare moments with the poets: Matthew Arnold. Wit and Wisdom 2:404-5 My 7 '87

Spaulding, Alice
Matthew Arnold's mind as revealed in his poetry. Masters essay, Univ. of Kansas, 1902. 37ff

Spedding, James
English hexameters. *In* Reviews and discussions. . . London, Kegan Paul, 1879. p316-43
[Concerned with "On Translating Homer"]

Spencer, Herbert
The study of sociology. Contemp 21:485-502 Mr '73

Splaine, James F.
Mr. Matthew Arnold's report on continental education. Month 58:185-96, 328-42, 549-63 O-D '86

Squire, John Collings
Matthew Arnold. *In* Essays on poetry. New York, Doran [1923?] p88-97

Squires, Vernon Purinton
The poetry of Matthew Arnold. Quarterly Journal of the Univ. of North Dakota 2:3-16 O '11

Starbird, R. S.
The ethnological in Matthew Arnold. Washington Univ. Bulletin 4:112

Starbuck, Charles C.
Religious thought in England. And R 10:473-91 N '88

The state of art in France. Blackw 135: 445-6 Ap '84

Stearns, Frank Preston
Matthew Arnold. *In* Modern English prose writers. London, Putnam, 1897. p310-30

Matthew Arnold's lecture. *In* Sketches from Concord and Appledore. . . New York, Putnam, 1895. p117-33

Stedman, Edmund Clarence
Matthew Arnold. *In* Victorian poets. London, Chatto & Windus, 1876. p90-100

A representative triad. Hood-Arnold-Proctor. Scribner's Monthly 7:463-78 F '74

Steinmetz, Martha Susanna
Die ideengeschichtliche bedeutung Matthew Arnolds. . . Schramberg, Gatzer, 1932. vii, 80p Thesis, Tübingen. bibl p77-80

Stephen, (Sir) Leslie
Matthew Arnold. Nat R 22:458-77 D '93; *same*. Ecl M 122:300-13 Mr '94; *same*. Liv Age 200:90-103 Ja 13 '94

Matthew Arnold. *In* Studies of a biographer. London, Duckworth, 1898. vol II p76-122

Mr. Matthew Arnold and the Church of England. Fraser ns 2:414-31 O '70

Stoddard, Francis Hovey
Tolstoi and Matthew Arnold. And R 10: 359-69 O '88; Congregational Review 3: 20 Ja '89

Stoddard, Richard Henry
The advent of Mr. Arnold. Harper W 27:679 O 27 '83

Matthew Arnold. Appleton J 3:46-8 Ja 8 '70

Matthew Arnold as a poet. No Am 146: 657-62 Je '88

Stone, George J.
Matthew Arnold. Notes & Q 7th ser 7: 287-8 Ap 13 '89; answer ibid:414-15 My 25 '89

Strachey, Giles Lytton
Dr. Arnold. *In* Eminent Victorians. London, Chatto & Windus, 1918. p181-214

Victorian critic. [Matthew Arnold] *In* Characters and commentaries. New York, Harcourt, Brace, 1933. p174-80

Sueur, William D. le
The poetry of Matthew Arnold. Canadian Monthly and National Review 1:219-29 Mr '72

Sullivan, Louis J.
The reception in England of Matthew Arnold's religious works. Masters essay, Columbia university, 1927. 34ff

Swanwick, Anna
Matthew Arnold. *In* Poets the interpreters of their age. London, Bell, 1892. p375-9

"Sweetness and light." Nation (NY) 5: 212-13, 238, 259 S 12, 19, 26 '67

Swinburne, Algernon Charles
Matthew Arnold's new poems. *In* Essays and studies. London, Chatto, 1875. p123-83; *also in* Fortn 8:414-45 O '67

Wordsworth and Byron. 19th Cent 15: 583-609, 764-90 Ap-My '84; *same in* Miscellanies. London, Chatto & Windus, 1886. p63-156

Swinburne, Louis Judson
Matthew Arnold in America. Lippinc 33: 90-6 Ja '84

The unrest of the age as seen in its literature. New Englander 38:612-36 S '79

Symonds, John Addington
Is poetry at bottom a criticism of life? *In* Essays, speculative and suggestive. New York, Scribner, 1907. 3d ed p315-34

Tait, C. J.
To Matthew Arnold; poem. Literary World (Lond) ns 61:511 Je 1 '00

Taunt, H. W.
The Oxford poems of Matthew Arnold, "The Scholar Gypsy" and "Thyrsis," with rambles in the country around Oxford to which the poems refer. Oxford, Alden [1929] 61p

Thayer, Stephen Henry
Matthew Arnold's influence on literature. And R 12:262-75 S '89

A theologian's estimate of Matthew Arnold. Critic (NY) 4:6 Ja 5 '84

Thirty-five years of school inspecting—Mr. Matthew Arnold's farewell. Pall Mall Gazette N 13 '86 p6

Thomas, Edward
Matthew Arnold. *In* A literary pilgrim in England. New York, Dodd, Mead, 1917. p68-81
(Rev in T L S O 12 '17 p489)

Thomas, Lula E.
Matthew Arnold as a literary critic. Masters essay, Columbia univ. 1915

Thompson, Alexander Hamilton
Tennyson and the Victorian poets. *In* A history of English literature. London, John Murray, 1901. p776-81

Thorndike, Ashley Horace
Introduction. *In* Matthew Arnold's Sohrab and Rustum. . . New York, Longmans, Green, 1910. pvii-xxii

Thorne, W. H.
Life of Matthew Arnold. *In* Modern idols. . . Philadelphia, Lippincott, 1887. p7-20

Thursfield, James R.
Arnold's "Signal Elm." T L S N 8 '17 p541

Thwing, Charles Franklin
Education according to Matthew Arnold. School and Society 3:338-46 Mr 4 '16

Tinker, Chauncey Brewster
Arnold's poetic plans. Yale R ns 22:782-93 Je '33

Tisdel, Frederick M.
The Victorian era. *In* Studies in literature. New York, Macmillan, 1913. p303-6

To Matthew Arnold in America; poem. Spec 57:442, 486 Ap 5, 12 '84; *same.* Liv Age 161:386 My 17 '84

Tours through literary England. Through the Matthew Arnold country. Sat R 150:9-10 Jl 5 '30

Townes, Mary Ella
An explanation of the allusions in "Culture and Anarchy." Masters essay, Columbia univ. 1930

Townsend, Walter
Matthew Arnold as a poet. Rose-Belford's Canadian Monthly and National Review 1:335-46 S '78

Traill, Henry Duff
The literature of the Victorian era. Fortn 67:828-9 My '97

Matthew Arnold. Contemp 53:868-81 Je '88; *same.* Liv Age 178:88-96 Jl 14 '88

Matthew Arnold. *In* The new fiction and other essays on literary subjects. London, Hurst, 1897. p76-103

Neo-Christianity and Mr. Matthew Arnold. Contemp 45:564-76 Ap '84

Translations of the Odyssey. Blackw 91:346-7 Mr '62

Tristram, Henry
Newman and Matthew Arnold. Cornhill 60:309-19 Mr '26

The **true** culture. National Observer 8:165-6 Jl 2 '92

Truman, Joseph
Laleham; poem. *In* Afterthoughts. London, Macmillan, 1889. p65-6
Victoria's poets; poem. Spec 78:476 Ap 3 '97

Tucker, T. G.
The foreign debt of English literature. London, Bell, 1907. p40-1, 56-7, 67-8

Tuell, Anne Kimball
Mrs. Meynell and her literary generation. New York, Dutton [c 1925]

Tweed, R. P. F.
[Matthew Arnold: his death] Notes & Q 150:269 Ap 10 '26

Tyrer, C. E.
In memoriam Matthew Arnold; sonnet. Manch Q 7:388 O '88
Matthew Arnold. Manch Q no 23:1-19 Ja '90
Matthew Arnold as poet. Manch Q no 36:358-85 O '90

Tyrwhitt, R. St. John
Art and culture. Contemp 13:362-80 Mr '70
An Oxford art-scheme. Contemp 8:161-77 Je '68

Vail, W. S.
Arnold and Emerson. Critic (NY) 4:198-9 Ap 26 '84

Van Ness, Mary Wickliffe
Arnold's life and character as shown in his letters. *In* Matthew Arnold and the spirit of the age, ed. by G. White. New York, Putnam, 1898. p31-43

Van Rensselaer, M. G.
Mr. Arnold and American art. Cent 36:314-16 Je '88

Veach, Prudence Melvina
Matthew Arnold's "Empedocles on Etna." Masters essay, Yale univ. 1931

The **Victorian** garden of song. Dial 19:238 N 1 '95

Virden, Bena M.
Notes to Matthew Arnold's "Discourses in America." Masters essay, Columbia univ. 1932

Waite, Richard Strodtman
Matthew Arnold, his critical vocabulary. Masters essay, Univ. of Arizona, 1930. 71ff

Walbrook, Henry Mackinnon
The "Marguerite poems." Lond Merc 5:414-15 F '22
The novel in Matthew Arnold's poems. Bookm [Lond] 78:109-12 My '30

Walker, Hugh
The age of Tennyson. (Handbooks of English literature) London, Bell, 1904. p203-9, 214-19
The dramas. *In* The greater Victorian poets. London, Swan Sonnenschein, 1895. p172-4

The English essay and essayists. London, Dent, 1915. p306-12
English satire and satirists. London, Dent, 1925. p305-7
Faith and doubt. *In* The greater Victorian poets. London, Swan Sonnenschein, 1895. p294-9
The influence of science. *In* The greater Victorian poets. London, Swan Sonnenschein, 1895. p241-5
The literature of the Victorian era. Cambridge, Univ. press, 1921. p465-80
Matthew Arnold. *In* The greater Victorian poets. London, Swan Sonnenschein, 1895. p122-49
(Rev in Literary World (Lond) ns 52:220 S 27 '95)
The poetry of nature. *In* The greater Victorian poets. London, Swan Sonnenschein, 1895. p220-30
The social and political aspects of the poets. *In* The greater Victorian poets. London, Swan Sonnenschein, 1895. p270-81

Walker, Hugh and Walker, (Mrs) Hugh
Outlines of Victorian literature. Cambridge, Univ. press, 1919. p76-8

Walsh, Joseph Lee
Matthew Arnold and his influence on English education. Masters essay, Yale univ. 1932

[Walsh, William Shepard] William Shepard [pseud]
Matthew Arnold. *In* Enchiridion of criticism. . . Philadelphia, Lippincott, 1885. p256-60
Matthew Arnold. *In* Pen pictures of modern authors. New York, Putnam, 1882. p325-6

Ward, Mary Augusta (Arnold)
A writer's recollections. *In* The family of Fox How. London, Harper, 1918

Ward, Thomas Humphry
Matthew Arnold. *In* The English poets... New York, Macmillan, 1907. vol IV p704-9

Warren, (Sir) Thomas Herbert
Matthew Arnold. *In* Essays of poets and poetry, ancient and modern. . . New York, Dutton, 1909. p44-84

Waters, W. G.
Arnold as a poet of nature. T L S N 2 '17 p529
Tristan and Iseult. Lit 6:247-8 Mr 24 '00

Watson, Robert A.
The counterfeit gospel of nature. British and Foreign Evangelical Review 35:627-50 O '86; *same in* Gospels of yesterday. London, Nisbet, 1888. p179-217

Watson, William
In Laleham churchyard; poem. Spec 65:278-9 Ag 30 '90; *same in* Poems. London, Lane, 1905. vol I p27-30

Waugh, Arthur
The poetry of reflection and doubt. *In* Reticence in literature, and other papers. London, Wilson [1915] p54-60

Weatherhead, Leslie D.
Arnold. *In* The after-world of the poets... London, Epworth press [1929] p124-43

Weet, Herbert Seeley
Characteristics and comparative excellence of Matthew Arnold's poetry. Hull prize essay, Univ. of Rochester, 1899. 15ff

Weitzel, S. W.
Matthew Arnold; poem. Lit W 19:200 Je 23 '88

Wellwood, John
Matthew Arnold as a poet. Ruskin Reading Guild Journal 1:12-16 Ja '89

West, (Sir) Algernon
Matthew Arnold. Contemporary portraits; men of my day in public life. London, Unwin [1920] p57-64

Weygandt, Cornelius
The muses in Germantown. *In* Tuesdays at ten. A garnering from the talks of thirty years on poets, dramatists and essayists. Philadelphia, Univ. of Penna. press, 1928. p97-102

What endures in poetry? Spec 63:236-7 Ag 24 '89

What Matthew Arnold means in the thought of to-day. Current Opinion 74:305-6 Mr '23

[Wheeler, Andrew Carpenter]
Has America outgrown Matthew Arnold, by Jay Paul Mowbray [pseud] Critic (NY) 40:409-13 My '02

Wheeler, C. B.
Matthew Arnold's poems. Notes & Q 11th ser 8:37 Jl 12 '13

Whipple, Edwin Percy
Matthew Arnold. *In* Recollections of eminent men, with other papers... With introd. by Rev. C. A. Bartol. Boston, Ticknor, 1887. p280-304; *also in* No Am 138:429-44 My '84

White, Greenough
Arnold's character as revealed in his poems. *In* Matthew Arnold and the spirit of the age. New York, Putnam, 1898. p17-30

Matthew Arnold and the spirit of the age. New York, Putnam, 1898. p1-7

White, Helen Constance
Matthew Arnold and Goethe. P M L A 36:436-53 S '21

White, W. Hale
Byron, Goethe, and Mr. Matthew Arnold. Appleton J ns 11:335-9 O '81; *same.* Contemp 40:179-85 Ag '81

Whitman, Walt
Our eminent visitors. Critic (NY) 3: 459 N 17 '83

Whitney, Elizabeth Boyce
The Oxford movement and its influence on English poetry. Masters essay, Univ. of Oklahoma, 1931

Whitridge, Arnold
Dr. Arnold of Rugby; with an introduction by Sir Michael Sadler. New York, Holt, 1928. 243p
(Rev by F. Marcham in Books Ag 26 '28 p12; F. Bartlett in Boston Transcript Jl 7 '28 p4; E. F. Edgett in Boston Transcript Jl 28 '28 p5; E. Boyd in Ind 121:43 Jl 14 '28; C. Wilkinson in Lond Merc 18:215-16 Je '28; Nation (NY) 127:sup 381 O 10 '28; Nat-Ath 43:213 My 19 '28; J. Orrick in New Adelphi Je 1 '28 p378-80; New Statesm & Nation 31:204 My 19 '28; C. Johnston in N Y Times Jl 8 '28 p6; O. W. Firkins in Sat R Lit 5:319 N 3 '28; Spec 140:686 My 5 '28; Springfield Republican S 2 '28 p7f; T L S Je 28 '28 p477

Letters of Cardinal Newman to Matthew Arnold. T L S Mr 10 '21 p160. Letters from Matthew Arnold to Cardinal Newman, ibid Mr 31 '21 p211

Wilcox, Helen Chapman
Matthew Arnold's use of the Greek classics. Masters essay, Columbia univ. 1911

Wilkins, A. S.
A Puritan's apology. Macmil 22:265-70 Ag '70

Wilkins, Ernest Hatch
The source of Arnold's Jacopone sonnet. Mod Philol 31:200-2 N '33

Wilkinson, William Cleaver
Matthew Arnold as poet: tried by his "Sohrab and Rustum." No Am 188: 666-81 N '08

Willcock, J.
Matthew Arnold's poems. Notes & Q 11th ser 7:478 Je 14 '13

Williams, Stanley Thomas
Arnold on men of his day. Literary Review 20:665-6 My 20 '22

A century of Matthew Arnold. No Am 217:107-16 Ja '23

Founding of Main Street; letters. No Am 216:411-16 S '22

Matthew Arnold and his contemporaries. *In* Studies in Victorian literature. New York, Dutton [c 1923] p95-108

Matthew Arnold as a critic of literature. Univ. of California Chronicle 26:183-208 Ap '24

The poetical reputation of Matthew Arnold. *In* Studies in Victorian literature. New York, Dutton [c 1923] p71-94

Some aspects of Matthew Arnold's poetry. Sewanee R 29:315-21 Jl-S '21

Theory and practice in the poetry of Matthew Arnold. *In* Studies in Victorian literature. New York, Dutton [c 1923] p123-60

Three aspects of Matthew Arnold's poetry. *In* Studies in Victorian literature. New York, Dutton [c 1923] p109-22

Williamson, Claude C. H.
Matthew Arnold. *In* Writers of three centuries, 1789-1914. Philadelphia, Jacobs [1915?] p241-4

Williamson, D. R.
To Matthew Arnold; poem. Great Thoughts 9:99 F 25 '88

Wilson, J. D.
Matthew Arnold and the educationists. *In* Hearnshaw, F. J. C. ed. The Social and political ideas of some representative thinkers of the Victorian age. (King's College lectures on social and political ideas, 1931-32) London, Harrap, 1933. p165-93

Wilson, P.
Matthew Arnold. *In* Leaders in literature. London, Oliphant, 1898. p193-216

Wilson, Richard
Helps to the study of Arnold's "Wordsworth." London, Macmillan, 1897. 88p

Winther, Sophus Keith
The literary reputation of Matthew Arnold in England and America. Diss. Univ. of Washington, 1927. For abstract see Univ. of Washington. . . Publications. . . Digest of theses 1914-1931. . . 1:135-8 D '31

Winwar, Frances [pseud]
see [Grebanier, (Mrs) Frances (Vinciguerra)]

Woodberry, George Edward
Makers of literature. New York, Macmillan, 1900. p1-26

Matthew Arnold. *In* Literary essays. New York, Harcourt, Brace and Howe, 1920. p73-89 [Reprinted from Makers of literature]

Matthew Arnold (1822-1888). *In* Warner, C. D. ed. Library of the world's best literature. . . Memorial ed. New York, Hill [c 1902] vol II p844-55

Woods, Margaret L.
Matthew Arnold. *In* English Association. Essays and studies. London, Oxford univ. press, 1929. vol XV p7-19

Poets of the 'eighties. *In* The eighteen-eighties, essays by fellows of the Royal society of literature, ed. by Walter De la Mare. Cambridge, Univ. press, 1930. p6-7

Worsfold, W. Basil
Matthew Arnold insists upon the interpretative [sic] power of literature. . . *In* The principles of criticism. New York, Longmans, Green, 1902. p136-61

Wragge, Walter
Religion of Matthew Arnold. Hibbert J 30:504-13 '32

Wright, Ichabod Charles
A letter to the Dean of Canterbury, on the Homeric lectures of Matthew Arnold. London, Macmillan, 1864. 35p

Wülker, Richard
Geschichte der englischen literatur. . . Leipzig, Bibliographischen instituts, 1907. p302-5

Wylie, Andrew Tennant
Matthew Arnold's conception of criticism. Masters essay, Indiana Univ. 1907

Yvon, Paul
L'inspiration poétique chez Matthew Arnold, à propos du "Scholar Gipsy." Revue A A 6:312-16 Ap '29

Zorn, Paul Wilhelm
Matthew Arnold und seine beziehungen zu deutschland. Diss. Hamburg, 1924. iii, 108p

Elizabeth Barrett Browning

NOTE

The compilers have here made no attempt to include items which are primarily concerned with Robert Browning. The student or general reader is referred to the many biographies and critical works about Robert Browning for further information relating to Elizabeth Barrett Browning. The publications of Baylor University and the compilations by Professor A. J. Armstrong in the Browning field should especially be noted.

Elizabeth Barrett Browning

I. Chronological Outline

1806. Born, March 6, Durham.

1826. An Essay on Mind, with Other Poems.

1833. Prometheus Bound, Translated from the Greek of Aeschylus, and Miscellaneous Poems.

1838. The Seraphim, and Other Poems.

1839. The Romaunt of the Page.

1844. Poems.

1846. Married Robert Browning.

1846-1851. Residence at Florence, Italy.

1850. Poems, second edition.

1851. Casa Guidi Windows.

1853. Poems, third edition.

1856. Poems, fourth edition.

1856-1857. Aurora Leigh.

1860. Poems Before Congress.

1861. Died, June 30, Florence.

1862. Last Poems.

1863. The Greek Christian Poets and the English Poets.

Elizabeth Barrett Browning

II. Bibliographical Material

American Art Association Anderson Galleries
A remarkable series of twenty-two unpublished letters by Elizabeth Barrett Browning and Robert Browning, addressed to Henrietta and Arabel Moulton-Barrett. *In* First editions, autograph letters and manuscripts . . . . public sale April 24 and 25 [1935] New York, American Art Association Anderson galleries, 1935.   p20-35 [Catalogue [no]4175]
(Noted by F. M. Hopkins in Pub W 127:1534-6 Ap 13 '35)

Armstrong, A. Joseph
Baylor university's Browning collection and other. Browning interests. Waco, Texas, Baylor univ. 1928. p5-51 [Baylor Bulletin 30:5-51 D '27]

Becker, (Mrs) May Lamberton
Reader's guide; best recent books on the Brownings. Sat R Lit 7: 277 O 25 '30

Brooks, Aurelia E.
Browningiana in Baylor University. [Waco, Texas, Baylor univ. press, 1921] vii,405p

Brown, G. A.
Elizabeth Barrett Browning. CHEL vol XIII p532-7

Browning, Robert Wiedemann Barrett
The Browning collections. Catalogue of autograph letters and manuscripts. . . . London, J. Tregaskis, 1913. 100p (Catalogue no 743)
The Browning collections. Catalogue of oil paintings. . . sold by auction by Sotheby, Wilkinson & Hodge. . . . May, 1913. [London] Dryden press [1913] viii,161p

Carter, John and Pollard, Graham
The sonnets from the Portuguese. *In* An enquiry into the nature of certain nineteenth century pamphlets. London, Constable, 1934. p361-8; see also p165-71

Clark, William Andrews, jr.
"Bibliographical" note. *In* Sonnets from the Portuguese. . . San Francisco, Nash, 1927.   pxvi-xxv

Dobell, Bertram
Browning memorials; a catalogue of books, drawings, autograph letters, and other relics. . . . London [R. Stockwell, 1913] 39p

Forman, Harry Buxton
Elizabeth Barrett Browning and her scarcer books; a bio-bibliographical note. London, Privately printed, 1896.   29p (30 copies only); same *in* Nicoll, W. R. & Wise, T. J. eds. Literary anecdotes of the nineteenth century. London, Hodder & Stoughton, 1896. vol II p81-101

Hodgkins, Louise Manning
Elizabeth Barrett Browning. *In* A guide to the study of nineteenth century authors. Boston, Heath, 1890. p49-53

Joyce, Hewette Elwell
Mrs. Browning's contributions to American periodicals. Mod Lang N 35:402-5 N '20

Livingston, Luther S.
The first books of some English authors. I. Robert and Elizabeth Barrett Browning. Bookm (NY) 10:76-81 S '99

Maggs Brothers, London
Rare and interesting autograph letters, signed documents and manuscripts. London, 1913. 2 vols

Mrs. Browning; collections toward a bibliography. Lit W 15:197 Je 14 '84

Mrs. Browning: some items of bibliography [list of poems which appeared in periodicals, 1825-1849] Ath 1:757-8 Je 14 '84; *same.* Lit W 15:251 Jl 26 '84

News for bibliophiles [ms at Sotheby sale] Nation (NY) 96:386 Ap 17 '13

Northup, Clark Sutherland
A register of bibliographies of the English language and literature. New Haven, Yale univ. press, 1925. p78

Page, Curtis Hidden
Elizabeth Barrett Browning. List of references. *In* British poets of the nineteenth century, ed. by

Page, Curtis Hidden—*Continued*
C. H. Page. New ed. by Stith Thompson. New York, Sanborn, 1930. p550

Pratt Institute, Brooklyn, School of Library Science
Elizabeth Barrett Browning. *In* Pratt Institute Library School Lectures on General Literature no 79:634-6 '93-'94

Quaritch, Bernard
A catalogue. . . . of books from the library of the late R. W. Barrett Browning. . . . London, 1913. 102p

Slater, J. H.
Early editions: a bibliographical survey of the works of some popular modern authors. London, Kegan Paul, Trench, Trübner, 1894
(Rev by T. J. Wise in Bookm (Lond) 6:49-50 My '94)

Sotheran, Henry, & co. London
Illustrated catalogue of engravings, etc. . . . of Robert and Elizabeth Barrett Browning. London, 1913. 130p

Wise, Thomas James
A bibliography of the writings in prose and verse of Elizabeth Barrett Browning. . . . London, Printed for private circulation only by R. Clay & sons, 1918. xv, 249p
(100 copies only)

A Browning library, a catalogue of printed books, manuscripts and autograph letters by Robert Browning and Elizabeth Barrett Browning, collected by Thomas James Wise. . . . London, Printed for private circulation only, 1929. xxxii,126p
(160 copies only)

Woods, George Benjamin
[Bibliography] *In* Poetry of the Victorian period. New York, Scott, Foresman [c1930] p980-2

Elizabeth Barrett Browning

III. Biographical and Critical Material

Abbot, Willis J.
Women of history. . . Philadelphia, Winston, 1913

Adams, Mildred
Mrs. Browning on Broadway. Woman's Journal 16:12-13 Mr '31

Albert, Edward
Elizabeth Barrett Browning. *In* A history of English literature, a practical text-book. New York, Crowell, 1924. p466-7

Alexander, Dorothy
Elizabeth Barrett Browning; an expression of her time. Masters essay, Columbia univ. 1928

Allingham, William
Letters from William Allingham [to Mr. and Mrs. Browning, 1853-1860] [np 1913?] 12p

Anderson, William
Elizabeth Barrett Browning. *In* Model women. London, Hodder and Stoughton, 1871. p188-200

Armstrong, A. Joseph
Baylor University's Browning collection and other Browning interests. Waco, Texas, Baylor university, 1928. p5-51 [Baylor Bulletin 30:5-51 D '27]
The Browning pilgrimage. Poet Lore 41: 72-90 Mr '30

Arnold, W. T.
Elizabeth Barrett Browning. *In* Ward, T. H. ed. The English poets. . . New York, Macmillan, 1907. vol IV p562-7

Askew, H.
Mrs. Browning: inscription. Notes & Q 147:289 O 18 '24

Auld, Thomas
Cowley and E. B. Browning. Notes & Q 9th ser 4:85 Jl 29 '99

Auslander, Joseph and Hill, Frank Ernest
The Brownings. *In* The winged horse. Garden City, N.Y. Doubleday, Doran, 1930. p316-32

Authors and artists at Florence. Eliza Cook's Journal 11:205 Jl 22 '54

Authorship of a poem. Notes & Q 3d ser 3:165 F 28 '63

Authorship of a poem: "Victoria's Tears." Notes & Q 3d ser 3:211 Mr 14 '63

Aynard, Joseph
Elizabeth Browning et le féminisme anglais. J Débats 125:1 My 20 '13

[Aytoun, William Edmondstoune and Martin, Theodore] Bon Gaultier [pseud]
The rhyme of Sir Lancelot Bogle. *In* The Book of ballads, ed. by Bon Gaultier. Edinburgh, Blackwood, 1870. 11th ed p179-92

Bailey, Ralph Sargent
Those Barretts of Wimpole street. Theatre Magazine 53:19-20 Mr '31

Bald, Marjory Amelia
Mrs. Browning. *In* Women-writers of the nineteenth century. . . Cambridge, England, University press, 1923. p209-32, 275-84

Bardi, Pietro
Elisabetta Barrett Browning. *In* Storia della letteratura inglese. Bari, Gius, Laterza, 1933. p169-70

Barlow, Jane
Against certain of our poets. Acad 71:161 Ag 18 '06

Barot-Odysse, François
Elizabeth Barrett Browning. *In* Histoire de la littérature contemporaine en Angleterre, 1830-1874. Paris, Charpentier, 1876. 2d ed. p167-76

Bates, Arlo
[Ingram's life of E. B. Browning] Book B ns 5:340 O '88

Bay, Jens Christian
A Tennyson-Browning association book . . . (np) 1929. 9ff Typed Ms. in New York Public Library

Bayne, Peter
Mrs. Barrett Browning. *In* Essays, biographical, critical, and miscellaneous. Edinburgh, Constable, 1859. p281-328
Mrs. Barrett Browning. *In* Essays in biography and criticism. Boston, Gould and Lincoln, 1857. 1st ser p146-210
Two great Englishwomen, Mrs. Browning and Charlotte Brontë. . . London, Clarke, 1881. lxxviii,340p

[Baynes, Dorothy Julia] Dormer Creston [pseud]
Andromeda in Wimpole street; the romance of Elizabeth Barrett Browning. New York, Dutton [c 1930] 287p (Rev in T L S N 7 '30 p893)

Beaunier, André
Miss Ba; avec extraits des lettres de Robert Browning et Elizabeth Barrett. Ann Pol et Litt 104:147-9 N 10 '34

Belpaire, Elisa
E. Barrett Browning. Dietsche Warande en Belfort 31:29-41, 114-39 Ja-F '31

Bensly, Edward
Mrs. Browning and Sappho. Notes & Q 11th ser 1:51 Ja 15 '10

Benson, Arthur Christopher
Elizabeth Barrett Browning. *In* Essays. New York, Macmillan, 1896. p205-37

Benson, Edward Frederic
"O lyric love half-angel and half-bird." Spec 141:31-2 N 3 '28

Besier, Rudolf
The Barretts of Wimpole street; a comedy in five acts. . . Boston, Little, Brown, 1931. x,165p

Bethune, George W.
Elizabeth B. Barrett. *In* The British female poets. Philadelphia, Lindsay & Blakiston [1848] p452-3

Bierbaum, Friedrich Julius
Elizabeth Barrett Browning. *In* History of the English language and literature till the Victorian age. Leipzig, Arthur Rossberg, 1922. 8th ed. p203-4

Blaze de Bury, Yetta
Élisabeth Browning. Révue Britannique 75:185-203 O '99

Élisabeth Browning. *In* Les romanciers anglais contemporains. Paris, Perrin, 1900. p159-94

Bleibtreu, Karl
E. Barret-Browning. *In* Geschichte der englischen literatur mit einschluss der amerikanischen. Bern & Leipzig, Ernst Bircher, 1923. p233-4

Boas, (Mrs) Louise Schutz
Elizabeth Barrett Browning. New York, Longmans, Green, 1930. vii,216p
(Rev by P. Allen in Bookm (NY) 71: 113-14 Mr '30)

Boase, Frederic
Browning, Elizabeth Barrett. *In* Modern English biography. Truro, Netherton & Worth, 1892. vol I p447

Böckel, F.
Robert und E. B. Browning. Tägliche Rundschau no 205-6 '08

Bolton, Sarah Knowles
Elizabeth Barrett Browning. *In* Lives of girls who became famous. New York, Crowell [c 1886] p194-212

Boothby, Edith Mortimer
The influence of personal and social environment upon the poetry of Elizabeth Barrett Browning. Masters essay, Boston Univ. 1932

Bower, H.
Mrs. Browning. Notes & Q 5th ser 7:356 My 5 '77

Bradfield, Thomas
The ethical impulse of Mrs. Browning's poetry. Westm 146:174-84 Ag '96

Bradford, Amory Howe
Spiritual lessons fror the Brownings. New York, Crowell, 1900. 38p

Brawley, B.
Elizabeth B. Browning and the Negro. Journal of Negro History 3:22-8 Ja '18

Breme, M. J.
E. B. Browning. Mädchenbildung auf Christliche Grundlage 4:282-8 '09

Brepohl, F. W.
Elizabeth Barrett Borwning. Der Alte Glaube no 40 '11

Bright, Norma K.
Elizabeth Barrett Browning. Bookm (NY) 24:460-3 Mr '06

Browning, Elizabeth Barrett
Alfred Tennyson: notes and comments; with a defence of the rhyme system of "The Dead Pan." [2 letters to R. H. Horne] London, Privately printed for T. J. Wise, 1919. 19p
(30 copies only)

The art of scansion. . . With an introd. by Alice Meynell [and foreword by Clement Shorter] London, Privately printed for Clement Shorter, 1916. ix,11p
(25 copies only)

Aurora Leigh. London, Chapman and Hall, 1856. vi,403p
(Rev in Blackw 81:23-41 Ja '57; Dublin University Magazine 49:460-70 Ap '57; T L S Jl 2 '31 p517-18; Westm 67: 168-9 Mr '57; Rivista di Firenze 2:204-13 Ap '58; Spec 82:53-4 Ja 14 '99; Ath 2:1425-7 N 22 '56; No Brit 26:450-62 F '57; Putnam's Magazine 9:28-38 Ja '57; New Quarterly Review 6:33-5 Ja '57; Spec 29:1239-40 N 22 '56; *same.* Liv Age 52:427-30 F 14 '57; Westm 67:306-10 Ja '57; Westm 68:399-415 O 1 '57; *same.* Ecl M 43:10-19 Ja '58; National Quarterly Review 5:134-48 Je '62; Ecl M 56:74-8 My '62; Nat R 4:239-67 Ap '57; Sat R 2:776-8 D 27 '56; National Magazine (Lond) 1:314-15 '57; E. Nencioni in Nuova Antol 75:5-18 My '84)

The book of the poets. New York, Miller, 1877. 226p
(Rev in Lit W 8:22-3 Jl '77)

Casa Guidi windows. A poem. London, Chapman and Hall, 1851. viii,140p
(Rev in American Whig Review 14: 462-6 D '51; Prospective Review 7:313-25 '51; Eclectic Review 94:306-17 S '51; Ath 1:597-8 Je 7 '51; Literary World (Lond) ns 65:17 Ja 3 '02)

Charles Dickens and other "Spirits of the Age" discussed and analyzed. [2 letters to R. H. Horne] London, Privately printed for T. J. Wise, 1919. 18p
(30 copies only)

A drama of exile: and other poems. New York, Langley, 1845. 2 vols xii, 264p; 279p [Issued in 1844. American edition of "Poems." London, Moxon, 1844]
(Rev in American Whig Review 1:38-48 Ja '45; Christian Examiner 38:206-7

Mr '45; R. C. Pitman in Meth R 28: 54-68 Ja '46; [E. A. Poe] in Broadway Journal 1:4-8, 17-20 Ja 4, 11 '45)

The earlier poems of Elizabeth Barrett Browning, 1826-1833. [Ed. by R. H. Shepherd] London, Robson, 1877. xiii,239p
(Rev in Lit W 8:201 Ap '78; Ath 2: 765-7 D 15 '77; Westm ns 53:289 Ja '78; Scribner's Monthly 15:741-3 Mr '78)

Edgar Allan Poe: a criticism; with remarks on the morals and religion of Shelley and Leigh Hunt. [2 letters to R. H. Horne] London, Privately printed for T. J. Wise, 1919. 15p
(30 copies only)

Elizabeth Barrett Browning. Letters to her sister, 1846-1859, ed. by Leonard Huxley. London, Murray [1929] xxv,344p
(Rev by C. Wilkinson in Lond Merc 21:278-9 Ja '30; D. M. Stuart in Nat-Ath 46:319 N 30 '29; T L S N 7 '29 p893; B. Dobreé in Nat R 94:931-40 F '30)

The Greek Christian poets and the English poets. London, Chapman and Hall, 1863. iv,211p [Reprinted from Ath, F 26 '42—Ag 27 '42]
(Rev in Ath 1:425 Mr 28 '63; Knickerbocker Monthly 62:212-16 S '63; Christian Examiner 75:24-43 Jl '63; Reader 1:311-12 Mr 28 '63)

A hitherto unpublished letter. . . Arena 6:296-9 Ag '92

Hitherto unpublished poems and stories, with an unedited autobiography. Boston, Printed exclusively for members of the Bibliophile society, 1914. 2 vols lxii,173p; 243p

Kind words from a sick room. [4 letters to A. P. Paton] Greenock, Privately printed by Wm. Hutchinson, 1891. 10p

Last poems. London, Chapman and Hall, 1862. xii,142p
(Rev in Brit Q 42:359-84 O '65; Eclectic Review ns 2:419-25 My '62; same. Ecl M 56:351-4 Jl '62; Dublin University Magazine 60:157-62 Ag '62; same. Ecl M 57:274-9 O '62; Ath 1: 421-2 Mr 29 '62; Sat R 13:472-4 Ap 26 '62)

Letters of Elizabeth Barrett Browning; ed. with biographical additions by Frederic G. Kenyon. . . London, Smith, Elder, 1897. 2 vols xiv,478p vi,464p
(Rev in Book Reviews 5:176-7 D '97; L. Monroe in Book Reviews 5:109-15 N '97; Church Q R 46:369-91 Jl '98; Good Words 39:43-6 '98; Critic (NY) 31:348-50 D 4 '97; Acad 52:382 N 6 '97; Lit 1:98-100 N 13 '97; Ath 2:627-9 N 6 '97; same. Liv Age 215:739-43 D 11 '97; Sat R 84:749 D 25 '97; Spec 79: 685-6 N 13 '97; A. Macdonell in Bookm (Lond) 13:99-100 D '97; Quar R 189:32-

57 Ja '99; same. Liv Age 221:26-34, 124-33 Ap 1, 8 '99; Bookm (NY) 6:463-6 Ja '98; L. J. Block in Dial 23:274-7 N 16 '97; V. L. Wentz in .Book B ns 16:243-4 Ap '98; Nation (NY) 66:112-13 F 10 '98; Ind 49:1618-19 D 9 '97; M. J. Minckwitz in Allgemeine Zeitung. Beilage O 13 '99 pl; A. MacMechan in Citizen (Phila) 4:84-5 Je '98)

Letters of Elizabeth Barrett Browning addressed to Richard Hengist Horne . . . with comments on contemporaries. Ed. by S. R. T. Mayer. London, Bentley, 1877. 2 vols x,272p; vi,296p
(Rev in Southern Review 23:34-46 Ja '78; H. James, jr. in Nation (NY) 24: 105-6 F 15 '77; Lit W 8:22-3 Jl '77; Sat R 43:25-6 Ja 6 '77; Atlan 39:629-30 My '77; International Review 4:565 Ag '77; Blackw 121:193-5 F '77)

The letters of Robert Browning and Elizabeth Barrett Barrett, 1845-1846. London, Smith, Elder, 1899. 2 vols viii,579p; vi,579p
(Rev in Lit 4:163-5 F 18 '99; Acad 56: 235-7 F 25 '99; Lit W 30:99-100 Ap 1 '99; Sat R 87:242-3 F 25 '99; A. B. McMahan in Dial 26:238-40 Ap 1 '99; Spec 82:308-10 Mr 4 '99; A. Meynell in Bookm (Lond) 15:168-70 Mr '99; A. Meynell in Bookm (NY) 9:162-5 Ap '99; Edin R 189:420-39 Ap '99; same. Liv Age 221:807-20 Je 24 '99; Liv Age 221:166-70 Ap 15 '99; Journal of Education 50:26 Je 29 '99; M. Dronsart in Le Correspondant 195:982-1011 Je 10 '99)

Letters to Robert Browning and other correspondents. . . Ed. by Thomas James Wise. London, Privately printed for T. J. Wise, 1916. 53p
(30 copies only)

New poems by Robert Browning and Elizabeth Barrett Browning, ed. by Frederic G. Kenyon. London, Smith, Elder, 1914. xxxii,184p
(Rev in Contemp 107:667-9 My '15; Nieuwe Gids 1:158-62 Ja '15; Dial 58: 268 Ap 1 '15)

A note on William Wordsworth; with a statement of her views on spiritualism. London, Privately printed for T. J. Wise, 1919. 17p
(30 copies only)

Poems. London, Moxon, 1844. 2 vols xvi,250p; iv,275p [other editions were issued in 1850, 1853, 1856, 1862, etc.]
(Rev in English Review 14:323-32 D '50; same. Ecl M 22:337-44 Mr '51; National Magazine (NY) 12:357-62 Ap '58; Brit Q 2:337-52 N 1 '45; Quar R 66:382-9 S '40; Blackw 56:621-39 N '44; Eclectic Review ns 20:573-85 N '46; Liv Age 28:552-5 Mr 22 '51; Colburn 107: 369-78 Jl '56; Fraser 43:178-82 F '51; No Brit 26:443-50 F '57; same. Ecl M 41:27-38 My '57; Brit Q 42:359-84 O 2 '65; Chamb J 20:361-3 D 3 '53; Prospec-

Browning, Elizabeth Barrett—*Continued*
tive Review 1:445 '45; Monthly Review
165:300 '44; Knickerbocker Monthly 25:
540-2 Je '45; Nation (NY) 3:517 D 27
'66; Tait's Edinburgh Magazine ns 11:
720-5 N '44; Brit Q 34:350-81 O 1 '61;
same. Ecl M 55:303-11 Mr '62; United
States Magazine & Democratic Review
ns 15:370-7 O '44; C. B. Conant in No
Am 94:338-56 Ap '62; C. C. Everett in
No Am 85:415-41 O '57; Ath 2:1242-4
N 30 '50; English Review 4:259-62 D
'45; Harper M 1:714 O '50; 3:280-1 Jl
'51; Edin R 114:513-34 O '61; Blackw
91:449-51 Ap '62; Southern Literary
Messenger 30:146-53 F '60; S. F. Adams
in Westm 42:381-92 D '44; No Brit 36:
514-34 My '62; Eclectic Review 93:295-
303 Mr '51; National Quarterly Review
1:173-201 Je '60; Christian Examiner
72:65-88 Ja '62; [H. F. Chorley] in
Ath 2:763-4 Ag 24 '44; New Quarterly
Review 4:570 O '44)

Poems before congress. London, Chapman and Hall, 1860. x,65p
(Rev in Blackw 87:490-4 Ap '60; Ath
1:371-2 Mr 17 '60; Sat R 9:402-4 Mr
31 '60; A. Wilson in Macmil 6:79-87
My '62; Edin R 114:513-34 O '61)

Poetical works
(Rev by H. D. Davray in Mercure Fr
50:266 Ap '04; Acad 53:117-18 Ja 29
'98; Sat R 85:497-8 Ap 9 '98; Lit W
29:13 Ja 8 '98; Eclectic Review ns 2:
189-212 Mr '62; Lit W 16:153-4 My 2
'85; W. M. Payne in Dial 9:243-4 Ja
'89; Lit W 31:216 N 1 '00; T L S F 5
'04 p33-4; Liv Age 241:312-16 Ap 30
'04; Ecl M 142:825-9 Je '04; M. J.
Minckwitz in Allgemeine Zeitung.
Beilage S 17 '04 p524-5)

The poet's record. [An interesting poem
of Mrs. Browning's stated to be unpublished—pref] *In* Conway, E.
Anthony Munday and other essays.
New York, Privately printed, 1927.
p105-12

The seraphim, and other poems. Lon-
don, Saunders and Otley, 1838. xxii,-
360p
(Rev in Monthly Review 147:119 '38;
Quar R 66:382-9 S '40; Museum of
Foreign Literature 41:195-7 F '41)

Some unpublished papers of Robert and
Elizabeth Barrett Browning, ed. by
G. S. Hellman. Harper M 132:530-9
Mr '16

Sonnets [from the Portuguese] [see
Carter, John and Pollard, Graham in
Section II, Bibliographical Material]
Rev in Lit W 17:419 N 27 '86; Ath
2:182 Ag 8 '03; Dublin Review 176:
148-9 Ja-Mr '25)

Browning, Elizabeth Barrett (transl)
Prometheus bound. Translated from the
Greek of Aeschylus. And miscel-
laneous poems, by the translator. . .
London, Valpy, 1833. xxvi,163p
(Rev in Acad 50:452 N 28 '96)

Browning, Robert
The death of Elizabeth Barrett Browning. London, Printed for private circulation only by Richard Clay, 1916. 21p

The last hours of Elizabeth Barrett
Browning. London, Printed for private
circulation only by Richard Clay, 1919.
12p

A **Browning** anniversary. Bookm (NY)
23:590-2 Ag '06

The **Browning** letters. T L S N 20, D 4 '30
p991, 1042

Browning relics. T. P.'s Weekly 25:21 Ja 2
'15

Browningana. [Note on discovery of
twenty-two unpublished letters] Sat R
Lit 11:612 Ap 6 '35

The **Browning's** love affair as a type of
legitimate romance. Cur Lit 53:348-51
S '12

Burdett, Osbert
The Brownings. London, Constable
[1928] ix,345p bibl p339
(Rev by R. M. Gay in Bookm (NY)
69:202-3 Ap '29; E. Boyd in Out 151:31
Ja 2 '29; D. MacCarthy in Sat R Lit 5:
657-8 F 9 '29; Spec 141:662-4 N 3 '28;
W. C. De Vane in Yale R 18:598-600
Mr '29)

Burton, Richard
The Brownings. *In* Little essays in literature and life. New York, Century,
1914. p287-91

Bury, Yetta Blaze de
see Blaze de Bury, Yetta

Butler, Francis H.
Sonnets from the Portuguese. Acad 66:
258 Mr 5 '04

Butler, Marion E[dwardine]
The child in English verse, William
Blake, Elizabeth Browning. Masters
essay, Columbia univ. 1914

Byron, Mary
A day with Elizabeth Barrett Browning.
London, Hodder & Stoughton [1911]
47p

Caclamanos, D.
Mrs. Browning's translations of the
Odyssey. Notes & Q 155:355, 396 N 16,
D 1 '28

Caine, Thomas Henry Hall, ed.
Sonnets of three centuries. . . London,
Stock, 1882. p129-37

Calverley, Charles Stuart
In the gloaming; poem. *In* The complete
works of C. S. Calverley. London,
Bell, 1902. p59-60
[A parody]

Carpenter, William Boyd
Mrs. Browning. Sun M 22:767-71 '93

Mrs. Browning. *In* In the footsteps of
the poets. New York, 1894. p279-95

Carter, John and Pollard, Graham
The sonnets from the Portuguese. *In* An enquiry into the nature of certain nineteenth century pamphlets. London, Constable, 1934. p8-37

Casa Guidi. Notes & Q 6th ser 6:406 N 18 '82

Casa Guidi Windows. Notes & Q 6th ser 11:238 Mr 21 '85

Charlotte Bronte: E. B. Browning. Notes & Q 5th ser 9:6 Ja 5 '78

Chauvet, Paul
E. B. Browning. *In* Sept essais de littérature anglaise. Paris, Figuière, 1931 (Rev in New Statesm 2:412 O 3 '31)

Chenery, Ruth Baldwin
At vesper times. [Poems] New York, Putnam, 1917. vii,89p [Several poems relate to E. Browning]

Chesterton, Gilbert Keith
Elizabeth Barrett Browning. *In* Varied types. New York, Dodd, Mead, 1903. p261-9

Great Victorian poets. *In* The Victorian age in literature. New York, Holt [1913] p176-81

Chorley, Henry Fothergill
Mrs. Browning. *In* Personal reminiscences by Chorley, Planché, and Young, ed. by R. H. Stoddard. New York, Scribner, Armstrong, 1876. p48-52

Chubb, Edwin Watts
Marriage of the Brownings. *In* Stories of authors, British and American. New York, Macmillan, 1926. p135-9

Clark, John Scott
Elizabeth Barrett Browning. *In* A study of English and American writers. New York, Row, Peterson [c 1916] p418-29

Clark, William Andrews, jr.
Some observations. *In* Sonnets from the Portuguese. . . San Francisco, Nash, 1927. p vi-xiv

Clarke, Isabel Constance
Elizabeth Barrett Browning; a portrait. London, Hutchinson [pref 1929] 304p (Rev by C. E. Lawrence in Bookm (Lond) 76:176 Je '29; T L S My 16 '29 p396)

Clever girls of our time and how they became famous women. London, Darton, 1863. vol. II

Cohen, Josef
Sonnetten vit het Portugeesch. Buiten p354, 480, 582 Jl, O 2, D 4 '15

Coleridge, Sara
Memoir and letters . . . ed. by her daughter [Edith Coleridge] London, King, 1873. vol I p301-5; vol II p446-8

A collection of portraits of Elizabeth Barrett Browning and a view of Casa Guidi, Florence. [London, 187-?]

Cone, Helen G. and Gilder, Jeannette L. eds.
Elizabeth Barrettt Browning. *In* Pen-portraits of literary women, by themselves and others, with biographical sketches by the former. New York, Cassell, 1887. vol II p93-127

Conway, Eustace
Elizabeth Barrett Browning. *In* Anthony Munday. . . New York, Privately printed, 1927. p105-12 (250 copies only)

Cook, Joseph
Preface. *In* Boston Monday lectures, January 8, 1883. London, Dickinson, 1883

Corkran, Henriette
A little girl's recollections of E. B. Browning. . . Ecl M 124:345-9 Mr '95; *same.* Liv Age 204:311-15 F 2 '95; *same.* Temple 103:551-8 D '94

Corner, Susanna
"The memorable lady." Notes & Q 11th ser 5:431 Je 1 '12

La correspondance amoureuse de Browning. R Pol et Litt 51:826-7 Je 21 '13

Corson, Hiram
The cost of a poet: Elizabeth Barrett Browning's "A musical instrument." Poet Lore 7:259-63 '95

Coupland, W. C.
Aurora Leigh. A discourse delivered in South Place Chapel, Finsbury. . . London, Allen [1886?] p93-104

Couthouy, Marion
Elizabeth Barrett Browning. Lippinc 21: 747-53 Je '78

Creston, Dormer [pseud]
see Baynes, Dorothy Julia

Crosse, (Mrs) Cornelia A. H.
The wedded poets. *In* Red letter days of my life. London, Bentley, 1892. vol I p225-80

Crow, (Mrs) Martha Emily (Foote)
Elizabeth Barrett Browning. (Modern poets and Christian teaching) New York, Eaton and Mains [c 1907] viii, 232p

Cruse, Amy
Bells and pomegranates: Aurora Leigh. *In* English literature through the ages. Beowulf to Stevenson. New York, Stokes [1914] p550-5

Cunliffe, John William
Early Victorian poets. *In* Leaders of the Victorian revolution. New York, Appleton-Century [c 1934] p118-30

Elizabeth Barrett's influence on Browning's poetry. P M L A 23:169-83 '08

Cunnington, S.
Sonnets from the Portuguese. Acad 66: 181 F 13 '04

Curtis, George William
[Reminiscences of the Brownings] Harper M 23:555-6 S '61

Darmesteter, Mary James
Grands écrivains d'outre manche: les Brontë, Thackeray, les Brownings, Rossetti. Paris, 1901

Darmesteter, Mary James—*Continued*
Ménage de poètes. Revue de P 5:295-317, 788-817 S 15, O 15 '98

[Date of Mrs. Browning's birth] Lit W 19:89 Mr 17 '88; Book B ns 7:288 Ag '90

Dawson, William James
Humanitarian movement in poetry—Thomas Hood and Mrs. Browning. *In* Makers of English poetry. New York, Revell, 1906. rev ed p164-77

Days with the Victorian poets: Mrs. Browning. London, Hodder & Stoughton, 1913

[Death of Elizabeth Barrett Browning] Harper M 23:563 S '61

Delaney, Honora
Alice Meynell as a critic of English literature. Masters essay, Univ. of Pittsburgh, 1932. *Abstract in* Univ. of Pittsburgh Bulletin 8:383-4 '32

Dennis, John
Elizabeth Barrett Browning. Leisure Hour 36:86-90 F '89; *same*. Liv Age 180:629-35 Mr 9 '89

Des Guerrois, Charles
Étude sur mistress Eliztbeth Browning, suivie de ses quarante-quatre Sonnets portugais et de quelques autres de ses poëmes traduits par Charles Des Guerrois. Paris, Lemerre, 1885

Dick, E.
Sonnets from the Portuguese. Acad 66:157 F 6 '04

Doerk, Agathe
Robert Browning und Elizabeth Barrett Browning. Die Frau 12:685-93 Ag '05

Doorn, Willem van
Theory and practice of English narrative verse since 1833. Amsterdam [1932?] p104-16

Dowden, Edward
Victorian literature. *In* Transcripts and studies. London, Kegan Paul, French, Trübner, 1896. 2d ed. p212-13

Drinkwater, John
Victorian poetry. (People's library) London, Hodder & Stoughton, 1923. p183-4

Druskowitz, H[elene] von
Drei englische dichterinnen; essays. Berlin, R. Oppenheim, 1885. 242p

Duclaux, Mary
see Darmesteter, Mary

Dye, Vincent
Die beziehung von Elisabeth Barrett Brownings leben zu ihrer dichtkunst. Leipzig, Zechel, 1905. 64p Diss. Leipzig

E. B. Browning. Notes & Q 3d ser 9:155-6 F 24 '66

E. B. Browning, the poetess. Notes & Q 3d ser 11:477 Je 15 '67

Eagle, Solomon [pseud]
see Squire, John Collings

Ein brief an Napoleon III. Dresdener Anzeiger Montagsbeilage no 21 '07

Eliot, R. F.
Elizabeth Browning and Christina Rossetti; a comparison. Masters essay, Columbia univ. 1927

Elizabeth B. Barrett. Southern Literary Messenger 11:235-43 Ap '45

Elizabeth Barrett. United States Magazine & Democratic Review ns 15:72-3 Jl '44

Elizabeth Barrett Browning. Ath 1:153 Ja 31 '63; Ath 2:19-20, 52-3 Jl 6, 13 '61; Atlan 8:368-76 S '61; Cornhill 29:469-90 Ap '74; Eclectic Review ns 2:189-212 Mr '62; Ecl M 32:423-7 Jl '54; Ecl M 67:247-8 Ag '66; Every Sat 16:510-18 My 9 '74; International Magazine 5:310 Mr 1 '52; Living Age 249:173-9 Ap 21 '06; Macmil 4:402-4 S '61; National Magazine (Lond) 10:210-13 '61; Notes & Q 7th ser 8:41-2 Jl 20 '89; T L S Mr 9 '06 p77-8; Scribner's Monthly 7:101-14 N '73; Ecl M 56:74-8 My '62; Atlan 8:368-76 S '61

Elizabeth Barrett Browning. *In* The Library of literary criticism of English and American authors . . . ed. by Charles Wells Moulton. . . Buffalo, New York, Moulton publishing company, 1904-05. vol VI p228-47

Elizabeth Barrett Browning (1809-1861) *In* Warner, C. D. ed. Library of the world's best literature. . . Memorial ed. New York, Hill [c 1902] vol VI p2523-7

Elizabeth Barrett Browning: a biographical and critical study. Madras, Sriniwasa, Varadachari, 1899. vi,79p

Elton, Oliver
The Brownings. *In* A survey of English literature, 1830-1880. London, Arnold, 1920. vol I p397-404

Emery, Fred Parker
Elizabeth Barrett Browning. *In* Notes on English literature. Boston, Ginn, 1891. p129-31

Engel, Eduard
Elisabeth Browning. *In* Geschichte der englischen literatur. Leipzig, Brandstetter, 1929. p410-13

Engels, Eleanor Perry
Elizabeth Barrett Browning: critic. Masters essay, Univ. of Notre Dame, 1933. 45ff

English singing-birds in Florence. Scribner's Monthly 4:616-17 S '72

Erdenberger, Gottfried G.
Popes einfluss auf die jugenddichtungen der Elizabeth Barrett Browning. Halle, John, 1916. 66p Thesis. Leipzig

Essay on Elizabeth Barrett Browning's "Sonnets from the Portuguese." London, Waters [pref 1878] 64p

Étienne, L.
La Littérature des femmes en Angleterre. Revue Contemporaine 2d ser 1:257-86 Ja F '58

Fallows, Joseph
Poem on the Italian wars. Notes & Q 9th ser 6:448 D 8 '00

Fawcett, (Mrs) Henry
Elizabeth Barrett Browning. *In* Some eminent women of our times. London, Macmillan, 1889. p111-16

Fehr, Bernhard
Die englische literatur des 19. und 20. Jahrhunderts. Wildpark-Potsdam, 1928. p215-16

[Field, Kate]
Elizabeth Barrett Browning. Atlan 8: 368-76 S '61

[Fitzgerald's dislike for Mrs. Browning]
Nation (NY) 49:111-12 Ag 8 '89

Fleckenstein, Edgar
Elizabeth Barrett Browning als kritiker englischer literatur. Heidelberg, Winter, 1912. viii,80p Diss. Würzburg. bibl pv

Die literarischen anschauungen und kritiken Elizabeth Barrett Brownings. (Würzburger beiträge zur englischen literaturgeschichte. v 3) Heidelberg, Winter, 1913. xii,124p

Fonblanque, Ethel Maude de (Mrs. Arthur Harter)
The influence of Italy on the poetry of the Brownings. Fortn 92:327-44 Ag '09

Forman, Elsa
Mrs. Browning: inscription. Notes & Q 147:228 S 27 '24

Forman, H[arry] Buxton
Elizabeth Barrett Browning: new data.... *In* Barrett, Elizabeth Barrett. The poets' enchiridion. Boston, The Bibliophile society, 1914. p9-34

Elizabeth Barrett Browning and her scarcer books; a bio-bibliographical note. London, privately printed, 1896. 29p [30 copies printed]

[Lines on "Aurora Leigh"] *In* Barrett (Browning), Elizabeth Barrett. The poets' enchiridion. Boston, Bibliophile society, 1914. p51-3

Fox, W. J.
Miss Barrett and Mrs. Adams. People's Journal 1:130-6 Mr 7 '46

Francis, John C.
Elizabeth Barrett Browning centenary. March 6th, 1906. Notes & Q 10th ser 5:204-5, 224-5 Mr 17, 24 '06

Frank, Maude Morrison
Elizabeth Barrett Browning. *In* Great authors in their youth. New York, Holt, 1915. p153-71

[French translations of her Sonnets] Acad 68:513-14 My 13 '05

Garnett, Richard
Elizabeth Barrett Browning. *In* English literature, an illustrated record, by Richard Garnett and Edmund Gosse. New York, Grosset & Dunlap [c 1904] vol IV p212-20

Gates, Lewis Edwards
English literature of the nineteenth century: a retrospect. Critic (NY) 36:177-80 F '00

Return to conventional life. *In* Studies and appreciations. New York, Macmillan, 1900. p38-44

Gaultier, Bon [pseud]
see Aytoun, William Edmondstoune and Martin, Theodore

Gaylord, Harriet
The Brownings and Gosse. Sat R Lit 11:220 O 20 '34

Gosse and the Reading sonnets. T L S N 8 '34 p775

The human side of E. B. B. Sat R Lit 12:9 Ag 24 '35

Pompilia and her poet ... with an introd. by Charles Hanson Towne. New York, Literary publications, 1931. [15]-190p [rev ed 1932. 205p]

Gilder, Richard Watson
A romance of the nineteenth century. Cent 70:918-27 O '05; *same.* Cur Lit 39:499-500 N '05

Gilfillan, George
Mrs. Elizabeth Barrett Browning. Tait's Edinburgh Magazine ns 14:620-5 S '47; *same.* Ecl M 12:249-56 O '47

Mrs. Elizabeth Barrett Browning. *In* Modern literature and literary men. New York, Appleton, 1857. 3d ed. p239-51

Gill, Helen Van Riper
The influence of Elizabeth Barrett Browning upon the poetry of Robert Browning. Masters essay, Univ. of California, 1922. 199ff

Gladstone, W. E.
British poetry of the nineteenth century. Speaker 1:34-5 Ja 11 '90

Goewey, Kate Severance (Spencer)
Descriptive catalogue of the Goewey collection of Browning pictures ... together with an introductory paper read before the San Francisco Browning society. San Francisco, Nash, 1917. xxii,40p [100 copies only]

Goforth, Alys Millsaps
Realism and idealism as exemplified in the works of Reverend George Crabbe and Elizabeth B. Browning. Masters essay, George Washington Univ. 1923. 34ff

Gosse, Edmund
The literature of the Victorian era. Engl Illus 17:487 Jl '97

The sonnets from the Portuguese. *In* Critical kit-kats. London, Heinemann, 1913. p1-17

Gothein, Marie
Eine dichterehe: Elizabeth Barrett Browning. Preussische Jahrbücher 109: 377-97 S '02

Gould, Elizabeth Porter
The Browning letters. Educa 20:214-20 D '99

The Brownings and America. Boston, Poet-lore company, 1904. 115p

The supremacy of Mrs. Browning. Unitar 21:43-50 Ja '84

Grappe, Georges
E. B. Browning. *In* Essai sur la poésie anglaise au XIXe siècle. Paris, Sansot, 1906. p65-8

[Grebanier, Mrs. Frances (Vinciguerra)] Frances Winwar [pseud]
Poor splendid wings. Boston, Little, Brown, 1933. p207

Greve, F. P. trans.
Briefe von Robert Browning und Elizabeth Barrett Browning. Berlin, 1905. 2 vols

Gribble, Francis
Robert Browning. 19th Cent 71:976-88 My '12

Griswold, Hattie Tyng
Elizabeth Barrett Browning. *In* Personal sketches of recent authors. Chicago, McClurg, 1898. p114-35

Robert and Elizabeth Browning. *In* Home life of great authors. Chicago, McClurg, 1887. p274-85

Guerrois, Charles des
see Des Guerrois, Charles

Guild, Marion Pelton
To Robert and Elizabeth Barrett Browning; poem. Atlan 86:420-1 S '00

Hamilton, Catherine Jane
Elizabeth Barrett Browning. *In* Women writers; their works and ways. London, Ward, Lock, 1893. 2d ser p142-65

Hamilton, Harry Wilson
The mind of Elizabeth Barrett Browning. Masters essay, Univ. of Texas, 1909. 184ff

Hanley, Constance E.
The Risorgimento in the works of Landor, Swinburne, Mrs. Browning and Meredith. Masters essay, Columbia univ. 1927

Harlan, Richard Davenport
A forgotten hymn of Mrs. Browning's. Out 133:499-50 Mr 14 '23

Havemann, J.
E. B. Browning. Der Türmer p378-81 Je '06

Hawthorne, Nathaniel
Passages from the French and Italian note-books. Boston, Osgood, 1873. vol II p9-13

Herridge, William T.
Elizabeth Barrett Browning. And R 7:607-23 Je '87

Hersey, Heloise E.
Introduction. *In* A selection from Mrs. Browning's poems. New York, Macmillan, 1903. pvii-xxi [Includes chronological list]

Herzfeld, M.
E. B. Browning in ihren Briefen. Österr Rundschau 6:286-95 '04

Hickey, Emily Henrietta
Elizabeth Barrett Browning; woman and poet. 19th Cent 74:164-84 Jl '13

Higginbotham, Elsie
An apology on reading the Browning love letters. Book-Lover (San Francisco) 2:127 '01

Higginson, Thomas Wentworth
A great poet in her prime. Bookn 24:457-9 Mr '06

Hillard, George Stillman
Robert and Elizabeth Browning. *In* Six months in Italy. Boston, Ticknor, Reed, & Fields, 1853. vol I p177-8

Hincks, Edward Y.
Elizabeth Barrett Browning. *In* Eminent women of the age. . . Hartford, Conn. S. M. Betts, 1868. p221-49

Holcombe, Samuel B.
Death of Mrs. Browning. Southern Literary Messenger 33:412-17 D '61

Homage français à Elizabeth Barrett Browning à l'occasion de son centenaire, mars 1806—mars 1906. Vals-les-Bains, Aberlen, 1906. 24,iii p

Hope, Eva
Queens of literature. London, 1886

Hopfenbeck, Franziska
Soziale zweckdichtung. Proben aus E. Gaskell, Kingsley und E. B. Browning. München, Kellerer, 1930. 63p

Hopkins, Annette Brown
The poet laureate of Hope End. So Atlan Q 30:290-308 Jl '31

Horne, Richard Hengist
Elizabeth Barrett Browning and her contemporaries. St J 36:138-50 Ap '75

Elizabeth Barrett Browning on some of her contemporaries. St J 3d ser 2:21-31 O '75

Letters from Elizabeth Barrett Browning to the author of "Orion" on literary and general topics. Contemp 23:146-61, 281-302, 447-61, 799-813 D '73, Ja, F, Ap, '74; *same*. Liv Age 120:281-90, 535-47 Ja '31, F 28 '74; 121:116-24 Ap 11 '74; 122:24-32 Jl 4 '74; *same*. Ecl M 82:213-21, 346-57 F, Mr '74

Miss E. B. Barrett and Mrs. Norton. *In* A new spirit of the age. New York, Harper, 1844. p265-70

Portraits and memories. Macmil 22:363-71 S '70; *same*. Liv Age 107:34-5 O 1 '70

Recollections of Elizabeth Barrett Browning. . . St J 35:466-80 F '75

Horne, Richard Henry
see Horne, Richard Hengist

Hosmer, Harriet G.
Recollections of the Brownings. Youth's Companion 74:388, 599-600 Ag 9, N 15 '00

[Hubbard, Elbert]
Elizabeth Barrett Browning. *In* Little journeys to the homes of famous women. (Little journeys vol 3, ser of 1897) London, Putnam [1897]

Humphrey, Grace
A poet and the wife of a poet. *In* The story of the Elizabeths. Philadelphia, Penn publishing co. 1924. p108-30

Hunt, Leigh
Aurora Leigh. Cornhill 76:738-49 N '97
Correspondence. London, Smith, Elder, 1862. vol II p264-8
A letter of Leigh Hunt's. Ath 2:15-18 Jl 7 '83

Hunt, Theodore W.
Elizabeth Barrett Browning. Presbyterian and Reformed Review 7:496-506 Jl '96
A study of Mrs. Browning. *In* English literary miscellany. Oberlin, Ohio, Bibliotheca Sacra co. 1914. Ser II p268-92

Hutton, Laurence
Literary landmarks of Florence. New York, Harper, 1897. p60-4

Huxley, Leonard
"The Barretts of Wimpole Street"; a comment. Cornhill ns 70:87-93 Ja '31
Mrs. Browning and her father's forgiveness. Cornhill ns 74:331-6 Mr '33
A visitor to the Brownings. From material supplied by O. S. Holt. Yale R 13:228-46 Ja '24
A visitor to the Brownings at Casa Guidi; letters of Walter Richard Cassels; ed. by L. Huxley. Cornhill ns 56:96-112 Ja '24

Ingram, John H.
Elizabeth Barrett Browning. . . (Famous women) Boston, Roberts, 1893. viii,[9]-264p bibl p[vii]-viii
Elizabeth Barrett Browning. (Eminent women ser) London, Allen, 1888. xii, 194p
(Rev in Critic (NY) 13:187-8 O 20 '88; J. A. Noble in Acad 34:265-6 O 27 '88; Sat R 66:466-7 O 20 '88; Lond Q R 72:22-42 Ap '89; *same.* Liv Age 181: 643-52 Je 15 '89)
Mrs. Barrett Browning's parentage. Ath 2:33, 255 Jl 7, Ag 25 '94
Mrs. Browning. Ath 1:146 F 4 '88

Innes, Arthur Donald
Elizabeth Barrett Browning. *In* Seers and singers. London, Innes, 1893
(Rev in Literary World (Lond) ns 48: 315 O 27 '93; Speaker 8:443 O 21 '93)

Innes, (Mrs) Kathleen Elizabeth
see Royds, Kathleen Elizabeth

Jacobi, Bernhard
Elizabeth Barrett Browning als übersetzerin antiker dichtungen. (Münstersche beiträge zur englischen literaturgeschichte. . . V) Münster, Schöningh, 1908. 94p Also: Diss. Münster, 1908. 85p

Jacottet, Henri
Poètes modernes de l'Angleterre; Élisabeth Barrett Browning. Bibliothèque Universelle et Revue Suisse 35:5-27, 352-74 Jl-Ag '87

James, Henry
William Wetmore Story and his friends . . . Boston, Houghton, Mifflin, 1904. 2 vols passim

Jiriczek, O.
Viktorianische dichtung. Heidelberg, 1907

Jones, Dora M.
English writers and the making of Italy. Lond Q R 118:85-90 Jl '12

Jones, (Sir) Henry
Robert Browning and Elizabeth Barrett Browning. *In* Essays on literature and education. . . ed. by H. J. W. Hetherington. London, Hodder and Stoughton [1924] p81-166; *also in* C H E L vol XIII p77-83

Jones, Marion Sheridan
Woman and genius. Outlook (Lond) 58: 284-5 S 25 '26

Kassner, Rudolf
Robert Browning und Elizabeth Barrett Browning. Neue Rundschau 15:769-804 Jl '04

Kearney, Edward P.
Elizabeth Barrett Browning; the development of her artistry in relation to her interests. Masters essay, Stanford Univ. 1933. 102ff

Kellner, Leon
Die englische literatur der neuesten Zeit. Leipzig, Tauchnitz, 1921. p187-96
Die englische literatur im zeitalter der königin Viktoria. Leipzig, Tauchnitz, 1909. p316-27

Kenley, Polk Macune
The influence of Elizabeth Barrett Browning on the works of Robert Browning. Masters essay, Univ. of Texas, 1928. 108ff

Kenyon, (Sir) Frederic George
The Brownings for the young. London, Smith, Elder, 1896. xii,203p
Of the Browning mss. Cornhill 108:166-74 Ag 13; *same.* Liv Age 278:733-8 S 20 '13

Kernahan, Coulson
Mrs. Browning and the "Ever-Womanly." *In* Wise men and a fool. New York, Brentano, 1901. p203-21

Key, Ellen
Elisabeth Barrett; Robert Browning och Elisabeth Barrett; Robert och Elisabeth Barrett Browning. *In* Människor. Stockholm, Bonnier [c 1913] p11-32, 43-80, 81-129

Kingsland, William G.
Mrs. Browning's "opinion" on Tennyson. Poet Lore 8:23-7 '96
Rare poems of Elizabeth Barrett Browning. Poet Lore 4:46-9 '92

Kingsley, Maud Elma
Outline studies in literature. [Elizabeth Barrett Browning] Boston, Palmer co. 1915

Kinney, Elizabeth Clementine
A day with the Brownings at Pratolino. Scribner's Magazine 1:185-8 D '70

[Krinitz, Elise] Selden, Camille [pseud]
Élizabeth Browning. *In* Portraits de femmes. Paris, Charpentier, 1877. p231-53

Kuhns, Oscar
Browning and Tennyson. *In* Dante and the English poets from Chaucer to Tennyson. New York, Holt, 1904. p234-8

Lambert, Lillian V.
The Brownings in Florence. Chautauquan 35:590-5 S '02

Landor, Walter Savage
To Elizabeth Barrett Browning and other verses. London, Privately printed, 1917. 22p
The late Elizabeth Barrett Browning. Liv Age 70:489-90 Ag 24 '61; *same.* Ecl M 54:55-7 S '61

Laughlin, Clara Elizabeth
The Brownings.—The most ideal of love stories. Good Words 44:474-85 '03; *same in* Stories of authors' loves. Philadelphia, Lippincott, 1902. vol II p9-45

Lee, Elizabeth
Mrs. Browning through Swedish eyes. Acad 65:721-2 D 26 '03

Leeuw, J. J. v. d.
Aurora Leigh. Minerva Mr 14, Ap 18, 25 '18

LeGallienne, Richard
A propos the Browning love-letters. *In* Sleeping beauty and other prose fancies. London, Lane, 1900. p191-8
The love story of Robert Browning and Elizabeth Barrett. *In* The loves of the poets. New York, Baker & Taylor, 1911. p1-57
Robert Browning and Elizabeth Barrett. *In* Old love stories retold. London, Lane, 1924

Lenanton, (Mrs) Carola Oman
Miss Barrett's elopement. London, Hodder & Stoughton, 1929. 368p

Letters of Elizabeth Barrett Browning in Cornhill Magazine, 1929. Notes & Q 156:309, 381 Ap 4, Je 1 '29; 157:19-20 Jl 13 '29

Le Vert, Octavia Walton
see Vert, Octavia Walton Le

Levy, Margaret Preston
The art of Elizabeth Barrett Browning. Masters essay, Univ. of Texas, 1912. 211ff

Ley, Wilfred R.
The Brownings in Paris. American Review 1:308-12 Je '33

Litchfield, Grace Denio
The publication of the Browning love-letters. Ind 51:1941-2 Jl 20 '99

The literature of the last fifty years. Blackw 141:745 Je '87

Loth, David Goldsmith
The Brownings; a Victorian idyll. New York, Brentano, 1929. xviii,289p bibl p287-9
(Rev by R. M. Gay in Bookm (NY) 69:202-3 Ap '29; W. C. DeVane in Yale R 18:598-600 Mr '29)

Lowell, James Russell
Swinburne's tragedies. *In* My study windows. Boston, Osgood, 1871. p212

Lubbock, Percy
Elizabeth Barrett Browning in her letters. London, Smith, Elder, 1906. 382p
(Rev in Acad 70:305-6 Mr 31 '06; E. Dowden in Bookm (Lond) 30:71-2 My '06; Spec 96:907-8 Je 9 '06; T L S Mr 30 '06 p118)

M. Taine on "Aurora Leigh." Every Sat ns 3:611 D 23 '71

McCandless, (Mrs) Lucy Bert
The modernity of E. B. Browning. Masters essay, Univ. of Pittsburgh, 1930. For abstract see Abstracts of Masters' theses, Univ. of Pittsburgh Bulletin 6: 330 '30

Macdonald, M.
Der dichterpaar Browning. Hamburg Correspondent no 5 '05

McFee, Inez Nellie Canfield
Elizabeth Barrett Browning. *In* Studies in American and British literature. Chicago, Flanagan [c 1905] p412-19

MacMahan, Anna Benneson
Elizabeth Barrett Browning. *In* Florence in the poetry of the Brownings. Chicago, McClurg, 1904. p21-102

Macpherson, Gerardine
Memoirs of the life of Anna Jameson. Boston, Roberts, 1878. p190-1

Maguire, Lillian Irma
The personality of Elizabeth Barrett Browning described by her contemporaries; a biographical study. Masters essay, Columbia univ. 1923

Mallock, E. B.
Prophets and poets. Dark Blue 1:152-62 Ap '71

Marshall, Andrew
Balaustion and Mrs. Browning. Cornhill 124:586-93 N '21; *same.* Liv Age 311:707-10 D 17 '21

Marshall, Edward H.
James Russell Lowell on "Aurora Leigh." Notes & Q 9th ser 4:95 Jl 29 '99

Martin, E. S.
[Note on the Browning letters] Harper W 43:493 My 20 '99

Martin, Theodore
see Aytoun, William Edmondstoune and Martin, Theodore

Massarini, Tullo
Poesie scelte di Elisabetta Barrett-Browning. Milano, 1898
(Rev in Nation (NY) 66:265 Ap 7 '98)

Matson, Esther
A practical memorial to a great woman. Craftsman 10:713 S '06

Maulsby, David Lee
Art phases of the Brownings' life in Italy. [Boston? 1906?] 16ff Typed ms. in the Boston Public Library

Meissner, Paul
Pessimistische strömungen im englischen geistesleben des 19. jahrhunderts. Engl Stud 64:434 '29

Memoir of Elizabeth Barrett Browning. *In* The poetical works of Elizabeth Barrett Browning. . . New York, Miller, 1876. vol I p5-23

[Memorial institute to Mrs. E. B. Browning at Ledbury] Bookm (NY) 3:6 Mr '96

Merlette, Germaine-Marie
La vie et l'oeuvre d'Elizabeth Barrett Browning. Paris, Colin, 1905. x,365p

Merrill, Flora
Flush of Wimpole Street and Broadway. New York, McBride, 1933. 120p

Meyerfeld, Max
Die Brownings. Das Litterarische Echo 7:1242-6 Je 1 '05

Michaelson-Jessen, Anna
Robert Browning and Elizabeth Barrett. Zukunft 28:555-9 S 23 '99

Milsand, Joseph Antoine
La poésie Anglaise. . . Elisabeth Browning, J.-E. Reade, Henry Taylor. R Deux Mondes 13:338-43 Ja 15 '52; *same in* Littérature anglaise et philosophie. Dijon, 1893. p147-72

Minckwitz, M. J.
Briefliche äusserungen der englischen dichterin. Beilage zur Allgemeinen Zeitung München no 234 '99
E. B. Browning's "Book of the poets." Beilage zur Allgemeinen Zeitung no 213 '04
E. Barrett-Browning. Glückauf no 25 '06
Einige beziehungen der englischen dichterin E. Barrett-Browning zu Frankreich, insbesondere zur französischen literatur. Zeitschrift für französische Sprache und Litteratur 30:332-42 '06
Zu den "Casa Guidi windows" der dichterin E. Barrett-Browning. Anglia 50:179-94 My '26

Mrs. Barrett Browning. Aurora Leigh. Blackw 81:23-41 Ja '57

Mrs. Barrett Browning's parentage. Ath 1:838 Je 30 '94

Mrs. Browning. Nation (NY) 48:7-8 Ja 3 '89; Macmil 59:138-45 D '88; *same.* Liv Age 179:802-8 D 29 '88; Sat R 12:41-2 Jl 13 '61; *same.* Liv Age 70:491-2 Ag 24 '61

Mrs. Browning and Christian poetry. Boston Review 1:154-64 Mr '61

Mrs. Browning and Miss Mitford. Lit 1:150-1 N 20 '97

Mrs. Browning as prophetess. Acad 61:345-6 O 12 '01

Mrs. Browning's birthplace. Acad 69:708-9 Jl 8 '05

Mrs. Browning's dog "Flush." Notes & Q 4th ser 11:104 F 1 '73

Mrs. Browning's early poem "The Battle of Marathon." Ath 2:618-19 N 7 '91

Mrs. Browning's religious opinions, as expressed in three letters, addressed to Wm. Merry, Esq. *In* Literary anecdotes of the nineteenth century . . . ed. by W. R. Nicoll and T. J. Wise. London, Hodder & Stoughton, 1896. vol II p123-42; also privately printed: London, 1896. 28p [30 copies]

Mrs. Browning's sonnet on Wordsworth. Notes & Q 155:374 N 24 '28

Mrs. Browning's translations of the Odyssey. Notes & Q 155:259, 355, 391 O 13, N 16, D 1 '28

Mrs. Elizabeth Barrett Browning. Ecl M 43:127-8 Ja '58

Mitford, Mary Russell
The friendships of Mary Russell Mitford. . . ed. by A. G. L'Estrange. London, Hurst & Blackett, 1882. vol II p15-19, 33-9, 66-78
Letters of Mary Russell Mitford. ed. by Henry Chorley. London, Bentley, 1872. 2d ser 2 vols passim
Married poets. *In* Recollections of a literary life. New York, Harper, 1852. p169-84

Moir, David M.
Sketches of the poetical literature of the past half-century. Edinburgh, Blackwood, 1852. 2d ed. p280-4

Molloy, J. Fitzgerald
Elizabeth Barrett Browning. Tinsley's 30:366-74 Ap '82

Molmenti, Pompeo
Elisabetta Barrett Browning. Nuova Antol 4th ser 73:276-84 Ja 16 '98; *same.* (translated) Liv Age 219:35-40 O 1 '98

Montégut, Émile
Mistress Browning. *In* Écrivains modernes de l'Angleterre. Deuxième série . . . Paris, Hachette, 1889. p133-92; *same.* R Deux Mondes 2d per 8:322-53 Mr 15 '57

Monti, Giulio
Elisabetta Barrett Browning. Emporium 3:354-63 My '96

Moore, Rebecca Deming
Famous men and women of March. Normal Instructor and Primary Plans 40:38 Mr '31

Moore, Virginia
Elizabeth Barrett Browning. *In* Distinguished women writers. New York, Dutton [c1934] p177-87

Morison, Jeanie
Robert Browning and Elizabeth Barrett Browning. *In* Chambers's cyclopaedia of English literature. New ed. by David Patrick. Philadelphia, Lippincott, 1904. vol III p549-59

Morris, George Perry
The Brownings in Italy. Their attitude towards its political evolution. [Boston] 1905. 30ff Typed MS. in the Boston Public Library. (Read before Boston Browning Society, December 1905)
Elizabeth Barrett Browning. Ind 60:501-4 Mr 1 '06

Municipio Della Città di Asolo Pel Cinquantesimo Anniversario Della Nozze di Roberto Browning con Elisabetta Barrett xii Dicembre MDCCCLXXXXVI. Asolo, Vivian, 1896. 8p

Murray, Henry
Lyric love. *In* Robert Buchanan. . . London, Wellby, 1901. p202-14

Myers, Jay Arthur
Elizabeth Barrett Browning. *In* Fighters of fate; a story of men and women who have achieved greatly despite the handicaps of the great white plague. . . Baltimore, Williams & Wilkins, 1927. p87-96

Nencioni, Enrico
Aurora Leigh (Poema di Elisabetta Barrett Browning) Nuova Antol 2d ser 45: 5-18 My 1 '84

Aurora Leigh. *In* Saggi critici di letteratura inglese. Firenze, 1897. p54-76

Nevinson, Henry Woodd
The poet lovers. *In* Books and personalities. New York, Lane, 1905. p99-115

Nicati, Mme. W.
Femme et poète, Elizabeth Browning. Paris, Perrin, 1912. 354p

Obituary. Gent M 211:215 Ag '61

O'Brien, (Mrs) William
Home affections. Irish Monthly 59:441-8 Jl '31

O'Hagan, Thomas
Mrs. Browning's "Sonnets from the Portuguese." *In* Studies in poetry, critical, analytical, interpretative. Boston, Marlier, Callanan, 1900. p38-50

Oliphant, Margaret
Elizabeth Barrett Browning. 1809-1861. *In* The Victorian age of English literature. New York, Tait [c 1892] vol I p227-34

Oliver, Eleanor
Poe and Mrs. Browning. Masters essay, Columbia univ. 1927

Ossoli, Sarah Margaret (Fuller) marchesa d'
Miss Barrett's poems. *In* Art, literature, and the drama. . . ed. by . . . Arthur B. Fuller. Boston, Brown, Taggard and Chase, 1860. p198-206

Pancoast, Henry S.
Mrs. Browning in poetry to-day. Bookn 24:464-6 Mr '06

Pape, Frederick J. "Aurora Leigh"; poem. Acad 36:39 Jl 20 '89

Parrott, Helen Louise
The literary and social significance of Mrs. Browning's "Aurora Leigh." Masters essay, Univ. of Iowa, 1931. 43ff

Parton, James
Elizabeth Barrett Browning. *In* Eminent women of the age. New York, Balden [188-?] p64-70

Peattie, Mrs. Elia (Wilkinson)
Love and death. Harper's Bazaar 45: 408-9 S '11

Pluviarmes, H.
Hommage français à Elizabeth Barrett Browning à l'occasion de son centenaire. Vals-les-Bains, 1906

Poe, Edgar Allan
Miss Barrett's "A drama of exile, and other poems." *In* The works of Edgar Allan Poe. . . ed. by E. C. Stedman and G. E. Woodberry. Chicago, Stone & Kimball, 1895. vol VI p288-320 (From Broadway Journal 1:4-8, 17-20 Ja 4-11 '45)

Poetesses. Sat R 25:678-9 My 23 '68; *same.* Liv Age 97:819-22 Je 27 '68

The **poetry** of Elizabeth Barrett Browning. Chamb J ns 20:361-3 D 3 '53; *same.* Liv Age 40:178-80 Ja 21 '54; Tait's Edinburgh Magazine ns 23:14-20 Ja '56; Westm 118:373-92 O 1 '82; *same.* Liv Age 155:416-26 N 18 '82

Pöling, Wilhelm Theodor Maria
Kritische studien zu E. B. Browning. (Münstersche Beiträge zur englischen literaturgeschichte. Heft 6) Münster, Schöningh, 1909. viii,90p bibl pvii-viii Diss. Münster

Porter, Laura Spencer
The world's greatest lovers. Woman's Home Companion 40:24 N '13

[Portraits]
Bookm (Lond) 64:12 Ap '23; Bookn 24: 457-8, 461, 463-5 Mr '06; Bookm (NY) 6:397 Ja '98; 17:603 Ag '03; Engl Illus 17:491 Jl '97; Bookm (Lond) 23:51, 55 N '02; Book B ns 16:208 Ap '98; Emporium 3:355, 358 My '96; Good Words 44:facing 457 '03

Powell, Thomas
Elizabeth B. Barrett. *In* The Living authors of England. New York, Appleton, 1849. p137-52

Preston, Harriet Waters
Robert and Elizabeth Browning. Atlan 83:812-26 Je '99

Proctor, Annie
A coincidence. Notes & Q 5th ser 4: 465-6 D 11 '75

Radecliffe, Noell
E. B. Browning. (First poem—"Battle of Marathon," published 1820) Notes & Q 3d ser 9:248 Mr 24 '66

Ratcliffe, S. K.
Mrs. Browning's birth-year. Spec 99:1049
D 21 '07

Reed, Myrtle
Elizabeth Barrett Browning. *In* Happy
women. London, Putnam, 1913. p61-74

Rehder, Helmut
Rilke und Elizabeth Barrett Browning.
J Engl & Germ Philol 33:547-59 '34

Relics of the Brownings. T L S N 26 '14
p527-8

Rendall, Vernon
Wild flowers in literature. London, Scholartis press, 1934

Ridley, Hilda M.
Great friendships; Mary Mitford and
Elizabeth Barrett. Canadian Magazine
60:515-20 Ap '23

Riesz, H.
E.-B. Browning und R. Browning; ein
dichterpaar. Dresdener Anzeiger no 11
'06

Ripon, W. B.
Mrs. Browning. *In* Masson, David, and
others. In the footsteps of the poets.
London, Isbister, 1893. p279-95

Ritchie, Anne Thackeray
Robert and Elizabeth Barrett Browning.
In Records of Tennyson, Ruskin,
Browning. New York, Harper, 1892.
p129-90; *same.* Harper M 84:832-55 **My**
'92
(Rev in Dial 13:339-42 D 1 '92; Literary
World (Lond) ns 46:299-300 O 21 '92;
National Observer 8:539-40 O 8 '92; Sat
R 74:545-6 N 5 '19; Speaker 6:447-8 O 8
'92)

Robbins, Reginald Chauncey
Mrs. Browning. *In* Poems of personality.
Cambridge, Mass. Riverside press, 1910.
2d ser p213-14

Robert Browning und Elizabeth Barrett
briefwechsel. Neue Rundschau 15:949-
74 Ag '04

Roberts, Elsie Williams
The social poetry of Elizabeth Barrett
Browning. Masters essay, Univ. of
North Carolina, 1933. 139ff

Robertson, Eric S.
English poetesses. . . London, Cassell,
1883. p255-320
"The Romaunt of the Page." Ath 1:825
Je 28 '84

Rockafellow, Ralph
The Brownings. Golden Book 13:64-6
My '31

Rossetti, William Michael
Some reminiscences. London, Brown
Langham, 1906. vol I p242-4
(Rev in Bookm (Lond) 31:156 D '06)

Roudabush, Lillie Alice
The influence of Elizabeth Barrett on
Robert Browning as seen in his poetry.
Masters essay, Columbia univ. 1928

Rowland, K. M.
The Brownings. Manhattan 3:553-62 Je
'84

Royds, Kathleen Elizabeth
Elizabeth Barrett Browning and her
poetry. (Poetry and life ser) London,
Harrap, 1912. 134p

Ruhrmann, Friedrich G.
Studien zur geschichte und charakteristik
des refrains in der englischen literatur.
(Anglistische forschungen, heft 64)
Heidelberg, Winter, 1927. p118-29

Russell, Frances Theresa
More about the Brownings. Dalhousie
Review 10:191-8 Jl '30
Two poets, a dog, and a boy; being a
selection of verse . . . a brief story of
their lives . . . sidelights on the poems.
Philadelphia, Lippincott [c 1933] 7-289p

Rutherford, Mildred
Elizabeth Barrett Browning. *In* English
authors. Atlanta, Ga. Franklin printing & publishing co. 1906. p537-43

Ryley, Emily
Reference wanted. ("Aurora Leigh")
Notes & Q 11th ser 11:230 Mr 20 '15

Saintsbury, George Edward Bateman
A history of English prosody from the
twelfth century to the present day.
London, Macmillan, 1910. vol III p241-
8
A history of nineteenth century literature.
London, Macmillan, 1931. p276-81

Sanders, H. M.
Other indiscretions and the Browning
letters. Temple 120:110-26 My '00

Sarrazin, Gabriel
Élisabeth Barrett Browning. *In* Poètes
modernes de l'Angleterre. Paris, Ollendorff, 1885. p155-230

Saunders, Frederick
Mrs. Browning. *In* The story of some
famous books. London, Elliot Stock,
1887. p176-9

Schelling, Felix E.
The English lyric. Boston, Houghton,
Mifflin, 1913. p206-8

Schinz, Albert
Victor Hugo, Napoléon III et Elizabeth
Browning. R Litt Comp 13:740-4 O-D
'33

Schuyler, Eugene
Mrs. Browning. *In* Italian influences.
New York, Scribner, 1901. p189-201

Selden, Camille [pseud]
see Krinitz, Elise

Shackford, Martha Hale
E. B. Browning: "Aurora Leigh." *In*
E. B. Browning; R. H. Horne; two
studies. [Wellesley, Mass.] The
Wellesley press [c1935] p5-27 bibl p73

Sharp, Amy
E. B. Browning. *In* Victorian poets.
London, Methuen, 1891. p103-20
(Rev in Speaker 4:206-7 Ag 15 '91)

Shepard, William [pseud]
see Walsh, William Shepard

Shepherd, Richard Herne
Mrs. Browning's earlier poems. Ath 2: 722 D 2 '76

Siebold, Erika von
Synästhesien in der englischen dichtung des 19. jahrhunderts. Engl Stud 53: 289-94 D '19

Sim, Frances Mary (Walters) Lady
Robert Browning and Elizabeth Barrett. London, Golden vista press, 1930. 64p

Smart, George Thomas
The influence of the kinship of Robert and Elizabeth Barrett Browning upon the world of books. [Boston, 1904] 20ff Typed Ms. in the Boston Public Library

Smiles, Samuel
Elizabeth Barrett Browning. *In* Brief biographies. Boston, Ticknor & Fields, 1861. p449-60

Smith, Arnold
E. Barrett Browning. *In* The main tendencies of Victorian poetry. . . London, Simpkin, Marshall, Hamilton, Kent, 1907. p42-58

Smith, Elsie Brown
Elizabeth Barrett Browning, humanitarian. Masters essay, Univ. of Vermont, 1934. 114ff

Smith, George Barnett
Elizabeth Barrett Browning. *In* Poets and novelists: a series of literary studies. New York, Appleton, 1876. p57-109

Snow, D. E.
Mrs. Browning's "Isabel's child." Religious Magazine and Monthly Review 48:253-60 S '72

Some poets of the Victorian era. IV. Elizabeth Barrett Browning. Acad 79:150-1 Ag 13 '10

Some recent women poets. Scribner's Monthly 10:100-1 My '75

Spence, R. M.
James Russell Lowell on "Aurora Leigh." Notes & Q 9th ser 3:244-5 Ap 1 '99

Spender, Harold
The Browning palace at Venice. Bookm (Lond) 2:81-2 Je '92

[Squire, John Collings] Solomon Eagle [pseud]
The new Browning poems. *In* Books in general. New York, Knopf, 1920. 2d ser p35-9 [From New Statesm]

Stanley, Hiram M.
The Browning-Barrett love-letters and the psychology of love. Open Court 13:731-41 D '99

Stedman, Edmund Clarence
Elizabeth Barrett Browning. Scribner's Monthly 7:101-14 N '73

Elizabeth Barrett Browning. . . (Modern classics, 12) Boston, Houghton, Mifflin [1881, c 1875] 96p

Elizabeth Barrett Browning. *In* Victorian poets. Boston, Houghton, Mifflin, 1896. p114-49

Steele, Eunice H.
The life together of the Brownings. Masters essay, Syracuse Univ. 1925. 93ff

Stephen, (Sir) Leslie
The Browning letters. *In* Studies of a biographer. London, Duckworth, 1902. 2d ser vol III p1-35

Stevenson, (Mrs) Hackett
Elizabeth Barrett Browning. Victoria Magazine 22:231-8 '73

Stöcker, Hel
Brownings. Vossische Zeitung no 33 '05

Stoddard, Richard Henry
Mrs. Browning in letters. Ind 40:737-8, 770-1, 803-4 Je 14, 21, 28 '88

Preface [and] Memoir. *In* Letters of Elizabeth Barrett Browning addressed to Richard Hengist Horne. New York, Miller, 1877. piii-xxxvii

Strachan, L. R. M.
Mrs. Browning: inscription. Notes & Q 147:289-90 O 18 '24

Mrs. Browning's sonnet on Wordsworth. Notes & Q 155:317 N 3 '28

Strugnell, G. Kenneth
Mrs. Browning's sonnet on Wordsworth. Notes & Q 155:317 N 3 '28

Swanwick, Anna
Elizabeth Barrett Browning. *In* Poets the interpreters of their age. London, Bell, 1892. p347-55

Swinburne, A. C.
Aurora Leigh. By E. B. Browning. . . With prefatory note by A. C. Swinburne. London, Smith, Elder, 1898. (Rev in Literary World (Lond) ns 58: 486 D 16 '98)

Taine, Hyppolite
Notes on England. . . trans. by W. F. Rae. New York, Holt, 1876. p89, 92

Tannenforst, Ursula
Divided. Elizabeth Barrett Browning buried at Florence, July 1, 1861, Robert Browning, buried in Westminster Abbey, December 31, 1889; poem. Poet Lore 2:193-5 '90

Tarr, Stambury R.
A priestess of liberty and her message. Canadian Magazine 8:176-8 D '96

Taylor, Bayard
At home and abroad. New York, Putnam, 1860. p444

The echo club, and other literary diversions. Boston, Osgood, 1876. p123-5

Texte, Joseph
Elisabeth Browning et l'idéalisme contemporain. *In* Études de littérature européenne. Paris, Colin, 1898

La Philosophie d'Elisabeth Browning. R Deux Mondes 3d per 112:834-57 Ag 15 '92

Thomas, Edith M.
Elizabeth Barrett Browning. Critic (NY) 37:516-17 D '00

Thompson, Alexander Hamilton
Tennyson and the Victorian poets. *In* A history of English literature. London, Murray, 1901. p774-6

Tiddeman, Lizzie Ellen
Elizabeth Barrett Browning, the woman and her work. Westm 167:82-92 Ja '07

Tilton, Theodore
Memorial [of E. B. Browning] *In* Browning, E. B. Last poems. New York, Miller, 1862. p11-75

Timlin, Constance J.
A study of Elizabeth Browning. Masters essay, Cornell Univ. 1931. 200ff

Tod, Alexandra Charlotte
Elizabeth Barrett Browning as a lyric poet. Master essay, Univ. of Manitoba, 1927. 44ff

Tours through literary England. . . Sat R 150:197-8 Ag 16 '30

Tuckerman, Henry Theodore
The poetry of Elisabeth Barrett Browning. *In* The poems of Elizabeth Barrett Browning. New York, Francis, 1850. vol I p[vii]-xv; *same in* Thoughts on the poets. New York, Francis, 1851. p281-9

Ulitz, Arnold
Die beziehung zwischen Erlebnis und gedicht in Elizabeth Barrett Browning's "Sonnets from the Portuguese." Breslau, Breslauer Genassensch.-Buchdr. 1914. 59p

Vert, Octavia Walton Le
Elizabeth Barrett Browning. New Eclectic Magazine 4:221-4 F '69

Verwey, M.
E. B. Browning. Minerva p171-3, 181-2, 194-6, 204-7 Ja 28, F 4, 11, 18 '15

Viterbi, Bona Benvenisti
Elizabetta Barrett-Browning. Bergamo, Instituto Italiano D'Arti Crafiche, 1913. 131p

Wagschal, Friedrich
E. B. Brownings "Sonnets from the Portuguese" und D. G. Rossettis "House of Life." Z F E U 13:207-17 '14

Walford, L. B.
Elizabeth Barrett Browning. *In* Twelve English authoresses. London, Longmans, Green, 1892. p169-83

Walker, Hugh
The age of Tennyson. (Handbooks of English literature) London, Bell, 1904. p233-6

The literature of the Victorian era. Cambridge, England, Univ. press, 1921. p366-72

Walker, (Mrs) Janie R.
Elizabeth Barrett Browning. *In* Stories of the Victorian writers. New York, Macmillan, 1922. p53-9

Walker, Mary Grace
Elizabeth Barrett Browning; poem. Acad 27:274 Ap 18 '85

[Walsh, William Shepard] Shepard, William [pseud]
The Brownings. *In* Pen pictures of modern authors. New York, Putnam, 1882. p216-35

[Walsh, William Shepard] Shepard, William [pseud] ed.
Mrs. Elizabeth Barrett Browning. *In* Enchiridion of criticism. . . Philadelphia, Lippincott, 1885. p234-7

Ward, Thomas Humphry
Browning, Elizabeth Barrett. *In* Men of the reign. London, Routledge, 1885. p125-6

Ward, Winfield Scott
The Brownings and social progress. [Boston? 1906?] 22ff Typed Ms. in the Boston Public library

Watkins, Alfred
Elizabeth B. Browning and Hope End. Transactions of Woolhope National Field Club (Lond) parts 1-2:105-9 '24-'26

Waugh, Arthur
The poetry of emotion. *In* Reticence in literature, and other papers. London, Wilson [1915] p64-6

Wedmore, (Sir) Frederick
The Brownings. *In* Certain comments. London, Selwyn & Blount [1925] p20-3

Weingärtner, Anton
Die textentwicklung von Elizabeth Barrett Browning's dramen "The Seraphim" und "A drama of exile." Heidelberg, Winter, 1915. 98p Diss. Würzburg

Wellington, Amy
The poet; Elizabeth Barrett Browning. *In* Women have told. Boston, Little, Brown, 1930. p23-33

Westwood, T.
Authorship of "Victoria's Tears." Notes & Q 3d ser 8:531 D 23 '65

"The like doth sway the like." Notes & Q 4th ser 11:191 Mr 8 '73

Mrs. Browning's dog "Flush." Notes & Q 4th ser 11:29-30 Ja 11 '73

Wharton, Anne Hollingsworth
[Biographical facts about Robert and Elizabeth Browning] Poet Lore 2:35-7 '90

The Brownings in Florence. Bookn 24:467-71 Mr '06

The Brownings in Italy. Lippinc 45:441-4 Mr '90

Wheeler, D. H.
Casa Guidi Windows, paraphrased. Chautauquan 11:282-6 Je '90

Whipple, Edwin P.
Essays and reviews. New York, Appleton, 1848. vol I p345-7

Whiting, Lilian
The Brownings; their life and art. Boston, Little, Brown, 1911. xiv,304p

E. B. Browning. *In* Women who have enobled life. Philadelphia, Union press [c 1915]

Elizabeth Barrett Browning. Bookm (NY) 3:35-9 Mr '96

Involuntary writing attributed to the Brownings. Unpopular Review 9:197-9 Ja-Mr '18

A study of Elizabeth Barrett Browning. Boston, Little, Brown, 1899. xxii,191p (Rev in Lit W 31:7 Ja 6 '00)

Williams, Stanley Thomas
Studies in Victorian literature. New York, Dutton [c 1923] passim

Willis, Irene Cooper
Elizabeth Barrett Browning. . . (Representative women) London, G. Howe [1928] 96p. *same in* Six brilliant English women. London, Howe [1930]

Wilson, A.
English poets in Italy: Mrs. Browning's last poems. Macmil 6:79-87 My '62

Wilson, P.
Mrs. Browning. *In* Leaders in literature. London, Oliphant, 1898. p127-52

Wingfield-Stratford, Esmé Cecil
Those earnest Victorians. New York, William Morrow, 1930

Winwar, Frances [pseud]
see Grebanier, (Mrs.) Frances

Wood, Benton Burdette
Ethics of the poetry of Mrs. Elizabeth Browning. Masters essay, Univ. of Nebraska, 1923. 74ff

Woolf, (Mrs) Virginia (Stephen)
Aurora Leigh. Yale R ns 20:677-90 Je '31

Flush; a biography. Atlan 152:1-12, 163-74, 326-37, 439-53 Jl-O '33; also published as book. New York, Harcourt, Brace [c 1933] 185p

Wotton, Mabel E.
Elizabeth Barrett Browning. *In* Word portraits of famous writers. . . London, Bentley, 1887. p34-6

Wülker, Richard
Geschichte der englischen literatur. . . Leipzig, Bibliographischen instituts, 1907. p269-70

Wyzewa, T. de
Un roman par lettres: The Letters of Robert Browning and Elizabeth Barrett Browning. R Deux Mondes 153: 456-67 My 15 '99

Zampini-Salazar, Fanny
L'Italia dal 1847 al 1861 nelle Lettre di Elisabetta Barrett Browning. Roma, Forzani, 1898. 27p *Also in* Nuova Antol 4th ser 76:686-708 Ag 16 '98

Roberto ed Elisabetta Browning. Con prefazione di A. Fogazzaro. Napoli, A. Tocco, 1896. vii-xvi,67p

La vita e le opere di Roberto Browning ed Elisabetta Barrett-Browning; con prefazione di Antonio Fogazzaro. Torino, Società tipografico-editrice nazionale, 1907. [viii]-xv,376p

Zeldenthius, J. J.
Literatur [Sonnets from the Portuguese] Groot-Nederland 13:647-8 '15

Arthur Hugh Clough

Arthur Hugh Clough

I. Chronological Outline

1819. Born, January 1, Liverpool.

1847. A Consideration of Objections Against the Retrenchment Association.

1848. The Bothie of Toper-na-Fuosich [title was later changed to: The Bothie of Tober-na-Vuolich].

1849. Ambervalia. Poems by Thomas Burbidge and Arthur Hugh Clough.

1850. Poems.

1858. Amours de Voyage.

1860. Greek History from Themistocles to Alexander in a Series of Lives from Plutarch. Revised and Arranged.

1861. Died, November 13, Florence.

1862. Poems.

1864. Plutarch's Lives. The Translation Called Dryden's, Corrected from the Greek and Revised.

1865. Letters and Remains.

1869. Poems and Prose Remains.

Arthur Hugh Clough

II. Bibliographical Material

Collections toward a bibliography of Arthur Hugh Clough. Lit W 15: 213-14 Je 28 '84

Brown, G. A.
Arthur Hugh Clough. *In* C H E L vol XIII p540-1

Page, Curtis Hidden
Clough; list of references. *In* British poets of the nineteenth century. . . . ed. by Curtis Hidden Page. new ed. by Stith Thompson. New York, Sanborn, 1930. p706

Stephen, (Sir) Leslie
[Bibliography] Dict N B vol IV p584

Woods, George Benjamin
[Bibliography] *In* Poetry of the Victorian period. New York, Scott Foresman [c1930] p991-2

Arthur Hugh Clough

III. Biographical and Critical Material

Allingham, H. and D. Radford, eds.
William Allingham, a diary. London, Macmillan, 1907. p57, 68, 72, 350

A[llingham] W[illiam]
Arthur Hugh Clough, 1819-1861. Fraser 74:525-35 O '66

Amiel and Clough. Spec 59:42-3 Ja 9 '86

Amy, Ernest F.
Religious influence upon Clough and Arnold as seen in their poetry. Masters essay, Wesleyan univ. 1911

Armstrong, Richard A.
Arthur Hugh Clough. . . *In* Faith and doubt in the century's poets. New York, Whittaker, 1898. p43-66
(Rev in Liv Age 219:67-70 O 1 '98)

Arnold, Matthew
The letters of Matthew Arnold to Arthur Hugh Clough. . . [see Lowry, Howard Foster, ed.]

On translating Homer. London, Murray, 1905. Section III p105-7

The scholar gypsy. *In* Poems. New York, Macmillan, 1883. vol II p199-211

Thyrsis; a monody to commemorate the author's friend, Arthur Hugh Clough, who died at Florence, 1861. *In* Poems. New York, Macmillan, 1883. vol II p212-24

Arnold, Thomas
Arthur Hugh Clough: a sketch. 19th Cent 43:105-16 Ja '98

[Arnold and Clough] Nation (NY) 3:372 Mr 22 '66

Arnold and Clough. T L S Ja 12 '33 p13-14

Arthur Hugh Clough. *In* Chambers's cyclopedia of English literature. Philadelphia, Lippincott; London, Chambers, 1903. vol III p511-13

Arthur Hugh Clough. *In* The library of literary criticism of English and American authors . . . ed. by Charles Wells Moulton. . . Buffalo, New York, Moulton publishing company, 1904-05. vol VI p248-56

Arthur Hugh Clough. Once a Week 21: 237-40 O 16 '69; Atlan 9:462-9 Ap '62; Lit W 15:279 Ag 23 '84

Arthur Hugh Clough, 1819-1861. Fraser 74:525-36 O '66

Bagehot, Walter
Mr. Clough's poems. *In* Literary studies . . . London, Longmans, Green, 1879. vol II p257-81

Beatty, Joseph Moorhead, jr.
Arthur Hugh Clough as revealed in his prose. So Atlan Q 25:168-80 Ap '26

Benn, Alfred William
The history of English rationalism in the nineteenth century. London, Longmans, Green, 1906. vol II p46-56

Bijvanck, Willem Geertrudes Cornelis
Hebbel, Clough, Baudelaire. *In* Poëzie en leven in de 19de eeuw. . . Haarlem, 1889. p151-262

Boase, Frederic
Clough, Arthur Hugh. *In* Modern English biography. Truro, Netherton & Worth, 1892. vol I p654-5

Brooke, Stopford Augustus
Arthur Hugh Clough. *In* Four Victorian poets. New York, Putnam, 1908. p30-55
(Rev in T L S My 21 '08 p161-2)

Burbidge, Thomas and Arthur H. Clough
see Clough, Arthur Hugh and Burbidge, Thomas

Butler, A. G.
The three friends: story of Rugby in the forties. London, Frowde, 1900. 134p
(Rev in Nation (NY) 72:92 Ja 31 '01)

Bynner, C. N.
Arthur Hugh Clough. Harv Mo 4:177-84 Jl '87

Byrde, Margaretta B.
(Memoir) Modern Churchman p80-93 My '20

Carlyle, Thomas
Arthur Clough. 1860. Lit W 16:187 My 30 '85

Cazamian, Louis
Arthur Hugh Clough. *In* Legouis, E. and Cazamian, L. A history of English literature. New York, Macmillan, 1930. p1222-4

Cazamian, Madeleine
Le roman et les idées en Angleterre; l'influence de la science (1860-1890). (Publications de la faculté des lettres de l'université de Strasbourg. Fascicule 15) Strasbourg, Librairie Istra, 1923. p260-1

Chapman, Edward Mortimer
The doubters and the mystics. *In* English literature in account with religion. Boston, Houghton, Mifflin, 1910. p426-32

Clark, John Scott
Arthur Hugh Clough. *In* A study of English and American writers. New York, Row, Peterson [c 1916] p512-21

Clough, Arthur Hugh
The Bothie of Toper-na-Fuosich, a long-vacation pastoral. Oxford, Macpherson, 1848. 55p
(Rev in Fraser 39:103-10 Ja '49; *same.* Liv Age 21:197-202 My 5 '49; W. M. Rossetti in Germ 1:36-48 Ja '50; Sat R 12:564-5 N 30 '61; Christian Remembrancer 45:61-89 Ja '63; *same.* Liv Age 76:391-407 F 28 '63; Literary World (Lond) ns 54:449 N 27 '96)

Letters and remains of Arthur Hugh Clough, sometime Fellow of Oriel College, Oxford. London, Privately printed by Spottiswoode, 1865. vi,328p
(Rev by C. E. Norton in No Am 105: 434-46 O '67; Macmil 15:89-102 D '66)

Poems of Clough, ed. by H. S. Milford. (Oxford library of prose and verse) London, Frowde, 1910. xiv,247p
(Rev by T. S. Omond in Mod Lang R 6:539-41 O '11; Ath 1:188 F 18 '11)

The poems and prose remains of Arthur Hugh Clough, with a selection from his letters and a memoir, ed. by his wife. London, Macmillan, 1869. 2 vols [iv], 426p; [v]-viii,502p
(Rev in Quar R 126:348-53 Ap '69; Spec 42:1073-5 S 11 '69; *same.* Liv Age 103:197-201 O 23 '69; *same.* Ecl M 73: 719-23 D '69; Every Sat 8:507-9 O 16 '69; Westm 92:363-87 O '69; Sat R 28: 383-5 S 18 '69; Ath 2:205-6 Ag 14 '69; Putnam's Magazine ns 4:752-4 D '69; Sat R 66:25-6 Jl 7 '88; noted in Ath 1: 826 Je 30 '88)

Poems, with an introduction by Charles Whibley. London, Macmillan, 1913. xxxvii, 459p
(Rev in Ath 2:724 D 20 '13; Spec 112: 230-1 F 7 '14; Contemp 105:285-8 F '14)

Poems, with a memoir [by Francis Turner Palgrave] London, Macmillan, 1862. xxvii,259p
(Rev in Spec N 23 '61; *same.* Eclectic Review ns 2:27-33 Ja '62; Spec 35:775-6 Jl 12 '62; Sat R 14:109-10 Jl 26 '62; National Review 13:310-26 O '62; Blackw 92:586-98 N '62; No Brit 37: 323-43 N '62; Ath 2:107-9 Jl 26 '62; Macmil 6:318-31 Ag '62; Eclectic Review ns 3:269-70 S '62; Christian Remembrancer 45:61-89 Ja '63; Critic (NY) 14:232 My 11 '89)

Selections from the poems of Arthur Hugh Clough. (Golden treasury ser) London, Macmillan, 1894. [v]-viii,208p
(Rev in Critic (NY) 25:106 Ag 18 '94; Literary World (Lond) ns 49:573-4 Je 22 '94; Lit W 25:221 Jl 14 '94; Nation (NY) 58:485 Je 28 '94)

Clough, Arthur Hugh (transl)
Greek history from Themistocles to Alexander in a series of Lives from Plutarch. Revised and arranged by A. H.

Clough, sometime Fellow of Oriel college, Oxford. London, Longman, Green, Longman, and Roberts, 1860. xvi, 481p

Clough, Arthur Hugh and Burbidge, Thomas
Ambarvalia; poems by Thomas Burbidge and Arthur H. Clough. London, Chapman and Hall, 1849. 155p [p[1]-64 are Clough's poems] Clough's poems of this volume were also issued separately: London, Chapman and Hall, 1849(?) 64p
(Rev in Fraser 39:580-5 My '49; Ath 1:135-6 F 10 '49)

Clough, (Mrs) Blanche M. (Smith)
Memoir [of Clough] *In* The poems and prose remains of Arthur Hugh Clough .... London, Macmillan, 1869. vol I p1-54

Clough and his defender. Acad 52:260-1 O 2 '97

Clough and Tennyson. Acad 66:205 F 20 '04

[Clough-Arnold memorial] Acad 63:51 Jl 12 '02

Clough's life and poems. Cornhill 14:410-21 O '66; *same.* Liv Age 91:259-66 N 3 '66; *same.* Every Sat 2:515-20 N 3 '66; *same.* Ecl M 67:735-43 D '66

Collins, J. C.
Clough and Tennyson. Acad 66:133 Ja 30 '04

Cunliffe, John W.
Mid-Victorian poets. *In* Leaders of the Victorian revolution. New York, Appleton-Century [c 1934] p155, 235-6

Curtis, George William
[Arthur Hugh Clough] Putnam's Magazine 11:6-7 Ja '68

[Death of Clough] Harper M 25:710-11 O '62

[Death of Clough's sister] Lit W 23:98 Mr 12 '92

"Dipsychus" and the letters of A. H. Clough. Macmil 15:89-102 D '66

Dixon, William Macneile
English epic and heroic poetry. London, Dent, 1912. p278

Doorn, Willem van
Theory and practice of English narrative verse since 1833. Amsterdam [1932?] p116-27

Dowden, Edward
The transcendental movement and literature. *In* Studies in literature, 1789-1877. London, Kegan, Paul, Trench, Trübner, 1902. p78-80

Victorian literature. *In* Transcripts and studies. London, Kegan, Paul, Trench, Trübner, 1896. 2d ed p205-6

Victorian literature. Fortn 47:855-7 Je '87

Dowden, John
Arthur Hugh Clough. Contemp 12:513-24 D '69; *same.* Liv Age 105:56-62 Ap 2 '70

Drinkwater, John
Victorian poetry. (People's library) London, Hodder & Stoughton, 1923. p82, 84

"Eminent Victorians" [Clough's defence of Florence Nightingale] Spec 121:10 Jl 6 '18

Fehr, Bernhard
Die englische literatur des 19. und 20. jahrhunderts. Wildpark-Potsdam, 1928. p189-90

Forster, E.
Arthur Hugh Clough. Acad 52:331 O 23 '97

Garrod, Heathcote William
Clough. In Poetry and the criticism of life. (The Charles Eliot Norton lectures for 1929-1930) Cambridge, Mass. Harvard univ. press, 1931. p109-27

Gates, Lewis Edwards
Return to conventional life. In Studies and appreciations. New York, Macmillan, 1900. p32-8; same. Critic (NY) 36: 174-7 F '00

Gill, W. K.
A. H. Clough. Spec 112:346 F 28 '14

Goodale, Ralph Hinsdale
Pessimism in English poetry and fiction, 1847-1900. In Abstracts of theses. . . Humanistic series Volume VI. . . . Univ. of Chicago. Chicago, 1927. p347-51

Gosse, (Sir) Edmund William
Clough. In Books on the table. London, Heinemann, 1921. p127-35

[Grebanier, Mrs. Frances] (Vinciguerra) Frances Winwar [pseud]
Poor splendid wings. Boston, Little, Brown, 1933. p324

Gredler, Hazel Rogers
Arthur Hugh Clough, a character study. Masters essay, Cornell Univ. 1931. 82ff

Guthrie, William Norman
Arthur Hugh Clough. In Modern poet prophets. . . Cincinnati, Clarke, 1897. p102-9

Guyot, Edouard
. . . Essai sur la formation philosophie de Arthur Clough (1819-61). Paris, Alcan, 1913. 170p Thesis, Paris

Hamilton, A. H. A.
Clough's "Bothie." Acad 23:11 Ja 6 '83

Hartwell, Robert Metcalf
Arthur Hugh Clough; an impression of a Victorian. Masters essay, McGill Univ. 1933. 119ff

Hayward, Edward F.
Clough and the poetry of reaction. Unitar 28:131-42 Ag '87

Hearn, Lafcadio
Pessimists. In Interpretations of literature. . . New York, Dodd, Mead, 1915. vol I p338-40

Hewlett, Maurice Henry
Teufelsdröckh in hexameters. 19th Cent 91:68-75 Ja '22

Hexameters. Notes & Q 7th ser 3:29-30 Ja 8 '87

Higgs, William
Arthur Hugh Clough. New Englander 51:241-55 O '89

Hodgson, Geraldine E.
Criticism at a venture. London, Macdonald [1919] p53-7

Holloway, Owen E.
Clough and Oriel. T L S Mr 23 '33 p200

Hoyt, Arthur S.
The spiritual message of modern English poetry. New York, Macmillan, 1924. p185-95

Hudson, William Henry
Arthur Hugh Clough. In Studies in interpretation. New York, Putnam, 1896. p77-149

Huth, Alfred O.
Über A. H. Clough's "The bothie of Tober-na-Vuolich." Leipzig, 1911. 76p Thesis, Leipzig

Hutton, Richard Holt
Amiel and Clough. In Brief literary criticisms. Edited by E. M. Roscoe. London, Macmillan, 1906. p304-25

Arthur H. Clough. In Literary essays. London, Macmillan, 1892. p286-309

Arthur Hugh Clough. In Essays in literary criticism. Philadelphia, Coates [pref 1876] p156-79

Arthur Hugh Clough. In Essays theological and literary. vol II Literary essays. London, Strahan, 1871. p368-91

The poetry of Arthur Hugh Clough. Fortn 39:790-807 Je '83; same. Liv Age 158:3-14 Jl 7 '83

Jerram, C. S.
"The Bothie of Tober-na-Vuolich." Notes & Q 5th ser 8:435 D 1 '77

Johnson, Rossiter
[Note on Clough and Hare] Book B ns 10:215 Je '93

Jones, Dora M.
English writers and the making of Italy. Lond Q R 118:92-3 Jl '12

Jones, W. Lewis
Arthur Hugh Clough. In C H E L vol XIII p114-18

Kellner, Leon
Die englische literatur der neuesten zeit. Leipzig, Tauchnitz, 1921. p230-1

Die englische literatur im zeitalter der königin Viktoria. Leipzig, Tauchnitz, 1909. p384-6

Kent, Muriel
A Balliol scholar. Criterion 9:675-88 Jl '30

Kimbro, Gladys Mae
Arthur Hugh Clough. Masters essay, Univ. of Oklahoma, 1924. 46ff

King, Carlyle
Arthur Hugh Clough: a critical study. Diss. Univ. of Toronto, 1931

Knickerbocker, William Skinkle
Creative Oxford. Its influence in Victorian literature. Syracuse, N.Y. University press [c 1925]

Semaphore: Arnold and Clough. Sewanee R 41:152-74 Ap '33

Krahmer, Alfred John
Arthur Hugh Clough in America. Masters essay, Columbia univ. 1930

Lewis, W. Aldersey
Clough and Tennyson. Acad 66:82, 205 Ja 16, F 20 '04

Lloyd, Richard John
Arthur Hugh Clough. Lit & Philos Soc 53:1-34 '99

Lowry, Howard Foster, ed.
The letters of Matthew Arnold to Arthur Hugh Clough. Doctor's thesis, Yale univ. 1931

The letters of Matthew Arnold to Arthur Hugh Clough. Edited with an introductory study by Howard Foster Lowry. New York, Oxford univ. press, 1932. xi,191p
(Rev in America 49:67 Ap 22 '33; Archiv 164:138-9 '33; D. Bush in Bookm (NY) 76:178 F '33; J. Zeitlin in Books My 21 '33 p14; M. D. Zabel in Commonweal 17:640-1 Ap 5 '33; H. Kingsmill in Engl R 56:227-30 '33; L. Trilling in Nation (NY) 136:211 F 22 '33; New Repub 74:139 Mr 15 '33; J. Eglinton in New Statesm & Nation 5:226 F 25 '33; L. Bonnerot in Revue A A 10:532-3 '33; K. Young in Sat R Lit 9:539 Ap 15 '33; W. S. Knickerbocker in Sewanee R 41:152-74 '33; D. Cecil in Spec 150:48 Ja 13 '33; T L S Ja 12 '33 p13-14; J. W. Dodds in Va Q R 9:453-6 Jl '33; S. Chew in Yale R 22:835-8 '33)

Lowry, Howard Foster and Rusk, Ralph Leslie, eds.
Emerson-Clough letters. . . Cleveland, The Rowfant club, 1934. ix[66]p [165 copies only]

Lucas, Frank Laurence
Clough. In Eight Victorian poets. Cambridge, England, Univ. press, 1930. p55-74
(Rev in T L S N 13 '30 p936)
Thyrsis. Life & L 2:344-60 My '29

Lutonsky, Paula
Arthur Hugh Clough. (Wiener beiträge zur englischen philologie. . . Bd. 39) Wien, Braumüller, 1912. 58p
(Rev in Acad 83:441 O 5 '12; by F. Asanger in Bei Anglia 24:51-2 F '13; H. Lötochert in Engl Stud 46:306-9 '13)

Lyttleton, Arthur Temple
The poetry of doubt. In Modern poets of faith, doubt, and other essays. London, Murray, 1904. p73-105

Mabie, Hamilton Wright
My study fire. New York, Dodd, Mead, 1899. 2d ser p101-14

McCabe, Joseph Martin
A biographical dictionary of modern rationalists. London, Watts, 1920. p169-70

MacCarthy, Desmond
Clough. In Portraits. London, Putnam [1931] 1st ser p63-7

McCormick, Mary Ellen
Arnold and Clough: a comparative study of religious thought. Masters essay, Cornell Univ. 1929. 57ff

Marble, Annie Russell
Messages of the nineteenth century poets. Dial 30:98 F 16 '01

Mayer, S. R. Townshend
Charles Kingsley and Arthur H. Clough. St J 40:265-76 '77

Mayhew, A. L.
The etymology of "Clough." Acad 36: 137-8, 154, 188 Ag 31, S 7, 21 '89

Meissner, Paul
Pessimistische strömungen im englischen geistesleben des 19. jahrhunderts. Engl Stud 64:445 '29

Miles, Alfred H.
Arthur Hugh Clough. In The poets and the poetry of the nineteenth century. (Humour) London, Routledge [190-?] p409-10

The modern poetry of doubt. Spec 43:166-7 F 5 '70; same. New Eclectic Magazine 6:490-4 Ap '70

Moggridge, M. W.
Idyllic poetry. Macmil 38:103 Je '78

Molloy, J.
"Clough." Acad 36:188 S 21 '89

Mordell, Albert
Introduction. In Symonds, J. A. Last and first. New York, N. L. Brown, 1919. p7-8

Mortimer, John
Concerning Arthur Hugh Clough. Manch Q 17:374-93 '98

Mount, C. B.
"There were giants in the land." Notes & Q 9th ser 8:186 Ag 31 '01

Murray, J. A. H.
"Clough," "Clow." Acad 36:341 N 23 '89

Nitchie, Elizabeth
Vergil and the English poets. New York, Columbia univ. press, 1919. p217 Diss. Columbia univ.

Noble, James Ashcroft
Arthur Hugh Clough. In Miles, A. H. ed. The poets and the poetry of the nineteenth century; Frederick Tennyson to Arthur Hugh Clough. London, Routledge, 1905 [vol IV] p645-52

Norton, Charles Eliot
Arthur Hugh Clough. In Warner, C. D. ed. Library of the world's best literature. Memorial ed. New York, Hill [c 1902] Vol IX p3821-8

Memoir of Clough. In Poems. . . ed. by C. E. Norton. Boston, Ticknor & Fields, 1862. pi-xxxvi

Oliphant, Margaret
Arthur Hugh Clough, 1823-61. *In* The Victorian age of English literature. New York, Tait [c 1892] vol II p436-7

Osborne, James Insley
Arthur Hugh Clough. London, Constable, 1919. 195p Diss. Columbia univ. (Rev in Ath 1:268-9 F 27 '20; R. E. Roberts in Bookm (Lond) 58:23-4 Ap '20; Nation (NY) 112:122-3 Ja 26 '21; T L S Mr 4 '20)

Palgrave, Francis Turner
Arthur Hugh Clough. Fraser 65:527-36 Ap '62

Patmore, Coventry
Arthur Hugh Clough. *In* Principle in art. London, Bell, 1912. p106-12

Peake, L. S.
A. H. Clough as a religious teacher. Modern Churchman p191-9 Jl '32

Perry, Thomas Sergeant
Arthur Hugh Clough. Atlan 36:409-18 O '75

Pickford, John
"The Bothie of Tober-na-Vuolich." Notes & Q 5th ser 8:88, 198-9, 435 Ag 4, S 8, D 1 '77

The poetry of doubt—Arnold and Clough. Liv Age 137:410-21 My 18 '78; *same.* Church Q R 6:117-39 Ap '78

Powell, Thomas
Thomas Burbidge and Arthur A. [sic] Clough. *In* The living authors of England. New York, Appleton, 1849. p86-94

Rhys, Ernest
Introduction. *In* The Bothie, and other poems: by Arthur Hugh Clough (Canterbury poets) London, Walter Scott publishing co. [nd] p[vii]-xxii

Rigaud, Gibbes
"The Bothie of Tober-na-Vuolich." Notes & Q 5th ser 8:394-5 N 17 '77

Robertson, John Mackinnon
Clough. *In* New essays towards a critical method. London, Lane, 1897. p301-32 (Noted in Acad 52:260-1 O 2 '97)

Russell Lowell on A. H. Clough. Spec 112: 263-4 F 14 '14

Rutledge, Rosa Dyer
The conflict of science and theology. Masters essay, George Peabody College, 1932

Saintsbury, George
A history of English prosody from the twelfth century to the present day. London, Macmillan, 1910. vol III p408-10

A history of nineteenth century literature. London, Macmillan, 1931. p309-10

Sams, Vera Emmaline
Arthur Hugh Clough: a study of his thought. Masters essay, Univ. of Texas, 1927. 118ff

Sass, G. H.
Arthur Hugh Clough. So M 9:72-88 Jl '71

Scepticism and modern poetry. Blackw 115:223-31 F '74; *same.* Ecl M ns 19: 488-95 Ap '74

Schackford, Martha Hale
The Clough centenary: his "Dipsychus." Sewanee R 27:401-10 O '19

Schelling, Felix E.
The English lyric. Boston, Houghton, Mifflin, 1913. p222-7

Scudder, Vida D.
Arthur Hugh Clough. *In* The life of the spirit in the modern English poets. Boston, Houghton, Mifflin, 1899. p265-8

Seeburg, L.
Über Arthur Hugh Clough. Göttingen, Bandenhoeck & Ruprecht, 1878. 22p

Shairp, John Campbell
Arthur Hugh Clough. *In* Portraits of friends. . . Boston, Houghton, Mifflin, 1889. p195-212

Sharp, Amy
Arthur Hugh Clough. *In* Victorian poets. London, Methuen, 1891. p121-37

Shepard, William [pseud]
see Walsh, William Shepard

Shindler, Robert
Tennyson, Arnold and Clough. *In* On certain aspects of recent English literature (Neuphilologische Vorträge und Abhandlung II) Leipzig, Teubner, 1902. p28-37

Sidgwick, Henry
The poems and prose remains of Clough. *In* Miscellaneous essays and addresses. London, Macmillan, 1904. p59-90

Smith, Arnold
Clough. *In* The main tendencies of Victorian poetry. London, Simpkin, Marshall, Hamilton, Kent, 1907. p105-15

Sonnet—On A. H. Clough [signed by "Z."] Spec 35:774 Jl 12 '62

Sprague, Janet Gilbertine
Arthur Hugh Clough in relation to the Victorian doubt. Williams memorial prize, Univ. of Rochester, 1926. 17ff

Statham, F. Reginald
Arthur Hugh Clough. Nat R 29:200-12 Ap '97

Stedman, Edmund Clarence
Victorian poets. Boston, Houghton, Mifflin, 1876. p243-4

Steede, M.
Arthur Hugh Clough. Temple 108:35-48 My '96

Stephen, (Sir) Leslie
Arthur Hugh Clough. *In* Dict N B vol IV p583-4

Stratton, Thomas
"The Bothie of Tober-na-Vuolich." Notes & Q 5th ser 9:114 F 9 '78

Swanwick, Anna
Arthur Hugh Clough. *In* Poets the interpreters of their age. London, Bell, 1892. p367-75

Symonds, John Addington
Arthur Hugh Clough. Fortn 10:589-617 D '68

Arthur Hugh Clough. *In* Last and first, being two essays. New York, Brown, 1919. p65-137

Taylor, Isaac
"Clough." Acad 36:154 S 7 '89

"Thyrsis." T L S Je 4 '14 p271-2

Tober-na-Fuosich. Notes & Q 5th ser 9: 199 Mr 9 '78

"Toper-na-Fuosich." Notes & Q 5th ser 8:395 N 17 '77

Turner, Albert Morton
A study of Clough's "Mari Magno." PMLA 44:569-89 Je '29

The **unpopularity** of Clough. Spec 55:1507-9 N 25 '82; *same.* Liv Age 155:764-7 D 23 '82

Waddington, Samuel
Arthur Hugh Clough, a monograph. London, Bell, 1883. x,333p
(Rev by E. D. A. Morshead in Acad 22:444-5 D 23 '82; Lit W 14:47 F 10 '83; Nation (NY) 36:259-60 Mr 22 '83)

Clough's "Bothie." Acad 23:11 Ja 6 '83

Walker, Hugh
The age of Tennyson. (Handbooks of English literature) London, Bell, 1904. p219-20

The literature of the Victorian era. Cambridge, Univ. press, 1921. p455-65

[Walsh, William Shepard] Shepard, William [pseud]
Arthur Hugh Clough. *In* Enchiridion of criticism. . . Philadelphia, Lippincott, 1885. p243-6

Ward, Thomas Humphrey
Arthur Hugh Clough. *In* The English poets. . . New York, Macmillan, 1907. vol IV p589-92

Waugh, Arthur
The poetry of reflection and doubt. *In* Reticence in literature, and other papers. London, Wilson [1915] p53-60

Victorian voices of doubt and trust. Cur Lit 31:556-9 N '01

Weatherhead, Leslie D.
Clough. *In* The after-world of the poets . . . London, Epworth press [1929] p144-53

Welby, Thomas Earle
Back numbers—LXXVIII. Sat R 145:805 Je 23 '28

Clough. *In* Back numbers. London, Constable, 1929. p106-10

Whibley, Charles
Introduction. *In* Poems of Arthur Hugh Clough. . . London, Macmillan, 1913. pi-xxxvii
(Rev in Contemp 105:285-8 F '14)

White, Greenough
Character of A. H. Clough as revealed in his poems. *In* Matthew Arnold and the spirit of the age. New York, Putnam, 1898. p8-16

Whitney, Elizabeth Boyce
The Oxford movement and its influence on English poetry. Masters essay, Univ. of Oklahoma, 1931.

Williams, Francis Howard
Clough and Emerson. . . Poet Lore 6: 348-56 '94

Williams, Stanley Thomas
Clough's prose. *In* Studies in Victorian literature. New York, Dutton [c 1923] p235-52

Winchester, Caleb Thomas
Arthur Hugh Clough. Meth R 88:716-32 S '06

Arthur Hugh Clough. *In* An old castle and other essays. . . New York, Macmillan, 1922. p362-80

Winwar, Frances [pseud]
see [Grebanier, (Mrs.) Frances] [Vinciguerra]

Wolfe, Humbert
Arthur Hugh Clough. *In* Royal society of literature of the United Kingdom. London. The eighteen-sixties. . . London, Macmillan, 1932. p20-50

Wright, H. G.
Clough and Wales. Welsh Outlook p194-5 Jl '30

Edward Fitzgerald

NOTE

In this bibliography two names will be spelled uniformly thruout: *Fitzgerald* will be given as one word, and *The Rubaiyat of Omar Khayyam* will be given without diacritical marks.

Edward Fitzgerald

I. Chronological Outline

1809. Born, March 31, Suffolk.

1848. Table-Talk of John Selden [includes many notes by Fitzgerald].

1849. Selections from the Poems and Letters of Bernard Barton, Edited by his Daughter [memoir by Fitzgerald, pages ix-xxxvi].

1851. Euphranor, a Dialogue on Youth.

1852. Polonius: a Collection of Wise Saws and Modern Instances.

1853. Six Dramas of Calderon, Freely Translated.

1856. Salámán and Absál. An Allegory. Translated from the Persian of Jámi.

1859. Rubaiyat of Omar Khayyam, First Edition.

1865. Such Stuff as Dreams are Made Of.

1868. Rubaiyat of Omar Khayyam, Second Edition.

1872. Rubaiyat of Omar Khayyam, Third Edition.

1876. Agamemnon, a Tragedy Taken from Aeschylus.

1879. [Readings in Crabbe].

1879. Rubaiyat of Omar Khayyam, Fourth Edition; and the Salámán and Absál of Jámi.

1880-81. The Downfall and Death of King Oedipus.

1883. Died, June 14, Norfolk.

Edward Fitzgerald

II. Bibliographical Material

Bentham, George
Bibliography chronologically arranged. *In* The variorum and definitive edition of the poetical and prose writings of Edward Fitzgerald... New York, Doubleday, Page, 1903. vol VII p135-57

[Bibliographical notes] Acad 38:30, 52 Jl 12, 19 '90

Bibliography. A list of English versions and editions of the Rubaiyat of Omar Khayyam. *In* Rubaiyat of Omar Khayyam rendered into English verse. (Old World ser) Portland, Maine, Mosher, 1900. 7th ed p123-41 (925 copies only)

Bibliography of Fitzgerald's version of the Rubaiyat. *In* Rubaiyat of Omar Khayyam of Naishapur the astronomer poet of Persia: rendered into English verse. Ashendene press, 1896. p[41]-6
[Reprinted from Mosher edition (1895) of the Rubaiyat]

Brockbank, James
Some editions of Omar Khayyam. Papers of the Manchester Literary Club 54:273-8 '28; *same.* Manch Q O '28

Brooklyn Public Library, New York
Edward Fitzgerald, 1809-1883. Brooklyn, New York, The Public Library, 1909. 10p

[**Brown, G. A.**]
Edward Fitzgerald. CHEL Vol XIII p549

Dole, Nathan Haskell
Bibliography of Omar Khayyam. *In* Rubaiyat of Omar Khayyam. Boston, Page, 1898. vol II p467+

Fitzgerald. Bookm (NY) 16:534-5 F '03

Glyde, John
A bibliography of the versions and editions of the Rubaiyat. *In* The life of Edward Fitzgerald. Chicago, Stone, 1900. p341-8

Heron-Allen, Edward
Bibliography. *In* The Rubaiyat of Omar Khayyam, being a facsimile of the manuscript. . . . London, Nichols, 1898. 2d ed p[281]-7

"Omar Khayyam": Fitzgerald's first edition, 1859. Notes & Q 10th ser 4:105 Ag 5 '05

Hill, Walter M.
A catalogue of first and rare editions of Fitzgerald's works, including many editions of the Rubaiyat of Omar Khayyam. . . The collection offered for sale by Walter M. Hill. Chicago, 1920 80p

Hopkins, Frederick M.
[Manuscript of the Rubaiyat] Pub W 126:1857 N 17 '34

Jackson, Holbrook
A bibliography of the English renderings of the Rubaiyat of Omar Khayyam. *In* Edward Fitzgerald and Omar Khayyam, an essay and a bibliography. London, Nutt, 1899. p35-41

Moreton, R. L.
Fitzgerald's "Omar Khayyam." Notes & Q 10th ser 6:453 D 8 '06

Mozley, William E.
Fitzgerald bibliography. Notes & Q 10th ser 2:214-15 S 10 '04

Nicholls, Norah
Some early editions of Fitzgerald's "Omar." Bookm (Lond) 79:320-1 F '31

Northup, Clark Sutherland
A register of bibliographies of the English language and literature. New Haven, Yale univ. press, 1925. p175

Page, Curtis Hidden
Fitzgerald; list of references. *In* British poets of the nineteenth century, ed. by C. H. Page. New ed. by Stith Thompson. New York, Sanborn, 1930. p696

Potter, Ambrose George
A bibliography of the Rubaiyat of Omar Khayyam. Together with kindred matter in prose and verse pertaining thereto. London, Ingpen & Grant, 1929. p1-100
(Rev in T L S D 12 '29 p1060)

Prideaux, William Francis
Fitzgerald bibliography. Notes & Q 10th ser 2:141-2 Ag 20 '04

Notes for a bibliography of Edward Fitzgerald. Notes & Q 9th ser 5:201-4, 221-4, 241-4 Mr 17, 24, 31 '00; Notes & Q 9th ser 6:61-2 Jl 28 '00; *same published*: [London]

Prideaux, William Francis—*Cont.*
Privately printed, 1900. 3-36p (50 copies only)
(Noted in Acad 59:126 Ag 18 '00; Ath 1:783 Je 23 '00)

Notes for a bibliography of Edward Fitzgerald. London, Hollings, 1901. x,88p
(Rev in Literary World (Lond) ns 64:386 N 15 '01)

Shorter, Clement K.
My bookshelves: Omar Khayyam. Bookm (Lond) 16:8-10 Ap '99

Way, W. Irving
Chronological list of the more important issues of Edward Fitzgerald's version of the Rubaiyat, and of other books written, translated, edited, or owned by him. Chicago, The Caxton club, 1899. 65p

Wheeler, Charles V. C.
A bibliography of Edward Fitzgerald. Washington, 1919. 3 vols

The important private library of C. V. Wheeler. Walpole Galleries. July 29, 30, 1919. 137p
(Most complete Fitzgerald collection ever offered for sale)

Woods, George Benjamin
[Bibliography] *In* Poetry of the Victorian period. New York, Scott, Foresman [c1930] p993-4

Wright, Thomas
Bibliography of Edward Fitzgerald. *In* The life of Edward Fitzgerald. London, Richards, 1904. vol II p241-3

Edward Fitzgerald

III. Biographical and Critical Material

Adams, Morley
In the footsteps of Borrow & Fitzgerald. London, Jarrold [1913] 3-262p

Omar's interpreter; a new life of Edward Fitzgerald. . . With an essay on the letters by Canon Ainger. London, Priory Press, 1909. 2d ed 174p

Aldrich, Thomas Bailey
A Persian poet. Atlan 41:421-6 Ap '78

Allingham, H. and D. Radford, eds.
William Allingham, a diary. London, Macmillan, 1907. p320-1

Altschul, Arthur
Anmerkungen. *In* Rubaiyat von Omar Chajjam . . . . Dresden, Köhler, 1910. p47-55

Armas, José de
Calderón en Inglaterra. *In* Ensayos críticos de literatura inglesa y española. Madrid, Librería general de Victoriano Suárez, 1910. p151-8

Arnold, William Harris
Ventures in book collecting. London, Scribner, 1923. p39-42

Ashley, W. J. B.
Edward Fitzgerald: a brief review of his life and character. Lit & Philos Soc 61:1-22 '10

Asquith, H. H.
[Address] *In* Rubaiyat of Omar Khayyam. . . New York, Mansfield, 1899. 67p [500 copies only]

Axon, William E. A.
Two of Edward Fitzgerald's early poems. Notes & Q 9th ser 3:441-2 Je 10 '99

Bacon, Thomas Rutherford
Edward Fitzgerald. New Englander 52:24-31, 117-29 Ja, F '90

Bailey, John Cann
Edward Fitzgerald. *In* Poets and poetry . . . Oxford, Clarendon press, 1911. p195-205

Edward Fitzgerald. *In* Studies in some famous letters. London, Burleigh, 1899

Baker, Ernest A.
Omarians. Readers' Review 3:35-7, 62-4 Ap, My '10

Batson, H. M.
Edward Fitzgerald. *In* The Rubaiyat of Omar Khayyam. . . . New York, Putnam, 1900. p69-82

Benn, Alfred William
The history of English rationalism in the nineteenth century. London, Longmans, Green, 1906. Vol II p292-4

Bensly, Edward
Antonio Urceo quoted by Burton and Fitzgerald. Notes & Q 10th ser 12:185 S 4 '09

Fitzgerald note. Notes & Q 158:319 My 3 '30

Benson, Arthur Christopher
Edward Fitzgerald. (English men of letters.) New York, Macmillan, 1905. vii, 207p
(Rev in Acad 69:677-8 Jl 1 '05; Nation (NY) 81:126-7 Ag 10 '05; J. L. Gilder in Critic (NY) 47:158-9 Ag '05; T L S Je 23 '05 p197-8; Ath 2:198 Ag '05; Sat R 100:500-1 O 14 '05; E. Clodd in Bookm (Lond) 28:162 Ag '05; Public Opinion (Lond) 87:801 Je 30 '05)

Edward Fitzgerald. March 31, 1809-June 14, 1883. Bookm (Lond) 35:251-7 Mr '09

Edward Fitzgerald at Woodbridge. Cornhill 99:535-47 Ap '09

The Upton letters. New York, Putnam [1910] 2d ed rev p97-100

Bhajiwala, Rustom Pestonji
. . . A succint account of the . . . [life] . . . of . . . Edward Fitzgerald. *In* Rubaiyat of Hakim Omar Khayyam. Bombay, The "News" printing press, 1927. p[1-25] (In Gujarati language)

Biographical preface. *In* Works of Edward Fitzgerald. New York, Houghton, Mifflin, 1887. vol I p[vii]-xxii

Birrell, Augustine
Edward Fitzgerald's letters. Empire Review 39:513-21 My '24

Bjerregaard, Carl Henrik Andreas
Sufi interpretations of the quatrains of Omar Khayyam and Fitzgerald. New York, Taylor, 1902. 126ff
(Rev in Literary World (Lond) ns 67:436-7 My 8 '03)

Sufism: Omar Khayyam and E. Fitzgerald. . . London, Sufi publishing society, 1915. 48p

Blake, Warren Barton
Poetry, time, and Edward Fitzgerald. Dial 46:177-80 Mr 16 '09

Blyth, James
Edward Fitzgerald and "Posh," "Herring Merchants". . . London, Long, 1908. 200p
(Rev in Blackw 184:150-2 Jl '08; M. A. Havens in Dial 45:162-3 S 16 '08; Acad

Blyth, James—*Continued*
75:32-3 Jl 11 '08; Ath 2:175-6 Ag 15 '08;
Sat R 106:210 Ag 15 '08; Spec 101:635
O 24 '08)

Boase, Frederic
Fitzgerald, Edward. *In* Modern English
biography. Truro, Netherton & Worth,
1892. vol I p1058

Bosis, Adolfo de
Su Omar Khayyam e su Elihu Vedder. Il
Convito 6:398-415 Je '95

Bowen, Katherine
Oriental pessimism in Fitzgerald and
Cazalis. Masters essay, Columbia univ.
1924

Bradford, Catherine Frances
Edward Fitzgerald as seen by his contemporaries. Masters essay, Columbia
university, 1931

Bradford, Gamaliel
Edward Fitzgerald. *In* Bare souls. New
York, Harper, 1924. p277-312
(Rev in Sat R 139:139 F 7 '25)

Bridges, Victor
Edward Fitzgerald and other verses.
London, Hodder & Stoughton, 1932.
21p
(Noted in T L S Je 23 '32 p467)

Brigham, Johnson
The many-sided Omar. (Rosemary press
brochures) [Des Moines, Iowa?] Rosemary press [c1925] 3-15p

Bromhead, H. W.
Fitzgerald's roses. T L S Ag 31 '16 p417

Brown, William Augustus
Introduction. *In* Rubaiyat of Omar
Khayyam. Boston, Houghton Mifflin,
1899

Browning, Robert
To Edward Fitzgerald. [Poem] Ath 2:64
Jl 13 '89 [A bitter 12-line poem in
answer to a remark included in "Let-
ters and Literary Remains of Edward
Fitzgerald," ed. by W. A. Wright]

Byron, May
A day with Omar Khayyam. London,
Hodder & Stoughton, 1914

C[adell, (Mrs)] J. E.
The true Omar Khayyam. Fraser ns 19:
650-9 My '79

Campbell, A. Y.
Edward Fitzgerald. *In* Massingham, H. J.
& Massingham, E. eds. The great Victorians. London, Nicholson and Watson [1932] p197-210

Cazamian, Madeleine
Le roman et les idées en Angleterre; l'influence de la science (1860-1890). (Publications de la faculté des lettres de
l'université de Strasbourg. Fascicule
15) Strasbourg, Librairie Istra, 1923.
p261

Chapman, Edward Mortimer
Doubters and the mystics. *In* English literature in account with religion. Boston, Houghton, Mifflin, 1910. p455-9

Charnwood, (Lady) Dorothea
Letters by ten literary men. Cornhill 45:
498-9 N '18

Chesley, Clair Vincent
A criticism of Fitzgerald. Masters essay,
Columbia univ. 1915

Chesterton, Gilbert Keith
Great Victorian poets. *In* The Victorian
age in literature. New York, Holt
[1913] p192-5

Christensen, Arthur
Critical studies in the Rubá'iat of 'Umar.
I-Khayyám. A revised text with English translation. Det kgl. danske Vi-
denskabernes Selskab. Historiskfilo-
logiske Meddelelser 14:1-180 '27

[Churchill, William]
The marvellous year. Introduction by E.
Markham. New York, Huebsch, 1909.
p14-16, 101-4

Clodd, Edward
Concerning a pilgrimage to the grave of
Edward Fitzgerald. London, Printed
for private distribution to the members
of the Omar Khayyam club, 1894. 18p

Edward Fitzgerald (1809-1883). *In* Memories. New York, Putnam, 1916. p92-8

Edward Fitzgerald. Engl Illus 11:529-33
F '94

Fitzgerald's roses. T L S S 21 '16 p453

Col. Hay on Omar Khayyam. Critic (NY)
31:401-2 D 25 '97

Conway, Moncure D.
The Omar Khayyam cult in England.
Nation (NY) 57:304-5 O 26 '93

Cook, (Sir) Edward
The second thoughts of poets. *In* Literary recreations. London, Macmillan,
1919. p270-7

Cooper, Ernest R.
A Suffolk coast garland. London, Heath
Cranton, 1928. p217-18

Davis, F. Hadland
Edward Fitzgerald: a centenary sketch.
Readers' Review 2:41-3 Ap '09

Dead poet pilloried; Robert Browning's
poem to the translator of Omar Khayyam. Book Notes 5:223-4 Je-Jl '27

"Dear Old Fitz, to be sure." Out 91:767-70
Ap 3 '09

Dennis, John
Edward Fitzgerald. Leisure Hour 44:32-
5 Ja '95

Dickson, L. M.
Rubaiyat of Omar Khayyam. Canadian
Bookman 15:100-1 Ag '33

Didden, R.
"The Omar Khayyam myth." Lit 6:502
Je 30 '00

Din, Siraj
Edward Fitzgerald. T L S Mr 9 '33 p167

Dobson, Austin
Verses read at the dinner of the Omar
Khayyam club. Bookm (NY) 5:198-9
My '97

Dole, Nathan Haskell

Edward Fitzgerald (1809-1883). *In* Warner, C. D. ed. Library of the world's best literature. . . Memorial ed. New York, Hill [c1902] vol XIV p5797-9

Fitzgerald and Omar Khayyam. *In* Rubaiyat of Omar Khayyam. . . Boston, Page, 1899. p9-23

Omar and his translators. *In* Rubaiyat of Omar Khayyam. Boston, Page, 1898. vol I p[ix]-cxxxii

Omar Khayyam Club of London. *In* Rubaiyat of Omar Khayyam. Boston, Page, 1898. vol II p594-615

Omar the tentmaker. London, Duckworth, 1899
(Rev in Literary World (Lond) ns 59: 223 Mr 10 '99)

Preface. . . *In* Rubaiyat. . . Portland, Me. Mosher, 1899. p i-xx

Dole, Nathan Haskell (ed)

Rubaiyat of Omar Khayyam. English, French, and German translations comparatively arranged in accordance with the text of Edward Fitzgerald's version; with further selections, notes, biographies, bibliography and other material, collected and edited by Nathan Haskell Dole. Boston, Knight, 1896. 2 vols
(Rev in Nation (NY) 63:391 N 19 '96)

Drinkwater, John

Victorian poetry. London, Hodder and Stoughton, 1923. p174-7

Dutt, William A.

Highways and byways in East Anglia. London, Macmillan, 1901. 428p

E. Fitzgerald. *In* The Library of literary criticisms of English and American authors. . . ed. by Charles Wells Moulton. . . Buffalo, New York, Moulton publishing company, 1904-05. vol VII p514-22

Edward Fitzgerald. T L S Mr 25 '09 p109-10; Nation (NY) 88:322-3 Ap 1 '09; Temple 88:331-44 Mr '90; *same.* Liv Age 184:815-23 Mr 29 '90

Edward Fitzgerald and T. E. Brown. Macmil 83:212-16 Ja '01; *same.* Book-Lover (San Francisco) 2:549-52 Ja-F '02

Edward Fitzgerald, 1809-1883. Bookn 26: 122-3 O '07

Edward Fitzgerald's "Omar Khayyam." Notes & Q 9th ser 3:395-6 My 20 '99

The **1859** edition of Fitzgerald's Omar Khayyam. Sat R 61:97-8 Ja 16 '86

Elton, Oliver

A survey of English literature, 1830-1880. London, Arnold, 1920. vol II p113-19

Elwin, Whitwell

Edward Fitzgerald. Monthly Review 15: 135-49 Ap '04

An **encyclopedic** "Rubaiyat." Book B ns 13:295-6 Je '96

The **ethics** of parody. Acad 64:513-14 My 23 '03

Fehr, Bernhard

Die englische literatur des 19. und 20. jahrhunderts. Wildpark-Potsdam, 1928. p188

Fernand, Henry

Les rubáiyát d'Omar Kheyyám traduits en vers français d'après la version anglaise d'Ed. Fitzgerald. . .
(Rev in Ath 1:140-1 Ja 31 '03)

Fitch, George Hamlin

Rubaiyat of Omar Khayyam. *In* Comfort found in good old books. New York, Grosset, 1911. p74-82

Fitzgerald, Edward

Edward Fitzgerald and Bernard Barton; letters written by Fitzgerald 1839-1856; with a foreword by Viscount Grey of Falloden; ed. by F. R. Barton. New York, Putnam, 1924. viii,190p
(Rev by A. Birrell in Empire Review 39:513-21 My '24)

Euphranor, a dialogue on youth. London, Pickering, 1851. [1]-81p
(Rev in Acad 69:1330-1 D 25 '05; Spec 90:982-3 Je 20 '03

A Fitzgerald friendship, being hitherto unpublished letters from Edward Fitzgerald to William Bodham Donne; ed. with an introduction and notes in collaboration with Mrs. Catherine Bodham, by Neilson Campbell Hannay. New York, Rudge, 1932. xvii,132[14]p
(Rev in T L S S 29 '32 p677; A. Waugh in Spec 149:452-4 O 8 '32; H. Moran in Lond Merc 27:83 N '32

A Fitzgerald medley, ed. by Charles Ganz. London, Methuen [1933] vii-xv,307p
(Rev in T L S Mr 4 '33 p309; A. Waugh in Spec 150:613 Ap 28 '33; New Statesm & Nation ns 5:698 My 27 '33; H. I.'A. Fausset in Bookm (Lond) 84: 153 Je '33)

Letters and literary remains of Edward Fitzgerald, ed. by W. A. Wright. London, Macmillan, 1889. 3 vols [v]-xii, 502p, 488p, 492p [same in 7 vols 1902-03]
(Rev in Sat R 68:44-5 Jl 13 '89; E. Dowden in Acad 36:63-4 Ag 3 '89; Ath 2:55-6 Jl 13 '89; Scots Observer 2:270-1 Jl 27 '89; Nation (NY) 49:112-14 Ag 8 '89; Critic (NY) 15:171-2 O 12 '89; Spec 63:211 Ag 17 '89; M. B. Anderson in Dial 10:161-4 N '89; G. E. Woodberry in Atlan 65:133-5 Ja '90; Temple 97:23-36 Ja '93; Edin R 180:365-91 O '94; Quar R 184:103-21 Jl '96; Liv Age 210: 771-83 S 26 '96; Out 74:523-4 Je 27 '03)

Letters from Edward Fitzgerald to Bernard Quaritch, 1853 to 1883, ed. by C. Quaritch Wrentmore. London, Quaritch, 1926. viii,135p
(Rev in T L S N 11 '26 p791)

Letters of Edward Fitzgerald, ed. by W. A. Wright. London, Macmillan, 1894. 2 vols [v]-xiv,350p, 368p
(Rev in Westm 142:112-13 Jl '94; Edin R 180:365-91 O '94; Liv Age 203:515-31

Fitzgerald, Edward—*Continued*

D '94; Lond Q R 84:318-31 Jl '95; Quar R 184:103-21 Jl '96; Liv Age 210:771-83 S 26 '96; Acad 59:75-6 Jl 28 '00)

Letters of Edward Fitzgerald to Fanny Kemble, 1871-1883, ed. by W. A. Wright. London, Macmillan, 1895. 263p
(Rev in Dial 19:174-5 O 1 '95; Nation (NY) 61:297-8 O 24 '95; Sewanee R 4: 73-9 N '95; Literary World (Lond) ns 52:429 N 29 '95; Ath 2:710-11 N 23 '95; Sat R 80:733-4 N 30 '95; R. C. Browne in Acad 48:451-2 N 30 '95; Edin R 183:329-32 Ap '96; Quar R 184: 103-21 Jl '96; Liv Age 210:771-83 S 26 '96; Acad 59:75-6 Jl 28 '00; Guardian 51:333 F 26 '96)

Letters to Frederick Tennyson, ed. by H. J. Schonfield. London, Hogarth press, 1930. 146p
(Rev in T L S O 16 '30 p831)

Miscellanies. London, Macmillan, 1900. 208p
(Rev in Acad 59:438 N 10 '00; Literary World (Lond) ns 62:408 N 23 '00; Lit W 21:307 S 13 '90; Lit 8:51 Ja 19 '01; M. Todhunter in Engl Stud 30:126-9 '02; Nation (NY) 72:92 Ja 31 '01)

More letters of Edward Fitzgerald, ed. by W. A. Wright. London, Macmillan, 1901. 295p
(Rev in Ath 2:810-11 D 14 '01; W. F. Prideaux in Acad 61:619-20 D 21 '01; Acad 61:583-4 D 14 '01; T L S Ja 17 '02 pl; Liv Age 232:445-7 F 15 '02; Spec 88:19-20 Ja 4 '02; Literary World (Lond) ns 65:28 Ja 10 '02; Ind 54:752-3 Mr 27 '02; Nation (NY) 74:256 Mr 27 '02; Ecl M 138:460-2 Ap '02; H. W. Boynton in Atlan 89:418-19 Mr '02; W. H. White in Ath 1:338 Mr 15 '02; Dial 33:164-5 S 16 '02; W. B. Gurdon in Bookm (Lond) 21:133-4 Ja '02)

New letters, ed. by N. C. Hannay. Atlan 146:628-37 N '30

Some new letters of Edward Fitzgerald... London, Williams & Norgate, 1923. viii,177p [Same as New York edition entitled "Edward Fitzgerald and Bernard Barton...."]

Three new letters from Edward Fitzgerald [to Thomas Constable; with a note by Archibald Constable] Ath 1:12 Ja 6 '12

Unpublished letters to Bernard Barton. Scrib 72:161-70, 326-32 Ag, S '22

Variorum and definitive edition of the poetical and prose writings of Edward Fitzgerald, including a complete bibliography and interesting personal and literary notes... New York, Doubleday, 1902-1903
(Rev by A. I. Coleman in Critic (NY) 43:561-3 D '03; Nation (NY) 75:462-3 D 11 '02; Nation (NY) 76:95 Ja 29 '03; Dial 34:204 Mr 16 '03; P. F. Bicknell in Dial 33:280-2 N 1 '02)

William Makepeace Thackeray and Edward Fitzgerald. Unpublished letters and verses. Introd. by Lady Ritchie. London, Privately printed by Clement Shorter, 1913

Works of Edward Fitzgerald. . . . Reprinted from the original impressions, with some corrections derived from his own annotated copies. . . . Boston, Houghton, Mifflin, 1887. 2 vols
(Rev in Lit W 18:294 S 17 '87; Spec 60: 1316-17 O 1 '87; Nation (NY) 47:501 D 20 '88)

Fitzgerald, Edward, trans.

Agamemnon. A tragedy taken from Aeschylus. London, Quaritch, 1876. [iii]-[vii], [1]-79p
(Rev by T. S. Perry in Atlan 39:736-8 Je '77; J. A. Symonds in Acad 12:4-6 Jl 7 '77; No Am 124:154-5 Ja '77)

Rubaiyat of Omar Khayyam, The Astronomer-poet of Persia. Translated into English verse. London, Quaritch, 1859. [iii]-xiii, [1]-21p
(Rev by C. E. Norton in No Am 109: 565-84 O '69; Fraser 81:777-84 Je '70; Nation (NY) 13:146-7 Ag 31 '71; J. W. Chadwick in Old & New 5:611-14 My '72; A. M. Machar in Canadian Monthly 10:399-404 N '76; T. S. Perry in Atlan 39:730-4 Je '77; F. J. Goldsmid in Acad 16:204-5 S 20 '79; Sat R 49:89-90 Ja 17 '80; Critic (NY) ns 2:230-1 N 15 '84; Harper M 70:324 Ja '85; A. B. Edwards in Acad 26:361-2, 399 N 29, D 13 '84; W. M. Payne in Dial 9:245-6 Ja '89; Ath 1:70-1 Ja 19 '01; Literary World (Lond) ns 59:296 Mr 31 '99; Literary World (Lond) ns 63:104 F 1 '01; Ath 2:784-5 D 25 '09; Lit W 8:165 F '78; A. B. Houghton in Harv Mo 1:102-18 D '85; Pilot 7:623-4 Je 27 '03)

Six dramas of Calderon. Freely translated by Edward Fitzgerald. London, Pickering, 1853. [1]-273p
(Rev in Ath 2:1063 S 10 '53; Sat R 2: 728-30 D 13 '56; T L S Je 5 '03 p178; Sat R 96:302-3 S 5 '03; T. S. Perry in Atlan 39:734-5 Je '77; Acad 64:536-7 My 30 '03)

Fitzgerald and Mme. de Sévigné. T L S Ja 21 '15 p23

Fitzgerald sans Omar. Acad 59:75-6 Jl 28 '00

[**Fitzgerald's** commonplace book] Dial 46: 181 Mr 16 '09

[**Fitzgerald's** dislike for Mrs. Browning] Nation (NY) 49:111-12 Ag 8 '89

[**Fitzgerald's** name on translations of the "Rubaiyat"] Critic (NY) 1:259 My 31 '84

Fitzgerald's "Omar." Bookm (Lond) 35: 257-63 Mr '09

Fitzgerald's "Polonius." Acad 59:471-2 N 17 '00

Fitzmaurice-Kelly, James

Omar Khayyam. Outlook (Lond) 2:372-3 O 22 '98

Foster, (Mrs) W. G.
Riddle of the Rubaiyat. Canadian Bookman 15:136-7 O '33

Fox, Duane Edwin
The depression Rubaiyat. Golden Book 20:258-74 S '34

Gabrieli, Francesco
Il vero Omar Khayyam. Nuova Antol 351:227-33 S 16 '30

Garnett, Richard and Gosse, Edmund
Edward Fitzgerald. *In* English literature, an illustrated record, by Richard Garnett and Edmund Gosse. New York, Grosset & Dunlap [c1904] vol IV p343-5

Gibb, William A.
"Old Fitz." Central Literary Magazine O '20 p295-303

Glyde, John
The life of Edward Fitzgerald, with an introd. by Edward Clodd. Chicago, Stone, 1900. xvi,358p bibl p349-52
(Rev in Nation (NY) 72:238-9 Mr 21 '01; Acad 58:327-8 Ap 21 '00; Ath 1:464 Ap 14 '00; Spec 84:635-6 My 5 '00; Literary World (Lond) ns 61:418 My 4 '00; Lit 6:331-2 Ap 28 '00; Speaker ns 2: 45-6 Ap 14 '00; W. B. Gurdon in Bookm (Lond) 18:47-9 My '00)
The personal characteristics of Edward Fitzgerald. Cur Lit 30:210-12 F '01

Goodale, Ralph Hinsdale
Pessimism in English poetry and fiction, 1847-1900. *In* Abstracts of theses. . . Humanistic series Volume VI. . . Univ. of Chicago, Chicago, 1927. p347-51

Gosse, (Sir) Edmund William
Edward Fitzgerald. Book-Lover (San Francisco) 2:97-105 '01
Edward Fitzgerald. Fortn 52:57-70 Jl '89; *same.* Liv Age 182:323-31 Ag 10 '89
Edward Fitzgerald. *In* Critical kit-kats. New York, Dodd, Mead, 1896. p65-92
Edward Fitzgerald. *In* The variorum and definitive edition of the poetical and prose writings of Edward Fitzgerald. . . New York, Doubleday, Page, 1902. vol I p ix-xxviii
Inscription; poem. Lit W 24:384 N 18 '93
The metrical form of Fitzgerald. Ath 1: 177 F 7 '03

Gray, Louis H.
An early allusion to Omar Khayyam. Nation (NY) 74:110-11 F 6 '02

Grendon, Felix
Fitzgerald on Tennyson; or, Tennyson before and after 1842. Sewanee R 14: 161-70 '06

Gribble, Francis Henry
Edward Fitzgerald. Fortn 85:647-57 Ap '09

Groome, Francis Hindes
Edward Fitzgerald. *In* Chambers's cyclopaedia of English literature. Philadelphia, Lippincott, 1910. vol III p424-8

Edward Fitzgerald: an aftermath. Blackw 146:615 N '89
Edward Fitzgerald; an aftermath; with miscellanies in verse and prose. Portland, Maine, Mosher, 1902. xxviii,156p
Two Suffolk friends. London, W. Blackwood, 1895. p67-133
(Rev in Sat R 80:175 Ag 10 '95)

Gurdon, W. Brampton
Omar Khayyam once more. Bookm (Lond) 22:176-7 Ag '02

Harris, May
A Victorian pagan. Sewanee R 34:309-17 Jl-S '26

Hay, John
An address delivered by the Hon. John Hay before the Omar Khayyam Club, London, December, 1897. *In* Fitzgerald, E. Rubaiyat of Omar Khayyam. . . New York, Brentano's [189 ?] p7-13; *also in* Fitzgerald, E. Rubaiyat of Omar Khayyam. . . New York, The Critic co. 1898. p3-6
Omar Khayyam. Book-Lover 5:157-61 F '04

Hearn, Lafcadio
Edward Fitzgerald and the "Rubaiyat." *In* Interpretations of literature; selected and ed. . . by John Erskine. New York, Dodd, Mead, 1915. vol I p304-20

Henry, Albert S.
Fitzgerald and Omar Khayyam. . . Bookn 23:912-17 Ag '05

Henry, Fernand
The metrical form of Fitzgerald. Ath 1: 240 F 21 '03

Heron-Allen, Edward
Edward Fitzgerald's Rubaiyat of Omar Khayyam, with their original Persian sources, collated from his own ms. and literally translated. London, Quaritch, 1899. 180p
(Rev in Ath 1:12 Ja 6 '00; Lit 4:305-6 Mr 25 '99; Sat R 87:466-7 Ap 15 '99; Spec 83:260 Ag 19 '99; Literary World (Lond) ns 59:212-13 Mr 10 '99)
The Rubaiyat of Omar Khayyam, being a facsimile of the manuscript in the Bodleian library. London, Nichols, 1898. 2d ed i-xlii,320p
(Rev in Literary World (Lond) ns 57: 82 Ja 28 '98)
Some side-lights upon Edward Fitzgerald's poem, 'The Rubaiyat of Omar Khayyam': being the substance of a lecture delivered at the Grosvenor Crescent club and Woman's institute, on March 22, 1898. London, Nichols, 1898. 36p

Holland, Bernard
The present popularity of Omar Khayyam. Nat R 33:643-52 Je '99

Hope, Henry Gerald
Edward Fitzgerald's "Omar Khayyam." Notes & Q 9th ser 3:326 Ap 29 '99
Thackeray and Edward Fitzgerald. Notes & Q 9th ser 3:4 Ja 7 '99

Hornby, C. H. St. John
To the gentle reader of the Rubaiyat of Omar Khayyam of Naishapur. *In* Rubaiyat of Omar Khayyam of Naishapur the astronomer poet of Persia: rendered into English verse. Ashendene press, 1896. p i-xiv

Hudson, A. H.
Fitzgerald and Omar Khayyam. Notes & Q 11th ser 7:370 My 10 '13

Hutchinson, Horace G.
Edward Fitzgerald. Quar R 256:279-301 Ap '31

Hutton, Richard Holt
A great poet of denial and revolt. *In* Brief literary criticisms. London, Macmillan, 1906. p334-47; *same.* Spec 49: 334-6 Mr 11 '76

Ince, Richard Basil
Edward Fitzgerald. *In* Calverley and some Cambridge wits of the nineteenth century. London, Richards & Toulmin [1929] p23-73
The influence of Omar Khayyam. Spec 82: 816-17 Je 10 '99

Jackson, Holbrook
Edward Fitzgerald and Omar Khayyam, an essay and a bibliography. London, Nutt, 1899. 41(1)p bibl p35-41

James, C. W.
Edward Fitzgerald on music and musicians. Macmil 85:330-7 Mr '02

James, Gilbert
Fourteen drawings illustrating Edward Fitzgerald's translation of the Rubaiyat of Omar Khayyám. London, 1898. unp

[John Hay on Omar Khayyam] Critic (NY) 33:484-5 D '98

Johnson, Catharine B. ed.
William Bodham Donne and his friends. New York, Dutton, 1905
(Rev by P. F. Bicknell in Dial 39:10-12 Jl 1 '05)

Johnson, Lionel Pigot
Lucretius and Omar. *In* Post liminium... New York, Kennerley, 1912. p58-63

Kearney, Michael
Biographical preface. Edward Fitzgerald. *In* Rubaiyat of Omar Khayyam... New York, Doran [1909?] p ix-xxiii
[This preface has been reprinted in many editions, sometimes unsigned]

Keene, H. G.
Omar Khayyam. Macmil 57:27-32 N '87

Kellner, Leon
Die englische literatur der neuesten zeit. Leipzig, Tauchnitz, 1921. p231-3
Die englische literatur im zeitalter der königin Viktoria. Leipzig, Tauchnitz, 1909. p386-9
Ein unsterblicher müssiggänger. Die Nation (Berlin) 16:24-6 O 8 '98

Kelman, John
Celtic revivals of paganism. *In* Among famous books. London, Hodder and Stoughton [1912] p89-97

Kerrich, Mary Eleanor FitzGerald
Edward Fitzgerald. A personal reminiscence by his great-niece. 19th Cent 65:461-70 Mr '09; *same.* Liv Age 261: 233-40 Ap 24 '09
Homes and haunts of Edward Fitzgerald. By his grand-niece. Blackw 174:439-52 O '03

Laban, Ferdinand
Ungelesene bücher als zeichen der zeit. [Omar Khayyam; with bibl] Deutsche Rundschau 111:433-9 '02

Lane-Poole, Stanley
[Comparison of Whinfield's and Fitzgerald's translation of the Rubaiyat] Acad 21:287-8 Ap 22 '82
Omar Khayyam as a bore. Critic (NY) 37:216-19 S '00

[Latin version of Fitzgerald's "Rubaiyat"] Book B ns 16:304-5 My '98

Laughlin, Clara Elizabeth
Two lights that failed: the stories of John Ruskin and Edward Fitzgerald. *In* Stories of authors' loves. Philadelphia, Lippincott, 1902. vol I p84-90; *same.* Delineator 58:418 S '01

Layard, G. S.
An Omar Khayyam curiosity. Bookm (Lond) 22:13-15 Ap '02

Le Gallienne, Richard
Rubaiyat of Omar Khayyam—a paraphrase. London, Richards, 1897 (Rev in Sat R 84:670 D 11 '97)

A letter of Edward Fitzgerald's. Nation (NY) 74:268 Ap 3 '02

Levey, Sivori
The ruby in the wine. A Persian allegory of the Old Omar Khayyam and his friends. . . Being Fitzgerald's 'Omar Khayyam.' Dramatised for costume presentation (Pilgrimage plays, no 7) London, Fountain publishing co. [n.d.] 17p

Literary haunts of East Anglia. Bookm (NY) 13:205-6 My '01

The literature of house-moving. . . T. P.'s Weekly 5:329-30 Mr 17 '05

Lowell, James Russell
In a copy of Omar Khayyam; poem. *In* The writings of James Russell Lowell in prose and poetry. Boston, Houghton, Mifflin, 1900. vol XI p123

Lyall, (Sir) Alfred
Studies in literature and history. London, Murray, 1915. p66-70

McCabe, Joseph Martin
A biographical dictionary of modern rationalists. London, Watts, 1920. p255

McCarthy, Justin Huntly, trans.
Rubaiyat of Omar Khayyam. London, Nutt, 1889
(Rev in Spec 63:215-16 Ag 17 '89)
[Compared with Fitzgerald]

Macfall, Haldane
The E. J. Sullivan Omar. T. P.'s Weekly 22:770 D 12 '13

McGill, Nettie Pauline
Fitzgerald's comments on his literary contemporaries as seen in the Letters. Masters essay, Columbia univ. 1913

McGovern, J. B.
Edward Fitzgerald and "N & Q." Notes & Q 11th ser 4:469 D 9 '11

McSweeney, Katherine Ella
Literary gossip in the letters of Edward Fitzgerald. Masters essay, Columbia univ. 1925

Mantell, A. M.
A modern view of Omar Khayyam. Quest 20:337-53 Jl '29

Maslen, B. J.
Celebrities and music. Edward Fitzgerald. Musical Opinion 55:830-1 Jl '32

Millar, A. H.
The Omar cult. Acad 59:77-8 Jl 28 '00
"The Omar Khayyam Myth." Lit 6:483 Je 23 '00; also see Lit 6:451 Je 16 '00

A **modern** pilgrimage. Blackw 185:723-6 My '09; *same*. Liv Age 261:696-700 Je 12 '09

More, Paul Elmer
Kipling and Fitzgerald. *In* Shelburne essays. New York, Putnam, 1905. 2d ser p104-25

The Seven seas and the Rubaiyat. Atlan 84:800-8 D '99

Moreton, R. L.
Fitzgerald's "Omar Khayyam." Notes & Q 10th ser 6:453 D 8 '06

Morley, Christopher Darlington
A friend of Fitzgerald. *In* Essays. Garden City, New York, Doubleday, Doran, 1928. p185-97

Morley, Henry
[Introduction] *In* Edward Fitzgerald, Miscellanies. London, Routledge, 1904. pi-vii

Murphy, Charles Perez
Rubaiyat of Omar Khayyam. National Magazine (Boston) 11:253-8 D '99

Murray, James A.
Omar Khayyam. Fortn 66:848-55 D '96

Musings without method. Blackw 167:694-7 My '00

Nagarkar, B. B.
Omar Khayyam. Indian Magazine Mr '98

Nevinson, Henry Woodd
If I were Fitzgerald. *In* Books and personalities. London, Lane, 1905. p196-203

An Omarian service. *In* Books and personalities. London, Lane, 1905. p204-12

A **new** Omar. Acad 78:513-15 My 28 '10

Newbolt, Henry
To Edward Fitzgerald; poem. *In* Poems: new and old. London, Murray, 1912. p134-5

Nicolas, J. B.
Les Quatrains de Khèyam.
(Rev in No Am 109:565-84 O '69)

Nicoll, William Robertson
Edward Fitzgerald and Bernard Barton. *In* A bookman's letters. London, Hodder and Stoughton, 1913. p183-91

An old commonplace book of Edward Fitzgerald's. *In* Literary anecdotes of the nineteenth century, contributions toward a literary history of the period by W. Robertson Nicoll and Thomas J. Wise, eds. London, Hodder & Stoughton, 1896. vol II p385-94

Nine letters from Edward Fitzgerald to Mrs. Kemble. Temple 131:537-48 My '05

[**Notes** on Fitzgerald] Literary World (Lond) ns 75:98-9 Ap 15 '09

Obituary. Acad 23:437 Je 23 '83

An **old** commonplace book of Edward Fitzgerald's. Bookm (Lond) 2:48-50 My '92 [See Nicoll, W. R.]

"**Old** Fitz." Vragen van den Dag 45:836-44 O '30

O'Leary, W. E.
Omar Khayyam: Fitzgerald's version. Notes & Q 12th ser 4:330 D '18

Omar and others. Acad 52:475-7 D 4 '97

Omar and the Fitzgerald centenary. Ath 1: 440-1 Ap 10 '09

The **Omar** cult. Acad 59:55-6, 77 Jl 21, 28 '00

Omar Khayyam. Lit 4:61-2 Ja 21 '99

Omar Khayyam Club of America. [Boston] Privately printed by the Rosemary press, 1921. (8),105,(2)p

Omar Khayyam's Rubaiyyat. A few of the quatrains untranslated by Fitzgerald. . . Cornhill 62:627-8 D '90

Page, Curtis Hidden
Answer to the Rubaiyat of Omar; poem. Bookm (NY) 8:573 F '99

[**Parody** of Fitzgerald's "Omar"] Ath 2:671 D 26 '14

The **personality** of "Omar" Fitzgerald. R of Rs (NY) 39:616-17 My '09

Phelps, William Lyon
Schopenhauer and Omar. *In* Essays on books. New York, Macmillan, 1922. p265-76; *same in* New Englander 49:328-36 N '88

Pickering, Charles J.
Rubaiyat from 'Umar. Acad 30:104-5 Ag 14 '86
'Umar of Nîshâpûr. Nat R 16:506-21 D '90

Pickford, John
Edward Fitzgerald. Notes & Q 10th ser 11:304-5 Ap 17 '09

Platt, Arthur
Edward Fitzgerald. *In* Nine essays. Cambridge, Univ. press, 1927. p23-42
(Rev by A. W. P[ollard] in Rev E S 4:488-9 O '28; F. H. Schwartz in Bei Anglia 40:177-8 Jl '29)

[Portraits of Fitzgerald] Book B 13:752 D '96; Critic (NY) 33:486 D '98; Engl Illus 11:530 F '94; Bookm (Lond) 35: 251, 256, 259 Mr '09; Bookm (NY) 11: 297 Je '00; Acad 58:327 Ap 21 '00; Ind 66:627 Mr 25 '09; Book Monthly 1: 225 Ja '04; Book-Lover (NY) 5:156 F '04; Bookm (Lond) 18:47 My '00; Delineator 58:418 S '01

Potter, A. G.
Fitzgerald and Omar Khayyam. Notes & Q 11th ser 7:437 My 31 '13

Prideaux, William Francis
Edward Fitzgerald and "N. & Q." Notes & Q 11th ser 5:17 Ja 6 '12

Fitzgerald's "Euphranor." Notes & Q 9th ser 1:302-3 Ap 16 '98

Fitzgerald's song in Tennyson's "Memoir." Notes & Q 10th ser 2:285 O 8 '04

Omar and his translator. Ely, 1909

Two of Edward Fitzgerald's early poems. Notes & Q 9th ser 4:15 Jl 1 '99

Propato, Francisco A.
Introduccion. *In* Ensayo crítico sobre las Rubaiyat de Umar-I-Khayyam. . . Paris, Bourdon, 1930. p 1-3

[Quatrain on Fitzgerald] Critic (NY) 17: 121 S 6 '90

A **query.** (My Omar Khayyam) [parody] Punch 109:73 Ag 17 '95

Quiller-Couch, (Sir) Arthur Thomas
Measure for measure; poem. *In* Green bays; verses and parodies. London, Oxford univ. press, 1930. new ed p35-6

Ralli, Augustus
Edward Fitzgerald and his times. *In* Critiques. London, Longmans, Green, 1927. p171-83

Ratcliffe, S. K.
Edward Fitzgerald and T. E. Brown. Lit 8:38 Ja 12 '01

The **real** facts in regard to Fitzgerald and "Omar Khayyam." Cur Lit 46:508-10 My '09

Rempis, C. H.
Die vierzeiler 'Omar Chajjams in der auswahl und anordnung Edward Fitzgeralds aus dem Persischen verdeutscht. Tübingen, Deutsche Chajjam Gesellschaft, 1934
(Noted in T L S My 17 '34 p360)

Rice, S. A.
The author of an immortal translation. Ind 66:627-9 Mr 25 '09

Robertson, John Mackinnon
The efficiency of Fitzgerald. Life & L 5:281-8 O '30

Rodgers, Cleveland
Who was Omar Khayyam? Mentor 16: 49-51 Mr '28

Rodwell, E. H.
Omar Khayyam. The Persian text, with paraphrase and the First and Fourth editions of Fitzgerald's translation. Ed.

by Brigadier-General E. H. Rodwell. London, Kegan, Paul, 1931
(Rev in T L S Je 18 '31 p484)

A **rose** from Omar's grave; poem. Dial 15: 275 N 1 '93

The **rose** in Fitzgerald's "Omar." Notes & Q 11th ser 9:509 Je 27 '14

Ross, Calder
Edward Fitzgerald in Shetland and Orkney. Scottish Notes and Queries 11: 161-2 N '33

Ross, E. D.
Biographical introduction. *In* The Rubaiyat of Omar Khayyam. . . with a commentary by H. M. Batson. London, Methuen, 1900
(Rev in Sat R 91:476-7 Ap 13 '01; Nation (NY) 71:509 D 27 '00)

Rutledge, Janette Cooper
Lumifar; the spiritual interpretation of Edward Fitzgerald's translation of the Rubaiyat of Omar Khayyam. London, Argo publishing company [1930?] 113p

Saintsbury, George
A history of nineteenth century literature. London, Macmillan, 1931. p207-9

Sargent, Frederick Le Roy
Omar and the Rabbi. . . Boston, Four seas company, 1919. 5-30p

Schmitt, Hermann
Edward Fitzgeralds Calderon—übersetzung von 1853. Diss. Würzburg, 1922. 163p

Scott, James B.
Introduction. *In* Edward Fitzgerald's Omar Khayyam with a prose translation from the French of J. B. Nicolas. Los Angeles, California, Parker, 1899 [500 copies only]

Scudder, Horace E.
Vedder's accompaniment to the song of Omar Khayyam. Cent 29:3-9 N '84

Sedgwick, Henry Dwight
"Omar" Fitzgerald. Putnam's Magazine 6:102-7 Ap '09

Shaylor, Joseph
Omar Khayyam. *In* Some favorite books and their authors. London, Richards, 1901. p196-200

Shorter, Clement K.
My bookshelves: Omar Khayyam. Bookm (Lond) 16:8-10 Ap '90

The story of the Omar Khayyam cult. Book-Lover 5:695-7 Je '04

Simpson, William
Omar Khayyam's grave. *In* Fitzgerald, E. The Rubaiyat of Omar Khayyam. . . Philadelphia, Coates, 1898. p xlv-li

Smith, Arnold
Fitzgerald-Swinburne. *In* The main tendencies of Victorian poetry. . . London, Simpkin, 1907. p135-47

Smith, G. C. M.
"Omar Khayyam." Acad 36:40 Jl 20 '89

[Source of title of Kipling's "The Seven Seas"] Critic (NY) 30:191 Mr 13 '97

Spence, Lewis
English translations of Calderon. Book-Lover's Magazine 7:104-7 '07-'08

[Squire, John Collings]
Fitzgerald's second thoughts. *In* Books in general. London, Heinemann, 1920. 2d ser p48-52

Starrett, Vincent
The man who made Omar. Haldeman-Julius Quarterly 1:122-7 Jl-S '27

Stockley, W. F. P.
Edward Fitzgerald. Queen's Q 18:1-13, 120-32 Jl-D '10

Stoddard, Richard Henry
Edward Fitzgerald. *In* Under the evening lamp. New York, Scribner, 1892. p245-62

Stokes, Whitley
A translation. Quatrains from Omar Khayyam. Acad 27:44 Ja 17 '85

The **Sufistic** quatrains of Omar Khayyam. In definitive form including the translations of Edward Fitzgerald. . . with Edward Heron-Allen's analysis, E. H. Whinfield, J. B. Nichols, with prefaces by each translator and a general introduction dealing with Omar's place in Sufism, by Robert Arnot. New York, M. Walter Dunne [c1903] xi-xxiii,1-127p

Sullivan, Edmund J.
Epilogia pro Opere suo. *In* Rubaiyat of Omar Khayyam. . . New York, Dutton [1913] p ix-[xvi]

Swinburne, A. C.
Letters on William Morris, Omar Khayyam and other subjects of interest. London, printed for private circulation, 1910. 31p (Printed for Thomas J. Wise. 20 copies only)

Tassy, Garcin J. H. de
Note sur les Ruba'yat de 'Omar Khaiyam. Journal Asiatique 5th ser 9:548-54 Je '57

Tennyson, Alfred
To E. Fitzgerald. New York, Gouverneur, 1900. (9)p Printed for L. C. Wordsworth. March 31 '00; *same in* Tiresias, and other poems. London, Macmillan, 1885. p1-4

Terhune, Alfred McKinley
Edward Fitzgerald's friendships with the major Victorians. Masters essay, Syracuse Univ. 1933. 270ff

Thomas, Edward
Edward Fitzgerald. Sat R 107:427-8 Ap 3 '09

Edward Fitzgerald. *In* A literary pilgrim in England. New York, Dodd, Mead, 1917. p236-43

Thompson, A. Hamilton
Edward Fitzgerald. *In* C H E L vol XIII p157-63

Thonet, Jeanne Marie H.
Etude sur Edward Fitz-gerald et la litterature persone, d'après les sources originales. (Bibliothèque de la faculté de philosophie et letters de l'université de Liège fasc XLI) Liège, H. Vaillant-Carmanne; Paris, Champion, 1929. 130, xivp bibl p[11]-13

To Omar Khayyam. Acad 59:78 Jl 28 '00

To the memory of the translator of Omar Khayyam; poem. Acad 36:55 Jl 27 '89

Todhunter, Maurice
Edward Fitzgerald. Westm 145:255-9 Mr '96

Torrey, Bradford
Edward Fitzgerald. Atlan 86:617-29 N '00

Edward Fitzgerald. *In* Friends on the shelf. Boston, Houghton, Mifflin, 1906. p43-87

Towle, Eleanor A.
Edward Fitzgerald and his friends. Longman's Magazine 46:310-22 Ag '05

[Translation of Omar Khayyam] Acad 52:449 N 27 '97

The **translations** of Omar Khayyam. Lit 2:208-9 F 19 '98

Trench, Richard Chenevix
Calderon; his life and genius. New York, Redfield, 1856. p111-12

The **true** Omar Khayam [sic] Fraser ns 19:650-9 My '79

Tutin, John Ramsden
A concordance to Fitzgerald's translation of the Rubaiyat of Omar Khayyam. London, Macmillan, 1900. vi,169p (Noted in Lit 6:260 Mr 31 '00; rev in Bookm (Lond) 19:31 O '00)

An **unhappy** recension [revisions of the Rubaiyat] Lit 4:383-4 Ap 15 '99

V. R. (Vernon Randall?)
Edward Fitzgerald: E.F.G. Notes & Q 12th ser 10:29 Ja 14 '22

Varma, S. P.
True and false orientalism in the English poetry of the nineteenth century. Diss. Univ. of London, 1927

Vedder, Elihu
The Rubaiyat of Omar Khayyam. . . With an accompaniment of drawings by E. Vedder. Boston, Houghton, Mifflin, 1884
(Rev in Nation (NY) 39:423 N 13 '84; Atlan 55:111-16 Ja '85; R Riordan in Book B ns 1:275-7 D '84)

Wales, H. L.
Andrew Lang and Omar. Book-Lover (San Francisco) 2:146 '01

Walker, Hugh
The age of Tennyson. (Handbooks of English literature) London, Bell, 1904. p236-9

The literature of the Victorian era. Cambridge, Univ. press, 1921. p480-90

Ward, Thomas Humphry
Edward Fitzgerald. *In* The English poets. New York, Macmillan, 1918. vol V p249-51

Fitzgerald, Edward. *In* Men of the reign. London, Routledge, 1885. p320

Watson, Francis
Omar the tent-maker: Fitzgerald's version of a heretic's poetry. Bookm (Lond) 79:293-4 F '31

Watts, Theodore
see Watts-Dunton, Theodore

Watts-Dunton, Theodore
Prayer to the winds; poem. *In* The coming of love. London, Lane [pref 1906] 9th ed p221-2

Toast to Omar Khayyam; poem. *In* The coming of love. London, Lane [pref 1906] 9th ed p217-20; *same.* Ath 1:609 My 11 '95

Way, W. Irving
Edward Fitzgerald. *In* Rubaiyat of Omar Khayyam rendered into English verse by Edward Fitzgerald. (Old world ser) Portland, Maine, Mosher, 1900. 7th ed p xvii-[xxxiii] [925 copies]

Omar Khayyam at the Caxton Club, Chicago. Bookm (NY) 8:446-8 Ja '99

Weekes, Charles
Fitzgerald's "Omar Khayyam." Acad 38: 73-4 Jl 26 '90

Weir, T. H.
Omar Khayyam. Quar R 245:63-81 Jl '25

Welby, Thomas Earle
Fitzgerald. *In* Back numbers. London, Constable, 1929. p190-3; *same in* Sat R 145:524 Ap '28

Whinfield, E. H.
Introduction. *In* The quatrains of Omar Khayyam. . . (Trübner's Oriental ser) London, Trübner, 1883. p xxi-xxii

"The quatrains of Omar Khayyam." Acad 21:340 My 13 '82

Whitmore, W. H.
Mr. Fitzgerald. Notes & Q 3d ser 4:27 Jl 11 '63

Whitten, Wilfred
Edward Fitzgerald. Bookm (Lond) 28: 83-9 Je '05

Whymant, Neville
Mystics and mysticism of Persia. Bookm (Lond) 79:292-3 F '31

Willett, E. V. Anson
Fitzgerald's "Omar Khayyam." Notes & Q 10th ser 6:388 N 17 '06

Williams, Talcott
Omar—fore-word and fore-plea. *In* Fitzgerald, E. The Rubaiyat of Omar Khayyam. . .   Philadelphia, Coates, 1898. p xi-xxiii

Williamson, Claude C. H.
Fitzgerald's "Omar Khayyam." *In* Writers of three centuries, 1789-1914. London, Richards, 1920. p167-9

Wilson, H. Schütz
Letters by Edward Fitzgerald. Ath 2: 635 N 9 '89

The Rubaiyat of Omar Khayyam. Contemp 27:559-70 Mr '76

Winterich, John Tracy
Edward Fitzgerald and his translation of the Rubaiyat of Omar Khayyam. *In* Books and the man. New York, Greenberg, 1929. p326-42

Woodberry, George Edward
Edward Fitzgerald. *In* Literary memoirs of the nineteenth century. New York, Harcourt, 1921. p189-200

Wright, Thomas
Edward Fitzgerald's "preacher." T. P.'s Weekly 6:551 N 3 '05

"Fitz." Acad 66:157 F 6 '04

The life of Edward Fitzgerald. New York, Scribner, 1904. 2 vols
(Rev in Nation (NY) 78:455-6 Je 9 '04; W. R. Browne in Dial 36:393-5 Je 16 '04; W. Meynell in Acad 66:118 Ja 30 '04; Spec 92:697-8 Ap 30 '04; T L S Ja 22 '04 p20; Sat R 97:428-9 Ap 2 '04; T.P.'s Weekly 3:213 F 12 '04; Literary World (Lond) ns 69:115-16 F 5 '04)

The life of T. R. Matthews. London, Farncombe, 1934. 250p

Wright, William Aldis
Edward Fitzgerald. *In* Dict N B vol VII p111-13

Mr. Edward Fitzgerald. Ath 1:795 Je 23 '83

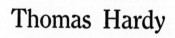

Thomas Hardy

Thomas Hardy

I. Chronological Outline

1840. Born, June 2, Dorsetshire.

1865. How I Built Myself a House. *In* Chambers's Journal, March 18.

1871. Desperate Remedies.

1872. Under the Greenwood Tree.

1873. A Pair of Blue Eyes.

1874. Far From the Madding Crowd.

1876. The Hand of Ethelberta.

1878. An Indiscretion in the Life of an Heiress. *In* New Quarterly Magazine, July.

1878. The Return of the Native.

1880. The Trumpet-Major.

1881. A Laodicean.

1882. Two on a Tower.

1886. The Mayor of Casterbridge.

1887. The Woodlanders.

1888. Wessex Tales.

1891. A Group of Noble Dames.

1891. Tess of the D'Urbervilles.

1894. Life's Little Ironies.

1896. Jude the Obscure.

1897. The Well-Beloved.

1898. Wessex Poems.

1902. Poems of the Past and the Present.

1903-04. The Dynasts, Part I.

1906. The Dynasts, Part II.

1908. The Dynasts, Part III.

1909. Time's Laughingstocks and Other Verses.

1913. A Changed Man.

1914. Satires of Circumstance.

1917. Moments of Vision.

1922. Late Lyrics and Earlier.

1923. The Famous Tragedy of the Queen of Cornwall.

1925. Human Shows, Far Phantasies, Songs, and Trifles.

1928. Died, January 11, Max Gate.

1928. The Short Stories of Thomas Hardy.

1928. Winter Words in Various Moods and Metres.

Thomas Hardy

II. Bibliographical Material

The Ashley library. A catalogue. . . . London, Printed for private circulation only by the Dunedin press, Edinburgh, 1922, 1926, 1927, 1930. vol II p168-78, vol VIII p143-4, vol IX p84-5, vol X p120-34

Beach, Joseph Warren
News for bibliophiles. Nation (NY) 94:82-3 Ja 25 '12
Notes for bibliophiles. Nation (NY) 94:107 F 1 '12

Bibliographies of modern authors. 2. Thomas Hardy (corrected by the author) New Age ns 6:259 Ja 13 '10

[Bibliography of Thomas Hardy's works] Lit 9:6-8 Jl 6 '01

Browne, P. H.
A collection of the writings of Thomas Hardy. [Chicago, 1927?] 14ff Typed ms in the Harvard College library

Cutler, B. D. and Villa Stiles (comps)
Thomas Hardy, 1840-1928. In Modern British authors. Their first editions. London, Allen & Unwin, 1930. p62-5 (Edition limited to 300 copies for Great Britain and 1050 copies for America)

Danielson, Henry
Bibliographies of modern authors. No 12—Thomas Hardy. Bookman's Journal and Print Collector 1:454, 469, 489 Ap 9-23 '20; ibid. 2:7, 24 Ap 30-My 7 '20
Criticism of [A. P. Webb's] "A bibliography of the works of Thomas Hardy." Publishers' Circular and Booksellers' Record 105:527, 552 N 11, 18 '16
The first editions of the writings of Thomas Hardy and their values. London, Allen & Unwin [1916] 38, [1]p

Elliott, Albert Pettigrew
Bibliography. In Fatalism in the works of Thomas Hardy. Philadelphia, 1935. p109-36. Diss. Univ. of Pennsylvania [1932]

Esdaile, Arundell
A short bibliography of Thomas Hardy's principal works. In H. H. Child, Thomas Hardy. New York, Holt, 1916. p119-25

Fabes, Gilbert H.
Modern first editions: points and values. London, Foyle [1929] p32 (750 copies only)
Modern first editions: points and values. London, Foyle, 1932. 3d ser

Fabes, Gilbert H. and Foyle, William A.
Modern first editions: points and values. London, Foyle [1931] 2d ser p39-41

Hopkins, Frederick M.
A check-list of the works of Thomas Hardy. (With prices) Pub W 113:292-4 Ja 21 '28

Hutchins, Margaret C.
A selected list of references on Thomas Hardy's works. Bulletin of Bibliography 12:25, 51-5 '23-'24

Lane, John
Thomas Hardy, a bibliography of first editions (1865-1922) In Lionel Johnson, The art of Thomas Hardy. London, Lane, 1923. new ed. p297-346

McCutcheon, George Barr
The renowned collection of first editions of Thomas Hardy, Rudyard Kipling, Robert Louis Stevenson. . . . New York, American art association [1925] p[1-23]

Millett, Fred B.
Thomas Hardy. In Contemporary British literature. . . New York, Harcourt, Brace, 1935. p261-8

Muir, Percy H.
Points, 1874-1930; being extracts from a bibliographer's notebook. (Bibliographia, no 5) New York, Smith, 1931. limited ed.

Northup, Clark Sutherland
A register of bibliographies of the English language and literature. New Haven, Yale univ. press, 1925. p193

Notes on sales of Hardy manuscripts and books. T L S Ag 9 '28 p584

Notes on sales of Hardy's and other first editions. T L S F 21 '29 p148

Purdy, Richard Little
A 1905 Dynasts. T L S F 14 '29 p118 [A single copy of the Dynasts, part second, published in 1906 with the title page in its uncancelled state and dated 1905 has turned up in the library of the Phillips Exeter Academy at Exeter, New Hampshire]

Purdy, Richard Little—*Continued*
Thomas Hardy, O. M., 1840-1928, catalogue of a memorial exhibition of first editions, autograph letters and manuscripts. New Haven, Yale univ. library, 1928. 41p
Thomas Hardy's works. T L S F 19 '31 p135 (Announces an authorized bibliography)

Quinn, John
The library of John Quinn. . . New York, Anderson galleries, 1924. part II p375-81

[Sale of Hardy first editions at Hodgson's] T L S D 30 '26 p964

Saxelby, F. Outwin
A Thomas Hardy dictionary; the characters and scenes of the novels and poems arranged and described. London, Routledge, 1911. pxi-xxii

Sotheby, firm, auctioneers, London
Catalogue . . . London, Davy [1928] p27-40

Thomas Hardy. Poetical works. Bibliographies of modern authors. Lond Merc 1:122 N '19

Thomas Hardy's first editions. Chicago Evening Post Literary Review Ap 8 '27

Troxell, Gilbert M.
[Exhibition of first editions and manuscripts of Thomas Hardy] Yale University Library Gazette 2:72-3 '28

Van Patten, Nathan
An index to bibliographies and bibliographical contributions . : . Stanford, Stanford univ. press, 1934. p110-11

Webb, A. P.
A bibliography of the works of Thomas Hardy, 1865-1915. London, Hollings, 1916. xiii,127p
(Rev in Spec 117:419 O 7 '16)
Hardy bibliography. Notes & Q 11th ser 11:228 Mr 20 '15

Weber, Carl J.
The Colby collection of Hardy letters. Colby Mercury 6:11-16 D 1 '34
Hardy at Colby. [In preparation]

Woods, George Benjamin
[Bibliography] *In* Poetry of the Victorian period. New York, Scott, Foresman [c1930] p1083-6

Zachrisson, Robert Eugen
A Swedish Hardy bibliography. Nyfilologiska Sällskapet i Stockholm. Studier i Modern Sprakvetenskap 10:157-9 '28; *also published*: Thomas Hardy as man . . . Uppsala, Almquist & Wiksell [1928] p29-31

Thomas Hardy

III. Biographical and Critical Material

Aas, L.
Thomas Hardy. Urd p33 '28
Thomas Hardy. Samtiden 34:337-58, 421-42, 470-82 '23
Thomas Hardy og hans digtning. Copenhagen, Haase, 1927. 112p
(Rev by W. Worster in Bookm (Lond) 74:220-1 Jl '28)

Abercrombie, Lascelles
The Dynasts. *In* The idea of great poetry. 1933. p154-7
Thomas Hardy, a critical study. London, Secker, 1912. 7-224p
(Rev in Ath 2:616 N 23 '12; D. Figgis in Bookm (Lond) 43:177-8 D '12; Spec 109:816 N 16 '12)
The war and the poets. Quar R 224:409-14 O '15

Abernethy, Julian W.
The invasion of realism. Educa 21:469-74 Ap '01

Adcock, Arthur St. John
Thomas Hardy. *In* Gods of modern Grub Street. New York, Stokes, 1923. p3-9 *Also in* Canadian Magazine 61:33-7 My '23
Thomas Hardy. Bookm (Lond) 73:263-6 F '28

Ahlin, Margaret Marie
Motivating forces in the works of Selma Lagerlöf and Thomas Hardy. Abstracts of theses, Univ. of Colorado, 1932. p2

Aldington, Richard
Conrad and Hardy. Literary Review 5: 8 S 6 '24

Alexander, Grace
Thomas Hardy, wizard of Wessex. New Repub 23:335-6 Ag '20

Alexander, Hooper
Hardy's "plagiarism." New Repub 54:71 F 29 '28

Amateurs who surpassed professionals in a great epic-drama. Current Opinion 68:643-5 My '20

Amy, Ernest F.
Introduction. *In* Thomas Hardy's The Mayor of Casterbridge. (Nelson's English ser.) New York, Nelson, 1933. pvii-xli

Anderson, John D.
Hardy, first of moderns. N Y Times My 28 '22 p10

Anthony, Henry
Romanticism in the novels of Thomas Hardy. Masters essay, Univ. of Pittsburgh, 1927

App, August J.
Lancelot in English literature; his role and character. Diss. Catholic univ. 1929. p215

Archer, William
Real conversations: I—with Thomas Hardy. Critic (NY) 38:309-18 Ap '01; *same.* Book League Monthly 1 no 2: 168-79 D '28
Real conversations. . . II—with Mr. Thomas Hardy. Pall Mall Magazine 23:527-37 Ap '01

Architecture and Thomas Hardy. Architect and Building News 119:119-121, 139, 147 Ja 20 '28

Arland, Marcel
Note sur [le pessimisme de] Thomas Hardy. Nouv R Fran 25:504-7 O 1 '25

Armstrong, Mary
The writings of Thomas Hardy considered as an illustration of the influence of the Darwinian ideas. Masters essay, Univ. of California, 1924. 149ff

Arns, Karl
Bemerkungen zu Hardys lyrik. Z F E U 22:264-77 '23
Hardys letzte gedichte. Z F E U 28: 612-16 '29
Hardys neue lyrik. Z F E U 26:175-86 '27

Aronstein, Philipp
Thomas Hardy. Germanisch-romanische Monatsschrift 6:160-76, 219-35 '14
Thomas Hardy. Magazin für Literatur 65:1316

The art of Thomas Hardy. Sewanee R 3: 447-56 Ag '95

Avancini, Bianca
L'arte di Thomas Hardy. Athenaeum (Pavia, Italy) ns 1:280-8 O '23

Aveling, E.
A propos d'un roman nouveau anglais par Thomas Hardy. L'Ere Nouvelle Mr '94

Aynard, Joseph
Thomas Hardy. Revue de P 4:98-128 Jl '03

Ayscough, John
Last giants. Cath World 100:779-82 Mr '15

Bagshaw, William
Thomas Hardy. Manch Q 42:99-114 Ap '23

Baillie, Alexander Stuart
English realism with special reference to Thomas Hardy. Masters essay, Univ. of Arizona, 1924. 52ff

Bangs, Nesbitt Hoyt
The element of chance in Hardy's fiction. Masters essay, Columbia univ. 1921

Barber, Elsa Jean
The Napoleonic legend in Chateaubriand, Tolstoy and Hardy. Masters essay, Stanford univ. 1926

Bardi, Pietro
Storia della letteratura inglese. Bari, Laterza, 1933. p197-8

Barker, A. L.
The poetry of Thomas Hardy. Masters essay, Boston Univ. 1926

Barrett, Albert S. L.
Thomas Hardy's novels; a critical appreciation. Masters essay, Columbia univ. 1915

Barrie, (Sir) James Matthew
Thomas Hardy: the historian of Wessex. Contemp 56:57-66 Jl '99; *same.* Ecl M 113:258-65 Ag '89

Barrie reviews Hardy. Lit Digest 100:22 F 2 '29

Bates, Ernest Sutherland
The optimism of Thomas Hardy. Int J Ethics 15:469-85 Jl '05; *same.* Cur Lit 39:154-5 Ag '05

Baugh, Albert C. (ed)
Introduction. *In* Hardy, Thomas. Return of the native. (Modern readers' series) New York, Macmillan, 1935. p i-xxiii

Baum, Paull F.
As to sources. Literary Review S 9 '22 p18

Beach, Joseph Warren
Bowdlerized versions of Hardy. P M L A 36:632-43 D '21

The technique of Thomas Hardy. Chicago, Univ. press [1922] ix,255p (Rev by J. Macy in the Nation (NY) 115:620-1 D 6 '22; Harvard Graduates Magazine 31:289-90 D '22; E. F. Edgett in the Bost Transcript O 18 '22 p6; T L S Jl 19 '23 p485)

Twentieth century novel. . . New York, Century [c1932] p140-4

Beale, Sophia
Woolbridge Manor, Dorsetshire: the home of the Turbervilles. Temple Magazine My '00

Beerbohm, Max
A sequelula to "The Dynasts." Thomas Hardy. *In* A Christmas garland. London, Heinemann, 1912. p59-73

"Tess", the footlights and the O.U.D.S. Sat R 89:264-5 Mr 3 '00

Bennett, Arnold
My literary heresies. III Concerning the living. T. P.'s Weekly 4:392 S 23 '04

The true greatness of Thomas Hardy. Evening Standard Ja 12 '28

Bennett, Richard
Wessex, the Hardy country. Four wood blocks. Book League Monthly 1 no 2:[143-8] D '28

Bense, J. F.
"Tess of the D'Urbervilles." Notes & Q 11th ser 2:96 Jl 30 '10

Benson, Arthur Christopher
Realism in fiction. No Am 195:830-1 Je '12

Bergmann-Jelgersma, T. J.
Thomas Hardy en H. G. Wells. Stemmen des Tijds p148-63 F '28

Berle, Lina Wright
George Eliot and Thomas Hardy; a contrast. . . New York, Kennerley, 1917. 174p

Bertrand, Julie
Thomas Hardy. Ath 2:900 D 31 '20

Thomas Hardy: a French view. Ath 2:739 N 26 '20

[Besant, Hardy, and Black] Bookm (NY) 35:121 Ap '12

Bescou, Yves
La tragédie de l'échec dans Jude l'Obscur et Tess d'Urbervilles. Revue de l'Enseignement des langues vivantes 49:337-43 Ag '32

Bestaux, Eugène
Thomas Hardy. Le Monde Nouveau 9:1036-9 Ja-F '28

Betts, Edward W.
Thomas Hardy: a French view. Ath 2:820 D 10 '20

Bickley, Francis
Hardy's poems. Bookm (Lond) 54:12-13 Ap '18

Biggs, John R.
Shaftesbury; the Shaston of Thomas Hardy; twelve wood-engravings by John R. Biggs and James E. Masters. Shaftesbury, At the High House Press, 1932. 28 leaves

Binyon, Laurence
The art of Thomas Hardy. Bookm (Lond) 47:143-4 F '15

The **birthplace** of Thomas Hardy. Bookm (Lond) 47:145 F '15

Bithell, Jethro
[Introduction to Hardy's poems] *In* Poèmes de Thomas Hardy, traduction Jeanne Fournier-Pagoire. Les Marges, 1925

Blanche, Jacques Émile
Souvenirs sur Thomas Hardy. *In* Mes modèles. . . . Paris, Librairie Stock, 1928. p77-90

Souvenirs sur Thomas Hardy par son peintre. Nouvelles Littéraires Ja 21 '28 p1-2

Blaze de Bury, Yetta
Thomas Hardy. *In* Les romanciers anglais contemporains. Paris, Perrin, 1900. p53-64

Bliss, Howard
Thomas Hardy inscriptions. T L S Ja 2 '30 p12

Blythe, Samuel G.
Great men who have met me. Saturday Evening Post 192:159 Ap 17 '20

Bogdonowitz, Jacob
Study of accident in Thomas Hardy's novels. Masters essay, State Univ. of Iowa, 1933. 70ff

Boice, Olive M.
Thomas Hardy's creed as a novelist. Masters essay, Univ. of Iowa, 1931

Bombe, Walter
Thomas Hardy. Deutsche Kunstwart 41:62-3 '28

Bopp, Dorothy Grey
"The famous tragedy of the Queen of Cornwall"; a study of Thomas Hardy's play. Masters essay, Columbia univ. 1925

Boughton, Rutland
A musical association with Thomas Hardy. Musical News and Herald F '28 p33-4

Bovitz, Mabel Doris
Marriage and morals in the novels of Thomas Hardy. Masters essay, New York Univ. 1931. 72ff

Bowker, R. R.
London as a literary centre. Harper M 77:8-9 Je '88

Boyd, Ernest [Augustus]
A new way with old masterpieces. VI— Thomas Hardy. Harper M 151:234-45 Jl '25

Thomas Hardy. *In* Literary blasphemies. New York, Harper, 1927. p227-55

Boyles, George H.
Thomas Hardy's versification. Masters essay, Vanderbilt Univ. 1930. 92ff

Brandl, Alois
Thomas Hardy und Rudyard Kipling. Cosmopolis 6:579-94 My '97

Brannon, Nelle Viola
The legend of Tristram in the works of Hardy, Masefield, and Robinson. Masters essay, Univ. of Nebraska, 1931. 155ff

Brash, W. Bardsley
Thomas Hardy: June 2, 1840-January 11, 1928. Lond Q R 149:145-57 Ap '28

Braybrooke, Patrick
Thomas Hardy. *In* Philosophies in modern fiction. London, Daniel, 1929. p35-40

Thomas Hardy and his philosophy. London, Daniel [1928] 167p
(Rev by F. Delatte in Revue Belge 8:600 Ap-Je '29; R. Kissack, jr. in Bookm (NY) 67:445 Je '28; S. C. Chew

in Books My 27 '28 p21; E. Boyd in Ind 120:459 My 12 '28; E. Blunden in Nat-Ath 42:816 Mr 3 '28; T L S F 2 '28 p82)

Brennecke, Ernest, jr.
The life of Thomas Hardy. New York, Greenberg, 1925. viii,259p
(Rev by F. Dublin in Nation (NY) 121:122 Jl 22 '25; by S. Chew in Forum ns 16:185-7 O '26; H. J. Forman in N Y Times Ap 12 '25 p7; B. Deutsch in Books My 24 '25 p5; E. F. Edgett in Bost Transcript My 16 '25 p4; Dial 79:262 S '25; Booklist 21:337 Je '25; L. Weitzenkorn in New York World Ap 12 '25 p6; Out 140:501 Ag 5 '25)

Thomas Hardy, to-day. N Y Times Je 5 '21 p12

Thomas Hardy's "Dynasts"; a reflection of the spirit of Aeschylus. Masters essay, Columbia univ. 1920

Thomas Hardy's universe: a study of a poet's mind. Boston, Small, Maynard, 1924. 153[1]p (Noted in T L S Ja 3 '24 p7)
(Rev by C. Aiken in New Repub 39: 332-3 Ag 13 '24; T L S My 15 '24; C. Aiken in Nat-Ath 35:264 My 24 '24; A. L. Carter in Mod Lang N 40:310-13 My '25; F. Dublin in Nation (NY) 121: 122 Jl 22 '25)

Thomas Hardy's universe, and The life of Thomas Hardy. New York, 1926. 7-153, [1], viii,259, [1]p plates (1 col) ports, facsims, genealogical table, coat of arms. (Thesis, Ph.D. Columbia univ. 1926) Each work has also special title page.

Bricker, Katharine
Criticism of Thomas Hardy in the major British reviews 1871-1930. A bibliography with excerpts. Masters essay, Columbia univ. 1932 [ii], 66p [typed]

The British novel as an institution. Edin R 206:126 Jl '07

Broderick, Clara
Nature in the novels of Thomas Hardy. Masters essay, State Univ. of Iowa, 1917. 47ff

Brodmerkel, Alexander H.
A comparison of the novels of Thomas Hardy and Theodore Dreiser. Masters essay, Columbia univ. 1932 [i], 174, 4 (bibl)p (typed)

Bronner, Milton
The art of Lionel Johnson. Bookm (NY) 36:184-5 O '12

Brown, Alec
Inward and outward dialogue. Dublin Magazine ns 7:33-9 Ap '32

Brown, Vincent
Thomas Hardy: an enthusiasm. Acad 58:208 Mr 10 '00

Brunius, August Georg
Thomas Hardy och hans nya diktsamlingar. *In* Ausikten och masker. Modern litteratur, konst och teater. Stockholm, Norstedt, 1917. p36-45

Brunnemann, Anna
Thomas Hardy. Aus fremden zungen '04
Thomas Hardy. Gegenwart 61:294-8 My 10 '02

Bryan, Adolphus Jerome
Two features in Thomas Hardy's stagecraft. Masters essay, Vanderbilt Univ. 1925. 140ff

Bryan, J. Ingram
The philosophy of English literature. Tokyo, Maruzen [1930] p256-9

Bryant, Lynwood Silvester
Fate in Hardy's novels. (Sohier prize essay, Harvard college, 1929) Typed MS. in Harvard College library. 24ff

Buchanan, Robert
The dismal throng; poem. Idler 3:607-12 Jl '93

Bullett, Gerald
Thomas Hardy, 1840-1928. Literary Guide ns no 380:32-3 F '28

Bulloch, J. M.
Hardy's "The three strangers." Notes & Q 12th ser 2:427 N 25 '16

Thomas Hardy and Aberdeen. Aberdeen University Review 15:141-2 Mr '28

Bullough, Geoffrey
The trend of modern poetry. Edinburgh, Oliver and Boyd, 1934. p3-5

Burchardt, Carl
Thomas Hardys livssyn. Vor Verden 6:500-4 O '29

Burdett, Osbert
The Beardsley period. . . London, John Lane [1925] p33-4

Burial of Thomas Hardy's heart in the country churchyard at Stinsford. Sat R Lit 4:613 F 18 '28

Burrell, Martin
Two English poets. *In* Betwixt heaven and Charing cross. Toronto, Macmillan, 1928. p 43-54

Burriss, Sarah Lucile
Characters in the fiction of Thomas Hardy. Raleigh, North Carolina, Meredith college [1929] 44p (Meredith college quarterly bulletin. Series 22, nos 1-2 N '28-Ja '29)

The fiction of Thomas Hardy. Masters essay, Cornell Univ. 1924. 138ff

Burrow, Ed. J. and Company, Ltd.
Burrow's guide to Wessex, the Hardy country, by Alison D. Murray . . . London, Burrow [1928] vi,66p

Burton, Richard
Hardy and Meredith. *In* Masters of the English novel . . . New York, Holt, 1909. p262-98

Bush, Douglas
Hobnobbing with eminent authors. Bookm (NY) 70:55 S '29

The varied hues of pessimism. Dalhousie Review 9:273-81 O '29

Busse, Kurt
Thomas Hardy und wir. Preussische Jahresbücher 211:359-61 Mr '28

Butler, A. J.
Thomas Hardy as a decadent. Nat R 27:384-90 My '96

Butler, Allen Dexter
The Bible in Thomas Hardy. Masters essay, Univ. of North Carolina, 1930. 99ff

Cage, Josefa Frances
Coincidence and fate in the six major novels of Thomas Hardy. Masters essay, Univ. of Texas, 1933. 193ff

Calverton, V. F.
Sex expression in literature. New York, Boni and Liveright, 1926. p244-6, 262-3

Campbell, Lucia Eugenia
The women in the novels of Thomas Hardy in their relation to the philosophy embodied in his work. Masters essay, Univ. of California, 1915. 71ff

Canby, Henry Seidel
He carried on. Sat R Lit 4:529, 532 Ja 21 '28; *also in* American estimates. New York, Harcourt, Brace [c1929] p53-6

Novelist of pity. *In* Definitions. New York, Harcourt [c1922] ser 1 p269-77; *same.* Literary Review Jl 9 '21 p1-2

Cantle, Christian [pseud]
see Kahn, Gilbert

A card from Mr. Hardy [concerning plagiarism in The Trumpet-Major] Critic (NY) 29:8 Jl 4 '96

The career of the novel. Puritan 6:342-3 Jl '99

[Caricature of Hardy "married to" Harper's Monthly Magazine] Bookm (NY) 3:1 Mr '96

Catalogne, Gérard de
Ce que fût la vie de Thomas Hardy. Nouvelles Littéraires Ja 14 '28 p7

Le message de Thomas Hardy; préface de F. Mauriac. Paris, Librairie de France, 1926. 135p

Cazamian, Louis
Le Sud: Hampshire, Berkshire, Wiltshire, Dorsetshire. *In* La grande Bretagne. Paris, Didier, 1934. p121-7

Thomas Hardy. *In* Legouis, E. and Cazamian, Louis. A history of English literature. . . New York, Macmillan company, 1930. p1283-90

Cazamian, Madeleine
Le roman et les idées en Angleterre; l'influence de la science (1860-1890). (Publications de la faculté des lettres de l'université de Strasbourg. Fascicule 15) Strasbourg, Librairie Istra, 1923. p86-9, 284-6, 367-8, 372-449

Cecil, David
Early Victorian novelists. . . London, Constable, 1934. p174-6, 226-8

Chamberlin, Jo Hubbard
Thomas Hardy: a study of the influence of the popular sensational novel, 1840-1880, upon his earlier works, including a brief analysis of the later and greater novels in which these sensational ele-

ments are changed, improved, and reduced in factual significance. Masters essay, New York Univ. 1932. 68ff

Chang, Hsin-Hai
A Chinese estimate of Hardy's poetry. Hibbert J 27:78-92 O '28

Chapman, Edward Mortimer
The newer fiction. *In* English literature in account with religion, 1800-1900. Boston, Houghton Mifflin, 1910. p533-62

Chapman, Frank
Hardy the novelist. Scrutiny 3:22-37 Je '34

Charteris, (Sir) Evan [Edward]
The life and letters of Sir Edmund Gosse. New York, Harper, 1931

Chase, Mary Ellen
Thomas Hardy from serial to novel. Minneapolis, Univ. of Minnesota press [c1927] [3]-210p bibl p[209]-10
(Rev by B. I. Evans in Rev E S 7:370 Jl '31; R. P. Boas in Mod Lang N 43:356 '28; S. B. Sloan in Philol Q 7:415-16 O '28; C. Rinaker in J E G P 28:144-7 '29)

"The Well-Beloved" from serial to novel. Diss. Univ. of Minnesota, 1918

Chassé, Charles
Un grand romancier anglais contemporain: Thomas Hardy. La Grande Revue 70:818-26 D 25 '11; 71:145-51 Ja 10 '12

A chat with Mr. Hardy. Book B 9:153 My '92

Chesson, W. H.
"Tess." Literary World (Lond) ns 48:38, 78 Jl 14, 28 '93

Chesterton, Gilbert Keith
[Death of Meredith] Illustrated London News 134:728 My 22 '09

Great Victorian novelists. *In* The Victorian age in literature. New York, Holt [1913] p143-5

On Thomas Hardy. *In* Generally speaking. . . London, Methuen [1928] p245-[250]

Thomas Hardy. Dietsche Warande p78-82 Ja-F '32

Chevalley, Abel
Le roman anglais de notre temps. London, Oxford, 1921. p24-7, 51-3, 65-71

Thomas Hardy. Revue de P 35pt 1:697-707 F 1 '28

Chew, Samuel Cloggett
Homage to Thomas Hardy. New Repub 23:22-6 Je 2 '20

Thomas Hardy, poet and novelist. (Bryn Mawr notes and monographs. III) Bryn Mawr, Pa. Bryn Mawr College, 1921. viii,257p
(Rev by E. Blunden in Lond Merc 6:662 O '22; C. Van Doren in Nation (NY) 114:19 Ja 4 '22)

Thomas Hardy, poet and novelist. [Rev and enl ed] New York, Knopf, 1928. 3-196, xiip bibl p[185]-196

Child, Harold Hannyngton
Thomas Hardy. New York, Holt [1916] 127[1]p bibl p119-25
(Rev in T L S Ja 27 '16 p42; Ath 1:75 F '16)

Thomas Hardy. Bookm (Lond) 58:101-3 Je '20

Chilton, Eleanor Carroll and Agar, Herbert
The garment of praise. . . Garden City, N. Y. Doubleday, Doran, 1929. p311-24

Chislett, William
The major note in Thomas Hardy. *In* The classical influence in English literature in the nineteenth century. Boston, Stratford co. 1918. p142-50

New Gods for old. *In* Moderns and near-moderns. . . New York, Grafton press [c1928] p171-80

Chudoba, František
Básnik slepé vule. [Thomas Hardy, poet of the blind will] Naśe Doba 32:400-17, 470-82 '24-'25

Básnik slepé vule, Pod listnatým stromem. II, Osobnost Th. Hardyho. *In* Pod listnatým stromem. [Under the greenwood tree] Prague, Melantrich, 1932. p221-[278]

Osobnost Thomase Hardyho. [The personality of Thomas Hardy] Naśe Doba 33:202 '31

Church, Richard
Thomas Hardy. Spec 140:71-2 Ja 21 '28

Clark, James M.
The English novel, 1870-1910. Germanisch-Romanische Monatsschrift 5:670-2 '13

Clark, John Scott
Thomas Hardy. *In* A study of English and American writers. New York, Row, Peterson [c1916] p599-613

Clark, Richard H.
"Georgia Scenes" and "Trumpet Major." *In* Memoirs of Judge Richard H. Clark, ed. by Lollie Belle Wylie. Atlanta, Georgia, Franklin Printing and Publishing Co. 1898. p235-42
[Indicates that Oliver H. Prince, not Longstreet, was author of "Militia Drill" to which Hardy is supposed by Clark to have referred for part of the 23d Chapter of "The Trumpet-Major"]

Clarke, George Herbert
Thomas Hardy. Dalhousie Review 8:1-15 Ap '28

Thomas Hardy and his biography. Queen's Q 38:280-305 '31

Clodd, Edward
Hardy's Waterloo lyric. [Cites a letter of Hardy] T L S F 2 '28 p80

Cockerell, Sydney
Early Hardy stories. T L S Mr 14 '35 p160

Cohen-Portheim, P.
Thomas Hardy und England. Frankfurt Zeitung '28 p64

Cole, Lettie
Thomas Hardy: a French view. Ath 2: 771 D 3 '20

Collins, H. P.
Modern poetry. London, Jonathan Cape [1925] p90-6

Collins, Norman
Meredith and Hardy. *In* The facts of fiction. London, Gollancz, 1932. p207-27

Collins, Vere Henry Gratz
Talks with Thomas Hardy at Max Gate, 1920-1922. . . New York, Doubleday, Doran, 1928. xv,84p *Also in* Bookm (NY) 67:1-6 Mr '28; *and in:* Book League Monthly 1 no 2:180-5 D '28 (these are both excerpts from her book and not all of it)
(Rev in T L S F 2 '28 p78; H. C. Minchin in T L S F 9 '28 p96; S. C. Chew in Books My 27 '28 p21; E. F. Edgett in Boston Transcript My 5 '28 p3; E. Blunden in Nat-Ath 42:816 Mr 3 '28; New Statesm 30:670 Mr 3 '28; N Y Times Ap 29 '28 p18)

Collison-Morley, Lacy
Pessimism and poetry. Edin R 237:338-9 Ap '23

Colum, Padraic
The poetry of Thomas Hardy. Book League Monthly 1 no 2:3-7 D '28
Robert Bridges and Thomas Hardy. New Repub 12:47-9 Ag 11 '17

Colvin, Ian
Thomas Hardy; an elegy. Liv Age 334: 337 F 15 '28; *same.* Lit Digest 96:32 F 18 '28

Compton, Charles H.
Who reads Thomas Hardy? Journal of Adult Education [American] 3:72-6 Ja '31; *same in* Who reads what? New York, Wilson, 1934. p[35]-52

Compton-Rickett, Arthur
Thomas Hardy. *In* I look back. . . London, Jenkins [1933] p176-86

Conacher, W. M.
Jude the obscure—a study. Queen's Q 35:529-40 Autumn '28
Thomas Hardy—Regional novelist. Queen's Q 35:271-87 F '28

Contemporary literature. Novelists. Blackw 125:338 Mr '79

Contre Thomas Hardy. La Nouvelle Revue Française 6:621-3 N 1 '11

Conyers, Pearl Howell
The causes of defeat in the characters of Thomas Hardy's novels. Masters essay, George Peabody College, 1928

Coope, Geoffrey Gainsborough
A study of irony in the works of Thomas Hardy. Masters essay, Univ. of California, 1923. 70ff

Copps, Abbie Maryette
The poetry of Thomas Hardy. Masters essay, Cornell Univ. 1929. 799ff

Corsen, Chester Russell
The immanent will in the poetry of Thomas Hardy. Masters essay, Syracuse Univ. 1926. 136ff

Courtney, William Leonard (Walter Lennard, pseud.)
Mr. Thomas Hardy and Aeschylus. Fortn 107:464-77, 629-40 Mr 1, Ap 2 '17; *also in* Old saws and modern instances. New York, Dutton, 1918. p1-30

Cramb, Meyrick G. H.
Thomas Hardy and his faith. T. P.'s Weekly 20:88 Jl 19 '12

Crawford, Jack R.
Thomas Hardy. *In* What to read in English literature. New York, Putnam, 1928. p285-8

Cristofaro, C.
Tommaso Hardy. Rassegna Nazionale 3d ser 1:11-15 Ja '28

Cross, W. L.
The contemporary novel. *In* Development of the English novel. New York, Macmillan, 1922. 7th ed p272-80

Crossman, Raymond Frank
Thomas Hardy as an antiquary. Masters essay, Syracuse Univ. 1931. 93ff

"Culture and anarchy." National Observer 7:555 Ap 16 '92

Cunliffe, John William
English literature during the last half century. New York, Macmillan, 1919. p40-58
English literature in the twentieth century. New York, Macmillan, 1933. p22-5
Mid-Victorian novelists. *In* Leaders of the Victorian revolution. New York, Appleton-Century [c1934] p215-27
Thomas Hardy. *In* English literature during the last half century. New York, Macmillan, 1923. 2d ed p42-62 bibl p61-2

Dalton, Arthur R.
Thomas Hardy and his novel "The Return of the Native." Bachelor's essay, Univ. of Buffalo, 1928

Danchin, F. C.
La biographie de Thomas Hardy. Revue de l'Enseignement des Langues Vivantes Ag '31 p337-47; O '31 p385-93
Les nouveaux poèmes de T. Hardy. Revue A A 3:481-93 Ag '26

Darton, Frederick Joseph Harvey
The soul of Dorset. Boston, Houghton Mifflin, 1922. p299-300, 247-8, 339-41
Thomas Hardy's birthplace. Liv Age 324:303-5 F 7 '25

Daudet, Léon
Ecrivains et artistes. 1928. vol IV p83-92

Davis, Frederick Hadland
The Hardy players. Drama 13:359-60 Ag-S '23
The music of Thomas Hardy. Musical Times 62:255-8 Ap 1 '21
The simplicity of Thomas Hardy. Literary Guide ns no 409:120 Jl '30

Davray, Henry D.
Thomas Hardy et son temps. Mercure
Fr 202:[5]-19 F 15 '28

Dawson, William James
Thomas Hardy. *In* The makers of English fiction. New York, Revell [c1905]
p213-40

Dawson, William James and Dawson, Coningsby W.
The great English novelists. (Reader's library) New York, Harper, 1911. vol
II p20-2

De Casseres, Benjamin
Thomas Hardy. *In* Forty immortals.
New York, Lawren [c1926] p34-50
Thomas Hardy's women. Bookm (NY)
16:131-3 O '02

Denvir, R. F.
The sentimental provincialism of Thomas
Hardy. Masters essay, Boston Univ.
1926

Dickinson, Thomas Herbert
Thomas Hardy's "The Dynasts." No Am
195:526-42 Ap '12

Did Hardy sham? Lit Digest 110 no 12:16
S 19 '31

Dobrée, Bonamy
Thomas Hardy. *In* The lamp and the
lute; studies in six modern authors.
Oxford, Clarendon, 1929. p21-44

Döll, Martha
Die verwendung der mundart bei Thomas
Hardy. Diss. Giessen, Selbstverl. d.
Engl. Seminars, 1923. 24p

Dolman, Frederick
An evening with Thomas Hardy. Young
Man 8:75 '92

Donnelly, Lillian
Thomas Hardy as a fatalistic novelist.
Masters essay, Univ. of South Dakota,
1927. 70ff

Douglas, (Sir) George
On some critics of "Jude the obscure."
Bookm (Lond) 9:120-2 Ja '96
Thomas Hardy. Some recollections and
reflections. Hibbert J 26:385-98 Ap '28
Wessex novels. Bookm (Lond) 18:110-12
Ja '00

Drake, Nell Davis
The problem of suffering; a comparison
of its treatment in Hardy and Eliot.
Masters essay, Vanderbilt Univ. 1928.
105ff

The drama. "Tess of the D'Urbervilles."
Critic (NY) 30:171-2, 185-6 Mr 6, 13 '97

Drinkwater, John
The loom of the poets, and To Thomas
Hardy. *In* Poems of men and hours.
London, Nutt, 1911
Mayor of Casterbridge; adapted by J.
Drinkwater. (Criticism by I. Brown in
Sat R 142:311 S 18 '26; N. G. Royde-
Smith in Outlook (Lond) 58:267 S 18
'26; H. Shipp in Engl R 43:470-1 O '26)

Dual personalities. Literary World (Lond)
ns 68:128-9 Ag 21 '03

Du Bos, Charles
Quelques traits du visage de Hardy. *In*
Approximations. Paris, Correa, 1930.
4th ser p125-64

Duffin, Henry Charles
Thomas Hardy; a study of the Wessex
novels. (Victoria univ. of Manchester,
English publications. English series 8)
London, Longmans, Green, 1916. 224p
Thomas Hardy: a study of the Wessex
novels. . . 2d ed. with an appendix on
the poems and *The Dynasts.* New
York, Longmans, Green, 1921. 240p
(Rev in T L S My 25 '16 p247)

Durrant, Wilfred S.
The disciple of destiny. Fortn 91:1117-24
Je '09; *same.* Liv Age 262:221-7 Jl 24
'09

"The Dynasts": a suggestion. T L S Ja 29
'04 p30; answered by Hardy, ibid. F 5
'04 p36-7

"The Dynasts" and the puppets. T L S
F 12 '04 p46; answered by Hardy, ibid.
F 19 '04 p53

[The **Dynasts** as performed on the stage]
T L S D 10 '14 p545-6; Oxford Magazine
F 13 '20 p210-11; T L S F 19 '20 p113-
14; Nation (Lond) 26:668-9 F 14 '20;
Cur Opin 68:643-5 My '20; Ath 1:251
F 20 '20

"The Dynasts" at the Kingsway. Spec
113:839-40 D 12 '14

"The Dynasts" at the Kingsway Theatre.
(Produced by H. Granville-Barker, November 25, 1914) Ath 2:572 N 28 '14

Edgar, Pelham
Thomas Hardy. *In* The art of the novel
from 1700 to the present time. New
York, Macmillan, 1933. p164-71

Edward, Ralph
Some emendations in the poetry of Mr.
Hardy. T L S D 18 '19 p767-8

Edwards, Lucile H.
The social status of woman as reflected
in realistic fiction of the late nineteenth
century, with particular reference to
the works of Thomas Hardy. . . Masters essay, Claremont Colleges, 1931.
102ff

Eliot, Thomas Stearns
[Thomas Hardy] *In* After strange gods:
a primer of modern heresy. (The Page-
Barbour lectures at the Univ. of Vir-
ginia, 1933) New York, Harcourt,
Brace, 1934. p 59-62
(Rev in N Y Times My 6 '34 p2)

Elliot, Robert Kerr
"Tess." Literary World (Lond) ns 48:62
Jl 21 '93

Elliott, Albert Pettigrew
Fatalism in the works of Thomas Hardy.
Diss. Univ. of Pennsylvania, 1932. [3]-
136p Published: Philadelphia, 1935.
bibl p109-36

Elliott, George Roy
Hardy's poetry and the ghostly moving-
picture. So Atlan Q 27:280-91 Jl '28

Elliott, George Roy—*Continued*
Spectral etching by Thomas Hardy. *In* The cycle of modern poetry. . . Princeton Univ. press, 1929. p91-111; *same.* P M L A 43:1185-95 D '28

Ellis, Havelock
Concerning "Jude the obscure." Savoy no 6:35-49 O '96; *also published*: London, Ulysses bookshop [1931] 37p (edition limited to 185 autographed copies)

Thomas Hardy and the human pair. *In* Views and reviews. . . Boston, Houghton, Mifflin, 1932. 2d ser p181-9

Ellis, Stewart Marsh
George Meredith: his life and friends in relation to his work. New York, Dodd, Mead, 1920. p208-10

Thomas Hardy: his lyrics. *In* Mainly Victorian. London, Hutchinson [pref 1924] p245-51

Thomas Hardy: some personal recollections. Fortn 129:393-406 Mr '28

Ellwanger, George H.
Landscape of Thomas Hardy. *In* Idyllists of the countryside. . . New York, Dodd, Mead, 1896. p83-119

Elsworth, Merle Margaret
Thomas Hardy in Germany. Masters essay, Columbia univ. 1933

The English novel and Mr. Hardy. Liv Age 270:650-6 S 9 '11; *same.* T L S Ag 3 '11 p281-2

The English novel in the nineteenth century. Edin R 196:495-6 O '02

The epic of tragic history [The Dynasts]. Nation (Lond) 26:668-9 F 14 '20

Erskine, John
The novels of Thomas Hardy. Evening Post Book Review Je 5 '20 p1

Evans, B[enjamin] Ifor
English poetry in the later nineteenth century. London, Methuen [1933] p178-94

Ewart, Wilfrid
Thomas Hardy and our own time. 19th Cent 90:427-37 S '21

Exideuil, Pierre d'
Le couple humain dans l'oeuvre de Thomas Hardy. . . Paris, La revue nouvelle, 1928. 224p bibl p222-[25] (Rev by A. Brulé in Revue A A 6:271-2 F '29)

The human pair in the works of Thomas Hardy; an essay on the sexual problem as treated in the Wessex novels, tales and poems. Translated from the French by Felix W. Crosse; introduction by H. Ellis. London, Toulmin, 1930. xxvii,219p bibl p212-19 (Rev in New Statesm 35:380 Je 28 '30; F. A. Clement in Sat R 150:152-3 Ag 2 '30)

Fägersten, A.
Thomas Hardys land. *In* Svenska Dagbladet Ja 21 '28

Fairley, Barker
Notes on the form of "The Dynasts." P M L A 34:401-15 S '19

Thomas Hardy's lyrical poems. Canadian Bookman 2:18-22 Jl '20

"Far from the madding crowd." [Dramatic production] Lit W 13:129 Ap 22 '82; Ath 1:293 Mr 4 '82

Fehr, Bernhard
Die englische literatur des 19. und 20. jahrhunderts. Wildpark-Potsdam, 1928. p358-66

Thomas Hardy. Neue Zürcher Zeitung '28 p84

Fenn, Alice Maude
The borderlands of Surrey. Cent 24:490 Ag '82

Firor, Ruth Anita
Folkways in Thomas Hardy. Philadelphia, Univ. of Pennsylvania press, 1931. 357p bibl p313-23 Thesis, Univ. of Pennsylvania
(Rev in T L S O 8 '31 p772; H. Moran in Lond Merc 25:311 Ja '32)

Firth, J. B.
Some aspects of sentiment. . . Westm 138:129-32 Ag '92

Fisher, E.
Thomas Hardy, novelist of country life. Holborn Review O '23 p433-43

Fitch, George Hamlin
Thomas Hardy and his tragic tales of Wessex. *In* Modern English books of power. San Francisco, Elder [c1912] p131-9

Fitzgerald, Eileen M.
Science in the poetry of Tennyson, Hardy, and Meredith. Masters essay, Mt. Holyoke college, 1929. 107ff bibl typed ms.

FitzGerald, Ellen
A modern epic of war. Poetry 5:288-93 Mr '15

Fletcher, John Gould
The Black rock: to Thomas Hardy; poem. Yale R ns 9:727-31 Jl '20; Yale R ns 17:447-51 Ap '28

The Spirit of Thomas Hardy. Yale R ns 13:322-33 Ja '24

Thomas Hardy; poem. Bookm (NY) 68: 621 F '29

Thomas Hardy's poetry. Poetry 16:43-9 Ap '20

Fogelquist, Torsten
Thomas Hardy. *In* Typer och tänkesätt. Stockholm, Bonniers [1927] p148-56

Follett, Helen Thomas and Follett, Wilson.
The historian of Wessex. Atlan 120: 356-66 S '17

Thomas Hardy. *In* Some modern novelists; appreciations and estimates. New York, Holt, 1919. p127-50

Forces. XVIII.—Thomas Hardy, novelist and poet. T. P.'s Weekly 5:813-14 Je 30 '05

Forsyth, Peter Taylor
The pessimism of Mr. Thomas Hardy. Liv Age 275:458-73 N 23 '12

Fournier-Pargoire, Jeanne
La poésie de Thomas Hardy. Revue de l'Enseignement des Langues Vivantes '24 p297-300

Fowler, John Henry
The novels of Thomas Hardy. (English Association Pamphlet no 71) Oxford, Oxford univ. press, 1928. 18p

Freeman, John
The poetry of Thomas Hardy. Bookm (Lond) 57:139-41 Ja '20

Poetry, prophecy and the war; Thomas Hardy's Dynasts. 19th Cent 77:644-7 Mr '15

Thomas Hardy. In The moderns; essays in literary criticism. London, Scott, 1916. p103-59

Thomas Hardy. Lond Merc 17:532-44 Mr '28

Friedlaender, Violet Helen
Early spring—and Hardy; poem. Fortn 131:265 F '29

Friend, G.
Thomas Hardy. Boekenschouw 19:231-3 O '25

Frierson, William C.
L'influence du naturalisme français sur les romanciers anglais de 1885 à 1900. Paris, Giard, 1925. p 15-18, 259-60

Frye, Prosser Hall
Nature and Thomas Hardy. Ind 54:1657-9 Jl 10 '02: also in Literary reviews and criticisms. New York, Putnam, 1908. p104-13

Fuess, Claude Moore
Thomas Hardy among the immortals. Boston Transcript Ja 28 '28

Furniss, Harry
Thomas Hardy. Strand Magazine 66:252-56 S '23

Gaggin, Richard Francis
Tragedy in the novels of Thomas Hardy and of Meredith. Masters essay, Syracuse Univ. 1933. 110ff

Gardiner, Alfred G.
Thomas Hardy. In Prophets priests and kings. London, Dent [pref 1914] p203-11

Gardner, W. H.
Some thoughts on "The mayor of Casterbridge." (English Association pamphlet no 77) [Oxford, University press] 1930. 29p

Garland, Hamlin
Thomas Hardy's birthplace. In Afternoon neighbors. New York, Macmillan, 1934. p85-99

Garrett, Lindsay S.
The essence of Hardyism. Monthly Review 27:59-67 Je '07

Garstang, A. H.
The humour of Thomas Hardy. Fortn 129:205-9 F '28

Garwood, Helen
Thomas Hardy, an illustration of the philosophy of Schopenhauer. Philadelphia, Winston, 1911. 91p Diss. Univ of Pennsylvania. bibl p90-1

Gaupp, O.
Thomas Hardy. Münchener neueste Nachrichten '03

George Meredith and Thomas Hardy. Bookm (NY) 9:146-9 Ap '99

Gilbert, Ariadne
In Thomas Hardy's world. St N 55:357-8 Mr '28

Gilbert-Cooper, Everard G.
The debt of Mr. Thomas Hardy to Indian philosophy. Hindustan Review 41:196-203 Mr '20

Goldstein, Henry M.
Thomas Hardy as a literary prose artist. Masters essay, New York Univ. 1911. 40ff

Gorman, Herbert Sherman
Hardy and Housman. In The procession of masks. Boston, Brimmer, 1923. p171-83

Poems and lyrics. Out 133:35-6 Ja 3 '23

Gosse, (Sir) Edmund William
Dedication. To Thomas Hardy. In Critical kit-kats. London, Heinemann, 1913. p[v]-vii

The historical place of Mr. Meredith and Mr. Hardy. International Monthly (Burlington, Vermont) 4:299-323 S '01

The lost novel of Thomas Hardy. Bookman's Journal 3d ser 15:194-8 '27

The lyrical poetry of Thomas Hardy. Edin R 227:272-93 Ap '18; also in Some diversions of a man of letters. London, Heinemann, 1919. p231-58; also in Selected essays. London, Heinemann, 1928. 1st ser p223-55

Mr. Hardy's new novel (Jude the obscure). Cosmopolis 1:60-9 Ja '96

The speaker's gallery—Thomas Hardy. Speaker 2:295-6 S 13 '90

Graves, Robert
Mr. Hardy and the pleated skirt. Nat-Ath 33:451-2 Jl 7 '23

Great houses of letters. II. Max Gate, Dorchester, where Thomas Hardy wrote his Wessex novels. Bookm (NY) 44:238-9 N '16

The **great** tragedian of modern English letters. Cur Opin 69:236-8 Ag '20

Greenwood, Frederick
The genius of Thomas Hardy. Illustrated London News 101:431 O 1 '92

Grenzow, Daisy B.
The last of the Victorians. World Review 5:261 Ja 30 '28

Grey, Rowland, pseud.
see Rowland-Brown, Lilian

Grimsditch, Herbert Borthwick
Character and environment in the novels of Thomas Hardy. London, Witherby, 1925. 188[1]p bibl p19-80 (Noted in T L S D 17 '25 p886; rev by G. Rouillot in Revue A A 4:169-71 D '26)

Groom, Bernard
A literary history of England. London, Longmans, Green, 1929. p354-6

Grove, Frederick Philip
Thomas Hardy. A critical examination of a typical novel and his shorter poems. University of Toronto Quarterly 1:490-507 Jl '32

Guedalla, Philip
Men of letters (People's library) London, Hodder and Stoughton, 1927
Mr. Thomas Hardy. *In* A gallery. London, Constable, 1924. p53-61

Guha-Thakurta, P.
Thomas Hardy. Calcutta Review 3d ser 36:376-85 S '30

Günther, Hildegard
Das verheimlichungs-, hochzeits- und brief-motiv in den romanen Thomas Hardys. Diss. Halle, 1933. 119p

Gutbier, Elisabeth
Psychologisch-Ästhetische studien zu Tristandichtungen der neueren englischen literatur. Erlangen, Döres, 1932. Diss. Erlangen 95p

Gwynn, Stephen
Literature portraits.—IX. Mr. Thomas Hardy [with bibliography] Lit 9:4-8 Jl 6 '01

Hall, Harold E.
Hardy and Powys. Sat R Lit 10:557, 606 Mr 17, Ap 7 '34

Hall, J. A.
The "thing" of Mr. Hardy's poetry. Adel 3:364-7 O '25

Halperin, Maurice
Le sort implacable—"The Queen of Cornwall" de Thomas Hardy. *In* Le roman de Tristan et Iseut dans la littérature anglo-americaine au XIXe et au XXe siècles. Paris, Jouve, 1931. p98-106 Diss. Paris

Hamilton, Cosmo
Thomas Hardy. . . *In* People worth talking about. New York, McBride, 1933. p245-52

Hankinson, Charles James [Holland, Clive, pseud]
In Thomas Hardy's country [illustrated] Black and White 22:192-3 Ag 10 '01
A pilgrimage to Wessex. Critic (NY) 39:136-44 Ag '01; *also published*: London, Lund, 1901. 28p
Thomas Hardy. The man, his books, and the land of Wessex. Bookm (Lond) 21:46-50 N '01
Thomas Hardy and Wessex. Bookm (Lond) 73:267-70 F '28
Thomas Hardy as I knew him. Landmark 10:75-7 Ja '28

Thomas Hardy, O. M., novelist and poet. The man, his country, and books. R of Rs (Lond) 65:498-503 My '22
Thomas Hardy, O. M., the man, his works and the land of Wessex. London, Jenkins [1933] 320p (Noted in T L S N 23 '33 p842)
Thomas Hardy's country. . . [illustrated] Bookm (NY) 9:328-40, 410-23, 519-27 Je-Ag '99
The work of Frederick Whitehead, a painter of Thomas Hardy's "Wessex." Studio 32:105-16 Jl '04

Hannigan, D. F.
Latest development of English fiction. Westm 138:655-9 D '96
Prospective transformation of the novel. Westm 140:258, 260 Mr '93
The tyranny of the modern novel. Westm 143:303, 306 Mr '95

Harding, Harry
Thomas Hardy and Dorchester. Wessex 2 no 2:37-9 Je '32
Thomas Hardy and Hardyland. British Archaelogical Association Journal ns 38:53-62 N '32

Harding, Henry
In Hardyland. "Egdon Heath" and "Rainbarrow." Educational Times 73:169-70 Ap '21

Hardy, Mrs. Florence Emily (Dugdale) (Mrs. Thomas Hardy) [comp]
The early life of Thomas Hardy, 1840-1891, compiled largely from contemporary notes, letters, diaries, and biographical memoranda, as well as oral information in conversations extending over many years. London, Macmillan, 1928. xii,327p
(Rev by W. Cross in Yale R ns 18:580-2 Mr '29; Sewanee R 37:381-2 Jl '29; R. M. Lovett in Bookm (NY) 69:96-8 Mr '29; E. Boyd in Out 150:1293 D 5 '28; Sat R 147:112-13 Ja 26 '29; C. K. Trueblood in Dial 86:150-4 F '29; V. Woolf in Nat-Ath 44:289-91 N 24 '28; V. Woolf in New Repub 57:70-2 D 5 '28; J. Freeman in Liv Ag 336:192-5 My '29; J. Freeman in Lond Merc 19:400-7 F '29; O. L. Jiriczek in Bei Anglia 41:321-7 N '30; O. Burdett in Lond Merc 22:250-7 Jl '30; J. M. Murry in New Adel 2:163-4 D '28-F '29; T L S N 8 '28 p827; New Statesm 32:ix-x D 1 '28; M. Van Doren in Nation (NY) 127:662 D 12 '28; D. MacCarthy in Sat R Lit 5:421-2 D 1 '28; S. C. Chew in N Y Times N 11 '28 p3; S. L. Bensusan in Quar R 253:313-29 O '29; E. Wagenknecht in Va Q R 6:621-4 O '30; O. Warner in Bookm (Lond) 85:17 O '33; S. C. Chew in Books D 2 '28 p3; F. Swinnerton in Chicago Daily Tribune D 8 '28 p21; New York Evening Post D 1 '28 p8; H. Walpole in Spec 141:657 N 3 '28; Springfield Republican D 23 '28 p7; Booklist 25:210 F '29; E. F. Edgett in Boston Transcript Ja 12 '29 p2; Cath World 129:374 Je '29; Chris-

tian Century 46:204 F 7 '29; Wisconsin Library Bulletin 25:30 Ja '29; John O'London's Weekly 20:256, 298 N 24, D 1 '28; W. L. Phelps in Scrib M 85: 221-3 F '29)

Early life of Thomas Hardy, 1840-1891 [and] The later years of Thomas Hardy, 1892-1928. London and New York, Macmillan, 1933. reissue. 2 vols xii,327p; x,286p

The later years of Thomas Hardy, 1892-1928. London, Macmillan, 1929. xi,286p (Rev in T L S My 1 '30 p367; O. Burdett in Sat R 149:559 My 3 '30; T. E. Welby in W E R '29 p267-8; O. L. Jiriczek in Bei Anglia 41:321-7 N '30; H. L. Morrow in Bookm (Lond) 78: 244-5 Jl '30; W. Cross in Yale R ns 20:175-7 S '30; E. Wagenknecht in Va Q R 6:621-4 O '30; A. R. Thompson in Bookm (NY) 71:553 Ag '30; M. Van Doren in Nation (NY) 130:680 Je 11 '30; O. Burdett in Lond Merc 22:250-7 Jl '30; O. Williams in Crit 10:339-42 Ja '31; J. Aynard in J Débats 37:559-60 O 3 '30; W. B. Brash in Lond Q R 154:246-8 O '30)

Hardy, Thomas

A changed man, The waiting supper, and other tales concluding with The romantic adventures of a milkmaid. London, Macmillan, 1913. viii,416p (Rev in T L S O 30 '13 p479; Ath 2: 488 N 1 '13; J. Bailey in Bookm (Lond) 45:143-4 D '13; Dial 56:74 Ja 16 '14; Current Opinion 56:47-8 Ja '14)

The Colby collection of Hardy letters [a list of 156 letters] compiled by C. J. Weber. Colby Mercury 6:11-16 D 1 '34

Collected poems (Rev in Lond Merc 1:333-4 Ja '20; C. K. Trueblood in Dial 82:522-5 Je '27; J. G. Fletcher in Sat R Lit 3:576-7 F 12 '27; Sat R 128:459-60 N 15 '19)

Desperate remedies. A novel. London, Tinsley, 1871. 3 vols vi,304p; v, 292p; vi,274p [Published anonymously] (Rev in Ath 1:399 Ap 1 '71; Sat R 32: 441-2 S 30 '71; Spec 44:481-3 Ap 22 '71; Harper M 49:136 Je '74)

The distracted young preacher. (Rev in Lit W 10:341 O 25 '79)

The dynasts, a drama of the Napoleonic wars. . . London, Macmillan, 1903, 1906, 1908. 3 vols xxiv,228, viiip; xvi,304p; xvi,356p (Rev in T. P.'s Weekly 3:149 Ja 29 '04; 7:231 F 23 '06; 11:299 Mr 6 '08; Cur Lit 40:522-3 My '06; Ind 61:807-9 Ap 5 '06; A. Macdonell in Bookm (Lond) 25:221-3 F '04; Nation (NY) 82:325 Ap 19 '06; W. M. Payne in Dial 40:325-6 My 16 '06; Spec 96:545 Ap 7 '06; Atlan 93:713 My '04; Literary World (Lond) ns 69:139-40 F 12 '04; Out 82:808 Ap 7 '06; Ath 1:123 Ja 23 '04; Acad 66:95 Ja 23 '04; Spec 92:293-4 F 20 '04; Ath 1:615

My 16 '08; T L S Ja 14 '04 p11-12; Nation (NY) 78:153-4 F 25 '04; J. P. Peabody in Critic (NY) 44:469-70 My '04; W. M. Payne in Dial 36:319-21 My 16 '04; Monthly Review 14:1-12 Mr '04; J. Pollock in Independent Review 4:149-55 O '04; W. P. Trent in Forum 38:86-94 Jl '06; T L S F 16 '06 p49-50; T L S F 27 '08 p65; Edin R 207:421-39 Ap '08; Westm 169:605-6 My '08; Nation (NY) 86:353-4 Ap 16 '08; Acad 74:555-7 Mr 14 '08; W. M. Payne in Dial 44:307-9 My 16 '08; H. W. Boynton in Bookm (NY) 27:486-8 Jl '08; H. Newbolt in Quar R 210:193-209 Ja '09; R. West in New Repub 1: 25-6 D 26 '14; A. Croom-Johnson in R of Rs (Lond) 51:70-1 Ja '15; M. Beerbohm in Sat R 97:136-8 Ja 30 '04; *same.* Liv Age 240:507-10 F 20 '04; W. De La Mare in Bookm (Lond) 34:110-12 Je '08; W. L. Randell in Acad 79:616-18 D 24 '10; R. Ross in Acad 70:206-7 Mr 3 '06; H. D. Davray in Mercure Fr 50:263 Ap '04 and in Mercure Fr 73: 166-7 My 1 '08; M. Meyerfeld in Das Litterarische Echo 7:474-5 Ja 1 '05)

The famous tragedy of the Queen of Cornwall at Tintagel in Lyonnesse. A new version of an old story arranged as a play for mummers in one act, requiring no theatre or scenery. London, Macmillan, 1923. 77p (Rev by L. Morris in Literary Digest International Book Review 2:111, 113 Ja '24; Nation (NY) 118:38 Ja 9 '24; L. Abercrombie in Nat-Ath 34:491 D 29 '23; S. C. Chew in New Repub 38:23-4 F 27 '24; F. L. Lucas in New Statesm 22:484-5 F 2 '24; I. Brown in Sat R 136:613-14 D 8 '23; M. Armstrong in Spec 131:904 D 8 '23; Theatre Arts Mo 8:281 Ap '24; A. Henderson in Forum 71:783-90 Je '24; H. MacAfee in Yale R ns 14:386-7 Ja '25; T L S N 15 '23 p767; Sat R 136:704-5 D 29 '23; J. C. Squire in Lond Merc 9:202 D '23)

Far from the madding crowd. London, Smith, Elder, 1874. 2 vols iv,336p; iv, 344p [Appeared in Cornhill Ja-D '74] (Rev in Lit W 26:282 S 7 '95; A. Lang in Acad 7:9-10 Ja 2 '75; Lit W 5:114-15 Ja '75; Dial 19:24 Jl 1 '95; H. James in Nation (NY) 19:423-4 D 24 '74; Harper M 50:598 Mr '75; Ath 2:747 D 5 '74; Sat R 39:57-8 Ja 9 '75; Spec 47:1597-9 D 19 '74; Spec 108:804 My 18 '12; O. Williams in New Adel 2:128-39 D '28-F '29; Scribner's Monthly Magazine 9:637 Mr '75; Westm ns 47:265-7 Ja '75; Brit Q 61:131 Ja '75)

A group of noble dames. London, Osgood, McIlvaine, 1891. viii,272p (Rev in Ath 2:35-6 Jl 4 '91; Sat R 71: 757 Je 20 '91; W. Wallace in Acad 40:153 Ag 22 '91; Lit W 22:257 Ag 1 '91; Spec 67:163-4 Ag 1 '91; Literary World (Lond) ns 43:556-8 Je 12 '91; Nation (NY) 53:72 Jl 23 '91; Harper

Hardy Thomas—A group of noble dames
—*Continued*
  M 83:641-2 S '91; Speaker 3:683 Je 6
  '91; Book B ns 8:262 Jl '91; Nat R
  17:845 Ag '91; Archiv 87:321-5 '91)
The hand of Ethelberta. A comedy in
  chapters. London, Smith, Elder, 1876.
  2 vols viii,324p; viii,320p [Appeared in
  Cornhill Jl '75-My '76]
  (Rev by G. Saintsbury in Acad 9:453-
  4 My 13 '76; Lit W 7:4 Je '76; Westm
  ns 50:281 Jl '76; Harper M 53:468 Ag
  '76; Scribner's Monthly 13:135-6 N '76;
  Ath 1:523 Ap 15 '76; Sat R 41:592-3
  My 6 '76; Spec 49:530-2 Ap 22 '76)
Human shows, far phantasies, songs, and
  trifles. London, Macmillan, 1925. v-x,
  279p
  (Rev by H. Goodspeed in New Repub
  46:52 Mr 3 '26; H. Allen in No Am
  223:360-2 Je-Ag '26; T L S D 3 '25
  p829; Boston Transcript Ja 2 '26; M.
  Van Doren in Nation (NY) 122:64 Ja
  20 '26; E. Shanks in Sat R 140:741 D
  19 '25; R. Herring in Lond Merc
  13:434-5 F '26; J. Freeman in Bookm
  (Lond) 69:197-9 Ja '26; Nat-Ath 38:354
  D 5 '25; K. Arns in Engl Stud 61:299-
  301 My '27; H. Wolfe in New Criterion
  4:384-6 Ap '26; W. S. Johnson in Sat
  R Lit 3:19 Ag 7 '26; Out 142:424-5 Mr
  17 '26; M. Moore in Dial 80:417-21 My
  '26; M. Wilkinson in Int Book 4:628,
  630 S '26; V. Moore in Atlantic Bookshelf Mr '26; N Y Times Ja 3 '26 p14;
  Spec 135:1145 D 19 '25; Liv Age 328:
  336-8 F 6 '26; E. Davison in Literary
  Review of New York Evening Post Ja
  23 '26 p1-2
An indiscretion in the life of an heiress.
  . . ed. . . by Carl J. Weber. Baltimore,
  Johns Hopkins Press, 1935. v-vii,146p
Jude the obscure. London, Osgood, Mc-
  Ilvaine, 1896. viii,520p [Appeared in
  Harper M D '94 under title of "The
  Simpletons" and from Ja-N '95 under
  title "Hearts Insurgent"]
  (Rev by J. B. Allen in Acad 49:134 F
  15 '96; R. Le Gallienne in Idler 9:114-16
  F '96; Lit W 27:3 Ja 11 '96; Nation
  (NY) 62:123-4 F 6 '96; Ath 2:709-10
  N 23 '95; Sat R 81:153-4 F 8 '96; by
  R. Y. Tyrrell in Fortn 65:859-64 Je 1
  '96; Blackw 159:137-42 Ja. '96; D. F.
  Hannigan in Westm 145:136-9 Ja '96;
  Our Day 16:101-4 F '96; Bookm (Lond)
  9:123-4 Ja '96; noted in Critic (NY)
  28:12, 29 Ja 4, 11 '95; Bookm (NY)
  2:427-9 Ja '96; W. M. Payne in Dial
  20:76-7 F 1 '96; Bookselling 1:142 D
  '95; Critic (NY) 27:437 D 28 '95)
A Laodicean; or, The castle of the De
  Stancys. A story of to-day. London,
  Sampson Low, Marston, Searle & Riv-
  ington, 1881. 3 vols iv,312p; iv,276p; iv,
  272p [Appeared in Harper M D '80-
  D '81]
  (Rev by A. Barker in Acad 21:5 Ja 7
  '82; Nation (NY) 34:18-19 Ja 5 '82;
  Critic (NY) ns 2:53-4 F 25 '82; Lit W

13:26-7 Ja 28 '82; Ath 2:899-900 D 31
  '81; Spec 55:296-7 Mr 4 '82; Sat R 53:
  53-4 Ja 14 '82)
Late lyrics and earlier, with many other
  verses. London, Macmillan, 1922. xxiv,
  288p
  (Rev by A. Williams-Ellis in Spec 129:
  54 Jl 8 '22; S. M. Ellis in Fortn 118:692-
  7 O 1 '22; J. C. Squire in Lond Merc
  6:317-18 Jl '22; A. W. Reed in Church
  Q R 95:344-7 Ja '23; L. Binyon in
  Bookm (Lond) 62:167-8 Jl '22; T L S
  Je 1 '22 p359; M. Van Doren in Nation
  (NY) 116:125 Ja 31 '23)
Life and art by Thomas Hardy; essays,
  notes and letters collected for the first
  time. Ed. with an introduction by
  Ernest Brennecke, jr. New York,
  Greenberg, 1925. vii-viii,140p [limited to
  2000 copies]
  (Rev in Boston Transcript F 21 '25 p3,
  My 16 '25 p4; S. Chew in Yale R
  ns 16:185-7 O '26; F. Dublin in Nation
  (NY) 121:122 Jl 22 '25; N Y Times
  Mr 1 '25 p7; N Y Tribune My 24 '25
  p5; N Y World Ap 12 '25 p6; Spring-
  field Republican Mr 23 '25 p6; Wiscon-
  sin Library Bulletin 21:168 Je '25;
  C. Taylor in World Tomorrow 8:88
  Mr '25; Atlantic Bookshelf Mr '26;
  Booklist [A. L. A.] 22:243 Mr '26; Books
  Ja 24 '26 p6; Sat R 140:740-1 D 19 '25)
Life's little ironies, a set of tales with
  some colloquial sketches entitled A few
  crusted characters. London, Osgood,
  McIlvaine, 1894. viii,304p
  (Rev by G. Saintsbury in Acad 45:453
  Je 2 '94; Critic (NY) ns 24:298-9 My 5
  '94; Spec 72:537-9 Ap 21 '94; W. M.
  Payne in Dial 16:367 Je 16 '94; National
  Observer 11:429 Mr 10 '94; G. St.
  George in Literary World (Lond) ns
  49:259-60 Mr 23 '94; Speaker 9:314 Mr
  17 '94; Ath 1:367 Mr 24 '94; Sat R 77:
  340 Mr 31 '94; W. Raymond in Bookm
  (Lond) 6:18-19 Ap '94; Book B ns 11:
  131-2 Ap '94; Archiv 93:350-1 '94)
The mayor of Casterbridge: the life and
  death of a man of character. London,
  Smith, Elder, 1886. 2 vols iv,316p; iv,
  316p [Appeared in Graphic Ja 2-My 15
  '86]
  (Rev by W. M. Payne in Dial 7:67-8
  Jl '86; Lit W 17:198 Je 12 '86; Lit W
  26:244 Ag 10 '95; Critic (NY) 9:5, 30-1
  Jl 3, 17 '86; Spec 59:752-3 Je 5 '86;
  Westm ns 70:300 Jl '86; Literary World
  (Lond) ns 48:74 Jl 28 '93; Harper M
  73:961-2 N '86; Book B ns 3:243 Jl
  '86; Ath 1:711 My 29 '86; Sat R 61:757
  My 29 '86)
Moments of vision, and miscellaneous
  verses. London, Macmillan, 1917. xii,
  256, 4p
  (Rev by E. Shanks in Dial 64:104-5 Ja
  31 '18; Sat R 124:507 D 22 '17; Spec
  120:287 Mr 16 '18; Ath 1:33-4 Ja '18;
  Liv Age 296:202-7 Ja 26 '18)

Pages from the works of Thomas Hardy. Arranged by Ruth Head, with an introduction by Henry Head. London, Chatto, 1922. x,243p
(Rev by E. Blunden in Lond Merc 6: 661-2 O '22)

A pair of blue eyes. A novel. London, Tinsley, 1873. 3 vols vi,304p; vi,312p; vi,262p [Appeared in Tinsley's Magazine S '72-Jl '73]
(Rev in Ath 1:820 Je 28 '73; Sat R 36: 158-9 Ag 2 '73; Spec 46:831-2 Je 28 '73; W. H. Browne in Southern Magazine 13:365-71 S '73; Lit W 26:282 S 7 '95)

Play of St. George; as aforetime acted by the Dorsetshire Christmas mummers; based on the version in The return of the native; together with a modernized version by Roger Sherman Loomis. New York, French, 1928. 36p

Poems of the past and the present. London, Harper, 1902. xii,264p
(Rev by W. M. Payne in Dial 32:314-16 My 1 '02; Lit W 33:23 F 1 '02; Speaker ns 5:342-3 D 21 '01; Nation (NY) 74:76 Ja 23 '02; E. M. Thomas in Critic (NY) 40:261 Mr '02; H. W. Boynton in Atlan 89:280-1 F '02; Ath 1:6-7 Ja 4 '02; Acad 61:475-6 N 23 '01; Spec 88:516-17 Ap 5 '02; G. Douglas in Bookm (Lond) 21: 131-3 Ja '02; W. D. Howells in No Am 174:140-1 Ja '02; Lit 9:604 D 28 '01; noted in Critic (NY) 39:292 O '01; Sat R 93:49 Ja 11 '02)

Poetical works
(Rev in Bookman's Journal 1:147 D 12 '19)

The return of the native. London, Smith, Elder, 1878. 3 vols viii,304p; viii,300p; viii,320p [Appeared in Belgravia Ja-D '78]
(Rev by W. E. Henley in Acad 14:517 N 30 '78; Atlan 44:672-4 N '79; Nation (NY) 28:155 F 27 '79; Harper M 58: 627-8 Mr '79; Lit W 10:37 F 1 '79; Westm ns 55:280 Ja '79; Brit Q 69:125-6 Ja '79; International Review 6:211-12 F '79; Ath 2:654 N 23 '78; Sat R 47: 23-4 Ja 4 '79; Spec 52:181-2 F 8 '79; Atlan 43:500-2 Ap '79; Blackw 125:338 Mr '79; Scribner's Monthly 17:910-11 Ap '79)

The romantic adventures of a milkmaid. (Harper's Franklin Square library) New York, Harper, 1883. [Appeared in Graphic Summer no '83]
(Rev in Lit W 14:245 Jl 28 '83; Nation (NY) 37:255 S 20 '83; noted in Nation (NY) 94:82-3 Ja 25 '12; Lippinc 32: 336 S '83)

Satires of circumstance: lyrics and reveries, with miscellaneous pieces. London, Macmillan, 1914. xii,232p
(Rev in Nation (NY) 100:139 F 4 '15; T L S N 19 '14 p514; Sat R 118:535-6 N 21 '14; Spec 114:19-21 Ja 2 '15; Ath 2:552 N 28 '14; L. Strachey in New

Statesm 4:269-71 D 19 '14; Liv Age 284:55-7 Ja 2 '15; Acad 87:476-7 N 28 '14)

Selected poems
(Noted in Lond Merc 5:43 F '22)

The short stories of Thomas Hardy. . . London, Macmillan, 1928. 1084p
(Rev by W. Gibson in Bookm (Lond) 74:148-9 Je '28; E. Shanks in Sat R 145: 495 Ap 21 '28; F. McGrath in Studies 17:504-5 S '28)

Tess of the D'Urbervilles. A pure woman faithfully presented. London, Osgood, McIlvaine, 1891. 3 vols viii, 264p; viii,280p; viii,280p [Appeared in Graphic Jl 4-D 26 '91]
(Rev by C. T. Copeland in Atlan 69: 697-702 My '92; Speaker 4:770-1 D 26 '91; J. Stanley-Little in Literary World (Lond) ns 45:412 Ap 29 '92; Lit W 23: 58, 192-3 F 13, Je 4 '92; Critic (NY) 21:13-14 Jl 9 '92, answered by Hardy in Critic (NY) 21:134 S 10 '92; Spec 68: 121-2 Ja 23 '92; R of Rs (Lond) 5:200 F '92; W. M. Payne in Dial 12:424 Ap '92; Ind 44:276 F 25 '92; Harper M 85: 152-3 Je '92; Edin R 192:211-12 Jl '00; Book B ns 9:68-9 Mr '92; Blackw 151: 464-74 Mr '92; J. S. Little in Library Review 1:62-71 Ap '92; Ath 1:49-50 Ja 9 '92; Sat R 73:73-4 Ja 16 '92; Quar R 174:319-26 Ap '92; Westm 137:347-8 Mr '92; noted in Spec 108:804 My 18 '12; A. Lang in Longman's Magazine 21: 100-6 N '92; W. Watson in Acad 41: 125-6 F 6 '92; A. Lang in New Review 6:247-9 F '92; Bookm (Lond) 1: 179-80 F '92; Gent M 273:321 S '92; Deutsche Rundschau 79:158-9 '94; Archiv 88:217-18 '92)

Three notable stories. London, Blackett, 1890. viii,216p
(Rev by G. Cotterell in Acad 38:88 Ag 2 '90; Literary World (Lond) ns 42:74 Jl 25 '90)

Time's laughingstocks and other verses. London, Macmillan, 1909. xii,212p
(Rev in Sat R 109:78 Ja 15 '10; Ath 1: 34-5 Ja 8 '10; Liv Age 264:306-10 Ja 29 '10; M. Hewlett in Engl R 4:639-43 Mr '10; Spec 104:155 Ja 29 '10; Acad 78:249-50 Mr 12 '10)

The trumpet-major. A tale. London, Smith, Elder, 1880. 3 vols viii,296p; viii,276p; viii,260p [Appeared in Good Words Ja-D '80]
(Rev by G. Saintsbury in Acad 18:420 D 11 '80; Lit W 12:25 Ja 15 '81; Nation (NY) 32:16-17 Ja 6 '81; Harper M 62: 474 F '81; Brit Q 73:227-8 Ja '81; Ath 2:672 N 20 '80; Sat R 50:588-9 N 6 '80)

Two on a tower. A romance. London, Sampson Low, Marston, Searle, & Rivington, 1882. 3 vols iv,248p; iv,240p; iv,224p [Appeared in Atlan vols 49 & 50 Ja-D '82]
(Rev in Ath 2:658 N 18 '82; Sat R 54: 674-5 N 18 '82; Spec 56:154 F 3 '83;

Hardy, Thomas—Two on a tower—*Cont.*
Lit W 13:461 D 16 '82; Nation (NY)
36:42-3 Ja 11 '83)

Under the greenwood tree. A rural
painting of the Dutch school. London,
Tinsley, 1872. 2 vols vi,216p; vi,216p
[Published anonymously]
(Rev in Nation (NY) 17:27 Jl 10 '73;
Literary World (Lond) ns 65:248 Mr 14
'02; Ath 1:748 Je 15 '72; Sat R 34:417-18
S 28 '72; Spec 45:1403 N 2 '72)

The well-beloved. A sketch of a temperament. London, Osgood, McIlvaine,
1897. xii,340p [Appeared in Illustrated
London News O 1-D 17 '92 under the
title "The pursuit of the well-beloved"]
(Rev by W. M. Payne in Dial 22:307-8
My 16 '97; Critic (NY) 30:300 My 1
'97; Lit W 28:156-7 My 15 '97; Literary
World (Lond) ns 55:283-5 Mr 26 '97;
Lit Digest 15:70-1 My 15 '97; Acad 51:
345-6 Mr 27 '97; G. Douglas in Bookm
(NY) 5:247-8 My '97; Ath 1:471 Ap 10
97; W. L. Phelps in Book B ns 14:410-
12 My '97)

The Wessex edition
(Rev by C. Whibley in Blackw 193:823-
31 Je '13; Edin R 215:93-112 Ja '12;
W. L. Randell in Acad 82:805 Je 29 '12;
83:535-6 O 26 '12; Ath 2:244, 414,
553, 689-90, 783 S 7, O 12, N 9, D 7, 28
'12; Ath 1:126 F 1 '13; Spec 109:335-7
S 7 '12; Sat R 113:781-2 Je 22 '12; Spec
108:804 My 18 '12; C. R. Meibergen in
Engl Stud 51:284-7 '17; Bookm (Lond)
8:50-1 My '95)

Wessex poems and other verses. London,
Harper, 1898. xii,228p
(Rev by W. M. Payne in Dial 26:274-5
Ap 16 '99; I. Zangwill in Cosmopolitan
26:582-3 Mr '99; E. Gosse in Lit 4:177-8
Mr 3 '99; Lit 3:615-16 D 31 '98; L. John-
son in Outlook (Lond) 2:822-3 Ja 28
'99; Lit W 30:86-7 Mr 18 '99; Nation
(NY) 68:479 Je 22 '99; A. Macdonell in
Bookm (Lond) 15:139-41 F '99; Ath 1:
41-2 Ja 14 '99; Sat R 87:19 Ja 7 '99;
W. B. Columbine in Westm 152:180-4
Ag '99; Acad 56:43-4 Ja 14 '99; noted in
Critic (NY) 34:127 F '99)

Wessex tales: strange, lively and com-
monplace. London, Macmillan, 1888.
2 vols viii,248p; viii,216p
(Rev in Spec 61:1037-8 Jl 28 '88; Lit W
27:367 O 31 '96; Westm 130:115 Jl '88;
Nation (NY) 46:530 Je 28 '88; Ath 1:825
Je 30 '88; Sat R 65:796 Je 30 '88;
Deutsche Rundschau 59:158-9 '89)

Winter words in various moods and
metres. London, Macmillan, 1928. xii,
202p
(Rev by M. Van Doren in Nation (NY)
127:662 D 12 '28; by R. Church in Spec
141:supp 443-5 O 6 '28; V. Sackville-
West in Nat-Ath 44:54 O 13 '28; C. K.
Trueblood in Dial 86:150-4 F '29; Books
D 23 '28 p3; New York Evening Post
D 8 '28 p10; N Y Times D 9 '28 p2;
Out 151:110-11 Ja 16 '29; T L S O 4

'28 p705; Sat R 146:610 N 10 '28; S. L.
Bensusan in Quar R 253:313-29 O '29;
W. Gibson in Bookm (Lond) 75:107-8
N '28; E. G. Twitchett in Lond Merc
19:203-5 D '28; E. Shanks in John O'
London's Weekly 20:103 O 27 '28; B.
Deutsch in Bookm (NY) 68:472 D '28)

The woodlanders. London, Macmillan,
1887. 3 vols iv,304p; iv,328p; iv,316p
[Appeared in Macmil My '86-Ap '87]
(Rev in Acad 31:251-2
Ap 9 '87; Spec 60:419-20 Mr 26 '87;
W. M. Payne in Dial 8:68 Jl '87; Westm
128:384 Je '87; Nation (NY) 44:430-1
My 19 '87; Harper M 75:317-18 Jl '87;
Lit W 18:149-50 My 14 '87; Ath 1:414
Mr 26 '87; Sat R 63:484-5 Ap 2 '87;
Lond Q R 68:382 Jl '87)

Works
(Rev in Literary World (Lond) ns 67:
107, 344, 609 Ja 30, Ap 10, Je 26 '03;
68:162 S 4 '03; Atlan 43:260-2 F '79;
H. D. Davray in Mercure Fr 46:264-5
Ap '03)

Hardy, Thomas (ed)
Select poems of William Barnes. Lon-
don, Frowde, 1908
(Rev in Ath 2:815-16 D 26 '08)

Hardy; poem. Atlan 118:855 D '16

Hardy and [George] Eliot. T. P.'s Weekly
20:120 Jl 26 '12

[**Hardy** "Bowdlerised"] Literary World
(Lond) ns 52:220-1 S 27 '95

The **Hardy** country. T. P.'s Weekly 26:188
Ag 21 '15

[**Hardy** in London] Lit W 17:249 Jl 24 '86

A **Hardy** note on a poem by Moule. Lond
Merc 6:631-2 O '22

Hardyana. Liv Age 250:189-91 Jl 21 '06

Hardy's Casterbridge. "The return of the
native" staged. Bookman's Journal 3:79
N 26 '20

Hardy's first book. Book-Lover (San
Francisco) 2:524 Ja-F '02

Hardy's first book—why it was never published and never will be. Munsey's
Magazine 26:596 Ja '02

Hardys gesellschaftskritik. *In* Anglica;
untersuchungen zur englischen philologie Alois Brandl zum siebzigsten geburtstage uberreicht. Leipzig, Mayer &
Müller, 1925. p461-74

[**Hardy's** hatred of "Sham optimism"] Dial
52:119 F 16 '12

[**Hardy's** New Year poem] Acad 72:3 Ja 5
'07

[**Hardy's** theory that immortals make sport
of humans] Bookm (Lond) 21:41 N '01

Harper, Charles George
The Hardy country; literary landmarks of
the Wessex novels. (Pilgrimage series)
London, Black, 1904. xvi,318p
(Rev in Bookm (Lond) 27:220-1 F '05;
Acad 68:16-17 Ja 7 '05)

Harper, George McLean
Hardy, Hudson, Housman. Scrib M 78: 151-4 Ag '25; *also in* Spirit of delight. London, Benn, 1928. p70-91

Harper and brothers, firm, publishers, New York
Thomas Hardy, notes on his life and work. New York, Harper [19-?] 32p

Harris, Frank
Thomas Hardy. *In* Latest contemporary portraits. New York, Macaulay [c1927] p150-61

Harris, R. B.
The curve of pessimism in Thomas Hardy. Masters essay, Vanderbilt Univ. 1925. 102ff

Hart, Ray H.
Thomas Hardy—a study of the romanticism and realism in his novels. Masters essay, New York Univ. 1912. 22ff

Hartmann, J.
Architektur in den romanen Thomas Hardys. Diss. Münster, 1934. vii,77p

Hazard, Lucy Lockwood
Thomas Hardy as a dramatic novelist. Masters essay, Univ. of California, 1917. 129ff

[Head of Thomas Hardy as captured in bronze by Youriévitch] Lit Digest 101: 23 Ap 27 '29

Heath, Frederick
A note on Thomas Hardy. Bermondsey Book 5:57-63 Mr-My '28
A stranger at Max Gate; poem. Lit Digest 89:34 Je 12 '26

Heath, Sidney
The heart of Wessex. . . Boston, Estes [1911] 64p

Heath, Sidney and Heath, F. R.
Dorchester (Dorset) and its surroundings. . . (Homeland handbooks series no 46) London, Homeland association, 1905

Hebb, John
Mr. Thomas Hardy and restoration. Notes & Q 10th ser 6:365 N 10 '06

Hedgcock, Frank Arthur
Thomas Hardy, penseur et artiste. . . Paris, Hachette, 1911. viii,508p Thesis, Paris. Bibl p491-8
(Rev by T. Seccombe in Bookm (Lond) 40:170-1 Jl '11; Sat R 111:747-8 Je 17 '11; Edin R 215:93-112 Ja '12; Acad 81: 171-2 Ag 5 '11)

Heely, Allan V.
The literary reputation of Thomas Hardy. Masters essay, Columbia univ. 1934

Hellström, Gustav
Thomas Hardy och odödligheten. Dagens Nyheter F 2 '28 p4-5

Heminger, Mary Margaret
Standardized romantic elements in the novels of Thomas Hardy. Masters essay, Univ. of Iowa, 1928

Henderson, Archibald
Mr. Hardy achieves a second immortality. Literary Digest International Book Review 2:372-4 Ap '24

Hener, O.
Goethe und Hardy. Beiträge z. sächs. Kirchengeschichte '16

Henkes, Eleanore Janet
Thomas Hardy's opinion of what a novel should be. Masters essay, State Univ. of Iowa, 1934. 94ff

Henneman, John Bell
The dramatic novel; George Meredith and Thomas Hardy. Reader 8:680-5 N '06

Henniker, Florence
The spectre of the real. *In* Scarlet and grey. London, Lane, 1896. p164-208

The **heroic** optimism of Thomas Hardy. Cur Lit 39:154-5 Ag '05

Hewlett, Maurice [Henry]
The root of poesy. *In* Extemporary essays. New York, Oxford univ. press, 1922. p72-6

Hickson, Elizabeth Cathcart
The versification of Thomas Hardy. Philadelphia, Privately printed, Univ. of Pa. 1931. 129p bibl p128-9; Thesis, Univ. of Pennsylvania
(Rev by J. W. Beach in J E G P 31: 627-9 O '32)

Hill, Mary Anderson
The tragedies of Thomas Hardy: an application of the principles of tragic drama to Hardy's tragic novels. Masters essay, Stanford Univ. 1922. 60ff

Hiller, Hedwig
Thomas Hardy, seine entwicklung als romancier. . . Tübingen, E. Göbel, 1933. 65p bibl p4-5 Diss. Tübingen

Hind, Charles Lewis
Thomas Hardy. *In* Authors and I. New York, Lane, 1921. p114-18

Two poets: Thomas Hardy and Flecker. Out 139:297 F 25 '25

Hirn, Yrjö
[Foreword] *In* En grupp förnäma damer [translated by] Karin Hirn. . . Stockholm, Björck & Börjesson, 1906. p i-xviii

Thomas Hardy. London, n.d.

Hitchcock, Helen
An aspect of Hardy. Vassar Journal of Undergraduate Studies 2:88-96 My '27

Hoare, Barnard George
Mr. Hardy and Tennyson. Acad 72:75, 100 Ja 19, 26 '07

Hodgson, W. Earl
A prig in the Elysian fields. National Review 19:191-9 Ap '92

Hogben, Launcelot
Thomas Hardy and democracy. Socialist Review 15:159-63 Ap-Je '18

Holcomb, Esther
The relation between Thomas Hardy's novels and his poetry. Masters essay, Univ. of Kansas, 1930. 154ff

Holland, Clive [pseud]
see Hankinson, Charles James

Holliday, Carl
Thomas Hardy. *In* English fiction from the fifth to the twentieth century. New York, Century, 1912. p361-6

Holmberg, Olle
Thomas Hardy. *In* Litterärt. Stockholm, Bonnier, 1924. p127-45

Hommage à Thomas Hardy. (La Revue Nouvelle, janv-févr 1928. A special number, with translations of various passages, p7-54; short articles or critical notes by M. Proust, R. Boylesve, E. Phillpotts, J. Joyce, J. M. Murry, E. Jaloux, J. Schumberger, J.-L. Vaudoyer, R. Fernandez, G. D'Hangest, P. D'Exideuil, F. Hellens, C. Du Bos, p55-139; and a short bibliography, p140-1)

Hone, Joseph Maunsell
The poetry of Thomas Hardy. Liv Age 313:52-7 Ap 1 '22; *same.* Lond Merc 5: 396-405 F '22

Hopkins, [Robert] Thurston
Dorset folk and Dorset ways. Thomas Hardy's characters in real life. Bookman's Journal 4:238 Ag 5 '21

Thomas Hardy's Dorset; with il. by E. Harries and from photographs. London, Palmer [c1922] 255p
(Rev by E. Blunden in Lond Merc 6: 663 O '22; Bookman's Journal 6:93 Je '22)

Houghton, M.
The women of the Wessex novels. Holborn Review 67:433-42 O '25

Houk, Gertrude Helen
A critical analysis of the works and ideas of Thomas Hardy. Masters essay, Cornell Univ. 1926. 259ff

Housman, Laurence
Sabrina Warham. London, Murray, 1904
(Rev in Sat R 98:iii-iv O 15 '04 supp under title "After Thomas Hardy")

Howells, W. D.
Mr. Thomas Hardy's Bathsheba Everdene and Paula Power. *In* Heroines of fiction. New York, Harper, 1901. vol II p193-210

Mr. Thomas Hardy's heroines. *In* Heroines of fiction. New York, Harper, 1901. vol II p177-92

Hsin-Hai, Chang
see Chang, Hsin-Hai

Hudson, Ruth
The relation of Thomas Hardy to Shakespeare, with particular reference to Hardy's eight major novels. Masters essay, Univ. of Texas, 1926. 229ff

In the D'Urberville country [signed "Y. Y."] Bookm (Lond) 6:46-8 My '94

In Thomas Hardy's country. Temple 108: 150-3 My '96; *same.* Ecl M ns 63:774-6 Je '96

Is Thomas Hardy overestimated? Cur Lit 43:290-2 S '07

Isogaya, Meizen
Naturalism and Mr. Thomas Hardy. Masters essay, Univ. of Washington, 1922. 36ff

Jackson, Holbrook
Thomas Hardy and the Dynasts. T. P.'s Weekly 24:595-6 D 5 '14

Jacobs, Charles P.
Will Mr. Hardy explain? Critic (NY) 2: 25-6 Ja 28 '82
[Parallel passages from Hardy's "Trumpet-Major" and Longstreet's "Georgia Scenes" suggest possible plagiarism. Hardy's passage is credited to Longstreet, and Longstreet's to Hardy. See also Critic (NY) 28:336 My 9 '96]

Jameison, Paul Fletcher
Nature and human morality; an ethical study of the novels of Thomas Hardy. Masters essay, Columbia univ. 1926

Japp, Alexander H.
Two pairs of novelists. Cassell's Family Magazine 21:530-1 Je '95

Jasienski, Alexander M.
Współczesni powiésciopisarze anglielscy. Warsaw, Paprocki, 1897
(Rev in Literary World (Lond) ns 56: 130 Ag 20 '97)

Jefferson, Ralph
Thomas Hardy's first love. [architecture] Country Life (Lond) 63::73-5 Ja 21 '28

Jiriczek, Otto Luitpold
Zum Thema "Maternal Impression." (An imaginative woman) Bei Anglia 39:87-8 Mr '28

Johnson, Lionel Pigot
The art of Thomas Hardy. With a portrait etched from life by W. Strang, and a bibliography by John Lane. London, Mathews and Lane, 1894. ix, 276,lxiiip
(Rev by A. Macdonell in Bookm (Lond) 7:85-6 D '94; Nation (NY) 60:225-6 Mr 21 '95)

The art of Thomas Hardy; to which is added a chapter on the poetry, by J. E. Barton and a bibliography by John Lane; together with a new portrait by Vernon Hill and the etched portrait by William Strang. New York, Dodd, Mead, 1923. xiii,357p bibl p297-346 2 por
(Rev in Lond Q R 140:107-10 Jl '23; T L S Jl 19 '23 p485; noted in T L S Je 14 '23 p406)

Mr. Hardy's later prose and verse. *In* Post liminium. . . New York, Kennerley, 1912. p142-50

Mr. Thomas Hardy. (portrait) Acad 55: 251-2 N 12 '98

Johnson, M.
Thomas Hardy's novels. Primitive Methodist Quarterly Review Ja '96

Thomas Hardy's poetry and philosophy of life. Primitive Methodist Quarterly Review Jl '02

Jones, Phyllis M. (ed)
English critical essays (20th century). (World's classics). London, Oxford univ. press, 1933

Jordan-Smith, P.
Thomas Hardy. *In* On strange altars. New York, Boni, 1924

[Jude the Obscure] Bookm (NY) 3:1-2 Mr '96

[Kahn, Gilbert]
The poetry of Thomas Hardy. By Christian Cantle [pseud] (Bowdoin prize essay, 1932) Typed ms. in Harvard college library. 33ff

Kammerer, Mary Caroline
Some aspects of Thomas Hardy's philosophy, as shown in the Wessex novels. Masters essay, Cornell Univ. 1931. 80ff

Kassner, Rudolf
Thomas Hardy. Corona 2:323-40 N '31

Kellner, Leon
Die englische literatur der neuesten zeit... Leipzig, Tauchnitz, 1921. p324-7

Die englische literatur im zeitalter der königin Viktoria. Leipzig, Tauchnitz, 1909. p561-4

Kendall, May
Pessimism and Thomas Hardy's poems. Lond Q R ns 1:223-34 Ap '99

Kennedy, Thomas J.
Novels of Thomas Hardy. Central Literary Magazine Ap '28 p219-26

Kilmer, Joyce
Introduction. *In* The mayor of Casterbridge, by Thomas Hardy. (Modern library) New York, 1917

Note on Thomas Hardy. *In* The circus, and other essays... New York, Doran, 1921. p268-74

King, George
Thomas Hardy: novelist and poet. Cornhill ns 64:278-91 Mr '28

King, Marianne
Temperamental pessimism in Thomas Hardy. Pacific Review 1:530-42 Mr '21

King, Robert Wylie
The lyrical poems of Thomas Hardy. Lond Merc 15:157-70 D '26

Kingsgate, John
"Tess"—and Thomas Hardy... Graphic 112:377 S 5 '25

Kipling, Rudyard
The rhyme of the three captains; poem. Ath 2:776-7 D 6 '90

Knickerbocker, Frances Wentworth
The Victorianness of Thomas Hardy. Sewanee R 36:310-25 Jl-S '28

Knight, Grant Cochran
The novel in English. New York, R.R. Smith, 1931. p233-48

Knowles, Dom David
The thought and art of Thomas Hardy. Dublin Review 183:208-18 O '28

Kornman, Lydia Weille
Thomas Hardy; antiquarian. Masters essay, Vanderbilt Univ. 1930. 132ff

Korten, Herta
Thomas Hardy's Napoleondichtung The Dynasts. Ihre abhängigkeit von Schopenhauer. Ihr einfluss auf Gerhart Hauptmann. Bonn, Georgi, 1919. 105p Diss. Rostock
(Rev by H. Hecht in Engl Stud 55:105-15 Ja '21; W. Fischer in Literatur 42:106-8 Mr-Ap '21; R. Petsch in Neue Jahrbücher für das Klassische Altertum 47:76 '21)

Kunstmann, Victor
Thomas Hardys Tristandichtung. 1928. ms in Archiv des Bayerischen Ministeriums für unterricht und kultur.

L [pseud]
Letters to eminent hands. (Moray library) London, Simpkin, 1892

Laing, Alexander
Hardy and Housman again. Sat R Lit 6:118 Jl 5 '30

Lalou, René
Panorama de la littérature anglaise contemporaine. Paris, Kra [c1926] passim

Lane, Harriet
Fate in the novels of Thomas Hardy. Essay for special honors in English, Smith College, 1925. 56ff typed ms. in Smith college library

Lang, Andrew
Tess of the D'Urbervilles. *In* Mordell, Albert, ed. Notorious literary attacks. New York, Boni and Liveright, 1926. p221-31

Lasselin, Georges
... Le couple humain dans l'oeuvre de Thomas Hardy... [Paris, Établissements Busson, 1928] bibl p222-[225] Thesis, Lille

Lawrence, David Herbert
Six novels of Thomas Hardy and the real tragedy. Book Collector's Quarterly no 5:44-61 Ja '32

Lawrence, Nevile Sherbrooke
The D'Urbervilles of Tess. Chamb J 7th ser 18:628-30 S 1 '28

Lea, Hermann
A handbook of the Wessex country of Mr. Hardy's novels and poems. London, Paul, 1906

Thomas Hardy's Wessex... London, Macmillan, 1913. 342p
(Rev by C. R. Meibergen in Engl Stud 52:133-4 '18)

Thomas Hardy's Wessex; illustrated from photographs by the author. (Highways and byways ser) London, Macmillan, 1925. xxiii,317p illus map
(Rev in Acad 85:655 N 22 '13; Ath 2:617 N 29 '13)

Lee, Vernon [pseud]
see Paget, Violet

Lefèvre, Frédéric
An hour with Thomas Hardy. Liv Age 325:98-103 Ap 11 '25; *same*. Les Nouvelles Littéraires F 21 '25 p1-2

Le Gallienne, Richard
[Jude the obscure] Idler 9:114-15 F '96

Lehmann, Karl
Die Auffassung und gestaltung des Napoleon-problems im englischen drama. Erlangen, K. Döres, 1931

Lemperly, Paul
Jude the obscure: a letter and a foreword. Lakewood, Ohio, 1917

[**Length** of Hardy's novels] T L S My 4 '22 p285

Lennard, Walter [pseud]
see Courtney, William Leonard

Letters to living authors—VII. Mr. Thomas Hardy. Good Words 43:672-8 S '02

Levy, Oscar
Thomas Hardy and Friedrich Nietzsche. Outlook (Lond) 61:217-18 F 18 '28

Lewis, Helen M.
Hardy's conception of nature. Masters essay, Univ. of Iowa, 1927

Lewis, (Mrs) Stella V. (McGuire)
The treatment of nature in the works of George Meredith and Thomas Hardy. Masters essay, Univ. of British Columbia, 1920. 124ff

Liddell, Katherine Forbes
Thomas Hardy, philosopher and poet. Masters essay, Yale univ. 1923

Ligo, Ida Louise
George Meredith and Thomas Hardy: a contrast. Masters essay, Columbia univ. 1919

Lillard, Richard Gordon
Irony; the integrant in the art and philosphy of Thomas Hardy and Joseph Conrad. Masters essay, Univ. of Montana, 1931. 167ff; condensed version *in* P M L A 50:316-22 Mr '35

Irony in Hardy and Conrad. P M L A 50:316-22 Mr '35

Linaker, Percy
Thomas Hardy in France. Ath 2:563 O 22 '20

Ling, William
Mr. Kipling and the pirate. Outlook (Lond) 4:277-8 S 30 '99

Linne, H.
Ein besuch bei Thomas Hardy. Gegenwart 49:307-9 My 16 '96

Liron, A.
La femme dans le roman de Hardy. Didier, 1919

The **literary** pages of the "Spectator." Spec 141:69 N 10 '28

Literary portraits. XII. Mr. Hardy. Daily Mail Jl 6 '07

Literature and journalism. Spec 108:900-1 Je 8 '12

Loane, George Green
"The Dynasts" and the N.E.D. T L S F 14 '29 p118
Hardy and N.E.D. T L S Ja 21 '32 p44; ibid. Ap 14 '32 p271

Loew, Joseph
The evolution of the art of Thomas Hardy. Masters essay, New York Univ. 1906. 23ff

Longstreet vs. Hardy. Bookm (NY) 23:121-2 Ap '06

Lösch, Olga
Das naturgefühl bei George Eliot and Thomas Hardy. Giessen, Christ, 1928. *In* Giessener beiträge zur erforschung der sprache und kultur Englands und Nord-amerikas 5:88-180 '28 Diss. Giessen
(Rev by K. Rhotert in Bei Anglia 41:330-5 N '30)

Love in fiction. (Turgénev and Hardy) T L S O 30 '13 p490-1

The **love** of good writing. Nation (NY) 94:608-9 Je 20 '12

Loveless, M. J.
Thomas Hardy's methods of characterizing women as developed in his novels. Masters essay, Univ. of Southern California, 1929. 187ff

Lowe, Orton
Thomas Hardy. Scholastic 9:12 S 18 '26

Lowes, John Livingston
Two readings of earth. Yale R ns 15:515-39 Ap '26; *also in* Of reading books. London, Constable, 1930
(Rev in T L S My 29 '30 p452; O. Barfield in Crit 10:155-8 O '30; Oxford Magazine Je 12 '30; Life & L 5:64-8 Jl '30)

Lucas, Frank Laurence
Hardy. *In* Eight Victorian poets. Cambridge, England, Univ. press, 1930. p133-51
(Rev in T L S N 13 '30 p936)

Lukavska, Ruzena Paula
The peasantry in the works of Thomas Hardy. Masters essay, Columbia univ. 1925
Románové a básnické dilo Tomáse Hardyho. [Thomas Hardy as poet and novelist] Nové Cechy 10:123-7, 156-9 '26-'27

Luttmer, Sister Mechtild
Eleusis did for Aeschylus what Wessex did for Hardy. Masters essay, Univ. of Notre Dame, 1930. 55ff

Lynd, Robert
Mr. Thomas Hardy. *In* Old and new masters. New York, Scribner, 1919. p234-49

Lyon, Harris Merton
A nineteen-act play. Green Book 13:595-8 Ap '15

Macarthur, Henry
Realism and romance: Thomas Hardy and Robert Louis Stevenson. *In* Realism and romance, and other essays. Edinburgh, Hunter, 1897. p1-23

MacArthur, James
[Literary work of Hardy] Harper W 49: 1486 O 14 '05

Macdonald, John F.
English life and the English stage. Fortn 103:350-5 '15

Macdonald, M.
Thomas Hardy. Hamburg Correspondent no 22 '01

Macdonell, Annie
Thomas Hardy... (Contemporary writers) New York, Dodd, Mead, 1895. vi, 232p
(Rev in Acad 47:123 F 9 '95; L. Johnson in Bookm (NY) 1:37-9 F '95; Literary World (Lond) ns 50:474 D 14 '94; L. Johnson in Bookm (Lond) 7:86-7 D '94)

McDowall, Arthur Sydney
Thomas Hardy, a critical study... London, Faber & Faber [1931] 11-283p bibl p277-9
(Rev in T L S My 28 '31 p423; T. E. Welby in W E R 3:852-4 Je 6 '31; R. A. Scott-James in New Statesm 2:17 Jl 4 '31; R. Watkins in Lond Merc 25:210-11 D '31; R. Church in Spec 146:941-2 Je 13 '31; O. Burdett in Sat R 151:833 Je 6 '31; M. E. Chase in Commonweal 16:355 Ag 3 '31; O. Williams in Nat R 97:267-75 Ag '31)

MacFall, Haldane
Thomas Hardy. Canadian Magazine 23: 105-8 Je '04

McGrath, Fergal
The pessimism of Thomas Hardy. Studies 17:29-38 Mr '28

Machen, Arthur
The Dorchester players. Acad 81:657-8 N 25 '11

McKenna, Donald
The naturalism of Thomas Hardy... Masters essay, Claremont Colleges, 1931. 134ff

Mackenzie, Compton
George Meredith and Thomas Hardy. In Literature in my time. London, Rich and Cowan, 1933. p51-2

McKie, George
Studies in the modern English novel... Chapel Hill, N.C. Univ. of N.C. press [c1924] p11-12

MacMichael, J. Holden
"Welter." Notes & Q 9th ser 12:74 Jl 25 '03

McMillan, James Benjamin
Thomas Hardy's views on sex. Masters essay, Univ. of North Carolina, 1930. 99ff

McNutt, Roy D.
A visit to Mr. Thomas Hardy. Dalhousie Review 6:51-5 Ap '26

Macy, John Albert
Thomas Hardy. In The critical game. New York, Boni and Liveright [c1922] p237-44

Two-fold genius of Hardy. Bookm (NY) 67:134-9 Ap '28
The world of Thomas Hardy. Book League Monthly 1 no 2:149-59 D '28

Magnus, Philip M.
Poetry and society since Tennyson. Edin R 249:303-5 Ap '29

Mainsard, Joseph
La pensée de Thomas Hardy. Études 191: 439-61 My 20 '27

Mais, Stuart Petre Brodie
Poetry of Thomas Hardy. In From Shakespeare to O. Henry... Revised ed. London, Richards, 1923. p282-99
Thomas Hardy. In Some modern authors. New York, Dodd, Mead, 1923. p227-37

Manly, John Matthews and Rickert, Edith
Thomas Hardy. In Contemporary British literature. New York, Harcourt, Brace [c1921] p75-80

Mantripp, J. C.
Thomas Hardy's "The Dynasts." Holborn Review 70:157-68 Ap '28

Marble, Annie Russel
Hardy again. Sat R Lit 2:796 My 15 '26

Margolies, Benjamin H.
Atmosphere in Thomas Hardy's novels. Masters essay, Columbia univ. 1922

Marks, Marjorie Cecile
Thomas Hardy as a poet and epic dramatist. Masters essay, Columbia univ. 1922

Marshall, Archibald
Under the greenwood tree. Literary Digest International Book Review 2:187, 236 F '24

Martin, Dorothy (Mrs. L. C. Martin)
Thomas Hardy's lyrics. Freeman 8:490-2, 515-16 Ja 30-F 6 '24

Martin, G. Currie
Thomas Hardy and the English Bible. Bookm (Lond) 74:24-6 Ap '28

Mason, Stuart
An unknown magazine article by Thomas Hardy. Ath 2:627 N 5 '20

Massingham, Henry William
The apology of Thomas Hardy. In H. W. M.; a selection from the writings of H. W. Massingham, ed. with a pref. and notes by H. J. Massingham. London, Cape [1925] p176-80
(From Nation Je 3 '22)

Maugham, W. Somerset
Cakes and ale: or the skeleton in the cupboard. New York, Doubleday, Doran, 1930. [i] 308p [Supposed by some to have reference to Hardy]

Mavrogordato, John
Thomas Hardy [with poem by Kostes Palamas] Ath 2:848 D 17 '20

Maxwell, Donald
The landscape of Thomas Hardy. London, Cassell [1928] vii-xii,80p

Maynard, Theodore
The poetry of Thomas Hardy. Cath World 123:46-54 Ap '26

Mayoux, J. J.
L'amour dans les romans de Thomas Hardy. Revue A A 5:201-18, 331-9 F, Ap '28
La fatalité intérieure dans les romans de Thomas Hardy. Revue A A 4:208-19 F '27

Meibergen, C. R.
The woodlanders. Engl Stud 51:226-47 '17

Meissner, Paul
Pessimistische strömungen im englischen geistesleben des 19. jahrhunderts. Engl Stud 64:448 '29

A **memorial** to Hardy; the houses of the dead; houses and spirits. Lond Merc 20:451-3 S '29

Meury, John Nicholas
Thomas Hardy—certain phases of several factors in his writing and his ideas with emphasis upon recently divulged biographical memoranda. Masters essay, New York Univ. 1933. 90ff

Miller, Margaret Pearl
Thomas Hardy, literary artist and deterministic philosopher. Masters essay, Univ. of Arizona, 1928

Milne, James
Mr. Hardy's birthday. . . Book Monthly 14:472-5 Je '19
Thomas Hardy at home. *In* A window in Fleet Street. London, Murray [1931] p253-67

Minto, Professor William
The work of Thomas Hardy. Bookm (Lond) 1:99-101 D '91

Mr. **Andrew Lang** and Mr. Thomas Hardy. Illustrated London News 101:579 N 5 '92

Mr. **Hardy** and our headlines. World's Work 24:385-6 Ag '12

Mr. **Hardy's** dominion. T. P.'s Weekly 4: 132 Jl 29 '04

Mr. **Hardy's** 80th birthday. Ath 1:737-8 Je 4 '20

[Mr. **Hardy's** home] Acad 56:5 Ja 7 '99

Mr. **Hardy's** lyrics. T L S N 27 '19 p681-2

Mr. **Hardy's** novels. Brit Q 73:342-60 Ap 1 '81

Mr. **Thomas Hardy.** Literary World (Lond) ns 63:588 Je 21 '01

Mr. **Thomas Hardy** and the mummers. Bookman's Journal 3:168 D 31 '20

Mr. **Thomas Hardy** [obituary] Sat R 145: 30-1 Ja 14 '28

Mr. **Thomas Hardy's** novels [Parallel passages of "Laodicean" Chapter V and Quarterly Review 49:381-2 1833, and of "The Trumpet-Major" Chapter XXIII and "Georgia Scenes"] Acad 21:120-1 F 18 '82

Modern men; Thomas Hardy. National Observer 5:301-2 F 7 '91

Modern pessimism. Quar R 196:636-40 O '02

Monroe, Harriet
Thomas Hardy. Poetry 31:326-32 Mr '28

Montfort, Eugène
Réflexions à propos de Thomas Hardy. Les Marges no. 9:165-70 Ja '06

Mooers, H. T.
Hardy's women and the spirit of the Wessex novels. Ex Libris 2:99-105 Ja '25

Moore, Cleo Bryan
Humor in the Wessex novels. Masters essay, George Peabody College, 1931

Moore, George
Conversations in Ebury street. London, Heinemann, 1924. p84-109 (Limited to 1030 copies)
(Rev by H. Hawthorne in Literary Digest International Book Review 2: 441 My '24)

Moosman, Emma Alice
Aspects of the philosophy of life expressed in Thomas Hardy's novels. Masters essay, Univ. of Nebraska, 1929. 84ff

[**Morality** of "Life's little ironies"] Literary World (Lond) ns 49:437 My 11 '94

Morley, Christopher
Touch wood. Sat R Lit 4:533 Ja 21 '28

Morris, Lloyd
Hardy, the great pagan. Open Court 42: 382-4 Je '28

Moss, Mary
The novels of Thomas Hardy. Atlan 98: 354-67 S '06

Muddiman, Bernard
The men of the nineties. London, Danielson, 1920. passim

Muir, Edwin
Novels of Mr. Hardy. Literary Review 4:801-2 Je 7 '24

Müller, [Otto] Karl
Das naturgefühl bei Thomas Hardy im zusammenhang mit seiner weltanschauung. Diss. Jena, 1923. vii,107p. *See also* Neuphilologische Monatsschrift (Leipzig) 4:253-68 '33

Murray, Alison D. [See Burrow, Ed. J. and co., ltd.]

Murray, David Christie
. . . Thomas Hardy (with portrait). Canadian Magazine 9:38-41 My '97
Under French encouragement—Thomas Hardy. *In* My contemporaries in fiction. London, Chatto and Windus, 1897. p71-84

Murry, John Middleton
The poetry of Mr. Hardy. *In* Aspects of literature. London, Collins [c1920] p121-38
The supremacy of Thomas Hardy. New Adel 1:219-24 Mr '28; Revue Hebdomadaire 1:413-23 année 37 Ja 28 '28
Thomas Hardy and the church of England. New Adel 1:193-9 Mr '28

Wrap me up in my Aubusson carpet. New York, Greenberg, 1924. 19p (ltd. ed. 500 copies) (Answer to Moore, G. and his criticism in Conversations in Ebury Street)

Myers, Lena Josephine
Typical pessimistic attitudes in English literature, 1880-1895. Urbana, Illinois, 1928. Diss. Univ. of Illinois [Abstract 16p]

Myers, Walter L.
The later realism. . . Chicago, Univ. of Chicago press [c1927] p60-1, 103-4, 141-3

Nairne, Alexander
The poetry of Thomas Hardy. Church Q R 87:150-4 O '18; same. Liv Age 302: 175-8 Jl 19 '19

Neel, Philippe
Thomas Hardy. Europe 16:398-404 Mr 15 '28

Neil, (Mrs) Alice C.
Style in the poetry of Thomas Hardy. Masters essay, Univ. of British Columbia, 1932. 123ff

Neville, (Mrs) Jean (Thompson)
Studies in The Dynasts. Masters essay, Univ. of Western Ontario, 1923. 67ff

Nevinson, Henry Woodd
Changes and chances. London, Nisbet [1923] p307-8
The Lilliput world. In Books and personalities. New York, Lane, 1905. p173-8
Son of earth (Hardy). In Essays in freedom and rebellion. New Haven, Conn. Yale univ. press, 1921. p93-9
Thomas Hardy. In Books and personalities. New York, Lane, 1905. p169-72

The new Hardy. National Observer 14:11-12, 82 My 18, Je 1 '95

Newbolt, (Sir) Henry John
My world as in my time, memoirs of Sir Henry Newbolt, 1862-1932. London, Faber and Faber [1932] p282-9
A new departure in English poetry. (Dynasts) In Studies, green and gray. New York, Nelson [1926] p90-101; same. Quar R 210:193-209 Ja '09; same. Liv Age 260:544-54 F 27 '09

Newton, Alfred Edward
[Facsimile of a letter from Hardy to Tinsley] In Amenities of book-collecting. Boston, Atlantic monthly press, 1918. p12
A Thomas Hardy memorial. "Oak Knoll," Daylesford, Berwyn P.O., Pennsylvania, 1931. (16)p (Privately printed) frontis por
Thomas Hardy, novelist or poet? [Philadelphia] Privately printed, 1929. 32p (Edition limited to 950 copies)

Newton, Joseph Fort
Christ on Egdon Heath. Christian Century 45:137-8 F 2 '28

Newton-Robinson, Janetta
A study of Mr. Thomas Hardy. Westm 137:153-64 F '92

Nicoll, William Robertson
Notes on English style in the Victorian period. Bookm (NY) 10:147-8 O '99
Thomas Hardy. In Chambers's cyclopedia of English literature. Philadelphia, Lippincott, 1903. vol III p680-3
Thomas Hardy. In History of English literature by W. Robertson Nicoll and Thomas Seccombe. New York, Dodd, Mead, 1907. vol III p1247-50

Nielson, Elizabeth Elsiemae
The influence of Thomas Hardy's philosophical preconceptions on his character delineation. Masters essay, Boston Univ. 1932

[**Nobel** prize and Hardy] Ath 2:509 O 15 '20

Norman, Sylva
Thomas Hardy [with recollection of visits to Thomas Hardy by Edmund Blunden] In Massingham, H. J. and Massingham, H. eds. The great Victorians. London, Nicholson and Watson [1932] p233-50

Norwood, Hayden Eugene
Studies in Victorian pessimism [Hardy, Gissing, and Thomson] Masters essay, Cornell univ. 1933

[**Note** on a manuscript of Hardy's presented to Aberdeen University Library] Aberdeen University Review 15:142 Mr '28

[**Note** on Hardy's "The house of hospitality"] Acad 76:701 Ja 23 '09

[**Note** on Hardy's life and works] Bookm (NY) 2:374-5 Ja '96

[**Note** on "The Dynasts"] Book Monthly 1:293-4 F '04

[**Note** on "The Woodlanders"] Lit W 18: 184-5 Je 11 '87

Notes about authors [sketch of Hardy's life and works] Literary World (Lond) ns 47:392 Ap 28 '93

Notes on English style in the Victorian period. Thomas Hardy. Bookm (NY) 10:147-8 O '99

The **novels** of Thomas Hardy. Sewanee R 1:1-25 N '92

Noyes, Alfred
The poetry of Thomas Hardy. No Am 194:96-105 Jl '11
To Thomas Hardy on his eighty-third birthday; poem. Lit D 78:34 Jl 14 '23; same. Liv Age 318:185 Jl 28 '23

Nutt, Constance Rose
Thomas Hardy's use of physical nature. Masters essay, Univ. of Montana, 1934. 48ff

[**Obituaries;** all are dated 1928] (L. Daudet in L'Action Française Ja 16; E. J. C. Squire in The Observer Ja 15; E. Jaloux in Candide Ja 19; R. Puaux in Le Temps Ja 13, 17; P. N. Van Eyck in Gulden Winckel Ja p26; P. W. Assmann in Boekenschouw 21:433-41 F; Die Nieuwe Rotterdamsche Courant Ja 12; Nation (NY) 126:84-5 Ja 25; New

Obituaries—*Continued*
Repub 53:260-1 Ja 25; Sat R 145:30-1
Ja 14; Blackw 223:429-32 Mr; P. Dorset
in National Historical Field Club
(Lond) 49:xxv-xxix; W. B. Brash in
Lond Q R 149:145-57 Ap; Oxford
Magazine Mr 18 p407-8; G. K. Chester-
ton in Illustrated London News 172:94
Ja 21; A. Chevalley in Revue de P 35:
697-707 F 1; H. D. Davray in Mercure
Fr 202:5-19 F 15; L. Gigli in Nuova
Antol 335:187-94 Ja 16; L. Gillet in R
Deux Mondes 43:704-5 F 1; S. Gwynn
in Fortn 123:416-22 Mr 1; H. Johnson
in Architectural Review F p58-9; G.
King in Cornhill 64:278-91 Mr; V. Ren-
dall in Engl R 46:192-5 F; N. K. Sidd-
hanta in Modern Review 43:191-5 F;
Dial 84:179-80 F; Lond Merc 17:337-40
F; L'Illustration 170:73 Ja 21; World
Today 51:244-5 F; R of Rs (NY) 77:
319-20 Mr; Lit Digest 96:36-41 F 4;
C. Van Doren in Out 148:154 Ja 25; J
Débats 35 pt 1:119-20 Ja 20; Litera-
rische Welt 4:1-2; Die Literatur 30:
333-4 Mr)

O'Conner, Thomas Power
Thomas Hardy as I knew him. Liv Age
334:454-7 Mr 1 '28

Oliphant, (Mrs) M.
The anti-marriage league. Blackw 159:
137-42 Ja '96

Olivero, Federico
An introduction to Hardy. Torino,
Bocca, 1930. 202p
(Rev by P. Aronstein in Literatur 53:
324-5 S-O '32; Quar R 255:208 Jl '30;
K. Arns in Engl Stud 66:292-3 N '31
Un'introduzione a Thomas Hardy. Tra-
duzione di a. Ramello. Torino, Bocca,
1931. 225p
On Thomas Hardy. Poetry Review 19:
107-15 F-Mr '28
The poetry of Hardy. Poetry Review 20:
1-22 Ja-F '29

On ugliness in fiction. Edin R 207:448-52
Ap '08

O'Neill, Burke
The pessimism of Thomas Hardy.
Thought 7:619-36 Mr '33

[Original of "Tess"] Notes & Q 149:109
Ag 15 '25

O'Rouke, James
The orthodoxy of Thomas Hardy. Irish
Ecclesiastical Record 5th ser 33:237-45
Mr '29

O'Rourke, M. R.
Thomas Hardy, O.M. 1840-1928. Month
152:205-12 S '28

Orr, Lyndon
Thomas Hardy and Longstreet. Bookm
(NY) 22:635-6; 23:121-2 F-Ap '06

Ortensi, U.
Letterati contemporanei: Thomas Hardy.
Emporium 20:100-8 '04

Overton, Grant Martin
Do you remember? [Tess of the D'Ur-
bervilles] Mentor 17:45 S '29

[Paget, Violet] Lee, Vernon [pseud]
Hardy. *In* The handling of words. . .
New York, Dodd, Mead, 1923. p222-41;
same. Engl R 9:231-41 S '11
Of Hardy and Meredith. Westminster
Gazette Jl 20 '05 p1-2

Palmer, Peter Fourie
Chance in Thomas Hardy. Masters
essay, Univ. of British Columbia, 1926.
67ff

Parker, W. M.
Christmas with Thomas Hardy; Christ-
mas readings. Fortn 122:804-16 D '24
The genius of Thomas Hardy. 19th Cent
88:63-71 Jl '20
The jubilee of "Far from the madding
crowd." Cornhill ns 56:119-26 Ja '24
My visit to Thomas Hardy. Cornhill 66:
149-57 F '29
On the track of the Wessex novels. A
guide to the Hardy country. Poole
[England] Looker, 1924. 52p
Thomas Hardy. Ath 2:848 D 17 '20
Thomas Hardy on anti-scrape. Note.
T L S Mr 1 '28 p150

Parrott, Thomas Marc and Thorp, Willard
(eds)
Poetry of the transition, 1850-1914. New
York, Oxford [c1932] p411-15

Paston, George
The art of portrait-painting in words.
Cornhill ns 3:213-16 Ag '97

Patmore, Coventry
Thomas Hardy. St. James' Gazette Ap 2
'87

Paul, Herbert
The apotheosis of the novel under Queen
Victoria. 19th Cent 41:787-8 My '97

Peacock, Margaret A.
Thomas Hardy, the poet. Bachelor's
essay, Univ. of Buffalo, 1925

Peek, Frederic Albert
The novels of Thomas Hardy. Diss.
Cornell Univ. 1910. 55ff

Pessimism of Thomas Hardy. Liv Age
255:180-2 O 19 '07; *same.* Nation (Lond)
1:795-6 Jl 27 '07

Phare, E. E.
Hardy as a humanitarian. Cambridge
Review My 3 '29 p410-11

Phelps, William Lyon
Meredith and Hardy. *In* The advance of
the English novel. New York, Dodd,
Mead, 1916. p163-91
The novels of Thomas Hardy. No Am
190:502-14 O '09
Some contrasts—Henley, Thompson,
Hardy, Kipling. *In* Advance of English
poetry in the twentieth century. New
York, Dodd, Mead, 1918. p1-34
Thomas Hardy. *In* Essays on modern
novelists. New York, Macmillan, 1910.
p33-55
Thomas Hardy. Sat R Lit 1:808 Je 6 '25
Thomas Hardy memorial. Sat R Lit 4:
785 Ap 21 '28
Thomas Hardy's fifteen novels. Forum
79:436-47 Mr '28

Using graphic algebra on Thomas Hardy. Literary Digest International Book Review 4:109-11 Ja '26

Phillips, Charles
The Hardy optimist. Cath World 108: 762-6 Mr '19

Phillpotts, Eden
To Thomas Hardy; poem. Liv Age 306: 173 Jl 17 '20

Pickering, Ernest Harold
Thomas Hardy. *In* A brief survey of English literature. London, Harrap [1932] p131-4, 152-3

[Pinero's "The Squire" and Hardy's "Far from the Madding Crowd"] Acad 21: 34 Ja 21 '82

Pinkham, R. V.
Thomas Hardy's use of the pathetic fallacy. Masters essay, Univ. of Southern California, 1931. 131ff

Pinto, Vivian De Sola
Thomas Hardy. Wessex 1 no 1:16-20 Je '28

[Plagiarism—Hardy and Longstreet] Critic (NY) 28:336 My 9 '96
See also: Alexander, H.; A card from Mr. Hardy; Clark, R. H.; Jacobs, C. P.; Longstreet vs. Hardy; Mr. Thomas Hardy's novels; Orr, L.; [Pinero's "The Squire"]; Spoor, C. T. F.; Wade, J. D.; Wedmore, F.

Podewils, C.
Thomas Hardy, ein rückblick. Abendland Monatshefte 5:200-3 '30

The **poetry** of Mr. Hardy. T L S N 23 '16 p553-4; T L S D 14 '17 p603; Liv Age 292:98-102 Ja 13 '17; Liv Age 296: 202-7 Ja 26 '18

The **poetry** of Thomas Hardy. Acad 80: 350-1 Mr 25 '11

The **popular** novel. Quar R 194:250-2 Jl '01

[A **portion** of the manuscript of "Tess"] Bookm (Lond) 21:40 N '01

[**Portrait** and brief sketch of his life and works] Critic (NY) 33:438-9 D '98

[**Portraits**] Book League Monthly 1 no 2: [2] D '28; Sat R Lit 4:529 Ja 21 '28; Bookm (NY) 23:11 Mr '06; Illustrated London News 101:424 O 1 '92; Bookm (NY) 67:facing 1 Mr '28; Bookm (Lond) 21:39, 41 N '01; Liv Age 336:193 My '29; World Today 51:245 F '28; Bookm (Lond) 69:197 Ja '26; Bookm (Lond) 74:25 Ap '28; Bookm (Lond) 57:139 Ja '20; Bookm (Lond) 73:265, 267, 271 F '28; Our Day 16:100 F '96; Out 125:369 Je 23 '20; Pall Mall Magazine 23:527, 537 Ap '01; Bookm (Lond) 38:122-3 Je '10; L'Illustration 170:73 Ja 21 '28; World's Work (Lond) 16:246 Ag '10; R of Rs (Lond) 65:497 My '22; Bookm (Lond) 85:252 D '33; N Y Times D 9 '28 p2; Colby Mercury 6:12 D 1 '34; Scholastic 9:12 S 18 '26; Bookm (Lond) 61:facing 136 D '21; Bookm (Lond) 43:134 D '12; Bookm (Lond) 45:143 D '13; Bookm (Lond) 78:244 Jl

'30; Bookm (Lond) 65:156 D '23; Harper M 77:6 Je '88; Bookm (NY) 2:374 Ja '96; Bookm (NY) 9:148 Ap '99; Bookm (NY) 14:548 F '02; Bookm (NY) 15:115 Ap '02; Book B ns 9:150 My '92; Critic (NY) 38:311 Ap '01; Critic (NY) 39:136 Ag '01; Ind 61:808 Ap 5 '06; World's Work (Lond) 16:246 Ag 10; Book Monthly 1:293 F '04; Bookm (Lond) 15:140 F '99; Harper M 151:235, 243 Jl '25

Posey, Margaret Grisham
The women in the novels of Hardy. Masters essay, Vanderbilt Univ. 1928. 130ff

Powell, G. H.
The weird of Wessex. Oxford and Cambridge Review no 22:55-70 Ag '12

Powys, John Cowper
Autobiography. London, Lane [1934] passim
Thomas Hardy. *In* Visions and revisions. New York, Shaw, 1915. p213-23
Thomas Hardy and his times. Current History 27:829-31 Mr '28
Weymouth sands. New York, Simon and Schuster, 1934. 579p
(Rev by E. S. Bates in Sat R Lit 10:557 Mr 17 '34; *see also* note on this review by H. E. Hall in Sat R Lit 10:606 Ap 7 '34)

Powys, Llewelyn
Glimpses of Thomas Hardy. Dial 72:286-90 Mr '22
Thomas Hardy. *In* Thirteen worthies. London, Richards, 1924. p181-92

[**Presentation** volume given to Hardy on 80th birthday by poets] Lond Merc 1: 135-6 D '19

Preston, George Parlin
The men and women of Thomas Hardy. Masters essay, McGill Univ. 1926. 48ff

Preston, Harriet Waters
Thomas Hardy. Cent ns 24:353-9 Je '93

Priestly, L. A. M.
Bathsheba Everdene in "Far from the madding crowd." Great Thoughts Jl '97

Prilipp, Beda
Thomas Hardy: echo über die zeitungen. Hochland 25:671-3 '28
Thomas Hardys Napoleonsdrama. Die Grenzboten 66:130-6 Ap 18 '07
Thomas Hardys Napoleonsdrama. Vossische zeitung Sonntags-beilage no 20 '07

The **prince** and the poet. Liv Age 318:516-19 S 15 '23 [from Times (Lond) Jl 20 '23]

The **prince** of pessimists. T. P.'s Weekly 20:205 Ag 16 '12

Puaux, René
Thomas Hardy. Revue de France 8:572-6 F 1 '28

Puccio, Guido
Il solitario del Wessex, Tommasso Hardy. Rassegna Italiana 21:212-18 Mr '28

Pugsley, Harriet May
Social philosophy of Thomas Hardy.
Masters essay, Univ. of Washington,
1928. 34ff

Pure, Simon [pseud]
see Swinnerton, Frank Arthur

Quillemin, B.
Thomas Hardy. Magdeburgh Zeitung
'28 p33

Quiller-Couch, (Sir) Arthur Thomas
The earlier novels of Thomas Hardy. *In*
The poet as citizen, and other papers.
New York, Macmillan, 1935. p197-217

Mr. George Moore. *In* Adventures in
criticism. New York, Putnam, 1925.
p196-9

The poetry of Thomas Hardy. *In* Studies in literature. New York, Putnam,
1918. 1st ser p189-211

Ralli, Augustus John
The heart of the Wessex novels. No Am
217:688-97 My '23; *also in* Critiques.
London, Longmans, Green, 1927. p37-
48

Randell, Wilfrid L.
The Hardy critic. Acad 73:656-7 Jl 6 '07
The modern Laureate. Acad 84:740 Je 14
'13
Mystic and realist. Acad 84:228 F 22 '13

Rann, Ernest H.
The Hardy country. *In* The homeland
of English authors. London, Methuen
[1927] p68-95

Raymond, E. T. [pseud]
see Thompson, Edward Raymond

Realism. Westm 158:339 S '02

Réflexions à propos de Thomas Hardy.
Les Marges 2:165-70 Ja '06

Reilly, Joseph John
Bazin and Hardy. A study in comparison
with a contrast. Cath World 114:629-40
F '22

Bazin and Hardy: some comparisons and
a contrast. *In* Dear Prue's husband.
New York, Macmillan, 1932. p237-62

The short stories of Thomas Hardy.
Cath World 128:407-15 Ja '29

Rendall, Vernon
Thomas Hardy, O.M. Engl R 46:192-5
F '28
Wild flowers in literature. London,
Scholartis press, 1934

Repplier, Agnes
Some aspects of pessimism. Atlan 60:766
D '87

[Return of the native] Lit W 10:61 F 15
'79

Rhodes, A. J.
The Wessex of the Hardy novels. Lis-
tener 5:supp xi-xii Je '31

[Rhymed criticism of Hardy's "Wessex
poems"] Bookm (NY) 9:106 Ap '99

Ricardo, S. L.
Thomas Hardy: his philosophy and creed.
Lit R 1:83-4 '29

Ridder-Barzin, Louise de
Le pessimisme de Thomas Hardy. ("Tra-
vaux de la faculté de philosophie et
lettres de l'Université de Bruxelles,"
Tome III) Bruxelles, Éditions de la
Revue de l'Université de Bruxelles,
1932. 192p bibl p189-92
(Rev by L. Cazamian in Revue A A
10:156-7 D '32)
La vie et l'oeuvre de Thomas Hardy.
Revue de l'Université de Bruxelles 33:
315-31 F-Ap '28

Rideing, William H.
Lady St. Helier and Thomas Hardy. *In*
Many celebrities and a few others.
Garden City, N.Y. Doubleday, Page,
1912. p280-8

Ritter, Otto
Thomas Hardy und Victorien Sardou.
Engl Stud 59:159-60 F '25

R[obinson], H[erbert] S[pencer]
Thomas Hardy. [Brief life] *In* Authors
today and yesterday. Edited by Stanley J. Kunitz. New York, Wilson, 1933.
p291-6 bibl p296

Rogers, Ruth
The conception of woman implicit in the
novels of Thomas Hardy. Masters
essay, Univ. of Kansas, 1927. 118ff

Rolleston, Thomas William
Life and death: considerations on a poem
of Thomas Hardy. Hibbert J 18:275-88
Ja '20

Rörig, H.
Thomas Hardy. Kölnische Zeitung '28
p256

Rosenbach, E.
Thomas Hardy. Hochschulwissen 6:602-5
'29

Rothenstein, William (ed)
Thomas Hardy, O. M. *In* Twenty-four
portraits . . . . with critical appreciations by various hands. London, Allen
and Unwin [1920] unpaged
(2000 copies only)

**[Rowland-Brown, Lilian Kate] R. Grey
[pseud]**
Certain women of Thomas Hardy. Fortn
118:677-91 O '22

Christmas in Wessex. Cornhill 58:26-33
Ja '25

The "Jeune Premier" and Thomas Hardy.
Bookm (Lond) 69:151-5 D '25

Woman in the poetry of Hardy. Fortn
119:34-46 Ja '26

[Royal Society of Literature gold medal
given to Hardy] Ath 1:656 Je 8 '12

Roz, Firmin
Thomas Hardy. R Deux Mondes 5th ser
34:176-207 Jl 1 '06

Thomas Hardy. *In* Le roman anglais
contemporain. Paris, Hachette, 1912.
p[59]-106

Russell, Constance
Mr. Thomas Hardy's "Queen of Cornwall." Notes & Q 13th ser 1:448-9 D 8
'23

Russell, J. A.
"The Dynasts." Thomas Hardy's epic-drama. Nieuwe Gids 44:158-66 Ag '29

The poetry of Thomas Hardy. Nieuwe Gids 43:611-25 D '28

Rutherford, Mildred
Thomas Hardy. *In* English authors. Atlanta, Ga. Franklin printing and publishing co. 1906. p713-14

Rutland, William R.
"Jude the obscure." T L S D 22 '32 p977

Thomas Hardy. Montreux, Corbaz [1932] 16p

Thomas Hardy. Conférence inaugurale faite séance publique le 14 Janvier 1932 à l'Université de Lausanne. 1932

Ryan, Marjorie Jones
A comparative study of Virgil and Hardy. Masters essay, Univ. of Montana, 1930. 44ff

Ryan, W. P.
A lunar elopement: the key to Allen Gaunt's defection. *In* Literary London, its lights and comedies. London, Smithers, 1898. p40-8

Sachs, Howard J.
"The harrowing contingencies of human experience." Some reflections on Hardy. *In* Quarto Club Papers, 1927-1928. New York, Printed for the members, 1929. p41-9

St. Clair, George
Is Hardy, the poet a pessimist? New Mexico Quarterly 1:307-21 N '31

Saintsbury, George Edward Bateman
The English novel. London, Dent, 1913. p274-6

Salberg, Gerda
Thomas Hardy's frauen im lichte seiner weltanschauung. . . Mulhouse, Éditions "Alsatia," 1927. iii,52p Thesis, Zürich

Salomon, Louis B.
The devil take her. . . Philadelphia, Univ. of Penna. 1931. p181-2

Salomon, Max
Zur naturbehandlung in Thomas Hardys romanen. Giessen, Engl. Sem. 1925. 42p Diss. Giessen

Salviris, Jacob
A reading of the Wessex novels. Westm 178:400-12 O '12

Sanden, G. von
Thomas Hardy, vater des modernen romans. Die Hilfe p367 '24

Sanders, Gerald de Witt (ed)
Chief modern poets of England and America. . . New York, Macmillan [c1929] p3-5

Saxelby, F. Outwin
A Thomas Hardy dictionary; the characters and scenes of the novels and poems alphabetically arranged and described. London, Routledge, 1911. lxxviii,238p 2 maps bibl pxi-xxii

Schelling, Felix E.
The English lyric. Boston, Houghton, Mifflin, 1913. p273

Schultheis, L. M.
Thomas Hardy. Der Türmer 30: '28

Schweikert, H. C. (ed)
Short stories. New York, Harcourt [c1925] p348-9 [Collection of short stories with brief sketch of author]

Scott-James, R. A.
The pessimism of Thomas Hardy. *In* Modernism and romance. London, Lane, 1908. p57-68

Scripture, E. W.
Versformeln und betonungsprinzipien bei Hardy und Kipling. Die Neueren Sprachen 38:122-6 F-Mr '30

Seccombe, Thomas
[The Dynasts] Readers' Review 2:25 Mr '09

Segrè, Carlo
L'ultimo romanzo di Thomas Hardy. Nuova Antol 147:620-40 Je 16 '96

Selby, Thomas G.
Thomas Hardy. *In* The theology of modern fiction, being the 26th Fernley lecture delivered in Liverpool, July 1896. London, Kelly, 1896. iv,192p

Shafer, Robert
Thomas Hardy. *In* Christianity and naturalism. . . New Haven, Yale univ. press, 1926. p235-81
(Rev in Sat R Lit 2:958 Jl 24 '26; L. Hayward in Out 143:111 My 19 '26; Bost Transcript My 15 '26 p6)

Shand, J.
Tess of the Melville Bros. New Statesm 25:662-4 '30

Shanks, Edward
The "new" poetry, 1911-1925. Quar R 246:143-5 Ja '26

Sharp, William
Thomas Hardy and his novels. Forum 13:583-93 Jl '92; *same.* Bookn 12:274-6 Mr '94; *also in* Papers critical and reminiscent . . . New York, Duffield, 1912. p241-64

Shaw, (Mrs) Will Rivers
Tragic figures in Thomas Hardy's major novels. Masters essay, Univ. of Texas, 1928. 155ff

Sheldon, Georgia
A study of the irony in the works of Thomas Hardy. Masters essay, Univ. of Oklahoma, 1925

Sheppard, Alfred Tresidder
A glimpse of Thomas Hardy. Bookm (Lond) 73:319-20 Mr '28

Sherman, Stuart P.
Thomas Hardy. *In* Men of letters. . . New York, Rudge, 1924. p75-6 (530 copies only)

Sherren, Wilkinson
Thomas Hardy, O.M.—86. R of Rs (Lond) 73:555-6 Je-Jl '26

Sherren, Wilkinson—*Continued*
Thomas Hardy, O.M. The man behind the books. T. P.'s Weekly 20:231 Ag 23 '12

The Wessex of romance. London, Chapman and Hall, 1903. xi,312p bibl p305-12 (Rev by G. Douglas in Bookm (Lond) 22:104-5 Je '02; Speaker ns 6:286-7 Je 7 '02)

. . . The Wessex of Thomas Hardy. T. P.'s Weekly 18:531 O 27 '11

Shindler, Robert
Thomson—Hardy. *In* On certain aspects of recent English literature (Neuphilologische Vorträge und Abhandlung II) Leipzig, Teubner, 1902. p64-71

Sholl, Anna McClure
The novels [of Thomas Hardy] *In* The Columbia university course in literature. New York, Columbia univ. press, 1929. vol XV p60-4

Thomas Hardy. *In* Warner, C. D. (ed) Library of the world's best literature... Memorial ed. New York, Hill [c1902] vol XVII p6933-8

Thomas Hardy [with selections] *In* The Columbia university course in literature, ed. by J. W. Cunliffe and others... New York, Columbia univ. press [c1929] vol XV p19-32

Shorter, Clement K.
Victorian literature... New York, Dodd, Mead, 1897. p68
(Rev in Literary World (Lond) ns 56: 431-2 N 26 '97)

Shouse, Mary Armstrong
Thomas Hardy's treatment of women. Masters essay, Columbia univ. 1913

Shurtliff, (Mrs) Ida (Agren)
Hardy's religion and moral standards as portrayed through his novels. Bachelors essay, Univ. of Utah, 1911. 51ff

Shuster, George Nauman
Thomas Hardy. Cath World 126:721-9 Mr '28

Sime, A. H. Moncur
Thomas Hardy and music. Musical Opinion 51:1178-9 S '28

Sime, Jessie Georgina
Thomas Hardy of the Wessex novels; an essay and biographical note. Montreal, Carrier, 1928. 58p

Skillington, S. H.
Thomas Hardy. T. P.'s Weekly 18:724 D 8 '11

Slaughter, Gertrude E. T.
Hardy's poetry. *In* The Columbia university course in literature. New York, Columbia univ. press, 1929. vol XV p87-91

Small, A. F.
The art of Thomas Hardy. Honor essay, Colorado College, 1926

Smith, Clarence Jack
The quality of Thomas Hardy's pessimism and its sources as shown in "Tess of the D'Urbervilles." Masters essay, Columbia univ. 1912

Smith, Fred
Hardy: the poet of life at its worst. Personalist 15:32-8 '34

Smith, Robert Metcalf
The philosophy in Thomas Hardy's poetry. No Am 220:330-40 D '24

Snyder, Raymond Martin
Influence of architecture in the literary work of Thomas Hardy. Masters essay, Univ. of Notre Dame, 1928. 42ff

Solberg, Victor
Poetry of Thomas Hardy. Masters essay, Univ. of Kansas, 1924. 214ff

The soldiers of Thomas Hardy. T L S Ag 27 '14 p401

Some forgotten first contributions. Bookm (Lond) 16:6 Ap '99

Some poets, old and new. Harper W 46:52 Ja 11 '02

Soupault, Philippe
[Thomas Hardy] Europe 16:404-6 Mr 15 '28

Spicer-Simson, Theodore
Men of letters of the British isles; portrait medallions from the life. . . New York, Rudge, 1924
(530 copies only)

Spoor, Charles T. F.
Plagiarism on a plagiarist. Nation (NY) 34:53 Ja 19 '82 [Parallel passages taken from Hardy's "A Laodicean" and an article in Quar R for 1833 suggest plagiarism]

Squire, John Collings
Kingsway Theatre: The Dynasts. New Statesm 4:224 D 5 '14

Mr. Hardy's old age. *In* Essays on poetry. New York, Doran [1923?] p140-51

Other people's books. *In* Books in general. London, Heinemann, 1919. 1st ser p168-72

Review of Hardy's "Tess of the D'Urbervilles" at the Barnes Theatre, 1925. Lond Merc 12:650-1 O '25

Thomas Hardy. Lond Merc 17:337-41 F '28

Thomas Hardy. *In* Sunday mornings. London, Heinemann, 1930

Stäglich, Hans
Verzeichnis der schriften zum thema pessimismus für die jahre 1872-1931. Leipzig, Stäglich, 1933. 26p

Stanbury, Walter Albert
Thomas Hardy and his magazine public, 1881-1891. Masters essay, Duke Univ. 1932. 160ff

Stanley, Carleton Wellesley
Poetry of Thomas Hardy. 19th Cent 108: 266-80 Ag '30

Steinbach, A.
Thomas Hardy und Schopenhauer. (Untersuchung zur englischen philologie. Alois Brandl zum 70. geburtstage) Leipzig, Mayer und Müller, 1925. vol II p434-47

Stephens, James
An essay in cubes. Engl R 17:89-90 Ap '14

Steuart, J. A.
Letters to living authors. London, Sampson Low, 1890
(Rev in Speaker 2:530-1 N 8 '90)

Stevenson, Lionel
Thomas Hardy. *In* Darwin among the poets. Chicago, Univ. of Chicago press [1932] p237-97

Stevenson, Robert Louis
. . . On himself and his contemporaries. Critic (NY) 22:408 Je 17 '93

Stewart, Agnes
"The Dynasts." A psychological interpretation. Engl R 38:666-80 My '24

Stewart, Herbert Leslie
Thomas Hardy as an artist of character. University Magazine 17:247-61 Ap '18

Thomas Hardy as a teacher of his age. No Am 208:584-96 O '18

Stone, Ruth R.
The influence of the Bible on the major novels of Thomas Hardy. Masters essay, Smith college, 1931. 187ff typed ms.

Stopes, Marie C.
To Thomas Hardy, O. M. [poem] Nat-Ath 46:893 Mr 29 '30

Strachey, Giles Lytton
Mr. Hardy's new poems. *In* Characters and commentaries. New York, Harcourt, Brace, 1933. p181-6

Strong, (Sir) Archibald Thomas
The poetry of Thomas Hardy. *In* Four studies. . . Ed. with a memoir by R. C. Bald. Adelaide, Preece, 1932. p81-101

Sturgeon, Mary C.
Thomas Hardy. *In* Studies of contemporary poets. London, Harrap, 1920. p368-80

Sturmer, Herbert H.
In Hardy's Wessex. Liv Age 227:260-1, 395-8, 457-9, 844-5 O 27-D 29 '00

In Hardy's Wessex—Dorchester. Speaker ns 2:643 S 15 '00

In Hardy's Wessex—the Isle of Portland. Speaker ns 2:670-1 S 22 '00

In Hardy's Wessex—The Isle of Purbeck. Speaker ns 3:61-2 O 20 '00

In Hardy's Wessex—Poole. Speaker ns 5:38-9 O 12 '01

In Hardy's Wessex—Sherborne. Speaker ns 4:497-8 Ag 3 '01

In Hardy's Wessex—Wareham. Speaker ns 3:8-9 O 6 '00

Swann, George Rogers
Hardy and the dualism of will and idea. *In* Philosophic parallelisms in six English novelists. . . Philadelphia, 1929. p110-37 Diss. Univ. of Pennsylvania

Sweetkind, Morris
The element of fate in the novels of Thomas Hardy. Masters essay, Yale univ. 1923

Swinnerton, Frank Arthur
The Londoner; Mr. Shaw, Mr. Hardy, and the Nobel prize. Simon pure [pseud] Bookm (NY) 64:720-1 F '27

Syers, (Mrs) Beatrice Bell
Folk-lore in Thomas Hardy's major Wessex novels. Masters essay, Univ. of Texas, 1933. 183ff

Symons, Arthur
A note on the genius of Thomas Hardy. Sat R 102:391-2 S 29 '06; *same.* Liv Age 251:634-6 D 8 '06; *also in* Figures of several centuries. New York, Dutton [1916?] p207-15

A study of Thomas Hardy. London, Sawyer, 1927. 69p [350 copies only]

Thomas Hardy. Dial 68:66-70 Ja '20

T. P.'s referendum: who shall be Laureate?
T. P.'s Weekly 22:73 Jl 18 '13

Talmadge, Irma
The treatment of nature in the works of Thomas Hardy. Masters essay, Columbia univ. 1921

Taufkirch, Richard
Die romankunst von Thomas Hardy. Marburg, 1912. xviii,58p Diss. Marburg

Taylor, C. Ralph
The philosophy of Thomas Hardy as revealed in his novels. Masters essay, Boston Univ. 1931

Taylor, Edith Belcher
The dramatization of nature in Hardy's novels. Masters essay, Columbia univ. 1919

[Tess of the D'Urbervilles] Book B ns 9: 107-8 Ap '92

"Tess of the D'Urbervilles." Spec 68:167 Ja 30 '92

Thom, Arthur F.
A tremendous genius. T. P.'s Weekly 20:172 Ag 9 '12

Thomas, Edward
Thomas Hardy. *In* A literary pilgrim in England. New York, Dodd, Mead, 1917. p144-54

Thomas Hardy of Dorchester. *In* Poetry and drama. London, 1913. vol I p180-4

Thomas, Elizabeth Wilkins
A critical study of Thomas Hardy's "Dynasts." Masters essay, Columbia univ. 1913

Thomas Hardy. Mercure Fr 141:278-9 Jl-Ag '20; Sat R 121:323-4 Ap 1 '16; Sat R 122:394-5 O 21 '16; Aus fremden Zungen 7:46; R of Rs (Lond) 65:504-7 My '22; Dorset Natural History and Antiquarian Field Club Proceedings 49:xxv-xxix '28; New Statesm 30:459-60 Ja 21 '28; Outlook (Lond) 61:74-5 Ja 21 '28; Liv Age 261:302-9 My 1 '09; Lit W 9:46 Ag '78; Lit W 12:25 Ja 15 '81; Bookn 26:775-7 Je '08; T. P.'s Weekly 12:764 D 11 '08; Acad 76:823-6 F 27 '09; T. P.'s Weekly 20:268 Ag 30 '12; Bookman's Journal 2: 84 Je 4 '20; Speaker 2:295-6 S 13 '90; Literary World (Lond) ns 67:223-4 **Mr**

Thomas Hardy—_Continued_
6 '03; Book B ns 9:151-3 My '92;
Christian Science Monitor (Bost) Je
30 '20 p14

Thomas Hardy. _In_ Men of the time: a dictionary of contemporaries. London, Routledge, 1879. 10th ed p488-9

Thomas Hardy: a coincidence. Notes & Q 11th ser 8:481 D 20 '13

Thomas Hardy: a French view. Ath 2:771 D 3 '20

Thomas Hardy; an appreciation. World Wide F 4 '28 p95

Thomas Hardy. An appreciation, on the occasion of his seventieth birthday. Bookm (Lond) 38:122-3 Je '10

Thomas Hardy and "anti-scrape." T L S F 23 '28 p129

Thomas Hardy and his criticism of life. T. P.'s Weekly 15:738, 740 Je 10 '10

Thomas Hardy and the Nobel prize. Liv Age 321:1212 Je 21 '24

Thomas Hardy—architect. Architects' Journal 68:593 O 31 '28

Thomas Hardy at home. Engl Illus 47:276-80 Je '12

Thomas Hardy at work. Liv Age 318:428 S 1 '23

Thomas Hardy from an Italian standpoint. R of Rs (NY) 14:229 Ag '96

Thomas Hardy: his genius in the Wessex novels. New York Tribune Je 7 '96 (Answered in Critic (NY) 28:429 Je 13 '96)

Thomas Hardy; his heart in Wessex; his ashes in the Abbey [illustrated] Illus London News 172:95-7 Ja 21 '28

Thomas Hardy in Russian translation. Adel ns 5:277-9 Ja '33

Thomas Hardy: last of the Victorians. Lit Digest 96:36 F 4 '28

Thomas Hardy, O. M. World's Work (Lond) 16:239-40 Ag '10

Thomas Hardy of Wessex. Out 125:369 Je 23 '20

Thomas Hardy—optimist or pessimist? Cur Lit 53:101-3 Jl '12

Thomas Hardy, poet. Nation (NY) 121:319 S 23 '25

Thomas Hardy. What is to be learnt from his works. T. P.'s Weekly 20:143 Ag 2 '12

Thomas Hardy writes to the American Red Cross. Biblio 5:857 N-D '25

[**Thomas Hardy's** birthplace] Liv Age 324:305 F 7 '25

Thomas Hardy's genius. Literary World (Lond) ns 70:88 Jl 29 '04

Thomas Hardy's latest production—magnum opus or monstrosity? Cur Lit 44:659-62 Je '08

Thomas Hardy's novels. Westm ns 63:334-64 Ap 1 '83; T L S Ja 19 '28 p33-4

Thomas Hardy's panoramic drama. Cur Lit 40:522-3 My '06

Thomas Hardy's poetry. T L S Ja 26 '28 p49-50

Thomas Hardy's Wessex (with map) Bookm (Lond) 1:26-8 O '91

[**Thomas Hardy's** women] Acad 63:384 O 11 '02

Thommen, E.
Ein führer in englischen dingen. Schweizerische lehrerzeitung no 7 '08

Thompson, Edward Raymond [Raymond, E. T. pseud]
Thomas Hardy. _In_ Portraits of the nineties. New York, Scribner, 1921. p211-20

Thompson, Maurice
Thomas Hardy. Bookn 6:223-4 Ja '88

Thouless, Priscilla
Thomas Hardy—the Dynasts. _In_ Modern poetic drama. Oxford, Blackwell, 1934. p115-25

Tilby, A. Wyatt
The philosophy of pessimism. Edin R 228:311 O '18

Tomlinson, Henry Major
England of Hardy. New Repub 25:190-2 Ja 12 '21

Hardy at Max Gate. Sat R Lit 4:585-7 F 11 '28

One January morning. _In_ Out of soundings. New York, Harper, 1931. p255-82

Thomas Hardy. London, Crosby Gaige, 1929. 30p [Limited to 761 copies, signed, of which 550 were distributed in America by Random House]

Tomlinson, May
Jude the obscure. So Atlan Q 23:335-46 O '24

Traill, H. D.
The literature of the Victorian era. Fortn 67:835 My '97

Trent, W. P.
Mr. Thomas Hardy. Citizen (Phila) 1:284-6 F '96

The novels of Thomas Hardy. Sewanee R 1:1-25 N '92

Treves, Frederick
Highways and byways in Dorset. New York, Macmillan, 1906
(Rev in Sat R 102:393-4 S 29 '06)

Truman, Joseph
Tess and Angel Clare; poem. Bookm (Lond) 2:11 Ap '92

Tugwell, Rexford Guy
Meditation in Stinsford churchyard. Columbia University Quarterly 25:[97]-106 Je '33

Turnbull, M. M.
[Thomas Hardy and William Barnes] Two delineators of Wessex. Gent M 295:469-79 N '03

Tyndale, Walter
Hardy country: water-colours. London, Black, 1920

Wessex, painted and described. London, Black, 1906. 292p
(Rev in Speaker ns14:291-2 Je 30 '06; *same.* Liv Age 250:189-90 Jl 21 '06)

Ufer, Hanna
Über die kompositionelle bedeutung der natur bei Thomas Hardy. Marburg, 1930. ix,100p Thesis, Marburg

Untermeyer, Louis
Modern British poetry. New York, Harcourt, Brace [c1930] 3d rev ed p128-31

Utter, Robert Palfrey
The work of Thomas Hardy. *In* Pearls and pepper. New Haven, Conn. Yale univ. press, 1924. p178-93; *same.* Sewanee R 25:129-38 Ap '17

V. R. [Vernon Rendall?]
Thomas Hardy: a coincidence. Notes & Q 11th ser 8:481 D 20 '13

Valakis, Apollon Panayotis Demosthenes
Lachyrmae rerum: The Moira of Aeschylus and the Immanent will of Thomas Hardy. (Susan Anthony Potter prize essay, Harvard college, 1928) 23ff Typed ms. in Harvard college library
The moira of Aeschylus and the immanent will of Thomas Hardy. Classical Journal 21:431-42 Mr '26

Van Doren, Carl
Anatole France and Thomas Hardy. Cent 109:418-23 Ja '25
Thomas Hardy. *In* American and British literature. New York, Century [c1925] p144-9, 242-7

Van Doren, Carl and Van Doren, Mark
American and British literature since 1890. New York, Century [c1925] p144-9, 242-7

Van Doren, Mark
Thomas Hardy, poet. Nation (NY) 126:151-2 F 8 '28; *also in* Piercy, J. K. ed. Modern writers at work. New York, Macmillan, 1930. p170-4

Van Dyke, Henry
Tess of the D'Urbervilles. *In* The man behind the book: essays in understanding. New York, Scribner, 1929. p283-305

Veldkamp, J.
Thomas Hardy. Stemmen des Tijds 2:394-408 Ag '24
Thomas Hardy. Stemmen des Tijds p390-407 Ap '28
The Tristram-legend and Thomas Hardy. Neophilologus 9:286-93 Jl '24

Vincent, Leon Henry
Thomas Hardy. *In* The bibliotaph, and other people. Boston, Houghton Mifflin, 1898. p80-112

Vinciguerra, Mario
Precursori: Thomas Hardy. *In* Romantici e decadenti inglesi. . . Foligno, Campitelli [1926] p[147]-154
Thomas Hardy. Il Concilio 1:59-62 '23

Vogt, Frieda
Thomas Hardys naturansicht in seinen romanen. Hamburg, Friederichsen, de Gruyter, 1932. vi,111p Diss. Hamburg

Vowinckel, Ernst
Der englische roman der neuesten zeit und gegenwart. Berlin, Herbig, 1926. p131-8

Wade, John Donald
Augustus Baldwin Longstreet. New York, Macmillan, 1924. p178-80
[Concerning "Georgia Scenes" and "The Trumpet-Major"]

Wais, Kurt K. T.
Die pessimistische literaturgeneration von 1880. Germanisch-romanische monatsschrift 19:376-7 '31

Waldock, A. J. M.
Thomas Hardy and the Dynasts; a lecture . . . the Australian English Association, Sydney, on May 11, 1933. (Australian English association. Sydney. Leaflet, July 1933, no 16) Sydney, Privately printed . . . by Australasian medical publishing co. 1933. 35p

Walkley, Arthur Bingham
The dynasts and the puppets. *In* Drama and life. New York, Brentano, 1908. p106-14

Walmsley, J. R.
Thomas Hardy and Victor Hugo. Notes & Q 11th ser 12:240 S 25 '15

Ward, A. C.
Thomas Hardy. *In* Twentieth-century literature. . . London, Methuen [1928] p112-25

Washburn, Helen Peavy
A study of Hardy's novels. Masters essay, Cornell Univ. 1929. 232ff

Watson, E. J.
Lionel Johnson and Mr. Hardy. T L S Jl 26 '23 p504

Watson, William
Mr. Hardy's "Tess of the D'Urbervilles." *In* Excursions in criticism. New York, Macmillan, 1893. p70-80
(Rev by A. Waugh in Literary World (Lond) ns 47:331-2 Ap 14 '93)

Waugh, Arthur
War poetry. Quar R 230:384 O '18

Webb, Flora
Nature in the novels of Thomas Hardy. Essay for special honors in English, Smith College, 1927. 76ff typed ms in Smith College Library

Weber, Carl Jefferson
Care and carelessness in Hardy. Mod Lang N 50:41-3 Ja '35
A careful chronology. Writer (Bost) 46:236-7 Jl '34
Casterbridge. Fairfield publishing co. 1932
Hardy's chosen poems. Scrib M 96:111 Ag '34
Hardy's lost novel. *In* Hardy, T. Indiscretion in the life of an heiress; Hardy's last novel, now first printed in

Weber, Carl Jefferson—*Continued*
America and ed. with introduction and notes by Carl J. Weber. Baltimore, Md. Johns Hopkins press, 1935. p1-20 (Rev by C. Morley in Sat R Lit 11:551 Mr 16 '35)

History as it is written. Colby Mercury 5:37-40 F 1 '34

In the land of the D'Urbervilles. Fairfield publishing co. 1933

In Thomas Hardy's workshop. (Colby monographs: no 6) Waterville, Maine, Colby college, 1934. 64p

Mrs. Grundy's wheel-barrow. Colby Mercury 5:56-7 My '34

A note on the manuscript names of Hardy's characters. Rev E S 10:456-9 O '34

Notes on Hardy's "Chosen poems." Scrib M 96:111 '34

On the dismemberment of Tess. Sat R Lit 11:308 N 24 '34

Shakespeare's twin-voice again. Shakespeare Association Bulletin 9:162-3 Jl '34

Thomas Hardy's Aeschylean phrase. Class J 29:533-5 Ap '34

Thomas Hardy's "Song in The Woodlanders." English Literary History S '35

Twin-voice of Shakespeare. Shakespeare Association Bulletin 9:91-7 Ap '34

Weber, Carl Jefferson (ed)
Colby notes on "Far from the Madding Crowd. . ." Waterville, Maine, Dept. of English, Colby College, 1935. [5]-63p

Webster, Harvey Curtis
Borrowings in "Tess of the D'Urbervilles." Mod Lang N 48:459-62 N '33

Wedmore, (Sir) Frederick
The acting in "The Squire." Acad 21: 91-2 F 4 '82 [Mentions connection between this Pinero play and "Far From the Madding Crowd"]

The stage. "Far from the madding crowd" at the Globe Theatre. Acad 21:348 My 13 '82 [Compares Pinero's "The Squire" with Hardy's dramatized novel]

Thomas Hardy's poems. *In* Certain comments. London, Selwyn & Blount [1925] p72-4

Weiner, Joyce
Four novels of Hardy; some second impressions. Contemp 142:229-36 Ag '32

Weltzien, Erich
Die gebärden der furcht in Thomas Hardys Wessexromanen. Berlin, Wilfried Deyhle, 1927. 53p Diss. Greifswald (Rev by F. Asanger in Literatur 48:267-8 Jl-Ag '27)

Thomas Hardys anschauung vom immanenten willen. Neue Jahrbücher für Wissenschaft und Jugendbildung 5:451-65 '29

Thòmas Hardys heimatkunst. Neue Jahrbücher für Wissenschaft und Jugendbildung 4:288-303 '28

The **Wessex** drama. Edin R 215:93-112 Ja '12

The **"Wessex"** Hardy [illustrated] Bookm (NY) 35:462-3 Jl '12

West, Rebecca
Blessed are the pure in heart. Out 157: 132-3 Ja 28 '31 (Rev in Lit Digest 108:18 F 21 '31)

Interpreters of their age. Sat R Lit 1: 41-2 Ag 16 '24

Two kinds of memory. *In* Strange necessity; essays. New York, Doubleday, Doran, 1928. p265-80

Westfall, Tipton Marshall
The influence of the King James version of the Bible upon the style of Thomas Hardy. Masters essay, Ohio Wesleyan univ. 1932. 121,lviiip [Contains classified list of Hardy's biblical allusions and quotations]

Westminster Abbey
The funeral service of the late Thomas Hardy, O. M. Monday, January 16, 1928. [London, Vacher and Sons ltd. 1928] 8, [1]p

"A **Westminster Abbey** irony." Lit Digest 96:29 F 11 '28

Weygandt, Cornelius
Mastery of Thomas Hardy. *In* Century of the English novel. New York, Century, 1925. p211-28

Wheeler, Harold L. (comp)
Contemporary novels and novelists: a list of references to biographical and critical material; Thomas Hardy. *In* School of mines and metallurgy. University of Missouri. Bulletin. June 1920. Rolla, Missouri, 1921. p61-2

Whibley, Charles
Thomas Hardy. Liv Age 278:96-103 Jl 12 13; *same.* Blackw 193:823-31 Je '13

White, J. William
In Mr. Hardy's country. Nation (NY) 55:184-5, 200-2 S 8, 15 '92

Whitefriars Club
A pilgrimage to Wessex. . . 1901. [London, Lund, 1901] 28p

Whitfield, Archie Stanton
Thomas Hardy: the artist, the man and the disciple of destiny; a lecture delivered before La Société internationale de philologie, science et beaux-arts. . . London, Richards, 1921. 48p

Whitmore, Charles E.
Mr. Hardy's "Dynasts" as tragic drama. Mod Lang N 39:455-60 D '24

Why Thomas Hardy did not get the Nobel prize. Liv Age 320:381-2 F 23 '24

Widdows, Margharita
Victorian prose. *In* English literature. London, Chatto and Windus [1928] p294-5

Wild, Friedrich
Thomas Hardy und die landschaft. *In* Die englische literatur der gegenwart seit 1870. Wiesbaden, Dioskurenverlag, 1928. p159-68

Willcocks, Mary Patricia
Thomas Hardy. *In* Between the old world and the new. London, Allen and Unwin [1925] p331-51

Willcox, (Mrs) Louise (Collier)
Thomas Hardy. No Am 201:423-9 Mr '15

William L. Phelps lines up Thomas Hardy. R of Rs (NY) 73:320 Mr '26

Williams, Charles
Thomas Hardy. *In* Poetry at present. Oxford, Clarendon press, 1930. p1-17

Williams, Duane
The teachings of Thomas Hardy. University Magazine 8:253-8 Je 1 '97

Williams, Harold
Modern English writers. . . London, Sidgwick and Jackson, 1918. p55-66

The passage of the centuries. *In* Outlines of modern English literature, 1890-1914. London, Sidgwick and Jackson, 1928. p66-73

Thomas Hardy. *In* Two centuries of the English novel. London, Smith, 1911. p283-303

The Wessex novels of Thomas Hardy. No Am 199:120-34 Ja '14

Williams, Orlo
On Thomas Hardy. Nat R 97:267-75 Ag '31

Williams, Randall
The Wessex novels of Thomas Hardy; an appreciative study. London, Dent, 1924. xi,157p (Noted in T L S Ja 1 '25 p11)

Williams, Rose Mary Urner
Thomas Hardy, John Masefield, and Wilfrid Wilson Gibson as poetic interpreters of life. Masters essay, Univ. of California, 1923. xii, 160ff

Williamson, Claude C. H.
Thomas Hardy. *In* Writers of three centuries, 1789-1914. Philadelphia, Jacobs [1915?] p314-21

Wilson, Samuel Law
The theology of Thomas Hardy. *In* The theology of modern literature. Edinburgh, Clark, 1899. p379-408

Windle, (Sir) Bertram Coghill Alan
The Wessex of Thomas Hardy. London, Lane, 1906. xxiv,332p (Rev in Literary World (Lond) ns 64: 545 D 27 '01; Nation (NY) 73:401-2 N 21 '01; H. H. Sturmer in Speaker ns 5: 617-18 Mr 1 '02; G. Douglas in Bookm (NY) 14:527-9 Ja '02 and in Bookm (Lond) 21:59 N '01)

Wolfe, Humbert
Dialogues and monologues. London, Gollancz, 1928. p86-9

Wood, Butler
. . . Song mentioned in "Tess of the D'Urbervilles." Notes & Q 13th ser 1:29 Jl 14 '23

Wood, William
More on Hardy. Sat R Lit 2:666 Mr 27 '26

Woolf, Leonard Sidney
Thomas Hardy. Nat-Ath 42:597-8 Ja 21 '28

Woolf, (Mrs) Virginia (Stephen)
Novels of Thomas Hardy. *In* Second common reader. New York, Harcourt, Brace, 1932. p266-80

Wright, Edward
The novels of Thomas Hardy. Quar R 199:499-523 Ap '04; *same.* Live Age 241: 456-71 My 21 '04

Wynd, Catherine
Fate and Hardy's women. Masters essay, Boston Univ. 1930

Yeager, Fannie Sophie
A psychological analysis of the characters in Hardy's novels. Masters essay, Univ. of Oklahoma, 1932. 86ff

Yendell, N. C.
On the pessimism of Thomas Hardy. Poetry Review 26:289-93 Jl-Ag '34

A young poet and an old one. Liv Age 314:367-8 Ag 5 '22

Zachrisson, Robert Eugen
Ett sammanträffande med Thomas Hardy och Wells. Dagens Nyheter N 9 '20 p5

Hardy. *In* Modern engelsk världsåskådning i litteraturers spegel. Stockholm and Uppsala, Almquist and Wiksells förlag, 1928. 176p

Stil och personlighet i Thomas Hardys diktning. Edda 20:57-98 '23

Thomas Hardy as man, writer, and philosopher; an appreciation, with a Swedish Hardy bibliography. Uppsala, Almquist and Wiksells förlag [1928] 31p bibl p29-31. *Also in* Nyfilologiska sällskapet i Stockholm. Studier i modern språkvetenskap 10:131-59 '28 (Rev by P. Aronstein in Bei Anglia 40: 174-5 Jl '28; T L S Ag 23 '28 p607; Lond Merc 18:348 Ag '28)

Thomas Hardy, en författare värd Nobelpris. Den engelska litteraturen konsekvent förbigången. . . Dagens Nyheter N 19 '19 p9

Thomas Hardy's twilight view of life. A study of an artistic temperament. Nyfilologiska sällskapet i Stockholm. Studier i modern språkvetenskap 11: 217-33 '31. *Also published:* Uppsala, Almquist and Wiksells förlag, 1931. 17p (Rev in T L S Ap 13 '33 p263)

Till frågan om årets litterära Nobelpris. Social-Demokraten N 30 '20

Trollkarlen från Wessex. *In* Studiekamraten. 1928

Zimmerman, (Mrs) I. C. M.
Thomas Hardy's theory of love. Diss. Univ. of Southern California, 1935. 312ff

Rudyard Kipling

Rudyard Kipling

I. Chronological Outline

Rudyard Kipling

II. Bibliographical Material

American Art Association, New York
An English collection of first editions of Rudyard Kipling. . . New York, American art association [1928] [109]p

Carter, John and Pollard, Graham
Rudyard Kipling. *In* An enquiry into the nature of certain nineteenth century pamphlets. London, Constable, 1934. p199-204

Chandler, Lloyd Horwitz
Index to Kipling library of Lloyd Horwitz Chandler. [Bryn Mawr? Pennsylvania. 1926] 68ff Typed ms in the New York Public Library

A Kipling problem. "Three and—an extra." Colophon part 4:[8 pages] D '30

List of magazines, newspapers, periodicals, etc. containing items of the work of Rudyard Kipling; items of work that have been attributed to him; and items written by others about him or about his work. [Washington ? D.C. 1933] 78ff Typed ms in the New York Public Library

A summary of the work of Rudyard Kipling, including items ascribed to him. . . New York, The Grolier club, 1930. xi-xxvii,465p (325 copies only)

[Clarke, William James] Monkshood, G. F. [pseud]
The less familiar Kipling and Kiplingiana. New York, Dutton, 1917. p59-[168]

The courting of Dinah Shadd: a contribution to a bibliography of the writings of Rudyard Kipling. New York, Marion press, 1898

Cripps, Matthew
Kipling in America. Notes & Q 9th ser 9:5-6 Ja 4 '02

Dalrymple, Cochrane M.
Bibliography. *In* Kiplings prosa. (Marburger Studien zur englischen Philologie. Heft 9) Marburg, Gleiser, 1905. p89-102 Diss. Marburg

Doubleday, Page and Company, New York
The Kipling index; being a guide to the authorized American trade edition of Rudyard Kipling's works. . . Garden City, New York, Doubleday, Page [c1919] iv,99p

Fabes, Gilbert H.
Modern first editions: points and values. London, Foyle [1929] p38-40
(750 copies only)

Fabes, Gilbert H. and Foyle, William A.
Modern first editions: points and values. London, Foyle [1931] 2d ser p47-8

Ferguson, J. De Lancey
Rudyard Kipling's letters of travel. Notes & Q 11th ser 9:325 Ap 25 '14

Uncollected Kipling items. [additions to and corrections of the bibliography compiled by A. W. Young in Notes & Q] Notes & Q 11th ser 9:134-5 F 14 '14

Firebrace, C. W.
Uncollected Kipling items. . . Notes & Q 12th ser 6:178 My 1 '20

First Edition Club, London
A bibliographical catalogue of the first loan exhibition of books and manuscripts held by the First Edition Club, 1922. London, The First Edition club, 1923. p178

Grolier Club, New York
Catalogue of the works of Rudyard Kipling exhibited at the Grolier Club from February 21 to March 30, 1929. New York, The Grolier club, 1930. [vii]-xi,201p 34 plates. (325 copies only)

Hopkins, Robert Thurston
Appendices [many bibliographical] *In* Rudyard Kipling; a literary appreciation. New York, Stokes [1916] p299-[349]

Lesser known Kiplingiana. Bookman's Journal 2:37-8 My 14 '20

Kipling's "American notes." Book-Lover (San Francisco) 2:14 '00

Kipling's correction of a biblical reference. Bookman's Journal 8:5 Ap '23

Knowles, Frederick Lawrence
Bibliography. *In* A Kipling primer. . . Boston, Brown, 1899

Lane, John
A bibliography of Rudyard Kipling. *In* Le Gallienne, Richard. Rudyard Kipling: a criticism. London, Lane, 1900. pi-xlvi

Livingston, Flora Virginia (Milner)
Bibliography of the works of Rudyard Kipling. New York, Wells, 1927. xviii,523p

A footnote to bibliography. Colophon part 7:[4 pages] S '31

Livingston, Luther Samuel
The first books of some English authors. IV. Rudyard Kipling. Bookm (NY) 10:329-37 D '99

Kipling's suppressed works. Bookm (NY) 9:62-3 Mr '99

The works of Rudyard Kipling: the description of the first editions of his books in the library of a New York collector. New York, Dodd, Mead, 1901. 92p

Lucas, Perceval
Uncollected Kipling items. Notes & Q 11th ser 9:416 My 23 '14

McCutcheon, George Barr
The renowned collection of first editions of Thomas Hardy, Rudyard Kipling, Robert Louis Stevenson. . . New York, American art association [1925]

Mansfield, Milburg Francisco and Wessels, A.
Kiplingiana. New York, Mansfield and Wessels [1899] p163-88

Martindell, Ernest Walter
A bibliography of the works of Rudyard Kipling (1881-1921). London, Bookman's Journal, 1922. xiii,111p (450 copies only)

A bibliography of the works of Rudyard Kipling (1881-1923). London, Lane, 1923. xvi,222p new ed
(Noted in T L S D 6 '23 p853; Bookman's Journal 9:115 D '23)

Fragmenta condita: the unrecorded portion of my Kipling collection; Appendix to A bibliography of the works of Rudyard Kipling. Ashford, Middlesex, Privately printed, 1922. 56p

A remarkable and comprehensive collection of the writings of Rudyard Kipling, the property of Captain E. W. Martindell. . . [London, 1921] 30p

Maybury, John
The Kipling bibliography. Book B ns 13:955 Ja '97

Millett, Fred B.
Rudyard Kipling. In Contemporary British literature. . . New York, Harcourt, Brace, 1935. p305-15

Mr. Kipling and others. Notes on sales. T L S My 5 '27 p324

Mr. Kipling's early work [with bibliography] Lit W 31:30-1 Ja 20 '00

Monkshood, G. F. [pseud]
see Clarke, William James

New Kipling collation ["Verses"] Bookman's Journal 13:184-5 F '26

News for bibliophiles [first editions] Nation (NY) 85:226-7 S 12 '07

North, Ernest Dressel
A bibliography of first editions of Kipling. Book B ns 13:593-5 N '96; same. R of Rs (NY) 15:183 F '97

Notes of rare books; a check list of first editions of Rudyard Kipling. Book B ns 19:191-2 O '99

Northup, Clark Sutherland
A register of bibliographies of the English language and literature. New Haven, Yale univ. press, 1925. p221-2

Norton, Charles Eliot
Books by Rudyard Kipling. McClure's Magazine 13:285 Jl '99; same. Windsor Magazine 11:68 D '99

Note on American Art Galleries, New York, sale. Notes & Q 154:38 Ja 21 '28

Notes on sales. T L S Mr 20 '24 p180

Overton, Grant Martin
Kipling's career [with bibliography of first editions] Bookm (NY) 61: 73 Mr '25

Page, Curtis Hidden
Kipling; list of references. In British poetry of the nineteenth century, ed. by Curtis Hidden Page; new ed. by Stith Thompson. New York, Sanborn, 1930. p968-9

Palmer, John Leslie
A short bibliography of Rudyard Kipling's principal writings. In Rudyard Kipling. New York, Holt [1915] p117-21

Petrie, James A.
Kipling's "Recessional." Bookman's Journal 9:72 N '23

Powell, F. York
Rudyard Kipling [bibliography of both works and criticism] Engl Illus 30:298, 429-32 D '03, Ja '04

Prideaux, William Francis
Kipling in America. Notes & Q 9th ser 9:89-91 F 1 '02

Mr. Kipling's Allahabad books: a bibliographical essay. Notes & Q 9th ser 1:101-3 F 5 '98

Quinn, John
The library of John Quinn. . . New York, Anderson Galleries, 1924. part III p501-15

A rare bit of Kiplingiana. Bookm (NY) 25:561 Ag '07

Rivett-Carnac, J. H.
Uncollected Kipling items. Notes & Q 11th ser 9:34-5, 309-10 Ja 10, Ap 18 '14; Notes & Q 12th ser 7:4, 216-17, 389 Jl 3, S 11, N 13 '20

Uncollected Kipling items: quatrain on G. W. Steevens. Notes & Q 12th ser 7:78 Jl 24 '20

Uncollected Kipling items: "With Number Three": "Surgical and Medical." Notes & Q 12th ser 6:258-9 My 29 '20

Roberton, William
Bibliography. *In* The Kipling guide book. Birmingham, Holland book co. 1899. p43-51

Sanborn, M. Ray
Uncollected Kipling items. Notes & Q 11th ser 9:416 My 23 '14

Sargent, G. H.
[Pirated "In Sight of Mount Monadnock"] Bookman's Journal 8: 6-7 Ap '23

Saxton, Eugene F. (compiler)
The Kipling index; being a guide to the authorized American trade edition of Rudyard Kipling's works. Garden City, New York, Doubleday, Page, 1911. 44p For later edition see: Doubleday, Page and Company, New York

Sidwell, Joseph (compiler)
Rudyard Kipling, poet and storyteller; a bibliography. [Coventry, Public libraries committee, 1925]

Sotheby, Wilkinson and Hodge, London
Catalogue of valuable books . . . and comprehensive collection of the writings of Rudyard Kipling. . . Monday, April 4, 1921. . . [London, Sotheby, Wilkinson and Hodge, 1921] 86p

Taylor, Harvey
Bibliography. *In* Norris, Frank. Two poems, and "Kim" reviewed. With a bibliography. . . San Francisco, Harvey Taylor, 1930. 21 leaves

Thompson, James Westfall
News for bibliophiles ["The Rhyme of the Three Captains"] Nation (NY) 94:130-1 F 8 '12

Uncollected Kipling items [signed "J. R. H."] Notes & Q 11th ser 9:309-10 Ap 18 '14

Williamson, G. M.
Collection of works of Rudyard Kipling. New York, 1915

Woods, George Benjamin
[Bibliography] *In* Poetry of the Victorian period. New York, Scott, Foresman [c1930] p1074-7

Young, Arthur W.
Uncollected Kipling items. Notes & Q 11th ser 8:441-2, 464-5, 485-6 D 6, 13, 20 '13

Rudyard Kipling

III. Biographical and Critical Material

A la manière de. . . Kipling. Mercure Fr 162:563-4 '23

A propos d'une visite incognito de Rudyard Kipling. Mercure Fr 170:567-8 '24

Aas, L.
Rudyard Kipling. En biografisklitteraer introduksjon. For Folkeoplysning 9: 11-14, 54-60 '24

Abbott, Lyman
Kipling and S. S. libraries. Lit W 30: 298 S 16 '99

"The **Absent-minded** Beggar." Argonaut 46:8 F 12 '00; Sat R 89:139-40, 173-4 F 3, 10 '00

The **accuracy** of Kipling. Liv Age 326:71-2 Jl 4 '25

Ackerley, Fred G.
Parodies of Kipling and the poet laureate. Notes & Q 10 ser 12:238 S 18 '09

Adams, Francis
The Anglo-Indian story-teller. *In* Essays in modernity. . . London, Lane, 1899. p85-115

Mr. Rudyard Kipling's verse. Fortn 60: 590-603 N '93; *also in* Essays in modernity. London, Lane, 1899. p187-216

Rudyard Kipling. Fortn 56:686-700 N '91; *same.* Ecl M 118:47-56 Ja '92

Adams, John D.
Rudyard Kipling. Book B ns 13:589-92 N '96

Adcock, Arthur St. John
Rudyard Kipling. Canadian Magazine 61:204-7 Je '23; *also in* Gods of modern Grub Street. New York, Stokes [c1923] p153-9

A. E. [pseud]
see Russell, George William

An **afternoon** at Rottingdean. Great Thoughts Ja '02

Ainger, Alfred
Mr. Kipling on Shakespeare. Spec 81: 82 Jl 16 '98

Alexander, E.
Kipling and his critics. Lit 6:192 Mr 3 '00

Allen, James Lane
Two principles in recent American fiction. Atlan 80:441 O '97

An **amateur** critic of Kipling. Argonaut (San Francisco) 41:8 Ag 16 '97

Anderson, J. D.
Rudyard Kipling and his critics. Lit 6: 191-2 Mr 3 '00

Anderson, W. Monro
[Poem answering Kipling's "The Islanders"] Bookm (NY) 12:14-15 Mr '02

Reply to Kipling's "Islanders." *In* Rhymes of a rouseabout. London, Heinemann, 1913

Anderton, Isabella M.
Un nuovo romanziere inglese; Rudyard Kipling. La Rassegna Nazionale 78: 535-50 Ag 16 '94

[**Anecdote** concerning Kipling] T. P.'s Weekly 26:79 Jl 24 '15

Angeli, Diego
Il poeta dell'impero. Rudyard Kipling. L'Italia Coloniale '00

Rudyard Kipling. Rassegna Contemporanea 1:44-58 Ja '08

Another betrothed [a parody signed "Hib"] Outlook (London) 8:271 S 28 '01; *same.* Bookm (NY) 14:215-16 N '01

Another great wax-work tableaux for Brussels [caricature] Punch 139:157 Ag 31 '10

[**Answer** to Kipling's poem "Tommy Atkins"] Critic (NY) 34:403 My '99

Archer, William
Rudyard Kipling. *In* Poets of the younger generation. London, Lane, 1902. p220-50

Arnauld, Michel
Kipling et Pierre Mille. La Nouvelle Revue Française 8:925-9 N 1 '12

Arnell, C. J.
The ideal laureate. Decachord 7:444-6 N-D '30

Aronstein, P.
Rudyard Kipling. Vossische Zeitung. Sonntagsbeilage Berlin no 14 '99

Around the world with Kipling. . . Garden City, N.Y. Doubleday, Page, 1926. 3-121p

Assmann, F. W.
Rudyard Kipling (por.) Boekenschouw 21:261-70 O '27

Aulhorn, Edith
Vom englischen Soldatenlied. Germanisch-Romanische Monatsschrift 8:29-44 Ja-F '20

Auslander, Joseph and Frank Ernest Hill
The winged horse. Garden City, N. Y. Doubleday, Doran, 1930. p390-5

Austin, Henry
The Kipling hysteria. Dial 26:327-8 My
16 '99

Autolycus [pseud]
see Bacon, Leonard

Babbitt, Irving
Romanticism and the Orient. Bookm
(NY) 74:352-4 D '31

Back numbers—CI. Sat R 146:727 D 1 '28

[Bacon, Leonard] Autolycus [pseud]
Rudyard Kipling. Sat R Lit 4:677-8 Mr
17 '28

Bacon, Thomas R.
Literary bondage. Impressions Quarterly 6:77-9 D '05

Baker, Harry T.
Kipling and his captains. Nation (NY)
94:183-4 F 22 '12
Poetry and the practical man. Forum
42:227-36 S '09
Will Kipling's poetry survive? Meth R
88:231-8 Mr '06

Balfour, A. J.
Truth and fiction [Royal society of liter-
ature award to Rudyard Kipling] Liv
Age 330:361-4 Ag 14 '26

A ballad (In the manner of R-dy-rd
K-pl-ng). Munsey's Magazine 16:755
Mr '97

The ballad of the young bard; poem.
Speaker 1:288-9 Mr 15 '90

Ballad poetry. Edin R 197:319-20 Ap '03

Bands for the million. Spec 114:187-8 F 6
'15

Bangs, John Kendrick
Bob La Follette (With apologies to the
author of "Danny Deever.") Life 70:
788 N 15 '17

Bannier, H.
Rudyard Kipling. . . Action Française F
28 '14

Banqueting with Barrie and Kipling. Liv
Age 326:427-8 Ag 22 '25

Barber, Cecil
Kipling as critic. Nat R 89:907-18 Ag '27

Barr, Amelia E.
Kipling and S. S. libraries. Lit W 30:
299 S 16 '99

Barrie, James M.
Mr. Kipling's stories. Contemp 59:364-72
Mr '91

Barroso, Gustavo
see Rudyard Kipling na Academia
Brasileira

Barry, John D.
[Popularity of Kipling] Lit W 30:120 Ap
15 '99

Bartels, A.
Rudyard Kipling. Deutsche Monats-
schrift für den Gesamte Leben den
Gegenwart p728-35 F '03

Batterham, Eric
A lost poem by Kipling. Notes & Q 12th
ser 2:409 N 18 '16

Baumgartner, A.
Rudyard Kipling. . . Stimmen aus Maria-
Laach 57:535-48 N 28 '99

[Bazley, Basil Mercer] Basil Mercer
[pseud]
Railways in art and literature. Railway
Magazine 42:244-5 Ap '18

Becher, Johannes Alexander
Untersuchungen über Kiplings erzäh-
lungskunst. . . Marburg an der Lahn,
Seidel, 1913. 71p Diss. Marburg

Beerbohm, Max
Kipling's entire. Sat R 95:198-9 F 14 '03
P.C., X, 36. By R*D**RD K*PL*NG.
In A Christmas garland. London,
Heinemann, 1921. p13-20

Bennett, Arnold
Rudyard Kipling. In Books and persons. . . London, Chatto and Windus,
1917. p160-6

Benson, Arthur Christopher
The Upton letters. New York, Putnam
[1910] 2d ed rev p100-8

Benson, Mary
Reminiscences of the Kipling family.
Sunday Magazine 28:822-6 D '99

Bentzon, T. [Blanc, Marie T.]
L'Armée anglaise peinte par Kipling. In
Questions américaines. Paris, Hach-
ette, 1901. p178-232
Un Roman de Rudyard Kipling. R Deux
Mondes 3d ser 110:612-45 Ap 1 '92

Beresford, G. C.
Kipling's schooldays. Book Notes 5:
173-7 Je-Jl '27

Berlage, Heinrich
Ueber das englische soldatenlied in der
zweiten hälfte des 19. jahrhunderts mit
besonderer berücksichtigung der solda-
tenlieder Rudyard Kiplings. Emsdet-
ten, Lechte, 1933. vi,50p Diss. Münster

Besant, Walter
Again on "The Hooligan." Lit 6:113 F
3 '00
Is it the voice of the Hooligan? Contemp
77:27-39 Ja '00
see also Buchanan, Robert and Besant,
Walter

[Besant, Hardy and Black] Bookm (NY)
35:121 Ap '12

Birch, Lionel
Rudyard Kipling. Manch Q 37:70-83, 197-
207 Ap, Jl '18; same. Papers of the
Manchester Literary Club 44:70-83,
197-207 '18

The birth of literature. Liv Age 249:701-3
Je 16 '06; Outlook (London) 17:647-8
My 12 '06

Bishop, William Henry
Mr. Kipling's work, so far. Forum 19:
476-83 Je '95

The black man's burden; poem. [signed
"G. F. B."] Speaker ns 7:491 F 14 '03

Blackburn, Vernon
Barrack-room ballads. National Observer 7:675 My 14 '92

Kipling. Literary Opinion Ag '91

Blacks and whites in South Africa. Public Opinion (Lond) 87:459 Ap 14 '05

Blair, Wilfred
A battle of the bards. *In* Poets on the Isis, and other perversions. Oxford, Blackwell, 1910

Stalky's school-song; poem. *In* Sa Muse, s'amuse. Oxford, Blackwell, 1913

Blakemore, Trevor
Rudyard Kipling: the poet of reality. Poetry Review 1:165-7 Ap '12

Blanc, Marie T.
see Bentzon, T.

Bland, John
Kipling's Norns. Acad 72:298 Mr 23 '07

Blaze de Bury, Yetta
Rudyard Kipling. *In* Les romanciers anglais contemporains. Paris, Perrin, 1900. p101-12

Bok, Edward K.
Authors who write too much. Ladies' Home Journal 8:15 My '91

Bolton, Sarah K.
Kipling and S. S. libraries. Lit W 30:298 S 16 '99

Books, books books; Rudyard Kipling. New Yorker 8:58-61 Ap 30 '32

Bordeaux, Henry
Un lauréat du prix Nobel—M. Rudyard Kipling. Le Correspondant 229:1164-82 D 25 '07

Rudyard Kipling. *In* Quelques portraits d'hommes. . . Paris, Fontemoing [1913] 2d ed p231-64; *same in* Portraits d'hommes. Paris, Plou-Nourrit [c1924] p83-119

Borgese, G. A.
Kipling e un suo critico. *In* La vita e il libro. 1913. 3d ser

Bosdari, Alessandro de
Rudyard Kipling; poeta e prosatore. Nuova Antol 163:443-63 F 1 '99

Studi di litterature straniere. 1929

Bragman, Louis J.
Laënnec and Culpeper as depicted by Kipling. Annals of Medical History 9:129-31 '27

Rudyard Kipling on public health. American Journal of Public Health 16:609-11 Je '26

Brandeis, Alois
Das englische heer und sein dichter [Rudyard Kipling] *In* Festschrift zum viii allgemeinen deutschen neuphilologentage. . . Wien, 1898. p159-78

Brandl, Alois
Thomas Hardy und Rudyard Kipling. Cosmopolis 6:579-94 My '97

Brandt, M. von
Rudyard Kipling. Deutsche Rundschau 100:384-401 S '99

Braybrooke, Patrick
Kipling and his soldiers. . . London, Daniel [1926] 180p

Rudyard Kipling. *In* Philosophies in modern fiction. London, Daniel, 1929. p47-51

Brenan, Gerald
Kipling's home at Rottingdean. Temple Magazine My '99

Brenner, Rica
Rudyard Kipling. *In* Ten modern poets. . . New York, Harcourt, Brace [c1930] p[193]-224

Bridges, Albert Foster
The British private in the colonies as portrayed by Kipling. Masters essay, George Peabody College, 1932. 232ff

Bridges, Robert
Kipling. Out 61:281-4 F 4 '99
. . Wordsworth and Kipling. *In* Collected essays, papers. . . London, Milford, 1933. [vol II] no XIII p27-38; *same.* T L S F 29 '12 p81-2; *same.* Liv Age 273:77-81 Ap 13 '12

Bridgman, Helen Bartlett
Rudyard Kipling. *In* Within my horizon. Boston, Small, Maynard [c1920] p89-94

Brie, Friedrich
Imperialistische strömungen in der englischen literatur. Halle, Niemeyer, 1928. p220-32

Brion, Marcel
Les romans de Kipling. Cahiers du Sud 15:332-44 Je '29

Rudyard Kipling. (Essais critiques, artistiques, philosophiques, littéraires. vol 14) Paris, La Nouvelle Revue Critique [1929]. [5th ed] 224p

Brodmann, C.
Rudyard Kipling in deutschem Gewande. Die Gegenwart 53:218-20 Ap 2 '98

Brodribb, C. W.
"Reward." Notes & Q 150:191 Mr 13 '26

Brown, E. I.
Burma and Kipling. Masters essay, Univ. of Southern California, 1926. 62ff

Brown, F. L. Rudston
The significance of Rudyard Kipling. Key to London 3:57-9 F '28

Brownell, George Hiram
Mr. Kipling sets us right. American Book Collector 5:43-7 F '34

Brulé, A.
Une leçon de style: les variantes du "Livre de la Jungle." Revue A A 9:417-28 Je '32

Bruno, A.
A proposito di un appello di Rudyard Kipling. La Rassegna Agraria, Industriale, Commerciale '06

Bryan, J. Ingram
The philosophy of English literature. Tokyo, Maruzen [1930] p267-70

Bryden, Robert
Some woodcuts of men of letters of the nineteenth century. London, Dent, 1899

Buchanan, Robert
The dismal throng; a poem. Idler 3:607-12 Jl '93

The ethics of criticism. A word to Sir Walter Besant. Contemp 77:221-30 F '00

The voice of "the Hooligan" [a criticism of Rudyard Kipling] Contemp 76:774-89 D '99

Buchanan, Robert and Besant, Walter
The voice of "the Hooligan"; a discussion of Kiplingism. (The Bacon library no 3) New York, Tucker publishing co. [1900] 59p

Bugbee, L. E.
The contribution of Rudyard Kipling to the short story. Masters essay, Boston Univ. 1925

Bullough, Geoffrey
The trend of modern poetry. Edinburgh, Oliver and Boyd, 1934. p10-11

Bury, Yetta Blaze de
see Blaze de Bury, Yetta

Business; poem [financial success of Kipling] Munsey's Magazine 26:593 Ja '02

Caine, T. H.
The mother of the man. Cleveland, Ohio, 1911. [A reply to Kipling's "The female of the species," from Cleveland *Plain Dealer,* November 7, 1911]

Cameron, Agnes Deans
Kipling and the children. Anglo-American Magazine 8:14-21 D '02; *same.* Engl Illus ns 30:470-4 Ja '04

Campbell, Bertha Belle
Kipling's women. Masters essay, State Univ. of Iowa, 1919. 56ff

Campbell, Mary Inez
The technique of Kipling's verse. Masters essay, Univ. of Texas, 1932. 114ff

Cant, G.
Bermuda en Rudyard Kipling. Buiten p177-8 Ap '31

Cantell, I. K.
A study of the moral implications in Rudyard Kipling's stories about and for children. Masters essay (Education), Univ. of Southern California, 1935. 68ff

[Caricature] Acad 57:663 D 9 '99

[Caricature by Beerbohm] Bookm (Lond) 40:209 Ag '11 (from "Poets' corner")

Carpenter, W. M.
Kipling's college, being an account of Kipling's school days at the United Services college, and giving a facsimile of pages of one of his school books, in which Kipling has made numerous crude sketches, extracts from the school magazine. . . 1929

Carping Kipling. Scholastic 9:14 O 16 '26

Carr, Kent
The Laureate of greater Britain. Atalanta O '97

Carter, John and Pollard, Graham
Rudyard Kipling. *In* An enquiry into the nature of certain nineteenth century pamphlets. London, Constable, 1934. p199-204

The **case** of Mr. Kipling. Sat R 87:776-8 Je 24 '99

Castellanos, Jesús
Rudyard Kipling. Cuba Contemporánea 1:11-37 Ja '13

Castelnuovo, Enrico
Un apostolo della forza. Atti del Reale Instituto Veneto di Scienze, Lettere ed Arti 60 pt 2:311-16 '00-'01

Cather, (Mrs) Katherine Dunlop
The lad who understood hearts. *In* Younger days of famous writers. New York, Century [c1925] p289-301

Cautley, L. R.
Kipling notes. Conservative Review 5: 78-83 Mr '01

Cecchi, Emilio
L'arte di Rudyard Kipling; dai "Plain Tales" a "The Light that failed." Nuova Antol 235:58-71 Ja 1 '11

Rudyard Kipling. Firenze, Casa editrice italiana, 1910. 75p

The **censorship** of poetry [amending Kipling] Ind 84:171 N 1 '15

Cestre, Charles
Rudyard Kipling et la plus grand Angleterre. Revue Internationale de l'Enseignement 69:37-50 Ja 15-F 15 '15

Chandler, Lloyd Horwitz
A summary of the work of Rudyard Kipling, including items ascribed to him. . . New York, The Grolier Club, 1930. xi-xxvii,465p

Chapman, Edward Mortimer
The newer fiction. *In* English literature in account with religion, 1800-1900. Boston, Houghton Mifflin, 1910. p533-61

Charles, Cecil
Rudyard Kipling; his life and works. London, Hewetson [1911] 19-49p

Chesterton, Gilbert Keith
On Mr. Rudyard Kipling and making the world small. *In* Heretics. London, 1909. 6th ed p38-53

Chevalley, Abel
The modern English novel; transl. from the French. . . by B. R. Redman. New York, Knopf [c1925] p149-56

Le roman anglais de notre temps. London, Oxford, 1921. p74-5, 145-52

Chevrillon, André
Le cas de Rudyard Kipling. Revue de P 15:817-30 F 15 '08

Nouvelles études anglaises. Paris, 1910. p191-211

La poésie de Rudyard Kipling. R Deux Mondes 6th ser 56:871-901 Ap 15 '20; ibid, 57:69-101, 371-411 My 1, 15 '20; *same in* Trois études de littérature

Chevrillon, André—*Continued*
anglaise. Paris, Plou-Nourrit [1921] 6th ed p1-162
(Rev by B. Fehr in Bei Anglia 32:269-70 D '21; T L S Je 5 '21 p383)

Rudyard Kipling. Revue de P 6:34-74, 621-53 Mr 1, Ap 1 '99

Rudyard Kipling. *In* Études anglaises. (Bibliothèque de littérature) Paris, Hachette, 1920. 4th ed p155-246

Rudyard Kipling as a Frenchman sees him. *In* Around the world with Kipling. Garden City, N.Y. Doubleday, Page, 1926. p61-76; *same in* Three studies in English literature. . . trans. from the French by F. Simmonds. London, Heinemann [1923] p1-152
(Rev by R. E. Roberts in Bookm (Lond) 64:89-90 My '23)

Chubb, Edwin Watts
Stories of authors: British and American. New York, Macmillan, 1926. rev ed

[City of brass; extract] Cur Lit 47:332 S '09

Clark, James M.
The English novel, 1870-1910. Germanisch-Romanische Monatsschrift 5:675-6 D '13

Clark, John Scott
Rudyard Kipling. *In* A study of English and American writers. New York, Row, Peterson [c1916] p634-45

[Clarke, William James] Monkshood, G. F. [pseud]
The less familiar Kipling and Kiplingana. London, Jarrold, 1917. 167p

Rudyard Kipling. An attempt at appreciation. . . (English writers of to-day. no 1) London, Greening, 1899. viii,11-236p
(Rev in Literary World (Lond) ns 59: 500-1 Je 2 '99)

Clarke, William James and Gamble, George
Rudyard Kipling. London, Greening, 1902. 3d ed with a new chapter [first issued c1899]

Clemens, William Montgomery
A ken of Kipling. Being a biographical sketch. . . with an appreciation and some anecdotes. New York, New Amsterdam book co. 1899. 141p

Cobb, Gerard F.
Rudyard Kipling. Lit 1:183 N 27 '97

Cobb, Irvin S.
Kipling at home. *In* Around the world with Kipling. Garden City, N.Y. Doubleday, Page, 1926. p13-15

Coffin, Harrison C.
Kipling and Horace [a note on splendide mendax] Classical Weekly 15:32 O 24 '21

Colby, Frank Moore
The writer who does not care. Bookm (NY) 15:85-7 Mr '02; *same in* Imaginary obligations. New York, Dodd, Mead, 1904. p25-32

Comerford, J.
The "Absent-minded beggar." Sat R 89:79-80 Ja 20 '00

Rudyard Kiplingism. Sat R 89:427-8 Ap 7 '00

The **contradictory** elements in Rudyard Kipling. Cur Lit 44:274-6 Mr '08

Cooke, Britton B.
Two talks with Kipling. Collier's 48:18 N 4 '11

Cooper, Anice Page
Rudyard Kipling. . . New York, Doubleday, Page, 1926. 100p
(Contains "Kipling index," p[47]-[99])

Rudyard Kipling—a biographical sketch. *In* Around the world with Kipling. Garden City, N.Y. Doubleday, Page, 1926. p19-41

Cooper, Belle
Kipling as the poet of ocean and empire. Masters essay, Univ. of Southern California, 1921. 88ff

Cooper, Frederic Tabor
Rudyard Kipling. *In* Some English story tellers. New York, Holt, 1912. p122-47
(Rev in Nation (NY) 96:311-12 Mr 27 '13)

Cope, Goring
The books of Rudyard Kipling. Gent M ns 49:136-46 Ag '92

Corelli, [Marie]
Patriotism—or self-advertisement? A social note on the present war. Philadelphia, Lippincott, 1900. 63p

Corfield, Wilmot
Parodies of Kipling. Notes & Q 10th ser 12:472 D 11 '09

Uncollected Kipling items: Padgett. Notes & Q 11th ser 9:93 Ja 31 '14

Cornford, L. Cope
Mr. Kipling's army of a dream. Spec 92: 1011 Je 25 '04

Cornwall, Charles Henry
The people of Rudyard Kipling's fiction. Masters essay, Univ. of Texas, 1931. 196ff

Coryell, Hubert V.
Authors every boy should know. Good Housekeeping 100:38-9, 98 Ja '35

[Couplet concerning Kipling and Haggard] Bookm (Lond) 1:30 O '91

[Criticism of "Captains courageous"] Bookm (NY) 5:183 My '97

Crockett, S. R.
On some tales of Mr. Kipling's. Bookm (NY) 1:23-5 F '95; *same.* Bookm (Lond) 7:139-40 F '95

Crooke, W.
Kipling and the swastika. Notes & Q 11th ser 2:239 S 17 '10

Ovington and Kipling. Notes & Q 10 ser 9:248 Mr 28 '08

Crosby, Ernest H.
The bugler in the rear. [To Rudyard Kipling]; poem. Arena 22:536-7 O '99

[Crosland, Thomas William Hodgson]
McNeill, Angus [pseud]
The egregious English. New York,
Putnam, 1903. p59-64, 104-6

Five notions. London, Richards, 1903.
94p

Crüwell, Gottlieb August
Kiplings ahnen. Die Zeit 24:56-8 Jl 28
'00

Kiplings gedichte. Die Zukunft 33:368-78
S 1 '00

Rudyard Kipling. Ueber Land und Meer
82:454-5 Ap '99

The cult of Kipling. Month 95:28-33 Ja '00

Cunliffe, John William
English literature in the twentieth cen-
tury. New York, Macmillan, 1933. p25-8
Late Victorian novelists. *In* Leaders of
the Victorian revolution. New York,
Appleton-Century [c1934] p295-301
Rudyard Kipling. *In* English literature
during the last half-century. . . New
York, Macmillan, 1919. p151-60 bibl
p160 *same* 2d ed rev and enlarged: New
York, Macmillan, 1923. p169-77

Currall, Howard S.
Kipling's poetry. Central Literary Magazine Jl '20 p246-57

Cury, Petty
"The new Kipling." Outlook (Lond) 2:
430 N 5 '98

Cushing, Harvey
The life of Sir William Osler. Oxford,
Clarendon press, 1925. 2 vols passim

Cutler, B. D.
Publishers and pirates. Bookm (NY)
75:172-5 My '32

Dalrymple, Cochrane M.
Kiplings prosa. (Marburger Studien zur
englischen Philologie. Heft 9) Marburg, Gleiser, 1905. 102p bibl p89-102
Diss. Marburg

Danchin, F. C.
Songs of the sea. Les Langues Modernes
Je '28 p314-24

Davis, P. R.
Rudyard Kipling. African Monthly 4:
457-71 O '08

Davray, Henry D.
Rudyard Kipling et son temps. Mercure
Fr 215:257-93 O 15 '29

Rudyard Kipling in France. Outlook
(Lond) 2:790 Ja 21 '99

The dawn of Rudyard Kipling. Bookm
(Lond) 16:5-6 Ap '99

Dawson, William James
Kipling. Young Man Ap '91

Quest and vision. London, Hodder &
Stoughton, 1892

Deane, (Canon) Anthony C.
Rudyard Kipling. British Weekly 88:
421 Ag 21 '30

Delmer, F. Sefton
Rudyard Kipling. Z F E U 1:281-5 '02

De Noailles, Comtesse
see Noailles, Comtesse de

Dickinson-Wildberg
Kiplings neues dschungelbuch. Litera-
turberichte Internationale 4:215 '97-'98

Diebow, Paul
Kiplings "Seven Seas" mit proben in
nachdichtungen. Ein beitrag zur
charakteristik des dichters. Oschers-
leben, Kreisblatt, 1904. 41p

Dilly Tante [pseud]
see Kunitz, Stanley J.

Dixon, James Main
Kipling's world message. Meth R 5th
ser 36:525-41 Jl '20

Wells versus Kipling. Personalist 2:97-
105 Ap '21

Dobell, Clarence M.
"The Rowers." Spec 90:14 Ja 3 '03

Dobrée, Bonamy
Modern prose style. Oxford, Clarendon
press, 1934. p24-8

Rudyard Kipling. Monthly Criterion 6:
499-515 D '27

Rudyard Kipling. *In* The lamp and the
lute; studies in six modern authors. . .
Oxford, Clarendon Press, 1929. p45-65

Dole, Nathan Haskell
Life of Rudyard Kipling. *In* Barrack
room ballads and other poems by
Rudyard Kipling. New York, Crowell
[c1899] p vii-xix

Life of Rudyard Kipling. *In* The poems
of Rudyard Kipling. . . New York,
Crowell [c1928] p vii-xxvi

[Dooley and Kipling] Bookm (NY) 38:587-
8 F '14

Douady, Jules
La mer et les poètes anglais. Paris,
Hachette, 1912. p309-31

Doubleday, Page and Company, New York
The life and works of the world's most
versatile author—Rudyard Kipling. . .
[192-?] [16]p

Dowden, Edward
The poetry of Mr. Kipling. Critic (NY)
38:219-24 Mr '01; *same*. New Liberal
Review F '01

Dowson, Herbert
Kipling: reference wanted. Notes & Q
12th ser 7:78 Jl 24 '20

Dual personalities. Literary World (Lond)
ns 68:128-9 Ag 21 '03

Dunsterville, Lionel C.
Rudyard Kipling als kind en jongeling.
De Nieuwe Rotterdamsche Courant D
10, 24, 31 '27

"Stalky" settles down. London, Jarrolds,
1932. [7]-288p

Stalky's reminiscences. London, Cape
[1928] 5-298p

Durand, Ralph Anthony
A handbook to the poetry of Rudyard
Kipling. . . Garden City, N. Y. Double-
day, Page, 1914. xix,386p
(Rev in Ath 2:605 D 5 '14; T. P.'s
Weekly 24:558 N 21 '14)

Eastgate, George
Rudyard Kipling and his critics. Lit 6: 248 Mr 24 '00

Eaton, Harriet P.
An American girl's reply to Kipling's criticisms. Bookman's Journal 3:404 Ap 1 '21

Edgar, Pelham
English poetry since Tennyson. University Magazine 7:263-5 Ap '08

Egan, Maurice Francis
Of Rudyard Kipling. Ind 51:2269-71 Ag 24 '99

Ehrentreich, Alfred
Kiplings Runenschrift. Archiv 160:89-90 S '31

English, John
Wireless; poem. Spec 119:385 O 13 '17

English amenities. Bookm (NY) 16:110, 113 O '02

The **English** novel in the nineteenth century. Edin R 196:503 O '02

Entwhistle, Joseph
Kipling and Freemasonry. Masonic Trestle Board (San Francisco) Je '32

Ernest-Charles, J.
Les samedis littéraires. 1905. vol III

Erstlingswerke von Rudyard Kipling in ihrer bedeutung für sammler. Börsenblatt für den deutschen Buchhandel no 118 '02

[**Estimate** of Kipling's work] Bookm (NY) 5:5-6 Mr '97

An **Eton** boy on "Stalky & co." Outlook (Lond) 4:368 O 21 '99

Eve stood at the garden gate. Notes & Q 9th ser 9:114 F 8 '02

Eves, Anna
Relation of Kipling's "Jungle book" and "Just so stories" to Indian folk-lore. Masters essay, Columbia univ. 1911

Eyre, (Lady) Alice
By the way: essays on various subjects. London, Nisbet, 1920

Fabulet, Louis
Les "Livres de la Jungle" et le scoutisme. Mercure Fr 209:745-53 F 1 '29

Une lettre. . . de Kipling. Mercure Fr 152:792-3 '21

Mr. Kipling and his French readers. World's Work 11:455-8 Ap '08

Mr. Kipling in French. World's Work 15:9925-7 F '08

Rudyard Kipling. Le Figaro D '07

Facsimile of a page of the original manuscript of Kipling's "The light that failed." Bookm (NY) 38:600 F '14

[The **fad** of Kipling] Harper M 81:801-2 O '90

Falls, Cyril
Rudyard Kipling: a critical study. (Martin Secker's ser of modern monographs) London, Secker, 1915. 11-207p
(Rev in Spec 114:373-4 Mr 13 '15; S. Butterworth in Bookm (Lond) 48:77-8

Je '15; T L S Mr 18 '15 p92; Ath 1: 326-7 Ap 10 '15; New Statesm 4:620 Mr 27 '15)

Fauley, Wilbur Finley
Rudyard Kipling's new home [at Rottingdean] Harper's Bazaar 33:2030-2 D 8 '00

Fehr, Bernhard
Die englische literatur des 19. und 20. Jahrhunderts. Wildpark-Potsdam, 1928. p325-6, 379-85

Ferguson, John De Lancey
The education of Rudyard Kipling. Educa 45:171-82 N '24

A note on The foreloper. Bookm (NY) 39:26-9 Mr '14

The poetry of Rudyard Kipling. Forum 50:396-411 S '13

Rudyard Kipling's letters of travel. Notes & Q 11th ser 9:134-5, 325 F 14, Ap 25 '14

Rudyard Kipling's revisions of his published work. J Engl & Germ Philol 22:114-24 Ja '23

Ferguson, Rachel
Celebrated sequels: a book of parodies. London, Cape, 1934

Firebrace, C. W.
Uncollected Kipling items: "With Number Three": "Surgical and Medical." Notes & Q 12th ser 6:178 My 1 '20

The **first** faint signs of a national awakening. R of Rs (Lond) 25:147-9 F '02

Fitch, George Hamlin
Kipling's best short stories and poems. *In* Modern English books of power. San Francisco, Paul Elder, 1912. p140-9

Fletcher, C. R. L. and Kipling, Rudyard
see Kipling, Rudyard and Fletcher, C. R. L.

Floyd, Isobel Henderson
The wisdom of the male; poem. Leslie's Weekly 113:613 N 30 '11

Folts, Grace Abbott
Analysis of Kipling's art in description. Masters essay, Univ. of Nebraska, 1914. 83ff

Forbes, Edgar Allen
Across India with Kim. World's Work 24:639-49 O '12

Foreign authors in America. Bookm (NY) 13:378 Je '01

Forster's notebook on Kipling. Birmingham, Holland co. [1898]
(Noted in Literary World (Lond) ns 58:453 D 9 '98)

France honors Kipling. Lit Digest 116:22 Jl 29 '33

Freeman, L. R.
The inimitable cruelty of Kipling. Overland Monthly ns 43:311-16 Ap '04

Frey, H.
Über ein unbekanntes weltberühmtes buch. Freimaurer-Zeitung 12:186 '30

Friedrich, Ernst
Kipling und die bewegung der "Boy Scouts." Neuphilologische Monatsschrift 4:333-6 S '33

Frierson, William C.
L'influence du naturalisme français sur les romanciers anglais de 1885 a 1900. Paris, Giard, 1925. p168-72

Frost, Edwin Collins
To the reader. *In* A letter from Rudyard Kipling on a possible source of The Tempest, with an epistle to the reader. . . Providence, Privately printed, 1906. p7-14

Furniss, Dorothy
Quiet Burwash where Kipling dwells. Country Life in America 38:67-8 Je '20

Furniss, Harry
A few new features for the House of Lords. Cassell's Magazine 35:663 My '03

Impressions of Rudyard Kipling. I. Strand Magazine 65:225-8 Mr '23

[The further adventures of "Stalky & co."] Bookm (NY) 8:186-8 N '98

Galbreath, D. L.
"Stalky and Co." by Rudyard Kipling. Notes Q 12th ser 7:118 Ag 7 '20

Gales, R. L.
Three jingle-makers [Belloc, Chesterton, Kipling] *In* Studies in Arcady. . . London, Herbert and Daniel, 1912. 2d ser p322-32

Galletti, Alfredo
Rudyard Kipling. *In* Studi di letteratura inglese. Bologna, Zanichelli, 1918. p291-347

Galsworthy, John
Times, tides, and taste. Sat R Lit 2:360 D 5 '25

Gamble, G.
see Clarke, William James and Gamble, G.

Gardiner, Alfred G.
Rudyard Kipling. *In* Prophets, priests and kings. London, Dent [pref 1914] p324-30; *also in* Taylor, Warner (ed) Essays of the past and present. . . New York, Harper [c1927] p444-50

Garland, Hamlin
A dinner with Kipling. *In* Roadside meetings. New York, Macmillan, 1930. p168-74

Kipling returns to America. *In* Roadside meetings. New York, Macmillan, 1930. p402-14

Roadside meetings of a literary nomad. . . Bookm (NY) 70:521-3 Ja '30; ibid 71: 306-7 Je '30

Genung, George F.
An apocalypse of Kipling. Ind 51:888-91 Mr 30 '99

German, Edward
The just so song book, being the songs from Rudyard Kipling's Just So Stories set to music. New York, Doubleday, Page, 1903. 62p

Gerould, Katharine (Fullerton) (Mrs. Gordon Hall Gerould)
The remarkable rightness of Rudyard Kipling. Atlan 123:12-21 Ja '19; *also in* Modes and morals. New York, Scribner, 1920. p254-78

Gilman, Frank Gaylord
Rudyard Kipling as a poet. Arena 20:312-22 S '98

Gilmer, Harold W.
The classical element in the poems of Rudyard Kipling. Classical Weekly 14: 178-81 Ap 25 '21

Glachant, Victor
Étude sur Rudyard Kipling, chantre de la grande guerre (1914-1918) Paris, Librairie de France, 1922. 60p

Glardon, A.
Romanciers anglais contemporains. Rudyard Kipling. Bibliothèque Universelle et Revue Suisse 3d period 58:492-526 Je '93; 59:46-78 Jl '93

Gleeson, J. M.
. . . An interpretation of Kipling's Jungle book; pictures. Outing 49:facing 288 D '06

Gorham, Wallace A.
Rudyard [a humorous poem on Kipling's verse] Midland Monthly 11:223 Mr '99

Gosse, (Sir) Edmund William
Mr. Rudyard Kipling's short stories. *In* Questions at issue. London, Heinemann, 1893. p255-93

Rudyard Kipling. Cent ns 20:901-10 O '91

Gould, Elizabeth Porter
Kipling and S. S. libraries. Lit W 30:299 S 16 '99

Graham, Erin
Kipling the colonial. Anglo-American Magazine 8:14-20 S '02

Graham, Stephen
Rudyard Kipling. *In* The death of yesterday. London, Benn [1930] p79-85

Grand, Sarah [pseud]
see MacFall, (Mrs) Haldane
Une **grande** voix d'Angleterre. J Débats 40 pt 1:439-40 Mr 17 '33

Graves, Robert
Rudyard Kipling. *In* Rickword, E. ed. Scrutinies. London, Wishart, 1928. p73-93

Graz, Friedrich
Beiträge zu einer kritik Rudyard Kiplings. Leipzig, 1898; *same.* Engl Stud 24:392-411 '98; *same* [translated]. Liv Age 221:139-50 Ap 15 '99

Der neue Kipling. Die Zeit 25:55-6 O 27 '00

The **great** interpreter. Spec 82:302-3 Mr 4 '99

Green, H. M.
Kipling as a journalist. Australian Quarterly no 13:111-20 Mr 14 '32

Kipling as a verse-maker. Australian Quarterly no 16:112-18 D 14 '32

Grey, Rowland [pseud]
see Rowland-Brown, Lillian Kate

Grieg, Nordahl
Rudyard Kipling and the British empire.
Edda 27:75-108, 196-249 '27

Griswold, Hattie Tyng
Rudyard Kipling. *In* Personal sketches
of recent authors. Chicago, McClurg,
1898. p266-80

Groom, Bernard
A literary history of England. London,
Longmans, Green, 1929. p359-60

Guedalla, Philip
The Irish guards. *In* Supers and super-
men. New York, Putnam, 1924. p307-
13

Mandalay. *In* A gallery. London, Putnam, 1924. p28-34

Gwynn, Stephen
Kipling as poet and prophet. Pilot O 10
'03

Hagemann, Gustav
Rudyard Kipling. Z F E U 25:50-4 '26

Hagen, Luise
Rudyard Kipling. Westermanns Illus-
trierte Deutsche Monatshefte 86:504-12
Jl '99

Haldeman-Julius, Emanuel
Rudyard Kipling's twelve immortals.
Haldeman-Julius Quarterly 1:119-23 Ja
'27

Hall, Frank O.
Kipling and S. S. libraries. Lit W 30:
298 S 16 '99

Hall, H. F.
Rudyard Kipling and his critics. Lit 6:
173-4, 212-13 F 24, Mr 10 '00

Hamilton, Cosmo
Rudyard Kipling. *In* People worth talking about . New York, McBride, 1933.
p21-8

The **handbooking** of Rudyard Kipling. Cur
Opin 58:48 Ja '15

Hankin, St. John
Lost masterpieces and other verses.
London, Constable, 1904. p30-1 [Paro-
dies of Kipling]

[Hankinson, Charles James] Holland, Clive
[pseud]
Rudyard Kipling and his critics. Lit 6:
153-4, 192-3 F 17, Mr 3 '00

Harris, Amanda B.
Kipling and S. S. libraries. Lit W 30:
299 S 16 '99

Harris, Frank
Contemporary portraits. New York, The
author [c1919] 2d ser p45-63; *same.*
Pearson's Magazine 37:412-17 My '17

Guy de Maupassant. Papyrus 3d ser, vol
2, no 2:3-4 Je '11

Hart, Walter Morris
Kipling, the story-writer. . . (Semi-
centennial publications, 1868-1918)
Berkeley, Univ. of California press, 1918.
225p
(Rev in Sat R 126:894-5 S 28 '18)

Has Kipling declined? Ind 63:522-4 Ag 29
'07

Haultain, [Theodore] Arnold
From Tennyson to Kipling. Canadian
Magazine 30:533-6 Ap '08

Hawthorne, Hildegarde
"Kim." St Nicholas 44:1032-4 S '17

Rudyard Kipling, maker of magic. St
Nicholas 42:348-50 F '15

Hearn, Lafcadio
Rudyard Kipling. *In* A history of English literature, in a series of lectures.
Tokyo, Hokuseido press, 1927. vol II
p795-809

Hegner, Wilhelm
Die impressionistische syntax bei Kipling. . . Borna-Leipzig, Noske, 1929.
viii,56p Thesis, Freiburg i. Br.

Heilborn, Ernst
Vom heiligen thier. Die Nation (Berlin)
15:55-8 O 23 '97

Hellier, William
Kipling and a literary mystery. Bookman's Journal 2:199 Jl 23 '20

Hellman, George S.
Animals in literature. Atlan 87:391-7 Mr
'01

Henderson, Archibald
Kipling. . . Bee-News (Omaha, Nebraska)
Ag 12 '28

Rudyard Kipling. *In* Contemporary immortals. . . New York, Appleton, 1930.
p194-[209]

Henderson, W. J.
Our "White man's burden"; poem.
Criterion 20:16 F 11 '99

Henley, William Ernest
Mr. Kipling and the "muddied oafs."
Sphere 8:88 Ja 25 '02

Hensel, P.
Rudyard Kipling. Die Wahrheit 7:116-
25 '97

Herzl, T.
Rudyard Kipling. Neue Freie Presse
no 3 '99

Heydrick, Benjamin A.
Echoes and growth in Rudyard Kipling.
Poet Lore 14:84-94 O '02

[Highlander's meeting with Kipling] Cur
Lit 28:141 My '00

Hilliard, John Northern
Where I discovered Rudyard Kipling.
Overland Monthly ns 81:20-2 Je '23

Hinchman, Walter Swain
Kipling, pioneer. *In* Pedestrian papers.
Boston, Houghton, Mifflin, 1928. p123-8

Hind, Charles Lewis
Rudyard Kipling. *In* Authors and I. New
York, Lane, 1921. p166-70

Hirsch, Charles Henry
[Kipling and Swinburne] Mercure Fr 41:
511-13 F '02

[History of the "Just So" stories] Book B
ns 20:185-6 Ap '00

Hoaxing wise editors; Jack London's experience; magazine competition. Town Talk 15:12 O 13 '06

Hodgson, A. J.
The philosophy of Rudyard Kipling. Liverpool Philamathic Society Proceedings 65:iii-xxxi '20

Holland, Clive [pseud]
see Hankinson, Charles James

Holthof, L.
Rudyard Kipling. Aus Fremden Zungen 9:383

The **home** of Rudyard Kipling, Batesman, Burwash, Sussex. House & Garden 41:36-7 Mr '22

Hooker, (William) Brian
The later work of Mr. Kipling. No Am 193:721-32 My '11

Hopkins, Robert Thurston
Kipling and the men of Sussex. Bookman's Journal and Print Collector 3: 110-11 D 10 '20

The Kipling country; with drawings by Irvine B. Bately and Gordon Volk. [London] C. Palmer [c1924] xii,263p (Noted in T L S My 15 '24 p308)

Kipling landmarks at Burwash. Bookman's Journal & Print Collector 3:18 O 29 '20

Kipling of today in his Sussex home. National Magazine 57:232 F '29

Kipling's Indian days. Bookman's Journal & Print Collector 3:349-50 Mr 11 '21

Kipling's Sussex. . . London, Simpkin, Marshall, Hamilton, Kent, 1921. viii,9-252p
(Rev by A. B. Maurice in New York Times My 22 '21 p4; E. F. Edgett in Bost Transcript My 7 '21 p6; Literary Review My 7 '21 p12; E. L. Pearson in Weekly Review 4:438 My 7 '21)

Kipling's Sussex revisited; [with line drawings by Godfrey T. Hopkins] London, Jenkins [1929] 255p

My first book. . . Bookm (Lond) 79:184 D '30

Rudyard Kipling; a character study; life, writings and literary landmarks. . . London, Simpkin, Marshall, Hamilton, Kent [1921] 3d ed 251p

Rudyard Kipling; a literary appreciation. New York, Stokes [1916] xiv,356p
(Rev in T.P.'s Weekly 27:51-2 Ja 15 '16)

Rudyard Kipling: a survey of his literary art. London, Digby, Long, 1914. x-xii, 13-192p
(Rev in Acad 87:259-60 Ag 29 '14; Bookm (Lond) 47:56 N '14)

Rudyard Kipling and Burwash. Bookm (Lond) 67:6-8 O '24; same. Liv Age 323:342-4 N 8 '24

Rudyard Kipling, the story of a genius. . . [London] Palmer [1930] 211p

Rudyard Kipling's world. . . London, Holden, 1925. 278p

The **horror** tales of Mr. Kipling. Bookm (NY) 12:330 D '00

Howells, William Dean
The laureate of the larger England. McClure's Magazine 8:453-5 Mr '97

The new poetry. No Am 168:582-4 My '89

Humières, (Vicomte) Robert d'
A visit to Rudyard Kipling. In Through isle and empire. transl. by A. T. De Mattos. New York, Doubleday, Page, 1905. p95-101

Humphry, H. Pearl
Mr. Kipling's "They." Acad 67:392 O 29 '04

Hutchison, Percy Adams
"The bridge builders"; poem. Bookm (NY) 9:259 My '99

Hutton, Maurice
Kipling. McGill University Magazine 17: 589-618 D '18

Kipling. In Many minds. New York, Holt, 1928. p110-42

The **Indian** mutiny in fiction. Blackw 161: 231 F '97

Is Kipling a plagiarist? [similarity between Emerson's "Woodnotes" and Kipling's "The Recessional"] J Ed 50: 304 N 9 '99

Jackson, Holbrook
Rudyard Kipling. In The eighteen-nineties. New York, Mitchell Kennerley, 1914. p280-95

James, Henry
Introduction. In Mine own people and In black and white, by Rudyard Kipling. Philadelphia, Wanamaker [189-?] p5-18

Mr. Kipling's early stories. In Views and reviews. Boston, Ball, 1908. p225-41

Jamieson, Herbert
Rudyard Kipling. Acad 57:463 O 21 '99

"Jane's marriage." Notes & Q 151:407 D 4 '26

Jasienski, Alexander M.
Wspólczesni powiesciopisarze Angielscy. Warsaw, Paprocki, 1897
(Rev in Literary World (Lond) ns 56: 130 Ag 20 '97)

Jeanroy-Felix, Victor
Rudyard Kipling. In Études de littérature étrangère. Paris, Bloud et Barral [1901] p169-223

Jesson, Thomas
A lost poem by Kipling. Notes & Q 12th ser 2:495 D 16 '16

Johnson, Lionel Pigot
Rudyard Kipling: Barrack-room ballads. In Reviews and critical papers. . . New York, Dutton, 1921. p32-40

Rudyard Kipling: Life's handicap. In Reviews and critical papers. . . New York, Dutton, 1921. p24-31

Rudyard Kipling: the light that failed. In Reviews and critical papers. . . New York, Dutton, 1921. p17-23

Johnson, M.
Kipling as a novelist. Primitive Methodist Quarterly O '99
Kipling as a poet. Primitive Methodist Quarterly Ap '00

Johnson, R. Brimley
A letter from England. Atlan 87:64 Ja '01

Johnston, Charles
The paganism of Kipling. Literary Era ns 8:161-4 Mr '01
Rudyard Kipling. Calcutta Review O '99

Jonius, Wilhelmus
A Spanish estimate of Kipling. Bookm (NY) 42:675-7 F '16

Jordan, Mary Augusta
Rudyard Kipling and clearness. Mod Lang N 5:417-23 N '90

Kellner, Leon
Die englische literatur der neuesten zeit. . . Leipzig, Tauchnitz, 1921. p340-54
Die englische literatur im zeitalter der königin Viktoria. Leipzig, Tauchnitz, 1909. p592-604

Kernahan, Coulson
Rudyard Kipling. *In* Six famous living poets. London, Butterworth, 1922. p53-93

Ketcham, Henry
Biographical sketch. *In* The poems of Rudyard Kipling. New York, Burt [c1900] p vii-xxiv

Kilman, Julian
Kipling and O. Henry. Editor 55:65-6 O 8 '21

Kim and the critics. Bookm (NY) 14:328 D '01

Kim and the letter-writer. Literary World (Lond) ns 64:329 N 1 '01

Kimball, Arthur Reed
A story of Rudyard Kipling. Ind 44:473 Ap 7 '92

Kingsley, Rannulph
Rudyard Kiplingism. Sat R 89:106-7, 204 Ja 27, F 17 '00

Kinnosuké, Adachi
A Japanese view of Kipling. Arena 21:699-715 Je '99

Kinsella, E. P.
Impressions of Rudyard Kipling. Strand Magazine 65:228-31 Mr '23

Kipling, Rudyard
Abaft the funnel. New York, Doubleday, Page, 1909. 323p
(Rev in Nation (NY) 89:460-1 N 11 '09)
Actions and reactions. London, Macmillan, 1909. 302p
(Rev in Ath 2:453-4 O 16 '09; Acad 77:681-2 O 30 '09; Cur Lit 48:225-6 F '10; Nation (NY) 89:460-1 N 11 '09; T.P.'s Weekly 14:519 O 22 '09; W. H. Hodgson in Bookm (Lond) 37:99-100 N '09)

Barrack-room ballads and other verses. London, Methuen, 1892. ix-xix,208p
(Rev in Nation (NY) 55:11 Jl 7 '92; Lit W 23:214-15 Je 18 '92; Critic (NY) 21:15 Jl 9 '92; W. M. Payne in Dial 13:186 S 16 '92; National Observer ns7:630-1 My 7 '92; Literary World (Lond) ns 45:475-6 My 20 '92; Spec 68:644-5 My 7 '92; G. A. Simcox in Bookm (Lond) 2:86-7 Je '92; Sat R 73:580-1 My 14 '92; Ath 1:629 My 14 '92; Edin R 178:498-9 O '93; L. Johnson in Acad 41:509-10 My 28 '92; A. T. Quiller-Couch in Engl Illus 10:901-3 '92-'93; Lond Q R 89:325-36 Ja '98; Ind 45:1761 D 28 '93)

A book of words. Selections from speeches and addresses delivered between 1906 and 1927. London, Macmillan, 1928. vii,299p
(Rev by A. Brulé in Revue A A 6:272-3 F '29; T L S Ap 26 '28 p301; A. Kinross in Bookm (Lond) 74:105-6 My '28; Contemp 133:803-4 Je '28)

Captains courageous. A story of the Grand Banks. London, Macmillan, 1897. 246p
(Rev in Nation (NY) 66:15-16 Ja 6 '98; Deutsche Rundschau 96:317-18 '98; Literary World (Lond) ns 56:349-50 N 5 '97; Spec 79:646-8 N 6 '97; Ath 2:589-90 O 30 '97; Acad 52:359 O 30 '97; Lit 1:81-2 N 6 '97; Dial 23:344 D 1 '97; Critic (NY) 31:264-5 N 6 '97; Atlan 80:855-7 D '97; Harper M 95:962-3 N '97; N. H. Dole in Book B ns 15:357-60 N '97; A. Macdonell in Bookm (Lond) 13:47-8 N '97; W. B. Parker in Atlan 80:855-7 D '97; Bookm (NY) 6:366-7 D '97; Ind 49:1622 D 9 '97; Lond Q R 89:389-90 Ja '98; Citizen (Phila) 3:239-40 D '97)

Collected verse
(Rev in T L S Ag 20 '08 p268; Nation (NY) 86:75-7 Ja 23 '08; Ath 2:655 N 30 '12; D. Scott in Bookm (Lond) 43:143-6 D '12; Ind 70:47 Ja 5 '11; Spec 109:905 N 30 '12)

The courting of Dinah Shadd and other stories. New York, Harper, 1890. 182p
(Rev in Lit W 21:378 O 25 '90; Ind 42:1458 O 16 '90)

The day's work. London, Macmillan, 1898. 381p
(Rev in Literary World (Lond) ns 58:253-4 O 14 '98; H. W. Preston in Atlan 83:136-7 Ja '99; Acad 55:76-7 O 15 '98; Cosmopolis 12:390 N '98; Die Nation (Berlin) 16:677-9 Ag 26 '99; Spec 81:526-8 O 15 '98; Ath 2:521-2 O 15 '98; Lit 3:350-1 O 15 '98; F. C. Mortimer in Book B ns 17:298-300 N '98; H. T. Peck in Bookm (NY) 8:350-1 D '98; Macmil 79:131-5 D '98; Out 60:492-3 O 22 '98; Nation (NY) 67:431-2 D 8 '98; Bookm (Lond) 15:52-3 N '98; Lit W 29:398 N 26 '98; J. von Keyserlingk in Das Litterarische Echo 1:324-5 D 1 '98; W. E. Henley in Outlook (Lond) 2:403-4 O 29 '98)

Debits and credits. London, Macmillan, 1926. vi,416p
(Rev by E. Wilson in New Repub 48: 194-5 O 6 '26; B. Matthews in Literary Digest International Book Review 4: 745-6 N '26; R. Wolf in Nation (NY) 123:509-10 N 17 '26; T L S S 16 '26 p611; M. H. Hirst in Central Literary Magazine Ja '27 p9-15; E. Rosenbach in Engl Stud 62:452 My '28)

Departmental ditties. Lahore, Civil and Military Gazette press, 1886. 29 leaves
(Rev in Nation (NY) 52:321 Ap 16 '91; Harper M 82:318 Ja '91; W. W. Hunter in Acad 34:128-9 S 1 '88; Acad 51:476-7 My 1 '97; Ath 1:527-8 Ap 26 '90; Critic (NY) 17:317 D 20 '90; Spec 65: 345-6 S 13 '90; W. M. Payne in Dial 11:312-13 F '91)

A diversity of creatures. London, Macmillan, 1917. 442p
(Rev by J. Macy in Dial 62:441-2 My 17 '17; Spec 118:461-2 Ap 21 '17; Nation (NY) 104:632 My 24 '17)

The eyes of Asia. New York, Doubleday, Page, 1918. 102p
(Rev in Dial 65:502 N 30 '18; Nation (NY) 107:629 N 23 '18)

Five nations. London, Methuen, 1903. 216p
(Rev in Literary World (Lond) ns 68: 227-8 O 2 '03; Sat R 96:548-9 O 31 '03; Spec 91:522-4 O 3 '03; Ath 2:474-5 O 10 '03; H. T. Peck in Bookm (NY) 18:307-9 N '03; B. Perry in Atlan 92: 843-7 D '03; Bookm (Lond) 25:90-4 N '03; C. A. Moody in Out West 20:297 Mr '04; W. M. Payne in Dial 35:355-6 N 16 '03; Acad 65:319-20 O 3 '03; Ind 55:2464-5 O 15 '03; W. Archer in Critic (NY) 43:436-9 N '03; F. T. Cooper in World's Work 7:4138-40 N '03; S. Gwynn in Liv Age 239:440-3 N 14 '03; same. Pilot 8:344-5 O 10 '03; same. Ecl M 142:44-7 Ja '04)

A fleet in being. London, Macmillan, 1898. 84p
(Rev in Lit 3:589-90 D 24 '98; Spec 81: 952 D 24 '98; Literary World (Lond) ns 58:503 D 23 '98)

The fox meditates. London, Medici Society, 1933. 8p
(Rev in T L S D 7 '33 p877)

France at war. London, Macmillan, 1915. 76p
(Rev by C. Merki in Mercure Fr 113: 728 F 16 '16; Ath 2:415 D 4 '15; Spec 115:698 N 20 '15; Nation (NY) 102:171-2 F 10 '16)

The fringes of the fleet. London, Macmillan, 1915. 74p
(Rev by J. B. Kerfoot in Life 67:354 F 24 '16; Spec 116:10-11 Ja 1 '16; Nation (NY) 102:171-2 F 10 '16)

From sea to sea and other sketches; letters of travel. London, Macmillan, 1900. 2 vols 498p; 438p
(Rev by L. S. Livingston in Bookm (NY) 9:429-32 Jl '99; Acad 58:219-20

Mr 17 '00; Ath 1:272 Mr 3 '00; Lit 6: 208-9 Mr 10 '00; Lit W 30:211 Jl 8 '99; H. M. Stanley in Dial 27:16 Jl 1 '99; Spec 84:415-17 Mr 24 '00; Literary World (Lond) ns 61:214-15 Mr 9 '00; Bookm (Lond) 18:19-20 Ap '00)

The harbour watch [a one-act play]
(Rev in Ath 2:292 S 20 '13)

His apologies. London, Medici Society, 1932
(Noted in T L S S 1 '32 p611)

In black and white. London, Sampson Low, Marston, Searle and Rivington [1890] 96p
(Rev in Ath 2:348 S 13 '90; Sat R 68: 165-6 Ag 10 '89; Speaker 2:251 Ag 30 '90; Literary World (Lond) ns 42:155-6 Ag 29 '90)

The islanders, a poem. New York, Doubleday, Page, 1902. 20 leaves
(Rev in Harper W 46:69 Ja 18 '02; Ind 54:412-13 F 13 '02)

The jungle-book. London, Macmillan, 1894. vi,212p
(Rev in Blackw 159:394 M '96; Nation (NY) 59:9 Jl 5 '94; Ath 1:766 Je 16 '94; P. Addleshaw in Acad 45:530 Je 30 '94; R. Le Gallienne in Idler 9:115-16 F '96; Critic (NY) 25:37-8 Jl 21 '94; I. Zangwill in Critic (NY) 25:252 O 20 '94; Sat R 77:639-40 Je 16 '94; Spec 72:747-8 Je 2 '94; Literary World (Lond) ns 49:547-8 Je 15 '94; Lond Q R 85: 382-3 Ja '96; Bookm (Lond) 6:116 Je '94; Book B ns 11:305 Jl '94)

Just-so stories for little children. London, Macmillan, 1902. 252p
(Rev by G. K. Chesterton in Bookm (Lond) 23:57-8 N '02 and Bookm (NY) 16:374-5 D '02; Speaker ns 7:103-4 O 25 '02; Book B ns 25:481-2 D '02; Literary World (Lond) ns 66:244-5 O 10 '02; Ath 2:447-8 O 4 '02; Out 72: 800 D 6 '02; Public Opinion (NY) 33: 507 O 16 '02; Nation (NY) 75:326 O 23 '02; Atlan 91:699-700 My '03; Spec 89:492-4 O 4 '02; Dial 33:408 D 1 '02; R of Rs (Lond) 26:427, 753 O, D '02)

Kim. London, Macmillan, 1901. 414p
(Rev in Literary World (Lond) ns 64: 219-20 O 4 '01; H. W. Preston in Atlan 88:845-7 D '01; Speaker ns 5:23-4 O 5 '01; Blackw 170:793-6 D '01; H. W. Boynton in Atlan 89:562 Ap '02; Outlook (Lond) 8:311, 377-8 O 5, 19 '01; Out 69:425-7 O 19 '01; J. D. Adams in Book B ns 23:232-3 O '01; A. B. Maurice in Bookm (NY) 14:146-9 O '01; World's Work 2:1341-2 O '01; Ind 53:2415-16 O 10 '01; C. A. Pratt in Critic (NY) 39:466-7 N '01; Nation (NY) 73:381 N 14 '01; Spec 87:484-5 O 5 '01; Acad 61:289-90 O 5 '01; Ath 2: 552-3 O 26 '01; W. M. Payne in Dial 31:368 N 16 '01; Lit W 32:209 D 1 '01; Literary World (Lond) ns 63:8-9 Ja 4 '01; Lit Digest 23:508 O 26 '01; W. Lee-Warner in Empire Review 2:437-41 N '01; Bookm (Lond) 21:18-20 O '01)

Kipling, Rudyard—*Continued*

The Kipling birthday book, compiled by Joseph Finn. London, Macmillan, 1896. 278p
(Rev in Acad 50:453 N 28 '96; Literary World (Lond) ns 54:458 N 27 '96)

A Kipling pageant. New York, Doubleday, Doran, 1935. v-xvii,936p
(Rev by B. R. Redman in Books D 1 '35 p32)

Land and sea tales for boys and girls. Garden City, N. Y. Doubleday, Page, 1923. 322p
(Rev by M. A. E. White in Literary Digest International Book Review 2: 604-5 Jl '24; T L S N 29 '23 p 819)

Letters of travel, 1892-1913. London, Macmillan, 1920. 284p
(Rev by H. D. Davray in Mercure Fr 142:793-4 '20; T L S Je 10 '20 p365; V. Woolf in Ath 2:75 Jl 16 '20; R. T. Hopkins in Bookman's Journal 2:152 Jl 2 '20; D. McCarthy in New Statesm 15:249-50 Je 5 '20; Spec 124:828-9 Je 19 '20)

Life's handicap: being stories of mine own people. London, Macmillan, 1891. 352p
(Rev in Blackw 150:729-35 N '91; L. Johnson in Acad 40:327-8 O 17 '91; Lit W 22:310 S 12 '91; Critic (NY) 19: 138-9 S 19 '91; Spec 67:417-18 S 26 '91; National Observer ns 6:381-2 Ag 29 '91; Literary World (Lond) ns 44:139-40 Ag 28 '91; Westm 136:457-8 O '91; Speaker 4:235-6 Ag 22 '91)

The light that failed. New York, United States Book co. [1890] 3-186p
(Rev in National Observer ns 5:592 Ap 25 '91; Lit W 22:72 F 28 '91; Ath 1:218 F 14 '03; Ath 1:497-8 Ap 18 '01; Critic (NY) 18:178-9 Ap 4 '91; L. Johnson in Acad 39:319-20 Ap 4 '91; Spec 66:174 Ja 31 '91; Literary World (Lond) ns 43: 318 Ap 3 '91; Speaker 3:111-12 Ja 24 '91)

Limits and renewals. London, Macmillan, 1932. 400p
(Rev by F. Kendon in John O'London's Weekly 27:161 Ap 30 '32; C. Morley in Sat R Lit 8:681 Ap 23 '32; Archiv 164: 139-40 S '33; Nat R 98:665-6 My '32; T L S Ap 7 '32 p245; E. Wilson in New Repub 71:50-1 My 25 '32)

Many inventions. London, Macmillan, 1893. ix,366p
(Rev in Literary World (Lond) ns 47: 595-6 Je 30 '93; Californian 4:719 O '93; Westm 140:460 O '93; Ath 2:55 Jl 8 '93; P. Addleshaw in Acad 44:7-8 Jl 1 '93; Critic (NY) 23:120 Ag 19 '93; Sat R 75:659-60 Je 17 '93; Spec 71:86-7 Jl 15 '93; Bookm (Lond) 4:113-14 Jl '93; W. M. Payne in Dial 15:94 Ag 16 '93; Ind 45:1453 O 26 '93; Nation (NY) 57: 199 S 14 '93; Lit W 24:206 Jl 1 '93; Speaker 7:726 Je 24 '93; Lond Q R 81: 185 O '93; Book B ns 10:285 Ag '93)

Mine own people. New York, United States Book co. [1891] vii-xxvi,9-268p
(Rev in Lit W 22:162 My 9 '91; Nation (NY) 52:483 Je 11 '91; Harper M 83: 641 S '91)

The new army in training. London, Macmillan, 1915. 64p
(Rev in Ath 1:141 F 13 '15; Spec 114: 232-3 F 13 '15)

The phantom 'rickshaw and other tales. Allahabad, Wheeler, 1888. 114p
(Rev in Lit W 21:306 S 13 '90; National Observer ns 5:411-12 Mr 7 '91; Literary World (Lond) ns 43:76-7 Ja 23 '91)

Plain tales from the hills. Calcutta, Thacker, Spink, 1888. 284p
(Rev in Lit W 21:155 My 10 '90; Critic (NY) 17:127 S 13 '90; Nation (NY) 51: 465-6 D 11 '90; J. Hawthorne in Lippinc 46:571-4 O '90; Literary World (Lond) ns 42:28-9 Jl 11 '90; Literary World (Lond) ns 60:34 Jl 14 '99; Deutsche Rundschau 68:478 '91; Archiv 85:333 '90; A. Glardon in Bibliothèque Universelle et Revue Suisse 3d period 49: 223-4 Ja '91)

Puck of Pook's hill. London, Macmillan, 1906. 306p
(Rev in Nation (NY) 83:286-7 O 4 '06; Contemp 91:760 Je '07; Ath 2:404 O 6 '06; Acad 71:327-8 O 6 '06; Liv Age 251:569-73 D 1 '06; Bookn 25:253 D '06; Sat R 102:430 O 6 '06; Cur Lit 41:699 D '06; Ind 61:820 O 4 '06; Spec 97:538-9 O 13 '06; H. T. Peck in Bookm (NY) 24:383 D '06; A. Noyes in Bookm (Lond) 31:81-2 N '06)

The recessional
(Rev in Spec 79:106-7 Jl 24 '97)

Rewards and fairies. London, Macmillan, 1910. 340p
(Rev by H. Murray in Bookm (NY) 32:489-90 Ja '11; Acad 79:347 O 8 '10; Ath 2:483 O 22 '10; Nation (NY) 91: 364-5 O 20 '10; H. A. Hinkson in Bookm (Lond) 39:97-8 N '10; Spec 105: 557-8 O 8 '10; T.P.'s Weekly 16:485 O 14 '10)

Sea warfare. London, Macmillan, 1916. 224p
(Rev in Dial 62:358-9 Ap 19 '17; H. D. Davray in Mercure Fr 119:743-5 F 16 '17)

The second jungle book. London, Macmillan, 1895. 240p
(Rev by J. C. Harris in Book B ns 12: 656-7 N '95; Ath 1:278 F 29 '96; Dial 19:339 D 1 '95; Literary World (Lond) ns 52:475-6 D 13 '95; Atlan 77:423 Mr '96; Bookselling 1:126-7 D '95; Critic (NY) 27:338-9 N 23 '95)

The seven seas. London, Methuen, 1896. 230p
(Rev in Literary World (Lond) ns 54: 419-20 N 20 '96; Nation (NY) 63:441 D 10 '96; R of Rs (Lond) 14:553-8 D '96; Lond Q R 89:325-36 Ja '98; Lit W 27:467 D 26 '96; C. Porter in Poet Lore

9:291-5 '97; Acad 50:377-8 N 14 '96;
J. O. Miller in Canadian Magazine 8:
456-9 Mr '97; Sat R 82:549-50 N 21 '96;
same. Liv Age 21:827-30 D 18 '96;
E. C. Stedman in Book B ns 13:596-8
N '96; W. M. Payne in Dial 22:87-8
F 1 '97; W. D. Howells in McClure's
Magazine 8:453-5 Mr '97; Spec 77:728-30
N 21 '96; Ind 49:153 F 4 '97; Bookm
(Lond) 11:65-7 D '96; A. Macdonnell in
Bookm (Lond) 11:67 D '96; S. Axson
in Citizen (Phila) 3:65-7 My '97)

Soldier tales. London, Macmillan, 1896.
172p
(Rev in Dial 21:339 D 1 '96; Literary
World (Lond) ns 54:458 N 27 '96)

Soldiers three, a collection of stories. . .
Allahabad, Wheeler, 1888. 97p
(Rev in Ath 1:527-8 Ap 26 '90; Spec 62:
403-4 Mr 23 '89; Literary World (Lond)
ns 42:28-9 Jl 11 '90; Westm 134:688-9
D '90)

A song of the English. London, Hodder
and Stoughton, 1914
(Rev by H. Jackson in T. P.'s Weekly
24:655-6 D 19 '14)

Songs from books. New York, Doubleday, Page, 1912. 250p
(Rev by E. E. Slosson in Ind 74:139-41
Ja 16 '13; P. Gibbon in Bookm (Lond)
45:146-7 D '13; Spec 111:657-8 O 25 '13)

Sons of Martha. [1907]
(Rev in Ind 62:1217-18 My 23 '07)

Souvenirs of France. London, Macmillan, 1933. 64p
(Rev in T L S Jl 20 '33 p 493)

Stalky & co. London, Macmillan, 1899.
272p
(Rev in Nation (NY) 70:17 Ja 4 '00;
Speaker ns 1:43-4 O 14 '99; Acad 57:
421-2 O 14 '99; Lit 5:372-3 O 14 '99;
Ath 2:515-16 O 14 '99; Lit W 30:405-6
N 25 '99; Dial 27:432 D 1 '99; R. Le
Gallienne in Idler 16:545-6 '99; Scottish
Review 35:214 Ap '00; Argonaut 45:8
O 23 '99; Spec 83:570 O 21 '99; Literary
World (Lond) ns 60:278-9 O 20 '99;
Outlook (Lond) 4:420-1 O 28 '99;
Mercure Fr 46:478-80 My '03)

The story of the Gadsbys. Allahabad,
Wheeler, 1888. 102p
(Rev in Ath 2:32-3 Jl 5 '90; Literary
World (Lond) ns 42:28-9 Jl 11 '90)

"They." London, Macmillan, 1905. 80
leaves
(Rev in Sat R 101:145 F 3 '06)

Traffics and discoveries. London, Mac-
millan, 1904. 394p
(Rev in T L S O 7 '04 p304; Ath 2:
476-7 O 8 '04; Acad 67:311 O 8 '04;
Monthly Review 17 no 2:170-3 N '04;
T. Jenks in Cur Lit 37:529-32 D '04;
H. T. Peck in Bookm (NY) 20:155-7
O '04; Cath World 30:401-2 D '04;
Reader Magazine 5:132-3 D '04; Critic
(NY) 45:472-3 N '04; Ind 57:921-2 O 20
'04; Sat R 98:494 O 15 '04; Spec 93:556-
8 O 15 '04; Lit W 35:326 N '04; Liter-

ary World (Lond) ns 70:284-5 O 14 '04;
H. D. Davray in Mercure Fr 52:808 D
'04)

Twenty poems from Rudyard Kipling.
London, Methuen [1918] 40p
(Rev in Sat R 125:510-11 Je 8 '18; *same.*
Liv Age 298:421-3 Ag 17 '18)

Under the deodars. Allahabad, Wheeler,
1888. 106p
(Rev in Ath 2:887 D 27 '90; noted in
Critic (NY) 18:179 Ap 4 '91; Sat R 68:
165-6 Ag 10 '89; National Observer
ns 5:411 Mr 7 '91; Literary World
(Lond) ns 42:405 N 14 '90)

Verse
(Rev in Mercure Fr 149:536 '21; T L S
D 14 '33 p892; R. E. Roberts in Bookm
(Lond) 61:134-5 D '21; Spec 124:80-1 Ja
17 '20; A. Williams-Ellis in Spec 127:639
N 12 '21; B. Brook in Bookm (Lond)
85:189 D '33)

Wee Willie Winkie. Allahabad, Wheeler,
1888. 104p
(Rev in Ath 2:886-7 D 27 '90; National
Observer ns 5:411 Mr 7 '91; Literary
World (Lond) ns 42:405-6 N 14 '90)

With the night mail: a story of 2000 A.D.
London, Macmillan, 1909. 3-77 leaves
(Rev in Nation (NY) 88:364 Ap 8 '09)

Works. London, Thacker, 1897
(Rev by E. E. Hale in Dial 23:42-4 Jl 16
'97; Blackw 164:470-82 O '98; Lit W 28:
92-3, 262, 431, 482 Mr 20, Ag 7, N 27,
D 25 '97; Dial 28:160 Mr 1 '00; Edin R
174:132-51 Jl '91; Edin R 187:203-26 Ja
'98; noted in Critic (NY) 30:83 Ja 30
'97)

The years between. London, Methuen
[1919] 160p
(Rev by F. Hackett in New Repub 19:
386-7 Ap 19 '19; Ath 1:297-8 My 9 '19;
T L S Ap 10 '19 p196; R. C. Macfie in
Bookm (Lond) 56:76-7 My '19; Dial 66:
571 My 31 '19; Spec 122:563-4 My 3 '19;
Nation (NY) 109:115 Jl 26 '19; C. H.
Towne in Bookm (NY) 49:618-19 Jl '19)

Kipling, Rudyard (ed)
The Irish guards in the great war. Ed.
and compiled from their diaries and
papers. London, Macmillan, 1923. 2
vols 344p; 312p
(Rev in T L S Ap 19 '23 p265; Bookman's Journal 8:88-9 Je '23; F. E.
Whitton in Bookm (Lond) 64:90-2 My
'23)

Kipling, Rudyard and Balestier, Wolcott
The Naulahka: a story of West and East.
London, Heinemann, 1892. 276p
(Rev by S. Kirk in Atlan 70:546-50 O
'92; Nation (NY) 55:262-3 O 6 '92; Edin
R 190:435-7 O '99; Speaker 6:118-19 Jl
23 '92; Book B ns 9:295-6 Ag '92; Liter-
ary World (Lond) ns 46:64 Jl 22 '92;
Ind 44:1229 S 1 '92; Westm 138:568-9
N '92; Spec 69:196-7 Ag 6 '92; Sat R
74:226-7 Ag 20 '92; Ath 2:154-5 Jl 30
'92; Lit W 23:258 Jl 30 '92; Bookm

Kipling, R. and Balestier, W.—*Continued*
(Lond) 2:152 Ag '92; W. M. Payne in
Dial 13:104 Ag '92; National Observer
ns 8:222-3 Jl 16 '92)

[Kipling, Rudyard and] Fletcher, C. R. L.
A history of England. London, Hodder
and Stoughton, 1911. 9-250p
(Rev in Ath 2:209 Ag 19 '11; Ind 71:
872-3 O 19 '11; Spec 107:214-15 Ag 5
'11; British Weekly 50:401 Jl 20 '11;
R. R. Buckley in T. P.'s Weekly 18:103
Jl 28 '11)

Kipling, Rudyard and Graves, C. (trans)
Quintus Horati Flacci Carminum Librum
Quintum. Oxford, Blackwell, 1920. 20
leaves, p21-34
(Rev in Spec 125:740-1 D 4 '20; H.
Straus in Nation (NY) 114:22-3 Ja 4
'22)

Kipling. Bookman's Journal 1:332 F 20
'20

Kipling Americanized. Town Talk 11:15
Ja 17 '03

[Kipling and Barrie] Bookm (NY) 9:395-7
Jl '99

Kipling and Chaucer. Atlan 84:714-16 N '99

Kipling and Dickens. Bookm (NY) 14:
327-8 D '01

Kipling and his pirates. Bookman's
Journal 11:42-3 O '24

Kipling and other critics. R of Rs (NY)
25:148 F '02

Kipling and Riley. Bookm (NY) 38:598-600
F '14

Kipling and the dictionary. . . Munsey's
Magazine 23:711 Ag '00

[Kipling and "The Islanders."] Bookm
(NY) 14:630-1 F '02

[Kipling and the Nobel prize] Mercure Fr
137:561 '20

Kipling and the swastika. Notes & Q 11th
ser 2:338, 395 O 22, N 12 '10

[Kipling and the war] Mercure Fr 134:318-
20 '19

Kipling and Westward Ho. T. P.'s Weekly
20:421 O 4 '12

Kipling as a futurist traveler. Lit Digest
48:620-1 Mr 21 '14

Kipling as a poet of patriotism. Out 64:18-
19 Ja 6 '00

Kipling as prophet. Bookm (NY) 31:234-5
My '10

Kipling as the greatest story-teller of our
time. Current Opinion 65:396 D '18

Kipling calendar. Garden City, Doubleday,
Page, 1923

Kipling caught again [plagiarism] Town
Talk 12:6 Ap 16 '04

Kipling city. T. P.'s Weekly 24:464 O 24
'14

Kipling: comparative psychologist. Atlan
81:858-9 Je '98

The **Kipling** curse. Bookm (NY) 26:6-9 S
'07

Kipling defends his rights. Argonaut 44:2
Je 12 '99

The "**Kipling** dictionary." Bookm (NY)
35:590-1 Ag '12

A **Kipling** exam. paper. Acad 62:121 F 1
'02

Kipling explained. T. P.'s Weekly 24:558
N 21 '14

[The **Kipling** "fad"] Harper M 81:801-2 O
'90

Kipling: "Father, we authors cannot tell a
lie," he says. News-Week 1:14-15 Jl
22 '33

A **Kipling** hoax. Lit Digest 58:37-8 Jl 6 '18

Kipling in America. R of Rs (NY) 19:419-
22 Ap '99

Kipling in fiction. Bookm (NY) 25:561 Ag
'07

Kipling in Italy. Bookman's Journal 3:348
Mr 11 '21

Kipling in the movies. Lit Digest 67:33
N 6 '20

The **Kipling** index. *In* Around the world
with Kipling. Garden City, N.Y.
Doubleday, Page, 1926. p79-121

The **Kipling** index; being a guide to the
Uniform and Pocket editions of Rudyard Kipling's works. . . London, Macmillan, 1914. 40p

Kipling interviewed at last. Lit Digest 47:
1277 D 27 '13

The **Kipling** Journal. London, 1927-1933,
nos. 1-25 [current]

A **Kipling** note book [a magazine issued
for twelve numbers between F '99 and
Ja '00]
see Mansfield, Milburg Francisco and
Wessels, A.

The **Kipling** of war-days. Lit Digest 50:
546-7 Mr 13 '15

Kipling on the stump. Lit Digest 45:904-5
N 16 '12

Kipling on woman suffrage. Ind 71:999 N
2 '11

Kipling out-Kiplinged. Cur Lit 12:360
Mr '93

Kipling: "Picaroon": "Barracoon." Notes
& Q 10th ser 9:234-5 Mr 21 '08

Kipling, pioneer. Forum 77:278-81 F '27

Kipling; poem. Atlan 118:856 D '16

Kipling, preaching individualism, denounces
tribe rule. Current Opinion 75:719-20
D '23

The **Kipling** procession. Punch 124:4 Ja 7
'03

Kipling still a best seller. Lit Digest 47:
816-17 N 1 '13

Kipling tells why Britons should fight. Lit
Digest 51:158-9 Jl 24 '15

Kipling to French eyes. Bookm (NY) 26:
584 F '08

Kipling to the younger generation. Lit Digest 79:28-30 N 10 '23

[Kipling *versus* Putnam's] Critic (NY) 42: 203-4 Mr '03

"Kiplingesque journalism." Sat R 126:1177 D 21 '18

The Kipling-Putnam controversy. Argonaut 44:11 Jl 3 '99

Kipling's attack on the British government. Lit Digest 48:1425-6 Je 13 '14

Kipling's blunders. Bookm (NY) 36:105-6 O '12

Kipling's commentators. Bookm (NY) 20: 2-3 S '04

Kipling's conception of India. Lippinc 94: 177-85 Ag '14

Kipling's early days. St James's Budget no 1013:6 N 24 '99

[Kipling's family] Bookm (NY) 9:496-7 Ag '99

[Kipling's "The female of the species"] Cur Lit 51:598-600 D '11

Kipling's half century. J Ed 83:148-9 F 10 '16

[Kipling's home at Rottingdean] Bookm (NY) 9:197-8 My '99

Kipling's influence. Argonaut 44:8 Ja 30 '99

Kipling's latest Jeremiad. Lit Digest 64:33-4 F 21 '20

[Kipling's lecture on travel] Ath 1:276 F 21 '14

[Kipling's life] Magazine of Music Ap '95; Cassell's Magazine 31:149 D '00

Kipling's popularity. . . Munsey's Magazine 26:593 Ja '02

[Kipling's "Recessional"] Lit W 29:59 F 19 '98

Kipling's 'Recessional': 'Dulce Domum.' Notes & Q 9th ser 3:236 Mr 25 '99

Kipling's "Retrocessional." Nation (NY) 67:292 O 20 '98

[Kipling's return to India] Bookm (NY) 1:291 Je '95

Kipling's scattered verse. Nation (NY) 95: 528-9 D 5 '12

Kipling's songs to music. T. P.'s Weekly 18:550 O 27 '11

Kipling's spiritual side. Harper's Bazaar 34:796-7 Mr 23 '01

[Kipling's suit against G. P. Putnam's sons] Dial 26:347 My 16 '99

[Kipling's "The Islanders"] Acad 62:663 Ja 11 '02

Kipling's "They." T. P.'s Weekly 23:182 F 6 '14

Kipling's "They" once more. Out 57:689-90 S 22 '04

Kipling's war poem. Bookm (NY) 40:121-6 O '14

Kipling's welcome to Americans. Lit Digest 58:21-2 Ag 24 '18

Knight, Beatrice M.
"Well-deserved" praise. T. P.'s Weekly 15:20 Ja 7 '10

Knowles, Frederick Lawrence
A Kipling primer. . . Boston, Brown, 1899
(Rev in Nation (NY) 69:297 O 19 '99; Literary World (Lond) ns 61:152 F 16 '00)

Koszul, André
Rudyard Kipling; sa doctrine. Revue Pédagogique ns 53:201-31 S 15 '08

[Kunitz, Stanley J.] Dilly Tante [pseud] (ed)
Rudyard Kipling. *In* Living authors. . . New York, Wilson, 1931. p210-11

Labouchère, Henry
The brown man's burden; poem. Argonaut 44:9 F 20 '99

Lacon [pseud]
Mr. Rudyard Kipling. *In* Lectures to living authors. London, Bles, 1925. p111-18

Laidlaw, Alaister K.
The hooligan of literature. T. P.'s Weekly 15:68 Ja 21 '10

Lalou, René
Rudyard Kipling et l'impérialisme. *In* Panorama de la littérature anglaise contemporaine. Paris, Kra [c1926] p138-49

Lamy, Etienne
Rudyard Kipling et la Guerre sur mer. R Deux Mondes 6th ser 48:251-71 N 15 '18

Lang, Andrew
Biographical sketch. *In* The courting of Dinah Shadd and other stories, by Rudyard Kipling. New York, Harper, 1890. p vii-xii
Mr. Kipling's stories. *In* Essays in little. New York, Scribner, 1891. p198-205

Lanier, Charles D.
A sketch of Rudyard Kipling. R of Rs (NY) 15:173-82 F '97

Lanier, Henry Wysham
Mr. Kipling's "cynical jingoism" toward the brown man. Dial 26:389-90 Je 16 '99

Larned, W. T.
Ballade of bitter regrets. Bookm (NY) 38:604 F '14

Laski, Harold Joseph
Four literary portraits. Liv Age 339:285-7 N '30

The later Kipling. . . Munsey's Magazine 32:600-1 Ja '05

The Laureateship. Illustrated London News 101:491 O 15 '92

Law, Arthur
The critics and Kipling. T. P.'s Weekly 15:68 Ja 21 '10

Lawton, William Cranston
Rudyard Kipling, the artist; a retrospect and a prophecy. New York, Morse, 1899. 30p

Leblond, Marius Ary
Rudyard Kipling, animalier et colonial. Mercure Fr 43:289-324 Ag '02

Lee, Vernon [pseud]
see Paget, Violet

Leeb-Lundberg, W.
Word-formation in Kipling; a stylistic-philological study. Lund, Lindstedt, 1909. vii,116p bibl p[viii]

Le Gallienne, Richard
A propos "The Absent-Minded Beggar." *In* Sleeping beauty and other prose fancies. London, Lane, 1900. p199-206

The books of two worlds ["Absent-Minded Beggar."] Idler 17:77-81 Mr '00

Rudyard Kipling. Cur Lit 29:136-9 Ag '00

Rudyard Kipling, a criticism. . . London, Lane, 1900. 163,xlvip bibl by John Lane, pi-xlvi
(Rev in Ath 1:810 Je 30 '00; Lit W 31: 115 Je 1 '00; Lit 6:370 My 12 '00; Literary World (Lond) ns 61:469 My 18 '00; Speaker ns 2:227-8 My 26 '00; Bookm (NY) 11:303 Je '00; Bookm (Lond) 18:84-7 Je '00)

Rudyard Kipling's place in literature. *In* Around the world with Kipling. Garden City, N.Y. Doubleday, Page, 1926. p45-51; *same.* Munsey's Magazine 68: 238-46 N '19

Legouis, Émile
Rudyard Kipling. R Pol et Litt 59:768-70 D 17 '21; ibid 60:8-11 Ja 7 '22

A **lesson** in fiction. Bookm (Lond) 21:162-3 F '02

Letters to living authors. II. Rudyard Kipling. Good Words 43:293-8 '02

Lewis, Austin
Kipling and women. Overland Monthly ns 42:357-60 O '03

[**Lines** to Admiral Evans] Bookm (NY) 34:584 F '12

Ling, William
Mr. Kipling and the pirate. Outlook (Lond) 4:277-8 S 30 '99

Lintot, Bernard
The poetry of Rudyard Kipling. T. P.'s Weekly 22:73 Jl 18 '13

The **literary** inspiration of imperialism. Scottish Review 35:262-78 Ap '00; *same.* Liv Age 225:807-11 Je 30 '00

A **literary** progenitress of Rudyard Kipling. Acad 65:444-5 O 24 '03

Living English poets: Rudyard Kipling. Cur Lit 30:363-4 Mr '01

Livingston, Flora V.
Kipling, his pirates, and "The light that failed." Bookman's Journal 11:92 N '24

Livingston, Luther Samuel
A lost poem by Kipling. Notes & Q 12th ser 3:173 Mr 3 '17

London, Jack
These bones shall rise again. *In* Revolution. New York, Macmillan, 1910. p217-34

Lord, Louis Eleazer
Two imperial poets: Horace and Kipling. Classical Journal 16:261-70 F '21

Lord Tennyson. Blackw 162:629 N '97

The **lordliest** life on earth. Monthly Review 6:1-6 F '02

Lost masterpieces. Punch 125:254 O 14 '03

Low, Mary C.
The vampire; poem. Bookm (NY) 9: 61 Mr '99

Löwe, Ernst
Beiträge zur metrik Rudyard Kiplings. (Marburger studien zur englischen philologie. heft 10) Marburg, Elwert, 1906. viii,103p Diss. Marburg, 1905
(Rev by A. Kroder in Engl Stud 40: 90-3 '08)

The **lower** deck [comparison of Bowles and Kipling] Acad 55:115-16 O 22 '98

Lucas, Perceval
Uncollected Kipling items. Notes & Q 11th ser 9:416 My 23 '14

Luquer, Lea Shippen
Kipling in America. Masters essay, Columbia univ. 1922

Lusk, Lewis
In Kipling's country. Art J 61:65-71, 111-16 Mr, Ap '09

Lynch, Arthur
Rudyard Kipling. *In* Human documents. . . London, Dobell, 1896. p203-31

Lynd, Robert
Mr. Rudyard Kipling. *In* Old and new masters. London, Unwin, 1919. p224-33

Ortheris: the heroic cockney soldier. John O'London's Weekly 27:113 Ap 23 '32

Lyndell, Noel
Rudyard Kipling. T. P.'s Weekly 18:724 D 8 '11

McAlpin, Edwin Augustus
The search for satisfaction. . . *In* Old and new books as life teachers. New York, Doubleday, Doran, 1928. p18-35

McCollin, Alice Graham
Rudyard Kipling. Ladies' Home Journal 11:5 Ag '94

McCulloch, Hugh, jr.
Impression of Mr. Kipling. Harv Mo 11:138-46 Ja '91

[MacFall, (Mrs) Haldane] Grand, Sarah [pseud]
Literary portraits. V. Rudyard Kipling. Canadian Magazine 23:404-6 S '04

MacGaffey, Ethel
My favorite character in fiction; Mulvaney. Scholastic 11:11 O 1 '27

McGinnis, Mabel
Cocktails from the hills (With apologies to Rudyard Kipling) Life 37:487-9 Je 6 '01

McGovern, A. F.
The poetry of Rudyard Kipling. Masters essay, Boston Univ. 1924

McKnight, George Harley
Kipling's view of Americans. Bookm
(NY) 7:131-5 Ap '98

MacMichael, J. Holden
Kipling and the swastika. Notes & Q
11th ser 2:239 S 17 '10

Macmillan, firm, publisher, London
The Kipling index. . . London, Macmillan,
1914. 40p
(Rev in T L S Ap 2 '14 p161)

MacMunn, (Sir) George Fletcher
Kipling's women. London, Sampson,
Low, Marston [1933] viii,215p

Some Kipling origins. Blackw 222:145-
54 Ag '27

Some origins of Kipling stories. India
1:21-3, 38 Ag '28

Macnaughten, Hugh
Flotsam and jetsam. Nat R 83:866-9 Ag
'24

McNeill, Angus [pseud]
see Crosland, Thomas William Hodgson
The madness of Mr. Kipling. Macmil 79:
131-5 D '98; same. Liv Age 220:91-6
Ja 14 '99

Magnus, Philip M.
Poetry and society since Tennyson. Edin
R 249:304-6 Ap '29

Malloch, D. Macleod
The engineering instinct. T. P.'s Weekly
15:44 Ja 14 '10

The man who was. Bookm (NY) 30:319-
22 D '09

Mangalore. Coincidence or copying? Notes
& Q 7th ser 12:206 S 12 '91

Manly, John Matthews
Contemporary British literature. New
York, Harcourt [c1921] p94-7

Mansback, Irving E.
Roster of the Kipling battalion. Bookm
(NY) 43:103-8 Mr '16

**Mansfield, Milburg Francisco and Wessels,
A.**
Glossary to accompany "Departmental
ditties" as written by Rudyard Kipling.
New York, Mansfield and Wessels,
1899. 63p

A Kipling notebook. New York, Mansfield and Wessels, 1899-1900 [Issued
also under the title of Kiplingiana]

Kiplingiana. New York, Mansfield and
Wessels [1899] 188p [taken from A
Kipling Note Book, a magazine which
ran for twelve numbers from F '99 to
Ja '00]
(Rev in Ind 51:2828 O 19 '99)

Marble, Annie Russell
A study of the modern novel. New York,
Appleton, 1928. p110-12

Writings of Kipling before and after the
award. In The Nobel prize winners in
literature. New York, Appleton-
Century, 1932. rev ed p85-103

Marcosson, Isaac F.
Rudyard Kipling. Bookn 25:203-6 D '06

Mark Twain and Kipling. Bookm (NY)
37:369-70 Je '13

Marquardt, Hertha
Kipling und Indien. . . (Sprache und
kultur der germanisch-romanischen
völker. Anglistische reihe. Bd 7)
Breslau, Priebatschs Buchhandlung,
1931. 167p bibl p161-5

Marshall, Archibald
Last century's literary favorites. IV.
Some Kipling stories. Literary Digest
International Book Review 2:375 Ap
'24

Marshall, Henry Rutgers
Rudyard Kipling and racial instinct. Cent
ns 36:375-7 Jl '99

Mason, Eugene
On the short story and two modern
exemplars. In A book of preferences
in literature. London, Wilson, 1914.
p58-66

Masterman, Charles Frederick Gurney
After the reaction. Contemp 86:816-20
D '04; same. Liv Age 244:194-7 Ja 28
'05

Matthews, Albert
A lost poem by Kipling. Notes & Q
12th ser 3:34 Ja 13 '17

Matthews, Brander
The gift of story-telling; Kipling & co.
In Aspects of fiction. . . New York,
Harper, 1896

Of Cervantes, Zola, Kipling and Co. In
Books and play-books. London,
Osgood, McIlvaine, 1895. p215-33;
same. Cosmopolitan 14:609-14 Mr '93

The story of the short-story from Esop
to Kipling. Munsey's Magazine 35:
545-6 Ag '06

Maurice, Arthur Bartlett
About the London of Rudyard Kipling.
Bookm (NY) 52:311-17 D '20; same.
Bookm (Lond) 59:151-5 Ja '21

Kipling's men. Bookm (NY) 32:199-200
O '10; same. Bookm (NY) 8:348-50 D
'98

Kipling's verse-people. Bookm (NY) 9:
57-61 Mr '99; same. Bookm (NY) 32:
539-40 Ja '11

Kipling's women. Bookm (NY) 8:479-81
Ja '99

Mr. Rudyard Kipling's "United States."
Bookm (NY) 38:156-63 O '13

More "Old Bookman days." Bookm
(NY) 70:64 S '29

A visit to Rudyard Kipling. Mentor 16:
18-19 F '28

Maurois, André
M. André Maurois on the Englishman of
today, translated by Mrs. R. Balfour.
Cornhill 3d ser 68:16 Ja '30

Maycock, Willoughby
"Bobs." Notes & Q 11th ser 10:472 D
12 '14

A lost poem by Kipling. Notes & Q 12th
ser 2:475 D 9 '16

Mr. Rudyard Kipling . . . will recite. . . The chantey of the nations. Punch 122:468 Je 25 '02

Mr. Rudyard Kipling's idea. Spec 88:40 Ja 11 '02

Mr. Rudyard Kipling's local colour. Lit 3:631 D 31 '98

Mr. Rudyard Kipling's poetry. Acad 75: 561-2 D 12 '08

Mr. Rudyard Kipling's prose writings. Scottish Review 34:291-309 O '99

Mr. Rudyard Kipling's tales. Quar R 175: 132-61 Jl '92

Monahan, Michael
The Kipling blue pill. Philistine 13: 129-36 O '01

[Note on Kipling] Papyrus 3d ser, vol 1, no 2:31 D '10

Style and the man. Papyrus 3d ser, vol 1, nos 3-4:25-7 F '11

To Villon; poem. Philistine 9:106-8 S '99

Monkshood, G. F. [pseud]
see Clarke, William James

Montgomery, M.
The nationality of Kipling's "Kim." Germanisch-Romanische Monatsschrift 6:587-8 O-N '14

Mood, Robert Gibbs
Rudyard Kipling and the Bible. Masters essay, Columbia univ. 1925

Moody, D. L.
Kipling and S.S. libraries. Lit W 30: 298 S 16 '99

Moore, George
Avowals. . . Lippinc 73:99-103 Ja '04; *same.* Pall Mall Magazine 33:375-9 Jl '04

Moore, Margaret D.
Getting acquainted with Kipling. Normal Instructor & Primary Plans 36:68-70 S '29

More, Paul Elmer
Kipling and Fitzgerald. *In* Shelburne essays. New York, Putnam, 1907. 2d ser p104-25

The Seven seas and the Rubaiyat. Atlan 84:800-8 D '99

Morley, Christopher
Horace, book five. Sat R Lit 3:155 O 2 '26

The **most** popular English poet of our day. Sphere 54:143 Ag 2 '13

A **mouth** of brass. Nation (Lond) 5:486-8 Jl 3 '09; *same.* Liv Age 262:314-17 Jl 31 '09

Muddiman, Bernard
The men of the nineties. New York, Putnam, 1921. passim

Mullin, E. H.
Stevenson, Kipling, and Anglo-Saxon imperialism. Book B ns 18:85-90 Mr '99

Munro, Neil
Mr. Rudyard Kipling. Good Words 40: 261-5 Ap '99

Rudyard Kipling. Bookm (NY) 9:258-9 My '99

Rudyard Kipling, "the laureate of English endeavor." Bookm (NY) 9:258-9 My '99

Munson, Arley Isabelle
Kipling's India. Garden City, N. Y. Doubleday, Page, 1915. xii,204p; *same in* Bookm (NY) 39:30-45, 153-71, 255-68 Mr-My '14

Murphy, J. F.
Kiplingesque journalism. Sat R 126: 1157 D 14 '18

Murray, David Christie
Guesses at truth: ethical, social, political and literary. London, Hurst and Blackett, 1908

Living masters, Rudyard Kipling. *In* My contemporaries in fiction. London, Chatto & Windus, 1897. p59-70; *same in* Canadian Magazine 8:475-8 Ap '97

Murray, Henry
Rudyard Kipling. *In* Robert Buchanan and other essays. London, Wellby, 1901. p153-62

Nazàri, Emilio
Rudyard Kipling: saggio critico. Palermo, Trimarchi, 1933. 263p

Nebraska University. Teachers' College. Department of English
Assignments on Kipling's "Captains courageous." Lincoln, Nebraska, Extension division, Univ. of Nebraska, 1925. 14p

. . . Lesson plans on Kipling's "Captains courageous," by Dept. of English of Teachers' College. Lincoln, Nebraska, Extension division, Univ. of Nebraska, 1925. 26p

Nencioni, Enrico
Plain tales. . . *In* Saggi critici di letteratura inglese. Firenze, 1897. p450-4

Neuendorff, B.
Kiplings schulroman und der englischen knabentypus. Zeitschrift für Jugendwohlfahrt p268 '10

A **new** indictment of Kipling's "poetic vulgarity." Current Opinion 67:256 O '19

Newbolt, Henry
An essay on criticism; poem. Monthly Review 10:1-5 F '03

Kipling the poet. Book Monthly 10:234-6 Ja '13

Newman, Ernest
Mr. Kipling's stories. Free Review 1: 236-48 D 1 '93

Nicoll, William Robertson and Wise, Thomas James (eds)
The suppressed works of Rudyard Kipling. *In* Literary anecdotes of the 19th century. . . London, Hodder & Stoughton, 1896. vol II p403-10

Niven, Frederick
The admirable Kipling. T.P.'s Weekly 16:891 D 30 '10

The **people's** Laureate; poem. Punch 145: 82 Jl 23 '13

Perry, Jennette Barbour
Mr. Kipling as an artist. Critic (NY) 33:473-5 D '98

Mr. Kipling as a moralist. Critic (NY) 33:360-2 N '98

Petrie, (Sir) Charles Alexander
Revaluations. Outlook (Lond) 61:405-6 Mr 31 '28

Phelps, William Lyon
As I like it. Scrib M 92:109 Ag '32

Rudyard Kipling. *In* Around the world with Kipling. Garden City, N. Y. Doubleday, Page, 1926. p55-7; *same in* Essays on modern novelists. New York, Macmillan, 1926. p208-28; *same.* Forum 42:217-26 S '09

Some contrasts. . . *In* The advance of English poetry in the twentieth century. New York, Dodd, Mead, 1918. p28-34

Pierpoint, Robert
"Bobs." Notes & Q 11th ser 10:473 D 12 '14

"Dust builds on dust": Kipling's "Recessional." Notes & Q 10th ser 8:385 N 16 '07

Kipling's "City of dreadful night." Notes & Q 9th ser 11:16-17 Ja 3 '03

Parodies of Kipling. Notes & Q 10th ser 12:297 O 9 '09

"Stalky and Co." by Rudyard Kipling. Notes & Q 12th ser 6:334-5 Je 26 '20

Pierre, André V.
Flaubert et Kipling. R Pol et Litt 67: 521-6 S 7 '29

Une politique d'après Kipling. Mercure Fr 210:257-91 Mr 1 '29

Pinkerton, Roy D.
The lost Kipling poem. Bookm (NY) 28:566-7 F '09

Pity the editor who "turned down" Kipling. Lit Digest 88:68-73 F 13 '26

Plater, C. D.
The cult of Kipling. Month 95:28-33 Ja '00

Platt, James, Jr.
"Ikona," South African term. Notes & Q 10th ser 6:46 Jl 21 '06

Kipling's "With Scindia to Delhi." Notes & Q 10th ser 6:32 Jl 14 '06

Pocock, Guy Noel
Mr. Rudyard Kipling's prose. *In* Pen and ink. London, Dent, 1925. p191-6

Mr. Rudyard Kipling's verse. *In* Pen and ink. London, Dent, 1925. p196-202

[A **poem** of Kipling's] Mercure Fr 158:680 '22

The **poet** in politics. R of Rs (Lond) 19: 107 F '99

[**Poetic** comments on "Islanders"] Bookm (NY) 15:14 Mr '02

Poetry revived in Kipling. Lit Digest 61: 34 My 31 '19

Poncetton, François
Kipling, poète. Le Figaro F 28 '14 p4

Pond, J. B.
Rudyard Kipling. *In* Eccentricities of genius. London, Chatto and Windus, 1901. p525-7

[The **popularity** of Kipling] Lit W 21:172 My 24 '90

[**Portraits**] Bookm (Lond) 64:89, 91 My '23; John O'London's Weekly 27:113, 161 Ap 23, 30 '32; Scholastic 11:11 O 1 '27; Everyman 8:717 D 31 '32; Bookm (Lond) 61:135 D '21; Bookm (Lond) 43:143 D '12; Bookm (Lond) 47:56 N '14; Sat R Lit 8:681 Ap 23 '32; Bookm (NY) 7:449 Ag '98; Bookm (NY) 22: 228 N '05; R of Rs (Lond) 14:552, 554 D '96; Bookm (NY) 2:294 D '95; Bookm (NY) 6:275 D '97; Bookm (NY) 13:374 My '01; Cur Lit 30:facing 257 Mr '01; Sat R Lit 4:679 Mr 17 '28; Canadian Magazine 23:406 S '04; Canadian Magazine 61:205 Je '23; Ladies' Home Journal 25:23 Mr '08; American Magazine 74:259 Jl '12; Ladies' Home Journal 26:7 Ja '09; Out 61:280 F 4 '99; World's Work 11: 459 Ap '08; World's Work 41:520 My '23; Book B ns 13:590-1 N '96; Bookm (NY) 30:24 S '09; Bookm (NY) 38:101 O '13; Bookm (NY) 29: 120 Ap '09; Book B ns 7:377 O '90; New England Magazine ns 20:518 Jl '99; Harper W 44:257 Mr 17 '00; Bookman's Journal 3:349 Mr 11 '21; McClure's Magazine 7:98, 101 Jl '96; McClure's Magazine 20:297 Ja '03; St N 44:1033 S '17; St N 42:349 F '15; Strand Magazine 65:225-30 Mr '23; Illustrated London News 101:491 O 15 '92; Idler 2:480 '92; Munsey's Magazine 68:239 N '19; National Magazine 22: 259 Je '05; National Magazine 57:232 F '29; National Magazine 10:77 Ap '99; Mentor 16:18-19 F '28; Windsor Magazine 11:65 D '99; Good Words 40:264 '99; Lit 8:facing 314 Ap 20 '01; World Review 8:56-7 F 25 '29; R of Rs (NY) 15:172, 175 F '97; Cosmopolitan 31:653-5, 657, 659 O '01; R of Rs (NY) 19:420-1 Ap '99; News-Week 1:15 Jl 22 '33; Bookm (NY) 15:506 Ag '02; Bookm (Lond) 40:209 Ag '11; Das Litterarische Echo 1:863 Ap 1 '99; E. O. Hoppé in Bookm (Lond) 77: Christmas number D '29; Sat R Lit 4:679 Mr 17 '28; Emporium 14:259-60, 263 O '01; Bookm (Lond) 17:38 N '99; Bookm (NY) 16:522 F '03; Book B ns 14:31 F '97; Bookm (Lond) 23: 143, 151-2, 154, 157-60 Ja '03; Bookm (Lond) 16:sup Ap '99; Bookm (Lond) 17:38, 45 N '99; Critic (NY) 34:304 Ap '99; Critic (NY) 33:414 D '98; Bookm (Lond) 80:5 Ap '31; Bookm (Lond) 23:143, 151-2, 157-60 Ja '03; Bookm (Lond) 64:89-91 My '23; Bookm (Lond) 71:15 O '26; Cent 58:facing 329 Jl '99; Critic (NY) 39: 135 Ag '01; Out 69:422 O 19 '01; Good

Portraits—*Continued*

Words 40:264 Ap '99; R of Rs (NY) 4:501 N '91; Cassell's Magazine 35:663 My '03; Idler 2:480 D '92; London Magazine 19:159 O '07; Punch 122:469 Je 25 '02; World's Work 25:frontispiece F '13; Cassell's Magazine 31:147 D '00; Vanity Fair 51:374 Je 7 '94; Bookn 25:140, 203-4, 206, 208-9, 786 N-D '06; Ag '07; Bookm (Lond) 29:195 F '06; Current Opinion 58:48 Ja '15; Current Opinion 65:396 D '18; Cent 58:facing 329 Jl '99; Pearson's Magazine 37:412 My '17; Illustrirte Zeitung 112:376 Mr 23 '99; Cent 42:802 O '91; Bookm (NY) 6:275 D '97; John O'London's Weekly 27:161 Ap 30 '32; Bookm (Lond) 43:143 D '12

Powell, F. York

Rudyard Kipling. Engl Illus 30:295-8 D '03

Power, William R.

Uncollected Kipling items: G. W. Steevens. Notes & Q 12th ser 7:136 Ag 14 '20

Pratt, G. W.

"Rare Kipling works." Bookman's Journal 4:16 Ap 29 '21

Prideaux, William Francis

Kipling's "With Scindia to Delhi." Notes & Q 10th ser 6:32 Jl 14 '06

Mr. Kipling's "Lucia." Notes & Q 9th ser 4:285-6 O 7 '99

Pulsford, W. Hanson

Kipling and his captains. Nation (NY) 94:183 F 22 '12

Punshon, E. R.

Mr. Kipling's "They." Acad 67:369 O 22 '04

Putnam, Frank

Kipling, body snatcher. National Magazine (Boston) 17:91-2 O '02

Quiller-Couch, (Sir) Arthur Thomas

From a Cornish window. London, Arrowsmith, 1906

R. Kipling: comparative psychologist. Atlan 81:858-9 Je '98

Ralph, Julian

Provincial letters and other papers. London, Smith, Elder, 1906

War's brighter side. . . New York, Appleton, 1901. vii-xvii,471p

Ramsay, Bernard Malcolm

The hooligan of literature. T.P.'s Weekly 15:20 Ja 7 '10

Randell, Wilfrid L.

The modern laureate. Acad 84:740 Je 14 '13

Rankin, Scott

People I have never met. Rudyard Kipling. Idler 3:511 Je '93

Ray, Bessie L.

Kipling's pictures of the relation of the two races in India. Masters essay, Columbia univ. 1931

Raymond, E. T. [pseud]

see Thompson, Edward Raymond

Really discovering Kipling. Bookm (NY) 38:99-101 O '13

The **recovery** of Rudyard Kipling. Ind 51:708-9 Mr 9 '99

The **red-dogs.** Spec 75:760-1 N 30 '95

Redman, H. Vere

Kipling's Englishman. Studies in English Literature (Japan) Ap '31

Two English journalist authors. Kipling and Wells in relation to the types of Englishmen they present. Studies in English Literature (Japan) Jl '29

Regnier, Henri François Joseph de

Figures et caractères. Paris, Mercure de France, 1901

Reilly, Joseph John

The passing of Kipling. Cath World 109:588-600 Ag '19

The **residence** of Rudyard Kipling. Country Life in America 14:552-5 O '08

The **rhyme** of the three captains. British Weekly 51:601 F 22 '12

Rice, Wallace

Introduction. *In* Kipling's poems. . . Chicago, Star publishing co. 1899. p i-xxvi

Richardson, Faithe

Kipling's types of Indian characters. Masters essay, Univ. of Colorado, 1932. 98ff

Rideing, William H.

The boyhood of famous authors. New York, Crowell [1897] p200-11

Ridpath, John Clark

The ascendency of Kipling. Arena 19:424-8 Mr '98

Rivett-Carnac, J. H.

"Stalky & co." by Rudyard Kipling. Notes & Q 12th ser 7:57, 298 Jl 17, O 9 '20

Roberton, William

The Kipling guide-book. A handy guide to Rudyard Kipling, his life and writings, with a bibliography of his works. Birmingham, Holland co. 1899. 52p

Roberts, Richard Ellis

Reading for pleasure, and other essays. London, Methuen, 1928

Rudyard Kipling. Empire Review 47:184-93 Mr '28

Robertson, T. M.

Rudyard Kipling. Madras, Natesan, 1905

(Rev in Calcutta Review 121:468 Jl '05)

Robinson, E. Kay

Kipling and the other two. Lit 4:445-6 Ap 29 '99

Kipling in India. . . McClure's Magazine 7:99-109 Jl '96

Rudyard Kipling as journalist. Lit 4:284-6 Mr 18 '99

Robinson, John P.

The ex-Kipling [with poem] Fishing Gazette (London) 47:282 O 31 '03

Rockingham
Kipling and the Swastika. Notes & Q
11th ser 2:338 O 22 '10

Rogers, Joseph M.
Kipling before he was famous. Bookn
25:209-10 D '06

Rollins, Alice W.
Mr. Kipling's "Recessional." Critic (NY)
31:115 Ag 28 '97

Romaine, Harry
The censor; poem. Lit W 22:256 Ag 1
'91

Roosmale-Cocq, Vivian
Is Kipling great? T.P.'s Weekly 15:68
Ja 21 '10

Rose-Soley, A. R.
To Rudyard Kipling; "Gentleman un-
afraid"; poem. Overland Monthly 2d
ser 33:354-5 Ap '99

Roth, L. von
R. Kipling der prophet der angelsächs.
weltherrschaft. Die Wahrheit p259-65
'99

**[Rowland-Brown, Lillian Kate] Rowland
Grey [pseud]**
The Kipling woman. Bookm (Lond) 80:
4-5 Ap '31

Roz, Firmin
Romanciers anglais contemporains. M.
Rudyard Kipling. R Deux Mondes 5th
ser 50:382-419 Ap 1 '09; *same in* Le
roman anglais contemporain. Paris,
Hachette, 1912. p167-223

Rudyard Kipling. New York, Scribner,
1899
(Issued in connection with the Outward Bound edition of Kipling)

Rudyard Kipling. *In* The Columbia university course in literature. New
York. Columbia univ. press, 1929.
vol XV p289-93

Rudyard Kipling. (1865-19) *In* Warner,
C. D. ed. Library of the world's best
literature... Memorial ed. New York,
Hill [c1902] vol XXII p8633-7

Rudyard Kipling. T.P.'s Weekly 22:858
D 26 '13; T.P.'s Weekly 27:331 Ap 1
'16; Lit 1:120, 248 N 13, D 11 '97;
Speaker 19:256-7 Mr 4 '99; *same.* Liv
Age 220:786-8 Mr 25 '99; Critic (NY)
16:212-13 Ap 26 '90; Liv Age 278:563-9
Ag 30 '13; J Ed 49:152-3 Mr 9 '99; Die
Umschau 3:242-6 Mr 25 '99; Everyman
8:721 D 31 '32; Out 61:490-1 Mr 4 '99

Rudyard Kipling and his stories. London,
Macmillan, nd; *same.* Book B ns 7:
377-9 O '90

Rudyard Kipling broadcasts. News-Week
1:14-15 Jl 22 '33

Rudyard Kipling na Academia Brasileira.
Revista da Academia Brasileira de
Letras anno 18 vol 23:427-47 Ap '27

Rudyard Kipling on the magic of words.
Cur Lit 41:42-3 Jl '06

Rudyard Kipling the man. New Voice 16:
13 Ap 1 '99

Rudyard Kiplingism. Sat R 89:237, 268 F
24, Mr 3 '00

Rudyard Kipling's first book. R of Rs
(NY) 7:229 Mr '93

Rudyard Kipling's latest move. Munsey's
Magazine 15:251-2 Ap '96

Rudyard Kipling's proof sheets. Liv Age
322:386 Ag 23 '24

Rumson, A.
Kipling's India. 1915

Russell, Charles Edward
Are there two Rudyard Kiplings?
Cosmopolitan 31:653-60 O '01; *same.*
Crampton F '02

[Russell, George William] A.E. [pseud]
"Ulster": an open letter to Mr. Rudyard
Kipling. *In* Imaginations and reveries.
New York, Macmillan, 1915. p80-5

Rutland, Arthur
Rudyard Kipling. Bookm (Lond) 71:14-
16 O '26

Saintsbury, George
Notes on a cellar-book. London, Mac-
millan, 1920. xxi,227p [Dedicated to
Kipling]

Salomon, Louis B.
The devil take her... Philadelphia, Univ.
of Penna. 1931

Salomon, Ludwig
Rudyard Kipling. Illustrirte Zeitung
112:375-6 Mr '99

Sanborn, M. Roy
Kipling poem. Notes & Q 11th ser 9:416
My 23 '14

Sandys, Sydney
Known on the tramp steamer. T.P.'s
Weekly 15:44 Ja 14 '10

Sarath-Roy, A. R.
Rudyard Kipling seen through Hindu
eyes. No Am 199:271-81 F '14

Sarfatti, M. G.
Il re del creato. Gerarchia '22

Saxton, Eugene F. (comp)
The Kipling index being a guide to the
authorized American trade edition of
Rudyard Kipling's works. Comp. by
Eugene F. Saxton, March, 1911. Garden City, New York, Doubleday, Page
[c1911] [iv]44p

The scene of Kipling's tales. Critic (NY)
18:22-3 Ja 10 '91

Schelling, Felix E.
The English lyric. Boston, Houghton,
Mifflin, 1913. p264-5

Schloesser, Frank
Kipling and the swastika. Notes & Q
11th ser 2:338 O 22 '10

Schmidt, Fredrik
A study in English school-life and school-
boy slang as represented by Kipling's
Stalky & co. Engl Stud 39:240-74 '08

Schultz, William Eben
Kipling's "Recessional." Mod Lang N
35:375 Je '20

Schuyler, Montgomery
Rudyard Kipling as a poet. Forum 22: 406-13 D '96

Schweikert, H. C. (ed)
Short stories. New York, Harcourt [c1925] p414-15 [Collection of short stories with brief sketch of authors]

The **scientific** spirit in Kipling's work. Popular Science Monthly 52:269-73 D '97

Scott, [W.] Dixon
The meekness of Mr. Rudyard Kipling. *In* Men of letters . . . with an introduction by Max Beerbohm. London, Hodder & Stoughton, 1916. p48-62

Rudyard Kipling. Bookm (Lond) **43:** 143-6 D '12

Scott-James, Rolfe Arnold
Living English poets. No Am 198:370-4 S '13

Personality in literature. London, Secker, 1913. p204-10

Scripture, E. W.
Kipling's lyrik. Archiv für die Gesamte Psychologie 65:66-76 '28

Verseformeln und betonungsprinzipien bei Hardy und Kipling. Die Neueren Sprachen 38:122-6 F-Mr '30

Seaman, (Sir) Owen
The rhyme of the Kipperling. *In* The battle of the bays. New York, Lane, 1896. p15-21

[Secret of Kipling's success] Cur Lit 50: 109-10 Ja '11

Ségur, Nicolas
Rudyard Kipling. La Revue 72:429-36 F 15 '08

Sencourt, Robert
India in English literature. London, Simpkin, Marshall, Hamilton, Kent [pref. 1923] p454-5

Serra, Renato
Rudyard Kipling. *In* Scritti inedite. Opere. Firenze, 1923. vol IV

Servajean, H.
Un discours sur Rudyard Kipling et la France. Revue A A 2:157-62 D '24

["Seven seas" as a title] Bookm (NY) 4: 413-14 Ja '97

Shanks, Edward
Mr. Rudyard Kipling. *In* Second essays on literature. London, Collins, 1927. p1-22

Rudyard Kipling. Lond Merc 7:273-84 Ja '23; *same.* Liv Age 316:410-17 F 17 '23

Sheldon, Walther Lorenzo
Two sides of Kipling. (Ethical addresses, ser 7 no 8) Philadelphia, Weston, 1900. p129-50

Sherman, Ellen Burns
Kipling's attitude. Sat R Lit 3:666 Mr 19 '27

Sherwood, Jessie B.
Kipling's women. Fine Arts Journal 37: 42-7 Mr '19

Shindler, Robert
The outlook—Rudyard Kipling. *In* On certain aspects of recent English literature. (Neuphilologische Vorträge und Abhandlungen II) Leipzig, Teubner, 1902. p96-112

The **sincerest** form of flattery. I. Of Mr. Rudyard Kipling. A slight inaccuracy. Cornhill ns 15:367-9 O '90

A **singer** of brave songs. Cent 58:163 My '99

Singh, Bhupal
Rudyard Kipling. *In* A survey of Anglo-Indian fiction. London, Oxford univ. press, 1934. p68-82

Rudyard Kipling and his school. *In* A survey of Anglo-Indian fiction. London, Oxford univ. press, 1934. p83-108

The **skyline** of the future. Rudyard Kipling's inspiring vision of the conquest of the air. Cartoons 5:450-2 My '14

Sladen, Douglas
Rudyard Kipling's poetry. Literary World (Lond) ns 47:319-21 Ap 7 '93

Slayton, W. H.
Kipling as an exponent of the modern spirit. J Ed 74:145-7 Ag 17 '11

Smalley, George Washburn
English men of letters. McClure's Magazine 20:296 Ja '03

Smith, M.
II. Kipling as a play-boy. Literary Digest International Book Review 4:303 Ap '26

Smith, Marion C.
Kipling's psychology; poem. Ind 71: 1445 D 28 '11

[Smoking room in "Captains courageous"] Bookm (NY) 18:9-12 S '03

Some opinions. Blackw 164:593, 601-2 N '98

Some recent verse. Edin R 210:395-6 O '09

[Source of title "The Seven Seas"] Critic (NY) 30:191 Mr 13 '97

Spee, Antonia, gräfin
Der sinnesimpressionismus bei Kipling. Diss. Bonn, 1934. 39p

Spruch, Christine
Die verwendung der mundart bei Rudyard Kipling. Breslau [Engl. Seminar Univ.] 1930. Diss. Breslau, 1930[1931] *In* Beiträge zur Erforschung der Sprache und Kultur Englands und Nordamerikas (Giessen) 6,heft 2:63-172 '30
(Rev by F. Karpf in Bei Anglia 42: 209-12 Jl '31; A. C. Dunstan in Engl Stud 66:260-1 '31)

Squire, John Collings
Mr. Kipling's later verse. *In* Books in general. London, Heinemann, 1921. 3d ser p194-9

Stabler, Marguerite
An inside light on Rudyard Kipling. Pacific Monthly 18:560-2 N '07

Stalky and co. Spec 83:607 O 28 '99

[Stalky & Co.] Bookm (NY) 10:300-1 D '99

Steckelberg, Anna Louise
The structure of the short story based on a study of the works of Kipling. Masters essay, Univ. of Nebraska, 1917. 13ff

Stedman, Edmund Clarence
Kipling's ballads of "The seven seas." *In* Genius, and other essays. New York, Moffat Yard, 1911. p268-73

Stephen, J. K.
Lapsus calami. Cambridge, Macmillan and Bowes, 1891. p3
(Noted in National Observer ns 6: 123 Je 20 '91)

Stephens, A. G.
The red pagan. Sydney, Bulletin co. [?]

Stephens, Henry Morse
Four phases of Kipling's work. University of California Chronicle 3:246-69 O '00

Stevenson, Lionel
Darwin among the poets. Chicago, Univ. of Chicago press [c1932] p316-23

The ideas in Kipling's poetry. University of Toronto Quarterly 1:467-89 Jl '32

Stevenson, Robert Louis
. . . On himself and his contemporaries. Critic (NY) 22:408 Je 17 '93

Stewart, Alexander G.
Rudyard Kipling, yeoman of Burwash. Literary Digest International Book Review 3:100-1 Ja '25

Stoddard, Charles Warren
Rudyard Kipling at Naulakha. National Magazine 22:259-68 Je '05

Stopford, Francis
Britain's living seer. Land and Water 65:15-16 Ag 21 '15

Stories of famous concert songs: "On the road to Mandalay" by Oley Speaks. Etude 51:82 F '33

Strachey, Henry
Kipling on Shakespeare. Spec 81:45-6 Jl 9 '98

Strang [William]
A series of thirty etchings by William Strang, illustrating subjects from the writings of Rudyard Kipling. London, Macmillan, 1901. 29 plates

Strange case of Mr. Rudyard Kipling. J Ed 82:372-3 O 21 '15

Stroke, Captain
The abolition of Rudyard Kipling. Fishing Gazette (London) 47:282 O 31 '03

Strunk, W.
Mr. Kipling justified. Nation (NY) 63: 472 D 24 '96

Sunderland, Jabez T.
The religion of Rudyard Kipling. New England Magazine ns 20:604-12 Jl '99

The **suppressed** works of Rudyard Kipling. Bookm (Lond) 3:116-18 Ja '93

Swaffer, Hannen
Rudyard Kipling. *In* Hannen Swaffer's who's who. London, Hutchinson [1929] p233-5

Swain, Corinne Rockwell
The traveller and the tramp royal. Nation (NY) 91:336-7 O 13 '10

T.P.'s portrait gallery—IV. Rudyard Kipling. T.P.'s Weekly 14:637 N 12 '09

T.P.'s Referendum: who shall be Laureate? T.P.'s Weekly 22:73 Jl 18 '13

Taking Kipling to task. Lit Digest 51:840-1 O 16 '15

Tapp, H. A.
Rudyard Kipling at Westward Ho! 1878-1882. *In* United Service College, 1874-1911. . . Aldershot, Printed for private circulation only by Gale and Polden [1934?] p13-14

"Stalky & Co." *In* United Service College, 1874-1911. . . Aldershot, Printed for private circulation only by Gale and Polden [1934?] p17

Tavenor-Perry, J.
Kipling and the swastika. Notes & Q 11th ser 2:292 O 8 '10; others on the same question, ibid 292-3 O 8 '10

Tenney, Mae Alice
Rudyard Kipling's literary relations with the French. Masters essay, Univ. of California, 1919. 155ff

Tennyson and Kipling. Bookm (NY) 22: 554-6 F '06

Thacker, J. G.
The seven seas. Notes & Q 11th ser 11: 502 Je 26 '15

That Kipling calendar. Town Talk 11:3 Ja 24 '03

That Kipling story. Bookm (NY) 38:475-6 Ja '14

A **theme** for an American play. Town Talk 23:5 F 21 '14

Thevenot, E.
Kipling et les instincts primitifs. Revue A A 6:421-8 Je '29

["They"] Lamp 29:226-31 O '04

Thompson, C. Patrick
The white-faced boy of Lahore. World Review 8:56-7 F 25 '29

[Thompson, Edward Raymond] E. T. Raymond [pseud]
Portraits of the new century. New York, Doubleday [c1928] p34-7

Thompson, Maurice
Theocritus, Weatherley and Kipling. Critic (NY) 22:45 Ja 28 '93

Thornbury, L. A.
The misquotations of Kipling. Cunard Daily Bulletin S 9 '12

Thundering dawn in Kipling and Francis Thompson. Notes & Q 11th ser 1:467, 2:113 Je 11, Ag 6 '10

Tille, Alexander
Kipling. Frankfurter Zeitung 170:19 '00
Rudyard Kipling. Die Zukunft 3:165-71 Ap 22 '93

Tinker, Chauncey Brewster
Caverns measureless to man: poetry and its sources. *In* Good estate of poetry. Boston, Little, Brown, 1929. p55-82
Xanadu [traffics and discoveries] Sat R Lit 3:815-17 My 14 '27

Tissot-Cantecor, Yvonne
Évolution du caractère de la nouvelle chez R. Kipling. Revue Germ 10:160-95 Mr-Ap '14

To Rudyard Kipling; poem. Bookm (NY) 10:337 D '99

Tomlinson, Henry Major
Kipling. *In* Waiting for daylight. New York, Knopf, 1922. p182-7

Tommy Atkins to Mr. Kipling; poem. Argonaut 46:10 Ja 15 '00

Traffics and mafficks. The strange case of Mr. Kipling. [signed "Y.Y."] Bookm (Lond) 27:76-8 N '04

Trevor, G. H.
Rudyard Kipling; poem. New Century Review 5:458 Je '99

Trevor, Philip C. W.
"Bobs" and Kitchener; poem [parody of Kipling's "Fighting Bobs"] Argonaut 46:9 F 12 '00
Thomas Atkins on Rudyard Kipling. Idler 14:136-41 Ag '98

Tuell, Anne Kimball
Mrs. Meynell and her literary generation. New York, Dutton [c1925]

Turnbull, T. E.
Mr. Kipling's titles. Acad 68:346 Mr 25 '05

A twelve-year-old critic of Kipling. Spec 110:536 Mr 29 '13

Über Kiplings aerzte. Münchner Medizinische Wochenschrift '08

Van Doren, Carl and Van Doren, Mark
American and British literature since 1890. New York, Century [c1925] p137-40, 171-7

Van Patten, Nathan
Kipling and his pirates. Bookman's Journal 11:43-4 O '24

Van Zile, Edward Sims
Kipling; poem. Lit Digest 88:32 Ja 30 '26

"A verray parfit Nobel Knight." Punch 133:435 D 18 '07

Vogüé, Vicomte Eugène-Melchoir de
La littérature impérialiste [Disraeli and Rudyard Kipling] R Deux Mondes 5th ser 3:196-212 My 1 '01; *same in* Pages d'histoire. Paris, Colin, 1902. p121-34
Le prix Nobel à Rudyard Kipling. Le Figaro D 11 '07 p1

Vowinckel, Ernst
Der englische roman der neuesten zeit und gegenwart. Berlin, Herbig, 1926. p157-9

Waddell, Milford Rhoades
Rudyard Kipling's reading with special attention to "Puck of Pook's Hill." Masters essay, Cornell Univ. 1929. 107ff

Waddington, R.
Kipling's charm. T.P.'s Weekly 15:20 Ja 7 '10

Wainewright, John B.
Gothaven. Notes & Q 11th ser 9:393-4 My 16 '14

Waldo, Fullerton Leonard
Kipling in Philadelphia. Out 130:138-9 Ja 25 '22

Walker, Arthur H.
Mr. Kipling's schoolmasters and schoolboys. Bookm (Lond) 17:46 N '99
The United Services college at Westward Ho! the school of Rudyard Kipling. Public School N '99

Wanamaker, John
Kipling and S.S. libraries. Lit W 30:298-9 S 16 '99

War and poetry. Edin R 196:48-9 Jl '02

Ward, Alfred C.
Rudyard Kipling: "Life's handicap." *In* Aspects of the modern short story. . . New York, Dial press, 1925. p116-28
Twentieth century literature. London, Methuen, 1928. p105-8

Ward, Harry Frederick
The religion of Kipling. Meth R 82:262-9 Mr '00

Warren, Algernon
French praise of Kipling as a fabulist. Bookman's Journal 2:232 Ag 6 '20

Waterhouse, Francis Asbury
The literary fortunes of Kipling. Yale R ns 10:817-31 Jl '21
Rudyard Kipling—primitivist. *In* Random studies in the romantic chaos. New York, McBride, 1923. p139-61

Watson, T. F.
Mr. Kipling's "Recessional" again. Critic (NY) 32:77 Ja 29 '98

Watson, William
Mr. William Watson and Mr. Rudyard Kipling. Acad 82:414 Mr 30 '12

Waugh, Arthur
The library edition of Kipling's poetry. Liv Age 304:428-30 F 14 '20
Mr. Kipling as poet. . . Book Monthly 1:90-5 N '03
One man's road. London, Chapman and Hall, 1931. p185-9, 199-200
The poetry of the South African campaign. Anglo-Saxon Review 7:46-58 D '00
Retrospect and prospect. *In* Reticence in literature, and other papers. London, Wilson [1915] p86-9

[The **way** in which Mr. Kipling's poem "Recessional" first reached the "Times"] Lit 8:279 Ap 13 '01

Webb, Alfred
Mr. Kipling's call to America. Nation (NY) 68:144 F 23 '99

Weird, Colin
Kipling as a story teller. Great Thoughts Mr '94

[**Welby, Thomas Earle**]
Mr. Kipling. *In* Back numbers. London, Constable, 1929. p55-8

Weld, Helen
Three Kipling boys. Scholastic 10:14 Ap 30 '27

Wells, Carolyn
A ballade of petition; poem. Bookm (NY) 8:423 Ja '99

The poets; poem. Judge F 17 '02

Wells, Herbert George
The new Machiavelli. London, Lane, 1913. 536p

Western stories of the East. Church Q R 56:96-118 Ap '03; *same.* Liv Age 238:193-206 Jl 25 '03

Weston, A. D.
An American girl's reply to Kipling's criticisms. Bookman's Journal and Print Collector 3:404 Ap 1 '21

Weynants-Ronday, Marie
Rudyard Kipling et l'Égypte. Chronique d'Égypte 6:59-73 Ja '31

Whatley, W. A.
Kipling influence in the verse of Robert W. Service. Texas Review 6:299-308 Jl '21

Wheeler, Harold L. (compiler)
Contemporary novels and novelists: a list of references to biographical and critical material. *In* School of mines and metallurgy. University of Missouri. Bulletin. June 1920. Rolla, Missouri, 1921. p77-8

Where Kipling found his new book ["Puck"] Bookn 25:141 N '06

Where Kipling stands. Bookm (NY) 29:120-2 Ap '09

Where Kipling wrote "The light that failed." Overland Monthly 79:67 Ap '22

White, Edward L.
"Rewards and Fairies." Notes & Q 158:82 F 1 '30

White, Michael Gifford
Kipling at school. Ind 51:752-4 Mr 16 '99; *same.* J Ed 50:93-4 Jl 27 '99

The **"White** Man's Burden." R of Rs (Lond) 19:139, 418 F, Ap '99; Spec 82:193-4 F 11 '99; *same.* Liv Age 220:663-5 Mr 11 '99

[The **white** man's burden] Explanation, parody and criticism of Rudyard Kipling's celebrated poem "The white man's burden." The cream of the daily press clippings since poem appeared. Chicago, Whipple [189-?] [20]p

Whitten, Wilfred
Mr. Kipling: where does he stand? Bookm (Lond) 23:141-5 Ja '03; *same.* Bookm (NY) 16:586-8 F '03

Why Kipling became a prohibitionist. Amethyst (Pittsburg) S '12

Wild, Friedrich
Die englische literatur der gegenwart seit 1870; drama und roman. Wiesbaden, Dioskuren-Verlag, 1928. p209-20

Wilhelm, M.
Kiplings niedergang. Das Freie Wort 2:278-83 '02

Wilkin, Lola
Literary treatment of the new material furnished by the life of the modern industrial age in the poetry and prose of Rudyard Kipling. Masters essay, Univ. of Kansas, 1928. 119ff

Willey, Day Allen
In Kipling's village. National Magazine 16:91-100 Ap '02

Williams, Charles
Rudyard Kipling. *In* Poetry at present. Oxford, Clarendon press, 1930. p40-55

Williams, Harold
Modern English writers. . . London, Sidgwick & Jackson, 1925. p56-62, 317-26

[**Williams, Jesse Lynch**]
Rudyard Kipling. New York, Scribner, 1899. 13p

Williams, Myrtle
Rudyard Kipling as an exponent of English ideals. Masters essay, Univ. of California, 1916. 90ff

Williams, Talcott
Kipling in prose and verse. Bookn 25:207-8 D '06

Williamson, Claude C. H.
Rudyard Kipling. *In* Writers of three centuries, 1789-1914. Philadelphia, Jacobs [1915?] p438-43

Wing, T. E.
Tommy Atkins' reply to Rudyard Kipling's fine poem ["The absent-minded beggar"] London, 1899

Wit, Augusta de
Actions and reactions. De Nieuwe Rotterdamsche Courant O 8 '10

Wolfe, F.
Mr. Kipling's titles. Acad 68:375 Ap 1 '05

Wolfe, Humbert
Dialogues and monologues. London, Gollancz, 1928. p90-2, 183-6

Epitaphs in advance. IV. Rudyard Kipling; poem. Spec 134:448 Mr 21 '25; *same.* Liv Age 325:505 Je 6 '25

Wolfe, Theodore Frelinghuysen
Kipling, Hartford authors. . . *In* Literary haunts and homes; American authors. Philadelphia, Lippincott, 1899. p207-14

Woollcott, Alexander
Another story. New Yorker 6:38 S 13 '30

On topographical errors. New Yorker 5:43 D 21 '29

Woolsey, Sarah C.
Kipling and S.S. libraries. Lit W 30:299 S 16 '99

The work of Rudyard Kipling. Bookm (Lond) 1:29-30, 63-5 O, N '91

The works of Mr. Rudyard Kipling. Edin R 187:203-26 Ja '98

Worster, W.
Merlin's isle; a study of Rudyard Kipling's England. . . London, Gyldendal [1920?] 75p

Worster, W. J. Alexander
Kiplings maend. Gads Danske Magasin p764-8 '11-'12

Wright, Edward
A literary causerie; glamour and vision. Acad 70:428-9 My 5 '06

Wyzewa, Teodor de
Le nouveau roman de M. Rudyard Kipling: Kim. R Deux Mondes 5th ser 5:936-46 O 15 '01

Rudyard Kipling, Stalky and co. *In* Écrivains étrangers. Paris, 1900. 3d ser

Yesterday's Kipling. Bookm (NY) 37:112-13 Ap '13

Young, William Arthur
A dictionary of the characters and scenes in the stories and poems of Rudyard Kipling, 1886-1911. . . London, Routledge [1911] xxx,231p
(Rev in Bookm (NY) 35:590-1 Ag '12)

The Sussex of Rudyard Kipling. Bookm (NY) 43:38-51 Mr '16

Zachrisson, Robert Eugen
Modern engelsk världsåskådning i litteraturens spegel. Stockholm, Almquist and Wiksells, 1928

Zangwill, I.
The autograph difficulty solved afresh. Pall Mall Magazine 7:152-3 S '95

Zilch, Rudyard [pseud]
If; poem [parody] Ballyhoo (Washington, D.C.) N 5 '32

Zweig, Arnold
Kiplings djungelbuch. Scheinwerfer 3:20-4 '30

Über ein unbekanntes, weltberühmtes buch. *In* Aus unbekannten schriften. Festgabe für Martin Buber zum 50. geburtstag. Berlin, Schneider, 1928. p184-90

William Morris

William Morris

I. Chronological Outline

1834. Born, March 24, Walthamstow.

1856. The Hollow Land, and other contributions to the *Oxford and Cambridge Magazine.*

1858. The Defence of Guenevere, and Other Poems.

1867. The Life and Death of Jason.

1868-1870. The Earthly Paradise.

1869. Grettis Saga. The Story of Grettir the Strong. Translated by Morris and Magnússon.

1870. Völsunga Saga. The Story of the Volsungs and the Niblungs, With Certain Songs from the Elder Edda. Translated by Morris and Magnússon.

1873. Love is Enough.

1875. Three Northern Love Stories, and Other Tales. Translated by Morris and Magnússon.

1875. The Aeneids of Virgil done into English Verse.

1877. The Story of Sigurd the Volsung, and the Fall of the Niblungs.

1882. Hopes and Fears for Art.

1884-1885. Chants for Socialists.

1886. The Pilgrims of Hope.

1887. The Odyssey of Homer done into English Verse.

1888. Signs of Change: Seven Lectures Delivered on Various Occasions.

1888. A Dream of John Ball, and A King's Lesson.

1888. A Tale of the House of the Wolfings.

1889. The Roots of the Mountains.

1891. The Story of the Glittering Plain.

1891. News from Nowhere.

1891. Poems by the Way.

1891. The Saga Library. Translated by Morris and Magnússon.

1893. Gothic Architecture: a Lecture for the Arts and Crafts Exhibition Society.

1893. Socialism: Its Growth and Outcome. By Morris and E. B. Bax.

1894. The Wood Beyond the World.

1894. Letters on Socialism.

1895. Child Christopher and Fair Goldilind.

1895. The Tale of Beowulf done out of the Old English Tongue. By Morris and A. J. Wyatt.

1896. The Well at the World's End.

1896. Old French Romances done into English.

1896. Died, October 3, Hammersmith.

1897. The Water of the Wondrous Isles.

1898. The Sundering Flood.

William Morris

II. Bibliographical Material

[Bibliography of the Kelmscott press with prices] Critic (NY) 35:918-19 O '99

Brown, G. A.
[Bibliography] *In* C H E L vol XIII p543-5

Carter, John and Pollard, Graham
William Morris. *In* An enquiry into the nature of certain nineteenth century pamphlets. London, Constable, 1934. p205-12

Cary, Elisabeth Luther
Bibliography. *In* William Morris, poet, craftsman, socialist. New York, Putnam [c1902] p269-90

Clark, William Andrews, jr.
The library of William Andrews Clark, jr. The Kelmscott and Doves presses . . . collated and compiled by R. E. Cowan assisted by Cora E. Sanders and Harrison Post. With an intro. by A. W. Pollard. San Francisco, Printed for J. H. Nash, 1921. xxxviii,123p (150 copies only)

Cleveland Public Library, The
William Morris: some books and periodicals in the Cleveland Public Library. [Cleveland] 1910. 15p

Cockerell, Sydney Carlyle
An annotated list of all the books printed at the Kelmscott Press. . . *In* A note by William Morris on his aims in founding the Kelmscott Press. [Hammersmith, Kelmscott press, 1898] p21-65

Cole, George Douglas Howard
[Bibliographical notes] *In* William Morris. Stories in prose, stories in verse, shorter poems, lectures and essays. (Centenary edition) New York, Random House, 1934. p[2, 283, 410,] 473-[474]

Colwell, Percy Robert
Bibliography. *In* The poems of William Morris. New York Crowell [c1904] pxi-xiv

Crow, Gerald H.
Bibliography. *In* William Morris, designer. New York, The Studio Publications, 1934. p118

Forman, Harry Buxton
The books of William Morris described, with some account of his doings in literature and in the allied crafts. London, Hollings, 1897. xv,224p

Henkels, S. V.
Publications of William Morris's Kelmscott press in the private library of L. T. Marshall. 1900

The **Kelmscott** press. A review and some statistics. Scottish Review 36:30-3 Jl '00

Kelmscott press books: their titles: the order of publication: sizes: number of copies printed. . . Book-Lover no 10:488-9 '02

[**Lists**, etc., of the Kelmscott Press publications] Hammersmith, Kelmscott Press, 1894-1897 [unpaged]

Loubier, Jean
Bibliographien von Morris's Schriften. Zeitschrift für Bücherfreunde 2:256-7 Ag-S '98

Manchester. Municipal Technical School and Municipal School of Art
Catalogue of an exhibition of the work of Willam Morris. Manchester, Municipal School of Art, 1908. 14p 11 plates

Morgan, John Pierpont
Catalogue of manuscripts and early printed books from the libraries of William Morris. . . London, Chiswick Press, 1906-1907. 4 vols

Morris, May
Bibliographical notes. *In* The collected works of William Morris. London, Longmans, Green, 1910-1915. 24 vols

The **Morris** exhibit at the Foreign Fair, Boston, 1883-84. Boston, Roberts, 1883. 5-30p

North, Ernest Dressel
A bibliography of the Kelmscott press publications. Book B ns 12: 550-4 N '95; Book B ns 13:923-4 Ja '97; Book B ns 16:423-4 Je '98

Northup, Clark Sutherland
A register of bibliographies of the English language and literature. New Haven, Yale univ. press, 1925. p259-60

Page, Curtis Hidden
Morris. List of references. *In* British poets of the nineteenth century, ed. by C. H. Page. New ed. by Stith Thompson. New York, Sanborn, 1930. p850-1

Perry, Marsden Jasiel
A chronological list of the books printed at the Kelmscott Press, with illustrative material from a collection made by William Mor-

Perry, Marsden Jasiel—*Continued*
ris and Henry C. Marillier, now
in the library of Marsden Jasiel
Perry of Providence, Rhode Island. [Boston, Merrymount press,
1928] vii,42p
(800 copies only)

Quinn, John
The library of John Quinn. . . New
York, Anderson galleries, 1924.
part IV p667-93

Ransom, Will
The Kelmscott press. *In* Private
presses and their books. New
York, Bowker, 1929. p325-31

Rinder, Frank
The Kelmscott press. [record of
copies and sales of books by the
press] Connoisseur 1:266-7 '01

Roden, Robert F.
Kelmscott books. Record prices in
England and America. New York
Times Saturday Review Ja 11 '02
p28 columns 3-4

Scott, Temple
A bibliography of the Kelmscott
press publications. Bookselling 1:
10-14 D '95

A bibliography of the original writings, translations and publications
of William Morris. *In* Vallance,
Aymer. The art of William Morris. London, Bell, 1897. appendix,
p[ii]-xxx
(220 copies only)

A bibliography of the works of
William Morris. London, Bell,
1897. vii,120p
(Rev in Ath 2:591-2 O 30 '97; Sat
R 83:621 Je 5 '97; Literary World
(Lond) ns 56:85 Jl 30 '97; Lit 1:
237 D 11 '97)

Slater, J. H.
Early editions. . . London, Paul,
1894. p198-208

(Rev by T. J. Wise in Bookm
(Lond) 6:49-50 My '94)

Steele, Robert
The Kelmscott press. *In* The revival of printing: a bibliographical
catalogue of works issued by the
chief modern English presses.
With an intro. by Robert Steele.
(Ricardi press books) London,
Warner, 1912. p11-23
(350 copies only)
(Rev by A. W. Pollard in Acad
82:615-16 My 8 '12)

Tomkinson, G. S.
The Kelmscott press. *In* A select
bibliography of the principal modern presses public and private in
Great Britain and Ireland. London, First edition club, 1928. p104-
31

Vallance, Aymer
Chronological list of the printed
works of William Morris. *In*
William Morris, his art, his writ-
ings, and public life. London,
Bell, 1897. p[447]-452

Vaughan, Charles Edwyn
Bibliography of the works of Wil-
liam Morris. *In* Bibliographies of
Swinburne, Morris and Rossetti.
(The English Association. Pam-
phlet no 29) [Oxford, Horace
Hart] 1914. p7-11

William Morris: biography and bibliography. Dial 21:211 O 16 '96

William Morris: printer and collector.
Lit 9:249 S 14 '01

Woods, George Benjamin
[Bibliography] *In* Poetry of the
Victorian period. New York,
Scott, Foresman [c1930] p1018-
21

William Morris

III. Biographical and Critical Material

Abbott, Leonard
The William Morris labour church at Leek. Book B ns 16:31-3 F '98
William Morris's Commonweal. New England Magazine ns 20:428-33 Je '99

Ackerman, Phyllis
Tapestry the mirror of civilization. New York, Oxford univ. press, 1933. p298-302
Wallpaper; its history, design and use. New York, Stokes, 1923. p61-4

Adams, Florence L.
The versification of William Morris. Masters essay, Columbia univ. 1911

Adams, Oscar Fay
Manuscripts, unpublished stories, clippings, etc., received from his literary executor, Miss Abbie Farwell Brown, May 16, 1925. Scrapbooks. 1. Notes on Morris's Earthly Paradise. 6 envelopes in portfolio. *In* Boston Public Library. Boston, Mass.

Adler, Georg
Geschichte des sozialismus und kommunismus von Plato bis zur gegenwart. Leipzig, 1899. vol I

Agresti, Antonio
Artisti e decoratori: William Morris e Walter Crane. Nuova Antol 216:621-35 D 16 '07

Allen, Ralph Bergen
Old Icelandic sources in the English novel. Doctor's essay, Univ. of Pennsylvania, 1933. p22-5

Allingham, H. and D. Radford (eds)
William Allingham, a diary. London, Macmillan, 1907. p75, 140-3, 153-4, 326

Anarchistische portraits: William Morris. Der Anarchist 1 no 4 O 23 '09

Apgar, Genevieve
Morris's "The Lady of the Land." Poet Lore 33:274-85 Je '22
Morris's "The Lady of the Land," its analogues, source and literary qualities. Masters essay, Stanford Univ. 1921. 49ff

App, August J.
Lancelot in English literature; his role and character. Diss. Catholic univ. 1929. p176-82

Arkell, Reginald
Kelmscott; a footnote to the William Morris centenary. Bookm (Lond) 86: 56-7 Ap '34

Arms, John Taylor
Handbook of print making and print makers. New York, Macmillan, 1934. p94

Arnot, Robert Page
William Morris versus the Morris myth. Labour Monthly 16:178-84 Mr '34

Aronstein, Philipp
William Morris. Zukunft 31:490-5 Je 16 '00

Arts and crafts in London. Nation (NY) 57:284-5 O 19 '93

Ashbee, Charles Robert
Business of Morris and company. House Beautiful 27:101-2 Mr '10
An endeavor towards the teaching of John Ruskin and William Morris. Being a brief account of the work, the aims, and the principles of the Guild of handicraft in East London. . . [London, E. Arnold, 1901] 52p (350 copies only)
The pre-Raphaelites and their influence upon life. House Beautiful 27:101-2 Mr '10

Auslander, Joseph and Hill, Frank Ernest
The winged horse. Garden City, N. Y. Doubleday, Doran, 1930. p371-80

Autograph letters and ms of Morris' speech on free trade. Recent accessions. Bodleian Quarterly Record (Oxford University. Bodleian Library) 2d quarter p71 '32

Backus, Truman J.
William Morris. *In* The outlines of literature, English and American. New York, Sheldon [c1897] p278-9

Bagster-Collins, Elijah William
The source of William Morris's poem, "The lovers of Gudrun." Masters essay, Columbia univ. 1898

Balderston, Elizabeth Grecian
William Morris and his sources. Masters essay, Univ. of California, 1921. 143ff

Baldry, A. L.
William Morris and George du Maurier. Art J 48:379 '96

Baldwin, M. H.
William Morris and his "News from nowhere." Masters essay, Indiana Univ. 1914. 26ff

Ball, A. H. R.
Introduction. *In* Selections from the prose works of William Morris. Cambridge, University press, 1931. pi-xl (Rev in T L S Ap 30 '31 p343; R. Church in Spec 146:412 Mr 14 '31; L. Wolff in Revue A A 9:159-60 D '31)

Ballod, Karl
Einiges aus der utopienliteratur der letzten jahre. Archiv für die geschichte des sozialismus und der arbeiterbewegung 6:114-28 '16

Balmforth, Ramsden
William Morris, poet and socialist. *In* Some social and political pioneers of the nineteenth century. London, Swan, 1900. p179-86

Bardi, Pietro
William Morris. *In* Storia della litteratura inglese. Bari, Gius, Laterza, 1933. p185-6

Barker, J. Ellis
British socialism. . . London, Smith, Elder, 1908. passim

Bart, Carol Spence (Prentice)
. . The influence of medieval French literature upon William Morris's "The defence of Guenevere, and other poems" . . . Chicago, 1914. 75f Diss. Univ. of Chicago. bibl f69-74

Bartels, Heinrich
William Morris, "The story of Sigurd the Volsung and the Fall of the Niblungs," eine studie über das verhältnis des epos zu den quellen. Münster, Schöningh, 1906. vi,80p bibl p[v]-vi

Barton, J. E.
The Morris note. Sat R 111:708-10 Je 10 '11

Barton, Willette Evelyn
The place of William Morris in the mediaeval movement. Masters essay, Univ. of Texas, 1933. 103ff

Bate, Percy H.
The English pre-Raphaelite painters. . . London, Bell, 1899. p79-80

Bates, Arlo
[Morris as a prospective Laureate] Book B ns 9:424 N '92

Bax, Ernest Belfort
Reminiscences and reflections. . . London, Allen, 1918. p117-22

Bayne, Thomas
Our modern poets [no xii] William Morris. St J 33:94-107 Ja '78

William Morris and a Scotch verger. Notes & Q 10th ser 11:144 F 20 '09

The beauty of England. T L S My 3 '34 p309-10

Beer, M.
A history of British socialism. London, Bell, 1920. p249-58

Beers, Henry Augustin
The pre-Raphaelites. *In* A history of English romanticism in the nineteenth century. New York, Holt, 1901. p314-40

Bell, A. F.
Rossetti, Morris, and Swinburne. *In* Leaders of English literature. London, Bell, 1915. p214-23

Bell, Mackenzie
William Morris. Lit 9:285 S 21 '01

William Morris: a eulogy. Fortn 66:693-702 N '96; *same.* Ecl M 127:777-84 D '96

Bell, Malcolm
Sir Edward Burne-Jones, a record and review. London, Bell, 1903. passim

Benn, Alfred William
The history of English rationalism in the nineteenth century. London, Longmans, Green, 1906. vol II p289-92

Benson, Arthur Christopher
Kelmscott and William Morris. *In* At large. New York, Putnam, 1908. p240-63; *same.* Putnam's Magazine 3:439-46 Ja '08

Bentley, Wilder
Morris influence. Pub W 125:1782-3 My 12 '34 [An answer to W. Bradley in Pub W 125:1373-6 Ap 7 '34]

Bernstein, E.
H. M. Hyndman's erinnerungen. Archiv für die geschichte des sozialismus und der arbeiterbewegung 4:105-15 '14

Bettmann, Otto
William Morris; with English translation. Gebrauchsgraph 11:50-7 Ap '34

Bettòli, Parmenio
William Morris. Emporium 4:330-4 N '96

Biber, Arthur Reinhold
Studien zu William Morris' prose romances. Greifswald, J. Abel, 1907. 97p Diss. Greifswald

Bierbaum, Friedrich Julius
William Morris. *In* History of the English language and literature till the Victorian age. Leipzig, Arthur Rossberg, 1922. 8th ed. p209-10

Binz, Gustav
William Morris als buchdrucker. Gutenberg gesellschaft. Jahresbericht 8:51-70 '09

Birkedal, Uffe
William Morris og hans betydning. En Levnetsskildring. Kjobenhavn, S. Bernsteen, 1908. 27p (675 copies only)

Blakey, Dorothy
A critical study of the romances of William Morris. Masters essay, Univ. of British Columbia, 1922. 105ff

Block, Louis J.
William Morris' last romances. Dial 24:320-2 My 16 '98

Bloomfield, Paul
Life and work of William Morris. (Cantor lectures, 1934) London, Royal Society of arts, 1934. 27p; *same.* Royal Society of Arts Journal 82:1103-16, 1119-32 S 21, 28 '34

William at Hammersmith. *In* Imaginary worlds. London, Hamish Hamilton [1932] p159-78, 269-83

William Morris. London, Barker, 1934. x,314p
(Rev in Spec 152:416-17 Mr 16 '34; T L S Mr 22 '34 p201; Royal Society of Arts Journal 82:534-5 Mr 23 '34; G. West in Bookm (Lond) 85:472-4 '34; Sat R p90 S 8 '34; O. Burdett in Lond Merc 29:565-7 '34; H. W. Nevinson in New Statesm & Nation p356-8 Mr 10 '34)

Blore, George Henry
William Morris, craftsman. *In* Victorian worthies. London, Oxford univ. press, 1920. p302-22

Blueher, Rudolf
Moderne Utopien; ein beitrag zur geschichte des sozialismus. (Bücherei der kultur und geschichte. Bd 9) Bonn, K. Schroeder, 1920. viii,117p

Blunt, Wilfrid Scawen
My diaries. . . New York, Knopf, 1921. Part one. passim

Boase, Frederic
Morris, William. *In* Modern English biography. Truro, Netherton & Worth, 1921. vol VI p250-1

Bodkin, Maud
Archetypal patterns in poetry. . . London, Oxford univ. press, 1934. p115-22

Bom, Emmanuel de
De tentoonstelling van het moderne boek in het Museum Plantin-Moretus te Antwerpen. . . 's Gravenhage, Nijhoff [1904] 40p

William Morris en zijn invloed up het boek; lezing gohouden Sept 1904. Amsterdam, Ipenbuur & Van Seldam, 1910. 45p

Bonnefont, G.
William Morris. Revue Britannique '96

Bottomley, Gordon
Foreword. *In* Two poems by William Morris. The defence of Guenevere and King Arthur's tomb, with eight decorations by Dante Gabriel Rossetti and a foreword by Gordon Bottomley. London, The Fanfrolico press, 1930. p[i-xvi] [450 copies only]
(Rev in T L S O 30 '30 p885)

Bowker, R. R.
London as a literary center. Harper M 76:820-1 My '88

Bowman, Florine Emily
Place of the individual in William Morris' social philosophy. Masters essay, State Univ. of Iowa, 1934. 66ff

Bradley, Will
William Morris. A review of his influence on the centenary of his birth. Pub W 125:1373-6 Ap 7 '34 [See above: Bentley, W.]

Braun, L.
Einer traum von William Morris. Die Neue Gesellschaft no 34 '06

Brewer, William F.
To William Morris; poem. Midland Monthly 7:18 Ja '97

Brief sketch of the Morris movement. Written to commemorate the firm's 50th anniversary. London, 1911

Bright, Norma K.
Social intercourse among the pre-Raphaelites. Bookn 24:691-5 Je '06

Brinton, Crane
Morris. *In* English political thought in the nineteenth century. London, Benn, 1933. p252-66

Brooke, Stopford Augustus
William Morris. *In* Four Victorian poets. New York, Putnam, 1908. p205-99
(Rev in Liv Age 258:244-9 Jl 25 '08; T L S My 21 '08 p161-2)

Browne, Anne Goodloe
William Morris and the matter of Iceland. Masters essay, Columbia univ. 1915

Bryden, Robert
Some woodcuts of men of letters of the nineteenth century. London, Dent, 1899

Buchhorn, Wilhelm
William Morris' Odyssee-übersetzung. Königsberg, Karg and Manneck, 1910. 66p Diss. Königsberg. bibl p65-6

Bullen, Henry Lewis
William Morris, regenerator of the typographic art. Inland Printer 69:369-74 Je '22 bibl p374

Burdon, Charles S.
Kelmscott press type. Notes & Q 11th ser 4:345, 435-6 O 28, N 25 '11

B[urne]-J[ones], G[eorgiana]
Memorials of Edward Burne-Jones. London, Macmillan, 1906. passim

Burns, Cecil Delisle
The principles of revolution: a study in ideals. London, Allen and Unwin, 1920

Butterfield, Lindsay P.
Floral forms in historic design. Mainly objects in the Victoria Albert Museum but including examples from designs by William Morris, etc. London, Batsford [1922] 18 plates

Byron, Mary C. [Gillington]
A day with William Morris. London, Hodder & Stoughton [1912] [46]p

Candee, Helen Churchill
The tapestry book. New York, Tudor publishing co. 1935. p257-61 [originally published by Stokes in 1912]

Carotti, Giulio
Della decorazione moderna in inghilterra. Emporium 2:121-9 '95

Le esposizioni d'arti e mestieri in inghilterra. Emporium 2:290-7 '95

Carr, Joseph William Comyns
Edward Burne-Jones. *In* Coasting Bohemia. London, Macmillan, 1914. p56-88

Carr, Joseph William Comyns—*Continued*
Some Victorian poets. *In* Some eminent Victorians... London, Duckworth, 1908. p208-10
(Rev by P. F. Bicknell in Dial 46:134-5 Mr 1 '09)

Cary, Elisabeth Luther
The handicraft of the pre-Raphaelites. Bookn 24:699-700 Je '06

"The real decorator makes the common thing pleasant to look upon and agreeable to use." Craftsman 30:207-8 My '16

William Morris and some of his books. Book B ns 22:309-13 My '01

William Morris in the making. Critic (NY) 41:195-208 S '02

William Morris, poet, craftsman, socialist. New York, Putnam, [c1902] ix,296p bibl p269-90
(Rev by I. Sargent in Craftsman 4:49-55 Ap '03; Nation (NY) 75:485 D 18 '02; Lit W 33:198 D 1 '02)

Cazalis, Henri (Jean Lahor) [pseud]
William Morris et le mouvement nouveau de l'art décoratif. Geneva [1897] 73p Diss. Geneva

Cazamian, Louis
A history of English literature, by Emile Legouis and Louis Cazamian. New edition... New York, Macmillan, 1929. p1210-16

Cazamian, Madeleine
Le roman et les idées en Angleterre; l'influence de la science (1860-1890). (Publications de la faculté des lettres de l'université de Strasbourg. Fascicule 15) Strasbourg, Librairie Istra, 1923. p291-2

Centenary exhibition at the Victoria and Albert museum. Burlington Magazine 64:188 Ap '34

Centenary exhibition in Victoria and Albert museum; with reproduction of the Bird hanging, a woolen fabric. Architectural Review 75:94a-b Mr '34

Centenary of William Morris. London Studio, American ed. of the Studio 7 (Studio 107):220 Ap '34; Art News 32:12 Mr 17 '34; Royal Society of Arts Journal 182:393-4 F 16 '34

Chalmers, R.
Lineage of "The Proud King." Royal Asiatic Society of Great Britain. Journal ns 24:39-52 '92

Chapman, Edward Mortimer
The doubters and the mystics. In English literature in account with religion, 1800-1900. Boston, Houghton Mifflin, 1910. p450-4

Charteris, (Sir) Evan [Edward]
The life and letters of Sir Edmund Gosse. New York, Harper, 1931

Chen, Karl C.
The sources of William Morris's "The Defence of Guenevere and other poems." Diss. Yale univ. 1934

Chesterton, Gilbert Keith
Great Victorian poets. *In* The Victorian age in literature. New York, Holt [1913] p196-200

The literary portraits of G. F. Watts, R. A. Bookm (Lond) 19:82 D '00

William Morris and his school. *In* Varied types. New York, Dodd, Mead, 1909. p15-28; *also in* Twelve types. London, Humphreys, 1902; *same.* Speaker ns 3: 315-16 D 22 '00
(Rev in Literary World (Lond) ns 66: 524-5 D 19 '02)

Child, Harold
Some English Utopias. Roy Soc Lit ns 12:49-53 '33

Chislett, William, jr.
The classical influence in English literature in the nineteenth century. Boston, Stratford co. 1918. p16-17

Clapp, Edwin Roosa
English literary criticism, 1830-1890, as exemplified in the works of the major critics. Harvard Univ. Summaries of Theses... Cambridge, Mass. 1931. p215-18

Clark, John Scott
William Morris. *In* A study of English and American writers. New York, Row, Peterson [c1916] p574-82

Clarke, William
William Morris. New England Magazine ns 3:740-9 F '91

William Morris. *In* Lee, F. W. William Morris—poet, artist, socialist. (Social Science library) New York, Twentieth century press [1891] p1-22

Clayton, Joseph
The rise and decline of socialism in Great Britain 1884-1924. London, Faber and Gwyer, 1926. passim

[Closing of Kelmscott press] Critic (NY) 30:391 Je 5 '97

Clutton-Brock, Arthur
The later poems of William Morris. Liv Age 251:241-5 O 27 '06; *same.* Acad 71: 228-9 S 8 '06

The prose romances of William Morris. *In* Essays on books. New York, Dutton [1920] p27-38

Waste or creation? *In* Essays on art. London, Methuen, 1919. p132-[144]

William Morris, his work and influence. (Home university library) London, Williams and Norgate [1914] viii,9-256p
(Rev in T L S Je 25 '14 p307; C. Bell in New Statesm 3:757-9 O 3 '14)

Cochrane, Robert
William Morris. *In* The treasury of modern biography. Edinburgh, Nimmo, Hay, and Mitchell, 1892. p529

Cockerell, Sydney Carlyle
The Kelmscott press. Acad 50:572 D 19 '96; Ath 1:244 F 23 '01

The printing of William Morris. Book B ns 14:168-9 Mr '97

A short history and description of the Kelmscott press. *In* A note by William Morris on his aims in founding the Kelmscott press. . . [Hammersmith, Kelmscott press, 1898] p7-20; *same in* William Morris. A note on his aims in founding the Kelmscott press. [New Rochelle, 1902] p5-14; *same in* Philobiblon 7[supp]:9-[22] '34

Cockerell, Theodore Dru Alison
William Morris and the world today. Dial 59:545-8 D 9 '15

Cole, George Douglas Howard
Biographical note [and] Introduction [to Morris] *In* William Morris. Stories in prose, stories in verse, shorter poems, lectures and essays. (Centenary edition) New York, Random house, 1934. pvii-xxiv
(Rev in T L S Mr 22 '34 p201; Spec 152:416-17 Mr 16 '34; K. John in New Statesm & Nation p489 Mr 31 '34; Life & L 10:251-2 '34)

William Morris. [London, Crosby Lockwood, 1913] (The Blue book, vol I no 5 p353-66)

William Morris. *In* Encyclopaedia of the social sciences. . . New York, Macmillan, 1933. vol XI p21

William Morris. *In* Revaluations; studies in biography by Lascelles Abercrombie (and others). . . Oxford, Oxford univ. press, 1931. p131-54

Colebrook, Frank
William Morris: master printer. Tunbridge Wells, Lewis Hepworth [1897] 39p

Colwell, Percy Robert
Introduction. *In* The poems of William Morris. New York, Crowell [c1904] pxv-xxxiv

Compton-Rickett, Arthur
The Morris circle. *In* I look back. . . London, Jenkins [1933] p157-71

William Morris; a study in personality. . . introduction by R. B. C. Graham. London, Jenkins, 1913. xxii,325p
(Rev by C. S. Northup in Dial 55:257-8 O 13; Acad 85:7-8 Jl 5 '13; Ath 1:585-6 My 31 '13; Spec 111:426 S 20 '13)

Contemporary poets and versifiers. Edin R 178:471-6 O '93

Contemporary portraits. New series. No. 11. William Morris. University Magazine 2:552-68 N '78

Cotton, Albert Louis
The Kelmscott press and the new printing. Contemp 74:221-31 Ag '98

Courtney, Helen F.
The influence of John Ruskin on William Morris. Masters essay, Northwestern Univ. 1934. 125ff

Courtney, W. L.
Poets of to-day. Fortn 40:726 N '83

Cox, Mabel
The arts and crafts exhibition. [Chiswick, Allen, 1896] 9-40p

Crane, Walter
An artist's reminiscences. New York, Macmillan, 1907. passim

Note on the work and life of William Morris. Mag Art 20:89-91 D '96

William Morris. Scrib M 22:88-99 Jl '97

William Morris. . . Die Neue Zeit 15:133-6 O 31 '96

William Morris: poet, artist and craftsman, and social reconstructor. Progressive Review 1:148-52 N '96

William Morris to Whistler. Papers and addresses on art and craft and the commonweal. . . London, Bell, 1911. x,277p
(Rev in Ath 2:634 N 18 '11; Acad 82:76-7 Ja 20 '12)

Crawford, Jack R.
William Morris. *In* What to read in English literature. New York, Putnam, 1928. p346-7

Cross, Allen Eastman
William Morris; a poem. *In* Lee, F. W. William Morris, poet, artist, socialist. New York, Twentieth century press [1891] pxx [From New England Magazine ns 3:731 F '91]

Crow, Gerald H.
William Morris, designer. New York, The Studio publications, 1934. 120p bibl p118 illustrated
(Rev in T L S Ja 3 '35 p7; C. P. Rollins in Sat R Lit 11:415 Ja 5 '35; I. Haas in American Book Collector 6:231 My-Je '35; Art Digest 9:21 D 15 '34)

Crowdy, Wallace L.
William Morris. Lit 9:243-8 S 14 '01

Cunliffe, John W.
Mid-Victorian poets. *In* Leaders of the Victorian revolution. New York, Appleton-Century [c1934] p248-52

Cunninghame-Graham, R. B.
With the north-west wind. Sat R 82:389-90 O 10 '96

Davies, Frank Joseph John
William Morris's "Sir Peter Harpdon's end." Philol Q 11:314-17 Jl '32

Davray, Henry D.
[Note on "News from nowhere"] Mercure Fr 113:343-4 Ja 16 '16

Dawson, William James
William Morris. *In* The makers of English poetry. New York, Revell, 1906. New ed revised. p368-79

William Morris. *In* The makers of modern English. . . New York, Whittaker, 1890. p363-75

Day, Lewis Foreman
Decorative art of William Morris and his work. (Easter Art Annual, 1899) London, Virtue [1899] 32p

A Kensington interior. Art J 55:139-44 '93

William Morris and his art. Art J 61 [extra no] 1-32 '99

Day, Lewis Foreman—*Continued*
William Morris and his art. *In* Great masters of decorative art. 1900. 32p plates

William Morris and his decorative art. Contemp 83:787-96 Je '03; *same.* Liv Age 238:102-9 Jl 11 '03

[Death of Morris] Critic (NY) 29:247 O 24 '96

Dennison, Baird
Great amateur. Architectural Review 75: 133 Ap '34

Destrée, Olivier Georges
Les Préraphaélites. . . Bruxelles, Dietrich [1894] p64-8

DeVinne, Theodore L.
The Kelmscott style. Bibliographer (NY) 1:1-10 Ja '02

The printing of William Morris. Book B ns 13:920-3 Ja '97

The diary of a literary wanderer. New Century Review 5:261-8 '99

Dickinson, Thomas
William Morris and esthetic socialism. Arena 36:613-17 D '06

Diehl, Karl
Über sozialismus, kommunismus und anarchismus. Jena, Fischer, 1911. 2d ed. p377

Dixon, William Macneile
English epic and heroic poetry. London, Dent, 1912. p315-25

Dodds, T. L.
William Morris; handicraftsman, socialist, poet and novelist. Liverpool Philomath. Society Proceedings 55:li-lxxx '10

Doherty, Helen Frances
A study of metrical form in the poetry of Rossetti, Swinburne, and Morris. Masters essay, New York Univ. 1909. 33ff

Dondore, Dorothy Anne
Morris' interpretation of primitive Germania. Masters essay, State Univ. of Iowa, 1917. 47ff

Doorn, Willem van
Theory and practice of English narrative verse since 1833. Amsterdam [1932?] p62-81

Douglas, James
William Morris. *In* Theodore Watts-Dunton. . . New York, Lane [1907?] p170-82

Dowden, Edward
Victorian literature. *In* Transcripts and studies. London, Kegan Paul, Trench, Trübner, 1896. 2d ed. p230-3

Victorian literature. Fortn 47:864-6 Je '87

Dowler, Minnabelle Anne
William Morris and his relation to Pre-Raphaelitism. Masters essay, Univ. of Manitoba, 1927. 128ff

Drinkwater, John
Victorian poetry. London, Hodder and Stoughton, 1923. p102-7, 135-8

William Morris; a critical study. New York, Mitchell Kennerley, 1912. 9-201p (Rev in Nation (NY) 96:155-6 F 13 '13; C. S. Northup in Dial 55:256-7 O 1 '13; Acad 83:439-40 O 5 '12; Ath 2:109-10 Ag 3 '12; Edin R 216:376-8 O '12)

William Morris and the state. *In* Prose papers. London, Mathews, 1917. p138-46

Durrant, William Scott
The influence of William Morris. Westm 169:542-9 My '08

Duryea, Minga Pope
Cobden-Sanderson's garden at Hammersmith, with glimpses of the gardens of William Morris and Rossetti. Scrib M 74:25-34 Jl '23

Dyce, Alan
William Morris. Sewanee R 22:257-75 '14

Earland, Ada
Edward Burne-Jones—William Morris. *In* Ruskin and his circle. London, Hutchinson, 1910. p108-25

[Editorial notes on centenary of Morris] Lond Merc 29:385-8 '34

Edmunds, Edward William and Spooner, Frank
William Morris. *In* The story of English literature. . . London, Murray, 1908. vol III p352-4

Einarsson, Stefán
Eiríkr Magnússon and his saga-translations. Scandinavian Studies & Notes 13:17-32 '34

Saga Eiríks Magnússonar. Reykjavik, 1933

Ellis, Frederick Startridge
The life-work of William Morris. Journal of the Society of Arts 46:618-28 '98

Elton, Godfrey
William Morris, 1883-1884. *In* "England, arise!" London, Jonathan Cape [1931] p56-72

Elton, Oliver
Poetic romancers after 1850. (Warton lecture on English poetry) *In* Proceedings of the British academy 1913-1914. London, Oxford univ. press [1915?] p413-31 *Also in* A sheaf of papers. Boston, Small, Maynard, 1923. p45-68

William Morris. *In* A survey of English literature, 1830-1880. London, Arnold, 1920. vol II p31-54

Emery, Fred Parker
William Morris. *In* Notes on English literature. Boston, Ginn, 1891. p136

The end of the Kelmscott press. Acad 50: 530 D 12 '96

Engel, Eduard
William Morris. *In* Geschichte der englischen literatur. Leipzig, Brandstetter, 1929. p426-7

William Morris. *In* A history of English literature (600-1900) London, Methuen, 1902. p433-4

English art in the Victorian age. Quar R 187:220-2 Ja '98

Evans, B[enjamin] Ifor
William Morris. *In* English poetry in the later nineteenth century. London, Methuen [1933] p81-101 bibl p101
William Morris and his poetry. (Poetry and life series) London, Harrap [1925] 9-[156]p bibl p155-[6]
(Rev in Sat R 139:390 Ap 11 '25)
William Morris, his influence and reputation. Contemp 145:315-23 Mr '34

Fabian Tract No.113. With introduction by George Bernard Shaw. Communism, a lecture by William Morris. London [1903]

Farmer, Albert J.
Le mouvement esthétique et "decadent" en Angleterre (1873-1900). Paris, Champion, 1931. p19-23

Fehr, Bernhard
Die englische literatur des 19. und 20. jahrhunderts. Wildpark-Potsdam, 1928. p172-3, 223-30

Fletcher, William Younger
English book-collectors. (English bookman's library) London, Kegan Paul, 1902. p423-7

Flower, B. O.
William Morris and some of his later works. Arena 17:42-52 D '96

Ford, Mary Bacon
The art socialists of London. Cosmopolitan 8:185-7 D '89

Forman, Harry Buxton
The books of William Morris described. London, Hollings, 1897. xv,224p
(Rev in Ath 1:80-1 Ja 15 '98; Sat R 85: 643 My 14 '98)
William Morris. Liv Age 211:380-2 N 7 '96; *same.* Illustrated London News 109:456 O 10 '96
William Morris. *In* Miles, A. H. The poets and the poetry of the nineteenth century. London, Routledge, 1905. vol VI p1-14
William Morris. *In* Our living poets . . . London, Tinsley, 1871. p375-426

Fotheringham, Jean Thornton
The possible influence of John Ruskin and William Morris on the dramas of George Bernard Shaw. Masters essay, Columbia univ. 1930

Frantz, Henri
Un rénovateur de l'art industriel; William Morris. Gazette des Beaux-Arts 39: 503-9 D 1 '97

Frantz, Nellie B.
William Morris and the Norse epic spirit as exemplified in Sigurd the Volsung. . . Masters essay, Claremont Colleges, 1930. 74ff

Frederich, John Towner
Relation of William Morris to the pre-Raphaelite movement. Masters essay, State Univ. of Iowa, 1917. 60ff

Frey, Eugen
William Morris, eine Studie. Programm Winterthur, 1901

Fritzsche, Gustav
William Morris' sozialismus und anarchistischer kommunismus. . . (Kölner änglistische arbeiten no 3) Leipzig, Tauchnitz, 1927. 132p bibl p[125]-132 Diss. Leipzig, 1925
(Rev by A. Walther in Bei Anglia 41: 309-13 '30)

Fuller, Edward
The work of William Morris. Bookm (NY) 37:577-81 Jl '13

Galton, Arthur
Mr. William Morris. *In* Urbana scripta. . . London, Stock, 1885. p[132]-55

Garnett, Richard and Gosse, (Sir) Edmund William
William Morris. *In* English literature, an illustrated record. New York, Grosset & Dunlap [c1904] vol IV p352-6

Gatch, Louise
Tristram, Launcelot, and the Holy Grail, as treated by Tennyson, Arnold, Morris, and Swinburne. Masters essay, Univ. of California, 1911. 130ff

Geoffrey Chaucer and William Morris. New Monthly Magazine 149:280-6 S '71

Gilchrist, Herbert Harlakenden (ed)
Anne Gilchrist, her life. . . London, Unwin, 1887. p90-1

Gilder, J. L.
William Morris. Critic (NY) 35:620-7 Jl '99

Gillis, Lois Isabel
Art in the great Victorian poets. Masters essay, Univ. of Oklahoma, 1921. 265ff

Glasier, John Bruce
["The Pilgrims of Hope."] A proletarian epic. Socialist Review 17:322-5 O-D '20
William Morris and the early days of the Socialist movement: being reminiscences of Morris' work as a propagandist, and observations on his character and genius, with some account of the persons and circumstances of the early socialist agitation; together with a series of letters addressed by Morris to the author. . . With a preface by May Morris. London, Longmans, Green, 1921. ix,208p
(Rev in T L S Mr 17 '21 p175)

Glass, Effie Mildred Kent
The medievalism of Morris. Masters essay, Univ. of Toronto, 1909

Golding, Louis
Evolution and William Morris. Sat R 133:253 Mr 11 '22

Goodale, Ralph Hinsdale
Pessimism in English poetry and fiction, 1847-1900. *In* Abstracts of theses. . . Humanistic series Volume VI. . . Univ. of Chicago. Chicago, 1927. p347-51 Diss. Univ. of Chicago

Gosse, (Sir) Edmund William
The literature of the Victorian era. Engl Illus 17:491 Jl '97

Goudy, Frederic W.
William Morris; his influence on American printing. Philobiblon 7:185-91 '34

Gould, Frederick J.
Hyndman, prophet of socialism. London, Allen and Unwin [1928] passim

Grappe, Georges
W. Morris. *In* Essai sur la poésie anglaise au XIXe siècle. Paris, Sansot, 1906. p54-7

Grautoff, O.
William Morris. Börsenblatt für den deutschen Buchhandel no 22 '02

[Grebanier, Mrs. Frances (Vinciguerra)] Frances Winwar [pseud]
Poor splendid wings. Boston, Little, Brown, 1933. p91-5, 99-101, 144-7, 152-4, 365-7

Green, A. Romney
William Morris: the craftsman as poet. Poetry Review 1:300-11 '12

Greenwood, George A.
William Morris: artist, poet, and reformer. Millgate Monthly 29:327-30 Mr '34

Gregg, Frederick James
The personality of William Morris. Book B 13:619-21 N '96

Greville, Frances Evelyn, Countess of Warwick
William Morris. His homes and haunts. With twelve drawings in crayon by A. Forestier. (The pilgrim books) New York, Dodge [1912] xi,68p

Groom, Bernard
William Morris. *In* A literary history of England. London, Longmans, Green, 1929. p330-2

Gruener, Gustav
The "Nibelungenlied" and "Sage" in modern poetry. PMLA 11:220-57 '96

Grünberg, Carl
Anarchismus. *In* Wörterbuch der Volkswirtschaft. Jena, 1911. 3d ed. vol I p92-7

Sozialismus und kommunismus. *In* Wörterbuch der Volkswirtschaft. Jena, 1898. vol II p527-76

Guyot, Edouard
L'idée socialiste chez William Morris. London, 1909

Le socialisme de William Morris. *In* Le socialisme et l'évolution de l'angleterre contemporaine. Paris, Alcan, 1913. p379-424

Gwynn, Stephen
William Morris. Macmil 78:153-60 Je '98

Hake, Thomas St. E.
How authors work best. T.P.'s Weekly 2:630 O 16 '03

Hall, Amy Violet
William Morris and "Main Street." Masters essay, Univ. of Washington, 1922. 73ff

Hamilton, Mary Agnes
William Morris and Bruce Glasier. Socialist Review 18:245-9 '21

Hamilton, Walter
Parodies of the works of English and American authors. . . London, Reeves and Turner, 1884. vol I p65

William Morris. *In* The aesthetic movement in England. London, Reeves and Turner, 1882. p58-61

Hanningan, D. F.
William Morris, poet and revolutionist. Westm 147:117-19 F '97

Haraszti, Zoltán
The centenary of William Morris. More Books 9:153-60 '34

Hazeltine, Mayo Williamson
William Morris's epic poem. *In* Chats about books. . . New York, Scribner, 1883. p272-86

Healy, Chris
William Morris and Prince Kropotkin. *In* Confessions of a journalist. London, Chatto and Windus, 1904. p1-18

Hearn, Lafcadio
Morris. *In* A history of English literature, in a series of lectures. Tokyo, Hokuseido press, 1927. vol II p691-4

William Morris. *In* Appreciations of poetry. . . New York, Dodd, Mead, 1916. p239-79

William Morris. *In* Pre-Raphaelite and other poets . . . selected and edited with an introduction by John Erskine. . . New York, Dodd, Mead, 1922. p262-310

Hellman, George S.
American and English poets. Dial 29:297-8 N 1 '00

Herford, Charles Harold
Norse myth in English poetry. Bulletin of the John Rylands Library 5:75-100 '18-'19

Hewlett, Henry Gay
Mr. Morris's "Sigurd" and the "Nibelunglied." Fraser 96:96-112 Jl '77

Modern ballads. Contemp 26:971-3 N '75

The poems of Mr. Morris. Contemp 25:100-24 D '74

Hodson, Laurence W.
The Birmingham group. . . Studio 70:3-4 Ap '20

The **home** of William Morris. Critic (NY) ns 27:119 Ag 24 '95

Hopkins, Frederick M.
[Note on Morris' effect upon Updike] Pub W 126:1856-7 N 17 '34

Horn, Angie
Chaucer and Morris. Masters essay, Univ. of Kansas, 1904. 36ff

Kellner, Leon
Englische epigonenpoesie. Beilage zur Allgemeinen Zeitung no 36 '89

Die englische literatur der neuesten zeit. Leipzig, Tauchnitz, 1921. p297-303

Die englische literatur im zeitalter der königin Viktoria. Leipzig, Tauchnitz, 1909. p518-27

The **Kelmscott** press. Bookworm 7:55-6 '93

The **Kelmscott** press. A review and some statistics. Scottish Review 36:19-35 Jl '00

The **Kelmscott** press—an illustrated interview with Mr. William Morris. Bookselling 1:3-10 D '95

Kent, Charles
[Kunsten og jordens skjønhed (William Morris)] *In* Dagdrømmen. Kristiania, H. Aschehong, 1919. 191p

Kenworthy, John C.
William Morris: a memory. . . New Century Review 1:77-82, 124-32 Ja, F '97

Kenyon, James B.
William Morris—poet, socialist, and master of many crafts. *In* Loiterings in old fields. New York, Eaton and Mains, 1901. p51-81

Kermode, H. Sybil
The classical sources of Morris's "Life and Death of Jason." *In* Primitiae. . . Liverpool, Univ. press, 1912. p158-82

Kingsland, William G.
A poet's politics: Mr. William Morris in unpublished letters on socialism. Poet Lore 7:473-7, 543-6 '95

[**Kisses** in "The Water of the Wondrous Isles"] Acad 52:549 D 18 '97

Knappert, E. C.
William Morris, 1834-1896. Leven en Werken p442-61 Jl-Ag '30

Knickerbocker, William Skinkle
Creative Oxford. . . Syracuse, New York, Univ. bookstore [c1925] p162-9

Koch, Adolf
Über eine neuenglische auffassung der Siegfried gestalt. Magdeburgh, Baensch, 1911. 26p

Koch, Rudolf
William Morris. Philobiblon 7: following p172 '34

Koeppel, Emil
William Morris nach A. Vallance. Beilage zur Allgemeinen Zeitung no 81 '98

Küster, Elisabeth Karola
Mittelalter und antike bei William Morris. . . Berlin, W. De Gruyter, 1928. vi, 239p Diss. Freiburg i. B. 1928 [1929] (Rev by F. Asanger in Literatur 52:358-9 Mr '31; H. Heuer in Bei Anglia 41: 51-6; H. Jantzen in ZFEU 28:471-3 '29; A. Ludwig in Die Literatur 32:54-5 O '29)

Lahor, Jean. See Cazalis, H.

Lalou, René
Panorama de la littérature anglaise contemporaine. Paris, Kra [c1926] passim

Lang, Andrew
Jubilee before revolution, by W. M. *In* The poetical works. . . ed. by Mrs. Lang. London, Longmans, Green, 1923. vol III p226-7

Mr. [William] Morris's poems. Longman's Magazine 28:560-73 O '96; *same*. Liv Age 211:323-30 N 7 '96

Mr. Morris's poems. *In* Adventures among books. London, Longmans, Green, 1905. p99-117

The poetry of William Morris. Contemp 42:200-17 Ag '82

William Morris. *In* History of English literature from "Beowulf" to Swinburne. London, Longmans, Green, 1921. p599-601

[**Lang** on Kelmscott press books] Acad 63: 53 Jl 12 '02

The **late** William Morris. R of Rs (NY) 14:732 D '96

The **later** English poets. . . Quar R 132: 575-85 Ja '72; *same*. Ecl M 78:390-4 Ap '72

The **later** labours of Mr. Morris. Tinsley's 7:457-65 N '70

Latouche, Peter
William Morris—artist, poet, and anarchist. *In* Anarchy! London, Everett, 1908. p187-90

The **Laureateship**. Illustrated London News 101:491 O 15 '92; Spec 69:517-18 O 15 '92; Critic (NY) 21:255-6 N 5 '92

Laurent, Raymond
Le préraphaélisme en angleterre; Introduction à l'étude du préraphaélisme anglais. *In* Études anglaises. Paris, Grasset, 1910. p31-138; *same*. Nouvelle Revue ns 40:180-5 My 15 '06

Lazarus, Emma
A day in Surrey with William Morris. Cent 32:388-97 Jl '86

Leatham, James
William Morris, master of many crafts. London, Twentieth century press, 1900 (Rev in Literary World (Lond) ns 61: 128 F 9 '00)

Lee, Donald Woodard
William Morris' "Sigurd the Volsung": a study. Masters essay, Duke Univ. 1933. 192ff

Lee, G. Francis Watt
Some thoughts upon beauty in typography suggested by the work of Mr. William Morris at the Kelmscott press. Knight Errant (Boston) 1 no 2:53-63 '92

LeGallienne, Richard
The romantic nineties. Garden City, New York, Doubleday, Page, 1925. p121-7

Leiblein, Emil
Prinzipien und anwendung des stabreims in W. Morris' "Sigurd the Volsung." Amorbach, Volkhardt, 1913. 102p Diss. Würzburg

Leisching, J.
Morris und sein ende. Mitteilungen d. Mährischen Gewerbemuseums in Brünn no 12:113-16 '02

Lethaby, W. R.
Philip Webb and his work. Builder 128: 42-3, 223-8, 381-3, 530-2, 676-7, 724-5, 870-2, 904-6, 943-4, Ja 9-Je 19 '25

[Lever, C. J.]
William Morris and Matthew Arnold. Fraser 79:230-44 F '69

Levetus, A. S.
Morris und. . . Kunst. Mitteilungen d. Erzherzog Rainenmuseums in Brünn p129-36 '13

The literary pages of the "Spectator." Spec 141:646 N 3 '28

Litzenberg, Karl
Contributions of the old Norse language and literature to the style and substance of the writings of William Morris 1858-1876. Diss. Univ. of Michigan, 1933. 400ff

The social philosophy of William Morris and the doom of the gods. *In* Essays and studies in English and comparative literature. . . (Univ. of Michigan publications, language and literature, volume X) Ann Arbor, Mich. Univ. of Michigan, 1933. p183-203

Lloyd, Henry Demarest
A day with William Morris. *In* Mazzini and other essays. New York, Putnam, 1910. p42-70

Loane, George G.
A mannerism of William Morris. T L S My 3, Je 14 '17 p214, 285

Lord, William S.
The silent singer; poem. Dial 21:262 N 1 '96

Loubier, Jean
Bibliographien von Morris's schriften. Zeitschrift für Bücherfreunde 2:256-7 Ag-S '98

Die kunst im buchdruck. Zeitschrift für Bücherfreunde 2:483-4 F '99

["Love is enough" dramatized] Ath 2:92 Jl 16 '20

Lovett, Robert Morss
A study of William Morris. Harv Mo 12: 149-61 Je '91

Lubbock, Percy
The poetry of William Morris. Quar R 215:482-504 '11

Lucas, Frank Laurence
William Morris. *In* Eight Victorian poets. . . Cambridge, Univ. press, 1930. p91-112
(Rev in T L S N 13 '30 p936)

Lüthi-Tschanz, Karl Jakob
Gutenberg, Bodoni, Morris, eine vergleichung ihrer Kunst; vortrag gehalten an der delegierten-versammlung des Bildungsverbandes schweiz. . . Bern, Büchler, 1925
[250 copies only]

Lux, Jacques
William Morris. R Pol et Litt 51:191-2 Ag 9 '13

Lynd, Robert
The personality of Morris. *In* The art of letters. New York, Scribner, 1921. p150-5

Lytton, Neville
A discussion about William Morris. Nat-Ath 34:793-4 Mr 8 '24

McAllister, Virginia
Nineteenth century interest in Northern antiquities. Masters essay, Univ. of Oklahoma, 1933. 103ff

McCabe, Joseph Martin
A biographical dictionary of modern rationalists. London, Watts, 1920. p535

McClelland, Nancy Vincent
The ideal home of William Morris. Bookn 24:701-3 Je '06

McCormick, James P. jr.
The social philosophy of William Morris reflected in his literary work. Masters essay, Northwestern Univ. 1934. 128ff

Macdonald, J. R.
William Morris. London, 1898

MacDonald, Louise
The social philosophy of William Morris. Masters essay, Univ. of Washington, 1926. 83ff

Macdonell, Annie
The poetry of William Morris. Bookm (Lond) 10:167-9 S '96

McDowell, George Tremaine
The treatment of the Volsunga saga by William Morris. Scandinavian Studies and Notes 7:151-68 '23

Mackail, John William
The genius of William Morris. Independent Review 11:51-7 O '06

The life of William Morris. London, Longmans, Green, 1899. 2 vols
(Rev in Lit W 30:227-8 Jl 22 '99; Edin R 191:356-79 Ap '00; Ath 1:587-8 My 13 '99; Acad 56:525-6 My 13 '99; Blackw 166:16-26 Jl '99; Church Q R 51:47-58 O '00; Bookm (NY) 9:498-9, 533-5 Ag '99; Spec 82:718-19 My 20 '99; Sat R 87:788-9 Je 24 '99; Speaker 19:692-3 Je 17 '99; R of Rs (Lond) 19:494-5 My '99; Bookm (Lond) 16:73-4 Je '99; Nation (NY) 69:228-9 S 21 '99; Literary World (Lond) ns 67:176 F 20 '03; Dial 27:90-3 Ag 16 '99; Lit 4:459-61 My 6 '99)

The parting of the ways; an address. . . Hammersmith, Hammersmith publishing society, 1903. 34p

William Morris. . . London, National home-reading union [1916] 32p bibl p31-2
(Rev in T L S My 25 '16 p245)

William Morris. *In* Dict N B vol XXII [supp] p1069-75

William Morris. *In* Studies of English poets. . . London, Longmans, Green, 1926. p173-97

Mackail, John William—*Continued*
William Morris. *In* Ward, T. H. ed. The English poets. New York, Macmillan, 1918. vol V p328-35

William Morris. Journal of the Royal Institute of British Architects 3d ser 41:557-65 Ap 14 '34

William Morris, an address. . . Hammersmith, Doves press, 1901. 27p

William Morris, an address delivered in the Town hall, Birmingham, at the annual meeting of the National home reading union, 28th October, 1910. London, Longmans, Green, 1910. 29p

William Morris and his circle. Oxford, Clarendon press, 1907

Mackall, Leonard
William Morris centenary. Books S 30 '34 p30

Mackenzie, Compton
Literature in my time. London, Rich and Cowan, 1933. passim

McMinn, Ney Lannes
The letters of William Morris to the press, 1868-1895. Diss. Northwestern Univ. 1928. 483ff

McMurtrie, Douglas C.
A typographical messiah. *In* The golden book. New York, Covici Friede, nd 3d ed. p276-90

McNally, Eva
The relation of William Morris to Geoffrey Chaucer. Masters essay, Univ. of Wisconsin, 1902. 52ff

Magnus, Laurie
William Morris. *In* English literature in the nineteenth century, an essay in criticism. New York, Putnam, 1909. p321-5

Magnússon, Eiríkr
William Morris. . . Cambridge, 1896. [6]p [Reprinted from Cambridge Review N 26 '96]

A **mannerism** of William Morris. T L S My 3, 10, 24, Je 14 '17 p214, 226, 250, 285

March-Phillips, L.
Pre-Raphaelitism and the present. Contemp 89:704-13 My '06

Marillier, Henry Currie
History of the Merton Abbey tapestry works, founded by William Morris. London, Constable, 1927. 37p
(Rev in T L S Je 23 '27 p439)

The Morris movement. London, Privately printed

Morris stained glass. London, Privately printed

Salutations of Beatrice. Art J 51:353

Marks, Jeannette [Augustus]
The beautiful for the people. So Atlan Q 7:143-54 Ap '08

Martin, Hugh
(Study) Congregational Quarterly Ap '26 p172-80

William Morris. *In* Christian social reformers of the nineteenth century, by James Adderley, A. Fenner Brockway. . . ed. by Hugh Martin. New York, Doran [1927] p168-81

Marx, Morris and Keir Hardie. [signed "R.R."] Adel 7:62-3 O '33

Mason, Eugene
The medievalism of William Morris. *In* Considered writers. . . London, Methuen [1925] p97-119

Masse, H. J. L. J.
William Morris as a craftsman. Architect 93:172-5 F 19 '15

Mavor, James
William Morris. *In* My windows on the street of the world. New York, Dutton, 1923. vol I p193-202

Maxwell, E.
Introduction. *In* Morris, William. Life and death of Jason. Oxford, Clarendon press, 1914. pvii-xxx

Maynadier, Howard
The Arthur of the English poets. Boston, Houghton, Mifflin, 1907. p357-63

Merington, Ruth
William Morris, his idealism and socialism. Masters essay, Columbia univ. 1914

Miller, Emily Huntington
William Morris; poem. Dial 21:262 N 1 '96

Mills, T. L.
William Morris and the Kelmscott press. Inland Printer 18:299-301 D '96

Mills College, Alameda County, California. 1834-1934. The Wm. Morris Centenary Exhibition. [Drawings, etc.] 1934

Mr. Morris. Temple 27:45-51, 175 Ag, S '69; Temple 28:35-48 D '69; *same.* Ecl M 73:551-9 N '69

Mr. Morris and his wall papers. Lit W 27:346 O 17 '96

Mr. Morris's "Sigurd." Spec 50:182 F 10 '77

Mr. William Morris. Tinsley's 3:262-77 O '68

Mr. William Morris at the Kelmscott press. Engl Illus 13:47-55 Ap '95

Modern developments in ballad art. Edin R 213:169-79 Ja '11

Modern men. William Morris. National Observer 5:142-3 D 27 '90

The **modern** poetry of doubt. Spec 43:166-7 F 5 '70; *same.* New Eclectic Magazine 6:490-4 Ap '70

The **modernity** of William Morris. Arts and Decoration 12:61 N '19

Moorhouse, E. Hallam
Aspects of William Morris. Fortn 98: 464-76 S '12

More, Paul Elmer
William Morris. Nation (NY) 88:243-6 Mr 11 '09

William Morris. *In* Shelburne essays. New York, Putnam's, 1910. 7th ser p95-118

Morgan, Mary Louis
Galahad in English literature. Diss. Catholic univ. 1932. p109-14

Morris, May
A Morris memorial hall. T L S Ap 26 '28 p313

Reminiscences about my father. Philobiblon 7:169-72 '34

Sonnets by William Morris. Ath 2:480 N 7 '14

[A talk broadcast by the British Broadcasting Corporation, February 9, 1934] Philobiblon 7: following p192 '34

William Morris. T L S My 17 '34 p360

Morris, William
Architecture, industry, and wealth: collected papers. London, Longmans, Green, 1902. viii,268p
(Rev in Critic (NY) 42:282 Mr '03; Dial 34:404 Je 16 '03; Ath 1:182 F 6 '04; Jugend p11-12 '03; Out 72:997 D 27 '02)

The collected works of William Morris, ed. by his daughter, May Morris. London, Longmans, Green, 1910-1915. 24 vols
(Rev in Spec 107:69-71 Jl 8 '11; Ath 1:5-6, 679-80 Ja 7, Je 17 '11; Ath 2:814 D 30 '11; Sat R 111:708 Je 10 '11; Lit Digest 44:217 F 3 '12; Nation (NY) 92:268 Mr 16 '11; Liv Age 284:812-16 Mr 27 '15; Bookm (Lond) 43:172-3 D '12; E. Thomas in Bookm (Lond) 41: 300-1 Mr '12; Ath 2:339-40 S 28 '12; Ath 2:619 N 29 '13; Nation (NY) 94: 64 Ja 18 '12; noted in Nation (NY) 93:125 Ag 10 '11)

The defence of Guenevere, and other poems. London, Bell and Daldy, 1858. 248p
(Rev in T L S Je 10 '04 p177-8; Westm 90:144-5 O '68; Lit W 5:183 Ap 1 '75; Ath 1:427-8 Ap 3 '58; Sat R 6:506-7 N 20 '58; W. D. Howells in Atlan 36:243-4 Ag '75)

A dream of John Ball, and A king's lesson. London, Reeves and Turner, 1888. 143p
(Rev in Literary World (Lond) ns 41: 11 Ja 3 '90; Westm 130:243-4 Ag '88)

The early romances of William Morris in prose and verse. (Everyman's library) London, Dent [1907] xix,303p
(Rev in T L S O 17 '07 p316)

The earthly paradise. A poem. London, Ellis, 1868-1870. 3 vols
(Rev in Sat R 28:771-3 D 11 '69; *same.* Ecl M 74:437-40 Ap '70; New Ecl 2: 478-9 Ag '68; Westm ns 39:581 Ap '71; Spec 44:103-5 Ja 28 '71; S. Colvin in Acad 2:57-8 D 15 '70; Once a Week 10:148 Ag 17 '72; Lit W 13:129-30 Ap 22 '82; G. A. Simcox in Acad 1:

121-2 F 12 '70; Spec 41:737-9 Je 20 '68; Spec 43:332-4 Mr 12 '70; Fortn 9: 713-15 Je '68; Contemp 8:631-3 Ag '68; Nation (NY) 7:33-4 Jl 9 '68; T. W. Higginson in Atlan 22:255 Ag '68; J. J. Piatt in Atlan 25:750-2 Je '70; Harper M 40:774-5 Ap '70; Harper M 42:777 Ap '71; Blackw 135:371-2 Mr '84; H. James, jr. in No Am 107:358-61 Jl '68; Ath 1:753-4 My 30 '68; Ath 2:868-9 D 25 '69; Ath 2:795-7 D 17 '70; Westm 90:147-9 O '68; Quar R 132:75-84 Ja '72; Edin R 133:243-64 Ja '71; Liv Age 98:74-8 Jl 11 '68; Ecl M 78:385-99 Ap '72; W. H. Browne in Southern Review 4:398-407 O '68; W. H. Browne in New Ecl 6:579-86 My '70; Blackw 106:56-73 Jl '69; Liv Age 102:399-412 Ag 14 '69; H. Morley in 19th Cent 2:704-12 N '77; Tinsley's 7:464-5 N '70; Sat R 25:730-1 My 30 '68; Christian Observer 69:196-208 Mr '70; New Englander 29:357-9 Ap '70; Lond Q R 36:251-8 Ap '71)

Gothic architecture: a lecture for the Arts and Crafts Exhibition Society. London, Kelmscott press, 1893. ii,68p
(Rev in Edin R 185:63-83 Ja '97)

The hollow land. Originally appeared in the Oxford and Cambridge Magazine in 1856. Reprinted in London at the Chiswick Press and published by Longmans, Green in 1903
(Rev by E. Radford in Bookm (Lond) 25:44-5 O '03)

Hopes and fears for art. . . London, Ellis and White, 1882. ii,217p
(Rev in Lit W 13:67 Mr 11 '82; Edin R 185:63-83 Ja '97; Spec 55:629-30 My 13 '82; Dial 2:292 Ap '82; Cent 24:464-5 Jl '82; E. Simcox in Fortn 37:771-9 Je '82; Ath 2:374-5 S 16 '82)

Letters to Reverend George Brinton, April 2, 4, 10, and May 6, 1888. [Privately printed for Thomas James Wise. London, 1894]

The life and death of Jason. A poem. London, Bell and Daldy, 1867. 363p
(Rev by A. C. Swinburne in Fortn 8: 19-28 Jl '67; *same.* Every Sat 4:115-18 Jl 27 '67; Westm 90:144-9 O '68; C. E. Norton in Nation (NY) 5:146-7 Ag 22 '67; H. James, Jr. in No Am 105:688-92 O '67; Blackw 106:56-73 Jl '69; *same.* Liv Age 102:399-412 Ag 14 '69; Edin R 133:243-66 Ja '71; Spec 40:668-70 Je 15 '67; Contemp 6:525-9 D '67; Ath 1:779-80 Je 15 '67; Christian Observer 69:196-208 Mr '70)

Love is enough, or The freeing of Pharamond. A morality. London, Ellis and White, 1873. 134p
(Rev by W. H. Browne in So M 12: 491-9 Ap '73; G. Fraser in Dark Blue 4:627-36 Ja '73; W. D. Howells in Atlan 31:359-60 Mr '73; G. A. Simcox in Acad 3:461-2 D 15 '72; Spec 46:49-50 Ja 11 '73; Ath 2:657-8 N 23 '72; Sat R 34:737-8

Morris, William—*Continued*

D 7 '72; Fortn 19:147-8 Ja 1 '73; Lond
Q R 40:243-6 Ap '73; Nation (NY) 16:
200 Mr 20 '73; Harper M 47:130 Je '73;
Scribner's Monthly 5:778-9 Ap '73)

News from nowhere; or, An epoch of
rest. Boston, Roberts, 1890. 7-278p
(Rev by M. Hewlett in Nat R 17:818-27
Ag '91; L. Johnson in Acad 39:483-4
My 23 '91; Ath 1:757-9 Je 13 '91; Nation
(NY) 53:241-2 S 24 '91; Speaker 3:561-2
My 9 '91; Critic (NY) 18:285 My 30 '91;
R of Rs (NY) 3:549-53 Je '91)

Poems by the way. London, Reeves and
Turner, 1891 [Printed at the Kelmscott
press] 197p
(Rev by C. Elton in Acad 41:197 F 27
'92; Ath 1:336-8 Mr 12 '92; Lit W 23:
162 My 7 '92; Sat R 73:154-5 F 6 '92;
W. M. Payne in Dial 13:51-2 Je '92;
Westm 138:101-2 Jl '92; Nation (NY)
55:11 Jl 7 '92; Speaker 5:149 Ja 30 '92)

The roots of the mountains. . . London,
Reeves and Turner, 1889. 424p
(Rev by C. Elton in Acad 36:397 D 21
'89; Spec 64:208-9 F 8 '90; Sat R 68:688
D 14 '89)

Signs of change: seven lectures delivered
on various occasions. London, Reeves
and Turner, 1888. xii,204p
(Rev in Westm 130:237-9 Ag '88; Sat R
65:607-8 My 19 '88)

Some hints on pattern designing
(Rev in Ath 1:280-1 Mr 2 '01)

Some thoughts on the ornamental manu-
scripts of the Middle Ages. New York,
Press of the woolly whale, 1934
(Rev by I. Hass in American Book
Collector 6:230-1 My-Je '35)

The story of the glittering plain. London,
Reeves and Turner, 1891 [Printed at the
Kelmscott press] 188p
(Rev in Critic (NY) 19:298 N 29 '91;
W. M. Payne in Dial 12:274-5 D '91;
Westm 138:102-3 Jl '92; Nation (NY)
53:472 D 17 '91)

The story of Sigurd the Volsung, and the
fall of the Niblungs. London, Ellis and
White, 1877. 392p
(Rev by H. Morley in 19th Cent 2:704-
12 N '77; H. G. Hewlett in Fraser ns 16:
96-112 Jl '77; E. W. Gosse in Acad 10:
557-8 D 9 '76; Scribner's Monthly 13:
724 Mr '77; No Am 124:323-5 Mr '77;
Lit W 7:136-7 F '77; Lit W 10:197-8
Je 21 '79; Spec 50:150-1 F 3 '77; Sat R
43:81-2 Ja 20 '77; Ath 2:753-5 D 9 '76;
Atlan 39:501-4 Ap '77; International Review 4:283, 696-9 Ap, O '77; Edin R
196:319-32 O '02)

The sundering flood. Hammersmith,
Kelmscott press, 1897. 507p
(Rev by L. J. Block in Dial 24:320-2
My 16 '98; Acad 53:304-5 Mr 19 '98;
Lit 2:352-3 Mr 26 '98; Bookm (Lond)
14:18 Ap '98; Lit W 29:147 My 14 '98)

A tale of the House of the Wolfings.
London, Reeves and Turner, 1888. 199p
(Rev in Book B ns 7:161-2 My '90; Lit
W 20:105 Mr 30 '89; Lit W 21:138 Ap
26 '90; Critic (NY) 15:13-14 Jl 13 '89;
W. M. Payne in Dial 11:67-9 Jl '90;
Westm 134:455-6 O '90; Nation (NY)
51:195 S 4 '90; G. E. Woodberry in
Atlan 65:851-4 Je '90; H. G. Hewlett in
19th Cent 26:337-41 Ag '89; C. Elton in
Acad 35:85-6 F 9 '89; Sat R 67:101-3
Ja 26 '89; Ath 2:347-8 S 14 '89)

Unpublished letters of William Morris to
Andreas Scheu, with an autobiography.
Ed. by Beresford Kemmis. Socialist
Review p24-36, 21-4, 34-8 Mr, Ap, My
'28

The water of the wondrous isles. Hammersmith, Kelmscott press, 1897. 340p
(Rev in Acad 52:343-5, 434 O 30, N 20
'97; Ath 2:777-9 D 4 '97; Critic (NY)
31:377-8 D 18 '97; A. Symons in Sat R
84:669-70 D 11 '97; Bookm (Lond) 13:
46 N '97; Lit W 28:389 N 13 '97; L. J.
Block in Dial 24:320-2 My 16 '98; Nation (NY) 66:136 F 17 '98)

The well at the world's end. Hammersmith, Kelmscott press, 1896. 496p
(Rev by A. C. Swinburne in 19th Cent
40:759-60 N '96; H. G. Wells in Sat R
82:413-14 O 17 '96; Ath 1:237-9 F 20 '97;
Lit W 27:375-6 N 14 '96; Nation (NY)
64:288-9 Ap 15 '97)

The wood beyond the world. Hammer-
smith, Kelmscott press, 1894. 261p
(Rev in Critic (NY) 27:337 N 23 '95;
Ath 1:273-4 Mr 2 '95; Spec 75:52-3 Jl 13
'95; Lit W 26:333 O 5 '95; Literary
World (Lond) ns 52:264-5 O 11 '95)

Works
(Rev in Ath 1:44-5, 233-4 Ja 16, Mr 13
'15; Spec 77:337-9 S 12 '96; Edin R 185:
63-83 Ja '97; Spec 114:272 F 20 '15; Edin
R 178:473-7 O '93; A. Macdonell in
Bookm (Lond) 19:67-9 S '96)

Morris, William and Bax, E. Belfort

Socialism: its growth and outcome. London, Swan Sonnenschein, 1893. viii,335p
(Rev in Ath 2:695 N 18 '93; Critic (NY)
24:107 F 17 '94; E. W. Bemis in Dial
16:306-7 My 16 '94; Nation (NY) 57:486
D 28 '93; Speaker 8:733 D 30 '93; Literary World (Lond) ns 48:503 D 22 '93;
Lond Q R 82:84-8 Ap '94)

Morris, William (prefacer)

Arts and crafts essays. London, Rivington, Percival, 1893
(Rev in Speaker 8:557-8 N 18 '93)

Morris, William (trans)

The Aeneids of Virgil done into English
verse. London, Ellis and White, 1876.
382p
(Rev by H. Nettleship in Acad 8:493-4
N 13 '75; Lit W 6:93 D '75; Ath 2:635-7
N 13 '75; Sat R 40:688-9 N 27 '75; Spec
48:1489-90 N 27 '75; Harper M 53:309
Jl '76)

The Odyssey of Homer done into English verse. London, Reeves and Turner, 1887. 2 vols 450p [continuous pagination]
(Rev by E. D. A. Morshead in Acad 31:299 Ap 30 '87; Sat R 63:587-8 Ap 23 '87; Sat R 64:738-9 N 26 '87; Spec 60: 1742-4 D 17 '87; Westm 128:380 Je '87; Westm 129:262-3 F '88; Macmil 56:130-5 Je '87; Church Review 49:706-7 Je '87)

Old French romances done into English by William Morris, with an introduction by Joseph Jacobs. London, Allen, 1896
(Rev by H. Oelsner in Acad 49:360-1 My 2 '96; Lit W 27:203 Je 27 '96; Dial 21:228 O 16 '96)

Morris, William and Magnússon, Eiríkr (translators)
Grettis Saga. The story of Grettir the strong. Translated from the Icelandic. London, Ellis, 1869. xxiv,306p
(Rev in Sat R 29:157-9 Ja 29 '70; Nation (NY) 71:509 D 27 '00; Tinsley's 7:457-9 N '70; Lond Q R 36:36-65 Ap '71)

The Saga library. London, Quaritch, 1891. vol I v-xlvii,227p
(Rev by C. Elton in Acad 40:448 N 21 '91; Spec 96:228 F 10 '06; Nation (NY) 53:220 S 17 '91; Lit W 22:36-7 Ja 31 '91)

The story of the ere-dwellers. . . (The Saga Library, vol II) London, Quaritch, 1892. lii,410p
(Rev in Lit W 23:39 Ja 30 '92)

Three northern love stories, and other tales. Translated from the Icelandic. London, Ellis and White, 1875. xi,3-243p
(Rev in Ath 2:75 Jl 17 '75; Spec 48: 1068-9 Ag 21 '75; Nation (NY) 22:251-2 Ap 13 '76)

Völsunga Saga. The story of the Volsungs and Niblungs, with certain songs from the Elder Edda. Translated from the Icelandic. London, Ellis, 1870. 275p
(Rev by G. A. Simcox in Acad 1:278-9 Ag 13 '70; Spec 43:983-4 Ag 13 '70; Sat R 30:81-3 Jl 16 '70; Tinsley's 7:459-64 N '70; Lond Q R 36:36-65 Ap '71)

Morris, William and Wyatt, A. J. (translators)
The tale of Beowulf done out of the Old English tongue. Hammersmith, Kelmscott press, 1895
(Rev in Literary World (Lond) ns 59: 3-4 Ja 6 '99; Speaker 19:56 Ja 14 '99; Ath 2:181-2 Ag 10 '95)

Morris and anti-scrape. T L S Mr 10 '27 p149-50

[Morris and the Earl of Surrey] Atlan 39: 621-2 My '77

Morris at Oxford. T L S My 17 '17 p236

Morris centenary. Art Digest 8:23 Ap 1 '34

Morris exhibition at the Victoria and Albert museum. Museums Journal 34:26-7 Ap '34

Morris in the present. T L S Ag 8 '12 p312

Morris Society, Chicago, Ill.
Bulletin [monthly] vol 1, 2 (no 1-4) November 1903-February 1905. Chicago, 1903-05. 71p
Inserted are By-laws; an editorial by Wm. Ellis, reprinted from The Philosopher; facsimile letter by Sydney C. Cockerell, a programme for the study of the life of Wm. Morris, by Martin Schütze; the poetry and fiction of Wm. Morris, syllabus by R. G. Moulton and reprint of the Circular of information of the South Park Workshop association.

Morris souvenir. Pub W 125:1376 Ap 7 '34

Morrison, Stanley and Jackson, Holbrook
A brief survey of printing. . . New York, Knopf, 1923. p18-20

[Morris's and Tennyson's treatment of mediaevalism] Atlan 39:102-3 Ja '77

Morris' opinion of the "dead level." Commonwealth (NY) 3:12 D '96

Morris's poetry. Lond Q R 33:330-60 Ja '70

Moss, Velma Catherwood
The socialism of William Morris, artist and poet. Masters essay, Columbia univ. 1924

Moulton, Charles Wells (ed)
William Morris. In The library of literary criticism. . . New York, Malkan, 1910. vol VIII p329-39

Moulton, Louise Chandler
Three English poets. Arena 6:46-8 Je '92

Moulton, Richard Green
The poetry and fiction of Wm. Morris, syllabus of private study or to accompany lectures. (Univ. extension lecture-study dept. no 186) Chicago, Univ. of Chicago press, 1904. 33p

Mourey, Gabriel
William Morris. In Passé le détroit. Paris, Ollendorff, 1895
William Morris. Revue Encyclopédique 6:805-10 N 21 '96

Muir, M. M. Pattison
The prose romances of William Morris. Oxford and Cambridge Review no 7:37-60 '09

Mumby, Frank Arthur
Publishing and bookselling. . . London, Cape [1930] p339-40

M[urry], John Middleton
The greatness of William Morris. Adel 4:774 '32

The return to fundamentals: Marx and Morris. Adel 5:19-29, 97-109 '32

William Morris. In Massingham, H. J. and Massingham, H. (eds) The great Victorians. London, Nicholson and Watson [1932] p325-41

Myers, Frederic William Henry
Modern poets and the meaning of life. 19th Cent 33:100-4 Ja '93

Nettlau, Max
Noticias de ninguna parte; O, Una era de reposo (capitulo para una novela utopica) prologo de Max Nettlau. (Los Utopistas (no) 2) Buenos Aires, Editorial la protesta, 1928. xxviii,30-219p

Nevinson, Henry Woodd
The last of romances. *In* Books and personalities. London, Lane, 1905. p66-72

The **new** printing. The mantle of Morris. Acad 54:127-8 Ag 6 '98; *see also* Acad 54:157 Ag 13 '98

New reminiscences of Oscar Wilde and William Morris. Current Opinion 71:226-9 Ag '21

Newdigate, B. H.
William Morris. Lond Merc 29:545-6 '34

The **next** Laureate. Pall Mall Budget 40:1514 O 13 '92

Nitchie, Elizabeth
Vergil and the English poets. New York, Columbia univ. press, 1919. p218-24 Diss. Columbia univ.

Nordby, Conrad Hjalmar
By the hand of the master. *In* The influence of old Norse literature upon English literature. (Columbia univ. Germanic studies vol I no iii) New York, Columbia univ. 1901. p37-73

[Note on "Earthly Paradise"] Atlan 39:489-90 Ap '77

[Note on Kelmscott press] Critic (NY) 36:305 Ap '00

[Note on Morris, with portrait] Critic (NY) 29:214 O 10 '96

[Note on Morris's death] Bulletin du Bibliophile p593 '96

Noyes, Alfred
William Morris. (English men of letters) (new ser) London, Macmillan, 1908. viii,156p
(Rev in Liv Age 260:368-72 F 6 '09; W. Clayton in Forum 41:175-7 F '09; Bookm (Lond) 35:224-6 F '09; T L S D 17 '08 p469-70; noted by H. D. Davray in Mercure Fr 77:736 F '09; Acad 76:684-5 Ja 16 '09; Sat R 107:629-30 My 15 '09; Spec 102:265-6 F 13 '09; Literary World (Lond) ns 75:39 F 15 '09)

Obituary. Bookn 15:113 N '96

O'Conor, Beatrice
G. B. S. and William Morris. New Statesm & Nation N 10 '34 p660

Ogilvy, Thomas
"Evolution and Wm. Morris." Sat R 133:285 Mr 18 '22

Oliphant, Margaret
William Morris, 1834. *In* The Victorian age of English literature. New York, Tait [c1892] vol II p445-8

Olivero, Federico
Sull' "Earthly Paradise" di William Morris. Rivista d'Italia 26:321-9 N 15 '23; *same in* Studi su poeti e prosatori inglesi. Torino, Fratelli Bocca, 1925. p361-76

Olivier of Ramsden, Sydney Olivier, 1st baron
William Morris, born March 24th, 1834. Spec 152:440-1 Mr 23 '34

"On the Wandle." Spec 56:1507-9 N 24 '83

Orage, Alfred Richard
Norse in English. *In* Readers and writers (1917-1921). London, Allen and Unwin, 1922. p136-8

Orcutt, William Dana
William Morris; the art of printing comes back. . . *In* Master makers of the book. . . Garden City, New York, Doubleday, Doran, 1928. p207-28

[**Organization** of the Morris society, Chicago, May 7, 1903] Craftsman 4:393-4 Ag '03

Originality in printing. Inland Printer 18:413-14 Ja '97

Osborn, (Mrs) Mamie (Hester)
William Morris's poetry; his resources. Masters essay, Louisiana State univ. 1933. 55ff

Parker, Orpha M.
The spirit of chivalry in the poems of Tennyson and William Morris. Masters essay, Univ. of Colorado, 1911. 92ff

Parks, Inez V.
Mediaevelism of William Morris. Masters essay, State Univ. of Iowa, 1918. 77ff

Parrott, Thomas Marc and Thorp, Willard (eds)
Poetry of the transition, 1850-1914. New York, Oxford [c1932] p98-100

Parry, John Jay
A note on the prosody of William Morris. Mod Lang N 44:306-9 My '29

Pascal, Georges
L'art décoratif; un précurseur trop oublié. Beaux Arts ns 73:2 Ap 20 '34

Pater, Walter Horatio
Aesthetic poetry. *In* Appreciations. London, Macmillan, 1889. p213-27

Some great churches in France, three essays. Portland, Maine, Mosher, 1905. viii,9-108p

Patmore, Coventry
"Distinction." Fortn 53:827 Je '90

Payne, William Morton
Editorial echoes. Chicago, McClurg, 1902
William Morris. *In* The Columbia university course in literature. New York, Columbia univ. press, 1929. vol XV p129-33

William Morris. *In* The greater English poets of the nineteenth century. New York, Holt, 1907. p316-47

William Morris (1834-1896). *In* Warner, C. D. (ed) Library of the world's best literature. . . Memorial ed. New York, Hill [c1902] vol XXVI p10337-42

Peck, Walter Edwin
Introduction. *In* Morris, W. Chants for socialists; with introductory appreciation, by W. E. Peck, and short biography of the author. (Library of social justice, no. 1) New York, Modern Books press, 1935

Pennell, Elizabeth Robins
Some memories of William Morris. American Magazine of Art 11:124-7 F '20

Pennell, Joseph and Pennell, Elizabeth Robins
Whistler as decorator, with an incidental comparison of the influence of Whistler and that of William Morris. Cent 83: 500-13 F '12

[The **personality** of William Morris] Citizen (Phila) 2:361 Ja '97

Phelan, (Mrs) Anna Augusta (Helmholtz)
The social philosophy of William Morris. . . Durham, North Carolina, Duke university press, 1927. (3)-207p bibl p(194)-7
(Rev by E. B. Burgum in Mod Lang N 43:548-50 D '28)

Pickering, Ernest Harold
William Morris. *In* A brief survey of English literature. London, Harrap [1932] p157-8

Plowman, Thomas F.
The aesthetes; the story of a nineteenth-century cult. Pall Mall Magazine 5: 37-9 Ja '95

Poet and artist. Harper W 22:1010-11 D 21 '78

The **poet** and the police. Critic (NY) ns 4: 176-7 O 10 '85

The **poet** in the police-court; poem. Sat R 60:417 S 26 '85; *same.* Critic (NY) ns 4:187-8 O 17 '85

Poetry and the intuition of immortality. T L S S 14 '16 p433-4

The **poetry** of the period. Temple Bar 28: 33-48 D '69; 27:45-51, 175 Ag, S '69

The **poetry** of William Morris. Cath World 12:89-98 O '70

Poets and politics. Critic (NY) ns 4:213-14 O 31 '85

The **policy** of the Socialist League. Commonweal 4:180 Je 9 '88

Pomeroy, Eltweed
A visit to the shop of William Morris. Craftsman no 5:43-8 F '02

[**Portraits** of Morris] Bookm (Lond) 85: 472 Mr '34; Cent 32:389 Jl '86; R of Rs (Lond) 14:413 N '96; Library ns 2: [113] Ap '01; Emporium 4:331 N '96; Bookm (Lond) 10:168 S '96; New England Magazine ns 3:740 F '91; Illustrated London News 101:491 O 15 '92; University Magazine 2: facing 552 N '78; Critic (NY) 35:620 Jl '99; R of

Rs (NY) 14:532 N '96; Critic (NY) 41:194 S '02; Bookm (NY) 29:379 Je '09; Book B ns 13:facing 918 Ja '97; Inland Printer 18:298 D '96; Bookm (NY) 2:296 D '95; Bookm (Lond) 40: 124 Je '11; Bookm (NY) 9:498 Ag '99; Harper M 76:818 My '88; Appleton J 7:673 Je 22 '72; Lit 9:243, 249 S 14 '01; Illustrated London News 109:456 O 10 '96; Once a Week 27:145 Ag 17 '72; Cosmopolitan 8:186 D '89; Pall Mall Magazine 5:36 Je '95; Bookm (Lond) 19:11, 82 O, D '00; Pall Mall Budget 40:1514 O 13 '92

Prance, C. R.
The collected edition of William Morris. T L S Ap 27 '22 p276

The **Pre-Raphaelite** Morris. Acad 65:111-13 Ag 1 '03

Pre-Raphaelitism in outline; William Morris. Bookn 24:698 Je '06

Prinsep, Valentine Cameron
. . . The Oxford circle: Rossetti, Burne-Jones, and William Morris. Mag Art 28:167-72 F '04

The **printing** of a book. Bookworm 7:21-3 '93

A **prophet** among the painters. Nation (NY) 39:240-1, 261-2 S 18, 25 '84

The **prose** romances of William Morris. T L S Ja 8 '14 p9-10

Pudor, Heinrich
William Morris, kaufmann. Gegenwart 64:156-7 S 5 '03

Pundt, Herbert
Dante Gabriel Rossetti's einfluss auf die gedichte des jungen William Morris. . . Diss. Breslau, 1920. Summary, Breslau, 1922. 2p

The **question** of the Laureateship. Bookm (Lond) 3:52-5 N '92

Quiller-Couch, (Sir) Arthur T.
Mr. William Morris. Speaker 14:391-2 O 10 '96

Radford, Ernest
The Kelmscott press; the beginnings of a great undertaking. Acad 66:150-1 F 6 '04

Rae, Frank B.
Those who followed. . . Ridgewood, New Jersey, 1902. 7p
(Reprinted from the Impressions Quarterly Mr '02)

Ralli, Augustus John
"The earthly paradise." *In* Critiques. . . London, Longmans, Green, 1927. p19-33; *same in* No Am 222:299-310 '26

Ransom, Will
The Kelmscott press. *In* Private presses and their books. New York, Bowker, 1929. p43-50

Rawson, Graham Stanhope
William Morris's political romance, "News from nowhere." . . . Borna-Leipzig, Noske, 1914. xiii,99p Thesis, Jena

Read, Elizabeth Fisher
The sources of William Morris's poem, The fostering of Aslaug. Masters essay, Columbia univ. 1899

Recollections of William Morris. Artist no 206:61-4 F '97

Rees, Richard
William Morris. Adel 3d ser 7:393-4 Mr '34

Rendall, Vernon
Wild flowers in literature. London, Scholartis press, 1934. p178-9

Rhys, Ernest
Lyric poetry. London, Dent, 1913. p348-9

Richardson, F.
William Morris. Primitive Methodist Quarterly Review 34:414 Jl '92

Richmond, (Sir) William Blake
Leighton, Millais, and William Morris: a lecture. . . London, Macmillan, 1898. 32p

Ricketts, Charles S. and Pissarro, L.
De la typographie et de l'harmonie de la page imprimée. William Morris et son influence sur les arts et métiers. Paris, En vente chez Floury. London, Sold by Hacon and Ricketts, 1898. 31p [256 copies only]

Riegel, (Julius)
Die quellen von William Morris' dichtung "The earthly paradise." (Erlanger beiträge zur englischen philologie. Bd 2 (no) 4) Erlangen, Deichert, 1890. 74p

Rinder, Frank
The Kelmscott press. Connoisseur 1:258-67 '01; same. Book-Lover (San Francisco) 2:481-4 Ja-F '02

Robertson, Lionel
Reviving the spirit of William Morris. House and Garden 41:43 Ap '22

Robertson, William Graham
Time was. London, Hamilton [1931] p92-7

Robinson, A. Mary F.
Zur geschichte der zeitgenössischen poesie Englands. William Morris. Unsere Zeit 2:457-67 S 15 '79

Roebuck, George Edward (ed)
William Morris: 1834-1934. Some appreciations. Edited for the William Morris Centenary celebrations. Walthamston museum and antiquarian society, 1934. 36p
(Rev in Spec 152:416-17 Mr 16 '34; Essex Review 43:124-6 '34)

Rogers, P.
A mannerism of William Morris. T L S My 24 '17 p250

Morris's "Summer dawn." T L S Je 21 '28 p468

Rollins, Carl Purington
New Morris item. Sat R Lit 11:151 S 29 '34

William Morris. Sat R Lit 11:119 S 15 '34

Rosenberg, W. L., Scheu, Andreas, and Mackay, J. H. (translators)
Gesänge fuer sozialisten von William Morris. Milwaukee, Wisconsin, Freidenker publishing co. 1889. 27p

Rosenblatt, Louise
L'idée de l'art pour l'art dans la littérature anglaise pendant la période victorienne. Paris, Champion, 1931. p115-18

Rossetti, William Michael
Some reminiscences. London, Brown Langham, 1906. vol I p214-18
(Rev in Bookm (Lond) 31:156 D '06)

Rothenstein, William
Men and memories. . . London, Faber and Faber [1931] vol I passim

Rowley, Charles
William Morris. In Fifty years of work without wages. London, Hodder and Stoughton [1912] p129-39

Ruhrmann, Friedrich G.
Studien zur geschichte und charakteristik des refrains in der englischen literatur. (Anglistische forschungen, heft 64) Heidelberg, Winter, 1927. p150-60

Ruskin, John; Morris, William, (etc)
Letters addressed to Algernon Charles Swinburne, by John Ruskin, William Morris, Sir Edward Burne-Jones and Dante Gabriel Rossetti. London, printed for private circulation only by Richard Clay, 1919. 16p

Rutherford, Mildred
William Morris. In English authors. Atlanta, Ga. Franklin printing and publishing co. 1906. p659-61

The Saga on the stage. William Morris's comment. T L S S 28 '22 p616

Saintsbury, George Edward Bateman
A history of English prose rhythm. London, Macmillan, 1912. p435-7

The prae-Raphaelite school. In A history of English prosody from the twelfth century to the present day. London, Macmillan, 1910. vol III p316-34

Poetry since the middle of the century. In A short history of English literature. New York, Macmillan, 1907. p783-5

William Morris. In Corrected impressions; essays on Victorian writers. . . New York, Dodd, Mead, 1895. p178-97; same in Critic (NY) 25:101-3 Ag 18 '94

William Morris. Critic (NY) 25:101-3, [115]-17 Ag 18, 25 '94

Sargent, Irene
Beautiful books. Craftsman 2 no 1:17-20 Ap '02

Life, art and influence of Morris. Craftsman 1 no 1:1-14 O '01

Morris and Burne-Jones. Craftsman 1 no 1:39-45 O '01

Morris and company, decorators. Craftsman 1 no 1:25-38 O '01

William Morris: his socialistic career. Craftsman 1 no 1:15-24 O '01

Schelling, Felix E.
The English lyric. Boston, Houghton, Mifflin, 1913. p236-8

Schleinitz, Otto von (freiherr)
Verkauf der "Morris Bibliothek" an Mr. Pierpont Morgan. Zentralblatt für Bibliothekswesen p471-4 '02

William Morris. . . Zeitschrift für Bücherfreunde 1:27-44, 59-78, 107-24, 146-65 Ap-Jl '07

William Morris, sein leben und wirken. I-IV [Bielefeld und Leipzig, Velhagen & Klassing, 1907-08]

Schnabel, B.
Nekrolog. Engl Stud 23:457 '97

Schur, Ernst
Ziele für die innere ausstattung des buches. Zeitschrift für Bücherfreunde 2:33-4 Ap '98

Scott, Ernest
William Morris and the relation of art to life. *In* Men and thought in modern history. Melbourne, Macmillan, 1920. p303-15

Scott, Frank Hope
The poetry of William Morris. Humberside 3:71-80 O '28

Scott, Nellie Mahaffay
Poetic treatment of the Arthurian legend since 1850. Masters essay, Univ of Oklahoma, 1929. 214ff

Scott, [W.] Dixon
The first Morris. *In* Men of letters. London, Hodder and Stoughton, 1916. p257-306

The first Morris. In Primitiae. . . Liverpool, Univ. press, 1912. p183-206

Scudder, Vida Dutton
Social ideals in English letters. Boston, Houghton, Mifflin, 1923. New ed passim

William Morris. *In* The life of the spirit in the modern English poets. Boston, Houghton, Mifflin, 1899. p274-7

Sélincourt, Ernest de
English poetry since 1815. *In* English poets and the national ideal. London, Oxford univ. press, 1915. p117-18

Sharp, Amy
Dante Gabriel Rossetti, William Morris, and Algernon Charles Swinburne. *In* Victorian poets. London, Methuen, 1891. p173-8
(Rev in Speaker 4:206-7 Ag 15 '91)

Sharp, William
William Morris: the man and his work. Atlan 78:768-81 D '96

Shaw, Albert
The versatile William Morris. Golden Book 20:168-70 Ag '34

Shaw, George Bernard
Morris as actor and dramatist. Sat R 82:385-7 O 10 '96

William Morris as a socialist. Daily Chronicle O 6 '96

[Shepard, Morgan] John Martin [pseud]
The Wolf's head and the queen. [A retelling of William Morris's "Child Christopher and Goldilind the fair."] New York, Scribner, 1931. xiv,244p
(Rev by S. K. Winther in Sat R Lit 8:478 Ja 23 '32)

Shepard, William [pseud]
see Walsh, William Shepard

Sherman, Francis
In memorabilia mortis [William Morris] [Cambridge, Univ. press] 1896. 11p (Privately printed)

Shinn, Charles Howard
The ideals of William Morris. Public 14:355-6 Ap 14 '11

Shipham, F. P. B.
A mannerism of W. Morris. T L S My 10 '17 p226

Shorter, Clement King
Victorian literature. New York, Dodd, Mead, 1897. p24-6

Sieper, E.
Das Evangelium der schönheit in der englischen literatur des 19. jahrhunderts. Dortmund, 1904. p339-63

Simcox, Edith
William Morris. Revue Britannique '79

Simond, Charles
William Morris. La Revue des Revues 19:321 '96

Sinclair, William
Socialism according to William Morris. Fortn 94:723-35 O '10

Singer, H. W.
Der Präraffaelismus in England. München, 1911

Smith, Arnold
William Morris. *In* The main tendencies of Victorian poetry. . . London, Simpkin, Marshall, Hamilton, Kent, 1907. p196-208

Smith, Louise
Indebtedness of William Morris to Chaucer. Masters essay, Univ. of Kansas, 1903. 40ff

Smith, Nowell
The poetry of Morris. Fortn ns 62:937-47 D '97

Smith, S. C. Kaines
Painters of England. London, Medici Society [1934] p93-6

Socialist League, London
The manifesto of the Socialist League, signed by the provisional council at the foundation of the league on 30th December 1884, and adopted at the general conference held at Farringdon Hall, London, on July 5, 1885. Annotated by William Morris and E. B. Bax. London, Socialist League office, 1885. New ed 14p

Sondheim, Moriz
William Morris. Zeitschrift für Bücherfreunde 2:12-20 Ap '98

Sondheim, Moriz—*Continued*
William Morris und die moderne stil. Berichte des freien deutschen Hochstifts p124-32 '98

Spargo, John
The socialism of William Morris. Westwood, Mass. Ariel press [1906?] 52p

Sparling, Henry Halliday
The Kelmscott press and William Morris master-craftsman. London, Macmillan, 1924. ix,176p
(Rev in T L S Ja 22, F 12 '25 p52, 104; Sat R 139:390 Ap 11 '25; E. Adler in Sat R Lit 2:48 Ag 15 '25; J. Hawthorne in Literary Digest International Book Review 3:177-8 F '25)

Speeches in commemoration of William Morris. Delivered at Walthamstow. By John Drinkwater, Holbrook Jackson, and H. J. Laski. Walthamstow, Public libraries, 1934. 21p

The state of art in France. Blackw 135:444 Ap '84

Stedman, Edmund Clarence
Latter day British poets. . . Morris. . . Scribner's Monthly 9:434-8 F '75

. . . William Morris. *In* Victorian poets. Boston, Houghton, Mifflin, 1896. p366-78

Steele, Richard
William Morris. Obituary. Acad 50:261-2 O 'O '96

Steele, Robert
The revival of printing. II.—The Kelmscott press. Acad 81:639-40 N 18 '11

William Morris. *In* Chambers's cyclopaedia of English literature. Philadelphia, Lippincott, 1904. New ed vol III p664-7

Stewart, Milroy Neil
William Morris, poet, artist and reformer. Hull prize essay, Univ. of Rochester, 1916. 10ff

Stillwell, Margaret Bingham
The heritage of the modern printer. New York, 1916. 15p (Reprinted from The Bulletin of the N. Y. Public Library 20:737-50 O '16)

The influence of William Morris and the Kelmscott press. . . Providence, Rhode Island, 1912. 16p (Exhibition of books from the later English presses)

Stirling, A. M. W.
William De Morgan and his wife. New York, Holt, 1922. passim

Stoddard, Richard Henry
William Morris. Appleton J 7:673-5 Je 22 '72

Streeter, A.
William Morris and Pre-Raphaelitism. Month 94:595-608 D '99

Stringer, Arthur
William Morris as I remember him. Craftsman 4:126-32 My '03

Stuart, G. B.
To William Morris; poem. Argosy 63:136 Ja '97

Swarzenski, Georg
William Morris und die entwicklung des modernen dekorativen stils in England. Neue Deutsche Rundschau 9:198-210 F '98

Sweet, Frederic Elmore
Archaic diction in William Morris's "The Sundering Flood." Masters essay, Brown Univ. 1929 61ff

Swinburne, Algernon Charles
Letters on William Morris, Omar Khayyám and other subjects of interest. London, printed for private circulation, 1910. 31p
(Printed for Thomas J. Wise. 20 copies only)

Morris's Life and death of Jason. *In* Essays and studies. London, Chatto, 1876. p110-22. *same.* Fortn ns 2:19-28 Jl '67

Swinburniana. T.P.'s Weekly 2:890 D 11 '03

Symons, Arthur
Morris as poet. Sat R 82:387-8 O 10 '96

William Morris. *In* Studies in two literatures. London, Smithers, 1897. p150-7
(Rev in Literary World (Lond) ns 56:443 D 3 '97)

William Morris's prose. *In* Studies in prose and verse. London, Dent [1910] p91-6

Szukiewicz, Wojciech
Apostof piekna. Biblioteka Warszawska 2:136-66 '00

Taylor, Bayard
The echo club, and other literary diversions. Boston, Osgood, 1876. p14-20

William Morris. *In* Critical essays and literary notes. New York, Putnam, 1880. p321-5

Taylor, George Robert Stirling
Leaders of socialism, past and present. New York, Duffield, 1910

Tea, Eva
William Morris e Giacomo Boni (with unpublished letters). I Libri del Giorno O '26

Tennyson: and after? Fortn 53:625 My '90

Thomas, Edward
William Morris. Bookm (Lond) 39:219-26 F '11

William Morris. *In* A literary pilgrim in England. London, Dodd, Mead, 1917. p82-8

Thompson, Alexander Hamilton
Tennyson and the Victorian poets. *In* A history of English literature. London, Murray, 1901. p783-5

William Morris. *In* C H E L vol XIII p137-43

Thompson, Tollef Bordsen
Beiträge zur entstehungsgeschichte des Earthly paradise. Germanisch-Romanische Monatsschrift 2:505-9 '10

Skandinavischer einfluss auf William Morris in den ersten Stadien (The earthly paradise). Berlin, Schade, 1910. 106p bibl p7-9 Diss. Greifswald

Tiffany, Francis
William Morris, craftsman and socialist. New World 9:103-14 '00

Tillotson, Geoffrey
Morris and machines. Fortn 141:464-71 Ap '34

Townshend, (Mrs)
William Morris and the communist ideal. (Fabian society. Fabian biographical series no 3. Fabian tract no 167) London, Fabian society, 1912. 23p

Tributes to Wm. Morris, on the publication of The earthly paradise. Boston [186-?] 36p

Triggs, Oscar Lovell
Morris and his plea for an industrial commonwealth. *In* Chapters in the history of the arts and crafts movement. 1902

The socialistic thread in the life and works of William Morris. Poet Lore 5:113-22, 210-18 Mr-Ap '83

William Morris. (New order ser no 1) Chicago [19-?] 46p

Tucker, T. G.
The foreign debt of English literature. London, Bell, 1907. p41, 67

Turner, Esther Hadassah
The implied social philosophy in the prose romances of William Morris. Masters essay, Univ. of Washington, 1931. 120ff

Turney, John Arthur
William Morris, poet, artist and reformer. Typed ms in Univ. of Rochester library. 1916. 11ff

Tynan, Katharine
Some memories of William Morris. Book B ns 13:925-6 Ja '97

Untermeyer, Louis
Modern British poetry. New York, Harcourt, Brace [c1930] 3d rev ed p66-8

Vallance, Aymer
The art of William Morris. . . London, Bell, 1897. xii,167,xxxp bibl piii-xxx (220 copies only) (Rev in Nation (NY) 66:111-12 F 10 '98)

The late Wm. Morris, artist, craftsman and poet. [Chiswick, Allen, 1896] 8p

The revival of tapestry—weaving. An interview with Mr. William Morris. Studio 3:99-101 Jl '94

William Morris: his art, his writings, and his public life; a record. London, Bell, 1897. xiv,462p (Later ed 1909) (Rev in Acad 52:394-5 N 13 '97; Critic (NY) 33:190-1 S '98; G. M. Twose in Dial 25:343-6 N 16 '98; Edin R 191:356-79 Ap '00; Sat R 84:749-50 D 25 '97; Spec 81:624-5 N 5 '98; Lit 1:36-8 O 30 '97; Studio 12:204-6 D '97)

Varnhagen, Hermann
Erlanger beiträge zur englischen philologie. [no 9] Erlangen, 1889

Velde, Henry van de
Kunstgewerbliche laienpredigten. Leipzig, Seemann [pref 1902] viii,195p

William Morris, artisan et socialiste. L'Avenir Social 3:35-48, 65-77 '98

[Vest, Eugene Bartlett]
The socialism of Ruskin and Morris, by Aurelius Prudentius Clemens [pseud] (Ruskin prize essay, Harvard college, 1932) Typed ms in Harvard College library, 1932. 32ff

The **Victorian** garden of song. Dial 19:238 N 1 '95

Vidalenc, Georges
Les idées de William Morris. Mercure Fr 92:5-21 Jl '11

La transformation des arts décoratifs au XIXe siècle; William Morris, son oeuvre et son influence. . . Caen, 1914. 335p Thesis, Caen

William Morris. Paris, Alcan, 1920. 166p (Rev by G. Binc in Literatur 43:177-8 My-Je '22)

The **vision** of William Morris. Cur Lit 46:515-18 My '09

Von Helmholtz-Phelan, Anne
see Phelan, (Mrs) Anna Augusta (Helmholtz)

Waddington, Samuel
Sonnets by William Morris. Ath 2:430 O 24 '14

Waentig, Heinrich
William Morris. *In* Handwörterbuch der staatswissenschaften. Jena, 1910. 3d ed vol VI p790-1

Wirtschaft und kunst. Jena, 1909

Walker, Harold E.
William Morris on Fascismo. Nat-Ath 32:233 N 11 '22

Walker, Hugh
The age of Tennyson. (Handbooks of English literature) London, Bell, 1904. p255-6

The literature of the Victorian era. Cambridge, Univ. press, 1921. p528-44

Walker, Hugh and Walker, (Mrs) Hugh
Outlines of Victorian literature. Cambridge, Univ. press, 1919. p85-8

[Walsh, William Shepard] Shepard, William [pseud]
William Morris. *In* Pen pictures of modern authors. New York, Putnam, 1882. p326-8

Ward, Sydney
William Morris and his papermaker, Joseph Batchelor. Philobiblon 7:177-80 '34

Wardle, George Young
William Morris as a man of business. Notes & Q 9th ser 6:495-6 D 22 '00

Wardrop, James
William Morris centenary exhibition. Apollo 19:206-9 Ap '34

Warwick, Frances Evelyn (Maynard)
William Morris, his homes and haunts. (Pilgrim books vol 6) London, Jack [pref 1912] xi,68p

Watkin, R. G.
Robert Browning and the English Pre-Raphaelites. Breslau, 1905

Watson, B. J. L.
William Morris from Oxford to the founding of the *Firm*, 1856-1861. Masters essay, Syracuse Univ. 1921. 61ff

Wattez, Omer
. . . William Morris. De Oud-Germaansche heldensage in de nieuwere engelsche letteren, door Omer Wattez, werkend lid der Koninklijke Vlaamsche Academie. Gent, W. Siffer, 1920. 23p

Watts-Dunton, Theodore
Mr. William Morris. Ath 2:487-8 O 10 '96

Rossettiana; a glimpse of Rossetti and Morris at Kelmscott. Engl R 1:323-32 Ja '09

William Morris. *In* Old familiar faces. London, Jenkins, 1916. p240-76

Webb, S.
Die wahre gesellschaft und die falsche von W. Morris. Protestant (Berlin) '98

Weekley, Montague
William Morris. (Great lives) London, Duckworth, 1934. 136p
(Rev in Spec 152:416-17 Mr 16 '34; T L S Mr 22 '34 p202; Apollo 19:216 Ap '34; G. West in Bookm (Lond) 85: 472-4 '34)

Weeks, Robert K.
The poetry of William Morris. New Englander 30:557-80 O '71

Welby, Thomas Earle
The Victorian romantics, 1850-70; the early work of D. G. Rossetti, W. Morris, Burne-Jones, Swinburne. . . and their associates. London, Howe, 1929. ix-x,161p
(Rev in T L S N 14 '29 p919)

West, Geoffrey
William Morris—man creative. Bookm (Lond) 85:472-4 Mr '34

Weygandt, Cornelius
Two pre-Raphaelite poets; William Morris and Dante Gabriel Rossetti. Bookn 24:687-90 Je '06

"What is the matter with the London poets and painters?" Critic (NY) 14:43-4 Ja 26 '89

Where are we now? Commonweal 6:361 '90

Whitaker, Charles Harris
William Morris, 1834-1896. American Magazine of Art 27:436-8 Ag '34

White, Greenough
[Mackail's Life of Morris] A study in biography. Conservative Review 2:347-63 N '99

Whitley, W. T.
Arts and crafts at the Royal Academy. International Studio 60:66-77 D '16

Whitney, Elizabeth Boyce
The Oxford movement and its influence on English poetry. Masters essay, Univ. of Oklahoma, 1931

Who will be Poet Laureate? Atlan 70:855-6 D '92

Wilde, Oscar
The English Renaissance. Boston, Luce, 1906. p1-17

Wiley, Edwin
William Morris, master-craftsman. *In* The old and new Renaissance. Nashville, Tennessee, 1903. 256p

Wilkes, J. A.
Memories of Kelmscott House. Socialist Review 14:325-31 '17

William Morris. Archiv für buchgewerbe 35:311; Once a Week 27:148 Ag 17 '72; Every Sat 13:429-34 O 19 '72; Book B ns 12:545-9 N '95; Critic (NY) 29: 207 O 10 '96; Spec 77:478-9 O 10 '96; Mitteilungen d. Mährischen Gewerbemuseum in Brünn 14:155 '97; Library 2d ser 2:[113]-19 Ap '01; Hohe Warte 146:7 '04; Expository Times 24:513-14 Ag '13; T L S My 22, 29 '19 p280, 296; T L S Mr 22 '34 p201-2; R of Rs (Lond) 14:413-15 N '96; Dial 21:209-11 O 16 '96; Speaker 2:623-5 D 6 '90

William Morris. *In* The Library of literary criticism of English and American authors. . . ed. by Charles Wells Moulton. . . Buffalo, New York, Moulton publishing company, 1904-05. vol VIII p329-39

William Morris. *In* Men of the time: a dictionary of contemporaries. . . London, Routledge, 1879. 10th ed p727

William Morris, 1834-1896. Craftsman, romancer, poet, prophet. San Francisco, Nash, 1934. 4p

William Morris [sketch] Nation (NY) 63: 306-7 O 22 '96

William Morris [with sketch and bibliography] Dial 21:[209]-11 O 16 '96

William Morris and anti-scrape. T L S Mr 10 '27 p149

William Morris and his provincial greatness. Current Opinion 66:120 F '19

Wlliam Morris and his wallpaper designs. Arts and Decoration 19:57 S '23

William Morris and the reviewers. Citizen (Philadelphia) 2:362-4 Ja '97

William Morris as a man of business. Notes & Q 9th ser 6:406 N 24 '00; ibid 7:54 Ja 19 '01

William Morris at work. American Architect and Building News 17:296-8 Je 20 '85

William Morris centenary exhibition. Apollo 19:167 Mr '34

William Morris: his tastes in art and literature. Craftsman 5:574 Mr '04

William Morris, poet and artist. Quar R 190:487-512 O '99

William Morris, poet and craftsman. Edin R 185:63-83 Ja '97

William Morris: "Sigurd the Volsung." Notes & Q 12th ser 2:448 D 2 '16

William Morris—the poet. Book B ns 13: 917-18 Ja '97

William Morris über seine zeile bei der begründung der Kelmscott press. Philobiblon 7:167-8 '34

The "William Morris window." Scribner's Monthly 6:245-6 Je '73

The William Morris works at Merton Abbey. Bookman's Journal 9:152 Ja '24

William Morris's great achievement [the Kelmscott press, with bibliography and prices] Critic (NY) 35:910-19 O '99

[William Morris's poetry] Ecl M 78:394-9 Ap '72

Williams, Stanley Thomas
Studies in Victorian literature. New York, Dutton [c1923] passim

Williamson, Claude C. H.
William Morris. In Writers of three centuries, 1789-1914. Philadelphia, Jacobs [1915?] p276-83

Wilson, Stella P.
William Morris and France. So Atlan Q 23:242-55 Jl '24

Windisch, Albert
William Morris als drucker. Gutenberg Jahrbuch 4:238-48 '29

Winslow, Bernice L.
Sources of the legend of Cupid and Psyche from William Morris' "The Earthly Paradise." Masters essay, Columbia univ. 1932

Winslow, W. Henry
William Morris, the artist. New England Magazine ns 16:161-77 Ap '97

Winwar, Frances [pseud]
see Grebanier, (Mrs) Frances

Witcutt, W. P.
William Morris: distributist. Am R 2:311-15 Ja '34

Wolff, Lucien
Le sentiment médiéval en angleterre au XIXᵉ siècle et la première poésie de William Morris. Revue A A 1:491-504 Ag '24; ibid 2:29-38 O '24

Wood, Esther
Morris, the man. An intimate memory of a prophet and song-smith. Book Monthly 11:231-5 Ja '14

Woods, Margaret L.
Poets of the 'eighties. In The eighteen-eighties, essays by fellows of the Royal society of literature, ed. by Walter De la Mare. Cambridge, Univ. press, 1930. p4-6

Wülker, Richard
Geschichte der englischen literatur. Leipzig, Bibliographischen instituts, 1907. p285-7, 296-8

Wyzewa, Teodore de
Écrivains étrangers. 1896
Un roman posthume de William Morris: The sundering flood. R Deux Mondes Ap 15 '98 p935-45

William Morris. In Le mouvement socialiste en Europe. Paris, Perrin, 1892. p[189]-205

William Morris. In (Le) Roman contemporain à l'étranger. Paris, Perrin, 1900. p87-107

Yeats, William Butler
Autobiographies. . . London, Macmillan, 1926. p172-84

The happiest of the poets (William Morris). Bibelot 18:112-28 '12; same. Fortn 79:535-41 Mr '03

Ideas of good and evil. In The happiest of the poets. London, Bullen, 1903. p70-89

Four years, 1887-1891. Lond Merc 4:129-40, 259-70, 364-77 Je-Ag '21; Dial 71: 70-6 Jl '21

Zabel, Morton Danwen
Two versions of the nineteenth century. Poetry 44:270-6 Ag '34

Zellerbach paper company
A Morris keepsake. . . sent out by the Zellerbach paper company. . . The portrait of Morris was specially painted by Henry Raschen. Text by Edward F. O'Day (American institute of graphic arts. . .) San Francisco, Printed by J. H. Nash, 1927. 3 leaves

Zueblin, Rho Fisk
A visit to William Morris's factory. Out 54:770-3 O 31 '96

Christina Georgina Rossetti

Christina Georgina Rossetti

I. Chronological Outline

1830. Born, December 5, London.

1847. Verses [privately printed].

1850. 7 Contributions to *The Germ* under pseudonym of Ellen Alleyne.

1862. Goblin Market, and Other Poems.

1866. The Prince's Progress, and Other Poems.

1870. Commonplace, and Other Short Stories.

1872. Sing-Song: a Nursery-Rhyme Book.

1874. Speaking Likenesses.

1874. Annus Domini, a Prayer for Each Day of the Year.

1879. Seek and Find.

1881. A Pageant, and Other Poems.

1881. Called to be Saints.

1883. Letter and Spirit. Notes on the Commandments.

1885. Time Flies: a Reading Diary.

1892. The Face of the Deep. A Devotional Commentary on the Apocalypse.

1893. Verses.

1894. Died, December 29, London.

1896. New Poems.

1897. Maude.

Christina Georgina Rossetti

II. Bibliographical Material

Anderson, J. P.
Bibliography. *In* Bell, Mackenzie. Christina Rossetti, a biographical and critical study. Boston, Roberts, 1898. p[377]-390

Brown, G. A.
[Bibliography] *In* C H E L vol XIII p548

Cary, Elisabeth Luther
Christina Rossetti's poems. *In* The Rossettis, Dante Gabriel and Christina. New York, Putnam, 1900. p282-7

Livingston, Luther Samuel
The first books of some English authors. III. Dante Gabriel and Christina G. Rossetti. Bookm (NY) 10:245-7 N '99

Northup, Clark Sutherland
A register of bibliographies of the English language and literature. New Haven, Yale univ. press, 1925. p333

Page, Curtis Hidden
List of references. *In* British poets of the nineteenth century, ed. by Curtis Hidden Page. new ed. by Stith Thompson. New York, Sanborn, 1930. p842

Quinn, John
The library of John Quinn. . . New York, Anderson galleries, 1924. part IV p797-800

Thomas, Eleanor Walter
Bibliography. *In* Christina Georgina Rossetti. (Columbia univ. Studies in English and comparative literature) New York, Columbia univ. press, 1931. p[213]-222

Woods, George Benjamin
[Bibliography] *In* Poetry of the Victorian period. New York, Scott, Foresman [c1930] p1009-11

Christiana Georgina Rossetti

III. Biographical and Critical Material

Agresti, Antonio
I Prerafaelisti. Torino, Società tipografico Editrice nazionale, 1908. (Noted in TLS S 10 '08 p292)

Agresti-Rossetti, Olivia
Cristina Giorgina Rossetti. Nuova Antol 207:37-52 My 1 '06

Alliaud, G. M.
Introduction. *In* Rossetti, Christina Georgina. Goblin market. . . Torino, Paravia, 1934

Angeli, Helen Rossetti
The wife of Rossetti. TLS O 27 '32 p789

Armytage, A. J. Green
C. G. Rossetti. *In* Maids of honour. . . London, Blackwood, 1906

Ashwell, Frances E.
Miss Christina Rossetti. Great Thoughts 23:288-90 F 2 '95

Bald, Marjory Amelia
Christina Rossetti. *In* Women-writers of the nineteenth century. Cambridge, England, Univ. press, 1923. p233-84

Bardi, Pietro
Cristina Georgina Rossetti. *In* Storia della letteratura inglese. Bari, Gius, Laterza, 1933. p184-5

Bary, Anna Bunston de
The poetry of Christina Rossetti. Poetry Review 1:203-10 My '12

Barzia, Elspeth H.
[Christina Rossetti] Sun Je '90 p615-18

Bates, Katherine Lee
The passing of Christina Rossetti; poem. Dial 18:135 Mr 1 '95

Beerbohm, Max
Rossetti and his circle. London, Heinemann, 1922. ixp,23 plates

Bell, Mackenzie
[Christina Rossetti] Author Mr '95 p269-70

Christina Rossetti, a biographical and critical study. Boston, Roberts, 1898. xvi,405p bibl p[377]-390
(Rev in Acad 53:88-9 Ja 22 '98; F. J. Greg in Book B ns 16:315-18 My '98; Ath 1:109-10 Ja 22 '98; Lit W 29:41-2 F 5 '98; Sat R 85:177-8 F 5 '98; Lit 2:66-8 Ja 22 '98; Bookm (NY) 7:73-5 Mr '98; Literary World (Lond) ns 57:43-4 Ja 21 '98; Nation (NY) 66:272-3 Ap 7 '98; Quar R 189:32-57 Ja '99; *same.* Liv Age 221:26-34, 123-33 Ap 1, 8 '99; W. R. Nicoll in Bookm (Lond) 13:154 F '98)

To Christina G. Rossetti; poem. Literary World (Lond) ns 51:21 Ja 4 '95

Benson, Arthur Christopher
Christina Rossetti. *In* Essays. New York, Macmillan, 1896. p268-91; *same.* Nat R 24:753-63 F '95; *same.* Liv Age 204:620-6 Mr 9 '95

Birkhead, Edith
Christina Rossetti and her poetry. (Poetry and life ser no 36) London, Harrap [1930] 126p
(Rev in TLS F 5 '31 p102; Oxford Magazine Je 18 '31 p887; O. Burdett in Sat R 151:24 Ja 3 '31)

Boase, Frederic
Rossetti, Christina Georgina. *In* Modern English biography. Truro, Netherton & Worth, 1901. vol III p306

Bourne, Anna Ruth
Christina Rossetti as exponent of the English pre-Raphaelite movement. Masters essay, Columbia univ. 1920

Bowker, R. R.
London as a literary center. Harper M 76:827-8 My '88

Breme, Ignatia
Christina Rossetti und der einfluss der bibel auf ihre dichtung. Eine literarisch-stilistische untersuchung. Münstersche beiträge zur englischen literaturgeschichte. . . [no] 4) Münster (Westf) Schöningh, 1907. xi,96p. bibl p[IX]-XI

Breme, M. I.
C. G. Rossetti. Mädchenbildung auf Christliche Grundlage 4:406-16 '09

Buck, Elizabeth Fleming
A comparison of the poetry of Christina Rossetti and Emily Dickinson. Masters essay, Univ. of Arizona, 1933. 98ff For abstract see Univ. of Arizona Bulletin 4 no 5:11 Jl 1 '33

Burke, Charles Bell
Sketch of Christina Rossetti. *In* Selected poems of Christina G. Rossetti. (Macmillan's pocket American and English classics) New York, Macmillan, 1913. pxix-xl

Caine, Lily Hall
A child's recollections of Rossetti. New Review 11:246-55 S '94

Cary, Elisabeth Luther
The Rossettis, Dante Gabriel and Christina. New York, Putnam, 1900. xi, 310p

Cazamian, Madeleine
Christina Rossetti. Revue de P 18:575-89 Ag 1 '11

Chapman, Edward Mortimer
The doubters and the mystics. *In* English literature in account with religion, 1800-1900. Boston, Houghton, Mifflin, 1910. p446-50

Christina Georgina Rossetti. Dial 18:37-9 Ja 16 '95; Book B ns 12:21-3 F '95; Critic (NY) 26:21 Ja 12 '95

Christina Georgina Rossetti. *In* The Library of literary criticism of English and American authors... ed. by Charles Wells Moulton... Buffalo, New York, Moulton publishing company, 1904-05. vol VIII p268-75

Christina Rossetti. Sat R 79:5-6 Ja 5 '95; Church Q R 59:58-75 O '04; TLS D 4 '30 p1021-2

Christina Rossetti, 1830-1894. Bookn 26: 369-72 Ja '08

Christina Rossetti's contributions to *Notes & Queries.* Notes & Q 155:127 Ag 25 '28

Clutton-Brock, Arthur
Christina Rossetti. *In* More essays on religion. New York, Dutton, 1928. p11-23

Coleridge, Christabel R.
The poetry of Christina Rossetti. Monthly Packet 89:276-82 Mr '95

Courten, Maria Luisa Giartosio de
...I Rossetti; storia di una famiglia. Milano, Alpes, 1928. 362p

Criticisms on contemporaries. No. VI The Rossettis.—Part I. Tinsley's 5:59-67 Ag '69

Cunliffe, John W.
Mid-Victorian poets. Christina Rossetti. *In* Leaders of the Victorian revolution. New York, Appleton-Century [c1934] p239-40

Davies, A. Morley
Christina Rossetti. Notes & Q 10th ser 6:397 N 17 '06

Death of Miss Rossetti. Critic (NY) 26: 16 Ja 5 '95

De La Mare, Walter John
Christina Rossetti. *In* Royal Society of literature. Essays by divers hands, being the Transactions of the society. Ed. by G. K. Chesterton. London, Milford, 1926. ns vol VI p79-116

Delaney, Honora
Alice Meynell as a critic of English literature. Masters essay, Univ. of Pittsburgh, 1932. Abstract in Univ. of Pittsburgh Bulletin 8:383-4 '32

Denans
La pensee et le sentiment religieux chez Christina Rossetti. Thesis for Diplome d'Etudes superieures. Univ. of Paris. Sorbonne, 1922

Dubslaff, Friedrich
Die sprachform der lyrik Christina Rossettis. (Studien zur Englischen philologie 77) Halle (Saale) Niemeyer, 1933. (iii)-vip bibl [v]-vi
(Rev by C. S. Northup in J Engl & Germ Philol 33:150-1 '34; P. de Reul in Engl Stud 16:120-1 '34; English Studies 69:140-2 '34)

Edwards, Matilda Barbara Betham
Tea with Christina Rossetti. *In* Friendly faces of three nationalities. London, Chapman, 1911. p129-35

Eliot, Ruth F.
Elizabeth Browning and Christina Rossetti; a comparison. Masters essay, Columbia univ. 1927

Ellis, Stewart Marsh
Christina Rossetti... Bookm (Lond) 79: 179-81 D '30

Elton, Oliver
The Rossettis. *In* A survey of English literature, 1830-1880. London, Arnold, 1920. p22-30

Evans, Benjamin Ifor
Christina Rossetti. *In* English poetry in the later nineteenth century. London, Methuen [1933] p65-80 bibl p80
The sources of Christina Rossetti's "Goblin Market." Mod Lang R 28:156-65 Ap '33

Ewing, Thomas J.
Paraphrase of poem wanted. Notes & Q 7th ser 12:337, 433 O 24, N 28 '91

Fehr, Bernhard
Die englische literatur des 19. und 20. jahrhunderts. Wildpark-Potsdam, 1928. p186

Field, Michael
To Christina Rossetti; poem. Acad 49: 284 Ap 4 '96

Ford, Ford Madox
see Hueffer, Ford Madox

Forman, Harry Buxton
Christina G. Rossetti. *In* Our living poets. London, Tinsley, 1871. p229-53

Frend, Grace Gilchrist
Great Victorians: some recollections of Tennyson, George Eliot and the Rossettis. Bookm (Lond) 77:9-11 O '29

Garnett, Richard
Christina Rossetti. *In* Dict N B vol XVII p282-4

Garnett, Richard and Gosse, (Sir) E. W.
Christina Georgina Rossetti. *In* English literature, an illustrated record, by Richard Garnett and Edmund Gosse. New York, Grosset & Dunlap [c1904] vol IV p349-52

Gilchrist, Grace
Christina Rossetti. Good Words 37:822-6 D '96

Gilchrist, Herbert Harlakenden (ed)
Anne Gilchrist, her life... London, Unwin, 1887. p145-7

Goodale, Ralph Hinsdale
Pessimism in English poetry and fiction, 1847-1900. *In* Abstracts of theses. . . Humanistic series. vol. VI. . . Univ. of Chicago. Chicago, 1927. p347-51

Gosse, (Sir) Edmund William
Christina Rossetti. *In* Critical kit-kats. London, Heinemann, 1896. p133-62; *same*. Cent ns 24:211-17 Je '93

Christina Rossetti. *In* Selected essays. London, Heinemann, 1928. 1st ser p83-110

Goyau, L. Félix-Faure
La nostalgie d'une conscience exilée, Christina Rossetti. *In* Vers la joie... Paris, Perrin, 1906

Grappe, Georges
C. G. Rossetti. *In* Essai sur la poésie anglaise au XIX° siècle. Paris, Sansot, 1906. p57-9

[Grebanier, (Mrs) Frances (Vinciguerra)] Frances Winwar [pseud]
Poor splendid wings. Boston, Little, Brown, 1933. p22-30, 35-7, 309-14

Greene, Kathleen Conyngham
Christina Georgina Rossetti; a study and some comparisons. Cornhill ns 69:662-70 D '30

Greenwell, Dora
To Christina Rossetti; poem. Good Words 17:824 '76

Griswold, Hattie Tyng
Christina Rossetti. *In* Personal sketches of recent authors. Chicago, McClurg, 1898. p281-97

Hearn, Lafcadio
Miss Rossetti. *In* A history of English literature, in a series of lectures. Tokyo, Hokuseido press, 1927. vol II p689-91

Hinkson, Katharine Tynan
London letter. Lit W 26:24 Ja 26 '95

The poetry of Christina Rossetti. Bookm (Lond) 5:78-9 D '93

Santa Christina. Bookm (Lond) 41:185-90 Ja '12; *same*. Liv Age 272:431-6 F 17 '12

Some reminiscences of Christina Rossetti. Bookm (NY) 1:28-9 F '95; *same*. Bookm (Lond) 7:141-2 F '95

Hubbard, Elbert
Christina Rossetti. *In* Little journeys to the homes of famous women. New York, Putnam, 1897. no V p147-72

Hueffer, Ford Madox
Christina Rossetti. Fortn ns 89:422-9 Mr '11

Christina Rossetti and pre-Raphaelite love. *In* Memories and impressions. London, Chapman and Hall, 1911. p54-69
(Rev by P. F. Bicknell in Dial 50:345-6 My 1 '11)

Hunt, Violet
The wife of Rossetti. New York, Dutton, 1932. xxx,339p

Hunt, William Holman
Pre-Raphaelitism and the Pre-Raphaelite brotherhood. New York, Macmillan, 1905-1906. 2 vols

Japp, Alexander H.
[Christina Rossetti] Cassell's Family Magazine F '95 p227

Johnson, M.
Christina Rossetti. Primitive Methodist Quarterly Review 37:469-81 '95

Kellner, Leon
Die englische literatur der neuesten zeit. Leipzig, Tauchnitz, 1921. p263-4

Die englische literatur im zeitalter der königin Viktoria. Leipzig, Tauchnitz, 1909. p473-4

Kent, Muriel
Christina Rossetti: a reconsideration. Contemp 138:759-67 D '30

Kenyon, James Benjamin
Rossetti and his sister Christina. *In* Loiterings in old fields. New York, Eaton, 1901. p149-71

Klenk, Hans
Nachwirkungen Dante Gabriel Rossetti's. Untersuchungen von werken von Christina Rossetti. . . Lauf a. d. Pegn. Bachmann, 1932. 62p Diss. Erlangen

Lang, Andrew
Christina Rossetti. Cosmopolitan Magazine (Lond) Je '95

Law, Alice
The poetry of Christina G. Rossetti. Westm 143:444-53 '95

Lawson, Malcolm
Music to song of Christina Rossetti. Notes & Q 12th ser 3:214 Mr 17 '17

Levy, Amy
The poetry of Christina Rossetti. Woman's World (Lond) 1:178-80 F '88

Lingo, June Inez
Study of the poetry of Christina Rossetti. Masters essay, State Univ. of Iowa, 1930. 68ff

Lowther, George
Christina Rossetti. Contemp 104:681-9 N '13

Lubbock, Percy
Christina Rossetti. *In* Ward, T. H. The English poets. New York, Macmillan, 1918. vol V p286-9

McGill, Anna Blanche
The Rossettis. Book B ns 20:378-82 Je '00

Mackenzie, Margaret
Fettered Christina Rossetti. Thought 7:32-43 Je '32

Marshall, Dorothy Vesta
The poetry of Christina Rossetti. Masters essay, Univ. of Nebraska, 1929. 171ff

Marshall, Louisville
The life of Christina Rossetti. Masters essay, Columbia univ. 1923

Martin, Helen Virginia
Christina Rossetti; a brief survey of her life and poetry. Masters essay, Columbia univ. 1915

Mason, Eugene
Two Christian poets, Christina G. Rossetti and Paul Verlaine. *In* A book of preferences in literature. New York, Dutton, 1915. p115-37

Mather, Frank Jewett, jr.
The Rossettis. Bookm (NY) 49:139-47 Ap '19

A **memorial** to Christina Rossetti. Sat R 86:601 N 5 '98

Meynell, Alice
Christina Rossetti. New Review 12:201-6 F '95; *same*. Liv Age 204:569-72 Mr 2 '95
Introduction. *In* Rossetti, Christina. Poems. (Red letter poets) London, Blackie, 1923

Miss Rossetti's poetry. Lond Q R 68: 338-50 Jl '87

Moore, Virginia
Christina Rossetti's centennial. Yale R ns 20:428-32 D '30; *same in* Distinguished women writers. New York, Dutton [c1934] p45-58

More, Paul Elmer
Christina Rossetti. Atlan 94:815-21 D '04; *also in* Shelburne essays. New York, Putnam, 1907. 3d ser p124-42

Morse, B. J.
Some notes on Christina Rossetti and Italy. Anglia 55:101-5 '31

Morse-Boycott, Desmond Lionel
Christina Rossetti. *In* Lead, kindly light; studies of the saints and heroes of the Oxford movement. New York, Macmillan, 1933. p121-7

Nash, Joseph John Glendinning
The Christina Rossetti Memorial. Critic (NY) 28:357 My 16 '96
Christina Rossetti's memorial. Nation (NY) 62:394 My 21 '96
A memorial sermon preached . . . for the late Christina G. Rossetti. . . London, Skeffington, 1895. 24p

Neenan, Mary Pius
Some evidences of mysticism in English poetry of the nineteenth century. Doctor's essay, Catholic univ. 1916

Noble, James Ashcroft
The burden of Christina Rossetti. *In* Impressions and memories. London, Dent, 1895. p55-64
Christina Rossetti. Literary Opinion D '91 p155-7

[**Note** on C. Rossetti] Lit W 6:181-2 My '76

[**Note** on Christina Rossetti] T. P.'s Weekly 2:491 S 18 '03

[**Note** on an unpublished story, "Maude"] Bookm (Lond) 11:57 D '96

Obertello, Alfredo
Christina Rossetti nel centenario della sua nascita. Rassegna Italiana 14:16-30 Ja '31

Obituary. Christina Rossetti. Acad 47:12 Ja 5 '95

O'Brien, (Mrs) William
C. G. Rossetti. *In* Unseen friends. London, Longmans, Green, 1912

Olivero, Federico
Poeti mistici, Christina Rossetti. *In* Nuova saggi di letteratura inglese. Torino, Libreria editrice internazionale [1918?] p289-95
(Rev in T L S S 19 '18 p451)

Osmond, Percy H.
The mystical poets of the English church. London, S.P.C.K. 1919. p401-10

Owen, Frances Mary
Goblin Market. *In* Essays and poems. London, Bumpus, 1888

Panels in the reredos in Christ Church. . . In memorial of Christina Rossetti. Critic (NY) 34:13 Ja '99

Paraphrase of poem wanted. Notes & Q 7th ser 12:135-6, 234-5 Ag 15, S 19 '91

Parker, Elizabeth
The love affairs of Christina Rossetti. McGill university. University Magazine 18:246-55 Ap '19

Payne, William Morton
Christina Georgina Rossetti. (1830-1894) *In* Warner, C. D. ed. Library of the world's best literature. . . Memorial ed. New York, Hill [c1902] vol XXXI p12397-9
Christina Rossetti. *In* Little leaders. Chicago, McClurg, 1902. p237-45

A **picture** of Christina Rossetti. Poetry Review 1:241 My '12

Poetesses. Sat R 25:678-9 My 23 '68; *same*. Liv Age 97:819-22 Je 27 '68

A **poetic** trio. Ath 2:193-4 Ag 7 '97

The **poetry** of Christina Rossetti. T. P.'s Weekly 3:675 My 20 '04

[**Portraits**] Bookm (NY) 3:14 Mr '96; Bookm (Lond) 41: facing 177 Ja '12; 41:185, 187, 192 Ja '12; Harper M 76: 823 My '88; Bookm (Lond) 79:180-1 D '30; 23 supp 1 D '02; 5:78 D '93; 7:141 F '95; Woman's World (Lond) 1:181 F '88; Cent ns 24:217 Je '93; Critic (NY) 26:34 Ja 12 '95

Proctor, Ellen A.
A brief memoir of Christina Rossetti. With a preface by W. M. Rossetti. London, S P C K. 1895. 84p
(Rev in Lond Q R 87:2-16 O '96)

Raleigh, Walter
Christina Rossetti. *In* Chambers's cyclopaedia of English literature. Philadelphia, Lippincott, 1903. vol III p646-8

The **Rambler.** Book B ns 12:20 F '95

Reid, Stuart J.
In memory of Christina Rossetti. Sunday Magazine 34:859-60 '05

Reilly, Joseph John
Christina Rossetti. America 44:460-1 F 14 '31

Christina Rossetti: poet of renunciation. *In* Dear Prue's husband. . . New York, Macmillan, 1932. p144-61

Robertson, Eric S.
English poetesses. . . London, Cassell, 1883. p338-48

Rossetti, Christina Georgina
Called to be saints: the minor festivals devotionally studied. London, S. P. C. K. 1881
(Rev by G. A. Simcox in Acad 20:341 N 5 '81)

Commonplace, and other short stories. London, Ellis, 1870. vi,[3]-329p
(Rev in Ath 1:734-5 Je 4 '70; Spec 43: 1292-3 O 29 '70; Lond Q R 36:258-9 Ap '71; G. A. Simcox in Acad 1:252 Jl 9 '70)

The face of the deep: a devotional commentary on the Apocalypse. London, Society for Promoting Christian Knowledge, 1892. 552p
(Rev in Ind 44:1524 O 27 '92; Ind 45:54 Ja 12 '93)

The family letters of Christina Georgina Rossetti, with some supplementary letters and appendices, ed. by William Michael Rossetti. New York, Scribner, 1908. xxii,242p
(Rev in No Am 189:618-21 Ap '09; Ath 2:601 N 14 '08; Bookm (Lond) 35: 140 D '08)

Goblin market, and other poems. Cambridge, Macmillan, 1862. 192p
(Rev by J. R. Dennett in Nation (NY) 3:47-8 Jl 19 '66; Mrs. C. E. Norton in Macmil 8:401-4 S '63; *same.* Liv Age 79:126-9 O 17 '63; Ath 1:557-8 Ap 26 '62; Sat R 13:595-6 My 24 '62; Brit Q 36:230-1 Jl '62; Eclectic Review ns 2: 493-9 Je '62; *same.* Liv Age 74:147-50 Jl 26 '62; T L S F 18 '32 p115)

Letter and spirit. Notes on the Commandments. London, Society for Promoting Christian Knowledge, 1883. 206p
(Rev by G. A. Simcox in Acad 23:395-6 Je 9 '83)

New poems, hitherto unpublished or uncollected. Ed. by William Michael Rossetti. London, Macmillan, 1896. xxiv,397p
(Rev by L. Johnson in Acad 50:59-60 Jl 25 '96; Ath 1:207-9 F 15 '96; Lond Q R 86:180-1 Ap '96; Bookm (NY) 3:55-6 Mr '96; Spec 76:309-10 F 29 '96; Lit W 27:85 Mr 21 '96; W. M. Payne in Dial 20:205-6 Ap 1 '96; Edin R 183: 514 Ap '96; Nation (NY) 62:437 Je 4 '96; Atlan 77:570 Ap '96; C. Porter in Poet Lore 8:149-50 Mr '96; Guardian 51:432 Mr 18 '96; Sat R 81:194-7 F '96)

A pageant, and other poems. London, Macmillan, 1881. ix,198p
(Rev in Ath 2:327-8 S 10 '81; *same.* Ecl M ns 34:708-12 N '81; Lit W 12: 372-3, 395-6 O 22, N 5 '81; Dial 2:241 F '82; Brit Q 74:480-1 O '81; Atlan 49:121 Ja '82; T. H. Caine in Acad 20:152 Ag 27 '81)

Poems
(Rev by R. Le Gallienne in Acad 39: 130-1 F 7 '91; F. A. Rudd in Cath World 4:839-46 Mr '67; Cath World 24:122-9 O '76; Lond Q R 68:338-50 Jl '87; Edin R 178:494-5 O '93; Literary World (Lond) ns 43:100 Ja 30 '91; International Review 4:109-10 F '77; H. Richter in Engl Stud 37:277-9 '07; Lond Q R 87:2-16 O '96)

Poetical works, ed. by William Michael Rossetti. London, Macmillan, 1904. 582p
(Rev in Ath 1:423-4 Ap 2 '04; T L S Ap 8 '04 p105-6; Spec 93:51-2 Jl 9 '04; F. M. Hueffer in Fortn ns 75:393-405 Mr. 1 '04; *same.* Liv Age 241:158-67 Ap 9 '04; Bookm (Lond) 26:31 Ap '04; H. D. Davray in Mercure Fr 50:548-9 My '04)

The prince's progress, and other poems. London, Macmillan, 1866. [vii]-viii,216p
(Rev in Ath 1:824-5 Je 23 '66; Spec 39:974-5 S 1 '66; Sat R 21:761-2 Je 23 '66; *same.* Ecl M ns 4:322-5 S '66; Reader 7:613 Je 30 '66; *same.* Liv Age 90: 441-2 Ag 18 '66; Eclectic Review 120: 124-30 Ag '64)

The Rossetti birthday book, ed. by Olivia Rossetti. London, Macmillan, 1896. 278p
(Rev by L. Johnson in Acad 50:60 Jl 25 '96)

Sing-song: a nursery-rhyme book. London, Routledge, 1872
(Rev by S. Colvin in Acad 3:23 Ja 15 72; Ath 1:11 Ja 6 '72; Harper M 44: 299 Ja '72; Scribner's Monthly 3:629 Mr '72)

Speaking likenesses. London, Macmillan, 1874. viii,96p
(Rev in Acad 6:606 D 5 '74; Ath 2:878 D 26 '74)

Time flies: a reading diary. London, Society for Promoting Christian Knowledge, 1885. 280p
(Rev in Book B ns 3:27 F '86)

Verses. London, Society for Promoting Christian Knowledge, 1893. 236p
(Rev by E. K. Chambers in Acad 45: 162-4 F 24 '94; Ath 2:842-3 D 16 '93; Speaker 8:588 N 25 '93; L. Watson in Sunday at Home no 2088:425-8 My 5 '94)

Rossetti, Christina Georgina. *In* Men of the time: a dictionary of contemporaries. . . London, Routledge, 1879. 10th ed p856

Rossetti, William Michael
Charles Cayley and Christina Rossetti. *In* Some reminiscences. London, Brown Langham, 1906. vol II p311-15 (Rev in Bookm (Lond) 31:156 D '06)

Memoir. *In* The poetical works of Christina Georgina Rossetti. London, Macmillan, 1914. pxlv-lxxi

Rossetti family in Bucks. Notes & Q 159: 176 S 6 '30

The **Rossettis.** Tinsley's 5:59-67, 142-51, 276-81 Ag-O '69

Rutherford, Mildred
Christina Rossetti. *In* English authors. Atlanta, Ga. Franklin printing and publishing co. 1906. p631-3

Saintsbury, George Edward Bateman
Poetry since the middle of the century. *In* A short history of English literature. New York, Macmillan, 1907. p779-83

The Prae-Raphaelite school. *In* A history of English prosody from the twelfth century to the present day. London, Macmillan, 1910. vol III p352-9

Sandars, Mary Frances
Life of Christina Rossetti. London, Hutchinson [1930] 291p
(Rev by E. Underhill in Spec 145:537-9 O 18 '30)

Seaman, (Sir) Owen
The links of love; poem. *In* The battle of the bays. New York, Lane, 1896. p69-70 [parody of "A Birthday"]

Serra, Beatrice
Christina G. Rossetti. Nuova Antol 344: 56-69 Jl 1 '29

Sharp, William
Christina Rossetti. Great Thoughts vol 23 '95

The Rossettis. Fortn 45:414-29 Mr 1 '86; *same.* Liv Age 169:161-70 Ap 17 '86; *same.* Ecl M 106:590-600 My '86

Some reminiscences of Christina Rossetti. Atlan 75:736-49 Je '95; *also in* Papers critical and reminiscent. . New York, Duffield, 1912. p66-103

Shipton, Irene A. M.
Christina Rossetti: the poetess of the Oxford movement. Church Q R 116: 219-29 Jl '33

Shove, (Mrs) Fredegond
Christina Rossetti; a study. New York, Macmillan, 1931. xvi,120p
(Rev in Notes & Q 161:18 Jl 4 '31; TLS Ag 27 '31 p650; Life & L 7:146-7 Ag '31; Oxford Magazine My 5 '32 p643; P. Meissner in Bei Anglia 43: 207-10 Jl '32; B. J. Morse in Engl Stud 67:287-9 N '32; R. Watkins in Lond Merc 25:210-12 D '31)

Shuster, George N.
The Catholic spirit in modern English literature. New York, Macmillan, 1922. p182-5

Smith, Ethel May
Christina Rossetti and her critics. Masters essay, Louisiana State Univ. 1934. 135ff

Snow, Florence L.
On first reading Christina Rossetti. Midland Monthly 7:120-7 F '97

Some notes on Christina Rossetti and Italy. Anglia 55:101-5 '31

Stewart, Bella Craig
Christina Rossetti "a singer of death." Masters essay, George Peabody College, 1933

Stuart, Dorothy Margaret
Christina Rossetti. (English association pamphlet no 78) London, Oxford, 1931. 70p (Noted in TLS Ag 27 '31 p650)

Christina Rossetti. (English men of letters, ns) London, Macmillan, 1930. viii, 200p
(Rev in Canadian Review Ap '30 p540; WER 2:886 D 13 '30; Spec 146:158 Ja 31 '31; Engl R 52:255-6 F '31; Quar R 256:411 Ap '31; O. Burdett in Sat R 151:24 Ja 3 '31; S. C. Chew in Yale R ns 21:209-10 S '31; B. J. Morse in Engl Stud 65:413-14 '31; M. U. Schappes in Symposium 3:123-8 Ja '32; M. Van Doren in Nation (NY) 132:508-9 My 6 '31)

Sutherland, D.
Christina Rossetti. Lit W 26:40 F 9 '95

Swinburne, Algernon Charles
A ballad of appeal. To Christina G. Rossetti. *In* A midsummer holiday and other poems. London, Chatto and Windus, 1884. p112-14

A new year's eve: Christina Rossetti died December 29, 1894. 19th Cent 37:367-8 F '95

Symons, Arthur
Christina G. Rossetti. *In* Miles, A. H. (ed) The poets and the poetry of the nineteenth century. London, Routledge, 1907. vol IX p1-16

Christina Rossetti. *In* Studies in two literatures. London, Smithers, 1897. p135-49
(Rev in Literary World (Lond) ns 56:443 D 3 '97)

Taylor, Bayard
Christina Rossetti. *In* Critical essays and literary notes. New York, Putnam, 1880. p330-2

Teasdale, Sara
Christina Rossetti. New York, Macmillan, 1932

Thirlmere, Rowland [pseud]
see Walker, John

Thomas, Edward
Christina Rossetti. *In* Last sheaf. London, Cape, 1928. p65-70

Thomas, Eleanor Walter
Christina Georgina Rossetti. (Columbia univ. studies in English and comparative literature) New York, Columbia univ. press, 1931. viii,229p bibl p[213]-222
(Noted in TLS N 19 '31 p918; rev in Lond Merc 24:xxii D '31; P. F. Baum in So Atlan Q 31:129-30 Ja '32; W. S. Knickerbocker in Sewanee R 40:254-6 Ap-Je '32; R. F. Russell in Lond Merc 25:501 Mr '32; M. U. Schappes in Symposium 3:123-8 Ja '32)

Thompson, Alexander Hamilton
Christina Rossetti. *In* C H E L vol XIII p153-6

Tennyson and the Victorian poets. *In* A history of English literature. London, John Murray, 1901. p785-6

Tooley, Sarah A.
Christina G. Rossetti. A character sketch. Young Woman N '94 p37-44

Tributes to Miss Rossetti. Dial 18:69-70 F 1 '95

Tuell, Anne Kimball
Christina Rossetti. *In* A Victorian at bay. Boston, Marshall, Jones, 1932. p49-60

Mrs. Meynell and her literary generation. New York, Dutton [c1925]

Tynan, Katharine
see Hinkson, Katharine Tynan

Untermeyer, Louis
Modern British poetry. New York, Harcourt, Brace [c1930] 3d rev ed p21-7

Wainewright, John B.
Music to song of Christina Rossetti. Notes & Q 12th ser 3:192 Mr 10 '17

Walker, Hugh
The age of Tennyson. (Handbooks of English literature) London, Bell, 1904. p244-6

The literature of the Victorian era. Cambridge, Univ. press, 1921. p501-8

Walker, Hugh and Walker, (Mrs) Hugh
Outlines of Victorian literature. Cambridge, Univ. press, 1919. p82-3

[Walker, John] Rowland Thirlmere [pseud]
In memoriam; poem. Manch Q Ja '96 p39-45

The lyrics of Miss Rossetti. Manchester, Heywood [1889] 12p
(Reprinted from Manch Q O '89)

Miss Christina Georgina Rossetti. *In* Eyles, F. A. H. ed. Popular poets of the period. London, Griffith, 1889. p234-40

Waller, Ross Douglas
The Rossetti family, 1824-1854. Manchester, Univ. press, 1932. xii,324p
(Rev in TLS My 19 '32 p364; note in TLS D 1 '32 p923; W. Browne in Bookm (Lond) 82:108 My '32; B. J. Morse in Engl Stud 67:283-7 '32; P. De Reul in English Studies 14:201-3 O '32)

Walters, Hildred A.
Comparison of Christina Rossetti and Emily Dickinson as poets of the inner life. Masters essay, Univ. of Colorado, 1931. 79ff

Watkin, Ralph Granger
Robert Browning and the English pre-Raphaelites. Breslau, Fleischmann, 1905. Diss. Breslau

Watson, Lily
Christina G. Rossetti. Leisure Hour 44:244-8 F '95

Watson, Mabel Madison
Over the bridge to Sing Song. Twenty-eight little piano sketches. Words by Christina Rossetti. Music by Mabel Madison Watson. Drawings by Ada Budell [c1915]

Watson (Sir) William
To Christina Rossetti. *In* A hundred poems. London, Hodder and Stoughton [1922] p179

To Christina Rossetti. *In* The poems of William Watson. New York, Lane, 1905. vol II p107

Watts, Theodore
see Watts-Dunton, Theodore

Watts-Dunton, Theodore
Christina Georgina Rossetti. Ath 1:16-18 Ja 5 '95

Christina Georgina Rossetti. *In* Old familiar faces. London, Jenkins, 1916. p177-206

Christina Rossetti; the two Christmas-tides. *In* The coming of love. London, Lane [pref 1906] 9th ed p253-5

Reminiscences of Christina Rossetti. 19th Cent 37:355-66 F '95

The two Christmastides; poem. Ath 1:49 Ja 12 '95

Waugh, Arthur
Christina Rossetti. December 5, 1830; December 5, 1930. 19th Cent 108:787-98 D '30

Christina Rossetti. *In* Reticence in literature. . . London, Wilson, [1915] p149-53

Welby, Thomas Earle
The Victorian romantics, 1850-70; the early work of D. G. Rossetti, W. Morris, Burne-Jones, Swinburne . . . and their associates. London, Howe, 1929. x,161p
(Rev in TLS N 14 '29 p919)

Westcott, Brooke Foss
An appreciation of the late Christina G. Rossetti. London, S.P.C.K. 1899. 24p

Whitney, Elizabeth Boyce
The Oxford movement and its influence on English poetry. Masters essay, Univ. of Oklahoma, 1931. 87ff

Wilde, Justine Fredrika de
Christina Rossetti, poet and woman. Nijkerk, Callenbach, 1923. 160p bibl p159-60 Diss. Amsterdam
(Rev by F. B[aur] in Leuvensche Bijdragen, Bijblad 21 nos 1-2:24-5)

Williamson, Claude C. H.
Christina Rossetti. *In* Writers of three centuries, 1789-1914. Philadelphia, Jacobs [1915?] p270-2

Winwar, Frances [pseud]
see [Grebanier, (Mrs) Frances Vinciguerra]

Wood, Esther
Dante Rossetti and the pre-Raphaelite movement. London, Sampson Low, Marston, 1894

Woods, Margaret L.
Poets of the 'eighties. *In* The eighteen-eighties, essays by fellows of the Royal society of literature, ed. by Walter de la Mare. Cambridge, Univ. press, 1930. p7-8

Woolf, Virginia (Stephen)
"I am Christina Rossetti." Nat-Ath 48: 322-4 D 6 '30; *also in* Second common reader. New York, Harcourt, Brace, 1932. p257-65

Wyzewa, Teodor de
Une femme-poète anglaise: Christina Rossetti. R Deux Mondes 5th ser 48: 922-33 D 15 '08

Zabel, Morton Dauwen
Christina Rossetti and Emily Dickinson. Poetry 37:213-16 Ja '31

Dante Gabriel Rossetti

Dante Gabriel Rossetti

I. Chronological Outline

1828. Born, May 12, London.

1843. Sir Hugh the Heron.

1850. Contributions to *The Germ*, including "The Blessed Damozel" and "Hand and Soul"

1857. Sister Helen, a Ballad.

1861. The Early Italian Poets from Ciullo d'Alcama to Dante Alighieri (translations)

1870. Poems.

1874. Dante and His Circle (translations)

1881. Ballads and Sonnets.

1882. Died, April 10, Birchington.

Dante Gabriel Rossetti

II. Bibliographical Material

Anderson, John P.
Bibliography. *In* Knight, Joseph. Life of Dante Gabriel Rossetti. London, Scott, 1887. pi-viii

Birmingham, England, Museum and Art Gallery
Catalogue of the collection of drawings and studies by Sir Edward Burne-Jones and Dante Gabriel Rossetti, presented to the city in 1903. Birmingham, Hudson, 1904. 78p

Brown, G. A.
Dante Gabriel Rossetti. C H E L vol XIII p541-3

Carter, John and Pollard, Graham
Dante Gabriel Rossetti. *In* An enquiry into the nature of certain nineteenth century pamphlets. London, Constable, 1934. p213-2I

Cary, Elisabeth Luther
Chronological list of paintings and drawings. . . *In* The Rossettis; Dante Gabriel and Christina. New York, Putnam, 1900. p288-301

Davies, Charles
Bibliography. *In* Dante Gabriel Rossetti. London, Merton press, 1925. p[148]-157

Garnett, Richard
[Bibliography] Dict N B vol XVII p289

A list of the principal paintings by Rossetti. Masters in Art 4:502-3 D '03

Livingston, Luther Samuel
The first books of some English authors. III. Dante Gabriel and Christina G. Rossetti. Bookm (NY) 10:245-7 N '99

Marillier, Henry Currie
List of works. *In* Dante Gabriel Rossetti; an illustrated memorial of his art and life. London, Bell, 1899. p233-66

Northup, Clark Sutherland
A register of bibliographies of the English language and literature. New Haven, Yale univ. press, 1925. p333

Page, Curtis Hidden
Dante Gabriel Rossetti; list of references. *In* British poets of the nineteenth century, ed by C. H. Page; new ed. by Stith Thompson. New York, Sanborn, 1929. p795-6

Philadelphia Academy of the Fine Arts, Philadelphia, Pennsylvania
Examples of the English Pre-Raphaelite school of painters, including Rossetti, Burne-Jones, Madox-Brown and others, together with a collection of the works of William Blake. Philadelphia, 1892

Prideaux, W. F.
Additions to the bibliography of the works of Dante Gabriel Rossetti. Bibliographer 2:243-7 '03
Rossetti bibliography. Notes & Q 10th ser 2:464-5 D 10 '04

Quinn, John
The library of John Quinn. . . New York, Anderson galleries, 1924. part IV p800-12

Rossetti, William Michael
Bibliography of the works of Dante Gabriel Rossetti. London, Ellis, 1905. [5]-53p (250 copies only) *same in* Bibliographer 1:420-30 '02; 2:34-44 '03
Classified lists of Dante Gabriel Rossetti's writings with the dates. [London] Privately printed, 1906

Rossetti bibliography. A list of the principal works and magazine articles dealing with Rossetti. Masters in Art 4:503-4 D '03

The **Rossetti** sale. Acad 22:49 Jl 15 '82

St. Johnston, Alfred
Rossetti's "Sudden light." Acad 25:279 Ap 19 '84

Slater, J. H.
Early editions. . . London, Kegan Paul, Trench, Trübner, 1894. p215-18
(Rev by T. J. Wise in Bookm (Lond) 6:49-50 My '94)

Toynbee, Paget J.
Chronological list, with notes, of paintings. . . by Rossetti. [Torino, Fratelli Bocca, 1912] [32]p

Vaughan, Charles E.
Bibliography of the works of D. G. Rossetti. *In* Bibliographies of Swinburne Morris and Rossetti. (The English Association pamphlet no 29) [Oxford, Horace Hart] 1914. p11-12

Woods, George Benjamin
[Bibliography] *In* Poetry of the Victorian period. New York, Scott, Foresman [c1930] p1005-7

Dante Gabriel Rossetti

III. Biographical and Critical Material

An **address** on the collection of paintings of the English pre-Raphaelite school: delivered at Birmingham, October 2nd, 1891. Birmingham, 1891

Agresti, Alberto
Dante Gabriele Rossetti. *In* I Prerafaellisti; contributo alla storia dell'arte. Torino, Società Tipografico-Editrice Nazionale, 1908. p163-90
(Noted in T L S S 10 '08 p292)

Poesie di Dante G. Rossetti tradotte, con uno studio su la pittura inglese e su l'opera pittorica e la vita dell'Autore. Firenze, Barbera, 1899

Allingham, H. and D. Radford (eds)
William Allingham, a diary. London, Macmillan, 1907. p74-5, 160-4

Angeli, Helen Rossetti
Dante Gabriele Rossetti. [Collezione di monogrifie illustrate. Artiste moderni 1] Bergamo, Instituto italiano d'arti grafiche, 1906. 143p

Ardagh, J.
Dante Gabriel Rossetti. Notes & Q 154: 280, 431 Ap 21, Je 16 '28

Armes, William Dallam
De Quincey and Rossetti. Critic (NY) 17:328 O 20 '90

Arnold, William Harris
Ventures in book collecting. London, Scribner, 1923. p209-15

Aronstein, P.
D. G. Rossetti und der preraphaelismus. *In* Verhandlungen des 10. allgemeinen deutschen neuphilologentages vom 20. bis 23. V. 1902 zu Breslau. Hannover, Meyer, 1903. p114-21

Arts and crafts in London. Nation (NY) 57:284-5 O 19 '93

Ashbee, Charles Robert
The pre-Raphaelites and their influence upon life. House Beautiful 27:75-7, 101-4, 112 F, Mr '10

Ashton, Algernon
Rossetti's tomb. Acad 84:31, 127 Ja 4, 25 '13

Auslander, Joseph and Hill, Frank Ernest
The winged horse. Garden City, N.Y. Doubleday, Doran, 1930. p371-5

Bachschmidt, Friedrich Wilhelm
Das italienische element in Dante Gabriel Rossetti. Breslau, Walter, 1930. 83p Diss. Münster

Baker, C. H. Collins
British painting. London, Medici society [1933] p201-6

Rossettis for the nation. Sat R 122:9-10 Jl 1 '16

Baker, Hugh M.
Rossetti: Samuel Butler. T L S D 4 '30 p1042; *see also* Doughty, Oswald

Ballad poetry. Edin R 197:318-19 Ap '03

Ballantyne, A. R.
What is pre-Raphaelitism? Edinburgh, Blackwood, 1856. 43p
(Rev in Fraser 53:686 Je '56)

Bangs, M. L.
Ballad-influence in the poems of Dante Gabriel Rossetti. Masters essay, Univ. of Southern California, 1912. 51ff

Barrington, Emilie Isabel (Wilson)
The painted poetry of Watts and Rossetti. 19th Cent 13:950-70 Je '83

Bassalik-de Vries, Johanna Christina Emerentia
William Blake in his relation to Dante Gabriel Rossetti. . . Basel, Brin, 1911. 58p Diss. Zürich. bibl p57-8

Bate, Percy H.
The English pre-Raphaelite painters, their associates and successors. London, Bell, 1899. xvi,126p
(Rev in Speaker 20:354 S 30 '99; Nation (NY) 69:352 N 9 '99; Sat R 88:836-7 D 30 '99; Edin R 191:356-79 Ap '00; Literary World (Lond) ns 64:531-2 D 27 '01; Mag Art 24:125-8 Ja '00)

Bateman, Arthur B.
Rossetti, the pre-Raphaelites, and a moral. Lond Q R 149:223-33 Ap '28

Bates, Herbert
A study of Rossetti's verse. Harv Mo 7:130-7 Ja '89

Baum, Paull Franklin (ed)
Dante Gabriel Rossetti. An analytical list of manuscripts in the Duke Univ. Library, with hitherto unpublished verse and prose. Durham, North Carolina, Duke univ. press, 1931. [ix] 122p

Introduction. *In* The house of life, a sonnet-sequence by Dante Gabriel Rossetti. Cambridge, Mass. Harvard univ. press, 1928. p[3]-62

Bayne, Thomas
Our modern poets. No. XI.-Dante Gabriel Rossetti. St J 32:415-30 O '77
The poetry of Dante Gabriel Rossetti. Fraser ns 25:376-84 Mr '82

Beavington-Atkinson, J.
Rossetti and Tadema—Linnell and Lawson. Blackw 133:392-411 Mr '83

Beerbohm, Max
Rossetti and his circle. . . London, Heinemann, 1922. ix p, 23 plates

Beers, Henry Augustin
The pre-Raphaelites. *In* A history of English romanticism in the nineteenth century. New York, Holt, 1902. p295-315

Bell, A. F.
Rossetti, Morris, and Swinburne. *In* Leaders of English literature. London, Bell, 1915. p214-23

Bell, (Mrs) Arthur (N. D'Anvers)
Gabriel Charles Dante Rossetti. *In* Representative painters of the XIXth century. London, Sampson, Low, Marston, 1899. p25-8

Bell, H. T. Mackenzie
At the grave of Dante Gabriel Rossetti; poem. Lit W 14:387 N 17 '83

Bell, Malcolm
Sir Edward Burne-Jones, a record and review. London, Bell, 1903. p7-13

Benelli, Zulia
Gabriel Rossetti, notizie biografiche e bibliografiche, raccolte e ordinate da... Firenze, Fratelli Bocca, 1898. xi,106p

Benson, Arthur Christopher
Rossetti. (English men of letters) London, Macmillan, 1904. ix,238p
(Rev in Sat R 98:173-4 Ag 6 '04; R. Pyke in Bookm (NY) 14:453-5 Ja '05; Literary World (Lond) ns 69:484-5 My 20 '04; Nation (NY) 78:418-19 My 26 '04; Atlan 94:270 Ag '04; Contemp 85:906-7 Je '04; Spec 93:224-5 Ag 13 '04; H. Hagen in Engl Stud 35:319-22 '05; T L S Ap 22 '04 p123-4; Ath 2:197-8 Ag 13 '04; Ind 57:919-20 O 20 '04; R. Garnett in Bookm (Lond) 26:51-3 My '04; E. A. Browne in Acad 66:397-8 Ap 9 '04; H. D. Davray in Mercure Fr 50:821-2 Je '04)

Benton, Joel
Dante Gabriel Rossetti. . . Manhattan 2:249-53 S '83

Berthet, A.
Rossetti sans son école. Nouvelle Revue d'Italie '20

Bickley, Francis Lawrence
The pre-Raphaelite comedy. . . London, Constable, 1932. x,276p

Binyon, Laurence
Zeichnungen Dante Gabriel Rossettis. Die Graphischen Künste 35:15-20 '12

Blee, Mary Edna
The romanticism of Dante Gabriel Rossetti. Masters essay, Univ. of California, 1911. 44ff

The blessed damozel. Acad 72:365-6 Ap 13 '07

"The blessed damozel" in French. Notes & Q 167:97 Ag 11 '34

Block, Lotte
Dante Gabriel Rossetti, der malerdichter. *In* Eine untersuchung für künstler. schaffens. Giessener beiträge zur erfor-

schung der sprache und kultur Englands und Nordamerikas. Giessen, Engl. Seminar, 1925. vol II p249-96 Diss. Giessen

Boas, Henrietta O'Brien (Owen) (Mrs. Frederick Samuel Boas)
Rossetti and his poetry. London, Harrap, 1914. 149p

Boase, Frederic
Rossetti, Gabriel Charles Dante. *In* Modern English biography. Truro, Netherton & Worth, 1901. vol III p306-7

A book and its story [The Family letters] Critic (NY) 28:463-4 Je 27 '96

Borchardt, Rudolf
Dante Gabriel Rossetti. Die Horen 6:53-62, 133-52 '30

Rossetti. Neue Zürcher Zeitung My 13, 15 '28 nos 871, 889

Bowker, R. R.
London as a literary center. Harper M 76:819-22 My '88

Boyle, J. R.
Rossetti's sonnets. Notes & Q 7th ser 7:258 Mr 30 '89

A brief account of the English pre-Raphaelites. . . New York, Dodd, Mead [nd] [5]p

Bright, Norma K.
Social intercourse among the pre-Raphaelites. Bookn 24:691-5 Je '06

Brocklehurst, J. H.
Dante Gabriel Rossetti. Manchester Literary Club Papers 55:94-115 '29

Brooke, Stopford Augustus
Dante Gabriel Rossetti. *In* Four Victorian poets. New York, Putnam, 1908. p145-204
(Rev in T L S My 21 '08 p161-2)

[Brown, James B.] Selkirk, James B. [pseud]
Ethics and aesthetics of modern poetry. London, Smith, Elder, 1878

Browning, Robert
[Critical comments on Algernon Charles Swinburne and Dante Gabriel Rossetti, by Robert Browning] [A series of letters privately printed by Thomas J. Wise] 1919

Bruyn, Jeanne de
D. G. Rossetti, 12 Mei 1828-9 April 1882. Dietsche Warande D '28 p957-91

Buchan, John
Morris and Rossetti. *In* Homilies and recreations. Boston, Houghton, Mifflin, 1926. p272-80

[Buchanan, Robert Williams] Maitland, Thomas [pseud]
[Admission that he wrote attack on Rossetti] Ath 2:794 D 16 '71

The fleshly school of poetry and other phenomena of the day. . . London, Strahan, 1872. p33-82; *same.* Contemp 18:334-50 O '71; *same in* Notorious lit-

Buchanan, R. W.—*Continued*
erary attacks, ed. by A. Mordell. New York, Boni and Liveright, 1926. p185-213
(Rev in Ath 1:650-1 My 25 '72) [Rossetti answered with "The stealthy school of criticism" in Ath 2:792-4 D 16 '71; Buchanan replied in Ath 2:887 D 30 '71]
God and the man: a romance. London, Chatto & Windus, 1881
[Dedicated to Rossetti]
"The martyrdom of Madeline." Acad 22:12 Jl 1 '82
Note on Rossetti. *In* Look round literature. London, Ward, 1887. p152-61
The stealthy school of criticism. Ath 2: 887 D 30 '71

Buchanan and Rossetti. Bookm (NY) 13: 524-6 Ag '01

Burgum, Edwin Berry
Rossetti and the ivory tower. Sewanee R 37:431-46 O '29

Burlington fine arts club. London
. . . Pictures, drawings, designs and studies by the late Dante Gabriel Rossetti. London, Printed. . . Burlington fine arts club, 1883. [15]-56p

Burne-Jones, G.
Memorials of Edward Burne-Jones. New York, Macmillan, 1906. passim

Butterworth, Walter
Dante Gabriel Rossetti in relation to Dante Alighieri. Manch Q 31:117-31 '12

Byron, Mary C.
A day with D. G. Rossetti. London, Hodder [1911] 48p

Caine, Lily Hall
A child's recollections of Rossetti. New Review 11:246 '94. *same.* Liv Age 203: 102-8 O 13 '94

Caine, (Sir) Thomas Henry Hall
D. G. Rossetti. Acad 21:304-5 Ap 29 '82
Dante Gabriel Rossetti. *In* Miles, A. H. ed. The poets and the poetry of the nineteenth century. London, Routledge, 1905. vol V p439-46
A disquisition on Dante Gabriel Rossetti's painting in oil, entitled "Dante's Dream". . . Liverpool, nd
My story. London, Heinemann, 1908. p75-240
(Rev by A. R. Marble in Dial 46:223-4 Ap 1 '09)
Obituary. Dante Gabriel Rossetti. Acad 21:266-8 Ap 15 '82
The poetry of Dante Rossetti. New Monthly Magazine 116:800-12 Jl '79
Recollections of Dante Gabriel Rossetti. London, Stock, 1882. xiii,297p
(Rev in Lit W 14:6 Ja 13 '83; J. A. Symonds in Acad 22:305-6 O 28 '82; Spec 55:1511-12 N 25 '82; Ath 2:590-1 N 4 '82; G. P. Lathrop in Atlan 51:549-53 Ap '83; Nation (NY) 36:67-8 Ja 18

'83; Quar R 184:185-214 Jl '96; F. Gregg in Book B ns 16:315-18 My '98; Lit W 29:42 F 5 '98; Art J 45:64 '83; Le Livre 4:4-5 Ja 10 '83; T L S O 4 '28 p705)
Rossetti; poem. Acad 23:310 My 5 '83

[Calverley, Charles S.]
The ballad of the period. Chamb J 46: 720 N 6 '69 [parody of Rossetti's "Sister Helen"]

Calverton, V. F.
Sex expression in literature. New York, Boni and Liveright, 1926. p249-52

Carducci, Giosuè
Il veggente in solitudine. In Opere. Bologna, Zanichelli, 1898. vol X

[Carnegie, Robert, Earl of Southesk]
Jonas Fisher: a poem in brown and white. London, Kegan Paul, Trench, Trübner, 1875. 243p

Carr, Joseph William Comyns
Dante Gabriel Rossetti. *In* Some eminent Victorians. London, Duckworth, 1908. p59-70
(Rev by P. F. Bicknell in Dial 46:134-5 Mr 1 '09)
The English school of painting at the Roman Exhibition. *In* Coasting Bohemia. London, Macmillan, 1914. p101-33
The ideals of painting. New York, Macmillan, 1917. p423-8
Rossetti's influence in art. *In* Papers on art. London, Macmillan, 1885; *same.* Engl Illus 1:28-40 '83
With Rossetti in Cheyne Walk. *In* Coasting Bohemia. London, Macmillan, 1914. p42-55

Cary, Elisabeth Luther
Dante Gabriel Rossetti, illustrator. Print-Collector's Quarterly 5:317-39 '15
The handicraft of the pre-Raphaelites. Bookn 24:699-700 Je '06
The new Rossetti water color in the Metropolitan Museum. International Studio 35:suppCXXV-CXXX O '08
Rossetti and the Pre-Raphaelites. Critic (NY) 27:320-6 O '00
Rossetti as an illustrator. Lamp (NY) 27:321-8 N '03
A Rossetti model. Scrip 1:286-8 Je '06
The Rossettis; Dante Gabriel and Christina. New York, Putnam, 1900. xi,310p
Rossetti's water colours. Scrip 3:173-8 Mr '08

Catalogne, Gérard de
Le centenaire de Dante-Gabriel Rossetti. Le Figaro Ap 14 '28 p3

Cecil, (Lord) E. C. David
Gabriel Charles Dante Rossetti. *In* Massingham, H. J. and Massingham, H. eds. The great Victorians. London, Nicholson and Watson [1932] p437-48

Un **centenaire** Dante-Gabriel Rossetti. J Débats 35 pt 1:951 Je 8 '28

Chapman, E. M.
The doubters and the mystics. *In* English literature in account with religion. Boston, Houghton, Mifflin, 1910. p448-50

Charteris, (Sir) Evan [Edward]
The life and letters of Sir Edmund Gosse. New York, Harper, 1931

Chesneau, Ernest
La peinture anglaise. Paris, Quantin [1882]

Peinture, sculpture. Les nations rivals dans l'art. . . Paris, Didier, 1868

Chesterton, Gilbert Keith
The literary portraits of G. F. Watts, R. A. Bookm (Lond) 19:81 D '00

Chiminelli, Piero
Gabriele Rossetti. *In* La fortuna di Dante nella Cristianità riformata. Roma, "Bilychnis," 1921. p101-28

Ciccotti, Ettore
. . . La fanciulla beata di Dante Gabriele Rossetti e un giudizio di Max Nordau . . . Milano, Kantorowicz, 1893. 29p

Clark, John Scott
Gabriel Charles Dante Rossetti. *In* A study of English and American writers. New York, Row, Peterson [c1916] p564-74

Colvin, (Sir) Sidney
Dante Gabriel Rossetti. *In* Memories and notes of persons and places. New York, Scribner, 1922. p60-75

Rossetti as a painter. Mag Art 6:177-83 '83

Signed articles. Ath 2:755 D 9 '71; see Buchanan's answer in Ath 2:794 D 16 '71

Some personal recollections. Scrib M 67:74-7 Ja '20

[Colvin preparing answer to Buchanan's attack on Rossetti] Ath 2:724 D 2 '71; see Colvin's reply in Ath 2:755 D 9 '71

Compton-Rickett, Arthur
Dante Gabriel Rossetti. *In* A history of English literature. London, Jack, 1918. p440-9

Cook, (Sir) Edward
The second thoughts of poets. *In* Literary recreations. London, Macmillan, 1919. p287-94

Cortissoz, Royal
Dante Gabriel Rossetti. Scrib M 84:617-25 N '28; *also in* The painter's craft. New York, Scribner, 1930. p301-13

Coterie glory. Sat R 33:239-40 F 24 '72 [probable author Robert Buchanan]

Courten, Maria Luisa Giartosio de
"La Beatrice di Dante" di Gabriele Rossetti; storia di un manoscritto e di un plagio. Nuova Antol 351:429-44 O 16 '30

. . . I Rossetti; storia di una famiglia. Milano, Alpes, 1928. 362p
(Rev by M. Muret in J Débats 35 pt1: 991-3 Je 15 '28)

Cowgill, Benjamin Ross
Keats and Dante Gabriel Rossetti; a study of the influence of Keats upon the Pre-Raphaelite brotherhood and the poetry of Rossetti. Masters essay, Columbia university, 1915

Cox, Kenyon
Ford Madox Brown and Preraphaelitism. *In* Old masters and new. New York, Fox, Duffield, 1905. p155-60

Crane, Walter
An artist's reminiscences. New York, Macmillan, 1907. p83, 100, 102

Criticisms on contemporaries. No. VII. The Rossettis.—Part II. Tinsley's 5:142-51 S '69

Cunliffe, John W.
Mid-Victorian poets. *In* Leaders of the Victorian revolution. New York, Appleton-Century [c1934] p236-8

D. G. Rossetti on art. Notes & Q 11th ser 3:407 My 27 '11

Dalziel, G. and E.
Record of 50 years' work in conjunction with many most distinguished artists of 1840-1890. Selected pictures by, and autograph letters from, Lord Leighton, P. R. A. and many others. London, Methuen, 1901

Dante Gabriel Rossetti. American Architect and Building News 60:35-7 Ap 30 '98; Die Literatur 30:588 Jl '28; Arts and Letters 1:243 '81-'82; Masters in Art 4:485-91 D '03

Dante Gabriel Rossetti. *In* Men of the time: a dictionary of contemporaries. . . London, Routledge, 1879. 10th ed p856-7

Dante Gabriel Rossetti, 1828-1882. Bookn 26:205-8 N '07; Boekenschouw 22:65-70 Je '28

Dante Gabriel Rossetti, poet. Tinsley's 8: 150-60 Mr '71

Darmesteter, Mary James
see Duclaux, Mary

Davies, Charles
Dante Gabriel Rossetti. London, Merton press, 1925. 157p bibl p[148]-57 (Rev in T L S D 13 '28 p982)

Preface. *In* Dante Gabriel Rossetti. (Augustan Books of English Poetry ser 2, no 27 [1927]) London, Benn [1927] p iii

Dawson, William James
Dante Gabriel Rossetti. *In* Makers of English poetry. New York, Revell [c1906] rev ed p347-58; *same in* Makers of modern English. . . New York, Whittaker, 1890. p341-52

Days with the Victorian poets; Rossetti. London, Hodder & Stoughton, 1913

De Bruyn, Jeanne
Dante Gabriel Rossetti herdacht. Dietsche Warande en Belfort 28:957-71 '28

De Catalogne, Gérard
see Catalogne, Gérard de

Des Garets, Marie-Louyse
Dante-Gabriel Rossetti, 1828-1882. La Revue Hebdomadaire 4:212-14 Mr 9 '12

Destrée, Olivier Georges
Les préraphaélites. Notes sur l'art décoratif et la peinture en Angleterre. . . Bruxelles, Dietrich [1894] p7-32, 73-90

De Vane, William Clyde
The harlot and the thoughtful young man: a study of the relation between Rossetti's Jenny and Browning's Fifine at the fair. Stud Philol 29:463-84 Jl '32

Die dichtungen des Dante G. Rossetti. Wiener Rundschau p1-6, 28-31 '01

Dick, Stewart
Our favourite painters. London, Davies, 1923

Rossetti and the Pre-Raphaelites. *In* Master painters, being pages from the romance of art. London, Foulis, 1911. p249-70

Dickens, Charles
Old lamps for new ones. Household Words 1:265-7 Je 15 '50

Dixon, J. B.
The relation between the poetry of Blake and the poetry of Rossetti. Masters essay, Northwestern Univ. 1930. 100ff

Doherty, Helen Frances
A study of metrical form in the poetry of Rossetti, Swinburne, and Morris. Masters essay, New York Univ. 1909. 33ff

Doughty, L. S.
Rest, Rossetti; response to Lost days; poem. Truth (NY) 34:18 F '30

Doughty, Oswald
Rossetti: Samuel Butler. T L S N 27 '30 p1014; see *ibid* D 4 '30 p1042, by H. M. Baker

Douglas, James
Dante Gabriel Rossetti. *In* Theodore Watts-Dunton. New York, Lane [1907?] p17-21, 138-69

Dowden, Edward
Victorian literature. Fortn 47:863-4 Je '87

Victorian literature. *In* Transcripts and studies. London, Kegan Paul, Trench, Trübner, 1896. 2d ed p226-30

Drawings of Rossetti. (Modern master draughtsmen series) London, Newnes, 1906
(Noted in Acad 70:558 Je 9 '06)

Draycott, Charles
A medley of voices. Temple 117:418 Jl '99

A dream of fair women. A study of some pictures by Dante Gabriel Rossetti. London, Kegan Paul, Trench and Trübner, 1883. 46p

Drinkwater, John
Victorian poetry (People's library) London, Hodder and Stoughton, 1923. p99-103, 183-5

Duclaux, Mary (Mary J. Darmesteter)
D. G. Rossetti. Revue de P 3:550-82 Je 1 '96

Grands écrivains d'outre-manche: les Brontë, Thackeray, les Browning, Rossetti. Paris, Levy, 1901

Dunn, Henry Treffry
Recollections of Dante Gabriel Rossetti and his circle. (Cheyne Walk life) Ed. and annotated by Gale Pedrick. London, Mathews, 1904. 96p
(Rev by R. Garnett in Acad 66:69 Ja 16 '04; Literary World (Lond) ns 69: 266 Mr 18 '04; Ath 2:197-8 Ag 13 '04; International Studio 24:sup xvi-xvii N '04)

DuPouey, Charles Marie Dominique-Pierre
Notes sur l'art et la vie de D. G. Rossetti. Paris, Chapelot, 1906. 81p

Dupré, Henri
Un Italien d'angleterre, les poète-peintre Dante Gabriel Rossetti; préface du Professeur Legouis. . . Paris, Dent, 1921. 148p

Duret, Théodore
Les expositions de Londres; Dante Gabriel Rossetti. Gazette des Beaux-Arts année 25, période 2, vol 28:49-58 Jl 1 '83

Duryea, Minga Pope
Cobden-Sanderson's garden at Hammersmith; with glimpses of the gardens of William Morris and Rossetti. Scrib M 74:25-34 Jl '23

Earland, Ada
Ruskin and the pre-Raphaelites. *In* Ruskin and his circle. London, Hutchinson, 1910. p73-89

Earle, Anne M.
Pre-Raphaelite ideals. Bookn 24:681-6 Je '06

Echo der zeitungen. Dante Gabriel Rossetti. Die Literatur 30:588 Jl '28

Edwards, Amelia B.
Dante Gabriel Rossetti. Lit W 14:94-5 Mr 24 '83; Acad 25:403 Je 7 '84

Elliott, Maurine Elder
Dante Gabriel Rossetti, the painter-poet; a study of the elements found in both his painting and poetry. Masters essay, Univ. of California, 1914. 50ff

Ellis, Stewart Marsh
George Meredith; his life and friends in relation to his work. New York, Dodd, Mead, 1920. p148-55

Elton, Oliver
Poetic romancers after 1850. (Warton lecture on English poetry. Read Oct. 28, 1914) Brit Acad Proc 6:413-31 '13-'14; *same in* A sheaf of papers. Boston, Small, Maynard, 1923. p45-68

The Rossettis. *In* A survey of English literature, 1830-1880. London, Arnold, 1920. vol II p1-22

English art in the Victorian age. Quar R 187:209-33 Ja '98

Evans, B[enjamin] Ifor
Dante Gabriel Rossetti. *In* English poetry in the later ninetenth century. London, Methuen [1933] p1-25 bibl p24-5

Farmer, Albert J.
Le mouvement esthétique et "décadent" en angleterre (1873-1900). Paris, Champion, 1931. p15-19

Fehr, Bernhard
Die englische literatur des 19. und 20. jahrhunderts. Wildpark-Potsdam, 1928. p216-23

Ferrazzi, Jacopo
Manuale Dantesca. Bassano, 1871. vol IV p442-3

Fish, Arthur
John Everett Millais. London, Cassell, 1923. passim

Flight the third. Punch 18:240 '50

Fontainas, André
Dante-Gabriel Rossetti, le poète. Mercure Fr 73:193-211 My 16 '08

Forbes-Robertson, (Sir) Johnston
A player under three reigns. London, Unwin, 1925

Ford, Ford Madox
see Hueffer, Ford Madox

Forman, Harry Buxton
Dante Gabriel Rossetti. *In* Our living poets. . . London, Tinsley, 1871. p185-228

The "Fleshly school" scandal. Tinsley's 10:89-102 F '72

The Rossettis. Tinsley's 5:142-51 S '69

Formichi, Carlo
Dante Gabriele Rossetti. Univ. of California Chronicle 31:267-80 Jl '29

Förster, M.
Die älteste fassung von D. G. Rossettis ballade "Sister Helen." Die Leipziger Neunundneunzig 25:116-39 '29

Forsyth, P. T.
Rossetti; or, The religion of natural passion. *In* Religion in recent art; being expository lectures on Rossetti, Burne Jones, Watts, Holman Hunt & Wagner. Manchester, Heywood, 1889

Foster, Nancy K.
A word for Rossetti. Poet Lore 21:322-9 Jl-Ag '10

Fox-Bourne, H. R.
Dante Gabriel Rossetti. Gent M ns 38: 596-610 Je '87

Franke, Lydia B.
Views on Rossetti (Dante Gabriel) as a mystic. Masters essay, Univ. of Colorado, 1928. 43ff

Fraser, Henry
Rossetti's tragic wife. Everyman 8:268 S 22 '32

Fred, W.
Die Prae-Raphaeliten. Eine episode. . . (Über Kunst der Neuzeit) Strassburg, Heitz, 1900. 152p

Frend, Grace Gilchrist
Great Victorians: some recollections of Tennyson, George Eliot and the Rossettis. Bookm (Lond) 77:9-11 O '29

Fry, Roger
Rossetti's water colours of 1857. Burlington Magazine 29:100-9 Je '16

Fuller, Edward
Arnold, Newman, and Rossetti. Critic (NY) ns 45:273-6 S '04

Gabriel Charles Dante Rossetti. *In* The Library of literary criticism of English and American authors. . . ed. by Charles Wells Moulton. . . Buffalo, New York, Moulton publishing company, 1904. vol VII p434-56

Galdemar, A.
La vie tragique de D. G. Rossetti. Gaulois D 27 '28

Galletti, Alfredo
Dante Gabriel Rossetti e il romanticismo preraffaellita. *In* Studi di letteratura inglese. Bologna, Zanichelli, 1918. p145-237 bibl p235-7

Studi di letterature straniere. D. Gabriele Rossetti e la poesia preraffaellita. Verona, Fratelli Drucker, 1903. viii, 215p

Gamberale, Luigi
Poeti inglesi e tedeschi moderni o contemporanei. Firenze, Barbèra, 1881. 275p

Gardner, Edmund G.
Poems unwritten and unended. Month 95:594 Je '00

Garnett, Richard
Dante Gabriel Rossetti. *In* Dict N B vol XVII p284-9

Geddes, Patrick
"The wood nymph" and "Silence." Scottish Art Review 1:155-6 O '88

Geisler, Friedrich
Dante Gabriel Rossetti: das romantische in persönlichkeit und dichtung. Diss. Marburg, 1923. 123p

A genius in private life. R of Rs (Lond) 19:90 Ja '99

The Germ. [In five parts, with an introduction by W. M. Rossetti] London, Stock, 1901. 5 vols

The Germ
(Noted in Spec 23:43 Ja 12 '50; Literary Gazette no 1722:47 Ja 19 '50; Builder 8:34 Ja 19 '50; E. W. Cox in Critic (Lond) F 15 '50 p94; S. C. Hall in Art J ns 2:96 Mr '50)

Gerwig, Henrietta
Dante Gabriel Rossetti. *In* Fifty famous painters. New York, Crowell, 1926. p310-17

Ghose, Sudhindra Nath
Dante-Gabriel Rossetti and contemporary criticism (1849-1882). Dijon, Darantière, 1929. 244p Diss. Strasbourg

Gilchrist, Herbert Harlakenden
Recollections of Rossetti. Lippinc 68: 571-6 N '01

Gilchrist, Herbert Harlakenden (ed)
Anne Gilchrist, her life and writings. London, Unwin, 1887. passim

Gillis, Lois Isabel
Art in the great Victorian poets. Masters essay, Univ. of Oklahoma, 1921. 265ff

Goodale, Ralph Hinsdale
Pessimism in English poetry and fiction, 1847-1900. *In* Abstracts of theses. . . Humanistic series Volume VI. . . Univ. of Chicago. Chicago, 1927. p347-51

Gosse, (Sir) Edmund William
D.G.R.; poem. *In* On viol and lute. London, Kegan Paul, Trench, Trübner, 1890. p181

Dante Gabriel Rossetti. Cent ns 2:718-25 S '82

The literature of the Victorian era. Engl Illus 17:491 Jl '97

Rossetti. Liv Age 334:1077-80 Jl '28

Graf, A.
Preraffaelliti, simbolisti ed esteti, nel volume Foscolo, Manzoni e Leopardi. Torino, Loescher, 1898. p401

Grappe, Georges
D. G. Rossetti. *In* Essai sur la poésie anglaise au XIX⁰ siècle. Paris, Sansot, 1906. p51-4

Grasé, J. C. G.
Dante Gabriel Rossetti. Onze Eeuw 14: 75-112 O '14

[Grebanier, (Mrs) Frances (Vinciguerra)] Frances Winwar [pseud]
Dante Gabriel's or William Michael's; attempt to establish authorship of some Rossetti sonnets. P M L A 48:312-15 Mr '33

Poor splendid wings. Boston, Little, Brown, 1933. xii,413p bibl p393-404 (Rev in American Magazine of Art 26: 561 D '33)

Greene, Richard Leighton
The English sonnet from Tennyson to the present time. Hull prize essay, Univ. of Rochester, 1925. 19ff

Gregg, Frederick James
Reminiscences of the Rossettis. Book B ns 16:315-18 My '98

Guthrie, William Norman
Dante Gabriel Rossetti. *In* Modern poet prophets. . . Cincinnati, Clarke, 1897. p116-23

Hake, Thomas Gordon
Memoirs of eighty years. London, Bentley, 1892. p213-36, 248-51

Hake, Thomas St. E.
"Aylwin." Notes & Q 9th ser 9:450-2 Je 7 '02

How authors work best. T. P.'s Weekly 2:630 O 16 '03

Hall, S. Elizabeth
Dante Gabriel Rossetti. Quest 19:367-84 Jl '28

Hamerton, Philip Gilbert
The reaction from pre-Raphaelitism. Fine Arts Quarterly Review 2:255-62 My '64; *same in* Thoughts about art. London, Macmillan, 1873. new ed. p184-91

Rossetti and Delacroix. Acad 31:130, 148 F 19 '87

Hamill, Alfred E.
Dante Gabriel Rossetti in America. Notes & Q 165:358-9 N 18 '33

Hamilton, George Rostrevor
Dante Gabriel Rossetti; a review of his poetry. Criterion 7:91-103 Je '28

Hamilton, Walter
Buchanan's attack on Rossetti. *In* The aesthetic movement in England. London, Reeves and Turner, 1882. 3d ed. p51-5

Dante Gabriel Rossetti. *In* The aesthetic movement in England. London, Reeves & Turner, 1882. 3d ed. p41-50; *see also* p1-12

"Jonas Fisher: a poem in brown and white," and Mr. Buchanan. *In* The aesthetic movement in England. London, Reeves & Turner, 1882. 3d ed. p70-81

Hancock, Thomas
Dante G. Rossetti. Acad 21:323 My 6 '82

Hannay, David
The paintings of Mr. Rossetti. Nat R 1:126-34 Mr '83

Hardinge, William M.
A note on the Louvre sonnets of Rossetti. Temple 91:433-43 Mr '91

A reminiscence of Rossetti. Universal Review (Lond) 6:398-411 Mr 15 '90

Harland-Oxley, W. E.
Houses of historical interest. Notes & Q 10th ser 5:484 Je 23 '06

Harper, Janet
Dante Gabriel Rossetti: artist and poet. Westm 146:312-21 '96

Harris-Bickford, E. L. T.
Rossetti; poem. Biblio 1:43 Ag '21

Hauser, Otto
Dante Gabriel Rossetti. Neue Freie Presse no 27 '00

Hearn, Lafcadio
Definitive Rossetti. *In* Essays in European and Oriental literature. New York, Dodd, Mead, 1923. p221-8

Note upon Rossetti's prose. *In* Life and literature. New York, Dodd, Mead, 1917. p188-99; *also in* Pre-Raphaelite and other poets. New York, Dodd, Mead, 1922. p108-21

Rossetti. *In* A history of English literature, in a series of lectures. Tokyo, Hokuseido press, 1927. vol II p646-61

Some human frailty. *In* Essays in European and Oriental literature. New York, Dodd, Mead, 1923. p229-35

Studies in Rossetti. *In* Appreciations of poetry. New York, Dodd, Mead, 1916. p37-125; *also in* Pre-Raphaelite and other poets. New York, Dodd, Mead, 1922. p1-107

Hellings, Emma L.
Rossetti's treatment of love. Poet Lore 16:76-9 Spring '05

Hengelhaupt, Margrit
Die personifikation bei George Meredith. Hannover, Küster, 1931. p22-4 Diss. Freiburg

Henry, Albert S.
Rossetti. Bookn 22:1032-3 My '04

Hewlett, Henry G.
Modern ballads. Contemp 26:976-8 N '75

Hodgkins, Louise Manning
D. G. Rossetti. *In* A guide to the study of nineteenth century authors. Boston, Heath, 1898. p66-70

Hodgson, Geraldine Emma
Dante Gabriel Rossetti. Church Q R 106:353-62 Jl '28

Holthausen, Ferdinand
Dante Gabriel Rossetti und die Bibel. Germanisch-Romanische Monatsschrift 13:310-12 Jl-Ag '25; 14:73-6 Ja-F '26

Hoppin, James Mason
Dante Gabriel Rossetti. *In* Great epochs in art history. Boston, Houghton, Mifflin, 1903. p210-19

Horn, Kurt
The "Staff and scrip" von D. G. Rossetti. Übertragung und erläuterung. Z F E U 26:575-91 '27

Studien zum dichterischen entwicklungsgange Dante Gabriel Rossettis. (Normannia. Germanisch-romanische bücherei. vol 5) Berlin, Felber, 1909. vii, 143p bibl p142-3

Zur entstehungsgeschichte von Dante Gabriel Rossettis dichtungen. Bernau, Grüner, 1909. 127(1)p bibl p126-7 Diss. Königsberg

Horne, Herbert P.
Thoughts toward a criticism of the works of Dante Gabriel Rossetti. Century Guild Hobby Horse 2:91-102 '86

Housman, Laurence
Pre-Raphaelitism in art and poetry. Roy Soc Lit ns 12:1-29 '33

The spirit of pre-Raphaelitism. Magazine of Fine Arts 1:406-15 Ap '06

Howe, Merrill Levi
Dante Gabriel Rossetti's comments on Maud. Mod Lang N 49:290-3 My '34

A dramatic skit by Dante Gabriel Rossetti. Mod Lang N 49:39-44 Ja '34

Some unpublished stanzas by Dante Gabriel Rossetti. Mod Lang N 48:176-9 Mr '33

Howell, Ruby
Poe's influence on the poetry of Rossetti. Masters essay, Louisiana State Univ. 1929. 42ff

Hubbard, Elbert
Little journeys to the homes of great lovers. . . East Aurora, New York, Roycrofters, 1906

Hueffer, Ford Madox
Ancient lights and certain new reflections, being the memoirs of a young man. London, Chapman and Hall, 1911. 320p

D. G. R. Bookm (Lond) 40:113-20 Je '11

D. G. Rossetti and his family letters. Longman's Magazine 27:465-74 Mr '96; *same.* Liv Age 209:53-9 Ap 4 '96

Ford Madox Brown, a record of his life and work. London, Longmans, Green, 1896. xx,459p

Memories and impressions. New York, Harper, 1911. passim
(Rev by P. F. Bicknell in Dial 50:345-6 My 1 '11)

The Millais and Rossetti exhibitions. Fortn ns 63:189-96 F '98

The pre-Raphaelite brotherhood; a critical monograph. London, Duckworth. 1907. 186p

Pre-Raphaelite epitaph. Sat R Lit 11: 417-19 Ja 20 '34

Rossetti, a critical essay on his art. (Popular library of art) London, Duckworth [1902] xvi,192p
(Rev in Speaker ns 6:415 Jl 12 '02; Literary World (Lond) ns 66:78-9 Ag 1 '02; Lit W 33:127 Ag 1 '02; Nation (NY) 75:136 Ag 14 '02)

Hueffer, Francis
Exhibitions of Rossetti's pictures. *In* Italian and other studies. London, Stock, 1883. p83-105

Memoir of Dante Gabriel Rossetti. *In* Rossetti, D. G. Ballads and sonnets. Leipzig, Tauchnitz, 1882. p7-24

Huhn, B.
Rossetti. Der Alte Glaube nos 1-2 '02

Hume, James Cleland
Rossetti, the poet, and the pre-Raphaelite brothers. Midland Monthly 7:42-52 Ja '97

Hunt, Violet
The wife of Rossetti, her life and death. . . London, J. Lane, 1932. xxx, 338p
(Rev in T L S S 22 '32 p655; F. Winwar in Sat R Lit 9:327 D 17 '32; H. Gregory in Nation (NY) 135:568 D 7 '32; M. D. Zabel in New Repub 73:78 N 30 '32; F. Shepard in Bookm (NY) 75:727-8 N '32; P. Crowley in Commonweal 17:249 D 28 '32; E. Waugh in Spec 149:449 O 8 '32; G. Rossetti in Bookm (Lond) 83:56 O '32; H. Moran in Lond Merc 27:83-4 N '32; H. Agar in Engl R 55:548-50 N '32; J. E. Courtney in Fortn 137:665-6 N '32; P. Quennell in Life & L 8:474-5 D '32; W. H. Chesson in Quar R 260:84-93 Ja '33; H. R. Angeli in T L S O 27 '32 p789)

Hunt, William Holman

Essay on the Newcomes. Oxford & Cambridge Magazine 1:53-4 Ja '56

The pre-Raphaelite brotherhood: a fight for art. Contemp 49:471-88, 737-50, 820-33 Ap, My, Je '86; *same.* Contemp 98:592-609, 702-25 N, D '10

Pre-Raphaelitism and the pre-Raphaelite brotherhood. New York, Macmillan, 1905. 2 vols vii-xxviii,512p; v-xiv,493p (Rev by E. K. Dunton in Dial 40:113-16 F 16 '06; T L S D 8 '05 p425-6; Spec 96:499-500 Mr 31 '06; Edin R 203: 450-70 Ap '06)

Hunziker, Marguerite

A century of Rossetti. Mentor 16:37-40 My '28

Hutton, Edward

"D. G. Rossetti": unauthorized additions. Ath 1:681 Je 4 '10

Mr. Arthur Symons's "D. G. Rossetti." Ath 1:741 Je 18 '10

Un Italien d'Angleterre. Le poète-peintre D. G. Rossetti. Preface by E. Legouis. Paris, Dent, 1922 (Rev in T L S My 11 '22 p304)

Jacottet, Henri

Poètes modernes de l'angleterre. Dante Gabriel Rossetti. Bibliothèque Universelle et Revue Suisse 3d period 62:503-24 Je '94; 63:95-114 Jl '94

Jay, Harriet

The fleshly school of poetry. *In* Robert Buchanan. London, Unwin, 1903. p159-68

Jessen, Jarno [pseud]

see Michaelson, R. Anna

Jiriczek, O. L.

D. G. Rossetti. Hochland p183-95 N '06

Viktorianische-Dichtung. Heidelberg, Winter, 1907. p265-79

Zum erstdruck von D. G. Rossetti's "Sister Helen." Germanisch-Romanische Monatsschrift 3:247 Ap '11

Johnson, Charles

English painting from the seventh century to the present day. London, Bell, 1932. p267-74

Jones, H. Foster

Dante Gabriel Rossetti, medievalist and poet. Quarterly Journal of the University of North Dakota 16:309-23 My '26

Jonson, G. C. Ashton

The house of life. Poetry Review 22:343-59 S '31

Kassner, Rudolf

Englische dichter. Leipzig, Insel, 1920. p106-23

Die mystik, die künstler und das leben. Leipzig, Diederichs, 1900. p132-58

Kellner, Leon

Die englische literatur der neuesten zeit. Leipzig, Tauchnitz, 1921. p256-63

Die englische literatur im zeitalter der königin Viktoria. Leipzig, Tauchnitz, 1909. p463-73

Kenyon, James Benjamin

Rossetti and his sister Christina. *In* Loiterings in old fields. New York, Eaton, 1901. p149-71

[Kernahan, Coulson]

A note on Rossetti. *In* Sorrow and song. Philadelphia, Lippincott, 1894. p47-66

Rossetti and the moralists. Fortn ns 49: 406-12 Mr '91

Ketrick, Paul John

The medievalism of Dante Gabriel Rossetti. Masters essay, Catholic univ. 1928

Kingsland, William G.

Rossetti's "Jenny." With extracts from an hitherto unpublished version of the poem. Poet Lore 7:1-6 '95

Kitchen, Paul Cliff

Influence of Dante on Rossetti. Diss. Univ. of Pennsylvania, 1913. xix,118ff

Klenk, Hans

Nachwirkungen Dante Gabriel Rossettis. Untersuchungen an werken von Christina Rossetti, Coventry Patmore, Philip B. Marston, T. Watts-Dunton, Arthur E. W. O'Shaughnessy, Ernest Dowson, John Davidson. Lauf a.d. Pegn. Bachmann, 1932. 62p. Diss. Erlangen

Klinnert, Adelheid

Dante Gabriel Rossetti and Stefan George. Würzburg, Mayr, 1933. 104p bibl p103-4 Diss. Bonn

Knickerbocker, Kenneth Leslie

Rossetti's "The Blessed damozel." St Philol 29:485-504 Jl '32

Knickerbocker, William Skinkle

Creative Oxford. Its influence in Victorian literature. Syracuse, New York, University press [c1925] passim

Knight, Joseph

Life of Dante Gabriel Rossetti. (Great writers ser) London, Scott, 1887. 186, xixp bibl and catalogue of pictures pi-xix (Rev by G. Cotterell in Acad 31:248-9 Ap 9 '87; Westm 128:781-2 '87; Quar R 184:185-214 Jl '96; Ath 2:432-5 O 1 '87; Critic (NY) ns 11:163 O 1 '87; Sat R 64:55 Jl 9 '87)

Our living authors. Pen 1:206-8 Jl '80

Knight, William

The pre-Raphaelites, especially Dante Gabriel Rossetti, with reminiscences. *In* Six lectures on some nineteenth century artists. . . (Scammar lectures, 1907) Chicago, Art institute, 1909. p95-123; *same in* Nineteenth century artists English and French. Edinburgh, Schulze, 1910. p95-123

Koszul, A.

Dante G. Rossetti; House of life, 18. Revue A A 10:331 Ap '33

Krapp, Lorenz
Dante Gabriel Rossetti. Die Kultur (Wien) 8:89-98 '07

Kuhns, Oscar
Matthew Arnold and Rossetti. *In* Dante and the English poets from Chaucer to Tennyson. New York, Holt, 1904. p202-17

Larg, David
Trial by virgins; fragment of a biography. London, Davies, 1933. vii,330p bibl p328-30
(Rev in T L S Ap 27 '33 p290)

La Sizeranne, Robert de
The germs of the pre-Raphaelite movement. *In* English contemporary art, trans. from the French. . . by H. M. Poynter. Westminster, Constable, 1898. p3-80
La peinture anglaise contemporaine. R Deux Mondes 125:562-96 O 1 '94; 126:326-57 N 15 '94; 127:372-412 Ja 15 '95; *same published*: Paris, Hachette, 1895
Ruskin et la religion de la beauté. Paris, Hachette, 1897

Las Vergnas, R.
Le britannisme de Rossetti. Revue A A 11:129-35 '33

The **late** Dante Rossetti. Lit W 13:129 Ap 22 '82

The **later** English poets. . . Quar R 132:569-75 Ja '72; *same.* Ecl M 78:390-4 Ap '72

Laughlin, Clara Elizabeth
Dante Gabriel Rossetti and "The House of Life." *In* Stories of authors' loves. Philadelphia, Lippincott, 1902. vol I p147-70; *same.* Book Lover (San Francisco) 2:512-16 Ja-F '02; *same.* Delineator 58:93-6 Jl '01

Laurent, Raymond
Le préraphaélisme en angleterre; Introduction à l'étude du préraphaélisme anglais. *In* Études anglaises. Paris, Grasset, 1910. p35-138; *same.* Nouvelle Revue ns 40:172-80 My 15 '06

Lawrence, Frederic
The romanticists around Dante Gabriel Rossetti. Lond Q R 108:269-82 O '07

Layard, George Somes
Rossetti. *In* Tennyson and his pre-Raphaelite illustrators. A book about a book. London, Stock, 1894. p49-65
(Rev in Sat R 77:370 Ap 7 '94; Literary World (Lond) ns 49:275 Mr 23 '94; Nation (NY) 59:270 O 11 '94; Studio 2:221-2 Mr '94; Critic (NY) 25:347-8 N 24 '94)

Le Gallienne, Richard
Dante Gabriel Rossetti and Elizabeth Siddal. *In* The loves of the poets. New York, Baker & Taylor, 1911. p145-80

Lemmermayer, Fritz
Dante Gabriel Rossetti, der romantiker. Das Goetheanum 7:404-6 D 16 '28

Linton, John
Dante Gabriel Rossetti. *In* The cross in modern art. . . London, Duckworth [1916] p41-66

The **literary** pages of the "Spectator." Spec 141:646, 691 N 3, 10 '28

The **literature** of the last fifty years. Blackw 141:744 Je '87

Littell, Philip
Books and things. New Repub 27:84 Je 15 '21
Poetry of Rossetti. *In* Piercy, J. K. ed. Modern writers at work. New York, Macmillan, 1930. p165-9

Low, Will H.
A century of painting. McClure's Magazine 7:71-2 Je '96

Lucas, Frank Laurence
Dante Gabriel Rossetti. *In* Eight Victorian poets. . . New York, Macmillan, 1930. p75-90
(Rev in T L S N 13 '30 p936)
Introduction. *In* Dante Gabriel Rossetti, an anthology. (Poets in brief) Cambridge, England, Univ. press. 1933. pxv-xxxiv

[Lushington, Vernon]
Two pictures. Oxford & Cambridge Magazine 1:479-84 Ag '56

Lynd, Robert
Rossetti and ritual. *In* Old and new masters. New York, Scribner, 1919. p137-41

Mabie, Hamilton Wright
The poetry of Dante Gabriel Rossetti. *In* Essays in literary interpretation. . . New York, Dodd, Mead, 1896. p71-98; *same.* And R 11:378-94 Ap '89

McCabe, Joseph Martin
A biographical dictionary of modern rationalists. London, Watts, 1920. p684-5

MacCarthy, Desmond
Rossetti. *In* Portraits. London, Putnam, 1931. vol I p226-33

MacColl, Dugald Sutherland
Dante Gabriel Rossetti. *In* Nineteenth century art. Glasgow, MacLehose, 1902. p137-41

McGill, Anna Blanche
The Rossettis. Book B ns 20:378-82 Je '00

MacIntyre, Carlyle Ferren
Der gebrauch der farbe in Rossettis dichtung. Diss. Marburg, 1923. 69p
Rossetti's use of colour in his poetry. Masters essay, Univ. of Southern California, 1920. 69ff

Mackail, John William
The life of William Morris. London, Longmans, Green, 1899. new ed 2 vols

McKillop, Alan Dugald
Festus and the Blessed damozel. Mod Lang N 34:93-7 F '19

McQuilland, Louis J.
Dante Gabriel Rossetti and the pre-Raphaelites. Bookman's Journal 11:60-2 N '24

Magee, S.
Rossetti and his friends. New Statesm 17:676 S 24 '21

Mahoney, A. L.
The interrelations of painting and poetry in the verse of Dante Gabriel Rossetti. Masters essay, Boston Univ. 1927

Maitland, Thomas [pseud]
see Buchanan, Robert Williams

Malmstedt, A.
Rossetti och "The aesthetic movement." Studier i Modern Sprakvetenskap utgivna av Nyfilologiska Sällskapet i Stockholm 6:193-229 '17

M[anson] J. B.
Dante Gabriel Rossetti. Apollo 7:257-8 Je '28

Marble, Annie Russell
Messages of the nineteenth century poets. Dial 30:99 F 16 '01

Marchbank, W.
A Rossetti ballad. T L S F 27 '30 p166; see *ibid* Mr 6 '30 p190 by G. C. M. Smith

March-Phillipps, L.
Pre-Raphaelitism and the present. Contemp 89:704-13 My '06

Marillier, Henry Currie
Dante G. Rossetti; an illustrated memorial of his art and life. . . London, Bell, 1899. v-xxiii,270p; list of works, p233-66
(Rev by W. M. Rossetti in Mag Art 24:217-23 Mr '00; N. Bell in Acad 67:357-8 O 22 '04; Nation (NY) 73:363 N 7 '01; Bookm (Lond) 21:145-6 Ja '02)

Rossetti. (Bell's miniature series of painters) London, Bell, 1906. 112p

The salutations of Beatrice: as treated pictorially by D. G. Rossetti. Art J 61:353-7 '99

Marks, Jeannette
Drugs and genius. *In* Genius and disaster, studies in drugs and genius. New York, Adelphi company, 1925. p22-5

Mather, Frank Jewett, Jr.
The Rossettis. Bookm (NY) 49:139-47 Ap '19

Mauclair, Camile
The influence of the pre-Raphaelites in France. Artist 32:169-80 '02

Mégroz, Rodolphe Louis
Dante Gabriel Rossetti (1828-1928). Dublin Magazine 3:39-49 Jl-S '28

Dante Gabriel Rossetti, painter poet of heaven in earth. . . London, Faber & Gwyer [1928] xi,15-[340]p bibl p319-21 (Rev in T L S D 13 '28 p982; New

Statesm 32:260-2 D '28; Criterion **8:**758-9 Jl '29; S. C. Chew in Sat R Lit 5:978 My 4 '29; W. Gibson in Bookm (Lond) 75:176-7 D '28)
Dante Gabriel Rossetti: the man and his poetry. Bookm (Lond) 74:4-10 Ap '28

Meldrum, D[avid] S[torrar]
Rossetti as painter. Bookm (Lond) 74:10-14 Ap '28

Memorabilia. [Rossetti's contributions to Notes and Queries] Notes & Q 155:127 Ag 25 '28

Meredith, George
A note on Cheyne Walk. Engl R 1:333 Ja '09

Merriman, Helen Bigelow
The English pre-Raphaelite and poetical school of painters. And R 1:594-612 Je '84

Meynell, Alice
Dante Gabriel Rossetti and contemporary poets. Acad 21:286 Ap 22 '82

[Michaelson, Anna] Jarno Jessen [pseud]
Rossetti. (Künstler-monographien. . . LXXVII) Bielefeld und Leipzig, Velhagen & Klasing, 1905. [3]-95p

Millais, John Guille
Pre-Raphaelitism: its meaning and its history. *In* The life and letters of Sir John Everett Millais. New York, Stokes, 1899. vol I p43-68

Miller, Joaquin (Cincinnatus Heine Miller)
Recollections of the Rossetti dinner. Overland Monthly 75:138-41 F '20

Milner, George
On some marginalia made by Dante G. Rossetti in a copy of Keats' poems. Engl Stud 61:211-19 My '27

Mr. Rossetti's new picture, "A vision of Fiammetta." Ath 2:439-40 O 5 '78

Mr. Rossetti's new pictures. Ath 2:566-7 N 1 '79; Ath 1:486-7 Ap 14 '77; Ath 1:304 F 26 '81

Mr. Rossetti's new pictures ["Venus Astarte"] Ath 1:486-7 Ap 14 '77

Mr. Swinburne's essays. Quar R 141:515-18 Ap '76

Modern developments in ballad art. Edin R 213:169-79 Ja '11

Monkhouse, William Cosmo
A Pre-Raphaelite collection. Mag Art 6:62-70 '83

"Rosa Triplex." Mag Art 6:271-2 '83

Rossetti at the Burlington Club. Acad 23:50-1 Ja 20 '83

Rossetti's pictures at the Royal Academy. Acad 23:14-15 Ja 6 '83

Monroe, Harriet
Rossetti. Poetry 32:270-7 Ag '28

Moore, Charles Leonard
The passionate Victorians. Dial 60:524 Je 8 '16

Morris, William
Address on the collection of paintings of the English pre-Raphaelite school delivered . . . in the Museum and Art Gallery, on Friday, October 2nd, 1891. Birmingham, Osborne [1891?] [3]-16p

Morris and Rossetti. Edin R 191:356-79 Ap '00

Morse, B. J.
Dante Gabriel Rossetti and Dante Alighieri. Engl Stud 68:227-48 S '33

Dante Gabriel Rossetti and William Blake. Engl Stud 66:364-72 Mr '32

A note on the autobiographical elements in Rossetti's "Hand and soul." Bei Anglia 54:331-7 N '30

Morse, Charles A. L.
Rossetti's poetry. Cath World 65:633-40 Ag '97

Mourey, Gabriel
D. G. Rossetti. *In* Passé le Détroit. . . Paris, Ollendorff, 1895

D. G. Rossetti et les Préraphaélites anglais. Paris, Laurens, 1909. 127p

Murphy, Sister Aurelia
Pre-Raphaelite effects in "The Blessed Damozel" of Dante Gabriel Rossetti. Masters essay, Univ. of Notre Dame, 1927. 28ff

Muther, Richard
The history of modern painting. New York, Macmillan, 1896. vol II p560-608, vol III p572-97

Rossetti, Burne Jones und Watts. Neue Deutsche Rundschau 13:859-65 Ag '02

Muthesius, H.
Dante Gabriel Rossetti. Kunst und Kunsthandwerk 4:373-89 '01

Myers, Frederic William Henry
Rossetti and the religion of beauty. Cornhill 47:213-24 F '83; *same.* Bibelot 8:337-67 '02; *same in* Essays: modern. London, Macmillan, 1883. p312-34

Nencioni, Enrico
Saggî critici di letteratura inglese. . . Firenze, Le Monnier, 1897. p317-21

The **New path.** [A periodical] Published by the Society for the advancement of truth in art. New York, 1864. nos 1-12, My '63-Ap '64 [much information about Pre-Raphaelitism]

Nicholson, Peter Walker
Dante Gabriel Rossetti, poet and painter. *In* The round table series, ed. by H. B. Baildon. Edinburgh, Brown, 1887. [no] VI 5-36p
(100 copies only)

Noble, James Ashcroft
At the grave of Rossetti. Bookm (NY) 1:170-3 Ap '95; *same.* Bookm (Lond) 8: 14-15 Ap '95

A pre-Raphaelite magazine. Fraser ns 25: 568-80 My '82; *also in* The sonnet in England and other essays. London,

Lane, 1896. p64-92; *same in* The Germ. . . Portland, Maine, Mosher, 1898. pxv-[xxx]

Noguchi, Yone
With Rossetti in London. National Magazine 23:157-60 N '05

Nordau, Max
Die Präraphaeliten. *In* Entartung. Berlin, Duncker, 1893. vol I p[123]-179

[**Note** on Rossetti's art] Ath 1:516 Ap 22 '82

Nothwang, Irene
Die frau, die liebe und der tod bei Dante Gabriel Rossetti. Fellbach-Stuttgart, Conradi [1932] 49p bibl p47-9 Thesis, Tübingen

Obituary. Art J 44:159 My '82

Olivero, Federico
Il ritornello nella poesia di D. G. Rossetti. *In* Saggî di letteratura inglese. Bari, Laterza, 1913; *same.* Archiv 125: 93-101 '10

Sul simbolismo di D. G. Rossetti. *In* Nuovi saggî di letteratura inglese. Torino, Libreria Editrice Internazionale [1918?] p[173]-210
(Rev in T L S S 19 '18 p451)

On a painting by Rossetti of snowdrops in an outlined hand; poem. Acad 23:401 Je 9 '83

Ortensi, Ulisse
Artisti contemporanei: Dante Gabriele Rossetti. Emporium 4:3-14, 83-95 Jl, Ag '96

The **P.-R. B.** Gent M 254:238 F '83

Pain, Barry
The poets at tea. VIII. Rossetti, who took six cups of it. *In* Playthings and parodies. New York, Cassell [c1892] p228

[**Paintings** by Rossetti] Ath 2:407 S 27 '73

[**Paintings** [10] by Rossetti] Masters in Art 4:465-83 D '03

Palgrave's "Golden Treasury." Notes & Q 10th ser 8:351-2 N 2 '07

Pàntini, Romualdo
La "Casa di Vita" di Dante Gabriele Rossetti. Italia Moderna anno 2 series 3 no 16:527-38 Ag '04

Parkes, Kineton
The pre-Raphaelite movement. London, Reeves and Turner [1889]

Ruskin and pre-Raphaelitism. New Century Review 7:133-43 F '00

Parrott, Thomas Marc and Thorp, Willard (eds)
Poetry of the transition, 1850-1914. New York, Oxford [c1932] p1-4

Pater, Walter Horatio
Dante Gabriel Rossetti. *In* Appreciations. London, Macmillan, 1913. p205-18

Dante Gabriel Rossetti. *In* The works of Walter Pater. . . London, Macmillan, 1901. vol V p205-18

Pater, Walter Horatio—*Continued*
Dante Gabriel Rossetti. *In* Ward, Thomas H. ed. The English poets. . . New York, Macmillan, 1910. vol IV p633-41

Patmore, Coventry K. D.
Rossetti as a poet. *In* Principle in art. London, Bell, 1912. p98-105

Walls and wall painting at Oxford. Sat R 4:583-4 D 26 '57

Payne, William Morton
Dante Gabriel Rossetti. *In* The greater English poets of the nineteenth century. New York, Holt, 1907. p284-315

Dante Gabriel Rossetti. *In* The Columbia university course in literature. New York, Columbia Univ. press, 1928. vol XIV p455-9

Dante Gabriel Rossetti (1828-1882) *In* Warner, C. D. (ed) Library of the world's best literature. . . Memorial ed. New York, Hill [c1902] vol XXXI p12411-15

Pennell, Elizabeth Robins
My glimpse of the pre-Raphaelites. American Magazine of Art 11:3-6 N '19

Pennell, Joseph
A golden decade in English art. Savoy no 1:112-14 Ja '96

Phelps, (Mrs) J. Q.
The mysticism of Rossetti. Fine Arts Journal 37:37-40 S '19

Picture exhibitions. Sat R 55:81-2 Ja 20 '83

Pissarro, Lucien
Rossetti; illustrated with eight reproductions in colour. (Masterpieces in colour) London, Jack [1908] vii,9-80p

Pius, Mary
Rossetti: God sought through beauty. *In* Some evidences of mysticism in English poetry of the nineteenth century. Diss. Catholic univ. 1916. p36-43

Placci, Carlo
Dante Gabriel Rossetti. La Rassegna Nazionale anno 4, vol 9:427-46 My 1 '82; *same published*: Firenze, 1882

Plowman, Thomas F.
The aesthetes; the story of a nineteenth-century cult. Pall Mall Magazine 5: 29-33 Ja '95

[**Poems** of Rossetti set to music]
A little while; music by F. A. Marshall. London [1870]

Love-lily and other songs; music by Edward Dannreuther. London [1884]

A New Year's burden; music by Eaton Faning. London [1879]

A New Year's burden; music by F. A. Marshall. London [1877]

A New Year's burden; music by Lord Henry Somerset. London [1876]

Poetry and the intuition of immortality. T L S S 14 '16 p433-4

The **poetry** of Dante Gabriel Rossetti. Lond Q R 82:104-12 Ap '94

The **poetry** of Rossetti. Brit Q 76:109-27 Jl '82

[**Portrait** of Swinburne by D. G. Rossetti] Book B ns 20:8-9 F '00

[**Portraits**] Cent ns 2:718 S '82; Bookm (Lond) 40:113-16, 125-6 Je '11; 35:140 D '08; 77:facing 8 O '29; 26:58, 64 My '04; 41:187, 192, 194-5 Ja '12; 19:81 D '00; 36:117 Je '09; Bookm (NY) 29: 377 Je '09; 3:14 Mr '96; 7:100 Ap '98; 75:691 N '32; Bookn 24:facing 681, 685, 688, 696 Je '06; Harper M 65:691 O '82; Critic (NY) 37:321, 325 O '00; John O'London's Weekly 27:858 S 17 '32; Mag Art 12:21-6, 57-61, 138-40 '89; Delineator 58:93-4 Jl '01; Pall Mall Magazine 5:29 Ja '95

The **pre-Raphaelite** brotherhood. Quar R 204:352-74 Ap '06

Pre-Raphaelite brotherhood; with a short biographical sketch by J. Ernest Phythian. . . (Newnes' art library no. 17) New York, Warne, 1906. 28;64p (Rev in Scrip 1:234-5 Ap '06)

A **pre-Raphaelite** exhibition. Sat R 4:11-12 Jl 4 '57

Pre-Raphaelites and peacocks. Bookm (NY) 75:691-3 N '32

Pre-Raphaelites at the Century Club. Critic (NY) 22:24-5 Ja 14 '93

Pre-Raphaelitism
(Noted in Blackw 68:82 Jl '50; Ath 1: 609 Je 9 '51; Art J ns 3:285-6 N '51; Spec My 4, 31, O 4 '51; Nation (NY) 1:273-4 Ag 31 '65; Guardian 5:396, 623 Je 1, Ag 28 '50; Brit Q 16:197-220 Ag '52)

Pre-Raphaelitism in outline; Dante Gabriel Rossetti. Bookn 24:696-7 Je '06

Preston, Margaret J.
Dante Gabriel Rossetti; poem. Lit W 14:77 Mr 10 '83; Literary World (Lond) ns 34:158 Ag 20 '86; *same*. Critic (NY) 10:9 Ja 1 '87

Prideaux, William Francis
D. G. Rossetti. Notes & Q 6th ser 8:364 N 10 '83
[Refers to a letter in the Ath 2:901-2 Ag 21 '52 signed "D. G. R." not yet noticed by biographers]

Dante Gabriel Rossetti. Notes & Q 7th ser 4:481-2 D 17 '87

Palgrave's "Golden Treasury." Notes & Q 10th ser 8:393, 454 N 16, D 7 '07

Prinsep, Valentine Cameron
Dante Gabriel Rossetti. Mag Art 28:281-6 Ap '04

The Oxford circle: Rossetti, Burne-Jones, and William Morris. Mag Art 28:167-72 F '04

The private art collections of London. The late Mr. Frederick Leyland's in Prince's Gate. First paper.—Rossetti and his friend. Art J 54:129-34 My '92

Proix, Jean
. . . Un mysticisme esthétique. (Cahiers de la quinzaine. sér 18 no 14) Paris, L'Artisan du livre [c1928] 52p
(1760 copies only)

Puaux, R.
Le dernier des préraphaélites. Le Temps 9:11 '10

Pundt, Herbert
Dante Gabriel Rossetti's einfluss auf die gedichte des jungen William Morris... Diss. Breslau, 1920. Summary, Breslau, 1922. 2p

Pyne, Evelyn
Rossetti's grave; poem. Acad 29:291 Ap 24 '86

Quesnel, Léo
La poésie au XIXᵉ siècle en angleterre. Le Correspondant 110:808-10 Mr 10 '78

Quilter, Harry
Dante Gabriel Rossetti as student and friend. In Preferences in art, life, and literature. London, Swan Sonnenschein, 1892. p15-22

The painting and the poetry of Dante Gabriel Rossetti. In Preferences in art, life, and literature. London, Swan Sonnenschein, 1892. p80-94; *same*. Contemp 43:190-203 F '83; *same*. Ecl M 100:448-57 Ap '83

Rossetti. In Sententiae artis. . . London, Isbister, 1886. p126-9, 244-60

Radford, Ernest
Dante Gabriel Rossetti (Newne's art library) With a biographical study by E. Radford. London, Newnes [1905] xxiip, 56 plates
(Rev by F. Bickley in Bookm (Lond) 36:42 Ap '09; noted in Ath 2:767 D 12 '08; rev in Ath 2:616 N 4 '05)

Raleigh, Walter
Dante Gabriel Rossetti. In Chambers's cyclopaedia of English literature. Philadelphia, Lippincott, 1904. new ed vol III p641-5

Ranftl, Johann
Dante Gabriel Rossetti. Historisch politische Blätter für das katholische Deutschland 139:477-500, 575-97 '07

Rawnsley, Hardwicke Drummond
Dante Gabriel Rossetti; poem. Acad 21: 285 Ap 22 '82

Recollections of Rossetti. T.P.'s Weekly 3:132 Ja 29 '04

Redgrave, Gilbert Richard
A history of water-colour painting in England. London, Sampson Low, Marston, 1892. p231-2
(Rev in Ath 2:489-90 O 8 '92)

Rees, J. Rogers
An odd corner in a book-lover's study. Bibliographer (Lond) 5:134 Ap '84

Reid, Forrest
The Moxon Tennyson. In Illustrators of the sixties. London, Faber and Gwyer [1928] p36-43

The pre-Raphaelite group. In Illustrators of the sixties. London, Faber and Gwyer [1928] p44-6

Rhys, Ernest
Lyric poetry. London, Dent, 1913. p346-8

Rickett, Arthur
Keats and Rossetti. In Personal forces in modern literature. London, Dent, 1906. p112-39

Rippingille, E. V.
Obsoletism in art. London, Bentley, 1852. 56p

Robertson, William Graham
The spell of Rossetti. In Time was. London, Hamilton [1931] p86-97

Robinson, Mary F.
Dante Gabriel Rossetti. Harper M 65: 691-701 O '82

Dante Gabriel Rossetti. Unsere Zeit ns 1:767-78 '79

Rod, Édouard
The English pre-Raphaelites. Connoisseur 2:109-23, 175-87 Mr, Je '88

Les préraphaélites anglais. Gazette des Beaux-Arts année 29, 2d période, vol 36:177-95, 399-416 S, N '87; *same in* Études sur le XIXᵉ siècle. Giacomo Leopardi. Paris, Perrin, 1888. p[47]-97

Roosbroeck, Gust. L. Van
Correspondence. Rossetti and Maeterlinck. Mod Lang N 34:439-41 N '19

Rosenblatt, Louise
L'idée de l'art pour l'art dans la littérature anglaise. pendant la période victorienne. Paris, Champion, 1931. p119-20

Rossetti, Dante Gabriel
The ballad of Jan van Hunks. . . With an introd. by Mackenzie Bell. London, Harrap [1929] 42p
(Rev in T L S D 5 '29 p1026)

Ballads and sonnets. London, Ellis and White, 1881. xii,335p
(Rev in Ath 2:457-60 O 8 '81; *same*. Ecl M ns 34:851-8 D '81; E. Dowden in Acad 20:285-6 O 15 '81; Lit W 12:396 N 5 '81; J. A. Symonds in Macmil 45: 318-28 F '82; Spec 55:269-70 F 25 '82; Edin R 155:322-37 Ap '82; J. Knight in Le Livre 2:722-3 D 10 '81; Dial 2:241 F '82; Nation (NY) 33:477 D 15 '81; Literary World (Lond) ns 60:34 Jl 14 '99; Harper M 64:473 F '82; Atlan 49: 119-21 Ja '82; A. Meynell in Art J 44: 85-7 Mr '82; Westm 117:284-6 Ja '82)

The blessed damozel. Introd. by William Michael Rossetti. London, Duckworth, 1898. xviiip [pages of the poem are unnumbered]
(Rev in Sat R 85:851-2 Je 25 '98; Lit 3: 150 Ag 20 '98)

Rossetti, Dante Gabriel—*Continued*

The collected works of Dante Gabriel Rossetti, ed. with preface and notes by William Michael Rossetti. London, Ellis and Scrutton, 1886. 2 vols xliv, 528p; xl,521p
(Rev in Sat R 63:172-3 Ja 29 '87; Ath 1:346-9 Mr 12 '87; E. Dowden in Acad 31:85-6 F 5 '87)

Dante Gabriel Rossetti. An anthology chosen by F. L. Lucas. (Poets in brief) Cambridge, England, Univ. press, 1933. vii-xxxiv,241p
(Rev in T L S Ap 27 '33 p290)

Dante Gabriel Rossetti: his family letters, with a memoir. London, Ellis and Elvey, 1895. 2 vols ix-xxx, 440p; 436p
(Rev in Spec 76:550-1 Ap 18 '96; Sat R 80:838-9 D 21 '95; Lit W 27:35 F 8 '96; Edin R 185:497-501 Ap '97; W. H. Chesson in Quar R 260:84-93 Ja '33; Quar R 184:185-214 Jl '96; W. Sharp in Acad 49:213-14 Mr 14 '96; Critic (NY) ns 28:463-4 Je 27 '96; Dial 20:164-7 Mr 16 '96; Edin R 191:356-79 Ap '00)

Dante Gabriel Rossetti: letters to Miss Alice Boyd. Chosen and arranged by John Purves. Fortn ns 123:577-94 My '28

Dramatic skit by Dante Gabriel Rossetti; with text. Ed. by M. L. Howe. Mod Lang N 49:39-44 Ja '34

The house of life. . .
(Rev by W. M. Payne in Dial 16:275 My 1 '94; Literary World (Lond) ns 58:485 D 16 '98; T L S D 13 '28 p982)

Letters from D. G. Rossetti to A. C. Swinburne regarding the attacks made upon the latter by Mortimer Collins and upon both by Robert Buchanan. London, Printed for Thomas James Wise for private circulation only, 1921. 15p
(30 copies only)

Letters of D. G. Rossetti, ed. by George Birkbeck Hill. Atlan 77:577-95, 744-54 My, Je '96; Atlan 78:45-57, 242-55 Jl, Ag '96

The letters of Dante Gabriel Rossetti to his publisher, F. S. Ellis; ed. with introd. and notes by Oswald Doughty. London, Scholartis press, 1928. xlviii, 150p (560 copies only)
(Rev by P. F. Baum in Mod Lang N 44:334-6 My '29; R. L. Megroz in Bookm (Lond) 74:214-15 Jl '28; T L S Je 7 '28 p427; Sat R 145:702 Je 2 '28; Nat-Ath 43:501 Jl 14 '28)

Letters of Dante Gabriel Rossetti to William Allingham, 1854-1870. Ed. by George Birkbeck Hill. London, Unwin, 1897. v-xxviii,307p
(Rev in Bookm (NY) 7:152-3 Ap '98; Nation (NY) 66:306 Ap 21 '98; T. de Wyzewa in R Deux Mondes 145:936-46 F 15 '98; Lit 1:264-5 D 18 '97; Sat R 84:717-18 D 18 '97; B. Schnabel in Engl Stud 27:134-5 '00; F. J. Gregg in Book B ns 16:315-18 My '98; Spec 80:238-9 F 12 '98; Ath 1:395-7 Mr 26 '98; Bookm (Lond) 13:128 Ja '98)

Pictures and poems of Dante Gabriel Rossetti. Arranged by Fitz Roy Carrington. New York, Russell, 1900. 27 leaves
(Rev in International Studio 11: supplement xvii S '00)

Poems. London, Ellis, 1870. x,282p
(Rev by Shirley [J. Skelton] in Fraser 81:609-22 My '70; *same.* Liv Age 105: 686-97 Je 11 '70; *same.* Ecl M ns 12: 143-54 Ag '70; No Brit 52:598-601 Jl '70; Spec 43:724-5 Je 11 '70; Sat R 29:651-2 My 14 '70; New Eclectic 7:110-17 Jl '70; Literary World (Lond) ns 63:522 My 31 '01; Harper M 41:463 Ag '70; J. R. Dennett in No Am 111:471-80 O '70; Lond Q R 87:2-16 O '96; New Englander 29:717 O '70; Ath 1:573-4 Ap 30 '70; W. D. Howells in Atlan 26:115-18 Jl '70; Old & New 2:92-4 Jl '70; Westm ns 38:226-7 Jl '70; Nation (NY) 11:29-30 Jl 14 '70; S. Colvin in Westm ns 39: 55-73 Ja '71; Edin R 155:322-37 Ap '82; N. Bell in Acad 67:478-9 N 19 '04; Ath 1:15 Ja 7 '05; W. Morris in Acad 1:199-200 My 14 '70; G. Hake in New Monthly Magazine 146:681-700 Je '70; Lakeside Monthly 4:320-3 N '70; Broadway 3d ser 1:286-8 O '70; Speaker 3:108-9 Ja 24 '91; W. J. Courthope in Quar R 132:69-75 Ja '72; *same.* Ecl M ns 15: 385-99 Ap '72; A. C. Swinburne in Fortn 13:551-79 My '70; H. B. Forman in Tinsley's 8:150-60 Mr '71; Lippinc 6:340-2 S '70; A. Pichot in Revue Britannique 267:560-1 Je '70; Contemp 14:480-1 Je '70; S. Colvin in Pall Mall Gazette Ap 21 '70; J. C. Earle in Cath World 19:263-72 My '74; Blackw 108:178-83 Ag '70)

Sir Hugh the heron. A legendary tale in four parts. By Gabriel Rossetti, Junior. London, Polidori's private press, 1843

Some unpublished stanzas by Dante Gabriel Rossetti; with poem "Border Song." Ed. by M. L. Howe. Mod Lang N 48:176-9 Mr '33

Rossetti, Dante Gabriel (illustrator)

Poems by Alfred Tennyson. London, Moxon, 1857. [contains 5 illustrations by Rossetti]
(Rev in Westm ns 12:591-2 O '57)

Two poems by William Morris. The defence of Guenevere and King Arthur's tomb, with eight decorations by Dante Gabriel Rossetti and a foreword by Gordon Bottomley. London, Fanfrolico press, 1930
(Rev in T L S O 30 '30 p885)

Rossetti, Dante Gabriel (painter)

Dante's dream.
(Rev in Ath 2:250 Ag 20 '81)

Ecce Ancilla Domini.
(Noted in Observer Ap 14 '50 p5;
Builder 8:184 Ap 20 '50; Ath 1:424 Ap
20 '50; W. M. Rossetti in Critic (Lond)
Jl 1 '50)

The girlhood of Mary Virgin.
(Noted in Builder 7:145 Mr 31 '49; Literary Gazette & Journal of Belles
Lettres no 1680:239 Mr 31 '49; Art J
11:147 '49; Observer (Lond) Ap 8-9
'49)

Rossetti, Dante Gabriel (trans)
Dante and his circle: with the Italian
poets preceding him. (1100-1200-1300)
A collection of lyrics, ed. and trans. in
the original metres. Rev. and re-
arranged ed. Part I. Dante's Vita
Nuova, etc. Poets of Dante's circle.
Part II. Poets chiefly before Dante.
London, Ellis and White, 1874. xxiv,
468p
(Rev in Nation (NY) 18:159-60 Mr 5
'74; Lond Q R 42:299-313 Jl '74; Critic
(NY) 11:26 Jl 16 '87)

The early Italian poets from Ciullo
d'Alcamo to Dante Alighieri (1100-
1200-1300) in the original metres together with Dante's Vita Nuova. Part I.
Poets chiefly before Dante. Part II.
Dante and his circle. London, Smith,
Elder, 1861. xxxvi,464p
(Rev in Ath 1:253-4 F 22 '62; Fraser
65:580-94 My '62; National Review 15:
60-95 Jl '62; Brit Q 35:500 Ap '62;
Westm (American ed) 77:316-17 Ap
'62; Spec 34:75-6 Ja 18 '62; Westm
ns 39:73-92 Ja '71; Sat R 13:449-51 Ap
19 '62; Reader 1:161-2 F 14 '63)

Lenore, by Gottfried August Bürger.
Trans. from the German by Dante
Gabriel Rossetti. London, Ellis and
Elvey, 1900. 36p
(Rev in Acad 58:504 Je 16 '00)

Rossetti, Helen M. M.
. . . The life and work of Dante Gabriel
Rossetti. . . London, Art Journal
office, 1902. 32p

Rossetti, William Michael
Dante Gabriel Rossetti as designer and
writer. London, Cassell, 1889. xv,302p
(Rev in Book B ns 6:566 D '89; Sat R
69:110-11 Ja 25 '90; Critic (NY) ns 16:
102 Mr 1 '90; Dial 10:289 F '90; J. T.
Nettleship in Acad 36:363-5 D 7 '89;
Ath 1:823-6 Je 28 '90; Scots Observer
3:158-9 D 28 '89; Igdrasil 1:113 Mr '90)

Dante Gabriel Rossetti as translator.
Sewanee R 17:405-8 O '09

Dante Rossetti and Elizabeth Siddal. *In*
Some reminiscences. London, Brown
Langham, 1906. vol I p192-200; *same.*
Burlington Magazine 1:273-95 My '03
(Rev in Bookm (Lond) 31:156 D '06;
Acad 71:466-7 N 10 '06)

Introduction. *In* The Germ. . . being a
facsimile reprint of the literary organ
of the pre-Raphaelite brotherhood,
published in 1850. London, Stock, 1901.
p[5]-30

Memoir of Dante Gabriel Rossetti. *In*
Dante Gabriel Rossetti, his family letters. London, Ellis and Elvey, 1895.
vol I p3-440

Mr. D. G. Rossetti's pictures. Ath 1:546
Ap 29 '82

Note. *In* A pre-Raphaelite collection.
[London] July, 1896. p[3]-6

Notes on Rossetti and his works. Art J
46:148-52, 165-8, 204-8 My, Je, Jl '84

The portraits of Dante Gabriel Rossetti.
Mag Art 12:21-6, 57-61, 138-40 '89

Praeraphaelite diaries and letters. . .
London, Hurst and Blackett, 1900. [3]-
328p
(Rev in Acad 57:741-2 D 23 '99)

Praeraphaelitism. *In* Fine art, chiefly
contemporary. . . London, Macmillan,
1867. p[168]-77

Preface. *In* The poetical works of Dante
Gabriel Rossetti. London, Ellis and
Elvey, 1903. p[xv]-xxx

Rossetti papers, 1862-1870; a compila-
tion. . . London, Sands, 1902. xxiii,
559p
(Rev in Dial 36:122-3 F 16 '04; Nation
(NY) 77:253-4 S 24 '03; Acad 65:78-9
Jl 25 '03; Ath 2:211 Ag 15 '03)

Ruskin: Rossetti: pre-Raphaelitism.
Papers 1854-1862, arranged and ed. . . .
New York, Dodd, Mead, 1899. xxi,327p
(Rev by T. de Wyzewa in R Deux
Mondes 157:935-46 F '00; Critic (NY)
35:651-5 Jl '99; Sat R 87:277 Mr 4 '99;
Nation (NY) 68:440-1 Je 8 '99; Argo-
naut 44:8 Je 12 '99; Literary World
(Lond) ns 59:40-1 Ja 13 '99; Speaker
19:82 Ja 21 '99; M. B. Anderson in Dial
26:336-8 My 16 '99; Acad 56:86-7 Ja 21
'99; Lit 4:61 Ja 21 '99)

Some reminiscences. . . London, Brown
Langham, 1906. 2 vols
(Rev in Acad 71:466-7 N 10 '06; Bookm
(Lond) 31:156 D '06)

Some scraps of verse and prose by Dante
Gabriel Rossetti. Pall Mall Magazine
16:480-96 D '98

Rossetti. Notes & Q 8th ser 2:29 Jl 9 '92;
Lit W 29:74 Mr 5 '98

Rossetti. (Masters in art. pt 48) Boston,
Bates and Guild [1903] 42p

Rossetti and Millais. Nation (NY) 66:65-6,
86-7 Ja 27, F 3 '98

Rossetti and the pre-Raphaelites. R of Rs
(Lond) 25:381 Ap '02

Rossetti and Swinburne [letters] T L S
O 16, 23 '19 p565-6, 591

Rossetti at Burlington House. Spec 56:14-
15 Ja 6 '83

Rossetti family in Bucks. Notes & Q 159:
176 S 6 '30

The **Rossettis.** Tinsley's 5:59-67, 142-51,
276-81 Ag, S, O '69

[Rossetti's career as a painter] Ath 1:481-2 Ap 15 '82; *same*. Liv Age 153:506-9 My 27 '82

Rossetti's Francesca. Nation (NY) 53:426-7 D 3 '91

[Rossetti's influence in America] Dial 3:16-17 My '82

Rossetti's love story. T.P.'s Weekly 3:500 Ap 15 '04

Rossetti's pets. T.P.'s Weekly 10:534 O 25 '07

Rossetti's pictures at the Royal Academy and the Burlington fine arts club. Art J 45:61-2 F '83

Rossetti's "Ruggiero and Angelica." Notes & Q 9th ser 9:425 My 31 '02

Rothenstein, William
Men and memories. . . London, Faber and Faber [1931] vol I passim

Rowley, Charles
The Rossettis. *In* Fifty years of work without wages. London, Hodder and Stoughton [1912] p113-25

Royal academy—winter exhibition. Ath 1: 22-3 Ja 6 '83

Ruhrmann, Friedrich G.
Studien zur geschichte und charakteristik des refrains in der englischen literatur. (Anglistische forschungen, heft 64) Heidelberg, Winter, 1927. p129-50

Ruskin, John
Pre-Raphaelitism. London, Smith, Elder, 1851. [v]-vi,68p
Pre-Raphaelitism. *In* Arrows of the chace. . . New York, Wiley, 1881. vol I p[59]-122
Pre-Raphaelitism. *In* Lectures on architecture and painting. . . New York, Wiley, 1882. p151-89
Realistic schools of painting. *In* The art of England. Orpington, Allen, 1884. p1-35
The three colours of pre-Raphaelitism. 19th Cent 4:925-31, 1072-82 N, D '78

Ruskin, John; Morris, William [etc.]
Letters addressed to Algernon Charles Swinburne, by John Ruskin, William Morris, Sir Edward Burne-Jones and Dante Gabriel Rossetti. London, Printed for private circulation only by Richard Clay and sons, 1919. 16p

Rutledge, Guy
Some notes on the life and work of Dante Gabriel Rossetti. Liverpool Philomathic Society Proceedings Session 80 vol 50:cxiii-cxxxix '04-'05

Rutter, Frank Vane Phipson
Art in my time. London, Rich and Cowan [1933] p27-8
Dante Gabriel Rossetti, painter and man of letters. London, Richards, 1908. xii, 157p
(Rev in Bookm (Lond) 35:283 Mr '09)

Saintsbury, George Edward Bateman
A history of nineteenth century literature. London, Macmillan, 1931. p288-92
The poetry of Dante Gabriel Rossetti. Bookm (Lond) 40:120-7 Je '11
The prae-Raphaelite school. *In* A history of English prosody from the twelfth century to the present day. London, Macmillan, 1910. vol III p308-16

Salomon, Solomon J.
Rossetti's tomb. Acad 84:63 Ja 11 '13

Sapori, Francesco
D. G. Rossetti. *In* I maestri dell' arte. Monographie d'artisti ital. mod. Torino, 1921. vol II no 27

Sarrazin, Gabriel
Dante Gabriel Rossetti. *In* Poètes modernes de l'Angleterre. Paris, Ollendorff, 1885. p231-71

Sartorio, G. A.
Nota su D. G. Rossetti pittore. Il Convito libro 2:121-50 F '95 *and* libro 3:261-86 Ap '95

Sawvel, Franklin B.
Dante's dream and Captive Andromache. Educa 21:32-6 S '00

Schäfer, Josy
Rosettis [sic] ansichten über kunst und künstler. Diss. Erlangen, 1925. 70p

Schelling, Felix E.
The English lyric. Boston, Houghton, Mifflin, 1913. p229-33

Schoepe, Max [W]
Der vergleich bei Dante Gabriel Rossetti. . . Berlin, Märkische buch- und kunstdruckerei, 1913. 64p bibl p62-3 Thesis, Kiel

Schücking, Levin Ludwig
Rossettis persönlichkeit. Engl Stud 51:189-225 '17

Schulte, W.
Dante Gabriel Rossetti. Kunst und Wissen '28 p19

Schuman, A. T.
Two poets: Rossetti; poem. Dial 21:179 O 1 '96

Scott, William Bell
Autobiographical notes of his life, ed. by W. Minto. London, Osgood, 1892. vol I p289; vol II p 115-16, 127
(Rev in Quar R 184:185-214 Jl '96)

Seddon, J. P.
King René's honeymoon cabinet. . . illustrated from photographs of the panels painted by D. G. Rossetti, etc. London, Batsford, 1898. x,16p, 8 plates

Seger, F.
D. G. Rossetti. Berliner Tageblatt no 7 '09

Seiler, Magdalene
D. G. Rossettis künstlerische entwicklung. Greifswald, Mitau, 1933. 126p Diss. Greifswald
(Rev by L. Wolff in Revue A A 12:153-4 '34)

Selkirk, J. B. [pseud]
see Brown, James Buchan

Shairp, J. C.
Aesthetic poetry: Dante Gabriel Rossetti. Contemp 42:17-32 Jl '82

Shanks, Edward
Dante Gabriel Rossetti. Lond Merc 18: 67-78 My '28

Sharp, Amy
D. G. Rossetti. *In* Victorian poets. London, Methuen, 1891. p157-73
(Rev in Speaker 4:206-7 Ag 15 '91)

Sharp, William
Dante Gabriel Rossetti, a record and a study. London, Macmillan, 1882. viii, 432p
(Rev by J. M. Gray in Acad 23:1 Ja 6 '83; G. P. Lathrop in Atlan 51:553-5 Ap '83; Nation (NY) 36:408 My 10 '83; Quar R 184:185-214 Jl '96; Le Livre 4:148 Mr 10 '83; Lit W 14:56-7 F 24 '83)

Dante Gabriel Rossetti and pictorialism in verse. Portfolio 13:176-80 '82

Rossetti in prose and verse. *In* Papers, critical and reminiscent. . . New York, Duffield, 1912. p38-65

The Rossettis. . . Fortn 45:414-29 Mr '86; *same.* Ecl M 106:590-600 My '86; *same.* Liv Age 169:161-70 Ap 17 '86

Sonnets for two pictures by Rossetti. Acad 22:242 S 30 '82

Shaw, Wilfred B.
Rossetti and Botticelli: a comparison of ideals and art. Craftsman 9:341-56 D '05

Shields, Frederic
Some notes on Dante Gabriel Rossetti. Century Guild Hobby Horse 1:140-54 '86

Shine, Wesley Hill
The influence of Keats on Rossetti. Masters essay, Univ. of North Carolina, 1925. 77ff
The influence of Keats upon Rossetti. Engl Stud 61:183-210 My '27

Shirley [pseud]
see Skelton, John

Shorter, Clement King
Victorian literature. New York, Dodd, Mead, 1897. p22-4

Shuster, George N.
The Catholic spirit in modern English literature. New York, Macmillan, 1922. p180-2

Siebold, Erika von
Synästhesien in der englischen dichtung des 19. jahrhunderts. Engl Stud 53: 295-303 D '19

Sieper, Ernst
Das evangelium der schönheit in der englischen literatur und kunst des XIX. jahrhunderts. Dortmund, Ruhfus, 1904. p250-64

Singer, Hans W[olfgang]
Dante Gabriel Rossetti. (Die kunst, 41) [Berlin] Bard, Marquardt, 1905. 66p
Gabriel Charles Dante Rossetti. *In* Von unsterblichen. Ein künstlerkalender. Rudolstadt, Müller, 1924

Sizeranne, Robert de la
see La Sizeranne, Robert de

[Skelton, John] Shirley [pseud]
Dante Rossetti and Mr. William Bell Scott. Blackw 153:229-35 F '93
Mainly about Rossetti. *In* The table talk of Shirley. London, Blackwoods, 1895. 3d ed p74-94
The poems of Dante Gabriel Rossetti. Fraser ns 1:609-22 My '70; *same.* Ecl M ns 12:143-54 Ag '70; *same.* Liv Age 105: 686-97 Je 11 '70

Smith, Arnold
Dante Gabriel Rossetti. *In* The main tendencies of Victorian poetry. . . London, Simpkin, Marshall, Hamilton, Kent, 1907. p183-95

Smith, Ashley Auburn
Dante Gabriel Rossetti; poem. Bookm (NY) 11:434 Jl '00

Smith, G. Barnett
Dante Gabriel Rossetti. Time (Lond) 7: 163-73 My '82
Rossetti's "Hand and Soul." Acad 21:341 My 13 '82

Smith, G. C. Moore
A Rossetti ballad. T L S Mr 6 '30 p190

Smith, Garnet
Dante Gabriel Rossetti. Contemp 133: 624-31 My '28

Smith, Harry Bache
Dante Gabriel Rossetti. Cent 117:245-53 D '28

Smith, Maurice
Dante Gabriel Rossetti. (Sohier prize, Harvard Univ. 1919) 36ff Typed Ms. in Harvard College library

Smith, S. C. Kaines
Painters of England. London, Medici Society [1934] p87-94

Smith, Simon Nowell
Rossetti manuscripts. T L S S 10 '31 p683

Some literary love stories. T.P.'s Weekly 5:300 Mr 10 '05

Some poets of the Victorian era. XI. Dante Gabriel Rossetti. Acad 79:317-18, 341-2 O 1, 8 '10

Spens, J.
The ethical significance of Rossetti's poetry. Int J Ethics 12:216-25 '02

Spielmann, Marion Harry
Millais and his works, with special reference to the exhibition at the Royal academy 1898. . . Edinburgh, Blackwood, 1898

Squire, John Collings
The newspaper pastoral [parody of "Sister Helen"?] *In* Collected parodies. London, Hodder and Stoughton [1921?] p182-3

Stedman, Edmund Clarence
Latter-day British poets. . . Scribner's Monthly Magazine 9:431-4 F '75; *also in* Victorian poets. Boston, Houghton, Mifflin, 1876. p357-66

Stephens, Frederic George
Beata Beatrix, by Dante G. Rossetti. Portfolio 22:[45]-47 '91; *same in* Modern paintings, ed. by Esther Singleton. New York, Dodd, Mead, 1911. p100-6

Dante Gabriel Rossetti. . . (Portfolio artistic monographs 5) London, Seeley, 1894. 96p
(Rev in Nation (NY) 59:89-90 Ag 2 '94; W. Sharp in Acad 46:72-3 Jl '94; Quar R 184:185-214 Jl '96)

The earlier works of Rossetti. Portfolio 14:87-91, 114-19 '83

Picture of lady in red. [The vision of Fiammetta] Notes & Q 10th ser 7:129, 193 F 16, Mr 9 '07

Pictures by Mr. Rossetti. Ath 2:219-21 Ag 14 '75

The private collections of England. Ath 2:407 S 27 '73

Rosa Triplex by Dante Gabriel Rossetti. Portfolio 23:197-9 '92

Stevens, W. B[ertrand]
Ecce ancilla Domini (Behold the handmaid of the Lord). Chautauquan 46:103-4 Mr '07

Stillman, William James
Dante Rossetti and chloral. Acad 53:333 Mr 19 '98

Rossetti, the painter and poet. Putnam's Magazine 16:95-101 Jl '70

Strahan and Co.
[Denial that Buchanan wrote "The Fleshly School of Poetry"] Ath 2:794 D 16 '71

Suddard, Mary
The house of life. *In* Studies and essays. Cambridge, England, Univ. press, 1912. p261-78

Sugimura, Kazue
Rossetti the man. Masters essay, Boston Univ. 1920

Sulman, Thomas
A memorable art class. Good Words 38:547-51 '97; *same.* Liv Age 214:889-93 S 18 '97

Mr. Linton and D. G. Rossetti. Acad 52:226 S 18 '97

Swalin, Benjamin Franklin
Rossetti and the pre-Raphaelites. Masters essay, Columbia univ. 1930

Swinburne, Algernon Charles
Notes on the Royal Academy exhibition. London, Privately printed, 1868. p45-51

The poems of Dante Gabriel Rossetti. *In* Essays and studies. London, Chatto, 1875. p60-109; *same.* Fortn 13:551-79. My 1 '70

Sonnet for a picture [parody] *In* The Heptalogia, or seven against sense. . . London, Chatto & Windus, 1880. p95-6

Swinburne, Louis Judson
Rossetti and the pre-Raphaelites. New Englander & Yale Review 44:502-22, 635-54 Jl, S '85; *same published:* [New Haven, Connecticut, 1885] 42p

Swinburne's letters to Rossetti and Watts-Dunton. Liv Age 297:498-500 My 25 '18; *same.* Spec 120:373-4 Ap 6 '18

Swinburniana. T.P.'s Weekly 2:890 D 11 '03

Symons, Arthur
Dante Gabriel Rossetti. . . (Kunst der Gegenwart. jahrg. 2 bd 3) Berlin, Verlagsanstalt für litteratur und kunst [1909] 6-59p

Dante Gabriel Rossetti. Paris, Librairie artistique et littéraire [1910] 59p

Dante Gabriel Rossetti. *In* Figures of several centuries. London, Constable, 1916. p201-6

Dante Gabriel Rossetti. *In* Studies in strange souls. London, Sawyer, 1929. p3-49
(Rev in T L S Je 13 '29 p471)

A note on Rossetti. No Am 204:128-34 Jl '16

Notes on two manuscripts. [A Swinburne manuscript and the original manuscript of Rossetti's Eden bower] Engl R 54:518-20 My '32

Rossetti on the Cornish coast. Bookm (NY) 57:604-9 Ag '23

The Rossettis. *In* Dramatis personae. Indianapolis, Bobbs-Merrill, 1923. p118-31

Talbot, Ethel
Tennyson, or another? Acad 73:654 Jl 6 '07

Taylor, Anne Richards
The ballad-poems of Dante Gabriel Rossetti. Masters essay, Yale univ. 1931

Taylor, Bayard
The echo club, and other literary diversions. Boston, Osgood, 1876. p65-8

Taylor, Jeannette Stuart
Medievalism in Coleridge, Keats, Swinburne and Rossetti. Masters essay, Columbia univ. 1908

Temple, A. G.
The art of painting in the Queen's reign. London, Chapman and Hall, 1897. p113-23

Tennyson: and after? Fortn 53:623 My '90

Terry, Ellen
My children and I. McClure's Magazine 29:585-6 O '07

Thomas, William Cave
Pre-Raphaelitism tested by the principles of Christianity. London, Wertheim, Macintosh, and Hunt, 1860. [5]-41p

Thompson, Alexander Hamilton
The Rossettis. *In* C H E L vol XIII p123-32

Thomson, Cora Marguerite
The earlier phase of pre-Raphaelitism: an attempt to distinguish between pre-Raphaelitism and the later work of Rossetti. Masters essay, Univ. of California, 1909. 56ff

Tietz, Eva
Das malerische in Rossettis dichtung. Bei Anglia ns 39:278-306 D '27

Das malerische in Rossettis dichtung. Diss. Königsberg, 1925 [1927] 89p

Tirebuck, William E.
Dante Gabriel Rossetti. Art J 45:27-8 '83

Dante Gabriel Rossetti: his work and influence, including a brief survey of recent art tendencies. London, Stock, 1882. 63p

Tisdel, Frederick Monroe
Rossetti's "House of life." Mod Philol 15:65-84 S '17

Trent, William Peterfield
Introduction. *In* Rossetti, Dante Gabriel. Henry the leper, paraphrased by. . . Boston, Bibliophile society, 1905. vol II pv-xx
(467 copies only)

Trombly, Albert Edmund
Rossetti the poet, an appreciation. (Univ. of Texas Bulletin no 2060:Oct. 25 '20) Austin, Texas, Univ. of Texas [1920] 86p

Rossetti studies. So Atlan Q 18:211-21, 341-9 Jl, O '19; 19:67-80 Ja '20; 20:33-40 Ja '21

A translation of Rossetti's. Mod Lang N 38:116-18 F '23

Tucker, T. G.
The foreign debt of English literature. London, Bell, 1907. p190-2

Tuell, Anne Kimball
Mrs. Meynell and her literary generation. New York, Dutton [c1925]

Turner, Albert Morton
Rossetti's reading and his critical opinions. P M L A 42:465-91 Je '27

Two drawings by Rossetti. Nation (NY) 3:501-2 D 20 '66

Tyrrell, R. L.
A literary causerie. The growth of a poem. [Rossetti's revisions of "The Blessed Damozel."] Acad 70:356-8 Ap 14 '06

Ulmer, Hermann
Dante Gabriel Rossettis verstechnik. Bayreuth, Ellwanger, 1911. 112p bibl p7-8 Diss. München

Underwood, Eric
A short history of English painting. London, Faber and Faber [1933] p168-80

Unwin, T. Fisher
Mr. Arthur Symons's "D. G. Rossetti." Ath 1:712, 769 Je 11, 25 '10

Urech-Daysh, C.
Dante G. Rossetti. . . Basel, Hirzen [1916] 137p bibl p136-7 Thesis, Lausanne

Zur entstehung und entwicklung der neuen dekorativen kunst. Basler Nachrichten 10:29 '09

Van Roosbrocck, Gustave L.
Rossetti and Maeterlinck. Mod Lang N 34:439-41 N '19

The **Victorian** garden of song. Dial 19:238 N 1 '95

Villard, Léonie
The influence of Keats on Tennyson and Rossetti. . . Saint-Étienne, Mulcey, 1914. 94p Thesis, Paris

Vincent, E. R. P.
Two letters from Mary Shelley to Gabriele Rossetti. Mod Lang R 27:459-61 O '32

Vinciguerra, Mario
Il preraffaellismo inglese. Bologna, Zanichelli, 1924

Vitale, Zaira
Le modelle di D. G. Rossetti. Rivista d'Italia anno 8 vol 2:448-59 S '05

Waddington, Samuel
The sonnets of Rossetti. Acad 25:385 My 31 '84

Wagschal, Friedrich
E. B. Brownings "Sonnets from the Portuguese" und D. G. Rossettis "House of Life." Z F E U 13:207-17 '14

Waldschmidt, Wolfram
Dante Gabriel Rossetti, der maler und der dichter. Die anfänge der praeraphaelit. Jena, Diederichs, 1905. 163p

Walker, Elizabeth B.
The ballads of Dante Gabriel Rossetti. Citizen (Phila) 4:76-7 Je '98

Walker, Hugh
The age of Tennyson. (Handbooks of English literature) London, Bell, 1904. p240-4

The literature of the Victorian era. Cambridge, Univ. press, 1921. p490-501

Walker, Hugh and Walker, (Mrs) Hugh
Outlines of Victorian literature. Cambridge, England, Univ. press, 1919. p79-82

Waller, Ross Douglas
"The Blessed damozel." Mod Lang R 26:129-41 Ap '31

Rossetti family, 1824-1854. Manchester, Univ. press, 1932. xii,324p
(Rev in T L S My 19 '32 p364; W. Browne in Bookm (Lond) 82:108 My '32; B. J. Morse in Engl Stud 67:283-7

Waller, Ross Douglas—*Continued*
N '32; P. de Reul in English Studies
14:201-3 O '32; Oxford Magazine p843
Je 16 '32; an error corrected by R. D.
Waller in T L S D 1 '32 p923)

Wallerstein, Ruth C.
The Bancroft manuscripts of Rossetti's
sonnets. [With text of two hitherto
unpublished sonnets] Mod Lang N 44:
279-84 My '29

Personal experience in Rossetti's House
of life. P M L A 42:492-504 Je '27

Walter, Jakob
William Blakes nachleben in der englischen literatur des 19. und 20. jahrhunderts . . . Schaffhausen, Bachmann,
1927. viii,99p

Ward, Julius H.
Rossetti in poetry and art. American
Church Review 41:371-9 Ap '83

Ward, Thomas Humphry
Rossetti, Gabriel Charles Dante. *In* Men
of the reign. London, Routledge, 1885.
p773-4

Ware, Lena
Rossetti as a Dante scholar. Masters
essay, Northwestern Univ. 1928. 72ff

Watkin, Ralph Granger
Robert Browning and the English pre-
Raphaelites. Breslau, Fleischmann,
1905. Diss. Breslau

Watts-Dunton, Theodore
Aylwin. London, Hurst and Blackett,
1898
(Rev in Cosmopolis 12:391 N '98) [The
character of D'Arcy may have been
drawn from the life of Rossetti]

Dante Gabriel Rossetti. *In* Old familiar
faces. . . London, Jenkins, 1916. p69-
119

The life of D. G. Rossetti. Spec 76:596-7
Ap 25 '96

Mr. D. G. Rossetti. Ath 1:480-1 Ap 15
'82; *same*. Liv Age 153:504-6 My 27
'82

Rossettiana. A glimpse of Rossetti and
Morris at Kelmscott. Engl R 1:323-32
Ja '09

Rossetti's unpublished poems. Ath 1:683
My 23 '96

The truth about Rossetti. 19th Cent 13:
404-23 Mr '83

Waugh, Evelyn Arthur St. John
Dante Gabriel Rossetti; a centenary criti-
cism. Fortn ns 123:595-604 My '28
Rossetti; his life and works. London,
Duckworth, 1928. 232p
(Rev in T L S My 10 '28 p341-2; J.
Purves in T L S My 24 '28 p396; A.
Whitridge in Sat R Lit Jl 28 '28; N Y
Times Je 24 '28 p5; Books S 2 '31;
Sat R 145:499 Ap 21 '28; R. A. Taylor
in Spec 140:719-21 My 12 '28; R. Camp-
bell in Nat-Ath 43:212 My 19 '28; P.
Quennell in New Statesm 31:160-1 My
12 '28; note by E. Waugh in T L S
My 17 '28 p379)

Wedmore, Frederick
The poetry of Mr. Rossetti. St J ns 9:
31-40 Ap '72

Weigand, Wilhelm
Dante Gabriel Rossetti. Die Gegenwart
35:38-40 Ja 19 '89

Welby, Thomas Earle
Rossetti and his publisher. *In* Back
numbers. London, Constable, 1929.
p94-7

The Victorian romantics, 1850-70; the
early work of D. G. Rossetti, W. Morris, Burne-Jones, Swinburne. . . and
their associates. London, Howe, 1929.
ix-x,161p
(Rev in T L S N 14 '29 p919)

West, Geoffrey
Revaluations. Dante Gabriel Rossetti.
Outlook (Lond) 61:596-7 My 12 '28

Weygandt, Cornelius
Two pre-Raphaelite poets; William Morris and Dante Gabriel Rossetti. Bookn
24:687-90 Je '06

Whiting, Mary Bradford
Beata Beatrix. Temple 126:270-82 S '02
Dante and Rossetti. Congregational
Quarterly (Lond) Ap '29 p206-14

Whitley, W. T.
Arts and crafts at the Royal Academy.
International Studio 60:66-77 D '16

Whitmore, Mary
The ballad poetry of Dante Gabriel Rossetti. Masters essay, Univ. of Kansas,
1930. 112ff

Whitney, Elizabeth Boyce
The Oxford movement and its influence
on English poetry. Masters essay,
Univ. of Oklahoma, 1931

Wiegler, Paul
Guggum. *In* Genius in love and death.
Transl. by C. Raushenbush. London,
Boni, 1929. p226-36

Wilde, Oscar
The English Renaissance. Boston, Luce,
1906. p1-17

Wilenski, Reginald Howard
Masters of English painting. Boston,
Hale, Cushman and Flint [1934] p220-8
An outline of English painting. . . (Cri-
terion miscellany—no. 41) London,
Faber and Faber [1933] p62-4

Wiley, Edwin
Dante Gabriel Rossetti and the pre-
Raphaelites. *In* The old and new
renaissance; a group of studies in art
and letters. Nashville, Tenn. Publishing house of the M.E. Church, South,
1903

Wilkins, W.
Dante Rossetti's "Hand and Soul." Acad
21:323 My 6 '82

Williams, Stanley Thomas
Rossetti's damosels: Blessed and otherwise. Texas Review 6:247-53 Ap '21

Two poems by Rossetti. *In* Studies in Victorian literature. New York, Dutton [c1923] p183-98

Williamson, Claude C. H.
Rossetti. *In* Writers of three centuries, 1789-1914. Philadelphia, Jacobs [1915?] p255-8

Williamson, George Charles
Dante Gabriel Rossetti. *In* Murray Marks and his friends; a tribute of regard. London, Lane [1919] p51-83

Willoughby, Leonard Ashley
Dante Gabriel Rossetti and German literature. A public lecture, 1912. . . London, Frowde, 1912. 32p; *same in* Oxford lectures on literature. London, Oxford univ. press, 1924
(Noted in Acad 83:176 Ag 19 '12)

Wilmersdoerffer, A.
Dante Gabriel Rossetti und sein einfluss. Westermanns Illustrierte Deutsche Monatshefte 85:592-610 F '99

Wiltse, Ernestine
The life of Dante Gabriel Rossetti from 1862-1882. Masters essay, Syracuse Univ. 1926. 148ff

Winwar, Frances [pseud]
see Grebanier, Mrs. Frances [Vinciguerra]

Wise, Thomas James
A Rossetti ballad. T L S D 12 '29 p1058

Withers, Percy
Blake, Shields and Rossetti. T L S Ag 18 '27 p561

Wolff, Lucien
Le centenaire de Dante Gabriel Rossetti. . . Rossetti et le moyen-age. Revue A A 5:452-8 Je '28

Dante Gabriel Rossetti. Paris, Didier, 1934. 320p
(Rev by A. Brulé in Revue A A 12:154-6 '34; Lond Q R 159:557 '34; Notes & Q 167:70 Jl 28 '34; K. John in New Statesm p155-6 Ag 4 '34)

Wood, Charles James
Dante Gabriel Rossetti. And R 8:573-92 D '87

Wood, Esther
Dante Rossetti and the pre-Raphaelite movement. London, Sampson Low, Marston, 1894. xii,323p

(Rev by W. Sharp in Acad 46:72-3 Jl 28 '94; Sat R 77:557-8 My 26 '94; Nation (NY) 59:89-90 Ag 2 '94; Speaker 9:727-8 Je 30 '94; Book B ns 11:300-1 Jl '94; Studio 3:supplement viii My '94)

Wood, T. Martin
The drawings of D. G. Rossetti. (Modern master draughtsmen) London, Newnes, 1905. p7-18

The true Rossetti. International Studio 60:3-15 N '16

Woodberry, George Edward
Literary portrait of Rossetti. *In* Studies of a littérateur. New York, Harcourt, Brace, 1921. p61-5

The works of Rossetti. Descriptions of the [10] plates. Masters in Art 4:34-40 D '03

Worsfold, W. Basil
The poetry of D. G. Rossetti. 19th Cent 34:284-90 Ag '93; *same.* Ecl M 121:851-4 D '93

Wotton, Mabel E.
Dante Gabriel Rossetti. *In* Word portraits of famous writers. London, Bentley, 1887. p256-62

Wyzewa, Teodor de
Peintres de jadis et d'aujourd'hui. . . deux préraphaélites. . . Paris, Perrin, 1903

Yeats, William Butler
Four years, 1887-1891. Lond Merc 4:129-40, 259-70, 364-77 Je-Ag '21

Young, Edward
Art: its constitution and capacities. Bristol, Chilcott, 1854. 106p

Pre-Raffaellitism; or, A popular enquiry into some newly-asserted principles connected with the philosophy, poetry, religion, and revolution of art. London, Longman, Brown, Green, Longmans, and Roberts, 1857. [vii]-xv,317p
(Rev in Sat R 3:332-4 Ap 11 '57)

Zakrzewska, M.
Untersuchungen über D. G. Rossettis sonettenzyklus. "The House of Life." Ms Diss. Freiburg i. B. 1922

Robert Louis Stevenson

Robert Louis Stevenson

I. Chronological Outline

1850. Born, November 13, Edinburgh.

1878. An Inland Voyage.

1879. Edinburgh: Picturesque Notes.

1879. Travels With a Donkey in the Cévennes.

1881. Virginibus Puerisque and Other Papers.

1882. Familiar Studies of Men and Books.

1882. New Arabian Nights.

1883. Treasure Island.

1883. The Silverado Squatters.

1884. Admiral Guinea, by Stevenson and Henley.

1885. More New Arabian Nights. The Dynamiter, by Robert Louis Stevenson and Fanny Van de Grift Stevenson.

1885. Prince Otto.

1885. A Child's Garden of Verses.

1886. Strange Case of Dr. Jekyll and Mr. Hyde.

1886. Kidnapped: Being Memoirs of the Adventures of David Balfour.

1887. Underwoods.

1887. Memoir of Fleeming Jenkin.

1887. Memories and Portraits.

1887. The Merry Men and Other Tales and Fables.

1888. The Black Arrow.

1889. The Master of Ballantrae.

1889. The Wrong Box, by Stevenson and Osbourne.

1890. Ballads.

1892. The Wrecker, by Stevenson and Osbourne.

1892. A Foot-Note to History: Eight Years of Trouble in Samoa.

1892. Across the Plains: With Other Memories and Essays.

1893. Catriona, A Sequel to "Kidnapped"

1893. Island Nights' Entertainments.

1894. The Ebb-Tide, by Stevenson and Osbourne.

1894. Died, December 3, Samoa.

1895. The Amateur Emigrant. From the Clyde to Sandy Hook.

1896. In the South Seas.

1896. Weir of Hermiston. An Unfinished Romance.

1897. St. Ives. Being the Adventures of a French Prisoner in England.

Robert Louis Stevenson

II. Bibliographical Material

Adcock, Arthur St. John
Notes. *In* Robert Louis Stevenson: his work and his personality, ed. by A. St. John Adcock. London, Hodder and Stoughton, 1924. p242-6

Arnold, William Harris
My Stevensons. *In* Ventures in book collecting. New York, Scribner, 1923. p259-98; *same.* Scrib M 71:53-65 Ja '22

Baildon, Henry Bellyse
Bibliography. *In* Robert Louis Stevenson, a life study in criticism. London, Chatto and Windus, 1901. p235-8
Robert Louis Stevenson. Engl Stud 25:218-19 Jl '98

Balfour, (Sir) Graham
Chronological list of the writings of Robert Louis Stevenson. *In* The life of Robert Louis Stevenson. New York, Scribner, 1901. vol II p248-61

Black, George F.
List of works in the New York Public Library relating to Scotland. Part XI. Bulletin of the New York Public Library 18: 1562-9 '14

Brown, George Edward
A book of R. L. S. works, travels, friends, and commentators. London, Methuen [1919] vii,298p

[Carlton, William Newnham Chattin]
Unique; or, A description of a proof copy of The Beach of Falesá, containing over a hundred manuscript changes, by Robert Louis Stevenson. Chicago, Privately printed, 1914. 40p
(27 copies only)

Carré, Jean Marie
Bibliography. *In* La vie de Robert Louis Stevenson. Paris, Gallimard, 1929. 8th ed p[243]-55

Carter, John and Pollard, Graham
Robert Louis Stevenson. *In* An enquiry into the nature of certain nineteenth century pamphlets. London, Constable, 1934. p245-66

Christie, M. and W., firm, booksellers, London
Catalogue of important unpublished autograph letters . . . and the manuscript of Stevenson's unpublished play "Monmouth." [London, Clowes, 1922] 12p

Colvin, (Sir) Sidney
The "Vailima" Stevenson. T L S Je 28, Jl 12 '23 p440, 472

Ellwanger, W. D.
Some of the rarer Stevensons, together with a list of Stevenson's contributions to English magazines, 1871-1891. Book B ns 12: 493-6, 820 O '95, Ja '96

Gosse, (Sir) Edmund William
Bibliographical notes. *In* The complete works of Robert Louis Stevenson. (Pentland ed.) London, Cassell, 1906-1907. 20 vols

Grolier Club, New York
First editions of the works of Robert Louis Stevenson, 1850-1894, with other Stevensonia exhibited at the Grolier club, November 5-28, 1914. New York, Grolier club, 1914. v-vi, 74p

Hamilton, Clayton
Bibliographical appendix. *In* Pinero, (Sir) Arthur Wing. Robert Louis Stevenson as a dramatist. Columbia Univ. Dramatic Museum Publications ser 1 no 4:73-8 '14. New York, Printed for the Dramatic Museum of Columbia Univ. 1914

Harvard University. Library. Widener Collection
A catalogue of the books and manuscripts of Robert Louis Stevenson in the library of the late Harry Elkins Widener, with a memoir by A. S. W. Rosenbach. Philadelphia, Privately printed [by E. Stern and Co.] 1913. xi, 266p
(150 copies only)

Hill, Walter M., firm, bookseller, Chicago
Robert Louis Stevenson; catalogue . . . of first editions . . . Chicago, Hill, 1916. 88p

Kebler, Leonard
The first edition of "Kidnapped." T L S Je 26 '24 p404

The late Robert Louis Stevenson's works. List of first editions. Scottish Notes & Queries 8:142 F '95

Lee, Albert
A unique bit of Stevensoniana. Book B ns 14:51-3 F '97

Literary Anniversary Club of San Francisco, California
Robert Louis Stevenson; catalogue of the Stevenson exhibition . . . [San Francisco, California, 1932] 22p

Livingston, Luther Samuel
The first books of some English authors. V. Robert Louis Stevenson. Bookm (NY) 10:437-40 Ja '00
The Harry Elkins Widener Stevenson collection. [np 1914?] 10p (50 copies only)

Lord, Isabel Ely
The best editions of Robert Louis Stevenson. Bulletin of Bibliography 3:11-13 Ap '02

McCutcheon, George Barr
The renowned collection of first editions of Thomas Hardy, Rudyard Kipling, Robert Louis Stevenson. . . New York, American Art Association, Inc. [1925] 80 leaves

News for bibliophiles [first editions] Nation (NY) 93:442 N 9 '11

News for bibliophiles ["Penny Whistle" pamphlet] Nation (NY) 96:126 F 6 '13

North, Ernest Dressel
A bibliography of Robert Louis Stevenson [first editions] Bookm (NY) 4:81-5 S '96

Northrup, Clark Sutherland
A register of bibliographies of the English language and literature. New Haven, Yale univ. press, 1925. p366-7

Notes on sales. T L S Ag 3 '22 p512

Prideaux, William Francis
A bibliography of the works of Robert Louis Stevenson. London, Hollings, 1903. xvi, 302p (600 copies only)
(Rev in Acad 65:327 O 3 '03; Ath 2:482 O 10 '03)
A bibliography of the works of Robert Louis Stevenson. . . A new and revised edition, ed. and supplemented by Mrs. Luther Samuel Livingston. . . London, Hollings, 1917. viii, 400p
The Widener-Stevenson collection. Notes & Q 11th ser 9:301-2 Ap 18 '14

The **quest** for Stevensoniana. Lit 9:86 Jl 27 '01

Quinn, John
The library of John Quinn. . . New York, Anderson galleries, 1924. part V p892-911

Radin, Herman T.
The Stevenson sale. Miscellany (Kansas City) 1:60-2 '14

Rosenbach, A. S. W.
see Harvard University. Library. Widener Collection

Safford, (Mrs) Clare (Wode)
Books from the library of R. L. Stevenson at Vailima . . . together with selections from two New York libraries. . . New York, Anderson Galleries, 1926. 62p

Slater, John Herbert
Early editions. . . London, Kegan Paul, Trench, and Trübner, 1894. p269-79
Robert Louis Stevenson; a bibliography of his complete works. (Bibliographers' handbooks [no 1]) London, Bell, 1914. v-vii, 45p
(Rev in Spec 112:617 Ap 11 '14)

Some rare Stevenson "finds." Bookman's Journal 3:111 D 10 '20

Sotheby, firm, auctioneers, London
Catalogue of valuable books . . . an extensive collection of the works of Robert Louis Stevenson. . . [London, Sotheby, 1921?] 86p

Stevenson and Shelley [sales] T L S Jl 20 '22 p480

[**Stevenson** first editions] Bookman's Journal 7:195-6 Mr '23

Stevenson in American periodicals. Book B ns 12:497 O '95

Stevensoniana. . . [sales] Ath 2:181-2 Ag 8 '14

Stevenson's "Records of a Family of Engineers." [note on sale] T L S Ag 4 '27 p536

Williams, (Mrs) Ignatius
Catalogue of books. . . Stevensoniana. . . property of Lloyd Osbourne. Auction by Sotheby, February, 1923. London [1923]

Williamson, George Millar
Catalogue of a collection of the books of Robert Louis Stevenson in the library of George M. Williamson, Grand View on Hudson. Jamaica, New York, Marion press, 1901. [96]p
Catalogue of a collection of the books of Robert Louis Stevenson in the library of George M. Williamson, Grand View on Hudson. Jamaica, New York, Marion press, 1903. 52p

Winship, George Parker
A rare Stevenson item collated ["Confessions of a Unionist"] Bookman's Journal 7:11 O '22

Wood, Arnold
Robert Louis Stevenson. First editions and some early pamphlets in the library of Arnold Wood. New York, Privately printed, 1898. 50p

Woods, George Benjamin
[Bibliography] *In* Poetry of the Victorian period. New York, Scott, Foresman [c1930] p1052-6

Robert Louis Stevenson

III. Biographical and Critical Material

Adair, Ward William
Stevenson's "Dr. Jekyll and Mr. Hyde"—
The fact of the dual nature. *In* Vital
messages in modern books. New York,
Doran [c1926] p1-11

Adams, P.
R. L. Stevenson. Die Bücherwelt 24:155-9
'27

Adcock, Arthur St. John
The man behind the books. *In* Robert
Louis Stevenson: his work and his
personality, ed. by A. St. John Adcock. London, Hodder and Stoughton, 1924. p 184-98

Notes. *In* Robert Louis Stevenson: his
work and his personality, ed. by A. St.
John Adcock. London, Hodder and
Stoughton, 1924. p229-51

The real Stevenson. Bookm (Lond) 67:
12-17 O '24

Stevenson and the juvenile drama.
Bookm (Lond) 65:9-12 O '23

Stevenson and the juvenile drama. *In*
Robert Louis Stevenson: his work and
his personality, ed. by A. St. John
Adcock. London, Hodder and Stoughton,
1924. p58-68

Alberts, Hermann
Der optimismus des englischen dichters
Robert Louis Stevenson. Marburg,
Hamel, 1928. 125p Thesis, Marburg

Allehoff, Julia Elizabeth
The influence of the Paston letters on
Stevenson's "The Black Arrow." Masters
essay, Univ. of Washington, 1930. 63ff

Allen, James Lane
Dr. Jekyll and Dr. Grimshawe. Critic
(NY) 9:17 Jl 10 '86

Allen, Maryland
South sea memories of R. L. S. Bookm
(NY) 43:591-603 Ag '16

Allison, Young E.
Robert Louis Stevenson. So M 5:599-
601 Mr '95

The American home of "R. L. S." National Magazine 56:77 O '27

Anderson, David
The enchanted galleon. [San Francisco,
Windsor press] 1930. 18p (Privately
printed for G. D. Merner . . . in appreciation of a Stevenson night . . . Rox-
burghe club of San Francisco, March
10, 1930. 60 copies)

Archer, William
In Memoriam. R. L. S. New Review
12:89-97 Ja '95
R. L. Stevenson: his style and his
thought. Critic (NY) 8:7-9, 19-20 Ja 2,
9 '86; Time (Lond) 2d ser 2:581-91
N '85
Robert Louis Stevenson at "Skerryvore."
Critic (NY) 11:225-7 N 5 '87

Ardagh, J.
Allusions in Stevenson. Notes & Q 153:
16 Jl 2 '27

Armour, Margaret
see Macdougall, Margaret Armour

Arnold, William Harris
My Stevensons. Scrib M 71:53-65 Ja '22;
also in Ventures in book collecting.
London, Scribner, 1923. p259-98

Arns, Karl
Robert Louis Stevenson. Der Gral 22:
367-70 '28

Assmann, P. W.
Robert Louis Stevenson. Boekenschouw
21:349-59 D '27

The author of "Dr. Jekyll." Book B ns 5:
59-60 Mr '88

Avellanus, Arcadius [pseud]
see Mogyoróssy, Árkád

Axson, Stockton
Approaches and reactions in six nineteenth
century fictionists. *In* The Rice Institute
Pamphlet. Houston, Texas, 1916. vol III
p101-24

Aydelotte, Frank
Robert Louis Stevenson darkening coun-
sel. *In* Oxford stamp, and other essays. Oxford, Milford, 1917. p149-73;
also in Engl J 1:340-50 Je '12

Babcock, Charlotte Farrington
Stevenson; poem. Educa 47:147 N '26

Baildon, Henry Bellyse
Robert Louis Stevenson; essayist, novelist and poet. Engl Stud 25:218-45 Jl
'98; 26:19-41, 27:399-411 '99; 28:246-93
'00; *same*. Ecl M 133:123-40 Jl '99;
same. Liv Age 221:671-88 Je 10 '99

Robert Louis Stevenson; a life study in
criticism. London, Chatto and Windus,
1901. xi,244p bibl p235-8
(Rev in Ath 1:431-2 Ap 6 '01; Lit 8:221
Mr 23 '01; Dial 30:345-6 My 16 '01; Sat
R 92:401 S 28 '01; G. K. Chesterton
in Five types. . . New York, Chatterton
[191-?] p35-45; *same*. Varied types.
New York, Dodd, Mead, 1909. p95-
105)

Baildon, Henry Bellyse—*Continued*
Some recollections of Robert Louis Stevenson. Temple 104:325-33 Mr '95; *same*. Liv Age 205:219-25 Ap 27 '95

Bailey, (Mrs) H. Somerville
A note on Robert Louis Stevenson, 1850-1894. London, Priory press, 1912

Bailey, J. C.
Stevenson's letters. Fortn ns 67:91-103 Ja '00

Bainville, Jacques
Vie romanesque d'un romancier. *In* Au seuil du siècle; études critiques. Paris, Editions du Capitole [1927] 4th ed p271-85

Baird, Mabel Anne
The mirror of romance in Stevenson's tales. Masters essay, Univ. of California, 1920. 140ff

Baker Cottage at Saranac Lake. Notes & Q 148:271 Ap 18 '25

Balfour (Sir) Graham
"Dumlicide." T L S Je 2 '21 p356

The life of Robert Louis Stevenson. . . London, Methuen, 1901. 2 vols [v]-x, 216p; 239p
(Rev in Out 69:689-92 N 16 '01; W. P. Trent in Book B ns 23:389-90 D '01; Sat R 93:supp v F 15 '02; Literary World (Lond) ns 64:291-2 O 25 '01; Speaker ns 5:103-4 O 26 '01; W. R. Nicoll in Bookm (Lond) 21:58-9 N '01; Church Q R 54:143-64 Ap '02; W. E. Henley in Pall Mall Magazine 25:505-14 D '01; *same in* Notorious literary attacks, ed. by A. Mordell. New York, Boni and Liveright, 1926. p232-55; Ath 2:549-50 O 26 '01; Blackw 170:613-23 N '01; R. Smith in Dial 31:356-9 N 16 '01; W. R. Nicoll in Bookm (NY) 14: 496-7 Ja '02; Overland Monthly ns 39: 560-2 Ja '02; Nation (NY) 74:54-5 Ja 16 '02; C. S. Northup in Dial 59:561-4 D 9 '15; J. B. Gilder in Critic (NY) 40:254-5 Mr '02; noted in Bookm (NY) 11:313-14 Je '00)

The life of Robert Louis Stevenson. . . New York, Scribner, 1915. abridged ed rev and illustrated 364p

Misprints of R. L. Stevenson. T L S F 2 '22 p77

Balfour, Marie C. (ed)
Mrs. M. I. Stevenson: letters from Samoa, 1891-95. New York, Scribner, 1906. x, 340p

Ballad poetry. Edin R 197:319 Ap '03

Barnett, David
A Stevenson study; "Treasure Island". . . Edinburgh, Macdonald, 1924. 30p

Barnouw, A.
Uit "De verzentuin van een kind." Groot-Nederland 2:360-5 S '11

Barratt, James
The essays of Robert Louis Stevenson. New Century Review 7:47-58 Ja '00

Barrie, (Sir) James Matthew
R. L. S. Liv Age 212:152-4 Ja 9 '97
Robert Louis Stevenson. *In* An Edinburgh eleven; pencil portraits from college life. London, The British Weekly, 1889. p97-108
Scotland's lament; poem. Bookm (Lond) 7:108 Ja '95; *same*. Bookm (Lond) 21:12 O '01; *same*. McClure's Magazine 4:286-8 F '95

Baxter, Charles
R. L. S. and L. J. R. T.P.'s Weekly 18: 86 Jl 21 '11

Bay, Jens Christian
Echoes of Robert Louis Stevenson. . . Chicago, Hill, 1920. 93p
(500 copies only)
(Rev in Ath 2:650 N 12 '20)

Bayne, Thomas
"Famous Scots." Notes & Q 9th ser 9:161-2 Mr 1 '02

Beach, Joseph Warren
The sources of Stevenson's "Bottle imp." Mod Lang N 25:12-18 Ja '10

Beeching, H. C.
Memories and portraits. Acad 33:1 Ja 7 '88
The works of Robert Louis Stevenson. *In* Robert Louis Stevenson: his work and his personality, ed. by A. St. John Adcock. London, Hodder and Stoughton, 1924. p93-111

Beer, Thomas
Frank Swinnerton. Bookm (NY) 58: 405-7 D '23

Beerbohm, Max
A puzzle in literary drama. Sat R 91: 600-1 My 11 '01

Bell, Howard Wilford
An unpublished chapter in the life of Robert Louis Stevenson. Pall Mall Magazine 24:267-71 '01

Bell, Mackenzie
Robert Louis Balfour Stevenson. *In* Half-hours with representative novelists of the nineteenth century. London, Routledge, 1927. vol III p312-13

Bennett, James O'Donnell
Stevenson's "Treasure Island." *In* Much loved books. . . London, Hutchinson, 1928. p15-22

Bensly, Edward
Allusions in Stevenson. Notes & Q 153: 16 Jl 2 '27
R. L. Stevenson problems. Notes & Q 163:316 O 29 '32

Benson, Edward Frederic
The myth of Robert Louis Stevenson. Lond Merc 12:268-83, 372-84 Jl, Ag '25

Binz, Arthur Friedrich
Robert Louis Stevenson. Orplid 3:71-7 '26
Von aufbruch und untergang. Aufsätze über dichter und dichtungen. Heidelberg, Meister, 1927. 95p

Zwei englische erzähler: R. L. Stevenson und J. Conrad. Orplid p95 '27

Biographical notes. McClure's Magazine 2:235 F '94

Biography with warts only. Lit Digest 84:28-9 Mr 28 '25

Black, Margaret Moyes
Robert Louis Stevenson. (Famous Scots ser) Edinburgh, Oliphant, Anderson, and Ferrier [pref 1898] 159p (Rev in Literary World (Lond) ns 58: 239 O 7 '98; Ath 2:446-7 O 1 '98; Bookm (NY) 8:592-3 F '99; Acad 54: 292 S 24 '98; Lit 3:316 O 8 '98; Bookm (Lond) 15:16 O '98)

Blackburn, Vernon
Mr. George Moore on Stevenson. Acad 51:476 My 1 '97

Blake, Rodney
Stevenson at Butaritari. Biblio 4:767-71 Ja '25

Bland, Henry Meade
Stevenson's California. San Jose, California, Pacific short story club [c1924] 9-36p

Bliss, William
Mr. Freeman and Robert Louis Stevenson. Lond Merc 6:303-4 Jl '22

Boase, Frederic
Stevenson, Robert Louis. *In* Modern English biography. Truro, Netherton & Worth, 1901. vol III p744-5

Bok, Edward William
The playful Stevenson. Scrib M 82:179-80 Ag '27

Bonet-Maury, Gaston
R. L. Stevenson voyageur et romancier. (1850-1894) R Deux Mondes S 1 '02 p164-201

Bonnerot, Louis
Quelques notes sur l'exotisme de Stevenson. Revue A A 5:439-51 Je '28

Boodle, Adelaide A.
R. L. S. and his sine qua non, flashlights from Skerryvore, by the gamekeeper... New York, Scribner, 1926. x, 168p; *also in* Cornhill ns 54:129-38 F '23; ns 55:732-41 D '23; ns 56:295-301 Mr '24; ns 56:513-20 My '24; ns 59:355-67 S '25 (Rev in Sat R Lit 3:39 Ag 14 '26)

The Bookman (Lond)
Robert Louis Stevenson. A Bookman extra number, 1913. London, Hodder & Stoughton. [1913] vii, 11-207p [To some extent an anthology compiled from back numbers of the Bookman]

Borchard, Ella H.
Stevenson's message to his age as it appears in his essays. Bachelor's essay, Univ. of Buffalo, 1924

[Borglum, Gutzon (John Gutzon de la Mothe)]
[Memorial tablet by G. Borglum] Cur Opin 60:47 Ja '16

Bosdari, A.
Robert Louis Stevenson. Nuova Antol 4th ser 82:601-18 Ag 16 '99

Bowker, R. R.
London as a literary centre. Harper M 77:15-16 Je '88

Boyd, Ernest Augustus
Readers and writers. Ind 115:714 D 19 '25

Bradley, Cornelius Beach
Stevenson and California. [Berkeley, 1909] 8p; *same in* Univ. of California Chronicle 11:114-21 Ap '09; *also in* Sierra Club Bulletin 8:110-17 Je '11

Braybrooke, Patrick
Treasure Island. *In* Great children in literature. London, Rivers, 1929. p257-68

Bremner, George St. G.
Robert Louis Stevenson. Scottish Notes and Queries 2d ser 1:63 O '99

Breuer, Wilhelm
Über R. L. Stevensons impressionistische technik. Göttingen, 1922. 86p MS. diss. Göttingen

Bridges, Robert
Robert Louis Stevenson. *In* The Columbia university course in literature. New York, Columbia univ. press, 1929. vol XV p252-9

Robert Louis Stevenson. *In* Warner, C. D. (ed) Library of the world's best literature. . . Memorial ed. New York, Hill [c1902] vol XXXV p13927-35

Brodribb, C. W.
Ben Gunn and Caliban. Notes & Q 156:46 Ja 19 '29

[Brown, Alice]
Robert Louis Stevenson, a study by A. B., with a prelude and a postlude by L[ouisa] I[mogen] G[uiney]. Boston, Copeland and Day, 1895. 46p (250 copies only)

Brown, George Edward
A book of R. L. S.; works, travels, friends, and commentators. New York, Scribner [1919] vii, 298p (Articles arranged in encyclopedic form)

Brown, Levi Ames
The personal essays of Robert Louis Stevenson. Masters essay, Univ. of North Carolina, 1911. 16ff

Brown, Vincent
Stevenson looks in. Acad 58:295-6 Ap 7 '00

Bryce, Catherine Turner
Robert Louis Stevenson reader. New York, Scribner, 1911. vii, 88p

Buchan, John
The country of Kidnapped. Liv Age 217:687-8 Je 4 '98; Acad 53:502-3, 612 My 7, Je 4 '98

Buell, Llewellyn Morgan
Eilean Earraid: the beloved isle of Robert Louis Stevenson. Scrib M 71:184-95 F '22

Bugbee, Lucius H.
Stevenson and his gospel of cheerful living. Meth R 89:916-25 N '07

Bullough, Geoffrey
The trend of modern poetry. Edinburgh, Oliver and Boyd, 1934. p8-9

Bunson, Marie von
Robert Louis Stevenson und seine schule. Das Litterarische Echo 1 no 14:887-92 Ap 15 '99

Burgess, Gelett
An interview with Mrs. Robert Louis Stevenson. Bookm (NY) 8:23-5 S '98

Burns, Shirley
The girl to whom Robert Louis Stevenson gave his birthday. Ladies Home Journal 32:19 Ap '15

Burriss, Eli Edward
The classical culture of Robert Louis Stevenson. Classical Journal 20:271-9 F '25

Burton, John W.
Robert Louis Stevenson and missions. Missionary Review 50:761-2 O '27

Burton, Richard
Robert Louis Stevenson. *In* Literary likings. Boston, Copeland and Day, 1898. p3-34

Stevenson. *In* Masters of the English novel. . . New York, Holt, 1909. p299-312

Stevenson's prayer book. *In* Little essays in literature and life. New York, Century, 1914. p269-81; *also in* No Am 189:869-76 Je '09

Bush, Bertha Evangeline
Story of Robert Louis Stevenson. (Instructor literature ser) Dansville, New York, Owen, n.d.

Campbell, Killis
Poe, Stevenson, and Béranger. Dial 47: 374-5 N 16 '09

Candler, Beatrice Post
Stevenson and Henley. Putnam's Magazine 7:367-8 D '09

The career of the novel. Puritan 6:343 Jl '99

Cargill, Alexander
The man of letters [Robert Louis Stevenson] Borderland Ja '95 p12-16

Carman, Bliss
A seamark; a threnody for Robert Louis Stevenson. Boston, Copeland and Day, 1895. [7-16]p

Carnall, Elizabeth E.
R. L. Stevenson as a critic of his contemporaries. Masters essay, Columbia univ. 1913

Carothers, Alva
Road of loving hearts. Saint Nicholas 54:14-18 N '26

Carr, Joseph William Comyns
A younger generation. *In* Some eminent Victorians. . . London, Duckworth, 1908. p215-19
(Rev by P. F. Bicknell in Dial 46:134-5 Mr 1 '09)

Carré, Jean Marie
The frail warrior [a life of Robert Louis Stevenson] transl. from the French by Eleanor Hard. New York, Coward, McCann, 1930. xii, 297p [Translation of: La vie de Robert Louis Stevenson] (Rev in T L S O 15 '31 p797; Quar R 256:410-11 Ap '31)

R. L. Stevenson et la France. (Mélanges . . . Baldensperger) Paris, Champion, 1930. vol I p105-20

Robert Louis Stevenson, the frail warrior. London, N. Douglas, 1931. xii,297p [American edition has title The frail warrior]

. . . La vie de Robert Louis Stevenson. . . (Vies des hommes illustres no 28) Paris, Gallimard, 1929, 8th ed 258p bibl p[243]-255

Carrington, James Beebee
Along the route of Stevenson's inland voyage. Book B ns 25:229-32 O '02

Another glimpse of R. L. S. Scrib M 82:180-3 Ag '27

Christmas at Silverado. Mentor 16:39-40 D '28

A visit to Stevenson's Silverado. Lamp 29:7-18 Ag '04

Cather, (Mrs) Katherine Dunlop
Velvet coat. *In* Younger days of famous writers. New York, Century [c1925] p207-34

Caufield, Sister Dolorosa
Craftsmanship of the short story as revealed by Stevenson in his essays. Masters essay, Univ. of Notre Dame, 1929. 28ff

Cecchi, Emilio
Il vero Stevenson. La Tribuna (Rome) Ag 20 '20

Chalmers, Stephen
Enchanted cigarettes; or, Stevenson stories that might have been. . . Boston, Houghton, Mifflin, 1917. vii, 43p

Letter on "The Bottle Imp." . . . Munsey's Magazine 61:633-5 S '17

The man in Portsmouth square. Overland Monthly ns 88:14 Ja '30

The Penny Piper of Saranac; an episode in Stevenson's life. . . With preface by Lord Guthrie. Boston, Houghton, Mifflin, 1916. xviii, 3-64p [First published in Out 102:314-20 O 12 '12] (Rev in Out 114:252-3 O 4 '16)

Chalmers, William P.
Charakteristische eigenschaften von R. L. Stevensons stil. (Marburger studien zur englischen philologie. Heft 4) Marburg, Elwert, 1903. 56p Diss. Marburg

Chamberlain, Essie
A Stevenson essay in a junior class [report of class discussion] Engl J 14: 790-5 D '25

Champion, Pierre
Marcel Schwob et Stevenson. Revue Universelle 27:528-41 D 1 '26

Chapin, Edward Whitman
Robert Louis Stevenson. *In* Evenings with Shakespeare, and other essays. Cambridge, Mass. Riverside press, 1911. p198-214

Chapman, Edward Mortimer
The newer fiction. *In* English literature in account with religion, 1800-1900. Boston, Houghton, Mifflin, 1910. p540-4

Chapman, John Jay
Robert Louis Stevenson. *In* Emerson and other essays. New York, Moffat, Yard, 1909. rev. ed. p215-47

Chapman, Livingston
The Stevenson memorial [at Saranac Lake, N.Y.] National Magazine 54:254 Ja '26

Charlesworch, Hector
Robert Louis Stevenson. Canadian Magazine 5:27-32 My '95

Charteris, (Sir) Evan Edward
The life and letters of Sir Edmund Gosse. London, Heinemann [1931] passim

Chesterton, Gilbert Keith
Break-up of the compromise. *In* The Victorian age in literature. New York, Holt [1913] p243-9

On R. L. S. *In* Generally speaking; a book of essays. London, Methuen [1928] p235-44

On the standardization of Stevenson. *In* All I survey. . . London, Methuen [1933] p6-10

Robert Louis Stevenson. . . London, Hodder and Stoughton [1927] vii-viii, 11-259p
(Rev by H. E. Woodbridge in Yale R ns 18:401-2 D '28; T L S D 8 '27 p928; C. Aiken in New Repub 54:169 Mr 21 '28; A Whitridge in Sat R Lit 4:864 My 12 '28; Dial 84:526 Je '28; S. A. Coblentz in Bookm (NY) 67:314-15 My '28; R. A. Taylor in Spec 140:21-2 Ja 7 '28; M. McLaren in Lond Merc 17:595-6 Mr '28; F. Swinnerton in Books Ap 1 '28 p7; H. I'A. Fausset in Bookm (Lond) 73:227-8 Ja '28; J. Panhuysen in Boekzaal S 1 '28)

Stevenson. *In* Varied types. New York, Dodd, Mead, 1903. p97-105; *also in* Twelve types. London, Humphreys, 1903. p107-20
(Rev in Literary World (Lond) ns 66: 524-5 D 19 '02)

Chevalley, Abel
Le roman anglais de notre temps. London, Oxford, 1921. p113-20

Chislett, William, jr.
Stevenson and the classics. J Engl & Germ Philol 15:267-81 Jl '16

Chrétien, L. E.
La vocation de Robert-Louis Stevenson; étude de psychologie littéraire. [Paris, Librairie Hachette] 1930. 370p Thesis, Paris

The "Christmas sermon" twenty years after. Scrib M 44:761-2 D '08

Chubb, Edwin Watts
Stevenson at Vailima. *In* Stories of authors, British and American. New York, Macmillan, 1926. p214-20

Churchill, William
Stevenson in the South sea. McClure's Magazine 4:278-85 F '95

The "Cigarette" and "Arethusa" of Stevenson's "An Inland Voyage." Bookm (NY) 7:472-6 Ag '98

Clapp, Edwin Roosa
English literary criticism, 1830-1890. . . Harvard univ. summaries of theses. . . Cambridge, Mass. 1931. p215-18

Clare, Maurice
A day with Stevenson. (Days with the great writers) London, Hodder & Stoughton, 1910. 44p

Clark, Evert Mordecai
The kinship of Hazlitt and Stevenson. Texas Studies in English 4:97-114 Mr 15 '24

Clark, John Scott
Robert Louis Balfour Stevenson. *In* A study of English and American writers. New York, Row, Peterson [c1916] p624-34

Clark, William Fordyce
"R. L. S. in the far north." *In* The Shetland sketch-book; folk-lore, legend, humour, incident. . . Edinburgh, Oliver and Boyd, 1930. p113-25

Clarke, W. E.
Robert Louis Stevenson in Samoa. Yale R ns 10:275-96 Ja '21

Claxton, A. E.
Stevenson as I knew him in Samoa. Chamb J 7th ser 12:627-30 S 2 '22

Clemens, Will M.
Stevenson at the Golden Gate. National Magazine 12:296-9 Jl '00

Clift, Denison Halley
"To remember Stevenson"; story. Saint Nicholas 43:290-9 F '16

Coates, Florence Earle
The burial of Robert Louis Stevenson at Samoa; poem. Out 69:137 S 14 '01

Colburn, Frona Eunice Wait (Smith) (Mrs. Frederick H. Colburn)
The women's side of the Robert L. Stevenson cult. Overland Monthly ns 88:51 F '30

Colby, F. M.
A debated charm. Bookm (NY) 14:620-1 F '02

Collins, Charles W.
To R. L. S.; poem. Book B ns 23:388 D '01

Collins, John Churton
Stevenson's letters. *In* Ephemera critica. New York, Dutton, 1902. p165-71

Collins, Joseph
The doctor looks at biography. New York, Doran [c 1925] p140-6

Colvin, (Sir) Sidney
Box Hill and its memories. Scrib M 60:197-8 Ag '16

More letters of Mrs. R. L. Stevenson. Scrib M 75:408-20 Ap '24

Robert Louis Stevenson. Royal Institution of Great Britain. Proceedings. 20:33-53 F 6 '11

Robert Louis Stevenson. *In* Dict N B vol XVIII p1132-41

Robert Louis Stevenson. *In* Memories & notes of persons & places. New York, Scribner, 1921. p98-152

Robert Louis Stevenson and Henry James. Scrib M 75:315-26 Mr '24

Robert Louis Stevenson at Hampstead. *In* The Hampstead annual. London, 1902. p144-54

Sir Sidney Colvin in Stevenson's defense. [A reply to G. S. Hellman's Stevenson myth in Cent 105:240-52 D '22] Liv Age 316:181-2 Ja 20 '23

Some personal recollections. Scrib M 67:338-54 Mr '20

Stevensoniana. Scrib M 52:593-606 N '12

When Stevenson was young. *In* Robert Louis Stevenson: his work and his personality, ed. by A. St. John Adcock. London, Hodder and Stoughton, 1924. p8-10

Colvin, (Sir) Sidney and others (ed)
The "Vailima" Stevenson. T L S Je 28 Jl 12 '23

Compton-Rickett, Arthur
Robert Louis Stevenson. *In* The vagabond in literature. London, Dent, 1906. p117-38

Copeland, C. T.
Robert Louis Stevenson. Atlan 75:537-46 Ap '95

Cordell, Richard Albert
The philosophy of life of Robert Louis Stevenson as revealed in his essays, letters, and prayers. Masters essay, Indiana Univ. 1925. 109ff

Cornford, Leslie Cope
Robert Louis Stevenson (Modern English writers) Edinburgh, Blackwood, 1899. vi,200p
(Rev in Book B ns 21:129 S '00; Nation (NY) 70:300 Ap 19 '00; A. Macdonell in Bookm (Lond) 17:86 D '99; noted in Lit 5:611 D 23 '99)

C[otton] J. S.
R. L. Stevenson [obituary] Acad 46:533-4 D 22 '94

Cougnenc, Lucienne H.
Francois Villon d'après Robert-Louis Stevenson et D. B. Wyndham Lewis. Masters essay, Columbia univ. 1933

Cowell, Henry J.
Robert Louis Stevenson and missions. Holborn Review ns 11:81-95 Ja '20

Uit het leven van R. L. Stevenson. Buiten p355-6 Jl '31

Crawshaw, Edith A. H.
"R. L. S." and music. Musical Times 73:705-7 Ag 1 '32

The **Crime** of Robert Louis Stevenson. Munsey's Magazine 60:552-5 My '17

Crockett, S. R.
The apprenticeship of Robert Louis Stevenson. *In* Robert Louis Stevenson. A Bookman (Lond) extra number, 1913. London, Hodder & Stoughton [1913] p67-72; *from* Bookm (Lond) 3:179-81 Mr '93

The apprenticeship of Robert Louis Stevenson. *In* Robert Louis Stevenson: his work and his personality, ed. by A. St. John Adcock. London, Hodder and Stoughton, 1924. p73-83

Mr. Stevenson's books. Bookm (Lond) 7:109-11 Ja '95

Robert Louis Stevenson. McClure's Magazine 4:288 F '95

Stevenson's books. *In* Robert Louis Stevenson. A Bookman (Lond) extra number, 1913. London, Hodder & Stoughton [1913] p155-9

Stevenson's books. *In* Robert Louis Stevenson: his work and his personality, ed. by A. St. John Adcock. London, Hodder and Stoughton, 1924. p118-27

Stevenson's letters. *In* Robert Louis Stevenson: his work and his personality, ed. by A. St. John Adcock. London, Hodder and Stoughton, 1924. p86-90

Cruse, Amy
Kidnapped. Catriona. *In* English literature through the ages. Beowulf to Stevenson. New York, Stokes [1914] p565-71

Robert Louis Stevenson. New York, Stokes [1915] ix, 13-190p
(Rev by C. S. Northup in Dial 59:561-4 D 9 '15)

Robert Louis Stevenson. *In* Boys and girls who became famous. New York, Harcourt, Brace, 1929. p133-42

Cunliffe, John William
English literature during the last half century. New York, Macmillan, 1919. p83-96

Late Victorian novelists. *In* Leaders of the Victorian revolution. New York, Appleton-Century [c1934] p284-90

Robert Louis Stevenson. *In* English literature during the last half-century. New York, Macmillan, 1923. 2d ed. rev. p87-100

Cunningham, Alison
Cummy's diary: a diary kept by R. L. Stevenson's nurse, Alison Cunningham, while travelling with him on the continent during 1863. With a pref. and notes by Robert T. Skinner. London, Chatto and Windus, 1926. xvi, 191p
(Rev in T L S O 14 '26 p692; T. Moult in Bookm (Lond) 71:126-7 N '26)

Dale, Dorothy F.
A comment and questionnaire on "An Inland Voyage" and "Travels with a Donkey." London, Pitman, 1927. 32p

Dalgleish, John
New lights on Stevenson. Outlook (Lond) 2:304-5 O 8 '98

Daplyn, A. J.
Robert Louis Stevenson at Barbizon. Chamb J 7th ser 7:525-8 Jl 14 '17

Dark, Sidney
Robert Louis Stevenson. . . London, Hodder and Stoughton [1931] vii,310p (Rev in T L S O 15 '31 p797; A. M. Mackenzie in New Statesm & Nation ns 2:xxviii D 5 '31; O. M. Green in Sat R 152:629 N 14 '31)

Dasent, Arthur Irwin
Herbert Spencer and R. L. Stevenson in Piccadilly. T L S O 28 '20 p702-3

Davidson, Mary Richmond
Sire de Maletroit's door; a dramatization of Robert Louis Stevenson's story of the same name . . . Boston, Baker [c 1927] 20p

Davies, Ada Hilton
Poet's tree. Sunset 60:37 F '28

Davies, Dudley G.
In Memoriam, R. L. S.; poem. Cornhill 148:745 D '33

Dawson, Nell Perkins
R. L. S. and the Fontainebleau trail. Bookm (NY) 36:265-70 N '12

Dawson, William James
The religion of Robert Louis Stevenson. Bookm (NY) 32:89-93 S '10; *same.* Bookm (NY) 4:35-9 S '96
Robert Louis Stevenson. *In* The makers of English fiction. New York, Revell [c1905] p241-67

[Death of Stevenson] Lit W 25:473 D 29 '94

DeCasseres, Benjamin
Stevenson's confession of faith. Critic (NY) 43:414-16 N '03

Dedication of Stevenson memorial [on Mt. St. Helena] Sierra Club Bulletin 8:133-6 Je '11

Delaney, William T.
Influence of "skeltery" on Stevenson. Masters essay, St. Louis Univ. 1933. 57ff

Delattre, Floris
Un dilettante de l'aventure: Robert-Louis Stevenson. Revue d'Histoire de la Philosophie et d'Histoire Générale de la Civilisation ns 2:355-75 O 15 '34

De Lautrec, Gabriel
Robert Louis Stevenson. Mercure Fr 94:673-91 D '11

Delebecque, Jacques
A propos du roman d'aventures: notes sur quelques ouvrages de R.-L. Stevenson. Mercure Fr 145:55-87 Ja 1 '21

Dewar, Alfred C.
Robert Louis Stevenson. Nat-Ath 36:358 D 6 '24

Dick, C. H.
Errors in Stevenson. T L S Ag 19 '26 p549

Dickie, Francis J.
Robert Louis Stevenson's famous boat Casco. St Nicholas 45:1032 S '18
The tragic end of Stevenson's yacht Casco. . . [New York, 1920] 8p

Diebold, Bernhard
R. L. Stevenson. Frankfurter Zeitung-Morgenblatt D 18 '25 p 1-2

Dobson, Austin
R. L. S. In Memoriam; a poem. Ecl M 137:89 Jl '01

Dr. Jekyll and Mr. Hyde
The untold sequel of the strange case of Dr. Jekyll and Mr. Hyde. Boston, Pinckney publishing co. [c 1890] 41p

Dodd, Loudon
Stevenson and Scott: "Hebdomadary." Notes & Q 10th ser 5:44-5 Ja 20 '06

Dorsenne, Jean
Vailima. J Débats 32:309-10 Ag 21 '25

Douady, Jules
R. L. Stevenson. *In* La mer et les poètes anglais. Paris, Hachette, 1912. p332-58

Doughty, Leonard
Answering R. L. S. The Reverend C. M. Hyde's reply to the Damien letter (as it might have been written). Southwest Review 14:21-37 Autumn '28

Douglas, A. Donald
R. L. S. New Repub 38:8-10 Ap 9 '24

Douglas, George Brisbane Scott
A cadger's creel, the book of the Robert Louis Stevenson club Bazaar. . . Edinburgh, Brown, 1925. xiii, 173p

Douglas, James
Mr. Watts-Dunton on Herbert Spencer and Robert Louis Stevenson. Bookm (Lond) 27:24-6 O '04; *same in* Theodore Watts-Dunton: poet, novelist, critic. London, Hodder and Stoughton, 1904. p215-21

Douglas, Robert B.
Stevenson at Fontainebleau. Macmil ns 1:340-7 Mr '06

Doyle, Arthur Conan
Mr. Stevenson's methods in fiction. Nat R 14:646-57 Ja '90

Drinkwater, John
To R. L. S.; poem. New Repub 46:298 Ap 28 '26

Droppers, Garrett
A letter from Stevenson, with a note. Scrib M 73:358-9 Mr '23
Robert Louis Stevenson. Harv Mo 4:20-33 Mr '87

Dual personalities. Literary World (Lond) ns 68:128-9 Ag 21 '03

Duffy, Richard
When they were twenty-one. Bookm (NY) 38:529-30 Ja '14

Duncan, William Henry, jr.
Stevenson's second visit to America. Bookm (NY) 10:454-64 Ja '00

Dunfield, Frank Freeman
Resemblances in the short stories of
Stevenson and Hawthorne. Masters
essay, Dartmouth college, 1912. 59ff

Dwight, H. G.
Of islands. Scrib M 43:99-100 Ja '08

Eagle, Solomon [pseud]
see Squire, John Collings

The **early** homes and haunts of Robert
Louis Stevenson. Pall Mall Budget
40:1068-9 Jl 21 '92

Eaton, Charlotte (Mrs. Wyatt Eaton)
The cottage [account of a visit with
R. L. Stevenson and his mother] Cath
World 123:320-5 Je '26

A day with Stevenson. Bookn 28:877-
81 Ag '10

A last memory of Robert Louis Stevenson. . . New York, Crowell [c 1916]
62p
(Rev in Dial 61:317-18 O 19 '16)

R. L. S. at Manasquan. Queen's Q 38:
678-90 O '31

Robert Louis Stevenson, an impression.
Craftsman 13:257-60 D '07

Stevenson at Manasquan; with a note on
the fate of the yacht "Casco," and 6
portraits of Stevenson by George
Steele Seymour. (Little bookfellow
ser) Chicago, Bookfellows, 1921. 48p

Echo der zeitungen. Stevenson. Die
Literatur 27:221-2 Ja '25

Edholm, Charlton Lawrence
In the shadow of the Stevenson monu-
ment. Overland Monthly ns 46:291-7
O '05

Ellis, Lilith
Robert Louis Stevenson. New Century
Review 5:347-53 My '99

Ellis, Stewart Marsh
George Meredith: his life and friends in
relation to his work. New York, Dodd,
Mead, 1920. passim

Ellwanger, William DeLancey
The collecting of Stevensons. Bachelor
of Arts 1:344-55 Jl-Ag '95

An incident in book collecting. In A
snuff-box full of trees and some apocryphal essays. New York, Dodd,
Mead, 1909. p75-91

England, George Allan
The real Treasure island. Travel 52:17-
21 Ja '29

The **English** novel in the nineteenth century. Edin R 196:499-500 O '02

Evans, Benjamin Ifor
William Ernest Henley and Robert Louis
Stevenson. In English poetry in the
later nineteenth century. London,
Methuen [1933] p265-78

Expert plagiarism by divine right and mere
literary theft. Munsey's Magazine 61:
623-8 S '17

Ewing, (Sir) James Alfred
The Fleeming Jenkins and Robert Louis
Stevenson. In An engineer's outlook.
London, Methuen [1933] p248-74

The Stevenson memorial, Edinburgh.
In An engineer's outlook. London,
Methuen [1933] p275-6

Fabre, Frédéric
R. L. Stevenson dans le Velay. Revue
d'Auvergne 46:1-18 Ja '32

Face to the front. Out 67:617-18 Mr 16 '01

Facsimile of Robert Louis Stevenson's
handwriting. Book B ns 6:103 Ap '89

Falconer, W. L.
Robert Louis Stevenson. Critic (NY)
13:323-4 D 29 '88

[**False** report of Stevenson's death] Lit W
20:161 My 11 '89

Fehr, Bernhard
Die englische literatur des 19. und 20.
jahrhunderts. Wildpark-Potsdam, 1928
p328-9, 346-53

Ferguson, A. S.
Stevenson the dreamer. Queen's Q 30:
26-36 Jl '22

Feuchtwanger, Lion
Über R. L. Stevenson. Die Weltbühne
22:465-8 '26

A **few** facts about Stevenson. Bookn 28:
892-4 Ag '10

Field, Benjamin Franklin
Robert Louis Stevenson and British
Samoa. Overland Monthly ns 92:63-4
Mr '34+ (to be continued)

Field, Isobel
Robert Louis Stevenson. . . Saranac
Lake, New York, Stevenson Society of
America Inc. 1920. 87p

'**Fifteen** men on a dead man's chest' [Dead
Man's Chest is an island in the Virgins
which has now lost its identity . . .
context] Liv Age 315:785-6 D 30 '22

Findlay, J. Patrick
In the footsteps of R. L. S. Edinburgh,
Nimmo, 1915. 64p

Finlayson, J. N.
The grandfather of Robert Louis Stevenson. Quarterly Journal of the Univ.
of North Dakota 17:211-20 Ap '27

Fitch, George Hamlin
Stevenson, prince of modern story tellers. In Modern English books of
power. San Francisco, Paul Elder
[c 1912] p123-30

A **fitting** memorial. Spec 79:275 Ag 28 '97

Fletcher, Charles Brunsdon
Stevenson's Germany; the case against
Germany in the Pacific. London,
Heinemann, 1920. xv,230p
(Rev in T L S Je 10 '20 p362; Weekly
Review 4:182 F 23 '21; Ath 1:735 Je 4
'20)

Flouton, Edna Thayer
The religious liberalism of Robert Louis
Stevenson. Masters essay, Columbia
univ. 1932

Ford, Richard Clyde
Modestine's shoes; a bit of Stevenson-iana. Atlan 137:527-31 Ap '26

Foreign authors in America. Bookm (NY) 13:371-7 Je '01

Forman, W. C.
Novelists' "Slips." Notes & Q 147:155 Ag 30 '24

Frank, Maude Morrison
Robert Louis Stevenson. *In* Great authors in their youth. New York, Holt, 1915. p31-66

Franklin, Viola Price
Stevenson in Monterey; or, An afternoon with Jules Simoneau... Salem, Oregon, Statesman publishing co. 1925. 3-18p

Fraser, Marie
In Stevenson's Samoa. London, Smith, Elder, 1895. vi,190p
(Rev in Nation (NY) 61:35 Jl 11 '95; Spec 74:853-4 Je 22 '95; Literary World (Lond) ns 51:289-90 Mr 29 '95; Bookm (Lond) 8:57 My '95; P. Addle-shaw in Acad 47:272 Mr 30 '95; Bookm (NY) 1:271 My '95; noted in Lit W 26:138 My 4 '95)

Freeman, John
English portraits and essays. London, Hodder and Stoughton, 1924. p33-59
Robert Louis Stevenson. Lond Merc 5: 617-27 Ap '22

French, Harold
How the home of Mrs. Robert Louis Stevenson was saved. Overland Monthly ns 48:137-8 S '06
Silverado—scene of Robert Louis Steven-son's honeymoon. Overland Monthly ns 48:129-37 S '06

A friendship; Robert Louis Stevenson, Jules Simoneau. [San Francisco, Printed for A. A. Brown by Taylor, Nash & Taylor, 1911] 8p
(400 copies only)

Fujisawa, Rikitaro
Robert Louis Stevenson and Yoshida Shoin. Trans-Pacific 16:5 D 1 '28

Galsworthy, John
Four more novelists in profile. *In* Candelabra... New York, Scribner, 1933. p249-69; *same in* Engl R 55:491-5 N '32

The garden ever young. T. P.'s Weekly 12:714 N 27 '08

Garnett, Richard
Symonds—Pater—Hamerton—Stevenson; poem. Lit W 26:24 Ja 26 '95

Garnett, Richard and Gosse, Edmund
Robert Louis Balfour Stevenson. *In* English literature, an illustrated record. New York, Grosset and Dunlap [c1904] vol IV p361-6

Garrod, Heathcote William
The poetry of R. L. Stevenson. *In* The profession of poetry and other lectures. Oxford, Clarendon press, 1929. p179-93

Geddie, John
The home country of R. L. Stevenson... Edinburgh, White, 1898. 2d ed xv, 219p

Geissinger, James Allen
Robert Louis Stevenson as an interpreter of life. Harvard Theological Review 2:85-94 Ja '09

The genius of Robert Louis Stevenson. [signed "Y. Y."] *In* Robert Louis Stevenson: his work and his person-ality, ed. by A. St. John Adcock. Lon-don, Hodder and Stoughton, 1924. p40-50; *same in* Robert Louis Stevenson. A Bookman (Lond) extra number, 1913. London, Hodder & Stoughton [1913] p11-16

Gentry, Parma
Robert Louis Stevenson; poem. Over-land Monthly ns 30:527 D '97

Genung, John Franklin
Stevenson's attitude to life; with read-ings from his essays and letters. New York, Crowell, 1901. vi, 44p
(Rev in Out 69:385-6 O 12 '01)

George, J. F.
Robert Louis Stevenson and the Garioch. Scottish Notes and Queries 2d ser 4: 154-5 Ap '03

Gerould, Katharine (Fullerton) (Mrs. Gor-don Hall Gerould)
Kalaupapa, the leper settlement on Molo-kai [Father Damien and Stevenson's Open letter] Scrib M 60:1-4 Jl '16

Gilbert, Ariadne
The lighthouse-builder's son. St Nicho-las 33:495-506 Ap '06

Gilder, Jeannette L.
Stevenson—and after. R of Rs (NY) 11: 186-90 F '95

Gilder, Joseph Benson
The first portrait of R. L. S. Putnam's Magazine 7:575-81 F '10

Gilman, Arthur
Damien, Stevenson and Dr. Hyde. Critic (NY) 17:109 Ag 30 '90

Gilroy, E. A.
R. L. S. and Edinburgh. New Statesm 13:346 Jl 5 '19

Glardon, A.
Romanciers anglais contemporains. Rob-ert-Louis Stevenson. Bibliothèque Uni-verselle et Revue Suisse 3d period 66: 493-521 Je '95; 67:80-111 Jl '95

Gooding, (David) Paul
Stevenson's Tahitian "brother." Over-land Monthly ns 66:64-9 Jl '15

Goodman, Jules Eckert
Treasure island; a play.... dramatized from the story of Robert Louis Steven-son. New York, French, 1933. 102p

Goodrich, Ruth
A comparative study of the narrative art of Nathaniel Hawthorne and Robert Louis Stevenson. Masters essay, Univ. of California, 1921. 289ff

Gordon, Alice
The first meeting between George Meredith and Robert Louis Stevenson. Bookm (Lond) 7:111-12 Ja '95; *also in* Robert Louis Stevenson: his work and his personality, ed. by A. St. John Adcock. London, Hodder and Stoughton, 1924. p53-7; *and in* Robert Louis Stevenson. A Bookman (Lond) extra number, 1913. London, Hodder & Stoughton [1913] p74-6

Gosse, (Sir) Edmund William
Biographical notes on the writings of Robert Louis Stevenson. London, Chiswick press, 1908. 150p
(50 copies only)

"Cummy." *In* Leaves and fruit. London, Heinemann, 1927. p325-33

Mr. R. L. Stevenson as a poet. *In* Questions at issue. London, Heinemann [1893] p237-54; *same.* Longman's Magazine 10:623-31 O '87

Robert Louis Stevenson, 1850-1894. *In* Clark, B. H. (ed) Great short biographies of the world. New York, McBride, 1929. p1300-14; *same in* Cent 50:447-54 Jl '95

Robert Louis Stevenson; an early portrait. *In* Robert Louis Stevenson. A Bookman (Lond) extra number, 1913. London, Hodder & Stoughton [1913] p32

Robert Louis Stevenson: an early portrait; poem. *In* Robert Louis Stevenson: his work and his personality, ed. by A. St. John Adcock. London, Hodder and Stoughton, 1924. p51-2

Robert Louis Stevenson; personal memories. *In* Critical kit-kats. London, Heinemann, 1896. p275-302

Stevenson's relations with children. Chamb J 76:449-51 Je 17 '99

To Tusitala at Vailima; poem. *In* Robert Louis Stevenson: his work and his personality, ed. by A. St. John Adcock. London, Hodder and Stoughton, 1924. p69-72

To Tusitala in Vailima. *In* Robert Louis Stevenson. A Bookman (Lond) extra number, 1913. London, Hodder & Stoughton [1913] p77-80

Gotch, T. C.
Robert Louis Stevenson, from a painter's point of view. St George 5:96-115 Ap '02

Gould, Gerald
A word for R. L. S. W E R 5:8-9 Ja 2 '32

Grant, Will
Robert Louis Stevenson and the Swanston shepherd. National Magazine 53:505-6 Jl '25

Graves, Clotilda Inez Mary
The pirate's hand. . . A romance of heredity. By the author of "Kneecapped," etc. [Pref signed "R. L. S."

and book appears to be parody of Stevenson] London, "Judy" office [1889] 122p

Greene, Henry Copley
The Puritan against Stevenson. Boston, 1898

Gregg, Frederick James
A unique Stevenson collection. Book B ns 18:200-3 Ap '99

Gregory, Angelina
Stevenson's development as a narrative writer. Masters essay, Columbia univ. 1915

Griswold, Hattie Tyng
Robert Louis Stevenson. *In* Personal sketches of recent authors. Chicago, McClurg, 1898. p191-208

Grove, Lily Mary
Robert Louis Stevenson, sa vie et son oeuvre, étudiée surtout dans les romans écossais. Paris, Bonvalot-Jouve, 1908. 216p bibl p209-14 Thesis, Paris

Grover, Edwin Osgood
My little book of Stevenson. Chicago, Volland [c1924] 141p

Gschwind, F. H.
Robert Louis Stevenson. Wissen und Leben 18:545-9

Guthrie, Charles John
"Cummy", the nurse of Robert Louis Stevenson. A tribute to the memory of Alison Cunningham. Edinburgh, Schulze, 1913. 32p

Robert Louis Stevenson; some personal recollections. . . Edinburgh, Green, 1920. 72p
(Rev by R. Lynd in Yale R ns 16:156-61 O '26; T L S S 23 '20 p610)

Robert Louis Stevenson 13th November 1850-4th December 1894. Juridical Review 31:89-109, 161-74 Jl, D '19; 32:7-26, 129-46 Mr, Je '20

Gwynn, Stephen
Grace after good words. Dalhousie Review 4:317-21 O '24

Mr. Robert Louis Stevenson; a critical essay. Fortn ns 56:776-92 N '94; *same.* Liv Age 204:67-79 Ja 12 '95; *same.* Ecl M 124:154-66 F '95

The posthumous works of Stevenson. Fortn ns 63:561-75 Ap '98

Haber, Tom Burns
Sharpening a tool in the "tool-course." Engl J (College ed) 23:472-6 Je '34

Hamilton, Clayton Meeker
Introduction. *In* Pinero, Arthur Wing. Robert Louis Stevenson as a dramatist. Columbia University Dramatic Museum. Publications ser 1 no 4:1-[22] '14

New aspects of Robert Louis Stevenson. Literary Digest International Book Review 2:270-1 Mr '24

On the trail of Stevenson. Bookm (NY) 40:140-53, 263-75, 396-410, 501-15, 621-35 S '14-F '15; 41:29-44 Mr '15; *same* with drawings by Walter Hale. New York, Doubleday, Page, 1915. ix,151p (Rev in T L S Jl 27 '16 p355)

Stevenson on the stage. Bookm (NY) 42:526-32 Ja '16

Hamilton, Cosmo
R. L. Stevenson and Edmund Gosse. *In* People worth talking about. New York, McBride [c1933] p255-61

Hammerton, John Alexander
'An Inland Voyage': a new note and an old memory. *In* Memories of books and places. Boston, Houghton, Mifflin, 1928. p222-48

In the track of R. L. Stevenson. . . Bristol, Arrowsmith [1907] xii,254p (Rev in Acad 74:539 Mr 7 '08; Spec 99:1101 D 28 '07)

A Stevenson pilgrimage. . . Critic (NY) 46:524-35 Je '05

Stevensoniana. . . New York, Wessels, 1903. xvi,350p

Stevensoniana; an anecdotal life and appreciation of Robert Louis Stevenson. Ed. from the writings of J. M. Barrie. . . [etc] Edinburgh, Grant, 1910. xviii, 350p
(Rev in T L S S 18 '03 p263-4; Acad 65:128 Ag 8 '03; Dial 36:15-18 Ja 1 '04; Ath 2:188 Ag 8 '03; Bookm (Lond) 33:182 Ja '08)

With R. L. S. through the land of war. Bookm (Lond) 54:169-75 S '18

With R. L. S. through the land of war. *In* Robert Louis Stevenson: his work and his personality, ed. by A. St. John Adcock. London, Hodder and Stoughton, 1924. p160-83

Hampden-Cook, E.
"Dr. Jekyll and Mr. Hyde." Ath 1:49 Ja 12 '95

Hankin, St. John
Stevenson as humorist. Acad 53:667-8 Je 18 '98

Harcourt, Betty
The unveiling of the Robert Louis Stevenson memorial. Overland Monthly ns 45:235-9 Mr '05

Hardwick, J. C.
The ideals of R. L. Stevenson. Modern Churchman Mr '19 p584-92

[Harper, Henry Howard]
Robert Louis Stevenson; an appreciation. [Boston, Bibliophile Society, 1921?] 36p

Harrington, Evaline
Why Treasure Island? Engl J 9:266-9 My '20

Harrison, Birge
With Stevenson at Grez. Cent 93:306-14 D '16

Harrison, E. S.
Stevenson's "Wrecker." Spec 107:1009 D 9 '11

Harrison, John S.
Nature [Stevenson's The Merry Men] *In* The vital interpretation of English literature. Indianapolis, Harrison, 1928. p69-72

Harvey, Alexander
Life of Robert Louis Stevenson. *In* Stevenson, R. L. A child's garden of verses and Underwoods. New York, 1911. pxv-lxiii

The literary history of Treasure island. . . *In* Stevenson, R. L. Treasure island. (Medallion ed.) New York, Current Literature Publishing co. 1910. p279-308

Hawkins, Lillian May
Stevenson's usage in syntax and in words. Masters essay, Columbia univ. 1919

Hawkins-Ambler, George A.
Stevenson's house at Monterey. Spec 109:302-3 Ag 31 '12

Hawthorne, Hildegarde
"Kidnapped." St. Nicholas 44:550-2 Ap '17

Robert Louis Stevenson, the great imaginer. St Nicholas 41:1030-2 S '14

Hearn, Lafcadio
R. L. Stevenson. *In* A history of English literature, in a series of lectures. Tokyo, Hokuseido press, 1927. vol II p782-91

Hecht, Hans
Deacon Brodie. Eine quellenstudie zu R. L. Stevenson. *In* Festschrift für Lorenz Morsbach. . . Halle, Max Niemeyer, 1913. p201-21

Hellman, George Sidney
"Cue" stories of Stevenson. Bookm (NY) 62:158-64 O '25

Stevenson and Henry James. The rare friendship between two famous stylists. Cent 111:336-45 Ja '26

The Stevenson myth. Cent 105:240-52 D '22

Stevenson's annotated set of Wordsworth. Colophon part 7:1-8 S '31

The true Stevenson: a study in clarification. . . Boston, Little, Brown, 1925. xiv, 253p
(Rev by W. H. Low in Bookm (NY) 62:340-2 N '25; Sewanee R 34:368-70 Jl-S '26; R. M. Lovett in New Repub 46:77-8 Mr 10 '26; L. Kronenberger in Literary Digest International Book Review 4:257-8 Mr '26; E. Pearson in Out 142:336-7 Mr 3 '26; R. Lynd in Yale R ns 16:156-61 O '26; E. Shanks in Sat R 142:339-40 S 25 '26; Spec 138:490-1 S 25 '26)

Henderson, James
Stevenson's beginnings. Acad 58:237-8 Mr 17 '00

Henley, William Ernest
Apparition. *In* The works of W. E. Henley. London, Nutt, 1908. vol I p40

A book of verses. London, Nutt, 1888. xi, 167p [Poems 25 and 28 relate to Robert Louis Stevenson]

"R. L. S." *In* Mordell, A. ed. Notorious literary attacks. New York, Boni and Liveright, 1926. p232-55

[Henley's attack on Stevenson]
Literary World (Lond) ns 64:437 N 29 '01; Acad 61:487-8, 596-7 N 23, D 14 '01

Henry, Brother
Robert Louis Stevenson and California. Masters essay, Catholic univ. 1923

[Herdam, R. A.]
A talk about Robert Louis Stevenson, being a lecture delivered to the brotherhood at Ancoats on November 10th, 1901. Westminster, Privately printed, 1901. 5-43p (50 copies only)

Hermansen, Ruth Hall
Robert Louis Stevenson; his first visit to America. Masters essay, Columbia univ. 1924

Heroism in life and art. Cur Lit 30:514-15 My '01

Hervier, Paul-Louis
Stevenson jugé par son beau-fils. Nouvelle Revue Français 59:3-13 My '22

Hesse, Hermann
A journey with Stevenson. Liv Age 333: 812-14 N 1 '27

Hills, Gertrude
Three letters from Robert Louis Stevenson. American Book Collector 2:209-11 O '32

Hind, Charles Lewis
Robert Louis Stevenson. *In* Authors and I. New York, Lane, 1921. p267-72

Hinkson, Katherine Tynan
London letter. Lit W 26:24 Ja 26 '95

Hirsch, L.
Profile: R. L. Stevenson. Berlin. Tageblatt '28 p411

Hitchcock, Champion Ingraham
The dead men's song: being the story of a poem and a reminiscent sketch of its author Young Ewing Allison. . . Louisville, Ky. [The Courier journal job printing company] 1914. 93p [The song in question is "Derelict," based upon "Fifteen men on the dead man's chest" from Stevenson's "Treasure Island."]
(250 copies only)

Hixson, Jerome Canady
Stevenson's literary principles as derived from the forces influencing him. Masters essay, Alleghany College, 1923

Hodges, Leigh Mitchell
The life worth while; an appreciation of Stevenson's creed. . . [Carthage, Mo] The author, 1904. [vii]-xvp

Hofmiller, Josef
Tolstoi und Stevenson. Süddeutsche Monatshefte 24:368-9

Hood, Robert Allison
Plot and character in Stevenson; a study with some reference to the influence of Scott and Dumas. Masters essay, Univ. of California, 1914. 67ff

Hopkins, Robert Thurston
Sidelights on R. L. Stevenson. Bookman's Journal 3:178-9, 194, 210, 225-6, 254, 266 Ja 7-F 11 '21

Horne, John
R. L. Stevenson in Wick. Chamb J 7th ser 13:749-50 O 20 '23

Housman, A. E.
R. L. S. [poem] Acad 46:533 D 22 '94

Hubbard, (Mrs) Alice (Moore)
Robert Louis Stevenson. *In* Life lessons: truths concerning people who have lived. . . East Aurora, N.Y. The Roycrofters [c1909] p87-104

Hubbard, Elbert
Little journeys to the homes of great geniuses: R. L. S. East Aurora, New York, The Roycrofters, 1911. vol XXXVIII no 4 Ap '11

R. L. Stevenson. *In* Little journeys to the homes of great Americans. East Aurora, New York, The Roycrofters, 1911. 2 vols in 1

Robert Louis Stevenson and Fanny Osbourne. . . East Aurora, New York, The Roycrofters [1916] 38p

Robert Louis Stevenson and Fanny Osbourne. *In* Little journeys to homes of great lovers. East Aurora, New York, The Roycrofters, 1906. vol XIX no 6 p161-93 D '06

Humphrey, Grace
"Treasure island." St. Nicholas 43:300-2 F '16

Hutchinson, Allen
Stevenson's only bust from life. [portraits] Scrib M 80:140-3 Ag '26

Hutchinson, Percy Adams
Stevenson; poem. Bookm (NY) 8:585 F '99

Ide, Marjorie
R. L. Stevenson; a Samoan memory. Liv Age 311:649-52 D 10 '21

Iles, George
A note upon Stevenson. Book B ns 12: 17 F '95

Robert Louis Stevenson. *In* Little masterpieces of autobiography. New York, Doubleday, 1908. vol IV p148-61

In memoriam Robert Louis Stevenson, Dec. 3d, 1894. [New York, 1895] 8p (Bookman Supplement to vol 1 no 1 1895)

Ireland, Ethel Alleyne
Some new letters by Leigh Hunt and Stevenson. Atlan 82:122-8 Jl '98

Ireland, F. G.
A letter from R. L. Stevenson. Spec 107:103 Jl 15 '11

Jacobs, Joseph
"Dr. Jekyll and Mr. Hyde." Ath 1:18, 87 Ja 5, 19 '95

Mr. Robert Louis Stevenson. Ath 2: 863-4 D 22 '94

Robert Louis Stevenson. *In* Literary studies. London, Nutt, 1895. 2d ed p175-85

Jaén, Ramon
Notes on Stevenson's "Olalla." Univ. of California Chronicle 25:376-84 Jl '23

James, George Wharton
Robert Louis Stevenson in California. National Magazine 35:389-405 D '11

James, Henry
The letters of Robert Louis Stevenson. No Am 170:61-77 Ja '00

Robert Louis Stevenson. *In* Notes on novelists with some other notes. New York, Scribner, 1914. p1-25

Robert Louis Stevenson. *In* Partial portraits. London, Macmillan, 1899. p135-74; *also in* Cent 35:869-79 Ap '88

Japp, Alexander Hay
Robert Louis Stevenson. Argosy 59:226-35 F '95

Robert Louis Stevenson; a record, an estimate, and a memorial. . . New York, Scribner, 1905. 2d ed ix-xii, 308p (Rev in Ath 1:143 F 4 '05)

Stevenson's beginnings. Acad 58:209-10 Mr 10 '00

Jeffords, E. Pearl
Friendship of Robert Louis Stevenson and William E. Henley. Masters essay, State Univ. of Iowa, 1930. 113ff

Jenks, James Lawrence
Address on Robert Louis Stevenson before St. Andrews society of Rhode Island, April 28, 1924. (St. Andrews pamphlets no 2) St. Andrews society of Rhode Island. Pawtucket, Rhode Island, 1924. 16p

Jenson, M. L.
Stevenson as a writer of narrative. Bachelors essay, Univ. of Utah, 1910. 29ff

Jessup, Alexander
The poetry of Robert Louis Stevenson. Poet Lore 18:396-401 S '07

Jessup, Alexander (ed)
The best of Stevenson. Boston, Page, 1902. 390p bibl p1-13 (Rev in Lit W 33:142 S 1 '02)

Johnson, Lionel Pigot
Reviews and critical papers; ed. with an introduction by Robert Shafer. New York, Dutton, 1921. p40-5

Johnson, R. Brimley
Story lives of nineteenth-century authors. London, Gardner, Darton, 1925

Johnstone, Arthur Giffard Whiteside
Recollections of Robert Louis Stevenson in the Pacific. . . London, Chatto, 1905. xix, 327p (Rev in Bookm (Lond) 28:174 Ag '05)

Keable, Robert
Bohemian and rebel in the world's garden; how Stevenson found a brother in the Tahitian and Gauguin sought in him living art. Asia 24:892-7 N '24

Keeler, Charles
To Stevenson; poem. Impressions Quarterly 5:97 D '04

Kellner, Leon
Die englische literatur im zeitalter der königin Viktoria. Leipzig, Tauchnitz, 1909. p542-53

Robert Louis Stevenson. *In* Die englische literatur der neuesten zeit von Dickens bis Shaw. Leipzig, Tauchnitz, 1921. p314-19

Kelman, John
The faith of Robert Louis Stevenson. . . Edinburgh, Oliphant, Anderson and Ferrier, 1903. ix-xii, 301p (Rev in Ath 2:86-7 Jl 18 '03; Ind 55: 2178-9 S 10 '03; Bookn 22:25-7 S '03; Acad 64:532-3 My 30 '03; Dial 35:215-17 O 1 '03; Pilot 8:91-2 Jl 25 '03)

Kenyon, James Benjamin
The letters of Robert Louis Stevenson. *In* Loiterings in old fields. New York, Eaton and Mains, 1901. p211-44

Kernahan, Coulson
The soul of an artist. *In* Wise men and a fool. New York, Brentano, 1901. p15-43; *same.* Lond Q R 93:25-37 Ja '00

Kimball, Ruth P.
Treasure Island; a dramatization in three acts, of R. L. Stevenson's novel of the same name. Boston, Baker [c1927] 69p

Kimber, Thomas
Stevenson and fine arts: the aesthetic career of a literary stylist. Masters essay, Univ. of Southern California, 1934. 101ff

Kingsley, Maude Elma
Examination questions for Stevenson's Treasure Island. Educa 30:525-6 Ap '10

Outline studies in literature. Inland voyage. Boston, Palmer, 1920. no 81 27p

Outline study of David Balfour. Educa 41:226-41 D '20

Kirk, Sophia
Robert Louis Stevenson. Atlan 60:747-55 D '87

Knight, Grant Cochran
The novel in English. New York, R. R. Smith, 1931. p226-33

Knowlton, Edgar C.
A Russian influence on Stevenson. Mod Philol 14:65-70, 449-54 '16

Kranendonk, A. G. van
R. L. Stevenson: "The master of Ballantrae." Nieuwe Gids 33:851-64 D '18

Lafleur, Paul T.
Poe: R. L. Stevenson.   Notes & Q 11th
ser 1:261-2 Ap 2 '10

Laird, Marjorie Evelyn
American interest in Robert Louis
Stevenson, 1879-1894.   Masters essay,
State Univ. of Iowa, 1930.   187ff

Lalou, René
Panorama de la littérature anglaise contemporaine.   Paris, Kra [c1926] p 100-5

Lancaster, W. J.
R. L. Stevenson's "painstakingness."   Lit
7:242 S 29 '00

Landau, M.
R. Louis Stevenson.   Nationalzeitung
no 565 '99

Lang, Andrew
"Dr. Jekyll and Mr. Hyde."   Ath 1:49,
186 Ja 12, F 9 '95

Mr. Stevenson's works.   *In* Essays in
little.   London, Henry, 1891.   p24-35

Recollections of Robert Louis Stevenson.
In Adventures among books.   London,
Longmans, Green, 1905.   p41-56; *also in*
No Am 160:185-94 F '95

Lanier, Charles D.
Robert Louis Stevenson.   R of Rs (NY)
11:181-6 F '95

Lansing, Ruth
Robert Louis Stevenson's French reading
as shown in his correspondence.   Poet
Lore 29:218-28 '18

The late Sir W. G. Simpson, Bart., and
Robert Louis Stevenson.   Bookm
(Lond) 14:92-5 Jl '98

The later course of English prose.   Acad
75:254 S 12 '08

Latham, Edward
Stevenson and Miss Yonge.   Notes & Q
12th ser 8:79 Ja 22 '21

Laurence, Perceval Maitland
Robert Louis Stevenson.   *In* Collectanea,
essays, addresses, and reviews.   London, Macmillan, 1899.   p222-5 [from
Diamond Fields Advertiser, D '94]

Lebeau, Henri
Au pays de Stevenson et du Gauguin.
Revue de P 16 no 4:125-48 Jl 1 '09

Lee, Vernon [pseud]
see Paget, Violet

LeGallienne, Richard
The dethroning of Stevenson.   *In* Sleep-
ing beauty and other prose fancies.
London, Lane, 1900.   p151-60

Robert Louis Stevenson; poem.   *In*
Robert Louis Stevenson: an elegy; and
other poems mainly personal.   London, Lane, 1895.   p1-10
(Rev in National Observer 14:87-8 Je
1 '95; Spec 76:573 Ap 25 '96; Westm
144:233 Ag '95; Bookselling 1:220-1 Jl
'95; Lit W 26:326-7 O 5 '95; P. Addle-
shaw in Acad 47:519-20 Je 22 '95; Atlan

78:425 S '96; A. Macdonell in Bookm
(Lond) 8:83-4 Je '95 and in Bookm
(NY) 1:408-9 Jl '95)
The romantic '90s.   Garden City, New
York, Doubleday, Page, 1925.   p104-14

Leigh, J. G.
Stevenson and imperialism.   Speaker
ns 2:69-70 Ap 21 '00

Leighton, Robert
Stevenson's beginnings.   Acad 58:189 Mr
3 '00

[Length of Stevenson's novels] T L S My
4 '22 p285

Leonhardy, Alma
Directed study guides for Stevenson's
"Treasure Island." . .   New York, Mac-
millan, 1930.   68p

Limedorfer, Eugene
The manuscript of Dr. Jekyll and Mr.
Hyde.   Bookm (NY) 12:52-8 S '00

Lipscomb, Herbert C.
Stevenson and the classics.   Classical
Journal 20:564-6 Je '25

Lisle, George
R. L. S. and some savages on an island.
Cornhill ns 51:706-12 D '21; *same.* Liv
Age 312:43-8 Ja 7 '22

Literary leprosy.   Sat R 92:672-3 N 30 '01

The literary pages of the "Spectator."   Spec
141:691 N 10 '28

Livingston, Luther S.
The first books of some English authors. . .   Bookm (NY) 10:437-40 Ja '00

Lockett, W. G.
R. L. S. and Mrs. MacMorland.   T L S
Ag 29, Ja 30, Jl 31, '29-'30 p668, 78, 628

Robert Louis Stevenson at Davos.   London, Hurst and Blackett, 1934.   304p
(Rev in T L S N 8 '34 p774)

Longstreth, Thomas Morris
Leslie takes tea with a friend of Long
John Silver.   St Nicholas 53:26-31 N
'25

Loudon, K. M.
East and West: Tagore and Stevenson.
In Two mystic poets and other essays.
Oxford, Blackwell, 1922.   p83-97

Low, Will Hicok
A chronicle of friendships, 1873-1900.
With illustrations by the author and
from his collections. . .   New York,
Scribner, 1908.   passim; *same in* Scrib
M 44:32-53, 324-44, 426-45 Jl, S, O '08

Concerning a painting of Robert Louis
Stevenson.   Bronxville, Bronx Valley
press, 1924.   17p

An epilogue to an epilogue.   *In* Morley,
C. D. compiler.   Modern essays.   New
York, Harcourt, Brace, 1924.   2d ser
p403-19

Exit R. L. S.   *In* A chronicle of friendships, 1873-1900.   New York, Scribner,
1908.   p419-29

Stevenson and Margarita. . .   New Rochelle, New York, Mayflower press,
1922.   20p

Lowe, Charles
Robert Louis Stevenson: a reminiscence. *In* Robert Louis Stevenson: his work and his personality, ed. by A. St. John Adcock. London, Hodder and Stoughton, 1924. p1-7; *same.* Bookm (Lond) 1:60-1 N '91; *same in* Robert Louis Stevenson. A Bookman (Lond) extra number, 1913. London, Hodder & Stoughton [1913] p16-20

Lucas, Edward Verrall
The Colvins and their friends. New York, Scribner, 1928. x,365p passim
Forbidden glimpses of R. L. S. Liv Age 301:308-10 My 3 '19

Lucas, F. J. E.
Stevenson's "The waif woman." Spec 118:15 Ja 6 '17

Ludwig, Albert
Dahn, Fouqué, Stevenson. "Das Galgenmännlein" und "The Bottle Imp." Euphorion 17:613-24 '10

Lyall, (Sir) Alfred
Studies in literature and history. London, Murray, 1915. p70-5

Lysaght, Sidney Royse
A visit to Robert Louis Stevenson. Liv Age 304:77-83 Ja 10 '20

Mabbott, Thomas Ollive
Allusions in Stevenson. Notes & Q 153: 53 Jl 16 '27

Mabie, Hamilton Wright
Introduction to Will o' the mill. Out 85:983-5 Ap 27 '07

Macalister, Robert Alexander Stewart
Textual errors in Stevenson. T L S Ag 5 '26 p525; cf. C. H. Dick, ibid, Ag 19 '26 p549

McAlpin, Edwin Augustus
Sin and its consequences. . . *In* Old and new books as life teachers. New York, Doubleday, Doran, 1928. p36-49

Macarthur, Henry
R. L. S. [a poem] *In* Realism and romance, and other essays. Edinburgh, Hunter, 1897. p287-91
Realism and romance: Thomas Hardy and Robert Louis Stevenson. *In* Realism and romance, and other essays. Edinburgh, Hunter, 1897. p23-32

MacArthur, James
"One who loved his fellow-men." Bookm (NY) 10:466-70 Ja '00

McCabe, Joseph
A biographical dictionary of modern rationalists. London, Watts, 1920. p763-4

McCabe, Lida Rose
Some Stevenson pictures. Book B ns 24: 373-8 Je '02

MacCarthy, Desmond
R. L. Stevenson. *In* Portraits. New York, Putnam, 1931. 1st ser p255-8

McClure, S. S.
My autobiography. McClure's Magazine 42:101-8 Mr '14 (noted in Cur Opin 56:295 Ap '14)

McClure, William J.
Father Damien and Dr. Hyde. Critic (NY) 17:120 S 6 '90

Macculloch, John Arnott
R. L. Stevenson and the Bridge of Allan, with other Stevenson essays. . . Glasgow, Smith, 1927. 95p
(Rev by M. McLaren in Out 17:596 Mr '28)
R. L. Stevenson: characteristics. Westm 149:631-47 Je '98

Macdonald, M.
Ein dichtergrab auf Samoa. Hamburg. Correspondent. Beilage no 8 '02

Macdougall, Margaret Armour
The home and early haunts of Robert Louis Stevenson. . . Edinburgh, White, 1895. 18-99p

McGovern, J. B.
"From pole to pole." Notes & Q 151:406 D 4 '26

Mackail, J. W.
Robert Louis Stevenson. *In* Chambers's cyclopaedia of English literature. Philadelphia, Lippincott, 1904. new ed vol III p699-705

Maclaren, Ian
In memoriam; R. L. S. *In* Robert Louis Stevenson: his work and his personality, ed. by A. St. John Adcock. London, Hodder and Stoughton, 1924. p112-15; *same.* Bookm (Lond) 7:111 Ja '95; *same.* McClure's Magazine 4:292 F '95; *same in* Robert Louis Stevenson. A Bookman (Lond) extra number, 1913. London, Hodder & Stoughton [1913] p149-51

MacLaren, Malcolm S.
"Cummy." [Robert Louis Stevenson's nurse] Bookm (Lond) 70:99-101 My '26
Robert-Louis Stevenson. Rouge et le Noir 8:1146-58 Mr '29
Théo Varlet: Author, poet and translator. French Quarterly 8:51-64 Mr '26

MacLaren, Margaret J. L.
Robert Louis Stevenson and romance; his attitude towards life and his confidence in the essential goodness of man as revealed in his romances. Masters essay, McGill Univ. 1926. 79ff

McLean, (Mrs) C. F.
Robert Louis Stevenson at Gretz. Midland Monthly 5:549-62 Je '96

Macnaughton, John
The art of Robert Louis Stevenson. Queen's Q 8:191-210 Ja '01

MacPherson, Harriet Dorothea
R. L. Stevenson. A study in French influence. . . (Publications of the Institute of French studies) New York, 1930. 76p bibl p74-6
(Rev by A. K. Davis, Jr. in Mod Lang N 47:135-6 F '32)

The **magic** initials, "R. L. S." Cur Opin 76:661-3 My '24

Mahaffy, A. W.
A visit to the library of R. L. Stevenson at Vailima, Samoa. Spec 75:762-3 N 30 '95

Mahoney, James
R. L. Stevenson and W. E. Henley, their literary relations. Masters essay, Columbia univ. 1915

Maier, Ludwig
Die Abenteuerromane Robert Louis Stevensons. Marburg, 1912. 88p Diss. Marburg

A maker of tales. Out 111:594-6 N 10 '15

Malcolm, F. A.
Count Nerli's portrait of R. L. S. Spec 134:325 F 28 '25

Mandel, Kurt
Die belesenheit von R. L. Stevenson mit hinweisen auf die quellen seiner werke. Erlangen, 1912. 138p Diss. Kiel

Marvin, Frederic Rowland
Stevenson and Father Damien. *In* The companionship of books. . . New York, Putnam, 1906. p31-7

Maslen, B. J.
Robert Louis Stevenson. Musical Opinion 55:116-17 N '31

Masse, Benjamin L.
Religion of Robert Louis Stevenson as revealed in his letters and essays. Masters essay, St. Louis Univ. 1932. 63ff

Masson, Flora
The Scottish homes and haunts of Robert Louis Stevenson. Liv Age 270:72-80 Jl 8 '11

Masson, Rosaline Orme
The life of Robert Louis Stevenson. . . New York, Stokes, 1923. xiv,358p
(Rev in T L S Ja 3 '24 p7; R. Lynd in Yale R ns 16:156-61 O '26)
R. L. S. at Pitlochry. Cornhill ns 62: 343-50 Mr '27
R. L. S. at Pitlochry *In* Poets, patriots and lovers. London, Clarke [1933] p171-82
The religion of Robert Louis Stevenson. *In* Poets, patriots and lovers. London, Clarke [1933] p159-70
Robert Louis Stevenson. (People's books) New York, Dodge, 1914. 94p bibl p91

Masson, Rosaline Orme (ed)
I can remember Robert Louis Stevenson. . . Edinburgh, Chambers, 1922. xii,292p
(Rev in T L S N 30 '22 p777; noted T L S My 18 '22 p323)

Mataafa, C. C.
The Stevenson fellowship. Impressions Quarterly 5:83[a] D '04

Mathews, C. E.
R. L. S. and Edinburgh. New Statesm 13:318 Je 28 '19

Matthews, (James) Brander
A moral from a toy theatre [Stevenson as a writer of plays] Scrib M 58:405-12 O '15
Mr. Robert Louis Stevenson. *In* Aspects of fiction. . . New York, Harper, 1896. p128-38
Mr. Robert Louis Stevenson. *In* Books and play-books. London, Osgood, McIlvaine, 1895. p161-71

Mee, Arthur
The hero of literature, R. L. S. *In* Arthur Mee's hero book. London, Hodder and Stoughton [1921?] p159-74

The memoirs of R. L. S. Cornhill Booklet 4:89-90 D '14

Memorable moments in connexion with R. L. S. Notes & Q 12th ser 11:27 Jl 8 '22

Memories and portraits. Monthly Review 6:1-10 Ja '02

The men that found the South seas. Mentor 10:18-31 F '22

Mew, Egan
Robert Louis Balfour Stevenson. Lit 9:76-84 Jl 27 '01

Middleton, Richard
"Treasure Island" as a book for boys. Liv Age 271:249-51 O 28 '11

Milbrandt, Ruth Victoria
A comparative study of the style of Stevenson and Pater. Masters essay, Columbia univ. 1927

Millard, (Frank) Bailey
How Stevenson discovered America. Bookm (NY) 39:539-44 Jl '14
Some rare glimpses of Stevenson. Bookm (NY) 28:442-9 Ja '09

Miller, Frank
R. L. Stevenson's friend, Mrs. MacMorland. T L S S 19 '29 p723

Mr. Gosse on Stevenson. Bookman's Journal 3:66 N 19 '20

Mr. R. L. Stevenson's novels. Church Q R 31:195-211 O '90

Mr. Stevenson on Father Damien. Critic (NY) 16:263-4 My 24 '90

Mr. Stevenson's books. McClure's Magazine 4:288-90 F '95

Mr. Stevenson's fables. Spec 75:299-300 S 7 '95

Modern men. Mr. R. L. Stevenson. Scots Observer 1:264-6 Ja 26 '89

[Mogyoróssy Árkád] Avellanus, Arcadius [pseud]
Impressio specialis prooemii ad versionem Latinam insulae thesaurariae Roberti Ludovici Stevenson. Brooklyn, New York, The author, 1922. 63p

Monahan, Michael
The defence of Damien. *In* An Attic dreamer. New York, Kennerley, 1922. p172-80

Moncrieff, C. K. Scott
Textual errors in Stevenson. T L S Ap 29 '26 p323

Montgomery, George Edgar
Stevenson; poem. Pall Mall Magazine 14:202-3 F '98

Montmorency, James Edward Geoffrey de
Romance [dramatization of Treasure Island] Contemp 123:525-7 Ap '23

Moore, Fanny Caroline
Robert Louis Stevenson's first visit to America. Masters essay, Stanford Univ. 1914. 110ff

Moore, Harry Jay
With Stevenson in Samoa. Boston, Small, Maynard [c1910] v-x,230p (Rev in Nation (NY) 91:500-1 N 24 '10; B. Bancroft in Bookm (NY) 33: 196-7 Ap '11; Ath 1:92 Ja 28 '11; Spec 106:186 F 4 '11)

Moore, Rebecca Deming
Famous men and women of November. Normal Instructor and Primary Plans 40:57 N '30
Treasure Island. Normal Instructor and Primary Plans 38:35 Je '29

Moorman, Lewis J.
Tuberculosis and genius: Robert Louis Stevenson. Annals of Medical History ns 6:540-56 '34

Morley, Christopher Darlington
A geometry notebook. Sat R Lit 3:663 Mr 19 '27
"Idolatry." In Essays. New York, Doubleday, Doran, 1928. p394-401
Nova et vetera; Conrad and Stevenson. Cath World 135:472-3 Jl '32
17 Heriot Row. In Essays. New York, Doubleday, Doran, 1928. p70-81
Two enthusiasms. Atlan 149:403-6 Ap '32

Morris, David Buchan
Robert Louis Stevenson and the Scottish Highlanders. . . Stirling, Mackay [1929] 158p (Rev by E. A. Baker in Mod Lang R 25:491-2 O '30)

Morse, Hiram Gardner
Robert Louis Stevenson as I found him in his island home. [Brooklyn, New York, 1902] 20p
The Mother of Robert Louis Stevenson. Chamb J 74:449-50 Jl 17 '97

Muir, Edwin
Robert Louis Stevenson. Bookm (NY) 74:55-60 S '31; same. Modern Scot 2: 196-204 O '31

Muirhead, John Henry
Robert Louis Stevenson's philosophy of life. In Philosophy and life, and other essays. London, Swan, Sonnenschein, 1902. p37-57

Mulder, J.
R. L. S. Vragen van den Dag 39:907-17 D '24

Mullin, E. H.
Stevenson, Kipling, and Anglo-Saxon imperialism. Book B ns 18:85-90 Mr '99

Munro, Neil
Robert Louis Stevenson. Liv Age 273: 399-405 My 18 '12
Stevenson: the man and his work. In Robert Louis Stevenson: his work and his personality, ed. by A. St. John Adcock. London, Hodder and Stoughton, 1924. p134-59; same in Robert Louis Stevenson. A Bookman (Lond) extra number, 1913. London, Hodder & Stoughton [1913] p179-92

Murdoch, W. G. Blaikie
The portraits of Robert Louis Stevenson. American Magazine of Art (Washington) 23:113-20 Ag '31
Stevenson relics and memories in Edinburgh. T. P.'s Weekly 20:13 Jl 5 '12

Murphy, Mabel Ansley
Tusitala, teller of tales. St Nicholas 48: 242-3 Ja '21

Murphy, Mary Agnes
The novel and the short-story contrasted in the works of Robert Louis Stevenson. Masters essay, Univ. of California, 1911. 114ff

Murray, David Christie
Robert Louis Stevenson. In My contemporaries in fiction. London, Chatto & Windus, 1897; also in Canadian Magazine 8:332-6 F '97

My ideal home. Country Life 40:35-7 O '21

Nencioni, Enrico
Saggi critici di letteratura inglese. Firenze, 1897. p313-16, 448-9

Neuman, B. Paul
Stevenson of the letters; poem. Spec 84: 140 Ja 27 '00

Nevinson, Henry Woodd
From Leith to Samoa. In Books and personalites. London, Lane, 1905. p149-61

New revelations of Robert Louis Stevenson. Cur Lit 51:316-18 S '11

A new tribute to Stevenson. Bookn 23: 85-6 O '04

Newton-Robinson, Janetta
Some aspects of the work of Mr. Robert Louis Stevenson. Westm 139:601-9 Je '93

Nicklin, J. A.
Mr. Henley and R. L. S. Lit 9:519 N 30 '01

Nicoll, (Sir) William Robertson
Home from the hill; poem. In Robert Louis Stevenson: his work and his personality, ed. by A. St. John Adcock. London, Hodder and Stoughton, 1924. p116-17; same. Blackw 157:256 F '95; same. Bookm (Lond) 21:13 O '01
Notes on English style in the Victorian period. Bookm (NY) 10:146-7 O '99
Robert Louis Stevenson. In Robert Louis Stevenson: his work and his personality, ed. by A. St. John Adcock. London, Hodder and Stoughton, 1924. p128-33; same. Bookm (Lond) 21:10-

Nicoll, W. R.—*Continued*
11 O '01; *same in* Robert Louis Stevenson. A Bookman (Lond) extra number, 1913. London, Hodder & Stoughton [1913] p152-4

Nicoll, William Robertson and Chesterton, Gilbert Keith
Robert Louis Stevenson. London, Hodder & Stoughton, 1906. 44p

Niven, Frederick
The Scotland of Robert Louis Stevenson. T. P.'s Weekly 18:594 N 10 '11

Nolan, James Bennett
A flight in the heather. On the trail of "Kidnapped." Bookn 28:886-91 Ag '10
The Stevenson museum. Mentor 16:50-3 My '28

Nordeck, Hans
Robert Louis Stevenson. Hochland 24: 106-7 Ap-S '27

[Note on "Weir of Hermiston"] Book B ns 13:221-2 My '96

Noyes, Alfred
Stevenson. *In* Robert Louis Stevenson: his work and his personality, ed. by A. St. John Adcock. London, Hodder and Stoughton, 1924. p199-228
Stevenson. *In* Some aspects of modern poetry. London, Hodder & Stoughton [1924] p96-117

Nutt, Alfred
"Stevenson looks in." Acad 58:337-8 Ap 21 '00

Obituary; R. L. Stevenson. Acad 46:533-4 D 22 '94

O'Connell, L.
Stevenson's word effects in "Virginibus Puerisque." Rosary 24:46-9 Ja '04

Odier, Henri Charles Agenor
Robert-Louis Stevenson. *In* Études de littérature anglaise contemporaine. . . Genève, Journal de Genève, 1913. p15-34

Une oeuvre inédite de R. L. Stevenson. Mercure Fr 158:283-4 Ag 15 '22

Oliphant, James
Robert Louis Stevenson. *In* Victorian novelists. London, Blackie, 1899. p208-28

Oliphant, Margaret
Mr. Robert Louis Stevenson. *In* The Victorian age of English literature. New York, Tait [c1892] vol II p502-3

Omond, George William Thomson
Notes on the art of Robert Louis Stevenson. No Am 171:348-58 S '00

O'Neill, Moira
The letters of Robert Louis Stevenson. Blackw 190:468-91 O '11; *same.* Liv Age 271:332-43, 398-407 N 11, 18 '11

Osborne, Maitland LeRoy
The last days of Robert Louis Stevenson. National Magazine 53:203-6 D '24

Osbourne, Katharine Durham
Robert Louis Stevenson in California. Chicago, McClurg, 1911. vii,112p
(Noted in Bookm (NY) 35:14-16 Mr '12)

Robert Louis Stevenson in San Francisco. Out West ns 6:3-15 Jl-Ag '13

Osbourne, Samuel Lloyd
Genius in exile, from an intimate portrait of R. L. S. *In* Keyes, R. K. ed. Lives of today and yesterday. . . New York, Appleton, 1931. p190-200
How I first saw Stevenson. *In* Robert Louis Stevenson: his work and his personality, ed. by A. St. John Adcock. London, Hodder and Stoughton, 1924. p33-9
An intimate portrait of Robert Louis Stevenson. . . New York, Scribner, 1924. 155p; *same in* Scrib M 74:515-24, 673-83 N, D '23; 75:66-73, 163-71 Ja, F '24
(Rev by R. Lynd in Yale R ns 16:156-61 O '26; Bookm (NY) 59:338 My '24; G. S. Hellman in Nation (N Y) 118:565 My 14 '24; No Am 219:716 My '24)
Introduction. *In* Stevenson, R. L. A child's garden of verses. New York, Scribner, 1901. p xi-xxiv
A letter to Mr. Stevenson's friends. Chicago, Howell [1895?]
Mr. Stevenson's home life at Vailima. Scrib M 18:458-64 O '95
[Note on: On the choice of a profession] Scrib M 57:66 Ja '15
Stevenson at play. Scrib M 24:709-19 D '98
[Osbourne on Stevenson] Dial 18:61 Ja 16 '95

O'Shea, James
Robert Louis Stevenson, the story teller. Rosary 22:284-95 Mr '03

Overton, Jacqueline Marion
The life of Robert Louis Stevenson for boys and girls. New York, Scribner, 1915. 3-180p bibl p175-80

Owen, Marie
Stevenson's use of allusion. Masters essay, Univ. of Iowa, 1926

[Paget, Violet] Lee, Vernon [pseud]
The handling of words. Stevenson. Engl R 9:441-8 O '11
Stevenson. *In* The handling of words... New York, Dodd, Mead, 1923. p213-22
The paradoxical optimism of Stevenson. Cur Lit 41:49-51 Jl '06

Parish, John Carl
Efficiency and Robert Louis Stevenson. Bookm (NY) 52:298-300 Ja '21

Parker, W. M.
Robert Louis Stevenson. *In* Modern Scottish writers. Edinburgh, Hodge, 1917. p27-41

Parks, Carrie Belle
Stevenson as a point of departure. Engl J 11:95-9 F '22

Parry, G. A.
The duel in "St Ives." T L S Ap 21 '32 p291; cf W. F. Alexander ibid, Ap 28 '32 p311

Parsons, Robert A.
R. L. S. the artist. American Catholic Quarterly Review 39:231-45 Ap '14

Paul, H.
At table with R. L. Stevenson. *In* Dinners with celebrities: anecdotal, descriptive, characteristic. n.p. Newton, 1896

Paul, J. Balfour
The portraits of Robert Louis Stevenson. Ath 2:328 S 7 '95

Robert Louis Stevenson. Ath 1:84 Ja 19 '95

Pearce, Charles E.
"Treasure Island" as a book for boys. Acad 81:457-8 O 7 '11

Pears, (Sir) Edmund Radcliffe
Some recollections of R. L. Stevenson, with a visit to his friend Ori, at Tahiti. Scrib M 73:3-18 Ja '23

Pearson, Hesketh
R. L. Stevenson and Oscar Wilde. *In* A Persian critic. London, Chapman & Dodd, 1923. p64-8

Pearson, Peter Henry
Treasure Island; questions for interpretative and literary study. . . Lindsborg, Kansas, Pearson [c1914] 8p

Pearson, T. S.
R. L. S.'s "New poems and variant readings." T L S F 6 '30 p102

Pease, Howard
Scott and Stevenson. Northern Counties Magazine 2:304-11 Ag '01

Peattie, T. Brunton
Tusitala of Vailima. Central Literary Magazine Jl '22 p248-58

Pendarvis, Susie
Position of the adverb only in the prose of Robert Louis Stevenson. Masters essay, Louisiana State Univ. 1930. 92ff 92ff

Pennell, Joseph
Robert Louis Stevenson, illustrator. The Studio. Winter no 1896-1897. p17-24

Perry, H. T.
Stevenson's impressionism. Harv Mo 8:144-52 Je '89

The personality of R. L. Stevenson. Quar R 191:176-97 Ja '00

Peterson, Meta
Robert Louis Stevenson. McGill University Magazine 4:152-60 Ja '05

Phelps, William Lyon
Introduction. *In* Stevenson, R. L. Essays. . . New York, Scribner, 1906. p ix-xx

The prayers of Stevenson. Ind 51:3350-2 D 14 '99

Robert Louis Stevenson. *In* Essays on modern novelists. New York, Macmillan, 1910. p172-90

The romantic revival, 1894-1904. *In* The advance of the English novel. New York, Dodd, Mead, 1916. p135-9; *same.* Bookm (NY) 43:30-2 Mr '16

Pierpoint, Robert
Allusions in Stevenson. Notes & Q 152:428 Je 11 '27

Pinero, (Sir) Arthur Wing
Robert Louis Stevenson: the dramatist. Critic (NY) 42:341-53 Ap '03; *same.* A lecture delivered by Arthur W. Pinero to the members of the Philosophical institution of Edinburgh, at the Music Hall in Edinburgh on Tuesday, 24th February, 1903. [London, Chiswick press, 1903] 31 numbered leaves; *same in* Columbia University Dramatic Museum. Publications. ser 1 no 4 '14

Piper, E. F.
An inquiry into some phases of the art of description as exhibited in the writings of Robert Louis Stevenson. Masters essay, Univ. of Nebraska [1900] 21ff

Pirates in a band box [dramatization of Treasure Island] Ind 84:521 D 27 '15

Pollard, Hugh
Treasure Island looted. Discovery 5:99-100 Je '24

Pomeroy, Leonard
A Stevensonian shrine. Acad 87:54-5 Jl 11 '14

Pope, Quentin
Robert Louis Stevenson; new sidelights on his life in Samoa. Overland Monthly ns 92:3 Ja '34

The popularity of Robert Louis Stevenson. Chamb J 82:673-6 S 23 '05

[Portraits]
Critic (NY) 25:430-1 D 22 '94; Book B ns 12:13 F '95; Book B ns 11:739-43 Ja '95; Book B ns 21:88 S '00; Book B ns 16:207 Ap '98; Canadian Magazine 8:333 F '97; Mentor 10:28 F '22; Putnam's Magazine 7:578-9 F '10; Engl Illus 11:768 My '94; Cosmopolitan 19:258 Jl '95; Cur Lit 41:50 Jl '06; Literary Digest International Book Review 2:270 Mr '24; Argosy 59:227 F '95; Book B ns 24:373 Je '02; Cent 35:868 Ap '88; McClure's Magazine 3:290-3 S '94; McClure's Magazine 4:274-7, 279-84 F '95; McClure's Magazine 2:218, 236-9 F '94; Sat R Lit 10:679 My 5 '34; Critic (NY) 25:430-1 D 22 '94; Critic (NY) 39:199 S '01; Critic (NY) 26:29 Ja 12 '95; Cur Lit 41:50 Jl '06; Engl Illus 21:123-5 My '99; Book B ns 12:125 Ap '95; Book B ns 11:739-41, 743 Ja '95; Bookm (Lond) 27:109 D '04; Harper M 77:11 Je '88; Bookm (NY) 2:375 Ja '96; Bookm (NY) 13:372 My '01; Bookm (Lond) 41:3 O '11; Book B ns 3: facing 59 Mr '86; Engl Illus 17:492 Je '97; Bookm (Lond) 23:139 Ja '03; Out 69:689-90 N 16 '01; Bookm (NY) 38:528 Ja '14; Bookm

Robert Louis Stevenson. T L S Ja 22 '25 p56; Spec 73:881-2 D 22 '94; Book B ns 3:75 Mr '86; Book B ns 11: 739-43 Ja '95; Critic (NY) 25:430-3 D 22 '94; Public Opinion (NY) 17:951 D 27 '94; Bookn 6:489-90 Jl '88; Bookn 13:210-11 Ja '95; Lit W 15:212 Je 28 '84; Sat R 78:675-6 D 22 '84; Bookm (Lond) 2:43-5 My '92; Dial 18:3-4 Ja 1 '95; National Observer 13:147-9 D 22 '94; Speaker 2:235-6 Ag 30 '90; Scottish Art Review 1:108-10 S '88

Robert Louis Stevenson. *In* The library of literary criticism of English and American authors. . . ed. by Charles Wells Moulton. . . Buffalo, New York, Moulton publishing company, 1904-05. vol VIII p234-54

Robert Louis Stevenson. By two of his cousins. Engl Illus 21:121-31 My '99

Robert Louis Stevenson: an anniversary chapter. Acad 50:562-4 D 19 '96

Robert Louis Stevenson and his wife. Cur Lit 39:47-8 Jl '05

Robert Louis Stevenson and Saranac. Bookm (NY) 42:116 O '15

Robert Louis Stevenson at Vailima, Samoa. Engl Illus 11:769-75 My '94

Robert Louis Stevenson Club, Edinburgh A cadger's creel; the book of the Robert Louis Stevenson club bazaar, ed. by Sir George Douglas, bart. Edinburgh, Pub. for the Bazaar book committee by W. Brown, 1925. xiii,173p

Robert Louis Stevenson: died Dec. 3d, 1894. McClure's Magazine 4:286 F '95

Robert Louis Stevenson, 1850-94. Bookn 26:684-8, 726 My '08

Robert Louis Stevenson memorial. Edinburgh, Skinner, nd 4p

Roberts, Morley A visit to R. L. Stevenson. A "personal view." Lit 9:85-6 Jl 27 '01

Roberts, Richard Ellis Reading for pleasure and other essays. London, Methuen, 1928

Roberts, W. Stevenson's Davos-Platz booklets. Ath 1:498 Ap 22 '99

Robertson, John Mackinnon Stevenson on Burns. *In* New essays towards a critical method. London, Lane, 1897. p273-99

Stevenson's minor works. *In* Criticisms. London, Bonner, 1903. vol II p46-59

Robertson, Stuart Sir Thomas Browne and R. L. Stevenson. J Engl & Germ Philol 20:371-84 Jl '21

Robinson, Charles Mulford Stevenson's literary work in college. Bookm (NY) 1:316-20 Je '95

Robinson, William Albert Secret of Robert Louis Stevenson's success. Meth R 90:912-26 N '08

Rodger, Hugh R. L. S. and the Scottish Convenanters. Bookm (Lond) 62:79-81 My '22

Rose-Soley, A. R. Vailima: the place of the five rivers. Overland Monthly 2d ser 33:389-99 My '99

Rosebery, Archibald Philip Primrose, 5th earl of Robert Louis Stevenson. *In* Miscellanies, literary and historical. London, Hodder and Stoughton [1921] vol II p22-9

Robert Louis Stevenson. *In* Wallace, Burns, Stevenson: appreciations. . . Stirling, Mackay, 1905. p65-80

Robert Louis Stevenson. Liv Age 212: 187-90 Ja 16 '97

Rosenblatt, Louise L'idée de l'art pour l'art dans la littérature anglaise pendant la période victorienne. Paris, Champion, 1931. p234-41

Ross, J. Calder R. L. Stevenson and Swanston cottage. Scottish Notes and Queries 11:[129] Mr '98

R. L. Stevenson and Swanston, Midlothian. Scottish Notes & Queries 9: 36-7 Ag '95

Ross, J. Edgar Silverado today. Overland Monthly ns 53:193-9 Mr '09

Ross, John A. The early home of Robert Louis Stevenson. Good Words 36:181-6 '95

Roughead, William The abduction of Jean Kay. Juridical Review 29:137-61 Je '17

Rouville, M. de R. L. Stevenson. Groot-Nederland 28: 536-46, 637-51 My, Je '30

Royal Institute of Great Britain. Weekly evening meeting, Friday, February 10, 1911. . . Robert Louis Stevenson. [London, Printed by William Clowes and Sons, 1911] 1-21p

Rutherford, Mildred Robert Louis Stevenson. *In* English authors. Atlanta, Ga. Franklin printing and publishing co. 1906. p676-81

Safroni-Middleton, A. Sailor and beachcomber. . . New York, Scribner, 1915. 7-304p (Rev by C. S. Northup in Dial 59: 564 D 9 '15)

A vagabond's Odyssey. London, Richards, 1916. passim

Saintsbury, George Edward Bateman The English novel. London, Dent, 1913. p293-5

A history of English prose rhythm. London, Macmillan, 1912. p440-1

Saintsbury, G. E. B.—*Continued*
Robert Louis Balfour Stevenson. *In* A history of nineteenth century literature. New York, Macmillan, 1910. p338-41
Stevenson and the problem of style. T L S Ja 20 '21 p43

Salmon, John
Two Stevenson queries. [i. "The dumlicide Justice." ii. "The licentiate Lucius."] T L S My 26 '21 p341

Sampson, George
On playing the sedulous ape. *In* Essays and studies by members of the English Association. Oxford, Clarendon press, 1920. vol VI p67-87

Sanchez, (Mrs) Nellie (Van de Grift)
In California with Robert Louis Stevenson. Scrib M 60:467-81 O '16
Some Stevenson legends. Overland Monthly ns 88:10 Ja '30

Sarolea, Charles
Robert Louis Stevenson and France. . . Edinburgh, Robert Louis Stevenson Fellowship [1923] 96p (Noted in T L S D 25 '24 p886)

Scheffauer, Herman
Stevenson and Simoneau. Cornhill 100: 459-65 O '09; Bookn 28:882-5 Ag '10

Schell, Sherril
Stevenson and the "Dead man's chest." Mentor 11:42 Jl '23

Schnack, Friedrich
Leben Stevensons. Der Wächter 10:77-9 '28
Robert Louis Stevenson. Der Kunstwart 42:195-7 D '28

Schuyler, Montgomery
The canonization of Stevenson. Cent ns 36:478-80 Jl '99

Schweikert, H. C. (ed)
Short stories. New York, Harcourt, Brace [c1925] p434-5 [Collection of short stories with brief sketch of authors]

Schwob, Marcel
R. L. S. New Review 12:153-60 F '95
R. L. S., an essay; done into English by . . . A. Lenalie. Portland, Maine, Mosher, 1920. xv,45p
Robert Louis Stevenson. *In* Spicilège. . . Paris, Au sans pareil, 1920. p39-48
Stevenson and Villon. Lit 5:449 N 4 '99

Scott and Stevenson and the supernatural. Acad 77:606-7 O 9 '09

Scribner, firm, publishers, New York
A little book of R. L. S. New York, Scribner [c1920] 15p
The shadow of Stevenson. Nation (NY) 78:448 Je 9 '04

Sharp, William
The country of Stevenson. *In* Literary geography. New York, Scribner, 1904. p20-36

In Stevenson's country. Harper M 105: 497-504 S '02

Sherman, Stuart Pratt
R. L. S. encounters the "Modern" writers on their own ground. *In* Critical woodcuts. New York, Scribner, 1926. p156-72
What is biographical truth? *In* Emotional discovery of America, and other essays. New York, Farrar and Rinehart, 1932. p196-212
Who made the Stevenson myth? *In* Emotional discovery of America, and other essays. New York, Farrar and Rinehart, 1932. p181-95

Shipman, Louis Evan
Stevenson's first landing in New York. Book B ns 13:13-15 F '96

Shorter, Clement King
Victorian literature. New York, Dodd, Mead, 1897. p59-60

Shuster, George Nauman
The surrender of Robert Louis Stevenson. Cath World 120:89-95 O '24

Simpson, E[velyn] Blantyre
Robert Louis Stevenson. (Spirit of the age ser no II) Boston, Luce, 1906. 72p
The Robert Louis Stevenson originals. New York, Scribner [1913] 3-213p (Noted in Bookm (NY) 36:605-6 F '13; rev in Spec 110:693-4 Ap 26 '13)
Robert Louis Stevenson's Edinburgh days. . . London, Hodder & Stoughton, 1898. vi,291p
(Rev in Lit W 30:374-5 N 11 '99; Nation (NY) 69:302-3 O 19 '99; Bookm (Lond) 15:79 D '98)
Some notes of Stevenson's childhood. Book B ns 18:298-303 My '99
Stevenson's hills of home. Liv Age 229: 255-9 Ap 27 '01
Stevenson's two mothers. *In* Robert Louis Stevenson: his work and his personality, ed. by A. St. John Adcock. London, Hodder and Stoughton, 1924. p11-21; *same.* Bookm (Lond) 12:143-6 S '97; *same in* Robert Louis Stevenson. A Bookman (Lond) extra number, 1913. London, Hodder & Stoughton [1913] p26-31

Sir Sidney Colvin in Stevenson's defense. A reply to G. S. Hellman's "The Stevenson myth." Liv Age 316:181-2 Ja 20 '23

Skerryvore. T L S D 4 '19 p711

Skinner, Helen
The development of Stevenson's prose style. Masters essay, Univ. of Texas, 1933. 262ff

Sladen, K.
R. L. S. in the second book. School (Toronto) 19:148-9 O '30

Smith, Frederic
The letters of Robert Louis Stevenson. Manch Q 22:297-322 '03

Smith, Frederick M.
Stevenson's essays. Poet Lore 14:70-83 O '02

Smith, Kate Leslie
Stevenson's view of woman. Booklover's Magazine 5:79-85 Ja '05

Smith, Lewis Worthington (ed)
Current reviews. New York, Holt [c1926] p62-8

Snyder, Alice D.
Paradox and antithesis in Stevenson's essays: a structural study. J Engl & Germ Philol 19:540-59 O '20

Stevenson's conception of the fable. J Engl & Germ Philol 21:160-8 Ja '22

Some tendencies of prose style. Edin R 190:369-70, 373 O '99

Spencer, W. T.
Books and the man. Bookman's Journal 2:85 Je 4 '20

Sprenger, Emil
Robert Louis Stevenson. Seine weltanschauung und seine kunst. Diss. Göttingen, 1923. vii,99p

[Squire, John Collings] Eagle, Solomon [pseud]
[Why has Edinburgh no monument to Stevenson?] (Books in general) New Statesm 13:292 Je 21 '19

Starrett, Vincent
The dead man's chest. Colophon, Part XVII '34

The history of a chanty. Freeman 6: 228-30 N 15 '22

In Inn of Aberhuern. . . Galleon 1:63-72 Jl '24

In praise of Stevenson; an anthology. . . Chicago, The Bookfellows, 1919. 142p

Stead, William Thomas
The man of dreams. Borderland Ja '95 p17-22

Stedman, Edmund Clarence
The work of Robert Louis Stevenson. In Modern eloquence; ed. by Thomas B. Reed. Philadelphia, Morris [c1900] vol IX p1098-1103

Stephen, J.
"Dumlicide." T L S Je 9 '21 p373

Stephen, (Sir) Leslie
Robert Louis Stevenson. Nat R 38:725-43 Ja '02; same. Liv Age 232:463-77 F 22 '02

Robert Louis Stevenson; an essay. (Ariel booklets) London, Putnam [1902] [2] 61p

Style and genius of Stevenson. In Studies of a biographer. New York, Putnam, 1907. vol IV p191-229

Steuart, John Alexander
The cap of youth, being the love-romance of Robert Louis Stevenson. . . Philadelphia, Lippincott, 1927. 394p

Robert Louis Stevenson. Nat-Ath 36: 357-8 D 6 '24

Robert Louis Stevenson. T L S N 6, 20 '24 p710, 776; see also ibid. D 11 '24 p850 and Ja 22 '25 p56

Robert Louis Stevenson, man and writer; a critical biography. . . Boston, Little, Brown, 1924. 2 vols xxi,418p; 352p
(Rev by R. Lynd in Yale R ns 16:156-61 O '26; C. Hamilton in Literary Digest International Book Review 3:110-11 Ja '25; Edin R 241:198 Ja '25; Dublin Review 176:292-3 Ap '25; Lond Q R 143:125-6 Ja '25; C. H. Gaines in No Am 221:567-70 Mr '25; American Mercury 4:125-7 Ja '25; Queen's Q 33:209-11 O-D '25; J. Freeman in Lond Merc 11:435-7 F '25; F. Swinnerton in Sat R Lit 1:344 D 6 '24; G. S. Hellman in Bookm (NY) 60:575-7 Ja '25; R. Church in Spec 133:696 N 8 '24; S. Colvin in Nat-Ath 36:268-70 N 15 '24; noted in T L S O 30 '24 p687)

To Mr. Robert Louis Stevenson. In Letters to living authors. London, Sampson Low, Marston, Searle and Rivington, 1890. p163-75
(Rev in Speaker 2:530-1 N 8 '90)

Stevenson, Fanny (Van de Grift) Osbourne (Mrs. Robert Louis Stevenson)
The cruise of the "Janet Nichol" among the South Sea islands; a diary. . . New York, Scribner, 1914. x,189p

Some letters of Mrs. R. L. Stevenson and one from Henry James; ed. by S. Colvin. Empire Review 39:238-55, 373-91 Mr-Ap '24

Stevenson, (Mrs) Margaret Isabella (Balfour)
From Saranac to the Marquesas and beyond; being letters written by Mrs. M. I. Stevenson during 1887-88, to her sister, Jane Whyte Balfour. . . New York, Scribner, 1903. xx,313p
(Rev in Ath 2:645-6 N 14 '03)

Letters from Samoa. . . New York, Scribner, 1906. x,340p
(Rev in Acad 70:426-7 My 5 '06)

Stevenson's baby book; being the record of the sayings and doings of Robert Louis Stevenson. . . San Francisco, Howell, 1922. 58p
(Noted by G. H. Sargent in Bookman's Journal 7:68-9 O '22)

Stevenson, Robert Louis
Across the plains: with other memories and essays. London, Chatto and Windus, 1892. x,317p
(Rev in Dial 13:83 Jl '92; National Observer 7:590-1 Ap 23 '92; Literary World (Lond) ns 45:356-7 Ap 15 '92; Nation (NY) 55:145 Ag 25 '92; Speaker 5:657-8 Mr 28 '92; Book B ns 9: 169-70 My '92; Gent M 272:638-9 Je '92; Sat R 73:630-1 My 28 '92; Spec 69:99-100 Jl 16 '92; R. Le Gallienne in Acad 41:462-4 My 14 '92; Ath 1:533 Ap 23 '92; Critic (NY) 20:312 Je 4 '92)

Stevenson, Robert Louis—*Continued*

Additional letters of Robert Louis Stevenson. London, Methuen [1901] 7p

The amateur emigrant. From the Clyde to Sandy Hook. Chicago, Stone and Kimball, 1895. viii,182p
(Rev in Bookm (NY) 1:46 F '95; Spec 74:165-7 F 2 '95; Dial 18:182 Mr 16 '95; Book B ns 12:151 Ap '95; noted in Lit W 26:90-1 Mr 23 '95)

Ballads. London, Chatto and Windus, 1890. viii,137p
(Rev in Nation (NY) 52:321 Ap 16 '91; Speaker 3:24-5 Ja 3 '91; Book B ns 7:662 Ja '91; National Observer 5:151 D 27 '90; Spec 66:17-18 Ja 3 '91; Lit W 22:39 Ja 31 '91; C. Monkhouse in Acad 39:108-9 Ja 31 '91; Ath 1:503 Ap 18 '91; Critic (NY) 18:108 F 28 '91; Sat R 71:331-2 Mr 14 '91; Dial 20:81-2 F 1 '96)

The black arrow. London, Cassell, 1888. viii,324p
(Rev in Lit W 19:230 Jl 21 '88; Acad 34:150 S 8 '88; Critic (NY) 12:303-4 Je 23 '88; Spec 61:1099-1100 Ag 11 '88; Book B ns 5:246-8 Jl '88; Deutsche Rundschau 64:318 '90)

Brave words about death. London, Chatto and Windus, 1916. 63p
(Rev in Spec 117:477-8 O 21 '16)

Catriona. A sequel to "Kidnapped." Being memoirs of the further adventures of David Balfour at home and abroad. . . London, Cassell, 1893. x, 371p
(Rev in Critic (NY) 23:180-1 S 16 '93; W. M. Payne in Dial 15:226 O 16 '93; Nation (NY) 57:451-2 D 14 '93; Lit W 24:307-8 S 23 '93; Book B ns 10:317, 505-6 S, D '93; Sat R 76:333 S 16 '93; A. Waugh in Acad 44:337 O 21 '93; Scottish Review 23:44-5 Ja '94; Ath 2:375-7 S 16 '93; Literary World (Lond) ns 48:163-4 S 8 '93)

A child's garden of verses. London, Longmans, Green, 1885. xii,101p
(Rev in Spec 58:382-3 Mr 21 '85; Lit W 16:228 Je 27 '85; Lit W 27:202 Je 27 '96; Dial 6:42 Je '85; Atlan 77:423 Mr '96; H. C. Bunner in Book B ns 2:103-4 My '85; Critic (NY) 27:425 D 21 '95; Bookselling 1:121-2 D '95)

Edinburgh: picturesque notes. London, Seeley, Jackson, and Halliday, 1879. viii,39p
(Rev in Critic (NY) 14:38 Ja 26 '89; Critic (NY) 30:76 Ja 30 '97; Ath 2:859 D 28 '78; Sat R 47:120-1 Ja 25 '79; Spec 77:152 Ag 1 '96; Lit W 27:243-4 Ag 8 '96; Sat R 82:608 D 12 '96)

Essays in the art of writing. London, Chatto and Windus, 1905. 160p
(Rev in Acad 69:918 S 9 '05; Ath 2:464 O 7 '05)

Essays of travel. London, Chatto and Windus, 1905. 254p
(Rev in Ath 1:781 Je 24 '05; Bookm (Lond) 28:166 Ag '05)

Fables. New York, Scribner, 1896. viii, 92p
(Rev in Dial 21:260 N 1 '96)

Familiar studies of men and books. London, Chatto and Windus, 1882. xxx, 397p
(Rev in Sat R 53:508-9 Ap 22 '82; W. E. Henley in Acad 21:224-5 Ap 1 '82; Ath 1:405 Ap 1 '82; Dial 8:44 Je '87; Nation (NY) 44:517 Je 16 '87; Lit W 18:179-80 Je 11 '87)

A foot-note to history: eight years of trouble in Samoa. London, Cassell, 1892. viii,322p
(Rev in Ind 44:1562-3 N 3 '92; Lit W 23:307 S 10 '92; Book B ns 9:301 Ag '92; Ath 2:343-4 S 10 '92; Critic (NY) 21:188-9 O 8 '92; Bookm (Lond) 3:28 O '92; Dial 13:217 O 1 '92; Literary World (Lond) ns 46:155-6 S 2 '92)

In the South Seas. . . London, Chatto and Windus, 1896. x,370p
(Rev in Acad 60:30-1 Ja 12 '01; Ath 1:69-70 Ja 19 '01; Book B ns 13:763-5 D '96; Lit W 27:341 O 17 '96; Literary World (Lond) ns 63:167-8 F 22 '01; Speaker ns 3:455-6, 539-40 Ja 26, F 16 '01; G. F. Scott in Bookm (Lond) 19:194-5 Mr '01)

An inland voyage. London, Kegan Paul, 1878. x,238p
(Rev by P. G. Hamerton in Acad 13:547-8 Je 22 '78; Spec 51:926-7 Jl 20 '78; University Magazine 2:127-8 Jl '78; Ath 1:694-5 Je 1 '78; Dial 4:67 Jl '83; Westm ns 54:524 O '78; Lippinc 32:439 O '83; J. B. Carrington in Book B ns 25:229-32 O '02)

Island nights' entertainments. . . London, Cassell, 1893. x,277p
(Rev in Literary World (Lond) ns 47:431-2 My 12 '93; A. Lang in New Review 8:714 Je '93; L. Johnson in Acad 43:473-4 Je 3 '93; *same in* Post liminium. New York, Kennerley, 1912. p106-11; P. Mille in Revue de P 1:143-61 Ja '95; Archiv 91:87-8 '93; Book B ns 10:107 Ap '93; Ath 1:468-9 Ap 15 '93; Critic (NY) 23:134 Ag 26 '93; Sat R 75:439-40 Ap 22 '93; Bookm (Lond) 4:82-3 Je '93; W. M. Payne in Dial 14:340 Je 1 '93; Ind 45:1154 Ag 24 '93; Nation (NY) 57:32 Jl 13 '93; Lit W 24:292 S 9 '93; Speaker 7:460-1 Ap 22 '93)

Kidnapped: being memoirs of the adventures of David Balfour. . . London, Cassell, 1886. viii,311p
(Rev in Lit W 17:259 Ag 7 '86; Critic (NY) 9:100 Ag 28 '86; Spec 59:990-1 Jl 24 '86; Dial 7:91 Ag '86; Westm ns 71:271-2 Ja '87; Nation (NY) 43:397 N 11 '86)

Lay morals and other papers. London, Chatto and Windus, 1911. 328p
(Rev in Acad 80:579-80 My 13 '11)

Letter to William Ernest Henley. Golden Book 19:748 Je '34

Letters of Robert Louis Stevenson, ed. by Sir Sidney Colvin. Scrib M 25: 29-48, 187-207, 327-40, 485-99, 599-613, 729-44 Ja, F, Mr, Ap, My, Je '99; Scrib M 26:20-33, 242-52, 338-50, 469-84, 570-87 Jl, Ag, S, O, N '99

The letters of Robert Louis Stevenson; ed. by Sir Sidney Colvin. New York, Scribner, 1911. new ed 4 vols vii-xli, 340p; v-xii,382p; v-ix,392p; v-ix,417p
(Rev by H. S. Canby in Dial 50:436-7 Je 1 '11; Nation (NY) 92:650-1 Je 29 '11; Liv Age 270:176-80 Jl 15 '11; C. Hamilton in Bookm (NY) 33:628-31 Ag '11; J. C. Adams in Yale R ns 1: 312-18 Ja '12; Ath 2:33-4 Jl 8 '11; Bookm (Lond) 40:174 Jl '11; Out 98: 765-6 Ag 5 '11; Acad 81:268-9, 298-9 Ag 26, S 2 '11; Ind 71:594-5 S 14 '11; Spec 107:549-50 O 7 '11; Book Monthly 8:719-22 Jl '11; J. St. Loe Strachey in Spec 133:466 O 4 '24)

The letters of Robert Louis Stevenson to his family and friends, selected and ed. with notes and introd. by Sir Sidney Colvin. London, Methuen, 1899. 2 vols xliv,375p; xiii,384p
(Rev by I. Strong in Critic (NY) 35: 1133-6 D '99; S. R. Crockett in Bookm (Lond) 17:74 D '99; Outlook (Lond) 4:512 N 18 '99; A. Birrell in Contemp 77:50-60 Ja '00; *same.* Ecl M 71:429-37 Ap '00; Acad 57:563-5 N 18 '99; Lit 5:479-80 N 18 '99; R. Le Gallienne in Idler 16:656-64 D '99; Sat R 88:681 N 25 '99; Spec 83:750-1 N 18 '99; T. de Wyzewa in R Deux Mondes D 15 '99 p921-32; Church Q R 54:143-64 Ap '02; Speaker ns 1:171-2 N 18 '99; Ath 2: 679-80 N 18 '99; Lit W 30:431-2 D 9 '99; B. Perry in Atlan 85:702-5 My '00; Nation (NY) 70:5-6 Ja 4 '00; W. H. Low in Book B ns 19:359-63 D '99; Macmil 81:182-7 Ja '00; Liv Age 224: 337-45 F 10 '00; H. James, jr. in No Am 170:61-77 Ja '00; Out 63:952-3 D 23 '99; Ind 51:3295-7 D 7 '99; Dial 27:416-18 D 1 '99; Literary World (Lond) ns 60: 395-6 N 24 '99; Book-Lover (San Francisco) 2:363-5 '01; Quar R 191:176-97 Ja '00)

The master of Ballantrae. A winter's tale. London, Cassell, 1889. viii,332p
(Rev in Book B ns 6:321, 440-1 O, D '89; Lit W 20:365 O 26 '89; Blackw 146:696-702 N '89; G. Saintsbury in Acad 36:284 N 2 '89; Critic (NY) 15: 183 O 19 '89; Spec 63:437-8 O 5 '89; Scots Observer 2:583-4 O 12 '89; Nation (NY) 50:225 Mr 13 '90; J. Zupitza in Archiv 84:192-4 '90)

Memoir of Fleeming Jenkin. New York, Scribner, 1887. viii,302p
(Rev in Ath 2:34 Jl 13 '12; Critic (NY) 12:77-8 F 18 '88; Spec 61:270-2 F 25 '88; Dial 8:274 Mr '88; Blackw 143: 841-5 Je '88; noted in Book B ns 4:339 N '87)

Memories and portraits. London, Chatto and Windus, 1887. x,299p
(Rev by H. C. Beeching in Acad 33: 1-2 Ja 7 '88; New Princeton Review 6: 389-90 N '88; Lit W 19:20 Ja 21 '88; Critic (NY) 11:309-10 D 17 '87; Dial 8:226 Ja '88; Westm 129:389-90 Mr '88)

The merry men and other tales and fables. London, Chatto and Windus, 1887. x,296p
(Rev in Critic (NY) 10:188 Ap 16 '87; Sat R 63:313 F 26 '87; Spec 60:358-9 Mr 12 '87; W. M. Payne in Dial 7:292 Ap '87; Nation (NY) 44:429-30 My 19 '87; Lit W 18:85 Mr 19 '87; Blackw 141:564-7 Ap '87; Book B ns 4:48 Mr '87; Archiv 87:466 '91)

New Arabian nights. London, Chatto and Windus, 1882. 2 vols xi,269p; vii, 234p
(Rev in Sat R 54:250-1 Ag 19 '82; Spec 55:1450-2 N 11 '82; Lit W 13:461 D 16 '82; Literary World (Lond) ns 50:372 N 16 '94; Cent 25:628-9 F '83; T. Bentzon in R Deux Mondes Ap 1 '80 p550-81; Quar R 173:488-92 O '91; Quar R 180:324-53 Ap '95)

New letters of Robert Louis Stevenson, ed. by Sir Sidney Colvin. Scrib M 49: 385-98 Ap '11; Scrib M 73:643-52 Je '23; Scrib M 74:3-11, 140-8 Jl, Ag '23

New poems and variant readings. London, Chatto and Windus, 1918. 156p
(Rev in Ath 1:26 Ja '19; Spec 121:732 D 21 '18)

On the choice of a profession. London, Chatto and Windus, 1916. 28p
(Rev in Spec 117:807-8 D 23 '16)

Poems
(Rev in T L S Mr 8 '07 p73-4; Liv Age 253:245-9 Ap 27 '07; Atlan 78:425 S '96)

Poems of Robert Louis Stevenson hitherto unpublished, with introd. and notes by G. S. Hellman and W. P. Trent. Boston, Bibliophile society, 1921
(Noted in Bookm (NY) 45:132-3 Ap '17; Dial 62:227 Mr 22 '17)

Prince Otto. A romance. London, Chatto and Windus, 1885. viii,300p
(Rev in Lit W 17:17 Ja 9 '86; E. Purcell in Acad 29:140-1 F 27 '86; T. Bentzon in R Deux Mondes Ap 1 '88 p550-81; Harper W 44:921 S 29 '00)

St. Ives. Being the adventures of a French prisoner in England. New York, Scribner, 1897. viii,438p
(Rev by E. O. U. Valentine in Bookm (NY) 6:251-3 N '97; Nation (NY) 66: 15 Ja 6 '98; Acad 50:391 N 14 '96; Literary World (Lond) ns 56:314-15 O 22 '97; Acad 52:307 O 16 '97; Lit 1:18-19 O 23 '97; R. Burton in Book B ns 15: 360-1 N '97; Critic (NY) 31:280 N 13 '97; Spec 79:603 O 30 '97; L. H. Vincent in Atlan 80:846-51 D '97; Bookm (Lond) 13:45 N '97; Lit W 29:3-4 Ja 8 '98; W. M. Payne in Dial 23:282-3 N 16 '97; Citizen (Phila) 4:40-1 Ap '98)

Stevenson, Robert Louis—*Continued*

Selected essays
(Rev in T L S Ja 3 '24 p7)

The Silverado squatters. . . London,
Chatto and Windus, 1883. viii,255p
(Rev in Lit W 15:51-2 F 23 '84; Critic
(NY) 1:52 F 2 '84; Spec 57:188-9 F 9
'84; Dial 4:261 F '84; Nation (NY) 38:
149 F 14 '84)

Some letters by Robert Louis Stevenson
[to A. Trevor Hadden] New York, In-
galls Kimball, 1902. 45p

Songs of travel and other verses. Lon-
don, Chatto and Windus, 1896. x,85p
(Rev in Ath 1:208-9 F 13 '97; Literary
World (Lond) ns 54:449-50 N 27 '96;
E. Purcell in Acad 50:253-4 O 10 '96;
Sat R 82:425 O 17 '96)

The Stevenson reader. . . ed. by Lloyd
Osbourne. London, Chatto and Win-
dus, 1898. viii,261p
(Rev in Ath 2:447 O 1 '98)

Stories
(Rev by R. A. Taylor in Spec 140:877-8
Je 9 '28; T L S Ja 5 '33 p1-2; O. Glöde
in Engl Stud 63:181 '28)

Strange case of Dr. Jekyll and Mr. Hyde.
London, Longmans, Green, 1886. viii,
143p
(Rev by T. Bentzon in R Deux Mondes
Ap 1 '88 p550-81; J. A. Noble in Acad
29:55 Ja 23 '86; Sat R 61:55-6 Ja 9 '86;
Dial 6:301 Mr '86; Literary World
(Lond) ns 54:80-1 Jl 24 '96; Harper M
72:972 My '86; Book B ns 3:23-4 F
'86; T L S N 20 '30 p983; noted in
Critic (NY) ns 5:68 F 6 '86; Literary
World (Lond) ns 33:108 Ja 29 '86)

Tales and fantasies. London, Chatto and
Windus, 1905. viii,237p
(Rev in Ath 2:238 Ag 19 '05; L. G.
Brock in Bookm (Lond) 28:209-10 S
'05)

Travels with a donkey in the Cévennes.
London, Kegan Paul, 1879. xii,227p
(Rev in Acad 15:563 Je 28 '79; Lit W
10:198-9 Je 21 '79; Spec 52:1224-5 S 27
'79; Ath 1:817-18 Je 28 '79; Brit Q 70:
258-9 O '79; H. M. Stanley in Dial 22:
57 Ja 16 '97; Nation (NY) 28:423 Je
19 '79; Westm ns 56:237 Jl '79; Atlan
44:652 N '79)

Treasure island. London, Cassell, 1883.
viii,292p
(Rev in Lit W 15:51-2 F 23 '84; Critic
(NY) 1:111 Mr 8 '84; Sat R 56:737-8 D
8 '83; Spec 57:318-19 Mr 8 '84; Dial 5:
19 My '84; Literary World (Lond) ns
60:504 D 22 '99; Nation (NY) 38:201-2
Ap 3 '84; L. Stevenson in Univ. of California Chronicle 27:422-3 O '25)

Underwoods. London, Chatto and Windus, 1887. xviii,138p
(Rev in Blackw 142:709-13 N '87; Sat
R 64:460-1 O 1 '87; Edin R 178:497 O
'93; Critic (NY) 11:112-13 S 3 '87; W.

M. Payne in Dial 8:184-5 O '87; Westm
128:1177-8 D '87; Lit W 18:367 O 29
'87; Ath 2:333-4 S 10 '87)

Unpublished Stevenson manuscripts. Liv
Age 314:368-9 Ag 5 '22

Vailima letters: being correspondence ad-
dressed by Robert Louis Stevenson to
Sidney Colvin, November 1890-October
1894. London, Methuen, 1895. xx,
366p
(Rev in Bookm (NY) 2:375-6 Ja '96;
Edin R 183:332-4 Ap '96; Nation (NY)
63:50-1 Jl 16 '96; Blackw 158:922-6 D
'95; Atlan 77:424 Mr '96; Bookselling
1:132 D '95; Sat R 80:689 N 23 '95;
Critic (NY) 27:360-1 N 30 '95; Nation-
al Magazine 4:103-4 Ap '96; R. Le
Gallienne in Idler 9:117-18 F '96;
McClure's Magazine 5:522-32 N '95;
Spec 75:663-4 N 16 '95; National
Observer 14:711 N 2 '95; D. Sladen in
Literary World (Lond) ns 52:379-80
N 15 '95)

Virginibus puerisque and other papers.
London, Kegan Paul, 1881. viii,296p
(Rev in Nation (NY) 46:33-4 Ja 12 '88;
Lit W 19:19 Ja 21 '88; Ath 1:589-90 Ap
30 '81; Sat R 51:528-9 Ap 23 '81; Spec
54:775-6 Je 11 '81)

Weir of Hermiston. An unfinished romance. London, Chatto and Windus,
1896. viii,289p
(Rev in Literary World (Lond) ns 53:
571-2 Je 19 '96; Atlan 78:717 N '96; Sat
R 81:603-4 Je 13 '96; E. Purcell in
Acad 49:521-2 Je 27 '96; Ath 1:673 My
23 '96; Book B ns 13:300 Je '96; Spec
76:843-5 Je 13 '96; Lit W 27:196-7 Je 27
'96; W. M. Payne in Dial 21:18 Jl 1 '96)

The will of Robert Louis Stevenson.
McClure's Magazine 5:176-8 Jl '95

The works of Robert Louis Stevenson.
Edinburgh, Constable, 1894-1898. 24
vols
(Rev in Church Q R 31:195-211 O '90;
Out 52:897-8 N 30 '95; Spec 73:813-14 D
8 '94; Ath 2:213-15, 245-7 Ag 14, 21 '97;
Edin R 182:106-31 Jl '95; Lit W 26:415-
16 N 30 '95; Spec 76:87-8 Ja 18 '96;
Dial 19:292 N 16 '95; Dial 21:47 Jl 16
'96; Nation (NY) 62:36-8 Ja 9 '96;
Lond Q R 85:1-20 O '95; H. E. Scudder in Atlan 77:274-5 F '96; Bookm
(NY) 2:528-9 F '96; Bookm (NY) 5:
244-7 My '97; Bookm (Lond) 8:21 Ap
'95; Bookselling 1:11 Ja '95; A. Macdonell in Bookm (Lond) 11:145 F '97
and Bookm (Lond) 12:17-18 Ap '97;
Ath 2:610 N 17 '06; Ath 1:409 Ap 6 '07;
Ath 2:68, 268, 791-2 Jl 20, S 7, D 21 '07;
H. C. Beeching in Bookm (Lond) 31:
179-81 Ja '07 and Bookm (Lond) 32:164,
166 Ag '07; Spec 107:902 N 25 '11; Spec
110:157 Ja 25 '13; Contemp 134:528-31
O '28; Quar R 180:324-53 Ap '95; Liv
Age 214:811-16, 870-6 S 18, 25 '97; C.
Van Doren in Cent 3:507-9 F '26; Sewanee R 34:368-70 Jl-S '26; E. Pearson
in Out 142:336-7 Mr 3 '26; R. Lynd in

Yale R ns 16:156-61 O '26; A. Macdonell in Bookm (Lond) 9:155-6 F '96 and 10:50-1 My '96; G. Keckeis in Literarischer Handweiser 61:626 Ag '25; H. D. Davray in Mercure Fr 71:551-2 F 1 '08; Mercure Fr 64:318 N 15 '06)

Stevenson, Robert Louis and Henley, William Ernest

Admiral Guinea. A melodrama in four acts. Edinburgh, Printed for private circulation only by R. and R. Clark, 1884. 62p
(Rev by G. B. Shaw in Sat R 84:620-1 D 4 '87)

Deacon Brodie, or, The double life: a melodrama. London, Heinemann, 1897. viii,182p [first separate issue]
(Rev in Critic (NY) 10:244 My 14 '87; F. Brock in Gent M 289:349-55 O '00)

Macaire. A melodramatic farce in three acts. Edinburgh, Printed for private circulation only, 1885. iv,40p
(Rev in Dial 20:51 Ja 16 '96)

Three plays. . . London, Nutt, 1892. xii, 250p
(Rev by L. Johnson in Acad 43:277-8 Ap 1 '93; Critic (NY) 22:125-6 Mr 4 '93; Bookm (Lond) 3:127-8 Ja '93; Nation (NY) 55:375 N 17 '92; Book B ns 9:543 D '92; A. Lang in New Review 8:247-8 F '93)

Stevenson, Robert Louis and Osbourne, Lloyd

The ebb-tide. A trio and quartette. London, Heinemann, 1894. viii,237p
(Rev in Ath 2:450-1 O 6 '94; Critic (NY) 25:88-9 Ag 11 '94; I. Zangwill in Critic (NY) 25:342-3 N 24 '94; Spec 73:443-4 O 6 '94; W. M. Payne in Dial 17:122-3 S 1 '94; Literary World (Lond) ns 50:203-4 S 28 '94; Nation (NY) 59:219 S 20 '94; Book B ns 11:445 O '94)

The wrecker. London, Cassell, 1892. viii,427p
(Rev by S. Kirk in Atlan 70:546-50 O '92; Literary World (Lond) ns 46:43-4 Jl 15 '92; W. M. Payne in Dial 13:104 Ag '92; Sat R 74:77-8 Jl 16 '92; Spec 69:132-3 Jl 23 '92; Lit W 23:255 Jl 30 '92; L. Johnson in Acad 42:103-4 Ag 6 '92; Ath 2:189 Ag 6 '92; Bookm (Lond) 2:149-50 Ag '92; National Observer 8:222-3 Jl 16 '92; Nation (NY) 55:263 O 6 '92; Speaker 6:89 Jl 16 '92; Book B ns 9:261-2 Jl '92; Pall Mall Budget 40:1036 Jl 14 '92)

The wrong box. London, Longmans, Green, 1889. iv,283p
(Rev in Book B ns 6:176, 214-16 Je, Jl '89; Lit W 20:236-7 Jl 20 '89; R. F. Littledale in Acad 36:51 Jl 27 '89; W. S. Walsh in Cosmopolitan 7:525-6 S '89; Critic (NY) 15:2 Jl 6 '89; W. M. Payne in Dial 10:57 Jl '89; Blackw 146:255-6 Ag '89)

Stevenson, Robert Louis and Stevenson, Fanny Van de Grift

More new Arabian nights. The dynamiter. London, Longmans, Green, 1885. vii,207p
(Rev by T. Bentzon in R Deux Mondes Ap 1 '88 p550-81; Book B ns 2:158 Jl '85; Lit W 16:209 Je 13 '85; J. W. Mackail in Acad 27:358 My 23 '85; Critic (NY) 6:304 Je 27 '85; Dial 6:121-2 S '85; Nation (NY) 41:158 Ag 20 '85)

Stevenson, a letter and a debt. Liv Age 312:431 F 18 '22

Stevenson again on the stage [dramatization of the Master of Ballantrae] Lit Digest 67:32-3 O 9 '20

[Stevenson and adventure] Book B ns 9:108 Ap '92

Stevenson and Bernard Shaw. Bookm (NY) 14:341 D '01

Stevenson and Hazlitt. Acad 57:768 D 30 '99

Stevenson and Hogg. Acad 78:419-21 Ap 30 '10

Stevenson and Samoa. Lit W 30:54 F 18 '99

Stevenson and Shelley. T L S Jl 20 '22 p480

Stevenson as progenitor of our neurotic literary optimism. Current Opinion 63:52 Jl '17

Stevenson as seen by his editor. Lit Digest 48:435 F 28 '14

[Stevenson at Saranac] Dial 59:88 Ag 15 '15

Stevenson at the Golden Gate. Biblio 3:483-7 Jl '23

[Stevenson autograph letter] Cosmopolitan 19:259 Jl '95

The Stevenson fountain. Lit W 28:458 D 11 '97; Book B ns 15:644-6 Ja '98

The Stevenson fountain in San Francisco. Critic (NY) 31:205 O 9 '97

Stevenson from a new point of view. Atlan 85:429-31 Mr '00

Stevenson gives away his birthday. Mentor 16:64 My '28

The Stevenson heritage. Bookm (NY) 39:113-14 Ap '14

Stevenson: his biographer and his critic. Lit 9:502 N 30 '01

Stevenson in extremis. Lit Digest 83:30-1 D 6 '24

Stevenson in his island home. Book B ns 10:641-2 Ja '94

Stevenson in his latest biography. Overland Monthly ns 39:560-2 Ja '02

Stevenson in Samoa. World Wide (Montreal) Ag 29 '31 p1387

A Stevenson letter. Bookm (NY) 43:369-70 Je '16

Stevenson letters; Sir Sidney Colvin's forecast of the new definitive edition. Book Monthly 8:560-4 My '11

A **Stevenson** memorial. Canadian Magazine 10:277 Ja '98

The **Stevenson** monument. . . Overland Monthly ns 30:528-30 D '97

A **Stevenson** portrait. T L S F 12 '25 p104

Stevenson remeasured by war standards. Cur Opin 68:241-2 F '20

Stevenson to-day. Liv Age 304:228-34 Ja 24 '20; *same in* T L S D 4 '19 p701-2

Stevenson unwhitewashed. Current Opinion 77:709-10 D '24

A **Stevensonian** hero. Spec 73:171-2 Ag 11 '94

Stevensoniana. Critic (NY) 26:160 Mr 2 '95; Critic (NY) 27:330-1 N 16 '95; Critic (NY) 26:16-17 Ja 5 '95; Critic (NY) 25:453 D 29 '94; Critic (NY) 26:16-17, 29-33 Ja 5, 12 '95

Stevensoniana, being a reprint of various literary and pictorial miscellany associated with Robert Louis Stevenson the man and his work. . . New York, Mansfield, 1900. 16p

Stevensoniana: the Trudeau dedications. Book B ns 12:12-14 F '95

[**Stevenson's** autobiography] Dial 52:303 Ap 16 '12

Stevenson's borrowed plot. Lit Digest 49:105-6 Jl 18 '14

Stevenson's fables. Acad 53:328-9 Mr 19 '98

Stevenson's gospel for these times. Scrib M 67:505-7 Ap '20

Stevenson's handwriting. Liv Age 311:681-2 D 10 '21

Stevenson's pirates lit up by footlights. Lit Digest 52:18-19 Ja 1 '16

[**Stevenson's** printing-press] Critic (NY) 46:495-6 Je '05

Stevenson's requiem [song put to music] Sunset 25:508-9 N '10

Stevenson's romances. Sat R 78:676 D 22 '94

[**Stevenson's** tomb] Book B ns 14:458-9 Je '97

[**Stevenson's** "Travels with a Donkey"] Edin R 210:321-2 O '09

Stevenson's tributes to his wife. Cur Opin 56:295 Ap '14

Stevenson's Trudeau. Bookm (NY) 42:632-5 F '16

Stevenson's use of "obliterated." Notes & Q 163:287 O 15 '32

Stevenson's wife. Lit Digest 48:508-9 Mr 7 '14

Stewart, George Rippey, jr.
[Introduction to an article by Stevenson] Scrib M 68:209-10 Ag '20

The real Treasure Island. University of California Chronicle 28:207-13 Ap '26

Stevenson in California: a critical study. Masters essay, Univ. of California, 1920. ii,100ff

Stoddard, Charles Warren
Stevenson in the South Seas. *In* Exits and entrances. New York, Lothrop, 1903. p13-37

Stevenson's Monterey. National Magazine 23:246-59 D '05

Stoessl, Otto
Zwei englische erzähler. Zeitwende 3:268-71 '27

Strate, Jessie B.
The part played by climate in Stevenson's life and works. Geographical Society of Philadelphia. Bulletin 28:89-100 '30

Stevenson and geography. Geographical Society of Philadelphia. Bulletin 29:14-25 '31

Stringer, Arthur
On a portrait of "R. L. S." the invalid. Bookm (NY) 17:420 Je '03

Strong, (Mrs) Isobel (Osbourne)
Autograph letters, original manuscripts, books, portraits. . . from the library of the late R. L. Stevenson. New York, Anderson auction co., Nov. 23-25, 1914; Jan. 25-27, 1915

In Samoa with Stevenson. Cent ns 41:657-68 Mr '02

Mr. Stevenson's relations with Mr. Colvin. Critic (NY) 35:886-8 O '99

Robert Louis Stevenson. New York, Scribner, 1911. 3-87p
(Rev in Bookm (Lond) 41:111 N '11)

. . . Robert Louis Stevenson in his home life. Scrib M 19:531-47, 736-47 My, Je '96

Stevenson and Mataafa. Argonaut 44:5 Je 12 '99

Stevenson in Samoa. Cent ns 36:476-8 Jl '99

"Tin Jack." Critic (NY) 38:431-4 My '01

Strong, Isobel and Osbourne, Lloyd
Memories of Vailima. New York, Scribner, 1902. viii,228p
(Rev in T L S S 18 '03 p263-4; Ath 2:252-3 Ag 22 '03)

Stubbs, Laura
Stevenson's shrine; the record of a pilgrimage. London, Moring, 1903. 58p

The **suggestion** of Jekyll and Hyde. Bookm (NY) 14:339-41 D '01

Sullivan, Thomas Russell
Robert Louis Stevenson at Saranac. Scrib M 62:242-6 Ag '17

Swinnerton, Frank Arthur
R. L. Stevenson, a critical study. . . New York, Doran [c1923] viii,13-195p bibl p193-5
(Rev by C. S. Northup in Dial 59:561-4 D 9 '15; Ath 2:644-5 D 19 '14; T. P.'s Weekly 24:667 D 19 '14)

Symons, Arthur
Un mot sur Robert Louis Stevenson. Traduit par Jack Colen et Louis Thomas. Mercure Fr 57:471-5 O 1 '05

Robert Louis Stevenson. *In* Studies in prose and verse. London, Dent, 1904. p77-82

Robert Louis Stevenson. *In* Studies in two literatures. London, Smithers, 1897. p241-7

The talk of R. L. Stevenson. Scrib M 28:507-8 O '00

Tennant, R. W.
R. L. S. and Edinburgh. New Statesm 13:346 Jl 5 '19

Testimonials in favor of Robert Louis Stevenson [Privately printed, 1881] 18p (Widener Collection Harvard college library)

Textual errors in Stevenson. T L S Ag 21 '30 p668

[Thayer's winged figure above Stevenson's grave] Critic (NY) 46:422-3 My '05

Thomas, Edward
R. L. Stevenson. *In* Literary pilgrim in England. New York, Dodd, Mead, 1917. p311-18

Thompson, D'Arcy W.
Misprints in R. L. Stevenson. T L S F 23 '22 p125

Thorogood, Horace
The Stevenson spirit today. Lit 7:455-6 D 8 '00

Tinker, Edward Larocque
Robert Louis Stevenson, illustrator. Arts and Decoration 17:303 Ag '22

To Prospero at Samoa; poem. [signed "Y. Y."] *In* Robert Louis Stevenson: his work and his personality, ed. by A. St. John Adcock. London, Hodder and Stoughton, 1924. p84-5

Tomlinson, Henry Major
Robert Louis Stevenson. *In* Massingham, H. J. and Massingham, H. eds. The great Victorians. London, Ivor Nicholson and Watson [1932] p479-88

Tompkins, H. W.
Robert L. Stevenson. Gent M ns 75:283-99 S '05

Torossian, Aram
Stevenson as a literary critic. University of California Chronicle 27:43-60 Ja '25

Torrey, Bradford
Robert Louis Stevenson. Atlan 89:89-99 Ja '02

Robert Louis Stevenson. *In* Friends on the shelf. Boston, Houghton, Mifflin, 1906. p151-93

Tourneur, N.
Grub street and R. L. S. Weekly Review 4:364-5 Ap 20 '21

The man who saved Stevenson. Quarterly Notebook (Kansas City, Mo.) 1:17-19 Je '16

R. L. Stevenson in Grub Street. Miscellany (Cleveland) 3:41-3 '16

Townsend, H. (ed)
New letters of R. L. Stevenson with introductory note and comment. Harper M 104:123-6 D '01

Traill, H. D.
The literature of the Victorian era. Fortn 67:835-6 My '97

"Travels with a donkey in the Cevennes" —a reminiscence of Stevenson. Spec 117:732 D 9 '16

"Treasure Island" and "King Solomon's Mines." Notes & Q 7th ser 6:345 N 3 '88

Tree carving by Robert Louis Stevenson. Scottish Notes and Queries 11: facing 129 Mr '98

Trent, William Peterfield
Stevenson's workshop. Boston, The Bibliophile society, 1921. 63p

Triggs, William Henry
Mr. R. L. Stevenson as a Samoan chief. Cassell's Family Magazine 21:183-7 F '95

Stevenson's life in Samoa. His own description of the days at Vailima. Bookm (NY) 73:158-63 Ap '31

Tuell, Anne Kimball
Mrs. Meynell and her literary generation. New York, Dutton [c1925]

Under the beard of Buchanan. Blackw 165:270-1 F '99

Unsworth, Basil
Hunting for Stevensoniana in the Hawaiian Islands. Chamb J 8th ser 1:527-8 Jl '32

Untermeyer, Louis
Modern British poetry. New York, Harcourt, Brace [c1930] 3d rev ed p189-90

Vale, Charles
R. L. S.—a biography. Biblio 4:700-2 Ag '24

Vallandigham, Edward N.
R. L. S. Book B ns 12:124-5 Ap '95

Vallings, Harold
Stevenson among the Philistines. Temple 122:205-9 F '01

Vance, Hiram Albert
Robert Louis Stevenson. Sewanee R 10:223-33 Ap '02

VanDyke, Henry
An adventurer in a velvet jacket. Scrib M 72:171-9 Ag '22

VanRensselaer, (Mrs) M. G.
Robert Louis Stevenson, and his writing. Cent 51:123-8 N '95

Vaughn, Arthur Peirce
The charmed pen of Stevenson. Overland Monthly ns 65:165-9 F '15

Veth, C.
De historische romans van Stevenson. Tijdspiegel 2:184-200 Je '12

Veth, C.—*Continued*
R. L. Stevenson. Mannen en Vrouwen van Beteekenis Ja '10
Stevenson's vertellingen. Gulden Winckel p97-102 '11

Vince, C. A.
Stevenson and Scott. Central Literary Magazine Ap '27 p64-71

Vincent, Leon Henry
Stevenson, the vagabond and the philosopher. Stevenson's St. Ives. *In* The bibliotaph, and other people. . . Boston, Houghton, Mifflin, 1898. p202-33

Vinciguerra, Mario
Precursori: R. L. Stevenson. *In* Romantici e decadenti inglesi. Foligno, Campitelli [1926] p155-64

Vrooman, Julia Scott
Stevenson in San Francisco. *In* Vrooman, C. and Vrooman, J. S. The lure and the lore of travel. Boston, Sherman, French, 1914. p284-91; *same.* Arena 38:526-9 N '07
The strange case of Robert Louis Stevenson and Jules Simoneau. *In* Vrooman, C. and Vrooman, J. S. The lure and the lore of travel. Boston, Sherman, French, 1914. p264-83; *same.* Cent 72:343-50 Jl '06

Walker, Edwin T.
J. M. B. and R. L. S. Acad 66:181 F 13 '04

Walker, Helen Osborne
Stevenson the story teller. Masters essay, Univ. of Arizona, 1922. 49ff

Walker, Hugh
The later fiction. *In* The literature of the Victorian era. Cambridge, Univ. press, 1921. p799-811
The latter half of the nineteenth century. *In* The English essay and essayists. London, Dent [1914] p291-301

Walker, Hugh and Walker, (Mrs) Hugh
Outlines of Victorian literature. Cambridge, Univ. press, 1919. p147-50

Walkley, Arthur Bingham
Literary document. *In* More prejudice. New York, Knopf, 1932. p242-6

Wallace, William
The life and limitations of Stevenson. Scottish Review 35:13-35 Ja '00
Scotland, Stevenson, and Mr. Henley. New Liberal Review 3:79-86 F '02

Ward, Alfred C.
Robert Louis Stevenson: "The merry men." *In* Aspects of the modern short story. New York, Dial press, 1925. p102-15

Was Robert Louis Stevenson a second-rate literary artist? Current Opinion 58:119-20 F '15

Was Stevenson a plagiarist? Out 116:252-3 Je 13 '17

Wassermann, J.
Stevenson und Fielding. Lebensdienst p251-8 '28

Watson, Henry Brereton Marriott
Robert Louis Stevenson: an appreciation. Fortn 80:501-15 S '03; *also in* Couch fires. London, K. Paul, Trench, Trübner, 1912

Watson, William
Written in a copy of Mr. Stevenson's "Catriona." *In* Robert Louis Stevenson. A Bookman (Lond) extra number, 1913. London, Hodder & Stoughton [1913] p73

Watt, Francis
The original Weir of Hermiston. *In* Terrors of the law. . . London, Lane, 1902
R. L. S. New York, Macmillan, 1913. v, 311p
(Rev in Ath 1:444-5 Mr 28 '14; Spec 112:357 F 28 '14)
Robert Louis Stevenson and Edinburgh, with original drawings by A. W. Henley. Art J 58:46-50 '96

Watt, Lauchlan MacLean
Robert Louis Stevenson's contribution to literature and life. Scrib M 68:641-53 D '20

Watt, William
A personal anecdote of Robert Louis Stevenson. Scottish Notes and Queries 3d ser 1:149-50 O '23

Waugh, Arthur
Charm of Stevenson. *In* Tradition and change. . . London, Dutton, 1919. p239-45

Waugh, Joseph Laing
"Honest John," the shepherd-friend of Robert Louis Stevenson. Chamb J 7th ser 4:81-5 Ja 10 '14

Weber, Wilhelm
R. L. Stevenson. Ein beitrag zur beurteilung des prosadichters und essayisten. . . [Heilbronn, A. Landerer, 1903] 62p

Wedgwood, Julia
Ethics and literature. Contemp 71:65 Ja '97

Weygandt, Cornelius
Stevenson and the old question of style. *In* Century of the English novel. New York, Century, 1925. p229-38

Wheeler, C. B.
Stevenson's "The wrong box." Notes & Q 12th ser 4:224-5 Ag '18

White, Eric W.
Misprints of R. L. Stevenson. T L S F 9 '22 p93

Whiting, Marie Louise
Robert Louis Stevenson: The man in his "Life" and "Letters." Sewanee R 10:385-405 O '02

Whitmee, S. J.
Tusitala; R. L. S.—a new phase. Atlan 131:344-53 Mr '23

Whyte, W. Farmer
More tales of Tusitala. Sunset 25:497-507 N '10

Wild, Friedrich
Die englische literatur der gegenwart seit 1870; drama and roman. Wiesbaden, Dioskuren-verlag, 1928. p226-30

Wilde, Oscar
The decay of lying. 19th Cent 25:35-56 Ja '89

Wiley, Edwin
The optimism of Robert Louis Stevenson. [San Francisco? 1915?] 5 leaves

Williamson, Claude C. H.
R. L. S. *In* Writers of three centuries, 1789-1914. Philadelphia, Jacobs [1915?] p352-9

Wilson, Rufus Rockwell
Foreign authors in America. Bookm (NY) 13:371-7 Je '01

Winterich, John Tracy
Romantic stories of books; Treasure island. Pub W 118:613-16 Ag 16 '30

Wister, Owen
In memoriam Stevenson; poem. Atlan 75:547 Ap '95

With R. L. Stevenson in Samoa. Cornhill 70:27-33 Jl '94; *same.* Ecl M 123:257-60 Ag '94; *same.* Liv Age 202:252-6 Jl 28 '94

With Stevenson last May. Sat R 79:38-9 Ja 12 '95

Wood, Charline Fender
A comparison of the descriptive passages in the writings of Carlyle, Pater, and Stevenson. Masters essay, Columbia univ. 1921

Woods, Margaret L.
Poets of the 'eighties. *In* The eighteen-eighties, essays by fellows of the Royal Society of literature, ed. by Walter de la Mare. Cambridge, England, Univ. press, 1930. p10-12

Woolf, Leonard Sidney
The fall of Stevenson. Nation (Lond) 34:517, 35:86 Ja 5, Ap 19 '24

Wright, Herbert G.
R. L. S.'s visit to Wales. Welsh Outlook Je '30 p165-7

Textual errors in Stevenson. T L S Ag 21 '30 p668

The **writers** of happiness. Liv Age 289· 412-18 My 13 '16

Wyzewa, Teodor de
Un livre nouveau de Robert Stevenson. Essays of Travel. R Deux Mondes Jl 15 '05 p457-68

Robert Louis Stevenson. Revue Britannique '95

Young, John P.
[A reply to Mr. H. W. Bell's "An unpublished chapter in the life of Robert Louis Stevenson" in Pall Mall Magazine 24:267-71 '01] Acad 61:3 Jl 6 '01

Zweig, A.
Ueber R. L. Stevenson. Tagebuch 9: 1093-8 '29

Algernon Charles Swinburne

Algernon Charles Swinburne

I. Chronological Outline

1837. Born, April 5, London.

1860. The Queen-Mother. Rosamond. Two Plays.

1865. Atalanta in Calydon.

1865. Chastelard.

1866. Notes on Poems and Reviews.

1866. Poems and Ballads [first series]

1867. A Song of Italy.

1868. William Blake.

1871. Songs Before Sunrise.

1874. Bothwell.

1875. Essays and Studies.

1875. George Chapman.

1876. Erechtheus.

1877. A Note on Charlotte Brontë.

1878. Poems and Ballads. Second Series.

1880. Songs of the Springtides.

1880. Studies in Song.

1880. A Study of Shakespeare.

1881. Mary Stuart.

1882. Tristram of Lyonesse, and Other Poems.

1883. A Century of Roundels.

1884. A Midsummer Holiday and Other Poems.

1885. Marino Faliero.

1886. Miscellanies.

1886. A Study of Victor Hugo.

1887. Locrine.

1889. Poems and Ballads. Third Series.

1892. The Sisters.

1894. Astrophel, and Other Poems.

1894. Studies in Prose and Poetry.

1896. The Tale of Balen.

1899. Rosamund, Queen of the Lombards.

1904. A Channel Passage, and Other Poems.

1905. Love's Cross-Currents: a Year's Letters.

1908. The Age of Shakespeare.

1908. The Duke of Gandia.

1909. Died, April 10, Putney.

Algernon Charles Swinburne

II. Bibliographical Material

[Bibliography of Swinburne's works]
Lit 9:315-16 O 5 '01

Brown, G. A.
[Bibliography] *In* C H E L vol
XIII p545-8

Butler, Edward K.
A catalogue of first editions of the
work of A. C. Swinburne in the
library of Edward K. Butler.
Boston, Privately printed, 1921.
24p

Carter, John and Pollard, Graham
Algernon Charles Swinburne. *In*
An enquiry into the nature of
certain nineteenth century pamphlets. London, Constable, 1934.
p267-92

Chew, Samuel Claggett
Swinburne's contributions to the
Spectator in 1862. Mod Lang N
35:118-19 F '20

**Dodd, Robert H., firm, booksellers,
New York**
A. C. Swinburne; first editions and
an autograph manuscript; offered
by R. H. Dodd. . . New York,
Dodd, 1915. 25p

The first American "Atalanta." T L S
F 5 '31 p99

Gosse, (Sir) Edmund William
A catalogue of the works of A. C.
Swinburne in the library of Mr.
Edmund Gosse. London, Pri-
vately printed at the Chiswick
press, 1919

Hill, Walter M., bookseller, Chicago
List of the original manuscripts of
A. C. Swinburne. . . Chicago,
Hill [19-?] 12p

Hyder, Clyde Kenneth
Bibliography. *In* Swinburne's literary career and fame. Durham,
North Carolina, Duke univ. press,
1933. p[333]-378

**Livingston, Flora (Milner) (Mrs.
Luther Samuel Livingston)**
Swinburne's proof sheets and
American first editions. Bibliographical data relating to a few
of the publications of Algernon
Charles Swinburne. With notes
on the priority of certain claim-
ants to the distinction of "Editio
princeps." Cambridge, Mass.
Privately printed, 1920. 31p

Livingston, Luther Samuel
First editions of Algernon Charles
Swinburne. The bibliographical
description of a collected set of
the first editions of the writings
of the last of the great Victorian
poets. With the manuscript of
"A Midsummer Holiday." Offered
for sale by Dodd and Livingston.
New York, Dodd and Livingston,
1913. 59p

Murdoch, W. G. Blaikie
Random recollections of Swinburne,
with notes toward a bibliography
of Swinburne criticism. Book-
Lover's Magazine 7:108-10, 144-52
'07, '08

Northup, Clark Sutherland
A register of bibliographies of the
English language and literature.
New Haven, Yale univ. press,
1925. p369-71

O'Brien, Edward J.
A bibliography of the works of
Algernon Charles Swinburne. *In*
A pilgrimage of pleasure; essays
and studies [by] A. C. Swinburne. Boston, Badger, 1913.
p153-81
(500 copies only)

Swinburne bibliography. Dial 55:
468 D 1 '13

Page, Curtis Hidden
Swinburne. List of references. *In*
British poets of the nineteenth
century, ed. by C. H. Page; new
ed. by Stith Thompson. New
York, Sanborn, 1930. p894-5

Payne, William Morton
Selected poems by Algernon
Charles Swinburne. (Belles-
lettres ser) Boston, Heath, 1905.
p359-62

Powell, Frederick York
Algernon Charles Swinburne [bib-
liography of works contributed to
periodicals] Engl Illus 29:84, 90,
213-14 Ap, My '03

Prideaux, William Francis
Swinburne's "Unpublished verses."
Ath 1:278 Mr 11 '11

Quinn, John
The library of John Quinn. . . New
York, Anderson galleries, 1924.
part V p926-60

Reul, Paul de
Bibliographie. *In* L'Oeuvre de Swinburne. Bruxelles, Sand, 1922. p[485]-490

Richter, Ludwig
Liste der benützten bücher. *In* Swinburnes verhältnis zu Frankreich und Italien. (Münchener beiträge zur romanischen und englischen philologie. Heft 51) Leipzig, Deichert, 1911. p[ix]-xiii

[Sargent, George Henry]
Writings of Swinburne. [Boston, 1909] [4]p broadside

Scribner's Sons, Charles, booksellers, New York
Superb collected sets of the first editions of Eliot, Milton, Coleridge, Swinburne, Wordsworth. New York, Scribner, 1914 [1913] p88

Shepherd, Richard Herne
The bibliography of Swinburne: a bibliographical list, arranged in chronological order, of the published writings in verse and prose of Algernon Charles Swinburne (1857-1883). London, Redway, 1883. 40p; 4th ed issued by Redway in 1887. 5-40p
(Rev in Notes & Q 6th ser 8:220 S 15 '83; noted in Acad 24:127 Ag 25 '83)

Slater, J. H.
Early editions. . . London, Kegan Paul, Trench, Trübner, 1894. p288-303
(Rev by T. J. Wise in Bookm (Lond) 6:49-50 My '94)

Sotheby, firm, auctioneers, London
Catalogue of the library of A. C. Swinburne. . . [London, Dryden press, J. Davy & sons, 1916] 82p
The Swinburne manuscripts. [regarding a controversy raised by T. J. Wise] [Boston, Bibliophile society, 191-?] 52p

Thomson, Joseph Charles
Bibliographical list of the writings of Algernon Charles Swinburne. Wimbledon, Thomson, 1905. [v]-viii,9-48p

Vaughan, Charles Edwyn
Bibliography of the works of Algernon Charles Swinburne. *In* Bibliographies of Swinburne, Morris and Rossetti. (The English Association. Pamphlet no 29) [Oxford, Hart] 1914. p3-6

Welby, Thomas Earle
A Swinburne library. Sat R 140: 306-7 S 19 '25

Wise, Thomas James
A bibliographical list of the scarcer works and uncollected writings of Algernon Charles Swinburne. London, Printed only for private subscribers by T. J. Wise, 1897. 112p; *same in* Literary anecdotes of the nineteenth century, ed. by W. R. Nicoll and T. J. Wise. London, Hodder and Stoughton, 1896. vol II p[291]-374

A bibliography of the writings in prose and verse of Algernon Charles Swinburne. . . London, Clay, 1919-20. 2 vols
(Rev by W. G. Partington in Bookman's Journal 4:6 Ap 29 '21)

A bibliography of the writings in prose and verse of Algernon Charles Swinburne. *In* The complete works of Algernon Charles Swinburne, ed. by Sir Edmund Gosse and Thomas James Wise. (Bonchurch ed) London, Heinemann, 1927. vol XX p 1-542

Privately printed works of Swinburne. Bookman's Journal 4:244-5 Ag 5 '21

A Swinburne library; a catalogue of printed books, manuscripts and autograph letters, by Algernon Charles Swinburne. London, Printed for private circulation only by T. J. Wise, 1925. xiv,295p
(Rev in T L S Ap 29 '26 p319)

Woods, George Benjamin
[Bibliography] *In* Poetry of the Victorian period. New York, Scott Foresman [c1930] p1025-9

Writings of Swinburne; little known facts of the poet's bibliography. Boston Transcript Ap 21 '09

Algernon Charles Swinburne

III. Biographical and Critical Material

A. Swinburne. Punch 104:221 My 13 '93

A. C. Swinburne. Notes & Q 10th ser 1:198 Mr 5 '04

An academy of letters. Acad 52:376 N 6 '97

Adams, Francis
The poetry and criticism of Mr. Swinburne. *In* Essays in modernity. London, Lane, 1899. p119-41

Addis, John
"Horsel." Notes & Q 4th ser 11:127 F 8 '73

Aesthetic. Punch 81:298 D 24 '81

Alden, Elizabeth E.
The poetical drama of Swinburne. Masters essay, Boston Univ. 1930

Algernon Charles Swinburne. Acad 76:5-7 Ap 17 '09; Nation (NY) 88:378-9 Ap 15 '09; Speaker 2:152-3 Ag 9 '90; Appleton J 3:378-81 Ap 2 '70; Once a Week 26:281 Mr 23 '72; Liv Age 261:556-61 My 29 '09; Bookn 26:533-6 Mr '08; T L S Ap 15 '09 p141-2

[Algernon Charles Swinburne] Galaxy 3:340 F 1 '67; Blackw 176:123-6 Jl '04

Algernon Charles Swinburne. *In* Men of the time: a dictionary of contemporaries. . . London, Routledge, 1879. 10th ed p942

Algernon Charles Swinburne; Born April 5, 1837: Died April 10, 1909. Engl R 2:193-4 My '09

Algernon Charles Swinburne—poet and critic. Lond Q R 31:370-401 Ja '69

Algernon Swinburne as the Peter Pan of the Victorian poets. Current Opinion 63:51-2 Jl '17

Allingham, H. and D. Radford (eds)
William Allingham, a diary. London, Macmillan, 1907. p143, 151

American views of Swinburne. Lit Digest 38:694-6 Ap 24 '09

Amram, Beulah B.
Swinburne and Carducci. Yale R ns 5: 365-81 Ja '16

A[nderson,] M[elville] B[est]
To Swinburne; poem. Dial 21:199 O 1 '96

Another ode to March. Punch 94:125 Mr 17 '88

App, August J.
Lancelot in English literature; his role and character. Diss. Catholic univ. 1929. p195-7, 207-8

The appreciations of Algernon. Punch 123: 79 Ag 6 '02

Archer, William
Webster, Lamb, and Swinburne. New Review 8:96-106 Ja '93

Armfield, Frank
Influences of Gautier and Baudelaire upon Swinburne. Masters essay, Univ. of North Carolina, 1934. 159ff

Armstrong, William
Mr. Swinburne and Mr. Watts-Dunton at "The Pines." Critic (NY) 39:512-22 D '01

Arvin, Newton
Swinburne as a critic. Sewanee R 32: 405-12 O '24

Asher, David
Miscellen [Algernon Charles Swinburne] Archiv 58:108-22 '77

Aubry, G. Jean
Baudelaire et Swinburne. Mercure Fr 124:265-81 N 16 '17

Auslander, Joseph and Hill, Frank Ernest
The winged horse. Garden City, N.Y. Doubleday, Doran, 1930. p379-88

Austin, Alfred
A. C. Swinburne. *In* Poetry of the period. London, Bentley, 1870

The autobiography of Alfred Austin, poet Laureate, 1835-1910. London, Macmillan, 1911. vol II p2-4

On a recent criticism of Mr. Swinburne's. Macmil 43:399-408 Mr '81; *same in* The bridling of Pegasus . . . London, Macmillan, 1910. p197-217

The poetry of the period. Mr. Swinburne. Temple 26:457-74 Jl '69; 28:35-48 D '69

An Austrian appreciation of Swinburne. Lit Digest 24:76-7 Ja 18 '02

Ayscough, John
Last giants. Cath World 100:776-9 Mr '15

Babydom. Punch 91:281 D 11 '86

Bailey, John Cann
Swinburne. Quar R 228:228-48 Jl '17
Swinburne's Scotch trilogy. *In* Poets and poetry. . . Oxford, Clarendon press, 1911. p181-6

Bailey, (Sir) William Henry
Swinburne and Shakespeare. (Inaugural address by the President, Manchester Shakespeare society, Autumn session, 1909) Manchester, 1909

Barlow, George
On the spiritual side of Mr. Swinburne's
genius. Contemp 88:231-50 Ag '05

Barre, André
Le symbolisme. . . Paris, Jouve, 1911.
p11

Barrus, Clara
The life and letters of John Burroughs.
Boston, Houghton, Mifflin, 1925. vol I
p288-9

Bausenwein, Joseph
Die poetischen bearbeitungen der Balin
und Balansage von Tennyson und Swinburne und ihr verhältnis zu Malory.
Würzburg, 1914. 47p Thesis, Heidelberg

Baxter, Frank Condie
Criticism and appreciation of the Elizabethan drama: Dryden to Swinburne.
Diss. Univ. of Cambridge, 1932-33. [For
abstract see Abstracts of Diss. . .
Univ. of Cambridge. . . 1932-33. Cambridge, 1933. p59-60]

Bayne, Peter
Mr. Arnold and Mr. Swinburne. Contemp 6:337-56 N '67; *same*. New Ecl 1:
144-64 F '68; *same*. Every Sat 4:753-61
D 14 '67

Bayne, Thomas
Algernon Charles Swinburne. St J 40:
436-47 '77

Carlyle, Coleridge and Swinburne. Notes
& Q 9th ser 10:296 O 11 '02

Mr. Swinburne's trilogy. Fraser ns 26:
469-79 O '82

Beatty, Richmond Croom
Swinburne and Bayard Taylor. Philol Q
13:297-9 Jl '34

Beerbohm, Max
No. 2. The Pines. *In* And even now.
London, Heinemann, 1921.   p55-88;
same. Fortn 114:246-61 Ag '20

Rossetti and his circle. London, Heinemann, 1922. v-ixp, plates 11 and 17

Beers, Henry Augustin
A history of English romanticism in the
nineteenth century. New York, Holt,
1901. p339-51

Bell, A. F.
Rossetti, Morris, and Swinburne. *In*
Leaders in English literature. London,
Bell, 1915. p214-23

Belloc, Hilaire
On a poet (Swinburne). *In* On anything.
New York, Dutton, 1910. p54-62

Benét, William Rose
On Swinburne. Sat R Lit 2:801-2 My
22 '26

Benn, Alfred William
The history of English rationalism in the
nineteenth century. London, Longmans, Green, 1906. vol II p286-9

Bennett, Arnold
Mallarmé, Bazin, Swinburne. *In* Books
and persons. . . London, Chatto and
Windus, 1917. p65-7

Poet and his people. *In* Lewisohn, Ludwig, ed. Modern book of criticism.
New York, Boni, 1919. p122-5

Swinburne. *In* Books and persons. . .
London, Chatto and Windus, 1917.
p123-9

Bensly, Edward
Swinburne and Maupassant. Notes & Q
10th ser 11:505 Je 26 '09

Swinburne as a polyglot author. Notes &
Q 11th ser 9:156-7 F 21 '14

Swinburne: T. Hayman. Notes & Q
148:122 F 14 '25

Swinburne translations. Notes & Q 10th
ser 9:375 My 9 '08

Benson, Arthur Christopher
The diary of Arthur Christopher Benson,
a selection by Percy Lubbock. London,
Hutchinson [19-?] 2d ed p64-8

Swinburne and Watts-Dunton. Liv Age
343:531-8 F '33

Benson, Edward Frederic
As we were; a Victorian peep-show.
London, Longmans, Green, 1930. pas-
sim

Bickley, Francis
Swinburnian byways. Acad 84:47-8 Ja 11
'13

"The big gun"; poem. Punch 98:114 Mr 8
'90
[Parody of "Dolores"]

Bird, Alice L. and Rhys, Ernest
Two evenings with Swinburne. Bibliophile 3:238-41 Jl '09

Blake, W. B.
Swinburne and Maupassant. Dial 47:63
Ag 1 '09

Blakeney, Edward Henry (ed)
A golden book of Swinburne's lyrics.
London, Hopkinson, 1927. viii, 52p
(Rev in T L S Ag 25 '27 p579)

Bleibtreu, Karl
Geschichte der englischen literatur im
neunzehnten jahrhundert. *In* Geschichte der weltlitteratur. . . Leipzig,
Friedrich [1887] vol II p507-9

Blunt, Wilfrid Scawen
My diaries. . . New York, Knopf, 1921.
part I p 114, 212, 333

Bombastes Swinburneoso. Critic (NY) 11:
104-5 Ag 27 '87; *same*. Pall Mall Gazette '87

Bonchurch, April 15, 1909; poem. Acad 76:
5 Ap 17 '09

Boni, Giacomo
Iris dalmatica. Nuova Antol 285:279-85
Je 1 '19

Bonnerjee, R. C.
Swinburne and Meredith; the last two
great Victorians. Hindustan Review
20:[72]-81 '09

Bowen, Adelaide Colvin
Poetic art and message of Swinburne.
Typed ms in the Univ. of Rochester
library. 1915. 9ff

Bowker, R. R.
London as a literary center. Harper M
76:820 My '88

Bradi, Lorenzi de
Swinburne—est-il obscur et sans pensée?
R Pol et Litt 68:184-7 Mr 15 '30

Bragman, Louis J.
The case of Algernon Charles Swinburne;
a study in sadism. Psychoanalytic Review 21:59-74 Ja '34

Brand, Wilhelm F.
Algernon Swinburne. Illustrirte Zeitung 132:803 Ap 22 '09

Brandes, Georg Morris Cohen
Algernon Charles Swinburne. In Crea-
tive spirits of the nineteenth century. . .
transl. by Rasmus B. Anderson. .
New York, Crowell [c 1923] p397-419
The genius and influence of Swinburne.
Bookm (Lond) 36:131 Je '09

Braybrooke, Patrick
Max Beerbohm, Swinburne and other
things. In Peeps at the mighty. Philadelphia, Lippincott [pref 1927] p43-58
On Swinburne. In Considerations on
Edmund Gosse. London, Dranes, 1925.
p9-26

Breymann, Hans
Algernon Charles Swinburne. Litera-
risches Centralblatt für Deutschland
51:640-1 Ap 7 '00

Brie, Friedrich
Imperialistische strömungen in der englischen literatur. Halle, Niemeyer, 1928.
p197-204

Brockbank, James
"Swinburne." Papers of the Manchester
Literary Club 52:175-81 '26

Brocklehurst, J. H.
Algernon Charles Swinburne. Manch Q
24:404-30 '05

Brooks, Van Tyne
The lyric origins of Swinburne. Poet
Lore 18:468-77 Winter '07

Brooks, Van Wyck
Swinburne in the flesh. In Sketches in
criticism. New York, Dutton, 1932.
p270-3

[Brown, James Bucham] J. B. Selkirk
[pseud]
Ethics and aesthetics of modern poetry.
London, Smith, Elder, 1878. p12

Browning, Oscar
Memories of 60 years. . . London, Lane
[nd] 2d ed p108-9

Browning, Robert
Critical comments on Algernon Charles
Swinburne and D. G. Rossetti, with an
anecdote relating to W. M. Thackeray
. . . Browning. London, Printed for
private circulation, by Richard Clay,
1919. 14p

Buchanan, Robert William
The fleshly school of poetry and other
phenomena of the day. . . London,
Strahan, 1872. ix, 97p; same. Contemp
18:334-50 O '71
(Rev in Sat R 33:700-1 Je 1 '72)
The monkey and the microscope; poem.
St P 11:240 Ag '72
The session of the poets.—August 1866;
poem. Spec 39:1028 S 15 '66

Budd, Doris May
Swinburne's life in his poetry; a study in
biography. Masters essay, Columbia
univ. 1922

Buisson, Benjamin [comp. and transl.]
Les Helléniques de Landor et autres
poèmes; avec des lettres inédites de
Swinburne. Paris, Lemerre, 1916. 237p

Bunner, Henry Cuyler
The great Swinburnian hoax. Bookm
(NY) 36:425-9 D '12
[Reprint of a review of supposed Swin-
burne volume of poems really written
by Bunner. Taken from N.Y. Daily
Graphic]
Home, sweet home, with variations. In
A century of parody and imitation, ed.
by Walter Jerrold and R. M. Leonard.
London, Oxford univ. press, 1913.
p365-7

Burne-Jones, Georgiana
Memorials of Edward Burne-Jones. New
York, Macmillan, 1904. 2 vols passim

Burton, Richard
The passing of Algernon Charles Swinburne and Frances Marion Crawford—
poet and novelist. Bellman 6:516 Ap 24
'09

Butchart, Montgomery
The concept of liberty in the poems of
Algernon Charles Swinburne. Masters
essay, Univ. of Pittsburgh, 1928

Buzzichini, M.
Swinburne o l'Italia. I Libri del Giorno
9:130-2 Mr '26

Caine, Hall
My story. London, Heinemann, 1908.
passim

Cairns, William Bateman
Swinburne's opinion of Whitman. American Literature 3:125-35 My '31

Calling a thing by its right name. Punch
51:189 N 10 '66

Calverton, V. F.
Sex expression in literature. New York,
Boni, 1926. p252-3

Campbell, Archibald Young
Swinburne's criticism. New Statesm 9:
110-11 My 5 '17

Caricature. Acad 56:686-7 Je 24 '99

[Caricature portrait by "Ape" 1874] Bookn
27:938 Ag '09

Carman, Bliss
Mr. Swinburne's poetry. In The poetry
of life. Boston, Page, 1905. p177-90

[Carnegie, Robert, Earl of Southesk]
Jonas Fisher: a poem in brown and white. London, Kegan Paul, Trench, Trübner, 1875. 243p

Carr, Joseph William Comyns
Some Victorian poets. *In* Some eminent Victorians. . . London, Duckworth, 1908. p208-12, 215-19
(Rev by P. F. Bicknell in Dial 46:134-5 Mr 1 '09)

Carroll, Charles Antoninus
Swinburne's dramatic works. Masters essay, Columbia univ. 1911

Carroll, Lewis [pseud]
see Dodgson, Charles Lutwidge
"Les Casquettes." Notes & Q 6th ser 9: 205-6 Mr 15 '84

Chapman, Edward Mortimer
Heyday of minor poetry. *In* English literature in account with religion. Boston, Houghton, Mifflin, 1910. p468-74

Charteris, (Sir) Evan [Edward]
The life and letters of Sir Edmund Gosse. New York, Harper, 1931

Chassé, Charles
Algernon Charles Swinburne. Mercure Fr 79:5-13 My '09

Cheney, John Vance
Six minutes with Swinburne. *In* The golden guess; essays on poetry and the poets. Boston, Lee and Shepard, 1892. p203-12

Chesterton, Gilbert Keith
Great Victorian poets. *In* The Victorian age in literature. New York, Holt [1913] p181-8
The literary portraits of G. F. Watts, R. A. Bookm (Lond) 19:82 D '00
On Algernon Charles Swinburne. *In* All is grist; a book of essays. New York, Dodd, Mead, 1932. p243-62

Chew, Samuel Claggett
Swinburne. Boston, Little, Brown, 1929. viii,335p bibl p[307]-311
(Rev by G. Lafourcade in Litteris 7: 165-75 D '30; T L S Jl 23 '31 p579; G. W. Stonier in New Statesm & Nation 1:658-60 Je 27 '31; O. Burdett in Sat R 151:576-7 Ap 18 '31; F. E. Pierce in Yale R ns 19:203-4 S '29; R. M. Lovett in New Repub 59:103-4 Je 12 '29; H. Leffert in Bookm (NY) 69:318-19 My '29; M. D. Zabel in Nation (NY) 128:536 My 1 '29; H. B. Fuller in Poetry 34:294-6 Ag '29; C. K. Hyder in Sat R Lit 5:1087, 1091 Je 8 '29; E. Ritchie in Dalhousie Review 9:405-6 '29)
Swinburne after ten years. Nation (NY) 108:659-60 Ap 26 '19
Swinburne's contributions to *The Spectator* in 1862. Mod Lang N 35:118-19 F '20

Chiarini, Giuseppe
A. Swinburne. *In* Ombre e figure: saggî critici. Roma, Sommaruga, 1884; *also in* Saggi di letterature straniere. Livorno, Vigo, 1905

Algernon Charles Swinburne 1879. *In* Studi e . . . letterari. Livorno, 1900. p219-39

Chilton, Eleanor Carroll and Agar, Herbert
The garment of praise. . . Garden City, N.Y. Doubleday, Doran, 1929. p303-11

Christmas waits [a caricature] Punch 87: 303 D 27 '84

Chudoba, Frantisek
A flying visit to Swinburne. *In* Pod listnatým stromen. [Under the Greenwood tree. A collection of essays] Prague, 1932. p203-18

Cippico, Antonio [conte]
Alice Galimberti, l'aedo d'Italia. Algernon Charles Swinburne, conversioni originali, ritratti e facsimile e una lettera del Senatore Prof. Cippico. Palermo, Roma [etc] Libraio dell real Casa. xv, 602p

Clapp, Edwin Roosa
English literary criticism, 1830-1890. . . Harvard univ. summaries of theses. . . Cambridge, Mass. 1931. p215-18

Clark, John Scott
Algernon Charles Swinburne. *In* A study of English and American writers. New York, Row, Peterson [c1916] p582-92

Clifford, William Kingdon
Cosmic emotion. 19th Cent 2:424-5 O '77; *same in* Lectures and essays, ed. by Leslie Stephen and Frederick Pollock. London, 1879. vol II p253-85; *same published separately*: (Humboldt library of science, vol 9, no 98) [New York, Humbolt publishing company, 1888] 30p

Clinton, Mary Elizabeth
Swinburne's dramas. Masters essay, Columbia univ. 1927

Clowning and classicism. Punch 82:10-11 Ja 7 '82

Clutton-Brock, Arthur
Algernon Charles Swinburne. *In* Essays on books. London, Methuen [1920] p54-66
The later poetry of Mr. Swinburne. Acad 71:397-8 O 20 '06

Cochrane, Robert
Algernon Charles Swinburne. *In* The treasury of modern biography. Edinburgh, Nimmo, Hay, and Mitchell, 1892. p541-2

Colles, Ramsay
Mr. Swinburne's early dramas and poems. Gent M 295:128-50 Jl '03
Mr. Swinburne's first drama. Gent M ns 68:301-10 Mr '02

Collette, C. H.
The suppression of vice. Ath 1:750 Je 5 '75
[*See also* Purnell, Thomas]

Collins, Churton
Mr. Swinburne and the "Quarterly Review." Ath 2:636 N 13 '86

Collins, L. C.
Life and memoirs of John Churton Collins, written and compiled by his son . . . London, Lane, 1912. passim

Collins, Mortimer
"If"; poem. *In* A century of parody and imitation, ed. by Walter Jerrold and R. M. Leonard. London, Oxford univ. press, 1913. p286

Salad; poem. *In* A century of parody and imitation, ed. by Walter Jerrold and R. M. Leonard. London, Oxford univ. press, 1913. p286-7

Two plunges for a pearl. A novel. New York, Appleton, 1872. 122p; *from* London Society '71

Collins, Nelson
The poet of this war. Cent 97:219-25 D '18

Colum, Padraic
Swinburne. New Repub 16:101-3 Ag 24 '18

The **coming** Laureate. Public Opinion (NY) 8:568 Mr 22 '90 [*from* Boston Advertiser]

Companions of the bath. Mask 1:193-5 Ag '68

Compton-Rickett, Arthur
Swinburne and Watts-Dunton. *In* I look back. . . London, Jenkins [1933] p143-57

Conrad, H.
A. C. Swinburne. Allgemeine Zeitung no 16 '09

Contemporary poets and versifiers. Edin R 178:471 O '93

Convers, Royall
A poet and a critic. Harper W 53:6 O 2 '09

Cook, E. T.
The life of John Ruskin. London, Allen, 1911. vol II p74-6

Cook, (Sir) Edward
The life of Florence Nightingale. London, Macmillan, 1913. vol II p95, 228

Cornish, Blanche Warre
Swinburne and Eton. Bookm (Lond) 36: 123-6 Je '09

Coterie glory. Sat R 33:239-40 F 24 '72

Courtney, W. L.
Mr. Swinburne's poetry. Fortn ns 37: 597-610 My '85; *same.* Ecl M 105:119-28 Jl '85; *same in* Studies new and old. London, Chapman, 1888. p124-49

Poets of to-day. Fortn 40:715-16 N '83

Crane, William
The genius and influence of Swinburne. Bookm (Lond) 36:128 Je '09

Cresswell, Lionel
Royal descent of Algernon Charles Swinburne. Genealogical Magazine (Lond) 6:358-60 D '02

Criticisms on contemporaries. no. 1. Mr. Algernon C. Swinburne. Tinsley's 3: 26-36 Ag '68

Crossing the channel. Punch 129:115 Ag 16 '05

Cunliffe, John W.
Mid-Victorian poets. *In* Leaders of the Victorian revolution. New York, Appleton-Century [c1934] p241-8

The **danger** of overdoing it. Punch 135: 244 S 30 '08

Davison, W. T.
Poetic agnosticism: Meredith and Swinburne. Lond Q R 112:127-30 Jl '09

Davray, Henry D.
[Swinburne] Mercure Fr 42:840-2 Je '02

Dawson, William James
Algernon Charles Swinburne. *In* Makers of English poetry. New York, Revell, 1906. rev ed p359-67

Dean, Jonathan
For an anthology of parody. Acad 57: 578 N 18 '99

The **death** of Mr. Swinburne. Literary World (Lond) ns 75:103 Ap 15 '09

[**Death** of Swinburne] Acad 76:3 Ap 17 '09; Dickensian 5:115-16 My '09

The **defence** of Mr. Swinburne. Sat R 22: 600-1 N 17 '66

De Gourcuff, Olivier
Un essai de Swinburne sur le "Roi Lear." Mercure Fr 115:373-6 My '16

Delattre, Floris
Charles Baudelaire et le jeune Swinburne. Paris, Champion, 1930. vol I p[199]-24. (Rev by G. Lafourcade in Litteris 7:165-75 D '30)

Swinburne et la France. Revue des Cours et Conférences 27:548-67 F 28 '26

Devey, Joseph
Androtheist school:—Swinburne. *In* A comparative estimate of modern English poets. London, Moxon, 1873. p337-54

DeWitt, Mary Montanya
A discussion of onomatopoeia in the poetry of Swinburne. Masters essay, Columbia univ. 1918

Dicey, Albert Venn
Memorials of Albert Venn Dicey, being chiefly letters and diaries, ed. by Robert S. Rait. London, Macmillan, 1925. p27-30

Die **dichtungen** des Dante G. Rossetti. (Algernon Charles Swinburne) Wiener Rundschau p1-6, 28-31 '01

Dingle, Herbert
Swinburne's "internal centre." Queen's Q 40:212-28 My '33

Dobson, Alban
Austin Dobson, some notes. . . London, Oxford univ. press, 1928

[**Dodgson, Charles Lutwidge**] Lewis Carroll [pseud]
Atalanta in Camden-town. *In* The collected verse of Lewis Carroll. London, Macmillan, 1932. p210-12; *same.* Punch 53:38 Jl 27 '67

Dodgson, L. C.—*Continued*
The little man that had a little gun; poem. *In* The collected verse of Lewis Carroll. London, Macmillan, 1932. p385

Doherty, Helen Frances
A study of metrical form in the poetry of Rossetti, Swinburne, and Morris. Masters essay, New York Univ. 1909. 33ff

Donkin, H. Bryan
Swinburne's Greek elegiacs on Landor. Spec 107:593 O 14 '11

Doorn, Willem Van
An enquiry into the causes of Swinburne's failure as a narrative poet. 1924; *also in* Neophilologus 10:36-42, 120-5, 199-213, 273-86 O '24-Jl '25
Theory and practice of English narrative verse since 1833. Amsterdam [1932?] p143-55, 179-96

Dottin, Paul
La littérature et l'histoire anciennes dans les poèmes de Swinburne. Revue de l'Enseignement des Langues Vivantes 52:145-54 Ap '25
Les poèmes de Swinburne et les légendes héroïques de la Grèce. Revue de l'Enseignement des Langues Vivantes 52: 9-15 Ja '25
Swinburne et les dieux. Revue A A 2: 419-27 Je '25
Swinburne, poète grec et latin. Revue A A 2:328-30 Ap '25

Douady, Jules
La mer et les poètes anglais. Paris, Hachette, 1912. p359-86

A **double-barrelled** hero. Punch 124:341-2 My 13 '03

Douglas, James
Algernon Charles Swinburne. *In* Chambers's cyclopaedia of English literature. Philadelphia, Lippincott, 1904. new ed vol III p672-80
Algernon Charles Swinburne. Ath 1:463-5 Ap 17 '09
Algernon Charles Swinburne. Bookm (NY) 11:435-9 Jl '00
English literature, Algernon Charles Swinburne. Philadelphia, Lippincott, 1903. 31p (25 copies only)
Mr. Swinburne as a metrist. Bookm (Lond) 18:75-9 Je '00
Swinburne and his circle. Bookm (Lond) 36:117-23 Je '09
Theodore Watts-Dunton. New York, Lane [1907?] p268-74, 279-84

Dowden, Edward
The letters of Edward Dowden and his correspondents, ed. by John Eglinton. London, Dent, 1914. p140-4
Mr. Swinburne's "Study of Shakespeare." Acad 17:48-9 Ja 17 '80
Victorian literature. Fortn 47:861-3 Je '87

Drew, Bernard
The passing of the master-singer. A threnody on the death of Algernon Charles Swinburne. London, Nutt [1909] 9p

Drinkwater, John
Swinburne, an estimate. London, Dent, 1913. 215p bibl p209-12
(Rev in Acad 84:715 Je 7 '13; Nation (NY) 97:510-11 N 27 '13; T. P.'s Weekly 21:647 My 23 '13)
Victorian poetry. (People's library) London, Hodder and Stoughton, 1923. p12-14, 107-13

Duffy, James O. G.
The first American "Atalanta." T L S F 5 '31 p99

Eagle, Solomon [pseud]
see Squire, John Collings

Earle, John Charles
The vices of agnostic poetry. Dublin Review ns 39:117-20 Jl '82

Ebsworth, Joseph Woodfall
Joseph Knight on the Laureateship. Notes & Q 10th ser 8:311 O 19 '07

Eliot, Thomas Stearns
Swinburne as critic. Swinburne as poet. *In* Sacred wood. London, Methuen, 1920. p15-22, 130-6

Ellis, Stewart Marsh
George Meredith: his life and friends in relation to his work. New York, Dodd, Mead, 1920. p148-51

Ellison, Lee Monroe
The non-dramatic poems of Algernon Charles Swinburne. Masters essay, Univ. of Texas, 1912. 218ff

Elton, Oliver
Algernon Charles Swinburne. *In* A survey of English literature, 1830-1880. London, Arnold, 1920. vol II p55-84
Frederick York Powell, a life and a selection from his letters and occasional writings. Oxford, Clarendon press, 1906. vol II passim
Mr. Swinburne's poems. *In* Modern studies. London, Arnold, 1907. p208-27

Emerson. A literary interview. Frank Leslie's Illustrated Newspaper 37:275 Ja 3 '74

England's reply. To Algernon Charles Swinburne, Esq. [As faintly heard by one of her children. (From the Northern Daily Express) London, 1867]

The **ethics** of Mr. Swinburne's poetry. Sat R 81:95-7 Ja 25 '96

Evans, B[enjamin] Ifor
A. C. Swinburne. *In* English poetry in the later nineteenth century. London, Methuen [1933] p26-64

Falk, Bernard
The naked lady: or storm over Adah; a biography of Adah Isaacs Menken. London, Hutchinson, 1934. 306p
(Rev by C. Wilkinson in Lond Merc 30:183-5 '34)

Falzon, Paul L.
Reminiscences of Swinburne in D'Annunzio. Notes & Q 11th ser 5:201-3 Mr 16 '12

Farmer, Albert J.
Le mouvement esthétique et "décadent" en angleterre (1873-1900). Paris, Champion, 1931. p22-7

Fashion in poetry. St P 1:703-5 Mr '68

Fehr, Bernhard
Auf Swinburnes spuren. *In* Studien zu Oscar Wilde's gedichten. (Untersuchungen und texte aus der deutschen und englischen philologie. Palaestra 100) Berlin, Mayer and Muller, 1918. p52-104

Die englische literatur des 19. und 20. jahrhunderts. Wildpark-Potsdam, 1928. p182-3, 230-40

Swinburne and Theodor Opitz. Zwei unveröffentlichte Swinburne-briefe. Engl Stud 62:243-9 N 10 '27

Zu Swinburnes literarischer biographie. Archiv 136:240-8 My '17

Fiedler, H. G.
Swinburne's mystifications. T L S Ag 19 '20 p536

Figgis, Darrell
On not seeing Swinburne. Lond Merc 4:254-8 Jl '21

The **first** of living poets. Cur Lit 40:268-70 Mr '06

Fisher, W. E. Garrett
Algernon Charles Swinburne. Lit 9:313-15 O 5 '01

Fitzgerald, Maurice H.
Swinburne on Emerson. Notes & Q 157:315 N 2 '29

Fitzhopkins
Pope Boniface VIII. Notes & Q 4th ser 11:361 My 3 '73

Fletcher, Robert Huntington
The metrical forms used by Victorian poets. J Engl & Germ Philol 7:87-91 '07

Fockens, Pieter
Maria Stuart, eine literarhistorische studie. Berlin, Schade, 1887. 104p Diss. Leipzig

Foote, G. W.
Swinburne as a free-thinker. Freethinker Ap 18, 25 '09

Forbes-Robertson, Johnston
Swinburne. *In* A player under three reigns. Boston, Little, Brown, 1925. p37-71

Ford, Ford Madox
see Hueffer, Ford Madox

Forman, Harry Buxton
A. C. Swinburne. *In* Our living poets. London, Tinsley, 1871. p333-73

Fountain, Lucy
An evening with Swinburne. Galaxy 12: 231-4 Ag '71

Franck, H.
A. C. Swinburne. Blaubuch no 17 '09

Franke, W[alther]
Algernon Charles Swinburne als dramatiker. Bitterfeld, Schencke [1900] 26p

Freeman, A. E.
The psychological basis of Swinburne's convictions. Poet Lore 38:579-89 D '27

Freeman, John
Swinburne. Spec 133:686-8 N 8 '24

A **French** critic. T L S Ja 1 '25 p9

Friswell, James Hain
Mr. Algernon C. Swinburne. *In* Modern men of letters honestly criticised. London, Hodder and Stoughton, 1870. p297-310

Friswell, Laura Hain
see Myall, (Mrs) Laura Hain Friswell

The **function** of poets. By Museus. Contemp 95: supplement 1-5 My '09

Furniss, Harry
Some Victorian men. London, Lane [1924] p81-2

Furniss, Henry
Fancy portrait of Algernon Charles Swinburne [cartoon] Punch 99:83 Ag 16 '90

Furnivall, Frederick James
Chaucer. Ath 1:417-18 Mr 31 '77

The "Co." of Pigsbrook & Co. [London, 1881] 6p
[Second issue, 8p, issued F '81]

Fletcher's and Shakspere's triple endings. Acad 18:27-8 Jl 10 '80

Mr. Swinburne and Fletcher's share in "Henry VIII." Acad 17:476 Je 26 '80

Mr. Swinburne and Mr. Spedding—Shakspere's "Henry VIII." Acad 9:34-5, 98-9 Ja 8, 29 '76

Mr. Swinburne and the New Shakspere society. Birmingham Weekly Post S 6 '79 p4

Mr. Swinburne and Shakespeare. Spec 52:1130, 1159 S 6, 13 '79

Mr. Swinburne's "Flat Burglary" on Shakespeare. Two letters from the "Spectator" of September 6th and 13th, 1879. London, Trübner, 1879. 4p

Mr. Swinburne's "Study of Shakespeare." Acad 17:28 Ja 10 '80

Gabrielson, Arvid
Rime as a criterion of the pronunciation of Spencer, Pope, Byron, and Swinburne. . . Uppsala, Almqvist & Wiksells, 1909. xvi, 211p

Gaines, C. H.
Algernon Charles Swinburne, an appreciation. Harper W 53:10 Ap 24 '09

Galimberti, Alice
L'Aedo d'Italia: A. C. Swinburne. (Biblioteca "Sandron," di scienze e lettere no 108) Palermo, Sandron, 1925. 589p bibl p583-9
Swinburne and Saffi. T L S N 5 '31 p866

Galland, René
Emerson, Swinburne et Meredith. Revue A A 6:37-43 O '28

Galletti, Alfredo
Algernon Carlo Swinburne. *In* Studî di letteratura inglese. Bologna, Zanichelli, 1918. p239-89
Carlo Algernon Swinburne. Nuova Antol 212:419-40 Ap 1 '07
Saggî e studi. Bologna, 1915

Galton, Arthur
Mr. Swinburne. *In* Urbana scripta. Studies of five living poets. . . London, Stock, 1885. p108-31

Gatch, Louise
Tristram, Launcelot, and the Holy Grail, as treated by Tennyson, Arnold, Morris, and Swinburne. Masters essay, Univ. of California, 1911. 130ff

Gilchrist, Herbert Harlakenden (ed)
Anne Gilchrist, her life. . . London, Unwin, 1887. p137

Gilder, Richard Watson
The genius and influence of Swinburne. Bookm (Lond) 36:130-1 Je '09

Gildersleeve, Basil Lanneau
The legend of Venus. *In* Essays and studies, educational and literary. Baltimore, Maryland, Murray, 1890. p[161]-205

Gillis, Lois Isabel
Art in the great Victorian poets. Masters essay, Univ. of Oklahoma, 1921

Gilman, Lawrence
The new Swinburne. Harper W 49:23 Ja 7 '05

Gladstone, W. E.
British poetry of the nineteenth century. Speaker 1:34 Ja 11 '90

Glücksmann, Hedwig Luise
Algernon Charles Swinburne. *In* Die gegenüberstellung von antike-christentum in der englischen literatur des neunzehnten jahrhunderts. Hannover, Küster, 1932. p8-41 Diss. Freiburg

Golther, Wolfgang
Tristan und Isolde in den dichtungen des mittelalters und der neuen zeit. Leipzig, 1907

Goodale, Ralph Hinsdale
Pessimism in English poetry and fiction, 1847-1900. *In* Abstracts of theses. . . Humanistic series. . . Volume VI. . . Univ. of Chicago. Chicago, 1927. p347-51

Gorman, Herbert Sherman
Swinburne's home life. *In* The procession of masks. Boston, Brimmer, 1923. p91-103

Gossaert, G.
A. C. Swinburne. Mannen en Vrouwen v. Beteekenis no 10 Ag '11

Gosse, (Sir) Edmund William
Algernon Charles Swinburne. *In* Ward, T. H. ed. The English poets. . . New York, Macmillan, 1918. vol V p368-75
The attack on "Poems and Ballads" in 1866. T L S D 20 '23 p896
The first draft of Swinburne's "Anactoria." London, Privately printed [?] 7p; *same.* Mod Lang R 14:271-7 Jl '19; *same in* Aspects and impressions. London, Cassell, 1922. p87-95
(Of the pamphlet only 10 copies were printed)
The genius and influence of Swinburne. Bookm (Lond) 36:126-7 Je '09
The life of Algernon Charles Swinburne. . . New York, Macmillan, 1917. xi,363p
(Rev by J. Bailey in Quar R 228:228-48 Jl '17; A. Quiller-Couch in Edin R 225:249-68 Ap '17; C. Kernahan in Lond Q R 128:91-101 Jl '17; L. Binyon in Bookm (Lond) 52:35-7 My '17; T L S Je 28, Jl 12 '17 p309, 333-4; Ath 1:256 My '17; E. Pound in Poetry 11:322-9 Mr '18; Spec 118:462-3, 490-1 Ap 21, 28 '17; B. I. Kinne in Dial 63:21-3 Je 28 '17; Nation (Lond) 21:42-4 Ap 14 '17; Contemp 111:651-3 My '17; S. C. Chew in Mod Lang N 33:224 Ap '18)
"Life of Swinburne." T L S Je 28 '17 p309; see *ibid.* Jl 17 '17 p333-4
The literature of the Victorian era. Engl Illus 17:491 Jl '97
Locrine. [London, Privately printed, 1899] 4p
Matthew Arnold and Swinburne. [Letters] T L S Ag 12 '20 p517
Mr. Swinburne. Cent 64:100-6 My '02
Poet among the cannibals. *In* Books on the table. New York, Scribner, 1921. p61-6
Snapshots at Swinburne. *In* More books on the table. New York, Scribner, 1923. p105-12
Swinburne. Traduit par Henry D. Davray. Mercure Fr 80:43-68 Jl '09
Swinburne, 1837-1909. *In* Portraits and sketches. London, Heinemann, 1912. p 1-58; *same.* Fortn 91:1019-39 Je '09; *same.* Liv Age 262:3-17 Jl 3 '09
(Rev by J. Bailey in Quar R 228:228-48 Jl '17; Nation (NY) 96:312-13 Mr 27 '13)
Swinburne, Algernon Charles. *In* The Encyclopaedia Britannica. London, Encyclopaedia Britannica co [c 1929] 14th ed. vol XXI p668-9
Swinburne. An essay written in 1875, and now first printed. London, Printed for private circulation, 1925. vi, 81p
(Rev in T L S Ja 7 '26 p9)
Swinburne and Kirkup. Lond Merc 3:156-65 D '20

Swinburne and music. Spec 118:516 My 5 '17

Swinburne at Etretat. Cornhill 3d ser 33:457-68 O '12

Swinburne's "Death of Franklin." T L S Jl 26 '17 p357

Swinburne's unpublished writings. Fortn 102:255-67 Ag '14

Gower, (Lord) Ronald Sutherland
My reminiscences. London, Kegan, Paul, Trench, 1883. p289-90

Old diaries, 1881-1901. New York, Scribner, 1902. p44

Graham, Clark James
The friends and heroes of Swinburne mentioned, referred to, or receiving dedications in the poems. Masters essay, Columbia univ. 1920

Graham, P. Anderson
Mr. Swinburne's poetry. Contemp 50: 401-11 S '86; *same.* Ecl M 107:607-14 N '86

Graham, Stephen
The island of Hugo and Swinburne. No one's island: Sark. *In* The death of yesterday. London, Benn [1930] p20-7

Granville-Barker, Harley Granville
Some Victorians afield. II. The poet as dramatist. Theatre Arts Mo 13:361-72 My '29

Tennyson, Swinburne, Meredith and the theatre. *In* The eighteen-seventies. Essays by fellows of the Royal society of Literature. . . Cambridge, England, Univ. press, 1929. p161-91; *same.* Fortn 131:655-72 My '29

Grappe, Georges
A. C. Swinburne. *In* Essai sur la poésie anglaise au XIXe siècle. Paris, Sansot, 1906. p59-65

Gray, George H. B.
The poetry of Algernon Charles Swinburne. Canadian Monthly and National Review 12:509-13 N '77

[Grebanier, Mrs. Frances (Vinciguerra)]
Frances Winwar [pseud]
Poor splendid wings. Boston, Little, Brown, 1933. passim

Greenblatt, Milton
A history and comparative study of the Tristram story in English literature (as treated by Malory, Arnold, Tennyson and Swinburne). Masters essay, Columbia univ. 1931

Grierson, Herbert John Clifford
Lord Byron: Arnold and Swinburne. (Warton lecture on English poetry. no 11. 1921) Brit Acad Proc 9:431-61 '19-'20; *same in* The background of English literature. New York, Holt, 1926. p68-114

Griggs, Earl Leslie
Swinburne on Coleridge. Mod Philol 30:215-16 N '32

Gutbier, Elisabeth
Psychologisch-ästhetische studien zu Tristan-dichtungen der neueren englischen literatur. Erlangen, Döres, 1932. 95p Diss. Erlangen

Guthrie, William Norman
Algernon Charles Swinburne. *In* Modern poet prophets. . . Cincinnati, Clarke, 1897. p110-15

Gwynn, Stephen
Experiences of a literary man. London, Butterworth [1926] p174-5

Mr. Swinburne on Boer tyranny. Sat R 92:622 N 16 '01

Hagberg, Karl August
Dolores. En af Swinburnes märkligaste dikter. Finsk Tidskrift 83:9-14 '17

Hake, Thomas St. E.
How authors work best. . . T. P.'s Weekly 2:630 O 16 '03

Hake, Thomas and Compton-Rickett, Arthur
The life and letters of Theodore Watts-Dunton. London, Jack, 1916. 2 vols passim

Hallard, James Henry
The poetry of Mr. Swinburne. *In* Gallica, and other essays. London, Longmans, Green, 1895. p128-42

Haller, William
The poetry of Swinburne. Kent prize essay, Amherst college, 1908. 50ff. Typed ms in Amherst College Library

Halperin, Maurice
Le triomphe de l'amour—Le "Tristram of Lyonesse" d'Algernon Swinburne. *In* Le roman de Tristan et Iseut dans la littérature anglo-américaine au XIXe et au XXe siècles. Paris, Jouve, 1931. p40-53 Diss. Paris

Hamilton, Cosmo
Algernon Charles Swinburne. . . *In* People worth talking about. New York, McBride, 1933. p227-34

Hamilton, Walter
Algernon Charles Swinburne. *In* The aesthetic movement in England. London, Reeves and Turner, 1882. 3d ed p61-8

Hankin, St. John
Swinburne. *In* Lost masterpieces, and other verses. London, Constable, 1904. p22-6; *same.* Punch 125:330 N 11 '03

Hanley, Constance E.
The Risorgimento in the works of Landor, Swinburne, Mrs. Browning and Meredith. Masters essay, Columbia univ. 1927

Hannigan, D. F.
Mr. Swinburne as a critic. Westm 142: 142-5 Ag '94

Harding, Anna Trail
Shelley's "Adonais" and Swinburne's "Ave atque Vale." Sewanee R 27:32-42 Ja '19

Hardman, (Sir) William
The Hardman papers. A further selection (1865-1868) from the letters and memoirs of Sir William Hardman, ed. and annotated by S. M. Ellis. London, Constable, 1930. p164-7, 191-2, 209-10, 291-2, 326-30

A mid-Victorian Pepys; the letters and memoirs of Sir William Hardman. . . annotated and ed. by S. M. Ellis. London, Palmer [c1923] p78-80

Hardy, Thomas
A singer asleep (Algernon Charles Swinburne, 1837-1909); poem. *In* Collected poems of Thomas Hardy. London, Macmillan, 1931. p304-5; *same*. Engl R 5:1-3 Ap '10

Harris, Frank
Swinburne, the poet of youth and revolt. *In* Contemporary portraits. New York, Brentano, 1915. 1st ser p228-39

Has England outgrown Swinburne? Lit Digest 34:763-4 My 11 '07

Hauser, Otto
Algernon Charles Swinburne. Westermanns Illustrierte Deutsche Monatshefte 90:796-805 S '01

Swinburne's lyrik. Z V L ns 15:206-32 '04

Havoc. Punch 93:61 Ag 13 '87

Hayne, Paul Hamilton
Sonnets to Algernon Charles Swinburne. Lit W 11:24 Ja 17 '80; *same in* Poems of Paul Hamilton Hayne. Boston, 1882. p269

Hazeltine, Mayo Williamson
Swinburne. *In* Chats about books, poets, and novelists. New York, 1883. p91-150

Hearn, Lafcadio
Studies in Swinburne. *In* Pre-Raphaelite and other poets; lectures . . . with an introduction by John Erskine. . . New York, Dodd, Mead, 1922. p122-79

Studies in Swinburne. *In* Appreciations of poetry. . . New York, Dodd, Mead, 1916. p126-71

Swinburne. *In* A history of English literature, in a series of lectures. Tokyo, Hokuseido press, 1927. vol II p675-86

Swinburne's "Hertha." *In* Interpretations of literature. New York, Dodd, Mead, 1915. vol I p362-70

Heilbrunn, Stella
. . . Elizabethan influence on Swinburne's dramas. . . Chicago, Ill. 1915. vi, 109ff Diss. Univ. of Chicago. bibl f[i]-vi

Heinemann, William
Swinburne, Watts-Dunton, and the new volume of Swinburne selections. Ath 1:25 Ja 2 '20

Hellman, George Sidney
The true Stevenson; a study in clarification. Boston, Little, Brown, 1925. p120

Helston, John
To Algernon Charles Swinburne; poem. Lit Digest 46:963-4 Ap 26 '13; *same*. Engl R 14:13-16 Ap '13

Henderson, Walter Brooks Drayton
Swinburne and Landor. A study of their spiritual relationship and its effect on Swinburne's moral and poetic development. London, Macmillan, 1918. viii, 304p
(Rev by S. Wheeler in Bookm (Lond) 54:96-7 Je '18; Ath 1:233-4 My '18; S. C. Chew in Mod Lang N 34:362-7 Je '19)

Hengelhaupt, Margrit
Die personifikation bei George Meredith. Hannover, Küster, 1931. p5-8, 22-4 Diss. Freiburg

Herlet, Bruno
Versuch eines kommentars zu Swinburnes Atalanta. Bamberg, Nagengast, 1909-1910. 2 vols 52p; 43p

Hewlett, Henry G.
Modern ballads. Contemp 26:973-6, 978-80 N '75

Hill, George Birkbeck
Letters of George Birkbeck Hill, ed. by Lucy Crump. London, 1906. p65-6

Hille, Peter
Algernon Swinburne. Gegenwart no 27 '08

Bei Algernon Swinburne. Die Gesellschaft 17:342-5 D '01

Hilton, Arthur Clement
Octopus, by Algernon Charles Sin-burn. *In* A century of parody and imitation, ed. by Walter Jerrold and R. M. Leonard. London, Oxford univ. press, 1913. p363-4

Hirsch, Charles Henry
[Kipling and Swinburne] Mercure Fr 41:511-13 F '02

Hoffman, Karl
Die Stuart-trilogie Swinburnes. (Eine krit. untersuchung d. drei Stuartdramen A. Ch. Swinburnes 'Chastelard,' 'Bothwell,' und 'Mary Stuart in prison' mit bes. Berücks. d. quellen) Diss. München, 1921. 99p

Hoffsten, Ernest Godfrey
Swinburne's poetic theory and practice. Sewanee R 13:54-60 Ja '05

Hood, Arthur
Is Swinburne a "great poet"? Lit 7:303 O 20 '00

Hoops, J.
Swinburnes Tale of Balen und Malorys Mort d'Arthur. *In* Festschrift zur Feier d. 50 jähr. Bestehens d. Gewerbevereins zu Suhl. Suhl, 1914. p1-44

Hoser, Josef
Freimaurerei, neuheidentum und umsturz, im hinblick auf ursprung und ziel der freimaurerei dargestellt an Swinburnes neuklassizismus. Regensburg, Manz, 1922. xii,171p Diss. München

Hueffer, Ford Madox
Ancient lights and certain new reflections, being the memoirs of a young man. London, Chapman and Hall, 1911. passim

Memories and impressions. . . New York, Harper, 1911

Hunt, Theodore Whitfield
The poetry of Swinburne. *In* English literary miscellany. Oberlin, Ohio, Bibliotheca Sacra co. 1914. ser II p293-316

Hutchinson, Horace Gordon
Swinburne and Meredith. *In* Portraits of the eighties. London, Unwin [1920] p188-93

Hutton, Richard H.
Tennyson. Macmil 27:143-67 D '72

Hyder, Clyde Kenneth
Emerson on Swinburne: a sensational interview. Mod Lang N 48:180-2 Mr '33

The medieval background of Swinburne's "The Leper." P M L A 46:1280-8 D '31

Swinburne and the popular ballad. P M L A 49:295-309 Mr '34

Swinburne's "Laus Veneris" and the Tannhäuser legend. P M L A 45: 1202-13 D '30

Swinburne's literary career and fame. Diss. Harvard univ. 1933. 520ff bibl ff474-520

Swinburne's literary career and fame. Durham, North Carolina, Duke univ. press, 1933. x,388p bibl p333-78 (Rev by C. Stillman in Books O 1 '33 p31; E. Walton in N Y Times O 15 '33 p2; S. Chew in Mod Lang N 50:59-60 '35; M. Colby in Harvard Graduates Magazine 42:246-7 '34; R. D. Waller in Mod Lang R 29:353-4 '34; W. S. Knickerbocker in Sewanee R 42:359-61 '34)

[If Mr. Swinburne is made Laureate] Critic (NY) 21:213 O 15 '92

An imaginary correspondence. Punch 123: 60 Jl 30 '02

An imitation of A. C. Swinburne's Ode on the proclamation of the French Republic, September 4, 1870. London, Provost, 1871. 24p

In earnest. Punch 82:12 Ja 7 '82

Irons, Phyllis Angeline
Mary Queen of Scots in European and American literature. Masters essay, Univ. of Pittsburgh, 1932. Abstract in University of Pittsburgh Bulletin 8: 393-4 '32

Jaggard, William
The children of the chapel. Notes & Q 10th ser 7:378 My 11 '07

James, Henry
Swinburne's "Chastelard." *In* Notes and reviews. Dunster House, Bookshop, 1921. p132-8; *same.* Nation (NY) 2: 83-4 Ja 18 '66

Swinburne's essays. *In* Views and reviews. . . Boston, Ball, 1908. p49-59; *same.* Nation (NY) 21:73-4 Jl 29 '75

[Japp, Alexander Hay] H. A. Page [pseud]
The morality of literary art. Contemp 5:172-6, 188-9 Je '67

Jay, Harriett
The fleshly school of poetry, 1870. *In* Robert Buchanan. . . London, T. Fisher Unwin, 1903. p159-68

Jelinek, Vladimir
The "Hymn to Proserpine." Masters essay, Columbia univ. 1920

Jewell, Alfred
"The Ancient Mariner." Notes & Q 5th ser 5:89 Ja 29 '76

Jiriczek, O.
Viktorianische dichtung. Heidelberg, 1907. p396-441

Johnson, Florence Maude
Swinburne: the critic. Masters essay, Univ. of Pittsburgh, 1927

Johnson, Harriet Moses
The sea in Swinburne's poetry. Masters essay, Columbia univ. 1920

Jones, Dora M.
English writers and the making of Italy. Lond Q R 118:98 Jl '12

Jones, Gwen Ann
Notes on Swinburne's "Song of Italy." Mod Lang N 32:200-7 Ap '17

Jonson, G. C. Aston
A plea for experiments. Drama 1:236-41 N '11
[Atalanta on the stage]

Kado, Maria
Swinburnes verskunst. Berlin, Felber, 1910. 67p Diss. Königsberg

Kassner, Rudolf
A. C. Swinburne. *In* Englische dichter. Leipzig, Insel, 1920. p124-42

Swinburne. *In* Die mystik die künstler und das leben. . . Leipzig, Diederichs, 1900. p159-92

Katscher, Leopold
Swinburne als dramatiker. Bühne und Welt 12:841-5 Jl '10

Kellett, Ernest Edward
Swinburne. *In* Reconsiderations; literary essays. Cambridge, University press, 1928. p219-42; *also in* Lond Q R 112: 8-24 Jl '09

Kellner, Leon
Die englische literatur der neuesten zeit. Leipzig, Tauchnitz, 1921. p271-80

Die englische literatur im zeitalter der königin Viktoria. Leipzig, Tauchnitz, 1909. p483-96

Kernahan, Coulson
A. C. Swinburne. *In* In good company. . . London, Lane, 1917. p1-31

Conversations with Mr Swinburne. Lond Q R 113:22-45 Ja '10

Swinburne and Emerson; reminiscences of a famous literary quarrel. Liv Age 336:257-62 Je '29

Kernahan, Coulson—*Continued*
Swinburne and Emerson. The story of, and a sequel to, an ancient enmity. Nat R 93:229-41 Ap '29

Swinburne and Watts-Dunton: a last chapter. Lond Q R 132:26-39 Jl '19

Swinburne as I knew him, with some unpublished letters from the poet to his cousin the Hon. Lady Henniker Heaton. . . London, Lane, 1919. xiii, 108p
(Rev in T L S D 11 '19 p730)

Keys, Florence V.
The Elizabethans and Mr. Swinburne. No Am 189:53-60 Ja '09

Kilmer, Joyce
Swinburne and Francis Thompson. *In* Circus, and other essays. . . New York, Doran, 1921. p253-67

[King Edward III] Spec 52:1019, 1043 Ag 9, 16 '79

Kipka, Karl
Maria Stuart im drama der weltliteratur vornehmlich des 17. und 18. jahrhunderts, ein beitrag zur vergleichenden literaturgeschichte. (Breslauer beiträge zur literaturgeschichte, IX) Leipzig, 1907

Kitchin, George
A survey of burlesque and parody in English. Edinburgh, Oliver and Boyd, 1931. p305-11

Knickerbocker, Kenneth Leslie
The source of Swinburne's "Les Noyades." Philol Q 12:82-3 Ja '33

Knickerbocker, William Skinkle
Creative Oxford. Its influence in Victorian literature. Syracuse, New York, University press [c1925] passim

Knight, William
Memoir of John Nichol. Glasgow, MacLehose, 1896. passim

Kok, Abraham Seyne
The genius and influence of Swinburne. Bookm (Lond) 36:128-9 Je '09

Lafourcade, Georges
Atalanta in Calydon. Le manuscrit, les sources. Revue A A 3:34-47, 128-33 O, D '25

La jeunesse de Swinburne (1837-1867). (Publications de la faculté des lettres de l'université de Strasbourg. Fascicules 44, 45) London, Oxford, 1928. 2 vols 272p; 618p
(Rev by P. Quennell in New Statesm 31:732 S 22 '28; C. K. Hyder in Mod Lang N 45:133-5 F '30; H. J. C. Grierson in Rev E S 6:77-87 Ja '30; E. A. Baker in Mod Lang R 24:485-8 O '29; B. Fehr in Bei Anglia 40:1-4 Ja '29; P. de Reul in Revue Belge 8:222-30 Ja-Mr '29; D. Saurat in Litteris 6:39-42 Ap '29; C. K. Hyder in Sat R Lit 5: 1087, 1091 Je 8 '29; R. Galland in Revue A A 6:508-15 Ag '29; H. M. Jones in Mod Philol 28:493-7 My '31; S. B. Liljegren in Engl Stud 65:415-18 '31)

Swinburne: a literary biography. London, Bell, 1932. xiv,314p
(Rev by W. C. De Vane in Yale R ns 22:633-4 Mr '33; S. B. Liljegren in Bei Anglia 44:211-12 '33; M. Praz in Rev E S 9:351-3 Jl '33; T L S Je 2 '32 p404, answered by Lafourcade in T L S Je 9 '32 p427; C. K. Hyder in Sat R Lit 9:122 S 24 '32; L. Trilling in Nation (NY) 135:594 D 14 '32; J. Sparrow in Spec 148:804 Je 4 '32; A. Waugh in Bookm (Lond) 82:154 Je '32; G. Grigson in Sat R 153:545 My 28 '32)

Swinburne and Lord Morley. T L S Jl 1 '26 p448

Swinburne and Walt Whitman. Mod Lang R 22:84-6 Ja '27

Swinburne et Baudelaire. Etude sur "Ave atque Vale" suivie d'une traduction en vers. . . Revue A A 1:183-96 F '24

Swinburne et Walt Whitman. Revue A A 9:49-50 O '31

Swinburne's "Death of Sir John Franklin." T L S F 9 '28 p9

Swinburne's Hyperion, and other poems, with an essay on Swinburne and Keats. London, Faber and Gwyer, 1927. xxi, 25-175p
(Rev in T L S S 20 '29 p663; L. Woolf in Nat-Ath 43:734 S 8 '28; P. Quennell in New Statesm 31:732 S 22 '28; A. Koszul in Revue A A 6:175-7 D '28; E. A. Baker in Mod Lang R 24:485-8 O '29)

Lang, Andrew
Ballade of cricket; poem. *In* A century of parody and imitation, ed. by Walter Jerrold and R. M. Leonard. London, Oxford univ. press, 1913. p354

Impressions of Swinburne. Nation (NY) 88:506-7 My 20 '09

Letters on literature. London, Longmans, Green, 1889. p20-3

Ode of jubilee, by A. C. S. *In* The poetical works. . . ed. by Mrs. Lang. London, Longmans, Green, 1923. vol III p224-5

The palace of bric-à-brac; poem. *In* A century of parody and imitation, ed. by Walter Jerrold and R. M. Leonard. London, Oxford univ. press, 1913. p355-6

To Lord Byron; poem. *In* Letters to dead authors. New York, Scribner, 1886. p205-15

The last of the giants. Harper W 53:6 Ap 24 '09

The later course of English prose. Acad 75:254 S 12 '08

The later English poets. . . Quar R 132: 563-9 Ja '72; *same.* Ecl M 78:390-4 Ap '72

Latham, F. L.
The Newdigate of 1858, and Swinburne's poem on the death of Sir John Franklin. T L S Jl 19, Ag 16 '17 p345, 393

The **Laureate** of the sea (Algernon Charles Swinburne). Bookm (Lond) 36:172-5 Jl '09

The **Laureateship.** Illustrated London News 101:491 O 15 '92; Spec 69:517-18 O 15 '92; Critic (NY) 21:255-6 N 5 '92

Laurent, Raymond
Le préraphaélisme en angleterre; introduction à l'étude du préraphaélisme anglais. *In* Études anglaises. Paris, Grasset, 1910. p35-138

Laus Veneris vs. Leaves of Grass. Public Opinion (NY) 3:407 Ag 20 '87 [*from* Philadelphia Telegraph]

Layard, George Somes
Mrs. Lynn Linton; her life, letters, and opinions. London, Methuen, 1901. p239-40

Leaf, K. S.
Swinburne and the "Spectator." Spec 134:531-2 Ap 4 '25

Leathes, (Sir) Stanley
Rhythm in English poetry. London, Heinemann [1935] p71-3, 133-43

Lee, E. D.
The papers of an Oxford man. London, Ingpen and Grant [1928] p166-72

Leffert, Henry
Algernon Charles Swinburne, lyric poet; an interpretation by means of his correspondence. Masters essay, Columbia univ. 1924

Le Gallienne, Richard
In a copy of Mr. Swinburne's "Tristram of Lyonesse." *In* English poems. London, Lane, 1895. p51

The romantic nineties. New York, Doubleday, Page, 1925. p20-34

Leith, (Mrs) Mary Charlotte Julia (Gordon) (Mrs. Disney Leith)
The boyhood of Algernon Charles Swinburne. Contemp 97:385-98 Ap '10

The boyhood of Algernon Charles Swinburne; personal recollections by his cousin, Mrs. Disney Leith, with extracts from some of his private letters. New York, Putnam, 1917. 4-250p (Rev by J. Bailey in Quar R 228:228-48 Jl '17; T L S Mr 22 '17 p139; Dial 63:275-6 S 27 '17; Nation (Lond) 21:42-4 Ap 14 '17)

The children of the chapel . . . including the Pilgrimage of pleasure, a morality play by Algernon Charles Swinburne. . . London, Chatto & Windus, 1910. vi, 182p

Swinburne's "Death of Franklin." T L S Ag 2, S 6 '17 p369, 429

[A **letter** from Swinburne] Acad 52:449 N 27 '97

Lindau, P.
A. C. Swinburne. Hamburg. Nachrichten no 48 '08

Linton, E. Knox
"A year's letters." Acad 63:275 S 13 '02

A **literary** curiosity [Swinburne's "A study of Victor Hugo's 'Les Misérables' "] Spec 112:732-3 My 2 '14

The **literary** pages of the "Spectator." Spec 141:645, 691 N 3, 10 '28

Littell, Philip
Swinburne. *In* Books and things. New York, Harcourt, Brace and Howe, 1919. p187-93

[Swinburne's poetry] Books and things. New Repub 8:145 S 9 '16

Living English poets. Cur Lit 29:268-9 S '00

Loewenberg, J.
The prophetic songs of Swinburne. Univ. of California Chronicle 20:106-15 Ja '18

Löhrer, Alfred
Swinburne als kritiker der literatur. Mit besonderer berücksichtigung seiner unveröffentlichten schriften. Weida i. Thür. Thomas und Hubert, 1925. 185p Diss. Zurich
(Rev by K. Horn in Z F E U 26:309-10 '27; S. B. Liljegren in Bei Anglia 37:137-8 My '26)

Lorenz, Emil Franz
Der politische mythus; beiträge zur mythologie der kultur. Leipzig, Internationaler psychoanalytischer verlag, 1923. 93p bibl footnotes

A **love** agony [parody beginning "Yea, lo!"] Punch 78:254 Je 5 '80

Lowell, James Russell
Letters of James Russell Lowell. New York, Harper, 1894. vol I p377

Swinburne's tragedies. *In* My study windows. Boston, Houghton, Mifflin, 1884. 20th ed p210-26; *same.* No Am 102:544-55 Ap '66

Lowry, James M.
Spasmodeus in Swinburnia. A fragment of Greek tragedy. *In* The Keys "At home," and Spasmodeus in Swinburnia. London, Simpkin, Marshall, 1897. p65-78

Lucas, Edward Verrall
At "The Pines." A visit to A. C. Swinburne. [London, Privately printed, 1916] 8p; *same.* New Statesm 6:593-5 Mr 25 '16
(25 copies only)

Reading, writing and remembering. New York, Harper, 1932. p140-4

Lucas, Frank Laurence
Enfant terrible: enfant gaté. *In* Authors dead and living. New York, Macmillan, 1926. p115-23

Swinburne. *In* Eight Victorian poets. Cambridge, England, Univ. press, 1930. p 115-31
(Rev in T L S N 13 '30 p936)

Lux, Jacques
Un ami de Swinburne. R Pol et Litt 52:32 Jl 4 '14

Lyall, (Sir) Alfred Comyn
Characteristics of Mr. Swinburne's poetry. *In* Studies in literature and history. London, Murray, 1915. p263-90; *same.* Edin R 204:468-87 O '06

Lynd, Robert
Swinburne. *In* Old and new masters. New York, Scribner, 1919. p188-99; *same.* Nation (Lond) 26:118 My 4 '18

Lyttleton, Arthur Temple
Modern pagan poetry. [Swinburne and James Thomson] *In* Modern poets of faith, doubt and paganism, and other essays. London, Murray, 1904; *same.* Church Q R 14:367-90 Jl '82

Lytton, Earl of
The life of Edward Bulwer, First Lord Lytton. London, Macmillan, 1913. vol II p431-9

MacArthur, Henry
A. C. Swinburne. *In* Realism and romance, and other essays. Edinburgh, Hunter, 1897. p165-203

McCabe, Joseph Martin
A biographical dictionary of modern rationalists. London, Watts, 1920. p774-5

MacCarthy, Desmond
The silent woman. New Statesm 24:203 N 22 '24

Swinburne's prose. Empire Review 44:458-61 N '26

McCarthy, Justin H.
How Jack Harris became an aesthetic. Belgravia 41:61-75 Mr '80

Macdonald, J. F.
The poetry of Swinburne. Queens Q 17:1-7 Jl-S '09

Macdonell, A. E.
Swinburne's methods. T L S Ja 8 '31 p28

McDowall, A. S.
Swinburne and Mary Stuart. T L S My 31 '17 p261; corrected in *ibid.* Je 14 '17 p285; *ibid.* Je 21 '17 p297

MacInnes, William A.
Introduction. *In* Ballads of the English border, by Algernon Charles Swinburne. London, Heinemann [1925] p vii-xii

Mackail, John William
Swinburne. *In* Studies of English poets. London, Longmans, Green, 1926. p201-5 (Rev in T L S Mr 11 '26 p179; J. St. Loe Strachey in Spec 136:1083 Je 26 '26; F. Bickley in Bookm (NY) 70:226 Jl '26; Nat-Ath 39:78 Ap 17 '26)

Swinburne; a lecture. Delivered before the university on April 30, 1909. Oxford, Clarendon press, 1909. 27p (Rev in Spec 102:865 My 29 '09)

McLeish, Jessie
Swinburne the appreciative critic. Masters essay, Stanford Univ. 1933-34. 115ff

McVarish, Duncan C.
Mr. Swinburne on Boer tyranny. Sat R 92:621, 642 N 16, 23 '01

Macy, John
Swinburne: thaumaturgist. Bookm (NY) 72:45-55 S '30

Magnus, Laurie
Algernon Charles Swinburne. *In* English literature in the nineteenth century, an essay in criticism. New York, Putnam, 1909. p327-32

Maitland, Thomas [pseud]
see Buchanan, Robert William

Mallarmé, Stephane
Five letters from Stephane Mallarmé to Algernon Charles Swinburne. With a note by de v. Payen-Payne. Privately printed, 1922. 16p

Mallock, William H.
A familiar colloquy. 19th Cent 4:289-302 Ag '78

Memoirs of life and literature. New York, Harper, 1920. p72-8

Malmstedt, A. ..
Om Swinburne's liv och diktning. Studier i Modern Språkvetenskap 5:47-86 '14

Mandin, Louis
[Swinburne's "Chastelard."] Mercure Fr 176:260-1 N 15 '24

Marble, Annie Russell
Messages of the nineteenth century poets. Dial 30:99 F 16 '01

Marks, Jeannette (Augustus)
Stigmata. *In* Genius and disaster, studies in drugs and genius. New York, Adelphi company, 1925. p129-52

Swinburne: a study in pathology. Yale R ns 9:349-65 Ja '20

Marquis, Don
Swinburne; poem. Putnam's Magazine 6:317 Je '09

Maupassant, Guy de
L'anglais d' Étretat. *In* Oeuvres complètes. Paris, Conard, 1909. vol XV p255-63

Maxwell, Patrick
Translations, good and bad. Notes & Q 9th ser 12:285 O 10 '03

Mazzini and Swinburne. T. P.'s Weekly 5:817 Je 30 '05

Medhurst, Francis
To Algernon Charles Swinburne; poem. Harper W 53:6 Ap 24 '09

Mehring, Sigmar
Algernon Charles Swinburne. Das Literarische Echo 8:1199-1212 Je '06

Men and matters: Swinburne and his contemporaries. Bookman's Journal 9:151 Ja '24

Men of the day.—No.XCI: Mr. Algernon Charles Swinburne. Vanity Fair 12:285 N 21 '74

Meredith, George
Letters from George Meredith to Algernon Charles Swinburne and Theodore Watts-Dunton. Pretoria, Printed for private circulation, 1922. 19p [30 copies only]

Letters of George Meredith, collected and ed. by his son. New York, Scribner, 1912. vol I p182-3, 188-90

Meynell, Alice Christina (Thompson) (Mrs. Willfrid Meynell)
Swinburne's lyrical poetry. Liv Age 262: 534-41 Ag 28 '09; same. Dublin Review 145:172-83 Jl '09; also in Hearts of controversy. New York, Scribner, 1917. p53-75

Michaelides, C. C.
Mr. Swinburne and the sea. Independent Review 8:69-80 Ja '06

A mid-Victorian literary tempest. Lit Digest 54:1851 Je 16 '17

Milner, George
On a recent poem by Mr. Swinburne: "The year of the rose." In Transactions of the Manchester Literary Club. London, Trübner, 1875. vol I p53-5

Minto, W.
Mr. W. B. Scott's autobiography. Acad 42:542 D 10 '92

Mr. Algernon C. Swinburne. Tinsley's 3: 26-36 Ag '68

Mr. Buchanan on immorality in authorship. Spec 39:1049-50 S 22 '66

Mr. Swinburne. Acad 60:267-8 Mr 23 '01

Mr. Swinburne among the fleas. Examiner p673-4 Jl 6 '72

Mr. Swinburne and his critics. Fraser 74: 635-48 N '66

Mr. Swinburne and Mary Stuart. Lippinc 32:506-12 N '83

Mr. Swinburne and the "Quarterly Review." Ath 2:636 N 13 '86

Mr. Swinburne as critic. Spec 40:1109-11 O 5 '67; same. Liv Age 95:397-400 N 16 '67; Acad 64:281-2 Mr 21 '03

Mr. Swinburne as a master of metre. Spec 102:605-6 Ap 17 '09; same. Liv Age 261: 372-6 My 8 '09

Mr. Swinburne, his crimes and his critics. Eclectic Review ns 11:493-508 D '66

Mr. Swinburne on Christianity. Sat R 81: 296-8 Mr 21 '96

Mr. Swinburne on Dickens. T L S Jl 25 '02 p219

Mr. Swinburne s'amuse. Punch 119:224 S 26 '00

Mr. Swinburne upon Charles Reade. Gent M 257:518-19 N '84

Mr. Swinburne's birthday. Spec 98:568-9 Ap 13 '07

Mr. Swinburne's debt to the Bible. Scottish Review 3:266-85 Ap '84

Mr. Swinburne's defense. Liv Age 91:661-4 D 15 '66; same. London Review 13: 482-3 N 3 '66

Mr. Swinburne's essay on "King Edward III." Spec 52:1043 Ag 16 '79

Mr. Swinburne's frenzy. Speaker 16:603 N 27 '97

Mr. Swinburne's lyrics. Edin R 171:429-52 Ap '90

Mr. Swinburne's "Mary Stuart." Ath 2:814 D 17 '81

Mr. Swinburne's new book. T. P.'s Weekly 12:341 S 2 '08

Mr. Swinburne's novel. Punch 129:2 Jl 5 '05

Mr. Swinburne's poetry. Westm 87:210-20 Ap '67

Mr. Swinburne's politics. Pall Mall Gazette p2-3 Ag 4 '87

Mr. Swinburne's tragedy. Acad 74:685-6 Ap 18 '08

Mrs. Boythorn and her canary [Swinburne-Lang controversy over Dickens] Acad 63:87-8 Jl 10 '02

Modern men. Algernon Charles Swinburne. Scots Observer 3:430-1 Mr 8 '90

A modern rhapsodist. Out 91:909-12 Ap 24 '09

Monroe, Will Seymour
Swinburne's recantation of Walt Whitman. Revue A A 8:347-51 Ap '31

Moore, Charles Leonard
The passionate Victorians. Dial 60:524 Je 8 '16

Poetic expression. Dial 56:131-2 F 16 '14

More, Paul Elmer
Algernon Charles Swinburne. Nation (NY) 88:378-9 Ap 15 '09

Swinburne. In Shelburne essays. New York, Putnam, 1907. 3d ser p100-23

More messages from the dead. Punch 135: 265 O 7 '08

Morley, John
Recollections by John, Viscount Morley. New York, Macmillan, 1917. vol I p40-4

Morton, Edward Payson
The technique of English non-dramatic blank verse. Chicago, Donnelley, 1910. p126-9 Diss. Univ. of Chicago

Motter, T. H. Vail
A new Arnold letter and an old Swinburne quarrel. T L S Ag 31 '33 p576

Moulton, Louise Chandler
An evening with Swinburne. Lippinc 21: 254-5 F '78

Mourey, Gabriel
Une visite à Algernon Charles Swinburne. In Passé le détroit: la vie et l'art à Londres. Paris, Ollendorff, 1895

Munro, John
Biography [of Furnivall]. In Frederick James Furnivall, a volume of personal record. London, Frowde, 1911. p lvi-lviii

Murdoch, W. G. Blaikie
Memories of Swinburne: with other essays. Edinburgh, Gray, 1910

Murdoch, W. G. B.—*Continued*
Random recollections of Swinburne; with notes towards a bibliography of Swinburne criticism. Book-Lover's Magazine 7:108-10, 144-52 '07, '08

Murray, Henry
Algernon Charles Swinburne. *In* Robert Buchanan; a critical appreciation and other essays. London, Wellby, 1901. p116-27
(Rev in Acad 61:50 Jl 20 '01)

Myall (Mrs) Laura Hain (Friswell)
In the sixties and seventies, impressions of literary people and others. Boston, Turner, 1906. p73-83
(Rev by P. F. Bicknell in Dial 40:188-90 Mr 16 '06)

Myers, Frederic W. H.
Modern poets and the meaning of life. 19th Cent 33:93-111 Ja '93; *same in* Science and a future life. London, Macmillan, 1901. p166-210

Nairn, John Arbuthnot
Mary queen of Scots in drama. Fortn 126:185-98 Ag '26

Nash, J. V.
The religion of Swinburne. Open Court 37:65-77 F '23

Neff, Marietta
Swinburne as a poet of enthusiasm. No Am 208:762-73 N '18

Nencioni, Enrico
Locrine di Swinburne. *In* Saggi critici di letteratura inglese. . . Firenze, Le Monnier, 1897. p346-8

Nevinson, Henry Woodd
A poet's youth. Nation (Lond) 1:267-8 Ap 13 '07; *also in* Essays in freedom. London, 1911. p37-42

A new poet. Blackw 134:435 O '83

A new Swinburne letter. Lond Merc 14:367 Ag '26

Newcomer, Alphonso G.
The Poe-Chivers tradition re-examined. Sewanee R 12:20-35 Ja '04

The Newdigate of 1858, and Swinburne's poem on the death of Sir John Franklin. T L S Jl 19, 26, Ag 2, 16, S 6 '17 p345, 357, 369, 393, 429

Newton, Adah L.
The immortal phrase applied in Swinburne's poetry. Masters essay, Univ. of Nebraska, 1913. 30ff

Newton, Theodore F[rancis] M.
The development of thought in the poetry of Algernon Charles Swinburne. Masters essay, McGill Univ. 1927. 139ff

The next Laureate. Pall Mall Budget 40:1514 O 13 '92

Nichols, Wallace Bertram
Date Lilia. An elegy on Algernon Charles Swinburne (obit 10th April, 1909) London, Burleigh [1909] 10p

Nicoll, (Sir) William Robertson
Algernon Charles Swinburne. *In* A bookman's letters. London, Hodder & Stoughton, 1913. p235-54; *same.* Contemp 95:527-38 My '09

Nicoll, William Robertson and Seccombe, Thomas
History of English literature. New York, Dodd, Mead, 1907. vol III p1250-7

[**Nicoll's** prediction concerning "Love's Cross Currents"] Critic (NY) 48:201-3 Mr '06

Nicolson, Harold George
Swinburne. New York, Macmillan, 1926. vii,207p
(Rev in T L S Ap 15 '26 p279; W. Gibson in Bookm (Lond) 70:149-50 Je '26; E. Shanks in Sat R 141:478 Ap 10 '26; H. Read in Nat-Ath 39:131-2 My 1 '26; W. R. Benét in Sat R Lit 2:801-2 My 22 '26; H. B. Fuller in Literary Digest International Book Review 4:545-6 Ag '26; E. Pearson in Out 143:417-18 Jl 21 '26; L. Mumford in New Repub 48:167 S 29 '26; G. Lafourcade in Revue A A 4:163-9 D '26; Contemp 131:804-8 Je '27; S. C. Chew in Yale R ns 16:612-16 Ap '27; G. H. Clarke in Va Q R 3:156-8 Ja '27; W. Van Doorn in English Studies 9:54-5 Ap '27; Spec 136:764 Ap 24 '26)

Swinburne and Baudelaire. (Zaharoff lecture, 1930) Oxford, 1930. 22p; *also in* Roy Soc Lit ns 6:117-37 '26
(Rev by J. O'Brien in Bookm (NY) 73:211 Ap '31; P. Meissner in Bei Anglia 43:25-6 Ja '32; G. Lafourcade in Litteris 7:165-75 D '30)

Nordau, Max
Degeneration. New York, Appleton, 1895. 7th ed p94-8

[**Note** on new and unexpurgated edition of Swinburne's *Poems and Ballads*] Ath 2:501 O 20 '66

[**Note** on Swinburne] Mercure Fr 157:514-15 Jl 15 '22; Rambler no. 230:1419-22 N 23 '01

Notes and news. Acad 6:480-1 O 31 '74

Novelties in poetry and criticism. Fraser ns 5:588-96 My '72

Noyes, Alfred
In memory of Swinburne. Cleveland, Ohio, Privately printed, 1909. 10p; *also in* Nation (NY) 88:460 My 6 '09; *same.* Blackw 185:733-4 My '09

Is Swinburne a "great poet"? Lit 7:241, 280-1 S 29, O 13 '00

A seventieth birthday [of A. C. Swinburne] No Am 184:740-1 Ap 5 '07; Fortn 87:571-2 Ap '07

Swinburne. Lit 7:328, 398 O 27, N 17 '00

Swinburne and conventional criticism. Liv Age 325:265-72 My 2 '25; *same.* Bookm (Lond) 47:195-200 Ja '25

Swinburne's tragedies. *In* Some aspects of modern poetry. London, Hodder and Stoughton, 1924. p261-72

Ofterning, Michael
A. C. Swinburne. Hochland 7:444-53 Jl
'09

Algernon Charles Swinburne. Festschrift
zum zwölften allgemeinen deutschen
neuphilologentage in München. . . Erlangen, Junge, 1906. p[146]-174

Oleo-margerine. Punch 80:174 Ap 16 '81

Oliphant, Margaret
Algernon Swinburne, 1837. *In* The Vic-
torian age of English literature. New
York. Tait [c 1892] vol II p437-42

Olivero, Federico
Atalanta in Calydon di C. A. Swinburne.
In Nuova saggi di letteratura inglese.
Torino, Libreria editrice internazionale
[1918?] p222-35
(Rev in T L S S 19 '18 p451)

On Swinburne's *Atalanta in Calydon.*
In Studies in modern poetry. London,
Milford, 1921. p[36]-53

Il paesaggio nei "Poems and Ballads" di
Algernon Charles Swinburne. Nuova
Antol 156:435-48 D 1 '11; *same in* Saggi
di letteratura inglese. Bari, Laterza,
1913

Ortensi, Ulisse
Letterati contemporanei. Algernon
Charles Swinburne. Emporium 13:202-
10 Mr '01

Oscar interviewed. Punch 82:14 Ja 14 '82

"Othello" V, ii, and Swinburne. Notes &
Q 10th ser 8:164 Ag 31 '07

The other Swinburne. T L S N 28 '18
p581

Oursler, Fulton
The world's delight. New York, Harper,
1929. 429p

Page, H. A. [pseud]
see Japp, Alexander Hay

Pain, Barry
The poets at tea. III. Swinburne, who
let it get cold. *In* Playthings and parodies. New York, Cassell [c1892] p226

Palgrave, Gwenllian F.
Francis Turner Palgrave. London, 1899.
p259-60

Pallis, Elisabeth Hude
Tennysons og Swinburnes Arthurdigte.
Edda 15:44-74 '21

Pancoast, Henry Spackman
A final word about Swinburne as "a love
poet." Dial 40:112-13 F 16 '06

Mr. Swinburne's poetry. Dial 40:36 Ja 16
'06

Parker, H. T.
A study in Swinburne. Harv Mo 6:30-9
Mr '88

Parmelee, Gertrude
The critical works of Swinburne. Masters essay, Univ. of Wyoming, 1924.
112ff

Parrott, Thomas Marc and Thorp, Willard
(eds)
Poetry of the transition, 1850-1914. New
York, Oxford [c1932] p 130-4

Partington, Wilfred George
Swinburne, Dickens, and the lovely cir-
cus-rider. Bookm (NY) 75:292-4 Je-
Jl '32

Patmore, Coventry
Mr. Swinburne's selections. *In* Principle
in art. London, Bell, 1889. p112-17

Payne, William Morton
Algernon Charles Swinburne. *In* The
Columbia university course in literature. New York, Columbia univ.
press, 1929. vol XV p105-8

Algernon Charles Swinburne. *In* Warner,
C. D. (ed) Library of the world's
best literature. . . (Memorial ed) New
York, Hill [c 1902] vol XXXVI p14289-
93

Introduction. *In* Mary Stuart, by Algernon Charles Swinburne. (Belles-lettres
ser) Boston, Heath, 1906. p[ix]-xlii

Personality and work of Swinburne. *In*
Greater English poets of the nineteenth century. New York, Holt, 1907.
p348-83

Payrn-Payne, De V.
Poèmes français de Swinburne. Mercure
Fr 134:765 Ag '19

Pearson, Edmund Lester
Swinburne. Nation (NY) 98:329-30 Mr
26 '14

Peck, Harry Thurston
Swinburne and the Swinburnians. Bookm
(NY) 29:374-84 Je '09

Pegasus on the war-path. Truth (Lond)
46:1329 N 30 '99

Pellegrini, Carlo
The eternal boy [caricature] Current
Opinion 63:52 Jl '17

Pennell, Elizabeth Robins and Pennell,
Joseph
The life of James McNeill Whistler.
Philadelphia, Lippincott, 1908. 2 vols
passim

The Whistler Journal. Philadelphia, Lippincott, 1921. p23-8

A performance of Swinburne's greatest
tragedy. Cur Lit 41:188-9 Ag '06

Perry, Bliss
Walt Whitman. (American men of letters) Boston, Houghton, Mifflin [c1906]
p260-1

Petit, Helen Ritchie
The influence of Baudelaire upon Swin-
burne in their attitude toward death.
Masters essay, Columbia univ. 1929

Phillips, Stephen
The poetry of Byron. Cornhill ns 4:20
Ja '98

Phillips, T. M.
Colour in George Meredith and other
modern English poets. Papers of the
Manchester Literary Club 44:193-5 '18

Phillips, T. M.—*Continued*
Nature in modern English poetry. Manch Q 37:271 O '18

Phillpotts, Eden
Swinburne; poem. Liv Age 261:706 Je 19 '09; *same.* Ath 1:496 Ap 24 '09

A phrase of Swinburne's: "The morn." Notes & Q 11th ser 6:216 S 14 '12

Pierce, Florence Helen
The poetic art and message of Swinburne. Williams memorial prize essay, Univ. of Rochester, 1915. 18ff

Pierpoint, Robert
Joseph Knight on the Laureateship. Notes & Q 10th ser 8:267 O 5 '07

"The pity of it." Acad 63:686 D 20 '02

Pizzagalli, A. M.
Il mito di Atalanta e Algernon Charles Swinburne. Atene e Roma 12:331-47 N-D '09

"Placing" Swinburne. Lit Digest 38:800-1 My 8 '09

Plowman, Thomas F.
The aesthetes; the story of a nineteenth-century cult. Pall Mall Magazine 5:27-44 Ja '95

["Poems and Ballads" 1st series withdrawn from circulation] Ath 2:211 Ag 18 '66; Illustrated London News 49:190 Ag 25 '66

A poet for poets. Dial 40:3-5 Ja 1 '06

The poet of pain. Nation (Lond) 5:82-3 Ap 17 '09

The poet Swinburne. Out 91:854-5 Ap 17 '09

Les poëtes s'amusent. Punch 83:261 D 2 '82

The poetry and criticism of Mr. Swinburne. Quar R 203:525-47 O '05

Poetry and the intuition of immortality. T L S S 14 '16 p433-4

Poetry and Italian politics. Tinsley's 2:95-100 F '68

The poetry of Praed and Lord Houghton. Quar R 118:417 O '65

A poet's day. Punch 82:58-9 F 4 '82

A poet's mind. Dial 47:5-7 Jl 1 '09

A poet's retrospect. Dial 38:111-13 F 16 '05

Pollock, Walter Herries
The Laureateship. National Observer 13:233-4 Ja 12 '95

Porter, Noah
Books and reading. Hours at Home 9: 47 My '69; *same in* Books and reading. New York, Scribner [1870]

[Portrait of Swinburne by D. G. Rossetti.] Book B ns 20:8-9 F '00

[Portraits] Bookm (Lond) 67:195, 197 Ja '25; Engl Illus 29:85 Ap '03; Out 132: 159 S 27 '22; 91:911 Ap 24 '09; Canadian Magazine 17:2-5 My '01; R of Rs (NY) 39:637 My '09; Open Court 37:facing 65 F '23; Pall Mall Magazine 43:688-91, 697 Je '09; 25:434, 436, 442 D '01; Literary Digest International Book Review 4: 545 Ag '26; Book B ns 20:8 F '00; Bibliophile 3:220 Jl '09; Illustrated London News 101:491 O 15 '92; Bookn 26:534 Mr '08; 24:697 Je '06; 25:786 Ag '07; 24:12 S '05; Cur Opin 54:233 Mr '13; Critic (NY) 48:202 Mr '06; Nuova Antol 212:419, 429 Ap 1 '07; Critic (NY) 39: 513-14 D '01; 24:375 Je 2 '94; Cent ns 42:100 My '02; Cur Lit 46:641 Je '09; Queens Q 17:facing 1 Jl-S '09; Bookm (Lond) 52:35, 147 My, Ag '17; 55:129 Ja '19; 70:149 Je '26; Critic (NY) 36:200 Mr '00; Bookm (Lond) 18:75, 77, 79 Je '00; 36:113-19 Je '09; 40:124 Je '11; 6:75 Je '94; Once a Week 26:279 Mr 23 '72; Appleton J 3:380 Ap 2 '70; R of Rs (NY) 26:363 S '02; Bookm (NY) 2:296 D '95; 3:395 Jl '96; 11:437 Jl '00; Engl Illus 17:489 Jl '97; Emporium 13:202, 210 My '01; Pall Mall Magazine 5:29 Ja '95; Book B ns 11:297 Jl '94; Pall Mall Budget 40:1514 O 13 '92

Poseidon and Athene. Notes & Q 11th ser 9:377-8 My 15 '15

Pot and kettle. Punch 92:245 My 21 '87

Pound, Olivia
On the application of the principles of Greek lyric tragedy in the classical dramas of Swinburne. Nebraska University. University Studies 13:341-60 '13

Powell, Charles
The poets in the nursery. . . London, Lane, 1920. p42-4

Powell, Frederick York
Algernon Charles Swinburne. Engl Illus 29:84 Ap '03; *same in* Frederick York Powell, a life and a selection from his letters and occasional writings, by Oliver Elton. Oxford, Clarendon press, 1906. vol II p311-13

Praz, Mario
Il manoscritto dell' "Atalanta in Calydon." La Cultura 8:405-15 Jl '29

Swinburne. La Cultura 1:536-53 S 15 '22

Swinburniana. La Cultura 9:11-23 Ja '30

Le tragedie "Greche" di A. C. Swinburne e le fonti dell' "Atalanta in Calydon." Atene e Roma ns 3:157-89 Jl-S '22

La trilogia di Maria Stuarda di A. C. Swinburne. Rivista di Cultura '21

The predecessors of Shakespeare. Quar R 161:335-7 O '85

Pre-Raphaelitism in outline; Algernon Charles Swinburne. Bookn 24:698 Je '06

Price, Warwick James
The last of the great poets. Sewanee R 17:409-17 O '09

Pughe, F. H.
Führende dichter im zeitalter der Königin Viktoria. Wien, Konegen, 1904. 104p

Purnell, Thomas
The suppression of vice. Ath 1:622 My 8 '75
[Followed by other letters, this finally precipitated Swinburne's letter in Ath 1:720 My 29 '75]

Purves, John
Swinburne and Aurelio Saffi. T L S S 24 '31 p729-30

Swinburne and Saffi. T L S N 26 '31 p960

The **Putney** pageant. Punch 132:251 Ap 3 '07

Quayle, William Alfred
Selfish womanhood. *In* Recovered yesterdays in literature. New York, Abingdon press, 1916. p74-87

Quesnel, Léo
Algernon Charles Swinburne, poète et prosateur. Bibliothèque Universelle et Revue Suisse 3d period 50:152-72 Ap '91

La poésie au XIX⁰ siècle en angleterre. Le Correspondant 110:808-9 Mr 10 '78

The **question** of the Laureateship. Bookm (Lond) 3:52-5 N '92

Quiett, M. C.
Swinburne as a critic. Masters essay, Colorado College, 1932

Quiller-Couch, (Sir) Arthur Thomas
Mr. Swinburne's "Astrophel." Speaker 9:500-2 My 5 '94

Swinburne. *In* Studies in literature. Cambridge, England, Univ. press, 1920. [ser 1] p246-73; *same.* Edin R 225:249-68 Ap '17

Unity put quarterly. *In* Green bays; verses and parodies. London, Oxford univ. press, 1930. new ed p76-7

Ralli, Augustus John
The soul of Swinburne. No Am 214:679-89 N '21; *same in* Critiques. London, Longmans, Green, 1927. p51-65

Ratchford, Fannie E.
The first draft of Swinburne's "Hertha." Mod Lang N 39:22-6 Ja '24

Swinburne at work. Sewanee R 31:353-62 Jl '23

Swinburne's projected triameron. Texas Review 9:64-74 O '23

Raymond, William O.
Introduction. *In* Selections from Swinburne. New York, Harcourt, Brace [c1925] p vii-xxxii

Reade, W. Winwood
Mr. Swinburne: a sketch. Galaxy 3:682-4 Mr '67

[Reade's letter about Swinburne] Galaxy 3:798-9 Ap 1 '67

Redesdale, Lord
Memories. London, Hutchinson, 1915. vol I p68-74

Reid, T. Wemyss
The life, letters, and friendships of Richard Monckton Milnes, first Lord Houghton. London, Cassell, 1890. 2d ed vol II passim

Reinach, S.
Thinking in French. Notes & Q 12th ser 1:207 Mr 11 '16

The **religion** of Swinburne. Cur Lit 47:179-82 Ag '09

Renauld, C.
A. C. Swinburne et l'Italie. Nouvelle Revue d'Italie '20

Reul, Paul de
L'oeuvre de Swinburne. . . London, Oxford, 1922. 502p bibl p485-90
(Rev by G. Lafourcade in Revue A A 1:542-8 Ag '24; W. van Doorn in English Studies 6:122-5 Je-Ag '24; J. F. C. Gutteling in Neophilologus 9:145-50 Ja '24; TLS My 4 '22 p288)

La poésie révolutionnaire et l'idéalisme de Swinburne. Revue de l'Université de Bruxelles 16:113-56 N-D '10

Swinburne and contemporary England. Liv Age 314:593-9 S 2 '22

Swinburne et la France. Essai de littérature comparée. Grande Revue 32:496-520 D 15 '04; *same.* Revue de l'Université de Bruxelles 9:267-322 Ja '04; *also published*: Bruxelles, Lefevre, 1904. 60p
(Rev in Sat R 98:828-9 D 31 '04)

Les tragédies antiques de Swinburne. Revue de l'Université de Bruxelles 17:369-407 F '12

Rhys, Ernest
Death of Swinburne. *In* Modern English essays. New York, Dutton, 1922. vol IV p178-95

Lyric poetry. London, Dent, 1913. p339-46

Swinburne's collected poems. Fortn 83:150-7 Ja '05; *same in* Poems by Algernon Charles Swinburne. (Modern library) New York, Boni and Liveright [nd] pvii-xvi

A tribute to Swinburne. 19th Cent 65:965-79 Je '09

Richter, Ludwig
Swinburne's verhältnis zu Frankreich und Italien. Naumburg, Lippert, 1910. vii, 52p bibl p iii-vii Diss. Munich

Swinburne's verhältnis zu Frankreich und Italien. (Münchener beiträge zur romanischen und englischen philologie. Heft 51) Leipzig, Deichert, 1911. xiii, 99p bibl p ix-xiii

The **riddle** of Swinburne. Cur Lit 47:411-12 O '09

Robinson, A. Mary F.
Zur geschichte der zeitgenössischen poesie Englands: Algernon Charles Swinburne. Unsere Zeit 2:181-99 Ag 1 '79

Robinson, Perry
Reminiscences of Swinburne. Bellman 6: 596 My 15 '09

Rolfe, W. J.
Swinburne on Shakespeare. Lit W 10:329 O 11 '79

Roman Catholic poets [with summary] Temple 27:170-86 S '69; 28:33-48 D '69

Ross, Robert
Swinblake: a prophetic book, with home Zarathrusts. Acad 71:307-9 S 29 '05

Rossetti, Dante Gabriel
Letters from D. G. Rossetti to A. C. Swinburne regarding the attacks made upon the latter by Mortimer Collins and upon both by Robert Buchanan. London, Printed for T. J. Wise for private circulation only, 1921. 15p
(30 copies only)

Rossetti, William Michael
The genius and influence of Swinburne. Bookm (Lond) 36:127-8 Je '09

Some reminiscences. London, Brown Langham, 1906. vol I p218-21
(Rev in Bookm (Lond) 31:156 D '06)

Swinburne's poems and ballads. A criticism. London, Hotten, 1866. vi,8-80p
(Rev in Spec 39:1311-12 N 24 '66; London Review 13:610-11 D 1 '66)

Rossetti and Swinburne. [letters] T L S O 16, 23 '19 p565-6, 591

Rothenstein, William
Men and memories. . . London, Faber and Faber [1931] vol I passim

Ruhrmann, Friedrich G.
Studien zur geschichte und charakteristik des refrains in der englischen literatur. (Anglistische forschungen, heft 64) Heidelberg, Winter, 1927. p160-75

Rummons, Constance
The ballad imitations of Swinburne. Poet Lore 33:58-84 Ja '22

Ruskin, John
Letters of John Ruskin to Charles Eliot Norton. Boston, Houghton, Mifflin, 1904. vol I p57
[Concerning Swinburne's "Atalanta"]

Ruskin, John; Morris, William [etc]
Letters addressed to Algernon Charles Swinburne, by John Ruskin, William Morris, Sir Edward Burne-Jones and Dante Gabriel Rossetti. London, Printed for private circulation only by Richard Clay, 1919. 16p

Russell, A. L. N.
Swinburnian foreknowledge. Spec 120: 562 Je 1 '18

Russell, Charles Edward
Swinburne and music. No Am 186:427-41 N '07

Rutland, William Rutland
Swinburne: a nineteenth century Hellene; with some reflections on the Hellenism of modern poets. Oxford, Blackwell, 1931. vii, 410p bibl p401-6
(Rev in T L S Jl 23 '31 p579; W. R.

Rutland in *ibid*. Ag 6, 20 '31 p609, 633; D. Bush in Philol Q 10:413-14 O '31; S. B. Liljegren in Bei Anglia 43:33-9 F '32; M. Praz in Rev E S 8:354-7 Jl '32; C. K. Hyder in Mod Lang N 47: 134-5 F '32; Oxford Magazine Ap 28 '32 p606; G. Lafourcade in R Litt Comp 12:464-7 Ap '32; G. W. Stonier in New Statesm & Nation 1:658-60 Je 27 '31)

Swinburne the Hellene. T L S Ag 8 '29 p624

Saintsbury, George Edward Bateman
Algernon Charles Swinburne. Bookm (Lond) 36:113-16 Je '09

A history of English prose rhythm. London, Macmillan, 1912. p427-35

Mr. Swinburne. *In* Corrected impressions. New York, Dodd, Mead, 1895. p60-78; *same in* The collected essays and papers of George Saintsbury 1875-1920. London, Dent, 1923. p220-30

Modern English prose. Fortn ns 19:255-6 F '76

The prae-Raphaelite school. *In* A history of English prosody from the twelfth century to the present day. London, Macmillan, 1910. vol III p334-52, 549-51

Salomon, Louis B.
The devil take her. . . Phila. Univ. of Penna. 1931

Salt, Henry S.
Swinburne at Eton. T L S D 25 '19 p781

Sarauw, Juliane Marie Auguste
Björnson's "Maria Stuart i Skotland," with comparisons of Schiller and Swinburne. Masters essay, Columbia univ. 1911

Sarrazin, Gabriel
Poètes modernes de l'Angleterre. Paris, Ollendorff, 1885. p273-348

La renaissance de la poésie anglaise, 1798-1889. Paris, Perrin, 1890. 2d ser

Sattler, Eduard
Algernon Charles Swinburne als naturdichter. Bonn, Foppen, 1910. 298p Diss. München

The **"Saturday"** and Swinburne. [On a criticism of Swinburne in Sat R 22:145-7 Ag 4 '66] Sat R 134:749-50 N 18 '22

Savage, Henry
A bookman's lost Atlantis. Bookman's Journal 1:142 D 12 '19

Scepticism and modern poetry. Blackw 115:223-31 F '74

Schaefer, Emma
Swinburnes "Tristram of Lyonesse." Eine quellenuntersuchung. Diss. Halle, 1923. 79p

Schelling, Felix E.
The English lyric. Boston, Houghton, Mifflin, 1913. p239-48

Schücking, L. L.
Besuch bei Swinburne. Die Leipziger Neunundneunzig 25:193-9 '29

Scott, Nellie Mahaffey
Poetic treatment of the Arthurian legend since 1850. Masters essay, Univ. of Oklahoma, 1929

Scott, Sally Helen
The poetry of Swinburne. Masters essay, Cornell Univ. 1929. 94ff

Scott, William Bell
Autobiographical notes of the life of William Bell Scott . . . ed. by W. Minto. London, Osgood, McIlvaine, 1892. vol II p14-20

Scudder, Vida D.
The life of the spirit in the modern English poets. Boston, Houghton, Mifflin, 1899. p278-80

Seaman, (Sir) Owen
Another poet of the channel. Punch 132: 326 My 8 '07

A channel record; poem. Punch 127:182 S 14 '04

[A parody of "A Channel Passage"]
In memoriam: Algernon Charles Swinburne. Punch 136:372 Ap 21 '09

A song of renunciation. *In* The battle of the bays. New York, Lane, 1896. p1-4

Sweet uses of obesity. Punch 126:290 Ap 27 '04

Watchman, what of the knight? Punch 120:26 Ja 9 '01

Seccombe, Thomas
Algernon Charles Swinburne. Readers' Review 2:55-6 My '09

The secret of Swinburne's power. Current Opinion 54:233-4 Mr '13

Sélincourt, Ernest de
English poetry since 1815. *In* English poets and the national ideal. London, Oxford univ. press, 1915. p107-8, 110-12

Selkirk, J. B. [pseud]
see Brown, James Bucham

Serner, Gunnar
The language of Swinburne's lyrics and epics. Lund, Sweden, Berlingska boktryckeriet, 1910. viii, 138p

Sewell, Elizabeth M.
The autobiography of Elizabeth M. Sewell, ed. by her niece, Eleanor L. Sewell. London, Longmans, Green, 1907. p105-9

Shackford, Martha Hale
Swinburne and Delavigne. P M L A 33: 85-95 '18

Sharp, Amy
Algernon Charles Swinburne. *In* Victorian poets. London, Methuen, 1891. p178-85
(Rev in Speaker 4:206-7 Ag 15 '91)

Sharp, William
Algernon Charles Swinburne. *In* Papers, critical and reminiscent. . . New York, Duffield, 1912. p281-320

Algernon Charles Swinburne. The story of a literary friendship. Pall Mall Magazine 43:689-97 Je '09

A literary friendship. Mr. A. C. Swinburne and Mr. Watts-Dutton at the Pines. Pall Mall Magazine 25:435-48 D '01

Shaw, George Bernard
The genius and influence of Swinburne. Bookm (Lond) 36:129 Je '09

[**Shelleyisms** of Swinburne] Dial 46:358-9 Je 1 '09

Shepard, William [pseud]
see Walsh, William Shepard

Sherman, Stuart Pratt
Core of Swinburne. *In* Emotional discovery of America, and other essays. New York, Farrar, 1932. p103-14

Shindler, Robert
Swinburne, Meredith. *In* On certain aspects of recent English literature. (Neuphilologische Vorträge und Abhandlungen II) Leipzig, Teubner, 1902. p38-47

The theology of Mr. Swinburne's poems. Ecl M 118:109-16 Ja '92; *same.* Gent M ns 47:459-71 N '91

Shirley [pseud]
see Skelton, John

Shorter, Clement King
A literary letter: chatter about Swinburne. Sphere 73:36 Ap 13 '18

From literary London. Dial 47:504-5 D 16 '09

Victorian literature. New York, Dodd, Mead, 1897. p16-17

Sichel, Walter
The sands of time. London, 1923. p109

Siebold, Erika von
Synästhesien in der englischen dichtung des neunzehnten jahrhunderts. Engl Stud 53:303-13 '19

Sigma [pseud]
Personalia. . . Blackw 174:304-7 S '03

Sillard, P. A.
Is Swinburne "a great poet"? Lit 7:262, 303 O 6, 20 '00

Swinburne. Lit 7:352 N 3 '00

Simcox, G. A.
Art and morality. Macmil 26:487-92 O '72

Mr. Swinburne's trilogy. Fortn ns 31: 166-79 F '82; *same.* Ecl M 98:498-506 Ap '82

Simpson, Selwyn G.
Algernon Charles Swinburne. East and West 13:30-44 Ja '14

[**Skelton, John**] Shirley [pseud]
The table-talk of Shirley . . . Edinburgh, Blackwood, 1895. p136-7

Smith, Arnold
Swinburne. *In* The main tendencies of Victorian poetry. . . London, Simpkin, Marshall, Hamilton, Kent, 1907. p147-82

Smith, Byron Caldwell
A young scholar's letters, being a memoir of Byron Caldwell Smith, ed. by D. O. Kellogg. London, Putnam, 1897. p73-5, 99-101

Smith, C[harles] Alphonso
Repetition in the poems of Algernon Charles Swinburne. *In* Repetition and parallelism in English verse. New York, University publishing co. 1894. p57-76

Smith, Lewis Worthington (ed)
Current reviews. New York, Holt [c1926] p288-94

Some poets of the Victorian era. VII.-Swinburne. Acad 79:221-4 S 3 '10

A song after sunset. Punch 67:45 Ag 1 '74

Spencer, W. T.
Books and the man. Bookman's Journal 2:85 Je 4 '20

Spiritual side of Swinburne's genius. Lit Digest 31:650-1 N 4 '05

Spiver, Gaynell Callaway
Elizabethanisms in Swinburne's tragedies. Masters essay, Univ. of North Carolina. 80ff

[Squire, John Collings] Solomon Eagle [pseud]
Delicate details. *In* Books reviewed. London, Heinemann, 1922. p276-83

If Swinburne had written "The Lay of Horatius." *In* Collected parodies. London, Hodder & Stoughton [1921?] p77-8; *also in* Tricks of the trade. New York, Putnam, 1917. p51-3

Mutual compliments. *In* Books in general. New York, Knopf, 1921. 2d ser p75-6

Swinburne's defects. *In* Books in general. London, Heinemann, 1921. 3d ser p26-32

Swinburne's vocabulary. *In* Books in general. New York, Knopf, 1921. 2d ser p66-8

Stead, William Taylor
The maiden tribute of modern Babylon. Pall Mall Gazette Jl 6-8, 10 '85 [Possibly had an effect on Swinburne's writing of "Rondeaux Parisiens" and "The Marquis of Stead"]

Stedman, Edmund Clarence
Algernon Charles Swinburne. Scribner's Monthly 9:585-96 Mr '75

Algernon Charles Swinburne. *In* Victorian poets. Boston, Houghton, Mifflin, 1896. p379-414

The nature and elements of poetry. Boston, Houghton, Mifflin, 1892. p131-3

Some London poets. Harper M 64:888-92 My '82

Stedman, Laura and Gould, George M.
Life and letters of Edmund Clarence Stedman. New York, Moffat, Yard, 1910. 2 vols passim

Steuart, J. A.
A. C. Swinburne. *In* Letters to living authors. London, Sampson Low, Marston, 1890 (Rev in Speaker 2:530-1 N 8 '90)

Stoddard, R. H.
Algernon Charles Swinburne. Appleton J 3:378-81 Ap 2 '70

Introduction. *In* Selections from the poetical works of A. C. Swinburne. New York, Crowell [c1884] p iii-xx

Strachey, James
Drama. Swinburne and Mr. Yeats. Ath 1:438 Je 6 '19

Stringer, Arthur
When closing Swinburne; poem. Bookm (NY) 17:159 Ap '03

Strodtmann, Adolf
A. C. Swinburne nach einer abhandlung von E. W. Gosse. *In* Dichterprofile. . . Berlin, Abenheim, 1879. vol II p43-90

Strong, (Sir) Archibald Thomas
Swinburne's Mary Stuart trilogy. *In* Four studies. Adelaide, Preece, 1933 (Rev in T L S Ap 27 '33 p291)

Svanberg, Harold
Swinburne. En studie. Göteberg, Vald Zachrissons boktrycheri, 1909. 127p Thesis, Lund

Swinburne, Algernon Charles
The age of Shakespeare. London, Chatto and Windus, 1908. x, 286p (Rev by F. T. Cooper in Forum 40:405-9 O '08; Cur Lit 45:661-3 D '08; Ath 2:674-5 N 28 '08; Dial 46:53-4 Ja 16 '09; Spec 101:502-3 O 3 '08; Sat R 106:422-3 O 3 '08; E. Dowden in Nation (Lond) 3:909-10 S 26 '08; Nation (NY) 87:445-6 N 5 '08; T L S S 24 '08 p305; J. H. Brocklehurst in Papers of the Manchester Literary Club 35:358-70 '09)

Astrophel, and other poems. London, Chatto and Windus, 1894. vii, 228p (Rev by E. D. A. Morshead in Acad 45:429 My 26 '94; Spec 72:828-9 Je 16 '94; Sat R 77:472-3 My 5 '94; Ath 1:701-3 Je 2 '94; Critic (NY) 25:36 Jl 21 '94; Literary World (Lond) ns 49:451-2 My 18 '94; Bookm (Lond) 6:74-6 Je '94; Book B ns 11:296-7 Jl '94; Gent M 276:640-4 Je '94; A. T. Quiller-Couch in Speaker 9:500-2 My 5 '94; W. E. Henley in Pall Mall Gazette p4 Je 13 '94; *same.* Critic (NY) 25:45-6 Jl 21 '94; Poet Lore 6:375 Je-Jl '94)

Atalanta in Calydon. A tragedy. London, Moxon, 1865. [xi]-xii, 111p (Rev by J. L. Warren in Fortn 1:75-80 My 15 '65; C. E. Norton in Nation (NY) 1:590-1 N 9 '65; De Bow's Review ns 6:231-9 Mr '69; Lord Houghton in Edin R 122:202-16 Jl '65; Christian Remembrancer ns 55:45-50 Ja '68; T L S D 11 '30 p1060; Mod Lang R 26:373 Jl '31; M. Praz in English Studies 13:34 F '31; L. Étienne in R Deux Mondes 2d ser 69:300-9 My 15 '67; Fraser 71:772-84 Je '65; Christian Examiner 79:

436 N '65; Spec 38:412-14 Ap 15 '65;
Ath 1:450-1 Ap 1 '65; Sat R 19:540-2
My 6 '65; Harper M 32:258 Ja '66; J. R.
Lowell in No Am 102:546-55 Ap '66;
M. Kaluza in Z F E U 1:441 '02; Examiner p440-1 Jl 15 '65; London Review
10:382-3 Ap 8 '65; Notes & Q 3d ser
7:272 Ap 1 '65; Reader 5:447-8 Ap 22
'65; Round Table 1:130-3 N 4 '65; Tablet p505 Ag 12 '65)

Bothwell: a tragedy. London, Chatto
and Windus, 1874. viii, 532p
(Rev by G. Saintsbury in Acad 5:651-3
Je 13 '74; Temple 41:545-51 Jl '74;
J. Morley in Macmil 30:521-9 O '74;
Cath World 20:346-53 D '74; Lord
Houghton in Fortn 22:76-88 Jl 1 '74;
same. Ecl M 83:302-9 S '74; *same.*
Canadian Monthly & National Review
6:174-82 Ag '74; Spec 47:724-6 Je 6
'74; Sat R 47 37:719-21 Je 6 '74; Ath
1:689-90 My 23 '74; Westm ns 46:296-7
Jl '74; Belgravia 23:516-28 Je '74; Lond
Q R 42:508-13 Jl '74; Examiner p568-
70 My 30 '74)

A century of roundels. London, Chatto
and Windus, 1883. xi, 100p
(Rev by J. A. Noble in Acad 23:429-
30 Je 23 '83; T. A. Schovelin in Dial
4:90-1 Ag '83; Spec 56:970 Jl 28 '83;
Ath 1:755-6 Je 16 '83; Le Livre 4:617
O 10 '83; American 6:248-9 Jl 28 '83;
Brit Q 78:227-8 Jl '83; Critic (NY) 3:
403-4 O 13 '83; W. P. Ker in Contemp
44:466-7 S '83; Lit W 14:222-3 Jl 14 '83;
Scottish Review 2:398-9 S '83; Pall Mall
Gazette p4-5 Jl 5 '83)

A channel passage, and other poems.
London, Chatto and Windus, 1904.
ix, 213p
(Rev by E. Rhys in Bookm (Lond)
27:23-4 O '04; Spec 93:393-4 S 17 '04;
Literary World (Lond) ns 70:195-6 S
16 '04; T L S S 2 '04 p265-6; Sat R
98:365-6 S 17 '04; Ath 2:475-6 O 8 '04;
Monthly Review 17 no 2:165-70 N '04;
F. Thompson in Acad 67:196 S 17 '04;
A. Agresti in Italia Moderna 3d ser
2, no 23:1679-86 D '04; H. D. Davray in
Mercure Fr 52:528-9 N '04; M. Meyer-
feld in Das Litterarische Echo 7:472-3
Ja 1 '05)

Charles Dickens. London, Chatto and
Windus, 1913. xx,84p; *from* Quar R Jl
'02
(Rev in Ath 1:277-8 Mr 8 '13; T. P.'s
Weekly 21:647 My 23 '13; Harper W
46:1237 S 6 '02; T. de Wyzewa in R
Deux Mondes 6th ser 15:457-68 My 15
'13; Bookm (Lond) 44:86-7 My '13;
G. K. Chesterton in Nation (Lond) 12:
1068 Mr 29 '13; T L S Jl 25 '02 p219;
Sat R 94:112-13 Jl 26 '02; Lit Digest
25:188-90 Ag 16 '02)

Chastelard; a tragedy. London, Moxon,
1865. viii, 219p
(Rev by Houghton in Fortn 4:533-43
Ap 15 '66; J. R. Lowell in No Am 102:
544-6 Ap '66; Spec 38:1342-4 D 2 '65;
Lond Q R 29:323-4 Ja '68; Ath 2:880-1

D 23 '65; Reader 6:621-2 D 2 '65; London Review 11:621-2 D 9 '65; H. James
in Nation (NY) 2:83-4 Ja 18 '66; Sat R
21:623-5 My 26 '66; Gent M 220:398-401
Mr '66 [S. Urban]; Pall Mall Gazette
p11-12 Ap 27 '66; Westm 86:277 Jl '66;
H. Morley in Examiner p597-9 S 22 '66;
Round Table 3:18-19 Ja 13 '66)

Christopher Marlowe and some minor
contemporaries. Fortn 105:764-9 My
'16; *same.* No Am 203:742-8 My '16

Collected works. London, Heinemann,
1924
(Rev by J. Freeman in Spec 133:686-8
N 8 '24; A. Noyes in Bookm (Lond)
67:196-200 Ja '25; F. L. Lucas in New
Statesm 24:420-1 Ja 17 '25)

Contemporaries of Shakespeare, ed. by
Sir Edmund Gosse and Thomas James
Wise. London, Heinemann, 1919. xii,
308p
(Rev in Spec 123:407-8 S 27 '19)

The duke of Gandia. London, Chatto
and Windus, 1908. 60p
(Rev in Liv Age 257:305-8 My 2 '08;
Sat R 105:532-3 Ap 25 '08; A. S. Henry
in Bookn 27:357-8 Ja '09; Ath 1:469-
70 Ap 18 '08; Nation (NY) 86:339 Ap
9 '08; W. M. Payne in Dial 45:60-1 Ag
1 '08; Bookm (Lond) 34:72-3 My '08;
H. de Davray in Mercure Fr 73:166 My
1 '08; Acad 74:685-6 Ap 18 '08)

Erechtheus: a tragedy. London, Chatto
and Windus, 1876. viii, 107p
(Rev in Edin R 144:147-68 Jl '76; J.
A. Symonds in Acad 9:23-4 Ja 8 '76;
Ath 1:13-14 Ja 1 '76; Sat R 41:50-1
Ja 8 '76; Westm ns 49:581 Ap '76; In-
ternational Review 3:552-3 Ag '76;
Blackw 126:419-20 O '79; Scribner's
Monthly 12:130-3 My '76; Brit Q 63:
568-71 Ap '76; Lond Q R 46:249-54 Ap
'76; Spec 49:15-17 Ja 1 '76; E. Gosse in
Examiner p41-3 Ja 8 '76; Pall Mall
Gazette p12-13 Ja 15 '76)

Essays and studies. London, Chatto and
Windus, 1875. xii, 380p
(Rev in American Bibliopolist 7:128-9
Je '75; G. Saintsbury in Acad 8:4-6 Jl
3 '75; Ath 1:681 My 22 '75; Sat R 40:54-
5 Jl 10 '75; Spec 48:855-7 Jl 3 '75;
H. James in Nation (NY) 21:73-4 Jl 29
'75; Westm ns 48:297-8 Jl '75; R. Gray
in No Am 123:220-1 Ap '76; Scribner's
Monthly 10:513-14 Ag '75; Quar R 141:
507-26 Ap '76; Brit Q 62:563-5 O '75;
J. Benton in Appleton J 14:628-9 N 13
'75; Examiner p665-6 Je 12 '75; Pall
Mall Gazette p11-12 Je 23 '75)

Four unpublished letters of Swinburne.
Yale University Library Gazette 4:
18-20 Jl '29

George Chapman: a critical essay. Lon-
don, Chatto and Windus, 1875. iv, 187p
(Rev by J. A. Symonds in Acad 7:442-3
My 1 '75; Spec 48:377-8 Mr 20 '75;
Westm ns 47:546-7 Ap '75; E. Gosse in
Examiner p214-16 F 20 '75)

Swinburne, Algernon Charles—*Continued*

Laus Veneris [For information see Carter, J. and Pollard, G. An enquiry. . . London, Constable, 1934. p272-7]
(Rev by T. Davidson in Radical 3:316-23 Ja '68; National Quarterly Review 14:150-8 D '66; No Am 104:287-92 Ja '67; Crescent Monthly F '67; Ecl M ns 4:765 D '66; R. G. White in Galaxy 2:665-70 D 1 '66; R. Gildersleeve in Southern Review 1:352-82 Ap '67; R. Sturgis, Jr. in Nation (NY) 3:446-7 D 6 '66; Round Table 4:307-8 D 8 '66)

Letters chiefly concerning Edgar Allan Poe, from Algernon Charles Swinburne to John H. Ingram. London, Printed for private circulation, 1910. 35p

The letters of Algernon Charles Swinburne, ed. by Edmund Gosse and Thomas James Wise. London, Heinemann, 1918. 2 vols xiv, 304p; iv, 296p
(Rev in Spec 122:13-14 Ja 4 '19; Sat R 126:1204 D 28 '18; B. Fehr in Bei Anglia 31:97-106 My '20; Liv Age 297:498-500 My 25 '18; Cur Opin 67:48-9 Jl '19; C. Kernahan in Bookm (Lond) 55:128-9 Ja '19; L. Gillet in R Deux Mondes 6th ser 57:890-901 Je 15 '20; Ath 1:22-3 Ja '19; Dial 66:612-14 Je 14 '19; Blackw 205:138-40 Ja '19; S. C. Chew in Nation (NY) 108:505-6 Ap 5 '19)

The letters of Algernon Charles Swinburne, with some personal recollections, by Thomas Hake and Arthur Compton-Rickett. London, Murray, 1918. xxii, 208p
(Rev by C. Kernahan in Bookm (Lond) 54:64-6 My '18; E. Shanks in Dial 64:396-8 Ap 25 '18; Ath 1:234 My '18; Nation (Lond) 23:118 My 4 '18)

Locrine: a tragedy. London, Chatto and Windus, 1887. viii, 138p
(Rev in Spec 61:16-17 Ja 7 '88; H. B. Garrod in Acad 32:381-2 D 10 '87; Lit W 19:54 F 18 '88; T. Watts-Dunton in Ath 2:856-9 D 24 '87; Sat R 64:763-4 D 3 '87; R. H. Shepherd in Gent M 263:608-14 D '87; Critic (NY) 13:242 N 17 '88; W. M. Payne in Dial 8:247 F '88; Westm 129:392 Mr '88; Nation (NY) 46:410-11 My 17 '88; Pall Mall Gazette p3 N 18 '87; Public Opinion 14:241 D 10 '92)

Love's cross-currents: a year's letters. London, Chatto and Windus, 1905. x, 258p
(Rev by W. Barry in Bookm (Lond) 28:159-60 Ag '05; Spec 95:157 Jl 29 '05; W. M. Payne in Dial 39:112-13 S 1 '05; C. H. Gaines in Harper W 49:1160 Ag 12 '05; Ath 2:165-6 Ag 5 '05; Acad 69:726-7 Jl 15 '05; Contemp 88:454-5 S '05; Critic (NY) 47:452 N '05; Nation (NY) 81:147 Ag 17 '05; Sat R 100:184-5 Ag 5 '05; Lit Digest 31:449 S 30 '05; Punch 129:90 Ag 2 '05)

Marino Faliero. A tragedy. London, Chatto and Windus, 1885. viii, 151p
(Rev by T. Watts-Dunton in Ath 1: 751-3 Je 13 '85; E. Robertson in Acad 27:412-14 Je 13 '85; Dial 6:248-9 Ja '86; Book B ns 2:150 Jl '85; Brit Q 82:207-8 Jl '85; W. P. Ker in Contemp 48:287-8 Ag '85)

Mary Stuart. A tragedy. London, Chatto and Windus, 1881. viii, 203p
(Rev in Lit W 13:3 Ja 14 '82; Dial 2:237-8 F '82; T. Watts-Dunton in Ath 2:771-2 D 10 '81; Sat R 52:702-3 D 3 '81; Nation (NY) 34:360 Ap 27 '82; Lippinc 32:506-12 N '83; Critic (NY) 1:351 D 17 '81; E. D. A. Morshead in Acad 20:427-8 D 10 '81; Westm 118:278 Jl '82; Brit Q 75:225-6 Ja '82; G. A. Simcox in Fortn ns 31:166-79 F '82; *same*. Ecl M 98:498-506 Ap '82; T. Bayne in Fraser ns 26:469-79 O '82; Pall Mall Gazette p19 D 17 '81)

A midsummer holiday and other poems. London, Chatto and Windus, 1884. [v]-vi, 189p
(Rev by G. E. Woodberry in Atlan 55:564-5 Ap '85; Lond Q R 65:247-50 Ja '86; E. D. A. Morshead in Acad 26:367-8 D 6 '84; Ath 2:651-3 N 22 '84; Spec 57:1584-5 N 29 '84; Dial 6:39-40 Je '85; Book B ns 2:19 F '85; Brit Q 81:212-14 Ja '85; Gent M 257:620 D '84; W. P. Ker in Contemp 47:144-5 Ja '85; Pall Mall Gazette p4-5 N 22 '84; Sat R 58:697-8 N 29 '84)

Miscellanies. London, Chatto and Windus, 1886. xii, 390p
(Rev by M. B. Anderson in Dial 7:156-8 N '86; T. Watts-Dunton in Ath 1:803-5 Je 19 '86; Sat R 62:100-1 Jl 17 '86; Spec 59:1248-9 S 18 '86; Literary World (Lond) ns 33:613-15 Je 25 '86; Notes & Q 7th ser 2:79 Jl 24 '86; Pall Mall Gazette p5 Je 7 '86)

Note of an English Republican on the Muscovite Crusade. London, Chatto and Windus, 1876. 24p
(Rev in Ath 2:827 D 23 '76; Acad 10:604 D 23 '76; Spec 49:1606-7 D 23 '76; Pall Mall Gazette p2-3 F 2 '77)

A note on Charlotte Brontë. London, Chatto and Windus, 1877. iv, 97p
(Rev by E. Dowden in Acad 12:233-4 S 8 '77; Spec 50:1095-7 S 1 '77; Brit Q 66:253 O '77; Ath 2:261-4 S 1 '77; G. E. Woodberry in Atlan 41:805-6 Je '78; Contemp 30:901-2 O '77; Examiner p1105-7 S 1 '77)

Notes on poems and reviews. London, Hotten, 1866. 23p
(Rev in Spec 39:1228-9 N 3 '66; Ath 2:564-5 N 3 '66; *same*. Liv Age 91:564-8 D 1 '66; Examiner p677 O 27 '66; Pall Mall Gazette p9-10 N 2 '66; Fun p99 N 17 '66; London Review 13:482-3 N 3 '66; Sat R 22:600-1 N 17 '66)

Ode on the proclamation of the French republic, September 4th, 1870. London, Ellis, 1870. 23p
(Rev in Ath 2:364 S 17 '70; Sat R 30: 403-4 S 24 '70; Lond Q R 35:517-19 Ja '71; Graphic 2:298-9 S 24 '70; Examiner and London Review p613-14 S 24 '70)

A pilgrimage of pleasure; essays and studies. Boston, Badger [1913] 181p
(Rev in Spec 105:561 O 8 '10; Dial 55: 364 N 1 '13)

Poems
(Noted in Literary World (Lond) ns 70:220 S 23 '04; rev in Edin R 134:71-99 Jl '71; R. G. White in Galaxy 2:665-71 D 1 '66; Liv Age 242:438-43 Ag 13 '04; T L S Jl 8 '04 p209-10; R. Le Gallienne in No Am 183:792-5 O 19 '06; Westm 87:210-20 Ap '67; Edin R 171:429-52 Ap '90; Acad 67:638 D 24 '04; Sat R 98: 699-700 D 3 '04; W. M. Payne in Dial 38:152-4 Mr 1 '05; G. Radford in Gent M 299:198-202 Ag '05; Out 80:388-90 Je 10 '05; J. Douglas in Bookm (Lond) 26:213 S '04; Ind 58:1420-1 Je 22 '05; E. Rhys in Fortn 83:150-7 Ja '05; H. D. Davray in Mercure Fr 52:803-4 D '04; H. D. Davray in Mercure Fr 53: 637 F 15 '05; O. Elton in Speaker ns 10: 541-3 S 10 '04 and ns 11:488-90 F 18 '05; W. M. Payne in Dial 5:136-9 O '84; Blackw 176:123-6 Jl '04; Ath 2:264-5 Ag 27 '04; F. Greenslet in Atlan 96:416 S '05; S. Urban in Gent M 297:309 S '04; Sat R 98:828-9 D 31 '04; Nation (NY) 80:292-3 Ap 13 '05)

Poems and ballads. [first series] London, Moxon, 1866. vii, 344p
(Rev by J. B. Taylor in No Am 104: 287-92 Ja '67; Liv Age 90:633-6 S 8 '66; Nation (NY) 3:446-7 D 6 '66; L. Étienne in R Deux Mondes 2d ser 69: 309-17 My 15 '67; J. Morley in Sat R 22:145-7 Ag 4 '66; same. Ecl M 67:556-60 N '66; R. Buchanan in Ath 2:137-8 Ag 4 '66; F. Thompson in Acad 66: 680-1 Je 25 '04; Lit W 9:37 Ag '78; Ecl M 143:555-60 O '04; Ath 1:775-6 Je 18 '04; Sat R 98:17-18 Jl 2 '04; J. Douglas in Bookm (Lond) 26:130-2 Jl '04; Spec 93:88-9 Jl 16 '04; Literary World (Lond) ns 69:580-1 Je 17 '04; H. D. Davray in Mercure Fr 51:818-20 S '04; Spec 39:1228-9 N 3 '66; Reader 7:675 Jl 28 '66; London Review 13:130-1 Ag 4 '66; Lit Digest 29:225-6 Ag 20 '04; Pall Mall Gazette p9-11 Ag 20 '66; Tablet p506 Ag 11 '66; Fun p236 Ag 18 '66; Notes & Q 10th ser 1:518-19 Je 25 '04; Liv Age 242:438-43 Ag 13 '04; H. Morley in Examiner p597-9 S 22 '66; Lord Houghton in Examiner p672 O 6 '66)

Poems and ballads. Second series. London, Chatto and Windus, 1878. ix, 240p
(Rev in Nation (NY) 27:45-6 Jl 18 '78; Edin R 171:429-52 Ap '90; G. Saintsbury in Acad 14:25-6 Jl 13 '78; Ath 2: 7-9 Jl 6 '78; Sat R 46:85-6 Jl 20 '78;

Brit Q 68:287-8 O '78; Westm ns 54:563 O '78; International Review 5:697-8 O '78; No Am 127:342-4 S-O '78; Appleton J ns 5:381-2 O '78; Notes & Q 5th ser 10:339 O 26 '78; Pall Mall Gazette p11-12 Jl 5 '78; Examiner p847-8 Jl 6 '78; Contemp 34:419 Ja '79)

Poems and ballads, third series. London, Chatto and Windus, 1889. viii, 181p
(Rev in Edin R 171:429-52 Ap '90; Spec 62:764-5 Je 1 '89; G. Cotterell in Acad 35:279-80 Ap 27 '89; Ath 1:655-8 My 25 '89; Lit W 20:223 Jl 6 '89; Critic (NY) 15:238-9 N 16 '89; Sat R 67:482-3 Ap 20 '89; W. M. Payne in Dial 10: 103-4 S '89; Scots Observer 1:639-40 Ap 27 '89; Nation (NY) 49:522 D 26 '89; Book B ns 6:280-1 S '89; Gent M 267: 103-4 Jl '89; O. Wilde in Pall Mall Gazette p3 Je 27 '89; Public Opinion 7:67 Ap 27 '89)

Poetical works
(Rev by W. M. Payne in Dial 5:136-9 O '84; H. D. Davray in Mercure Fr 58: 299-301 N 15 '05; H. W. Boynton in Critic (NY) 47:58-61 Jl '05)

Posthumous poems by Algernon Charles Swinburne, ed. by Edmund Gosse and Thomas James Wise. London, Heinemann, 1917. xxvi, 194p
(Rev in T L S Je 21 '17 p295; Ath 2: 362 Jl '17; C. Aiken in Dial 65:70 Jl 18 '18; Spec 118:701-2 Je 23 '17; L. Binyon in Bookm (Lond) 52:145-7 Ag '17; J. Bailey in Quar R 228:228-48 Jl '17; Contemp 112:106-7 Jl '17; Studies 6:708-9 D '17; P. Colum in New Repub 16:101-3 Ag 24 '18)

The Queen-Mother. Rosamond. Two plays. London, Pickering, 1860. x, 217p
(Rev in Ath 1:595 My 4 '61; Nation (NY) 2:549 My 1 '66; National Quarterly Review 13:183-8 Je '66; Fraser 51: 781-4 Je '65; Ecl M ns 3:772 Je '66; New Englander 25:594 Jl '66; Spec 34: 42 Ja 12 '61)

Rosamund, Queen of the Lombards. London, Chatto and Windus, 1899. vi, 88p
(Rev by A. Macdonell in Bookm (Lond) 17:86 D '99; Speaker ns 1:118-20 N 4 '99; same. Public Opinion 27: 723-4 D 7 '99; Nation (NY) 70:361 My 10 '00; Lit 5:431-2 N 4 '99; Ath 2:579 O 28 '99; E. M. Thomas in Critic (NY) 36:152-3 F '00; Sat R 88:619-20 N 11 '99; Spec 84:173-4 F 3 '00; W. M. Payne in Dial 28:48-9 Ja 16 '00; Literary World (Lond) ns 60:351-2 N 10 '99; Ind 51: 3431-2 D 21 '99; Bookm (NY) 10:495 Ja '00; W. C. Brownell in Book B ns 20:54-5 F '00; E. M. Thomas in Critic (NY) 36:152-3 F '00; Acad 57: 534-5 N 11 '99; Gent M 288:101-3 Ja '00; Sewanee R 8:106-9 Ja '00; Lit Digest 19:737 D 16 '99; Poet Lore 12:134-6 Ja-Mr '00)

Sappho. Liv Age 280:817-18 Mr 28 '14

Swinburne, Algernon Charles—*Continued*

Selections from A. C. Swinburne. Ed. by Edmund Gosse and Thomas James Wise. London, Heinemann, 1919. 299p
(Rev in T L S D 11 '19 p732; Nation (Lond) 26:652 F 7 '20)

Selections from poetical works
(Rev in Lit W 15:307 S 20 '84; T. Watts-Dunton in Ath 1:727-9 Je 4 '87; E. D. A. Morshead in Acad 32:145-6 S 3 '87; Critic (NY) 5:207 N 1 '84; W. M. Payne in Dial 8:185 D '87; Nation (NY) 39:527 D 18 '84; Nation (NY) 45:97 Ag 4 '87; Critic (NY) 11:162 O 1 '87; Lit W 18:329 O 1 '87; Nation (NY) 81:96 Ag 3 '05)

Shakespeare: written in 1905 and now first published. London, Frowde, 1909. [5]-83p
(Rev in Ath 2:289-90 S 11 '09; Nation (NY) 89:411 O 28 '09)

Siena
(Rev in American Quarterly Church Review 20:461-3 O '68)

The sisters: a tragedy. London, Chatto and Windus, 1892. x, 107p
(Rev in National Observer 8:43-4 My 28 '92; Bookm (Lond) 2:88 Je '92; Sat R 73:602 My 21 '92; Ath 2:31-2 Jl 2 '92; Lit W 23:239-40 Jl 16 '92; Spec 69:19-21 Jl 2 '92; G. Cotterell in Acad 42:5 Jl 2 '92; Critic (NY) 21:308 D 3 '92; W. M. Payne in Dial 13:185-6 S 16 '92; Gent M 273:212 Ag '92; Lit Digest 5:187 Je 18 '92; Public Opinion 14:193 N 26 '92)

A song of Italy. London, Hotten, 1867. 66p
(Rev in Westm 88:148-9 Jl '67; Spec 40:415-16 Ap 13 '67; Ath 1:446-8 Ap 6 '67; Sat R 23:503-4 Ap 20 '67; C. E. Norton in No Am 105:324-5 Jl '67; Contemp 5:385 Jl '67; Pall Mall Gazette p11 Ap 13 '67; Examiner p230 Ap 13 '67; T. Purnell in Every Sat 3:551-3 My 4 '67; Round Table 6:9-10 Jl 6 '67)

Songs before sunrise. London, Ellis, 1871. viii, 287p
(Rev in Edin R 134:71-99 Jl '71; Westm ns 39:579-80 Ap '71; A. Hayward in Quar R 132:59-69 Ja '72; *same.* Ecl M 78:385-90 Ap '72; F. Hüffer in Acad 2:87-9 Ja 15 '71; Ath 1:41-2 Ja 14 '71; Sat R 31:54-5 Ja 14 '71; Tinsley's 8:561-8 Je '71; H. D. Davray in Mercure Fr 51:818-20 S '04; S. Amos in Fortn 15:281-2 F 1 '71; Graphic 3:87 Ja 28 '71; Examiner p45-6 Ja 14 '71; Lit W p154-5 Mr 1 '71; Notes & Q 10th ser 2:240 S 17 '04; Ath 2:264-5 Ag 27 '04)

Songs of the springtides. London, Chatto and Windus, 1880. x, [3]-135p
(Rev by R. Lowell in Lit W 11:239 Jl 17 '80; Dial 1:59 Jl '80; G. Saintsbury in Acad 17:378-9 My 22 '80; Sat R 49:698-9 My 29 '80; T. Watts-Dunton in Ath 1:655-7 My 22 '80; *same.* Appleton J ns 9:178-82 Ag '80; Nation (NY)

30:458-9 Je 17 '80; Scribner's Monthly 20:943 O '80; Brit Q 72:121-2 Jl '80; C. T. Congdon in No Am 131:183-4 Ag '80; Gent M 246:752-3 Je '80; 19th Cent 8:332-3 Ag '80; Notes & Q 6th ser 1:427 My 22 '80; W. Sharp in Modern Thought p458-9 Ag 1 '80; Westm 114:291-3 Jl '80; Examiner p610-11 My 15 '80)

Songs of two nations. London, Chatto and Windus, 1875. viii, 78p
(Rev in Acad 7:371 Ap 10 '75; H. D. Davray in Mercure Fr 51:818-20 S '04; E. Gosse in Examiner p354-5 Mr 27 '75)

The springtide of life. Poems of childhood by Algernon Charles Swinburne, with a preface by Edmund Gosse. New York, Doubleday, Page, 1926. v-xi, 132p
(Rev in Sat R Lit 3:242 O 23 '26; J. Morley in Liv Age 329:587-92 Je 12 '96)

Studies in prose and poetry. London, Chatto and Windus, 1894. vi, 298p
(Rev by St. J. Hankin in Acad 46:547-8 D 29 '94; C. Coupe in Dublin Review 116:338-62 Ap '95; T. Watts-Dunton in Ath 2:853-5 D 22 '94; Sat R 78:539-40 N 17 '94; National Observer 13:427 Mr 2 '95; Literary World (Lond) ns 50:491-2 D 21 '94; Bookm (Lond) 7:83-4 D '94; Gent M 278:105-8 Ja '95)

Studies in song. London, Chatto and Windus, 1880. vi, 212p
(Rev in Lit W 12:72 F 26 '81; Congregationalist 10:152-9 F '81; T. Watts-Dunton in Ath 1:90-2 Ja 15 '81; Spec 54:316-17 Mr 5 '81; Dial 1:192 Ja '81; Nation (NY) 32:98-9 F 10 '81; Brit Q 73:500-2 Ap '81; American 1:288-9 F 12 '81; E. Dowden in Acad 19:20-1 Ja 8 '81; Westm 115:615-16 Ap '81)

A study of Ben Jonson. London, Chatto and Windus, 1889. vi, 181p
(Rev by J. Davidson in Acad 36:331-2 N 23 '89; Lit W 21:88-9 Mr 15 '90; Dial 10:341-2 Ap '90; Critic (NY) 16:101-2 Mr 1 '90; Nation (NY) 50:208-9 Mr 6 '90; F. E. Schelling in Mod Lang N 5:183-5 Je '90; S. Urban in Gent M 267:631-2 D '89)

A study of Shakespeare. London, Chatto and Windus, 1880. viii, 309p
(Rev by E. Dowden in Acad 17:1-2 Ja 3 '80; Spec 53:850-2 Jl 3 '80; Sat R 49:159-60 Ja 31 '80; Brit Q 71:262-3 Ap '80; Ath 1:146-8 Ja 31 '80; Notes & Q 6th ser 1:368 My 1 '80; Westm 113:615-16 Ap '80; Examiner p49-50 Ja 10 '80)

A study of Victor Hugo. London, Chatto and Windus, 1886. vi, 148p
(Rev by T. Watts-Dunton in Ath 1:351-3 Mr 13 '86; Lit W 17:114 Ap 3 '86; E. D. A. Morshead in Acad 29:211-12 Mr 27 '86; Critic (NY) ns 5:192-3 Ap 17 '86; Dial 6:305 Mr '86; Nation (NY)

42:175 F 25 '86; H. C. O. Huss in Mod Lang N 1:59-60 Ap '86; S. Urban in Gent M 261:103 Jl '86; Pall Mall Gazette p5 F 27 '86)

Swinburne letters. [unpublished letters to Edmund Clarence Stedman] Liv Age 262:154-65 Jl 17 '09

The tale of Balen. London, Chatto and Windus, 1896. vi, 132p
(Rev by E. D'Esterre-Keeling in Acad 49:481-2 Je 13 '96; Sat R 82:166-7 Ag 15 '96; Ath 1:799-800 Je 20 '96; Book B ns 13:307 Je '96; W. M. Payne in Dial 21:119-20 S 1 '96; Literary World (Lond) ns 53:536-7 Je 5 '96; Bookm (NY) 3:395-6 Jl '96; Nation (NY) 63: 274 O 8 '96; Guardian 51:905 Je 10 '96; A. Macdonell in Bookm (Lond) 10:112 Jl '96; Atlan 78:569-70 O '96; Critic (NY) 29:4-5 Jl 4 '96; Gent M 281:106-8 Jl '96; A. Lang in Cosmopolis 3:69-70 Jl '96)

Thomas Nabbes. Fortn 105:769-72 My '16

Three plays of Shakespeare. London, Harper, 1909. xvi,85p
(Rev in Ath 1:254 F 27 '09)

The tragedies. . . London, Chatto and Windus, 1905
(Rev in T L S Je 30 '05 p208; T L S F 2 '06 p33-4; Dial 40:330-1 My 16 '06; Sat R 100:54-5 Jl 8 '05; Sat R 101: 238-9 F 24 '06; A. Noyes in Bookm (Lond) 30:57-62 My '06; G. Murray in Speaker ns 12:570-2 S 16 '05; same. Liv Age 247:244-8 O 28 '05; Out 83:483 Je 23 '06; H. D. Davray in Mercure Fr 58:299-301 N 15 '05; Notes & Q 10th ser 4:39, 418, 497 Jl 8, N 18, D 16 '05; 10th ser 5:118 F 10 '06)

Tristram of Lyonesse, and other poems. London, Chatto and Windus, 1882. xi, 361p
(Rev in Dial 3:255 Mr '83; Sat R 54: 156-7 Jl 29 '82; American 1:75-6 N '82; Lit W 13:293-4 S 9 '82; Spec 55:1055-7 Ag 12 '82; Brit Q 76:476-8 O '82; J. A. Symonds in Acad 22:93-4 Ag 5 '82; T. Watts-Dunton in Ath 2:103-5 Jl 22 '82; Critic (NY) 2:210 Ag 12 '82; Westm 118:586-7 O '82; S. Urban in Gent M 253:384 S '82; Pall Mall Gazette p4 Jl 29 '82)

William Blake. A critical essay. London, Hotten, 1868. viii, 304p
(Rev by M. D. Conway in Fortn 9: 216-20 F '68; Ath 2:149-50 Ag 11 '06; Ath 1:12-13 Ja 4 '68; Spec 41:320-2 Mr 14 '68; Westm 89:587-8 Ap '68; Broadway Annual p723-30 '68; Examiner p84-6 F 8 '68)

Works
(Rev in T L S Ja 7, N 25 '26 p9, 855)

Swinburne, Algernon Charles (ed)
Ballads of the English border. Ed. by A. C. Swinburne. With an introd. by W. A. MacInnes. London, Heinemann [1925] xviii, 264p
(Rev in T L S Jl 15 '26 p476; H. Read in Nat-Ath 39:131-2 My 1 '26)
Christabel and the lyrical and imaginative poems of S. T. Coleridge. Arranged and introduced. . . London, Sampson Low, 1869. xxvii, 150p
(Rev in Contemp 13:296-8 F '70; Ath 2:237 Ag 21 '69)
Joseph and his brethren: a dramatic poem by Charles Wells with an introduction. . . London, Chatto and Windus, 1876. xix, 252p
(Rev in Ath 1:191-2 F 5 '76; Westm 105:580-1 Ap '76; Scrib M 12:276-8 Je '76)
A selection from the works of Lord Byron. Ed. and prefaced by . . . (Moxon's miniature poets) London, Moxon, 1866. xxxii, 244p
(Rev in Spec 39:356-8 Mr 31 '66; Ath 1:359 Mr 17 '66; Westm 86:277 Jl '66)

Swinburne, Algernon Charles (prefacer)
Aurora Leigh. By Elizabeth Barrett Browning. . . With prefatory note. . . London, Smith, Elder, 1898. xiv, 375p
(Rev in Literary World (Lond) ns 58:486 D 16 '98)

Swinburne, Evelyn C.
Swinburne's ancestry. Spec 118:516 My 5 '17

[Swinburne, Isabel and Gosse, (Sir) Edmund William]
[Letters regarding Swinburne's Juvenilia] T L S Ap 5 '13 p11-12, 14-16

Swinburne. Harper W 49:269 F 25 '05; Sat R 107:484-5 Ap 17 '09; Dial 46:281-3 My 1 '09; Lit 7:352-3 N 3 '00; Literary World (Lond) ns 67:175 F 20 '03

Swinburne again. Ind 66:878 Ap 22 '09

Swinburne and the "little folk." Speaker 9:529 My 12 '94

Swinburne and Mary Stuart. T L S Je 14, 21 '17 p285, 297

Swinburne and Meredith. Westm 172:29-35 Jl '09

Swinburne and Meredith: the last Victorians. Chautauquan 55:160-2 Jl '09

Swinburne and Mr. Yeats. Ath 1:438 Je 6 '19

Swinburne and Morley. Liv Age 327:378 N 14 '25

Swinburne and water. Punch 81:26 Jl 23 '81

Swinburne and Watts-Dunton. T L S N 27 '19 p696

Swinburne as a metrician. Acad 76:32-3 Ap 24 '09

[Swinburne as a possible Laureate] Critic (NY) 21:213 O 15 '92

[Swinburne as a thinker] Acad 57:529 N 11 '99

Swinburne as critic. T L S S 11 '19 p483

Swinburne copyrights. T L S Ap 5 '17 p166

Swinburne letters. T L S My 27, Je 3, 10 '09 p196, 204, 214

Swinburne on Emerson. Notes & Q 157: 411 D 7 '29

Swinburne on Emerson; philosophaster. Notes & Q 157:463 D 28 '29

[Swinburne on poets] Appleton J 7:637 Je 8 '72

[Swinburne on the English Academy] Acad 52:449 N 27 '97

Swinburne, the improvisatore. Collier's 43: 29-30 My 8 '09

Swinburne; the last of the giants. Cur Lit 46:640-3 Je '09

Swinburne, the last of the Victorian poets. R of Rs (NY) 39:637-8 My '09

Swinburne versus Carlyle. Spec 49:1606-7 D 23 '76

[Swinburne's "Dirae"] Spec 46:655, 697 My 24, 31 '73

Swinburne's "Hymn of Man" and Carducci's "Inno a Satana." New Age ns 6:210-11 D 30 '09

Swinburne's mania for alliteration. Lit Digest 11:100 My 25 '95

Swinburne's methods. T L S Ja 8 '31 p28

[Swinburne's poems] Lit 6:74 Ja 20 '00

Swinburne's prose. Acad 76:7-10 Ap 17 '09

[Swinburne's seventieth birthday] Acad 72: 355 Ap 13 '07

[Swinburne's sonnet on the Transvaal crisis] Acad 57:417 O 14 '99

Swinburne's swat at Lowell and Emerson. Boston Transcript O 16 '18 p4

Swinburne's visit to Paris in 1882. T L S Ap 26 '17 p203

[Swinburne's work] Critic (NY) 45:196 S '04

Swinburniana. Pall Mall Gazette S 15 '66 p13

Symonds, John Addington
A. C. Swinburne. *In* Letters and papers of John Addington Symonds, collected and ed. by Horatio F. Brown. New York, Scribner, 1923. p51-2

A note on Whitmania. Fortn ns 42:459-60 S '87

Symons, Arthur
Algernon Charles Swinburne. *In* Figures of several centuries. New York, Dutton [1916?] p153-200

Algernon Charles Swinburne. *In* Miles, A. H. (ed) The poets and the poetry of the nineteenth century. London, Routledge, 1905. vol VI p281-8

Algernon Charles Swinburne. *In* Studies in strange souls. London, Sawyer, 1929. p50-[83]
(Rev in T L S Je 13 '29 p471)

Algernon Charles Swinburne: with some unpublished letters. Fortn 107:795-804 My '17; *same.* Liv Age 293:666-73 Je 16 '17

Notes on two manuscripts [a Swinburne manuscript and the original manuscript of Rossetti's Eden Bower] Engl R 54: 514-20 My '32

Tabb, John Bannister
Swinburne; poem. *In* Litz, Francis A. The poetry of Father Tabb. London, 1928. p411

Talbot, Ethel
Tennyson, or another? Acad 73:654 Jl 6 '07

Taylor, Bayard
The echo club, and other literary diversions. Boston, Osgood, 1876. p37-43; *same.* Atlan 29:171-2 F '72

Taylor, (Sir) Henry
Correspondence of Henry Taylor, ed. by Edward Dowden. London, Longmans, Green, 1888. p398-9, 406-7, 417-18

Taylor, Jeannette Stuart
Medievalism in Coleridge, Keats, Swinburne and Rossetti. Masters essay, Columbia univ. 1908

Taylor, Marie Hansen
On two continents. London, Smith, Elder, 1905. p174

Teall, Gardner C.
Whistler and Swinburne. Bookm (NY) 18:69-70 S '03

Teasdale, Sara
On the death of Swinburne; poem. Cur Lit 46:687 Je '09

Tennyson: and after? Fortn 53:625-9, 637 My '90

Thomas, Edward
Algernon Charles Swinburne: a critical study. London, Secker, 1912. 238p
(Rev in No Am 197:281-3 F '13; Ath 2: 684 D 7 '12; Spec 110:131 Ja 25 '13; T. P.'s Weekly 21:647 My 23 '13)

Swinburne. *In* Literary pilgrim in England. New York, Dodd, 1917. p263-9

Thomas Dekker. Notes & Q 7th ser 3: 324-5 Ap 23 '87

Thompson, Alexander Hamilton
Algernon Charles Swinburne. *In* CHEL vol XIII p143-53

Thompson, Silvanus P.
Swinburne's use of bouts-rimés. Sat R 107:529 Ap 24 '09

Thomson, James
The Swinburne controversy. *In* Satires and profanities. London, Progressive publishing co. 1884. p[99]-104; *same.* National Reformer p403-4 D 23 '66

Three representative poets:—Mr. Tennyson, Mr. Swinburne, and Mr. Browning. Scottish Review 2:343-9 S '83

Tilghman, Tench Francis
The literary ballad in English poetry of the nineteenth century. Diss. Univ. of Virginia, 1933. [For abstract see Univ. of Virginia Abstracts of diss. 1932-1933 p20-1]

Tilley, Arthur
Two theories of poetry. Macmil 44:268-79 Ag '81

"Time with a gift of tears." Notes & Q 12th ser 10:219 Mr 18 '22

Tinsley, William
Random recollections of an old publisher. London, Simpkin, Marshall, Hamilton, Kent, 1900. vol I p232-4

To Mr. Swinburne; poem [signed "B.M.R."] Acad 57:578 N 18 '99

Todhunter, John
The genius and influence of Swinburne. Bookm (Lond) 36:129-30 Je '09

Tollemache, Lionel A.
Swinburne. Spec 118:488 Ap 28 '17

Swinburne and Gladstone. Spec 102:662-3 Ap 24 '09

Swinburne, the Laureateship, and Tennyson. Guardian 64:763 My 12 '09

Torossian, Aram
Stevenson as a literary critic. University of California Chronicle 27:43-60 Ja '25

Traill, H. D.
Recaptured rhymes: political and other fugitives arrested. London, Blackwoods, 1882

Traubel, Horace
With Walt Whitman in Camden. New York, Kennerley, 1914. 3 vols passim

Turner, W. J.
Algernon Charles Swinburne. *In* Massingham, H. J. and Massingham, H. eds. Great Victorians. London, Nicholson & Watson [1932] p489-502

Turquet-Milnes, Gladys
Swinburne. *In* The influence of Baudelaire in France and England. London, Constable, 1913. p222-9

Tyrwhitt, R. St. John
Ancilla domini: thoughts on Christian art. VI.—The immoral theory of art. Contemp 5:418-36 Ag '67

Underhill, George F.
The philosophical poetry of Mr. Swinburne. Book-Lore 6:121-5 O '87

Untermeyer, Louis
Modern British poetry. New York, Harcourt, Brace [c1930] 3d rev. ed. p94-8

Urban, Sylvanus [pseud]
The Laureate and Mr. Swinburne. Gent M 268:431 Ap '90

Mr. Swinburne as a poet. Gent M 297:312 S '04

Mr. Swinburne's dedicatory epistle. Gent M 297:311-12 S '04

Mr. Swinburne's poetic awards. Gent M 267:632 D '89

Mr. Swinburne's praise of Northumberland. Gent M 273:212-13 Ag '92

A **valediction** to St. Valentine; poem. Punch 108:95 F 23 '95 [Parody of "Dolores"]

Vettermann, E.
Balen-dichtungen und ihre quellen. (Zeitschrift für Romanische Philologie. Beih. 60) Halle a.S. 1918

The **Victorian** garden of song. Dial 19:238 N 1 '95

Viereck, George Sylvester
Freudian glimpses of Swinburne. Stratford Monthly 4:3-10 Ja '25

To Swinburne; poem. Cent 73:464 Ja '07; *same.* Nation (NY) 85:36 Jl 11 '07; *same in* Nineveh and other poems. N.Y. Moffat, Yard, 1907

Wakefield, Mildred
Varieties of metrical and stanzaic form in Swinburne's verse. Masters essay, Columbia univ. 1920

Walford, L. B.
London letter ["The Sisters"] Critic (NY) 20:317-18 Je 4 '92

Walker, Hugh
The literature of the Victorian era. Cambridge, England, Univ. press, 1931. p545-61

Walker, Hugh and Walker, (Mrs) Hugh
Outlines of Victorian literature. Cambridge, Univ. press, 1919. p88-91

[Walsh, William Shepard] Shepard, William [pseud]
Algernon Charles Swinburne. *In* Enchiridion of criticism. . . Philadelphia, Lippincott, 1885. p260-2

Swinburne and Oscar Wilde. *In* Pen pictures of modern authors. New York, Putnam, 1882. p202-15

"Wan Legends." Mr. Swinburne [Locrine] on the stage. Acad 56:362-3 Mr 25 '99

Watson, William
Some literary idolatries. *In* Excursions in criticism. . . London, Mathews and Lane, 1893. p[1]-22

Watts-Dunton, Clara Jane (Reich) (Mrs. Walter Theodore Watts-Dunton)
Christmas with Swinburne. 19th Cent 90:1007-17 D '21

The home life of Swinburne. . . London, Philpot, 1922. 288p
(Rev by H. S. Gorman in Out 132:158-9 S 27 '22; T L S Mr 23 '22 p189; Bookman's Journal 6:54 My '22)

My recollections of Swinburne. 19th Cent 90:219-29, 438-47 Ag, S '21

Waugh, Arthur
Reticence in literature. *In* Reticence in literature, and other papers. London, Wilson [1915] p17-20; *same.* Yellow Book 1:213 Ap '94
(Rev in T L S Ap 16 '15 p123)

Waugh, Arthur—*Continued*
The Swinburne letters and our debt to
the Victorian era. 19th Cent 84:1021-34
D '18; *same.* Liv Age 300:102-12 Ja 11
'19; *same in* Tradition and change.
London, Chapman and Hall, 1919. 2d
ed p180-203

Weatherhead, Leslie D.
Swinburne. *In* The after-world of the
poets. . . London, Epworth press
[1929] p153-70

Welby, Thomas Earle
The Victorian romantics, 1850-70; the
early work of D. G. Rossetti, W. Morris, Burne-Jones, Swinburne . . . and
their associates. London, Howe, 1929.
ix-x, 161p
(Rev in T L S N 14 '29 p919)

A study of Swinburne. . . New York,
Doran, 1926. viii, 17-289p
(Rev in T L S D 16 '26 p931; Sat R
142:649 N 27 '26; E. Muir in Nat-Ath
40:390 D 11 '26; S. C. Chew in Sat R
Lit 3:358 D 4 '26)

Swinburne. A critical study. London,
Elkin Mathews, 1914. 191p
(Rev in Spec 115:114-15 Jl 24 '15;
Ath 1:113 F 6 '15)

Wesley, Edmund Alfred
The poetical works of Algernon Charles
Swinburne critically considered. [24p]
Lit & Philos Soc 58: paged separately
'05

Weygandt, Cornelius
The last of the Victorian poets. . .
Bookn 27:839-43 Jl '09

Wheeler, Alfred A.
Swinburne on art and life. Californian
3:129-31 F '81

Wherein the clergy have failed. R of Rs
(Lond) 20:444 N '99

Whistler, James Abbott McNeill
"Ten o'clock." Portland, Me. Mosher,
1916. xii, 54p

White, Richard Grant
[Letter answering Swinburne] Galaxy 3:
114 Ja 1 '67

Whiting, Lilian
Louise Chandler Moulton, poet and
friend. Boston, Little, Brown, 1910.
p85-6, 114

Whitney, Elizabeth Boyce
The Oxford movement and its influence
on English poetry. Masters essay,
Univ. of Oklahoma, 1931

Who should be Laureate? [by various au-
thors] Idler 7:400-19 '95

Who will be Poet Laureate? Atlan 70:855-
6 D '92

Wier, Marion Clyde
The influence of Aeschylus and Euripides
on the structure and content of Swinburne's Atalanta in Calydon and Erechtheus. Ann Arbor, Michigan, Wahr,
1920. 46p Diss. Univ. of Michigan,
1918

Wilde, Oscar
The English Renaissance. Boston, Luce,
1906. p1-17

Willcox, (Mrs) Louise (Collier)
The fortifying principle in Swinburne.
No Am 190:93-100 Jl '09

Williams, Francis Howard
Mr. Swinburne as "a love poet." Dial
40:79 F 1 '06

Williamson, Claude C. H.
Algernon Charles Swinburne. *In* Writers
of three centuries, 1789-1914. Philadelphia, Jacobs [1915?] p284-303

Williamson, George Charles
Swinburne. *In* Behind my library door;
some chapters on authors, books and
miniatures. New York, Dutton, 1921.
p201-8

Wilson, W. E.
A phrase of Swinburne's: "The morn."
Notes & Q 11th ser 6:147 Ag 24 '12

A **wizard** of words. Ind 66:822-3 Ap 15
'09

Wollaeger, Hermann Wilhelm Franz
Studien über Swinburne's poetischen stil.
Heidelberg, Geisendörfer, 1899. vi, 106p
Diss. Heidelberg

Wood, Joanna E.
Algernon Charles Swinburne; an appre-
ciation. Canadian Magazine 17:3-10
My '01

Woodberry, George Edward
Late Victorian verse: Browning, Swinburne, Tennyson. *In* Studies of a littérateur. New York, Harcourt, Brace,
1921. p37-60

Literary essays. New York, Harcourt,
Brace and Howe, 1920. p289-338

Swinburne. (Contemporary men of letters ser) New York, McClure, Phillips,
1905. 3-117p
(Rev by F. Greenslet in Nation (NY)
82:58-9 Ja 18 '06)

Woods, Margaret L.
Poets of the 'eighties. *In* The eighteen-
eighties, essays by fellows of the Royal
society of literature, ed. by Walter de
la Mare. Cambridge, England, Univ.
press, 1930. p3-4

[Work of Swinburne]   Blackw 176:123-6 Jl '04

Wratislaw, Theodore
Algernon Charles Swinburne, a study. London, Greening, 1900. viii,212p
(Rev in Ath 1:330 Mr 16 '01; Literary World (Lond) ns 63:205-6 Mr 1 '01; Bookm (Lond) 19:200 Mr '01; Lit 8:119 F 16 '01; Acad 60:267-8 Mr 23 '01)

Wright, Herbert G. (ed)
Unpublished letters from Theodore Watts-Dunton to Swinburne. Rev E S 10:129-55 Ap '34

Wright, Thomas
The life of John Payne. London, Fisher Unwin [1919] passim

Wynne, D. Annette
Swinburne as critic of the drama and Jonson. Masters essay, New York Univ. 1916. 83ff

The **young** men [signed "A Fogey"] Contemp 65:178 F '94

Zangwill, I.
The genius and influence of Swinburne. Bookm (Lond) 36:128 Je '09

Alfred Lord Tennyson

Alfred Lord Tennyson

I. Chronological Outline

1809. Born, August 6, Somersby in Lincolnshire.

1827. Poems by Two Brothers, by Alfred and Charles Tennyson.

1829. Timbuctoo: A Poem Which Obtained the Chancellor's Medal at the Cambridge Commencement.

1830. Poems, Chiefly Lyrical.

1832. Poems.

1842. Morte D'Arthur, Dora, and Other Idyls.

1847. The Princess; A Medley.

1850. In Memoriam.

1850. Appointed Poet Laureate.

1852. Ode on the Death of the Duke of Wellington.

1855. Maud.

1859. Idylls of the King.

1864. Enoch Arden.

1869. The Holy Grail, and Other Poems.

1872. Gareth and Lynette.

1875. Queen Mary. A Drama.

1876. Harold. A Drama.

1879. The Lover's Tale.

1880. Ballads and Other Poems.

1884. The Cup and the Falcon.

1884. Becket.

1885. Tiresias and Other Poems.

1886. Locksley Hall Sixty Years After.

1889. Demeter and Other Poems.

1892. The Foresters.

1892. Died, October 6, Aldworth.

1892. The Death of Oenone, Akbar's Dream, and Other Poems.

Alfred Lord Tennyson

II. Bibliographical Material

Adkins, Nelson F.
Tennyson's "Charge of the heavy brigade": a bibliographical note. Notes & Q 167:189-90 S 15 '34; *see also:* ibid. 266 O 13 '34

Alfred, Lord Tennyson, August 5, 1809-1909. St. Louis. Public Library Monthly Bulletin ns 7: 100-1 Je '09

Americana and Tennyson. T L S My 10 '28 p364

Anderson Auction Co. New York
The choice collection of the works of Alfred, Lord Tennyson, formed by A. E. Jack. New York, Ja 28, 1907. 17p

Austin, Alfred
[Bibliography] Dict N B vol XIX p555

Beck, Georg
Bibliography. *In* Alfred Tennysons ethische anschauungen. . . Erlangen, Döres, 1930. p85-6 Diss. Erlangen

Benson, Arthur Christopher
Bibliography. *In* Alfred Tennyson. New York, Dutton, 1904. p ix-x

Biography and bibliography. Dial 13:235-6 O 16 '92

Blair, D.
Tennyson's early poems. Notes & Q 3d ser 12:98 Ag 3 '67

Bouchier, Jonathan
Tennysoniana. Notes & Q 5th ser 9:508 Je 29 '78

Bowden, Marjorie Moreland (Sansom)
Bibliography. *In* Tennyson in France. (Manchester Univ. pub. French ser. no. 5) Manchester, Univ. press, 1930. p155-62

Brooklyn Public Library
Tennyson, a list of works with references to periodicals in the Brooklyn public library. Brooklyn, New York, The library, 1909. 19p

Brown, G. A.
[Bibliography] *In* C H E L vol XIII p524-30

The **building** of the Idylls: a study in Tennyson. *In* Literary anecdotes of the nineteenth century.

. . ed. by W. Robertson Nicoll and Thomas J. Wise. London, Hodder & Stoughton, 1896. vol II p217-72

Carter, John and Pollard, Graham
Alfred, Lord Tennyson. *In* An enquiry into the nature of certain nineteenth century pamphlets. London, Constable, 1934. p293-343

Choisy, Louis Frédéric
Bibliography. *In* Alfred Tennyson, son spiritualisme, sa personalité morale. . . Genève, Kündig, 1912. p287-9

Clark, J. Scott
Bibliography of criticism on Tennyson. *In* A study of English and American poets. . . New York, Scribner, 1900. p764-6

Collins, John Churton (ed)
Bibliography of the poems of 1842. *In* The early poems of Alfred Lord Tennyson; ed. with a critical introduction, commentaries and notes, together with the various readings, a transcript of the poems temporarily and finally suppressed and a bibliography . . . London, Methuen, 1900. p315-17

DeTabley, J. B. L. Warren, 3d Baron
see Warren, J. L.

Dixon, James Main
Bibliography. *In* The spiritual meaning of "In Memoriam." Interpretation for the times. Introduction by James M. Campbell. New York, Abingdon press [1920] p167-70

Dixon, William Macneile
List of dates and bibliography. *In* A primer of Tennyson, with a critical essay. London, Methuen, 1896. p145-89

First editions of Tennyson. Bookworm 6:26 '93

Fischer, Thomas A.
Quellen [also lists of German translations and the chronology of the English editions] *In* Leben und werke Alfred Lord Tennysons. Gotha, Perthes, 1899. p281-6

Gordon, William Clark
Bibliography. *In* . . . The social ideals of Alfred Tennyson as

Gordon, William Clark—*Continued*
related to his time. . . Chicago, Univ. of Chicago press, 1906. p251-2

Griggs, Edward Howard
Book list. *In* The poetry and philosophy of Tennyson; a handbook of six lectures. . . New York, Huebsch [c1906] p40-4

Grolier club, New York
A chronological list of the works of Alfred, Lord Tennyson with some few items of Tennysoniana and a series of portraits of the poet laureate. . . New York, The Grolier club, 1897. 24p

Haney, John Louis
Tennyson bibliography. Notes & Q 10th ser 11:322 Ap 24 '09

Tennysoniana. Ath 2:153-4 Ag 7 '09

Holmes, Mabel Dodge
Books referred to in the preparation of the foregoing discussion. *In* . . . The poet as philosopher; a study of three philosophical poems: Nosce teipsum; The Essay on man; In Memoriam. . . Philadelphia, 1921. p187-90
Thesis (Ph.D) Univ. of Pennsylvania

Jack, Albert E.
Tennyson bibliographies. Dial 26: 329 My 16 '99

[Livingston, Luther Samuel]
Bibliography of the first editions in book form of the works of Alfred, Lord Tennyson. . . New York, Dodd, Mead, 1901. ix,95p (Noted in Nation (NY) 74:52 Ja 16 '02)

The first books of some English authors. The Tennysons. Bookm (NY) 10:123-7 O '99

Luce, Morton
Chronological table. *In* A handbook to the works of Alfred, Lord Tennyson. London, Bell, 1895. p439-44

Mr. Tennyson's chief works. Lit W 13:281 Ag 26 '82

Möllman, Adelheid
Literaturnachweis. *In* Alfred Tennysons künstlerische arbeit an seinen gedichten. Münster, Helios, 1930. p79-81

North, Ernest Dressel
A Tennyson bibliography. Critic (NY) 21:211-12 O 15 '92

Northup, Clark Sutherland
A register of bibliographies of the English language and literature. New Haven, Yale univ. press, 1925. p373-5

Page, Curtis Hidden
Tennyson. List of references. *In* British poetry of the nineteenth century, ed. by C. H. Page. New ed. by Stith Thompson. New York, Sanborn, 1930. p442-4

Parsons, Eugene
Bibliography of first editions. *In* The poetical works of Alfred, Lord Tennyson, Poet Laureate. New York, Crowell [c1900] p xvii-xviii

"Poems, chiefly lyrical." Bookworm 7:48 '93

Pollard, Graham
Tennyson's "A Welcome," 1863. T L S F 15, Mr 15 '34 p112, 200

Postma, J.
Bibliography. *In* Tennyson as seen by his parodists. . . New York, Stechert, 1926. p198-9

Pratt Institute, Brooklyn. School of Library Service
Alfred Tennyson: [bibliography] *In* Pratt Institute, Library school lectures on general literature, no. 82. [Brooklyn, 1893-94] p643-9

Quinn, John
The library of John Quinn. . . New York, Anderson galleries, 1924. part V p1009-11

Ratchford, Fannie E.
The Tennyson collection in the Wrenn Library. Texas Review 7:95-105 '22

Rolfe, William James (ed)
Bibliography of Tennyson's works. *In* The poetic and dramatic works of Alfred Lord Tennyson. (Cambridge ed) Boston, Houghton, Mifflin [c1898] p875-6

Tennyson and his works. *In* The young people's Tennyson. Boston, Houghton, Mifflin [c1886] p87-118

Tennyson's revisions of his poems. Nation (NY) 88:460-1 My 6 '09

Schmitt, Karl
Alfred Tennyson in Deutschland. Deutsches Museum 3:905-8 D 15 '53

[Shepherd, Richard Herne]
The bibliography of Tennyson. A bibliographical list of the published and privately-printed writings of Alfred (Lord) Tennyson, poet Laureate, from 1827 to 1894 inclusive, with his contributions to annuals, magazines, newspapers, and other periodical publications, and a scheme for a final and definitive edition of the poet's works. London, Printed for subscribers only, 1896. vii,88p (Rev in Literary World (Lond) ns 53:170 F 21 '96)

The genesis of "In Memoriam." Walford's Antiquarian Magazine 11:407-12 Je '87

The lover's tale. A supplementary chapter to Tennysoniana. [London, 1870] 8p
(50 copies only)

Tennysoniana. London, Pickering, 1879. 2d ed. rev. and enlarged viii,208p
(Noted by A. L. Mayhew in Notes & Q 6th ser 8:337 O 27 '83)

Tennysoniana. Notes bibliographical and critical on Early poems of Alfred & C. Tennyson. . . London, Pickering, 1866. xii,170p
[Correct pagination is x,140p Errors made in the numbering of pages]

Slater, J. H.
Early editions. . . London, Kegan Paul, Trench, Trübner, 1894
(Rev by T. J. Wise in Bookm (Lond) 6:49-50 My '94)

Smith, Jean Pauline
Bibliography. *In* The aesthetic nature of Tennyson. New York, White, 1920. p61-2

Sotheran, H. & co. firm, booksellers, London
Illustrated catalogue of rare Tennyson items. . . London, Sotheran [1902] 29p

Tennyson, Hallam
Chronology of the books of poems. *In* Alfred Lord Tennyson: a memoir. . . London, Macmillan, 1897. vol I p xviii-xxii

Tennyson manuscripts. T L S Jl 17 '30 p596

Tennyson reference list. Providence Public Library Monthly Bulletin 3:280-3 O '97

Tennysonian and Thackerayan rarities. Walford's Antiquarian Magazine 12:79-83 Ag '87

Tennysoniana. Acad 45:57-8, 81 Ja 20, 27 '94; Leisure Hour 16:653-5 O 1 '67; Ath 2:517 O 15 '92; Notes & Q 3d ser 12:283 O 12 '67

Tennysoniana: Cleopatra. Notes & Q 10th ser 9:121-2 F 15 '08

[Tennyson's "Princess"] Acad 59:46 Jl 21 '00

Thomson, Joseph Charles
Bibliography of the writings of Alfred, Lord Tennyson. Wimbledon, Thomson, 1905. viii,10-72p

"Timbuctoo" [Notes on sales] T L S D 1 '27 p916

Traductions de Tennyson. L'Intermédiaire des Chercheurs et Curieux 39:507, 662, 978, 40:163 Ap 10, My 7, Je 30, Jl 30 '99

Troxell, Gilbert M.
Tennyson emergent; sale of autograph manuscripts. Sat R Lit 7:60 Ag 16 '30

Van Dyke, Henry
A chronology of Tennyson's life and works. *In* The poetry of Tennyson. New York, Scribner, 1907. 10th ed. rev and enlarged with a new preface. p351-87

A chronology of Tennyson's life and works. *In* Studies in Tennyson. New York, Scribner, 1920. p239-73

Wace, Walter E.
The bibliography of Tennyson. *In* Alfred Tennyson, his life and works. Edinburgh, Macniven and Wallace, 1881. p176-203

Walters, John Cumings
A note on Tennysonian volumes and manuscripts. *In* Tennyson: poet, philosopher, idealist. Studies of the life, work and teaching of the poet Laureate. London, Paul, Trench, Trübner, 1893. p341-8

Warren, J. Leicester
The bibliography of Tennyson. Fortn 2:385-403 O '65; *same.* Ecl M 66:159-70 F '66; *same.* Liv Age 87:289-99 N 18 '65

Wells, John Edwin
Variations in the "Idylls of the King." Nation (NY) 88:557 Je 3 '09

Wise, Thomas James
A bibliography of the writings of Alfred, Lord Tennyson. . . London, Printed for private circulation [by R. Clay] 1908. 2 vols [vii]-xv,363p; [v]-vi,209p
(100 copies only)
(Rev in Ath 1:557 My 8 '09)

Tennyson bibliography. Ath 1:417-18, 479-80, 543-4, 681-2 Mr 27, Ap 10, 24, My 22 '97; 2:388-9, 419-20 S 18, 25 '97

Tennyson's "A welcome," 1863. T L S Mr 8 '34 p168

Woods, George Benjamin
[Bibliography] *In* Poetry of the Victorian period. New York, Scott, Foresman [c1930] p952-8

Alfred Lord Tennyson

III. Biographical and Critical Material

Abbott, C. Colleer
A short view of the case against Tennyson. Humberside 1:5-26 O '23

Abercrombie, Lascelles
Tennyson. *In* Revaluations: studies in biography. London, Oxford univ. press, 1931. p60-76

[**Absence** of the Prince of Wales from Tennyson's funeral] Critic (NY) 21:288 N 26 '92

Adam, Graeme Mercer
Alfred (Lord) Tennyson. The spirit of modern poetry. *In* Lord, John. Beacon lights of history. New York, Clarke [c1896] vol XIII p437-77

Adams, Francis
Tennyson. New Review 10:311-23 Mr '94

Tennyson. *In* Essays in modernity. London, Lane, 1899. p3-39

Adapting Tennyson to the stage ["Elaine"] Critic (NY) 10:192-3 Ap 16 '87

Addis, John
"In Memoriam." Notes & Q 4th ser 11: 388 My 10 '73

After reading Maud; poem. *In* Ionica [unsigned volume of poems] London, 1855

An **afternoon** with Tennyson. Temple 126: 216-21 Ag '02

Agresti, A.
Alfred Tennyson. Rassegna Contemporanea 2:77-87 O '09

Ainger, Alfred
Alfred Lord Tennyson. *In* Dict N B vol XIX p546-55

The death of Tennyson. *In* Lectures and essays. London, Macmillan, 1905. vol II p114-26; *same.* Macmil 67:76-80 N '91

Tennyson for the young. London, Macmillan, 1891. xiii,120p

Albee, John
"Learn" for "teach" in Tennyson. Dial 22:177 Mr 16 '97; *see also* Dial 22:209 Ap 1 '97

Alden, Raymond MacDonald
Alfred Tennyson; how to know him. Indianapolis, Bobbs-Merrill [c1917] [vii],376p
(Rev in New Repub 13:24 N 3 '17)

Aldrich, Thomas Bailey
Tennyson; poem. Critic (NY) 21:289 N 26 '92; Atlan 65:412 Mr '90

Alfred Baron Tennyson. Gent M 273:535-7 N '92

Alfred, Lord Tennyson, 1809-1892. Bookn 25:846-54 Ag '07

Alfred, Lord Tennyson. *In* The Library of literary criticism of English and American authors. . . ed. by Charles Wells Moulton. . . Buffalo, New York, Moulton publishing company, 1904-05. vol VIII p64-111

Alfred Tennyson. Bookn 11:68-9 N '92; Every Sat 9:2 Ja 1 '70; Liv Age 62: 195-201 Jl 23 '59; Scrib M 8:100-7, 160-70 My, Je '74; Lit W 23:372-3 O 22 '92; Dial 13:231-3 O 16 '92; Leisure Hour 12:119-24, 136-40 F 21, 28 '63; Ecl M 13:289-95 Mr '48; L'Europe Littéraire Mr 6, 15 1833; Le Voleur D 20 1834; Vanity Fair 6:27 Jl 22 '71; National Observer 8:521-2 O 8 '92; Lit W 23:372-3 O 22 '92; National Magazine (Lond) 1:3-5 '57; New Monthly Magazine 120:47-68, 131-47, 241-51 Jl, Ag, S '81

Alfred Tennyson. *In* Men of the time: a dictionary of contemporaries. . . London, Routledge, 1879. 10th ed p952-3

Alfred Tennyson. The poetry of sorrow. *In* Essays from the London Times. (Appleton's popular library 2d series) New York, Appleton, 1852. p38-59

Alger, George W.
Tennyson as poet of the English people. Poet Lore 8:325-9 '96

Allen, G. C.
Tales from Tennyson. London, Constable, 1900. 112p
(Rev in Literary World (Lond) ns 62: 235 O 5 '00)

Allen, Grant
Tennyson's homes at Aldworth and Farringford. Engl Illus 10:145-56 '92

Allingham, H. and D. Radford (eds)
William Allingham, a diary. London, Macmillan, 1907

Allison, William Talbot
Tennyson's treatment of the worth of life. Canadian Magazine 33:319-26 Ag '09

Althaus, Friedrich
Alfred Tennyson. Ein dichterleben. Nord und Süd 73:206-30 My '95

Ambler, B. G.
Alfred, Lord Tennyson, his homes and haunts. London, Jack, 1911. 96p
(Rev in Ath 2:295 S 9 '11)

Andrews, Samuel
Our great writers; or, popular chapters on some leading authors. London, Stock, 1884

Annis, Mary
Nature in Wordsworth and Tennyson. Masters essay, Univ. of Toronto, 1904

Another and a better Tennyson. Sat R 84:582-4 N 27 '97

Anti-Maud. By a poet of the people. London, Churton, 1855. 23p; [2d ed issued in 1856 by Booth. 30p]
[A reply to "Maud" by Tennyson]

App, August J.
Lancelot in the poetry of Tennyson. In Lancelot in English literature; his role and character. Diss. Catholic univ. 1929. p151-75

Apparatus for the study of Tennyson [an annotated list] Lit W 31:136 Jl 1 '00

Archer, William
Mr. Alfred Tennyson. In English dramatists of today. London, Sampson Low, 1882. p334-51

Argyll, Duke of
At the Laureate's funeral; poem. Nat R 20:581-6 Ja '93

Armstrong, Richard A.
Alfred Tennyson. . . In Faith and doubt in the century's poets. New York, Whittaker, 1898. p67-90

Armstrong, T. Percy
Tennyson portraits by Watts. Notes & Q 153:394 N 26 '27

Arnold, (Sir) Edwin
A day with Lord Tennyson. In Forum papers. Ed. by C. R. Gaston. New York, Duffield, 1925. 2d ser p192-211; same. Forum 12:536-48 D '91
Poem. Critic (NY) 21:210 O 15 '92

Arnold, William Harris
My Tennysons. Scrib M 71:589-601 My '22; same in Ventures in book collecting. London, Scribner, 1923. p227-58
Readings in Tennyson. Nation (NY) 88:534 My 27 '09

Aronstein, P.
Tennyson's welt- und lebensanschauung. Engl Stud 28:54-91 '00

Art and architecture in Tennyson's poetry. American Architect and Building News 38:87-90 N 5 '92

An Arthurian journey. Atlan 65:811-29 Je '90

Ashe, Leslie
Tennyson's rhythms. Spec 119:713 D 15 '17

Asher, David
Tennysons erhebung in den pairstand. Die Gegenwart 25:41 Ja 19 '84

Atkins, Gaius Glenn
The entangled soul—"Idylls of the King" and Faith and doubt—"In Memoriam." In Reinspecting Victorian religion. New York, Macmillan, 1928

Auld, William Muir
The mount of vision. . . New York, Macmillan, 1932. viii,3-197p
[A study based on Tennyson's "The Ancient Sage"]

Auslander, Joseph and Hill, Frank Ernest
Lord Tennyson. In The winged horse. Garden City, N. Y. Doubleday, Doran, 1930. p303-15

Austin, Alfred Lamia [pseud]
The autobiography of Alfred Austin, poet Laureate, 1835-1910. London, Macmillan, 1911. vol II p219-31
Lord Tennyson's new volume. [Demeter] Nat R 14:694-702 Ja '90
"The passing of Merlin"; poem. Critic (NY) 21:210-11 O 15 '92
Tennyson. In Poetry of the period. London, Bentley, 1870; same. Temple 28:35-48 D '69
Tennyson at eighty; poem. Spec 63:175 Ag 10 '89
Tennyson's literary sensitiveness. Nat R 20:454-60 D '92; same. Ecl M 120:230-4 F '93
A vindication of Tennyson. In The bridling of Pegasus. . . London, Macmillan, 1910. p197-217

Austin, D. M.
A study of the aesthetics of the Idylls of the king in the light of their sources and their development. Masters essay, Univ. of Southern California, 1921. 116ff

Authors and artists at Florence. Eliza Cook's Journal 11:205 Jl 22 '54

Axon, William Edward Armitage
An Italian translator of Tennyson. Notes & Q 9th ser 1:503-4 Je 25 '98
Tennysoniana. Notes & Q 7th ser 11:326 Ap 25 '91
Tennyson's "Confessions of a sensitive mind." Notes & Q 5th ser 11:49, 355 Ja 18, My 3 '79
Tennyson's "Lover's tale"—its original and analogues. Roy Soc Lit ser 2, 24:61-79 '03
Tennyson's "Northern Farmer." Notes & Q 5th ser 10:466 D 14 '78

Axson, Stockton
Syllabus of a course of six lectures on Browning and Tennyson. [Philadelphia, American society for the extension of university teaching, 1894] 11p

Axtell, Elizabeth
Tone-color in the poetry of Tennyson with an appendix on his stanzaic rhyme-schemes. Masters essay, Univ. of Southern California, 1927. 152ff

Aytoun, William Edmondstoune
The Laureate, by Alfred Tennyson [a parody] Tait's Edinburgh Magazine 10: 275 My '43; *same in* The book of ballads, ed. by Bon Gaultier. . . New York, Worthington, 1890. p129-31

Maud, by Alfred Tennyson. *In* Mordell, G. (ed) Notorious literary attacks. New York, Boni, 1926. p138-61

La mort d'Arthur. A fragment—not by Tennyson. Tait's Edinburgh Magazine 10:651-2 O '43; *same in* The book of ballads, ed. by Bon Gaultier. . . New York, Worthington, 1890. p191

[Aytoun, William Edmondstoune and Martin, Theodore] Bon Gaultier [pseud]
The biter bit. *In* The book of ballads, ed. by Bon Gaultier. . . New York, Worthington, 1890. p68-70

Caroline. *In* The book of ballads, ed. by Bon Gaultier. Edinburgh, Blackwood, 1870. 11th ed p239-41 [generally attributed to Martin]

The lay of the lovelorn. *In* The book of ballads, ed. by Bon Gaultier. Edinburgh, Blackwood, 1870. 11th ed p102-11

Azarias, Brother
see Mullany, Patrick Francis

Babson, Herman
Tennyson's touch with humanity. Kent Prize, Amherst college, 1893. 36ff Ms in Amherst college library

Bacon, George B.
Mr. Tennyson and the Idyls of King Arthur. New Englander 18:1-42 F '60

Bacon, Thomas R.
Locksley Hall sixty years after. New Princeton Review 3:265 Mr '87

Bagehot, Walter
Wordsworth, Tennyson, and Browning; or, pure, ornate, and grotesque art in English poetry. *In* Literary studies. London, Longmans, Green, 1879. vol II p338-90; *same.* National Review ns 1:27-67 N '64

Bailey, Albert Edward
Notes on the literary aspects of Tennyson's Princess. Worcester, Press of C. F. Laurence, 1897. 21p

Bailey, William Whitman
Flowers of Tennyson. Educa 24:96-101 O '03

Baker, Arthur Ernest
A concordance to "The Devil and the Lady. . ." Being a supplement to the concordance to the works of the late Lord Tennyson. . . London, Golden vista press, 1931. viii,247p
(Rev in T L S D 10 '31 p1001; P. E. More in Nation (NY) 100:220-1 F 25 '15; H. I'A. Fausset in Bookm (Lond) 81:227 Ja '32; noted in Notes & Q 158: 343 My 17 '30)

A concordance to the poetical and dramatic works of Alfred, Lord Tennyson. . . London, K. Paul, Trench, Trübner, 1914. xvi,1212p
(Rev in Ath 2:280 S 19 '14)

Tennyson dictionary; the characters and place names contained in the poetical and dramatic works of the poet, alphabetically arranged and described. . . London, Routledge [1916] vii,296p bibl p295-6
(Rev in Ath 2:318 Jl '16)

Baker, Myron Eugene
Tennyson and Browning: a study in the conflict of personality and art. Diss. Univ. of Wisconsin, 1898. 233ff

Ballad poetry. Edin R 197:317 Ap '03

"Ballads and other poems." Notes & Q 6th ser 3:158 F 19 '81

Barera, Eugenio
A critical essay on the works of Alfred, Lord Tennyson. Venice, Visentini, 1896. iv,108p

Baret, Adrien
Tennyson. *In* Morceaux choisis des classiques anglais. . . Paris, Garnier, 1886

Barry, E. Milner
Tennyson's Arthurian poem. Notes & Q 4th ser 11:183-4 Mr 1 '73

Barry, William
Tennyson—a fragment. Bookm (Lond) 37:13-19 O '09

Barthélemy, A.
Tennyson. Revue Hebdomadaire Mr '98

Bates, Charlotte Fiske
To the Laureate; poem. Lit W 16:272 Ag 8 '85

Bateson, Frederick W.
English poetry and the English language. Oxford, Clarendon press, 1934. p101-4, 124-6

Batson, Winifred Creamer
Classical influence upon the poetry of Tennyson. Masters essay, Univ. of South Dakota, 1922. 71ff

Bausenwein, Joseph
Die poetischen bearbeitungen der Balin und Balansage von Tennyson und Swinburne und ihr verhältnis zu Malory. Würzburg, 1914. 47p Diss. Heidelberg

Baxter, Wynne E.
Tennyson's "Enoch Arden": bigamy and desertion. Notes & Q 3d ser 6:258 S 24 '64

Bay, Jens Christian
A Tennyson-Browning association book. . . [np] 1929. 9ff Typed ms in New York Public Library

Bayne, Peter
Alfred Tennyson. *In* Lessons from my masters. Carlyle, Tennyson and Ruskin. New York, Harper, 1879. p203-364
(Rev in National Quarterly Review 40: 234-40 Ja '80; Spec 52:1044-6 Ag 16 '79)

Alfred Tennyson—his first volume. Literary World (Lond) ns 18:200-2 S 27 '78

The compass and scheme of In Memoriam. Literary World (Lond) ns 18:344-7 N 29 '78

M. Taine on Tennyson and Alfred De Musset. Literary World (Lond) ns 18:216-18 O 4 '78

The religious philosophy of In Memoriam. Literary World (Lond) ns 18:328-30 N 22 '78

Tennyson and his teachers. *In* Essays in biography. Boston, Gould and Lincoln, 1857. 1st ser vol I p50-145

Tennyson as a people's poet. Literary World (Lond) ns 18:280-2 N 1 '78

Tennyson—the Dream of fair women and Palace of art. Literary World (Lond) ns 18:264-7 O 25 '78

Tennyson—the two versions of Maud. Literary World (Lond) ns 18:248-51 O 18 '78

Tennyson—the two voices. Literary World (Lond) ns 18:296-8 N 8 '78

Tennyson's diction. The Idylls of the King. Literary World (Lond) ns 18:360-2 D 6 '78

Tennyson's Oenone, Lotos Eaters, Ulysses, Simeon Stylites, and In Memoriam. Literary World (Lond) ns 18:312-15 N 15 '78

Tennyson's poems on marriage. Literary World (Lond) ns 18:232-4 O 11 '78

Bayne, Thomas
Carlyle and Lord Tennyson. Notes & Q 7th ser 11:204 Mr 14 '91

Charles Lamb and Lord Tennyson. Notes & Q 8th ser 2:206 S 10 '92

Tennyson and Grindrod. Notes & Q 12th ser 3:253 Mr 31 '17

Tennyson's "J. S." Notes & Q 7th ser 7:55-6 Ja 19 '89

Tennyson's "The Ancient Sage." Notes & Q 9th ser 3:376 My 13 '99

Bayne, W.
Tennyson's rhymes. Spec 119:446 O 26 '17

Beach, Constance Louise
The use of Anglo-Saxon material by Scott, Bulwer-Lytton, Kingsley, and Tennyson in relation to the Anglo-Saxon revival in England. *In* Chicago, University of Chicago, Abstracts of theses. Humanistic ser. . . 1930-32 vol IX p443-5

Beale, Dorothea
Tennyson; poem. Spec 69:595 O 29 '92

Beattie. Blackw 128:34-6 Jl '80

Beatty, Arthur
Tennyson's "In Memoriam." Mod Lang N 9:257-60 My '94

Beaver, Dorothy M.
Mr. Tennyson. Sat R Lit 11:108 S 15 '34

Beck, Georg
Alfred Tennysons ethische anschauungen. . . Erlangen, K. Döres, 1930. 5-87p bibl p85-6 Diss. Erlangen

"Becket" at the Lyceum. Spec 70:253-4 F 25 '93; Sat R 75:146-7 F 11 '93

Bede, Cuthbert [pseud]
see Bradley, Edward

Beerbohm, Max
Rossetti and his circle. London, Heinemann, 1922. plate 9

Beers, Henry Augustin
Diffused romanticism in the literature of the nineteenth century. *In* A history of English romanticism in the nineteenth century. New York, Holt, 1901. p264-75

From Chaucer to Tennyson. . . (Chautauqua reading circle literature) New York, Flood and Vincent, 1898 p244-9

An outline sketch of English literature. New York, Chautauqua press, 1886. p284-9

Beljame, Al (ed)
. . . Enoch Arden. Texte anglais, publié avec une notice sur la vie et les oeuvres de Tennyson, une étude sur la versification du poème, des notes grammaticales et littéraires et des appendices, par Al. Beljame. Paris, Librairie Hachette, 1901. 5th ed 120p

Bell, A. F.
Tennyson and Browning. *In* Leaders of English literature. London, Bell, 1915. p182-94

Bellezza, Paolo
Iuando nacque e quando mori Alessandro Manzoni, con un appendice relativa ad A. Tennyson. *In* Anniversari Manzoniani. Firenze, 1895-97. 3 pts in 1 vol

La vita e le opere di Alfredo Tennyson. La Rassegna Nazionale 75:60-89, 246-70, 398-423, 636-49 Je 1-F 16 '94; *same published*: Firenze, Uffizio della Rassegna nazionale, 1894. 225p (Rev in Archiv 93:454-7 '94; Ath 2:486-9 O 13 '94)

Belrose, Louis, Jr.
To the poet Laureate. [Tennyson, a poem] Washington, Brentano [1887] 4p

Benn, Alfred William
The history of English rationalism in the nineteenth century. London, Longmans, Green, 1906. vol II p296-300

Bennett, W. C.
"Locksley Hall." An appeal from "Locksley Hall Sixty Years After" to "Locksley Hall." London, Hart, 1887. 3-14p [From "Liberal Home Ruler" Ja 15-29 '87]

B[ense] J. F.
Alfred Lord Tennyson. Vragen en Mededeelingen 1:226-9 My 20 '10

Bensly, Edward
Literary queries: Tennyson. . . Notes & Q 158:319 My 3 '30

"Memmian Naphtha-pits" in Tennyson. Notes & Q 11th ser 9:137 F 14 '14

Tennyson on tobacco. Notes & Q 12th ser 6:280 Je 5 '20

Benson, Arthur Christopher
Alfred Tennyson. New York, Dutton, 1904. x,243p bibl p ix-x
(Rev in Contemp 85:754-6 My '04; Literary World (Lond) ns 69:249 Mr 11 '04; Acad 66:191 F 20 '04)

At the sign of the hollyhock. *In* Rambles and reflections. New York, Putnam [c1926] p110-17

Benson, Edward Frederic
As we were; a Victorian peep-show. London, Longmans, Green, 1930. passim

Benson, M. Eloise
"In memoriam," "Adonais," and "Thyrsis" in relation to the thought of their time. Masters essay, Univ. of Iowa, 1929. 75ff

Benton, Ralph
Tennyson's philosophy as reflected in "In Memoriam" in the light of recent thought. Masters essay, Univ. of Southern California, 1914. 46ff

Biblical allusions in Tennyson. Chautauquan 45:375-6 F '07

Bidwell, Alice Townsend
Tennyson's adaptation of medieval romance to nineteenth century ideals. Masters essay, Columbia univ. 1911

Bihn, Sister Ross
Spiritual message of Tennyson's "Idylls of the King" to the youth of today. Masters essay, Univ. of Notre Dame, 1927. 40ff

Biographical sketch [of Lord Tennyson]. London, Chatto, 1884

Biography and bibliography. Dial 13:235-6 O 16 '92

Bird, W. H. B.
Tennyson in 1833. T L S S 21 '33 p631

Birrell, Augustine
Tennyson. *In* Collected essays and addresses, 1880-1920. New York, Dent, 1922. vol II p140-3

Bixby, James T.
Alfred Tennyson and the questionings of our age. Arena 2:57-71 Je '90

Black, William George
Tennysoniana. Notes & Q 6th ser 9:26 Ja 12 '84

Blackburn, Henry
Tennyson and M. Doré. Ath 1:64 Ja 11 '68

Blair, D.
Tennysoniana. (A plea that Tennyson indicate "final additions and alterations.") Notes & Q 4th ser 9:467 Je 8 '72

Tennyson's "Idylls of the King." Notes & Q 4th ser 5:537 Je 4 '70

Blake, Warren Barton
On Tennyson's centenary. Ind 67:398-402 Ag 19 '09

Tennyson's "Poet's song." Spec 108:436 Mr 16 '12

Blakeney, E. H.
The teaching of Tennyson. [London, 1893] 8p [*From* Churchman D '92]

Tennysoniana. Acad 42:461 N 19 '92

Blanloeil, A.
Les grands poètes anglais. Paris, Delhomme et Briguet, 1883

Bleibtreu, Karl
Die Victoria-poesie. *In* Geschichte der englischen literatur mit einschluss der amerikanischen. Bern, Bircher, 1923. p226-33

Tennyson. Zukunft 1:169-73 O 22 '92

Blémont, E.
Tennyson. La Renaissance Artistique et Littéraire My 11 '72

Blennerhassett, (Lady) [C de L]
Alfred Lord Tennyson. Deutsche Rundschau 98:257-90 F '99

Alfred Lord Tennyson. Literarhistor p189-236 '16

Bliss, Elvira Englund
Tennyson's versification. Masters essay, Univ. of South Dakota, 1932. 90ff

Block, Louis James
The dramatic sentiment and Tennyson's plays. Poet Lore 8:512-27 '96

Tennyson's songs. Poet Lore 7:127-33 '95

Blore, George Henry
Alfred Tennyson. *In* Victorian worthies. London, Milford, 1920. p150-76

Blos, Ernst
Die politischen auschauungen Tennysons. Erlangen, Döres, 1930. [5]-63p bibl p62 Diss. Erlangen

Blue, Eliza
Common folk in Tennyson. Masters essay, Tulane univ. 1926. 58ff

Blunden, Edmund
Nature in English literature. (Hogarth lectures no 9) London, Hogarth press, 1929. p101-4

Boas, Frederick Samuel
"Idylls of the King" in 1921. 19th Cent 90:819-30 N '21; *same*. Roy Soc Lit ns 2:23-42 '22

Boas, Guy
Tennyson and Browning contrasted. New York, Nelson, 1925

Boase, Frederic
Tennyson, Alfred Tennyson. *In* Modern English biography. Truro, Netherton & Worth, 1901. vol III p913

Bodley, Edith May
The pronouns of address in Tennyson's dramas. Masters essay, Stanford univ. 1915. 134ff

Boedeker, Augusta
Tennyson's "Idylls of the King." Educa 18:355-61, 403-13, 476-81 F, Mr, Ap '98

Boegner, André
La pensée religieuse de Tennyson dans "In Memoriam." Cahors, 1905. 108p Thesis, Montauban. Also published as English monograph 93

Boguslawsky, Amalie K.
Tennyson's women. Bookn 27:826-31 Jl '09

Bolton, Sarah (Knowles)
Alfred Tennyson. In Famous English authors of the nineteenth century. New York, Crowell [c1890] p256-310

Boodle, R. W.
The Idylls of the King: their growth and meaning. Rose-Belford's Canadian Monthly & National Review 6:379-98 Ap '81

Tennyson's Idylls. Rose-Belford's Canadian Monthly & National Review Ap '88

Bordes, Elsie M.
Tennyson's "Poet's song." Spec 108:230 F 10 '12

Boss, Eleanor
In quest of the Grail. . . London, Marshall [1930] 60p

Boswell, R. Bruce
Lord Tennyson and Mr. Churton Collins: "The Miller's Daughter." Notes & Q 8th ser 1:359 Ap 30 '92

Bouchier, Jonathan
Literary coincidence: Scott and Tennyson. Notes & Q 7th ser 5:170 Mr 3 '88

Literary parallel: Addison—Tennyson. Notes & Q 9th ser 6:45 Jl 21 '00

The metre of "In Memoriam." Notes & Q 4th ser 10:293 O 12 '72

Mistral and Tennyson. Notes & Q 9th ser 2:487 D 17 '98

Sir Walter Scott and Tennyson. Notes & Q 7th ser 2:128 Ag 14 '86

Tennyson and Oliver Cromwell. Notes & Q 5th ser 10:105 Ag 10 '78

Tennyson queries. Notes & Q 7th ser 6:513 D 29 '88

Tennyson's "Elaine." Notes & Q 3d ser 11:336 Ap 27 '67

Tennyson's "Palace of Art." Notes & Q 4th ser 1:364 Ap 18 '68

Bouchor, Maurice
Becket, un drame historique de Tennyson. Revue Hebdomadaire 10:275-87 Mr 11 '93

Bourdillon, Francis William
Sursum corda. London, Unwin, 1893 [Only 50 copies printed]

Tennyson; poem. Critic (NY) 21:256 N 5 '92

Bowden, Marjorie Moreland (Sansom)
Tennyson in France. . . (Manchester Univ. pub. French ser no 5) Manchester univ. press, 1930. viii,166p bibl p155-62
(Rev in Mod Lang R 26:126 Ja '31; Bookm (Lond) 80:31 Ap '31; A. Brule

in Revue A A 8:262-3 F '31; K. R. Gallas in English Studies 14:40-1 F '32)

Bowen, Robert Adger
Tennyson; poem. Bookm (NY) 5:46 Mr '97

Bowerman, Elma M.
Tennyson as a descriptive artist. Masters essay, Northwestern univ. 1903. 69ff

Bowker, R. R.
London as a literary center. Harper M 76:816-17 My '88

Boynton, Henry Walcott
Tennyson. Putnam's Magazine 6:598-603 Ag '09

Brachvogel, Udo
Poe, Longfellow und Tennyson. Nord und Süd 77:87-96 Ap '96

Bradby, Godfrey Fox
Tennyson's "In Memoriam." In The Brontës and other essays. London, Oxford univ. press, 1932. p90-112

Bradley, Andrew Cecil
A commentary on Tennyson's "In Memoriam." New York, Macmillan, 1901. xvi,223p
(Rev in Speaker ns 4:559-60 Ag 17 '01)

The reaction against Tennyson. In A miscellany. London, Macmillan, 1929. p1-31; same. English Association. Pamphlet no. 39. Oxford, Univ. press, 1917. 19p; same in Jones, P. M. (ed) English critical essays (twentieth century). New York, Oxford univ. press, 1933. p59-87

Bradley, E. T.
The burial of Tennyson. Critic (NY) 21:286-8 N 26 '92

[Bradley, Edward] Bede, Cuthbert [pseud]
Early poetry of Alfred Tennyson. Notes & Q 3d ser 9:206 Mr 10 '66

In immemoriam; poem. In A century of parody and imitation, ed. by Walter Jerrold and R. M. Leonard. London, Oxford univ. press, 1913. p273

"Locksley Hall" [Parody on] Notes & Q 4th ser 9:518 Je 22 '72

A passage in Tennyson's "Lotos-Eaters." Notes & Q 5th ser 12:307 O 18 '79

Stanzas by Alfred Tennyson. Notes & Q 7th ser 5:283 Ap 14 '88

Tennyson's "Ancle" and "Ankle." Notes & Q 6th ser 9:326 Ap 26 '84

Tennyson's "Death of the Old Year." Notes & Q 4th ser 9:92 F 3 '72

Brahm, Claudia Cecilia
The treatment of nature in the poetry of Alfred Tennyson. Masters essay, Univ. of Texas, 1907. 67ff

Brandl, Alois
Zur quellenkunde von Tennysons "Enoch Arden." Archiv 126:103-8 '11

Tennysons bruder. Allgemeine Zeitung. Beilage 4:289-90 '92-'93

Breachan
The bar of Michael Angelo. Notes & Q 2d ser 12:56 Jl 20 '61

Bremond, Henri
Le centenaire de Tennyson. Le Correspondant 236:248-69 Jl 25 '09

Brewer, E. Cobham
"Gareth and Lynette." Notes & Q 5th ser 9:41-2, 122-3, 201-2 Ja 19, F 16, Mr 16 '78

"Morte D'Arthur. . ." Notes & Q 5th ser 10:21-2 Jl 13 '78

Tennyson and Elaine. Notes & Q 5th ser 11:101-2 F 8 '79

Tennyson's Idylls. . . Notes & Q 5th ser 12:1-2, 142-4 Jl 5, Ag 23 '79

Bricard, Georges
Alfred Tennyson. La Quinzaine 22:259-77 My 16 '98

[Brief sketch] Lit W 23:376-7 O 22 '92

Brightwell, D. Barron
A concordance to the entire works of Alfred Tennyson. . . London, Moxon, 1869. xiv,477p

Concordance to the works of Alfred Tennyson, Poet Laureate. London, Strahan, 1870. 542p

Tennyson and Washington Irving. Notes & Q 5th ser 12:65 Jl 26 '79

Brimley, George
Alfred Tennyson's poems. *In* Cambridge essays. . . London, Parker, 1855. p226-81; *same in his own* Essays. New York, Rudd and Carleton, 1861. p[13]-128

Broadus, E. B.
A study of the Tennyson flora. Masters essay, George Peabody college, 1926

Broadus, Edmund Kemper
Alfred Tennyson. *In* The Laureateship . . . Oxford, Clarendon press, 1921. p184-96

Brodribb, C. W.
Tennyson and Froude. T L S O 15, D 17 '31 p802, 1028

[Brody, George M.] Walter Irving [pseud]
Tennyson. Edinburgh, Maclachlan and Stewart, 1873. 28p

Tennyson's "Queen Mary": a criticism. Edinburgh, Maclachlan and Stewart [1875] iv,44p

Brooke, Stopford Augustus
Browning and Tennyson. *In* The poetry of Robert Browning. London, Isbister, 1903. p1-56

Tennyson. Contemp 62:761-85 D '92

Tennyson, his art and relation to modern life. London, Isbister, ·1894. [v]-vi,[7]-490p
(Rev in Book B ns 11:300 Jl '94; Critic (NY) 24:369-70 Je 2 '94; Edin R 181:485-513 Ap '95; Spec 73:18-19 Jl 7 '94; Acad 46:24-5 Jl 14 '94; Sat R 77:450 Ap 28 '94; P. Bayne in Literary World (Lond) ns 49:436-7 My 11 '94;

Speaker 9:615-16 Je 2 '94; Nation (NY)58:471 Je 21 '94; Bookm (Lond) 6:86-7 Je '94; Lond Q R 82:381-3 Jl '94)

Brookfield, Frances Mary (Mrs. Charles Hallam Elton Brookfield)
Alfred Tennyson. *In* Cambridge apostles. New York, Scribner, 1906. p308-30

Brooks, Elbridge Streeter
Out doors with Tennyson. Boston, Lothrop, Lee and Shepard, 1900

Tennyson remembrance book: a memorial for the poet's reader friends. Boston, Lothrop, 1893. 118p [Selections from Austin Dobson, Henry Van Dyke, Carroll Burton and others]

Brooks, Mabel Frances
The poetic vocabulary and grammar of Tennyson's poems. Masters essay, Columbia univ. 1912

Brotherton, Mary
Lord Tennyson. *In* Chambers's cyclopaedia of English literature. Philadelphia, Lippincott, 1904. new ed vol III p540-3

Brown, Anna Robertson
Celtic element in Tennyson's "Lady of Shalott." Poet Lore 4:408-15 '92

Brown, Calvin S.
Tennyson's fondness for archaic words. Dial 22:209 Ap 1 '97

[Brown, James Bucham] Selkirk, J. B. [pseud]
Ethics and aesthetics of modern poetry. Cornhill 37:580-3 My '78

Brown, Stephen J.
Homeric simile after Homer. Thought 4:597-8 Mr '30

Browne, Irving
Elucidating Tennyson. Critic (NY) 20:25 Ja 9 '92

Browning, Elizabeth Barrett
Alfred Tennyson: notes and comments; with a defence of the rhyme system of "The Dead Pan." [2 letters to R. H. Horne] London, Privately printed for T. J. Wise, 1919. 19p (30 copies only)

An opinion on Tennyson. *In* Literary anecdotes of the nineteenth century. . . ed. by Nicoll, W. R. and Thomas J. Wise. London, Hodder and Stoughton, 1895. vol I p33-41

Browning, Oscar
Memories of 60 years. . . London, Lane [nd] p112-18

Browning and Tennyson. Leisure Hour 39:231-4 '90; Spec 63:879-80 D 21 '89

Bruce, Harold
Tennyson and death. Sewanee R 25:443-56 O '17

Bryan, J. Ingram
The philosophy of English literature. Tokyo, Maruzen [1930] p218-20

Bryant, Maggie May
Tennyson's patriotism. Masters essay, Columbia univ. 1926

Bryden, Robert
Tennyson. *In* Some woodcuts of men of letters of the nineteenth century. London, Dent, 1899

Buchan, T. Winter
Tennyson's "To-Morrow"—a coincidence. Acad 36:270-1 O 26 '89

Buchanan, Robert Williams
From Pope to Tennyson. *In* A look round literature. London, Ward, 1887. p347-58

"The Galahad of song"; poem. Critic (NY) 21:210 O 15 '92

Tennyson, Heine, and De Musset. *In* Master-spirits. London, King, 1873. p54-88

Tennyson's charm. St P 10:282-303 Mr '72

Buckley, Reginald R.
Survivors of popularity. II.—Tennyson. T.P.'s Weekly 22:527 O 24 '13

Buckley, W. E.
"Aylmer's Field." Notes & Q 7th ser 12:509-10 D 26 '91

"Dream of Fair Women." Notes & Q 6th ser 2:470 D 11 '80

Gwydion: Flur. Notes & Q 7th ser 10: 409-10 N 22 '90

"Palace of Art." Notes & Q 6th ser 2:492 D 18 '80

Parallel passages. Notes & Q 6th ser 7: 325-6 Ap 28 '83

Tennyson's "In Memoriam." Notes & Q 6th ser 1:499-500 Je 19 '80

Buckner, Mabel Claire Stovall
Tennyson's attitude towards women. Masters essay, Columbia univ. 1925

Bullen, A. H.
Tennyson and Shelley. Notes & Q 5th ser 4:464 D 11 '75

Bulwer-Lytton, (Sir) Edward
The new Timon, a poetical romance. London, Colburn, 1845 [Generally considered an attack on Tennyson]

The **burial** of Tennyson. Pall Mall Budget 40:1502-5 O 13 '92

Burke, Margaret Mary
Leadership and Tennyson. Journal of Applied Sociology 11:344-50 Mr '27

Burne-Jones, Georgiana
Memorials of Edward Burne-Jones. New York, Macmillan, 1904. 2 vols passim

Burritt, Phoebe
The philosophy of Tennyson in the Idylls of the King. Masters essay, George Washington univ. 1917. 34ff

Burroughs, John
Whitman's and Tennyson's relations to science. Dial 14:168-9 Mr 16 '93

Burton, Katherine
Hallam's review of Tennyson. Mod Lang N 45:224-5 Ap '30

Burton, Richard
Tennyson; poem. Critic (NY) 22:24 Ja 14 '93

Bush, Douglas
The personal note in Tennyson's classical poems. University of Toronto Quarterly 4:201-18 '34

Bussmann, Ernst
Tennysons dialektdichtungen nebst einer übersicht über den gebrauch des dialekts in der englischen literatur vor Tennyson. Weimar, Wagner, 1917. 67p Diss. Münster
(Rev by E. Eckhardt in Engl Stud 53: 445-7 F '20)

Butcher, S. H.
Presidential address, and "Tennyson," by the president. . . Brit Acad Proc 4:24-7 '09-'10

Butler, Arthur G.
A walk with Tennyson; poem. Spec 97: 263 Ag 25 '06; *same.* Ecl M 147:394 N '06; *same.* Liv Age 251:514 D 1 '06

Butler, H. Montagu
. . . A sermon preached in the Chapel of Trinity College . . . in reference to the death of Lord Tennyson. Cambridge, Macmillan and Bowes, 1892. 16p

Butler, May Jaqueline
Psychology of the dreams in the poetry of Tennyson. Masters essay, Stanford univ. 1914. 87ff

Byron and Tennyson. Quar R 131:354-92 '71; *same.* Ecl M 78:1-20 Ja '72

Caine, Hall
My story. London, Heinemann, 1908. passim

Callender, G.
Tennyson and Froude. T L S O 22, D 31 '31 p820, 1053; *see also* T L S Ja 21 '32 p44

Calverley, Charles Stuart
First love [parody of "Locksley Hall"] *In* Fly leaves. London, 1873. 3d ed p32-5

Wanderers; poem. *In* A century of parody and imitation, ed. by Walter Jerrold and R. M. Leonard. London, Oxford univ. press, 1913. p296-8

Camerini, E.
Alfred Tennyson. Nuova Antol F '70

Cameron, Julia Margaret
Alfred, Lord Tennyson and his friends. A series of 25 portraits and frontispiece in photogravure from the negatives of Mrs. Julia Margaret Cameron and H. H. H. Cameron. Reminiscences by Anne Thackeray Ritchie with introduction by H. H. Hay Cameron. London, Unwin, 1893. 16p 25 portraits
(Rev in Nation (NY) 57:356 N 9 '93; Sat R 76:473 O 21 '93)

Illustrations to Tennyson's Idylls of the King and other poems. London, King, 1875. vi,24p

Victorian photographs of famous men and fair women. London, Hogarth press, 1926. plate 4

Cameron, P.
Idyll of Guinevere.- Cath World 63:328-42 Je '96

Canebrake, Thomas
The philosophy of Locksley Hall. Southern Bivouac ns 2:704-8 Ap '87

Cann, Bertha
Tennyson's "Idylls of the King." An introductory essay for a school edition. Masters essay, Columbia univ. 1904

Canton, William
The life of Lord Tennyson. Good Words 38:785-92 '97

Tennyson. *In* Masson, David, and others. In the footsteps of the poets. London, Isbister, 1893. p333-81

Tennyson's early poems. Liv Age 227:187-92 O 20 '00; *same.* Ecl M 135:778-83 D '00

Capen, S. H. R.
The source of "Enoch Arden." Book-Lover (San Francisco) 2:458 N-D '01

Carlson, Alma S.
The influence of the English Bible on the diction of Alfred Tennyson. Diss. Northwestern univ. 1903. 76ff

Carlyle, Thomas
Alfred Tennyson. 1840. Lit W 16:187 My 30 '85

Tennyson. *In* Moore, J. R. ed. Representative essays. English and American. New York, Ginn, 1930. p108-9

Carpenter, William Boyd
Tennyson. *In* The religious spirit in the poets. New York, Crowell, 1901. p162-81
(Rev in Nation (NY) 72:518-19 Je 27 '01)

Tennyson—In Memoriam. *In* The religious spirit in the poets. New York, Crowell, 1901. p182-201

Carr, Joseph William Comyns
Some eminent Victorians. London, Duckworth, 1908. p112-13, 193-8
(Rev by P. F. Bicknell in Dial 46:134-5 Mr 1 '09)

Carr, Thomas
Tennyson twenty-five years after. Spec 119:384 O 13 '17

Carroll, Lewis [pseud]
see Dodgson, Charles Lutwidge

Carruth, William Herbert
Pronouns of address in "The Idylls of the King." Kansas University Quarterly. vol VI B p159-70

Carruthers, Adam
A Tennysonian interpretation. Canadian Magazine 39:526-9 O '12

Cary, Elisabeth Luther
Tennyson, his homes, his friends, and his work. New York, Putnam, 1898. viii,312p
(Rev in Critic (NY) 34:71-4 Ja '99; Lit W 29:434 D 10 '98)

Caswell, C. J.
A comitia of errors. Birmingham Weekly Mercury Ap 11 '91

Lord Tennyson's birthday. Notes & Q 7th ser 11:201-2 Mr 14 '91

Tennyson's schooldays. Pall Mall Gazette Je 19 '90

Catholic musings on Tennyson's "In Memoriam." Cath World 34:205-11 N '81

Cattle, Frederic
Some less-known Tennysoniana. Bookworm 2:263-4 '89

Cazamian, Madeleine
Le roman et les idées en Angleterre; l'influence de la science (1860-1890). (Publications de la faculté des lettres de l'université de Strasbourg. Fascicule 15) Strasbourg, Librairie Istra, 1923. p77-8

Cécilia, Jean la
Tennyson. Notes & Q 155:44 Jl 21 '28

Le **centenaire** de Tennyson. Le Temps Ag 11 '09

A **centenary** study of Alfred Tennyson. Acad 77:391-2 Ag 7 '09

Challsteth, A.
American edition of Tennyson's poems. Notes & Q 3d ser 9:48 Ja 13 '66

Chamberlain, N. H.
Tennyson's new battle piece. Lit W 13:97 Mr 25 '82

Chapman, Edward Mortimer
The great twin brethren: Tennyson and Browning. *In* A history of English literature. London, Murray, 1901. p349-93

Chapman, Elizabeth Rachel
A companion to "In Memoriam." London, Macmillan, 1888. 72p

Talks with Tennyson. Putnam's Magazine 7:546-52, 746-52 F, Mr '10

Charteris, (Sir) Evan [Edward]
[Tennyson] *In* The life and letters of Sir Edmund Gosse. London, Heinemann [1931] passim

Chase, Jane
The Idyls [sic] of the King. Masters essay, Northwestern univ. 1900. 15ff

Chaucer and Tennyson. National Observer 11:428 Mr 10 '94

Chauvet, Paul
Tennyson. *In* Sept essais de littérature anglaise. Paris, Figuière, 1931. p151-95
(Rev in New Statesm 2:412 O 3 '31)

Cheetham, Samuel
The Arthurian legends in Tennyson. Contemp 7:497-514 Ap '68

Cheney, John Vance
Tennyson. Chautauquan 11:173-8, 308-12 My, Je '90

Tennyson and his critics. *In* The golden guess; essays on poetry and the poets. Boston, Lee & Shephard, 1892. p161-201

Chesson, Nora Hopper
Tales from Tennyson. . . London, Tuck
[190-?] 96p

Chesterton, Gilbert Keith
Great Victorian poets. *In* The Victorian
age in literature. New York, Holt
[1913] p160-9
The literary portraits of G. F. Watts,
R. A. Bookm (Lond) 19:81 D '00
Tennyson. *In* The uses of diversity. . .
New York, Dodd, Mead, 1921. p25-33
Tennyson. *In* Varied types. New York,
Dodd, Mead, 1909. p249-57
The two great Victorian poets. I.
Tennyson. Bookm (NY) 16:349-51 D
'02

Chesterton, Gilbert Keith and Garnett,
Richard
Tennyson. (Bookman biographies) London, Hodder and Stoughton [1903]
[iii]-iv,40p

Chesterton, Gilbert Keith and Williams, J.
E. Hodder
Literary pictures of the year. I.
Shakespeare, Tennyson, Dickens.
Bookm (NY) 11:427-34 Jl '00

Chestnutt, J.
"In Memoriam." Notes & Q 8th ser 2:
430 N 26 '92

Chignell, T. W.
Tennyson: a lecture, delivered before
the Exeter Literary Society. Exeter,
Printed at the office of the "Devon
Weekly Times," 1881. 15p

Child, Margaret Sykes
A statistical investigation of the
"Artistic Temperament" and its appli-
cation to a group of nineteenth cen-
tury English artists. Masters essay,
Vassar college, 1923. 105p

Child, Mary
The weird of Sir Launcelot. No Am
188:903-9 D '08

Chimenti, Francesco
Alfredo Tennyson e la sua poesia. *In*
Larghi orizzonti. Bari, Petruzzelli,
1897. p75-93

Choisy, Louis Frédéric
Alfred Tennyson, son spiritualisme, sa
personalité morale. . . Genève, Kündig,
1912. iv-vii,289p bibl p287-9
(Rev in Ath 1:283-4 Mr 8 '13)

Christianity in Tennyson's poetry. Pall
Mall Budget 40:1659 N 10 '92

Christmas waits [a caricature] Punch 87:
303 D 27 '84

Chubb, Edwin Watts
Emerson on Carlyle and Tennyson. *In*
Stories of authors, British and American. New York, Macmillan, 1926.
p150-5
Tennyson. *In* Masters of English literature. Chicago, McClurg, 1914. p398-
420

Tennyson. *In* Stories of authors, British
and American. New York, Macmillan,
1926. p144-9

Church, Alfred John
The Laureate's country. . . London,
Seeley, 1891. viii,111p

[Churchill, William]
The marvellous year. Introduction by
E. Markham. . . New York, Huebsch,
1909. p65-8

Chynoweth, Edna
English life as seen in the works of
George Crabbe and Alfred Tennyson.
Masters essay, Univ. of Wisconsin,
1897. 132ff

Clark, Henry William
A reconsideration and appreciation.
Fortn 92:223-38 Ag '09

Clark, Thomas Arkle
Alfred Tennyson. *In* Biographies of
great English authors. . . Taylorville,
Ill. Parker, 1901-02. 2d ser

Clark, William
Tennyson's "Crossing the Bar." Canadian
Magazine 8:420-2 Mr '97

Clarke, George Herbert
Browning and Tennyson. Canadian
Magazine 39:120-32 Je '12

Clarke, Helen A.
How to study Tennyson's "In Memoriam." Poet Lore 5:574-82 N '93

Clarke, Henry V.
Alfred Tennyson. Munsey's Magazine
7:189-94 My '92

Clarke, Hyde
Tennyson's "Enoch Arden. . ." Notes
& Q 5th ser 5:255-6 Mr 25 '76

Clarke, Marcus
Gray's "Elegy." Notes & Q 5th ser 5:
29-30 Ja 8 '76

Cleopatra. Notes & Q 4th ser 10:499
D 21 '72

Clifford, John R. S.
"In Memoriam." Notes & Q 5th ser
8:514 D 29 '77
Parallelism in Tennyson's "In Memoriam." Notes & Q 5th ser 6:66 Jl
22 '76

Clough, Arthur Hugh
The poems and prose remains . . . ed.
by his wife. London, Macmillan, 1869.
vol I p264-9

Clough and Tennyson. Acad 66:205 F 20
'04

Clugston, Phil R.
Chapters on Tennyson's art, with special
reference to the epithet. Diss. Univ.
of Wisconsin, 1927. 309ff

Cobbe, Frances Power
Lord Tennyson. Spec 69:527 O 15 '92

Cochrane, Robert
Lord Tennyson. *In* Great thinkers and
workers. London, Chambers, 1888
p50-72

Cogswell, B. L.
Tennyson's "In Memoriam": a study. Masters essay, Boston univ. 1895

Cole, Samuel Valentine
The return; poem. Critic (NY) 21:223 O 22 '92

A salutation; poem. Critic (NY) 5:268 D 6 '84

Coleman, A. I. de P.
Mr. Lang's side glance at Tennyson. Critic (NY) 40:153 F '02

Collier, John
Lord Tennyson. *In* Massingham, H. J. and Massingham, H. eds. The great Victorians. London, Nicholson & Watson [1932] p503-16

Collier, William Francis
Alfred, Lord Tennyson. *In* A history of English literature in a series of biographical sketches. London, Nelson, 1900. p472-9

Collins, John Churton
Clough and Tennyson. Acad 66:133 Ja 30 '04

Illustrations of Tennyson. London, Chatto and Windus, 1891. [v-xi],186p (Rev in Spec 67:849-50 D 12 '91; R. Le Gallienne in Acad 41:55-7 Ja 16 '92)

Introduction. *In* The early poems of Alfred Lord Tennyson; ed. with critical introduction, commentaries and notes, together with the various readings, a transcript of the poems temporarily and finally suppressed and a bibliography. . . London, Methuen, 1900. p vii-xlii

A new study of Tennyson. Cornhill 41:36-50 Ja '79; 42:17-35 Jl '80; 44:87-106 Jl '81; *same*. Liv Age 146:483-92, 544-54 Ag 21, 28 '80

Tennyson. *In* The posthumous essays of John Churton Collins, ed. by L. C. Collins. London, Dent, 1912. p242-55

Collins, L. C.
Life and memoirs of John Churton Collins, written and compiled by his son... London, Lane, 1912. passim

Collins, Mortimer
Hair; poem. *In* A century of parody and imitation, ed. by Walter Jerrold and R. M. Leonard. London, Oxford univ. press, 1913. p287-8

Colvin, (Sir) Sidney
Box Hill and its memories, Keats, Meredith, Tennyson. Scrib M 60:195-209 Ag '16

The coming Laureate. Public Opinion (NY) 8:568 Mr 22 '90 [*from* Boston Advertiser]

Compton-Rickett, Arthur
Prophets of the century. London, Ward, Lock, 1898

Concerning cutting and carving. Fraser 67:213 F '63

Congreve and Wycherley. Notes & Q 4th ser 7:486 Je 3 '71

Conway, Moncure Daniel
Autobiography. . . Boston, Houghton, Mifflin, 1904. vol II p32-8

Laureate despair, a discourse given at South Place Chapel, December 11th, 1881. London [Privately printed, 1882(?)] 19p

Tennyson's pilgrimage. Open Court 6: 3455-9 N 17 '92

Cook, Albert S.
Literary factors in Tennyson's "St Agnes' eve." Poet Lore 3:10-17 Ja '91

The literary genealogy of Tennyson's Ulysses. Poet Lore 3:499-504 '91

Cook, E. Wake
Appreciations and depreciations of Tennyson. Acad 77:473-4 Ag 28 '09

Cook, (Sir) Edward
The second thoughts of poets. *In* Literary recreations. London, Macmillan, 1919. p259-70

Cooke, George Willis
Tennyson. *In* Poets and problems. Boston, Ticknor, 1886. p55-169

Cooledge, Charles Edwin
The sunny side of bereavement as illustrated in Tennyson's "In Memoriam." Boston, Badger [1913] xiii,56p

Cooper, Alfred B.
Tennyson. The formative influences of his first twenty years. Bookm (Lond) 37:20-8 O '09

Cornish, (Mrs) Blanche (Ritchie) Warre
Memories of Tennyson. Lond Merc 5: 144-55, 266-75 D '21, Ja '22

Personal memories of Tennyson. Liv Age 313:404-9, 472-8, 511-17 My 13, 20, 27 '22

Coupe, Charles
Tennysonian sea-echoes. American Catholic Quarterly Review 28:455-63 Jl '03

Courthope, William John
Byron and Tennyson. *In* Life in poetry; law in taste. . . London, Macmillan, 1901. p388-418

Craggs, John
Tennyson's "To the Queen." Notes & Q 5th ser 7:205 Mr 17 '77

Cranch, Christopher Pearse
On re-reading Tennyson's Princess. *In* The bird and the bell, with other poems. Boston, Osgood, 1875. p283-4 (Rev in International Review 3:113-15 F '76)

Crane, Walter
An artist's reminiscences. New York, Macmillan, 1907. p182-3

Crawford, A. W.
Tennyson's "Maud." A study of social conditions. Canadian Magazine 43: 29-36 My '14

Crespi, Angelo
Alfredo Tennyson. Nuova Antol 143:
569-89 O '09

Cressman, Edmund Dresser
The classical poems of Tennyson. Classical Journal 24:98-111 N '28

Cross, Ethan Allen
. . . Tennyson's dramas; a technical and critical study. . . [Chicago] 1906. 112f Diss. Univ. of Chicago

Cross, Tom Peete
Alfred Tennyson as a Celticist. Mod Philol 18:485-92 Ja '21

Crum, Ralph B.
Nature red in tooth and claw. Tennyson's problem. *In* Scientific thought in poetry. New York, Columbia univ. press, 1931. p157-90

Cruse, Amy
The idylls of the king. *In* Famous English books. New York, Crowell, nd p274-[284]

A crux in Tennyson. Spec 107:344, 379-80, 415-16 S 2, 9, 16 '11

Cunliffe, John W.
Early Victorian poets. *In* Leaders of the Victorian revolution. New York, Appleton-Century [c1934] p130-40

"The Cup" at the Lyceum. Sat R 51:48-9 Ja 8 '81

Currier, Mary M.
Affectation in Tennyson's poetry. Writer (Boston) 14:52-3 Ap '01

Curzon, George Nathaniel
Lord Tennyson. *In* Subjects of the day. . . London, Allen & Unwin [1915] p239-42

Cusins, W. G. ed.
Tennyson's songs set to music by various composers. London, Kegan Paul, 1879
(Rev in Spec 52:1652 D 27 '79; Nation (NY) 30:160-1 F 26 '80)

Cuthbertson, Evan J.
Tennyson, the story of his life. London, Chambers, 1898. 128p
(Rev in Literary World (Lond) ns 58:436 D 2 '98)

D'Albeville, J. W.
The origin of Tennyson's "Rizpah." Bookm (Lond) 3:78 D '92

Daniels, Earl
The younger generation reads Browning and Tennyson. Engl J 18:653-61 O '29

Darch, Alice Maddeford
A comparison of Tennyson's In Memoriam with Carlyle's Sartor Resartus. Masters essay, Univ. of Western Ontario, 1927. 59ff

Darmesteter, Mary James
Tennyson. R Pol et Lit 50:619-23 N 12 '92

Davidson, (Mrs) H. A.
The study of the Idylls of the King. Albany, N. Y. Williams, 1901. 51p

Davidson, Thomas
Prolegomena to "In Memoriam." Boston, Houghton, Mifflin, 1889. vi,177p

Davies, James
Tennyson's Ode on the Death of the Duke of Wellington. Notes & Q 4th ser 11:407 My 17 '73

Davies, Joseph J.
Tennyson's Lincolnshire farmers. Westm 136:132-7 '91; *same.* Liv Age 191:183-6 O 17 '91
Tennyson's turncoat. Westm 142:558-66 '94

Davies, Samuel D.
Shakespeare's "Miranda" and Tennyson's "Elaine." Poet Lore 5:15-25 Ja '93

Davies, Trevor H.
Tennyson: "In Memoriam." A poet's plea for faith. *In* Spiritual voices in modern literature. New York, Doran [c1919] p101-28

Davies, W. W.
Lord Tennyson's "The Foresters." Notes & Q 8th ser 1:432 My 28 '92

Davray, Henry D.
La biographie d'Alfred, Lord Tennyson. L'Ermitage D '00

Dawson, Edwin Collas
Morals of the round table; Malory's Morte d'Arthur compared with the Idylls of the king. Liv Age 267:606-10 D 3 '10

Dawson, George
Enoch Arden. *In* Shakespeare and other lectures, ed. by G. St. Clair. London, Kegan Paul, Trench, 1888. p481-5
The "Idylls of the King." *In* Shakespeare and other lectures. . . London, Kegan Paul, Trench, 1888. p471-80

Dawson, Samuel Edward
A study; with critical and explanatory notes, of Lord Tennyson's poem "The princess". . . Montreal, Dawson bros. 1882. vi,120p
(Rev by E. Myers in Macmil 47:492-8 Ap '83; Harper M 66:963-4 My '83; Lit W 15:332 O 4 '84)

Dawson, William James
Idylls and the Idylls of the King. *In* Makers of English poetry. New York, Revell, 1906. rev ed p229-39
Lord Tennyson: general characteristics; etc. *In* Makers of English poetry. New York, Revell, 1906. rev ed p178-228, 240-50
Tennyson. *In* Makers of modern English. New York, Whittaker, 1890. p169-269
Tennyson's In Memoriam. *In* Makers of English poetry. New York, Revell, 1906. rev ed p251-74

The **"De profundis"** of Alfred Tennyson. Remodelled by Metamorphosis. London, Allen [1882] 7p

Dearmer, Geoffrey
Tennyson; poem. Lit Digest 85:40 Ap 4 '25

The death of Tennyson. Spec 69:484-5 O 8 '92

Deatrick, W. Wilburforce
The religious significance of Tennyson's "In Memoriam." Reformed Quarterly Review 58:481-98 O '09

De Blowitz
Le poète-lauréat. Le Gaulois O 7 '92

Dees, R. R.
Tennyson's "Gareth and Lynette." Notes & Q 4th ser 11:207 Mr 8 '73

Déjob, Ch.
Les pauvres gens de Victor Hugo et Enoch Arden. Revue des Cours et des Conférences '00 p751

Delaney, Honora
Alice Meynell as a critic of English literature. Masters essay, Univ. of Pittsburgh; abstract *in* Univ. of Pittsburgh Bulletin 8:383-4 '32

Dessommes, Georges
Un poète heureux: Tennyson. Revue de P 1:777-805 F 15 '01

De Vere, Aubrey
see Vere, Aubrey de

Devey, Joseph
The art school:- Tennyson. *In* A comparative estimate of modern English poets. London, Moxon, 1873. p275-336

Dewey, Lenard Valess
Tennyson's doctrine of immortality; as illustrated in "In Memoriam" and lesser poems. Masters essay, Univ. of South Dakota, 1924. 64ff

Dhaleine, L.
. . . A study on Tennyson's "Idylls of the king." Bar-le-Duc, Jacquet, 1905. 112p Diss. Univ. of Paris

Dhruva, A. B.
Kant and Tennyson and Kant and Browning. . . Bombay, 1917. iv,50p

Dialect of Tennyson's "Northern Farmer." Reader 4:189, 233, 328, 383 Ag, S '64

Dickinson, Thomas H.
Contemporary drama of England. Boston, Little, Brown [c1917] p27-9

Didier, Eugene L.
An illustrious plagiarist. Literary Era ns 8:228-30 Ap '01; *same*. Book-Lover (San Francisco) 2:374-6 '01

Is Tennyson a plagiarist? Lit W 14:272-3 Ag 25 '83

Dieter, Ferdinand
Alfred Tennyson. Die Gegenwart 42: 309-12 N 12 '92

Dixon, James Main
The "Rubaiyat" and "In Memoriam": a comparison. Meth R 104:353-68 My '21

The spiritual meaning of "In Memoriam." An interpretation for the times. Introduction by James M. Campbell. New York, Abingdon Press [c1920] [5]-173p bibl p167-70

Tennyson and Treitschke: a spiritual forecast. Meth R 101:524-38 Jl '18

Dixon, William Macneile
Narrative poetry in the nineteenth century—Tennyson, Morris, Arnold. *In* English epic and heroic poetry. London, Dent, 1912. p309-29

A primer of Tennyson, with a critical essay. London, Methuen, 1896. [iv], 189p bibl p145-89
(Rev in Literary World (Lond) ns 53: 343 Ap 10 '96; Lond Q R 86:178-9 Ap '96)

Tennyson, Arnold, Browning. *In* English poetry from Blake to Browning. London, Methuen, 1894. p188-200

Dobson, Alban
Austin Dobson, some notes. . . London, Oxford univ. press, 1928

Dobson, Austin
Alfred, Lord Tennyson; poem. Ath 2: 483 O 8 '92; *same*. Critic (NY) 21: 224-5 O 22 '92

The metre of Tennyson's "In Memoriam." Notes & Q 4th ser 10:338 O 26 '72

[Dodgson, Charles Lutwidge] Lewis Carroll [pseud]
An index to "In Memoriam." London, Moxon, 1862. iv,40p

The three voices; poem. *In* A century of parody and imitation, ed. by Walter Jerrold and R. M. Leonard. London, Oxford univ. press, 1913. p314-21

A visit to Tennyson. Book-Lover (San Francisco) 2:476-7 N-D '01

Döllen, Dr.
Alfred Tennyson. Archiv 17:73-82 '55

Donegan, Sylvia Eugenie
The failure of the poetical drama in the Victorian period, with special attention to Browning, Bulwer-Lytton, and Tennyson. Diss. Boston univ. 1932

Dooley, Bertha Rosetta
Tennyson's Queen Mary and Aubrey De Vere's Mary Tudor: a study in Tennyson's sources. Masters essay, Univ. of Washington, 1929. 100ff

Doorn, Willem van
Tennyson and the encroachment of lyricism. *In* Theory and practice of English narrative verse since 1833. Amsterdam [1932?] p163-79

"Dora." Notes & Q 4th ser 10:8 Jl 6 '72

Dorchester, Daniel, Jr.
Alfred Tennyson, the man and the poet; a syllabus with questions topics and bibliographies. Boston, Skinner, Bartlett, nd 43p

Doré, Gustave
. . . Illustrations to Elaine. Tennyson. London, Moxon, 1867
Illustrations to Enid. London, Moxon, 1868
. . . Illustrations to Guinevere. Tennyson. . . London, Moxon, 1867
Illustrations to the Idyls of the king. London, 1867-68. Four parts
. . . Illustrations to Vivien. Tennyson. . . London, Moxon, 1867
(Rev in Ath 2:845 D 21 '67)

Dorsey, Anna Vernon
Tennyson's idyls: their sources and significance. Am M 7:737-43 Ap '88

Douady, Jules
Enoch Arden. *In* La mer et les poètes anglais. Paris, Hachette, 1912. p262-83

Douglass, W. W.
The didactic element in Tennyson. Masters essay, Univ. of Kansas, 1908. 25ff

Doveton, F. B.
Tennyson—or another. Acad 73:709 Jl 20 '07

Dowden, Edward
Mr. Tennyson and Mr. Browning. *In* Afternoon lectures on literature. Dublin, McGee, 1869. 5th ser p139-79; *same in* Studies in literature, 1798-1877. London, Kegan Paul, Trench, Trübner, 1906. p191-239

Tennyson as a teacher. Illustrated London News 101:490 O 15 '92

Victorian literature. Fortn 47:852-5 Je '87

Victorian literature. *In* Transcripts and studies. London, Kegan Paul, Trench, Trübner, 1896. 2d ed p201-5

Doyle, Kathrine H.
Poetic truth—Tennyson. Bachelor's essay, Univ. of Buffalo, 1928
The drama. "Becket" [performed] Critic (NY) 23:326 N 18 '93

Draycott, Charles
A medley of voices. Temple 117:418 Jl '99

"A dream of fair women." Notes & Q 8th ser 2:478 D 10 '92

Drew, Mary (Gladstone)
Tennyson and Laura Tennant. *In* Acton, Gladstone and others. London, Nisbet, 1924. p119-30

Drinkwater, John
Poetry of Tennyson. Toronto, Musson book shop
[Tennyson] *In* Victorian poetry. London, Hodder and Stoughton, 1923. p54-71, 140-68

Drury, Charles
Tennyson's "Lord of Burleigh." Notes & Q 9th ser 11:4-5 Ja 3 '03

[Duboc, C. E.] R. Waldmueller [pseud]
Alfred Tennyson. Illustrirte Deutsche Monatshefte 25:214-24 N '68

Alfred Tennyson. Unsere Zeit 1:522-43 '68

Duclaux, Mary
see Darmesteter, Mary James

Duncan, Bertha Chandler
Tennyson's old age; a study in biography. Masters essay, Columbia univ. 1924

Dunne, Marie Aloysia
The eschatology of the poets: a study in optimism. American Catholic Quarterly Review 34:622-6 O '09

Dupuy, Ernest
Alfred Tennyson poète-lauréat. Revue Hebdomadaire 1:128-44 Ja '15

Dutoit, M.
La vie de Tennyson. Revue des Jeunes Filles F '00

Dyboski, Roman
Tennysons sprache und stil. (Wiener beiträge zur englischen philologie. 1907. no 25). . . Wien, Braumüller, 1907. xxxvii,544p

Wortbildung und wortgebrauch bei Tennyson. Bausteine 1:165-223 '04

Dyneley, Mortimer
Locksley Hall and liberalism. Nat R 8:641-7 D '86

Eagle, Solomon [pseud]
see Squire, John Collings

Earls, M.
Wilfrid Ward and Tennyson; reply. Commonweal 21:124 N 23 '34; *see also* Sheed, M.

An **early** French estimate of Tennyson. Ath 2:554-5 O 22 '92

Early recollections. Bookm (Lond) 3:50-1 N '92

Early recollections of Tennyson. Temple 101:203-7 F '94; *same.* Liv Age 200: 618-21 Mr 10 '94

An **early** sonnet by the poet Laureate. Notes & Q 6th ser 9:205, 333 Mr 15, Ap 26 '84

Echoes of the Tennyson centenary. Dial 47:116 S 1 '09

Edgar, Pelham
English poetry since Tennyson. University Magazine 7:259-61 Ap '08

Egan, Maurice Francis
Imitators of Shakespeare. [Tennyson's "Becket" and S. De Vere's St. Thomas of Canterbury] *In* Ghost in Hamlet. Chicago, McClurg, 1906. p203-33

Of Tennyson. Cath World 56:149-57 N '92

"Saint Thomas of Canterbury" and "Becket." Cath World 42:382-95 D '85

Ehrsam, Theodore George
Tennyson's two sonnets on Poland. Nowy Swiat Niedzielny Dodatek Ilustrowany (NY) Ja 5 '36 p11

Elkin, Sallye Martha
Sources of Tennyson's attitude toward the English caste system. Masters essay, Univ. of Iowa, 1926-1927

Ellacombe, H. N.
Tennyson's "Flower in the crannied wall." Notes & Q 11th ser 3:167 Mr 4 '11

Ellias, Laura Lillian
Tennyson's musical sense. Masters essay, Stanford univ. 1916. 93ff

Elliott, J. J.
"Poems by two brothers." Literary World (Lond) ns 47:612-13 Je 30 '93

Ellis, A. S.
Tennyson family. Notes & Q 9th ser 1: 312-13 Ap 16 '98

Ellis, Harold Milton
Tennyson's use of Malory's Morte d'Arthur and the Mabinogion in the Idylls of the King. Masters essay, Univ. of Maine, 1908. 44ff

Ellison, Edith Nicholl
A child's recollections of Tennyson. New York, Dutton, 1906. 112p (Rev in Out 84:428 O 20 '06)

Elsdale, Henry
Studies in the Idylls. An essay on Mr. Tennyson's "Idylls of the King." London, King, 1878. [v-viii],197p

Studies on Tennyson's "Idylls of the King." London, Kegan, Paul, Trench, Trübner, 1877

Elton, Oliver
Alfred Tennyson and Matthew Arnold. London, Arnold, 1924. 96p

Poetic romancers after 1850. (Warton lecture on English poetry. Read Oct. 28, 1914) Brit Acad Proc 6:413-31 '13-'14; *same in* A sheaf of papers. Boston, Small, Maynard, 1923. p45-68

Tennyson. *In* A survey of English literature, 1830-1880. London, Arnold, 1920. vol I p330-63

Tennyson: an inaugural lecture. . . London, Nutt, 1902. 25p; *same in* Modern studies. London, Arnold, 1907. p183-207

"Elucidating" Tennyson. Critic (NY) 20: 357 Je 25 '92

Emerson, G. R.
[A singular coincidence] Ath 2:211-12 Ag 18 '66

Emerson, Oliver Farrar
Light upon the wind. [Tennyson's use of the word "wind"] Nation (NY) 101:15 Jl 1 '15

Thackeray and Tennyson. Nation (NY) 102:592-3 Je 1 '16

Eminent persons. Lord Tennyson, 1809-1892. Obituary notice, Friday, October 7, 1892. *In* Eminent persons. Biographies reprinted from The Times. London, Macmillan, 1896. vol V p272-90

Engel, H.
Taines urteil über Tennyson. Z F E U 20:8-12 '21

"Enoch Arden." Notes & Q 5th ser 5:166 F 26 '76

Enoch Arden, by C. H. P. Not by the "Laureate," but a timid hand that grasped the Poet's golden lyre, "and back recoil'd—e'en at the sound herself had made." np 1866. 12p [blank verse]

Escott, Thomas Hay Sweet
Cornish colour in Tennyson's poetry. New Century Review 3:52-8 Ja '98

Evans, Benjamin Ifor
Tennyson and the origins of the Golden Treasury. T L S D 8 '32 p941

Evans, Howard
Tennyson's "Holy Grail." Congregationalist 13:463-71 Je '84

Evans, Jessie Ruth
The religious philosophy of Alfred Lord Tennyson. Masters essay, George Washington univ. 1925. 51ff

Evans, Lillian Elizabeth
Tennyson and contemporary poets. Masters essay, Columbia univ. 1913

Evans, Morris Owen
The healing of the nations. Boston, Badger [c1922]

Everett, Charles Carroll
Tennyson and Browning as spiritual forces. *In* Essays theological and literary. Boston, Houghton, Mifflin, 1901. p304-27; *same*. New World 2:240-56 Je '93

Ewing, Thomas J.
Tennyson's "Voyage of Maeldune." Notes & Q 7th ser 9:475-6 Je 14 '90

Faguet, Émile
The centenary of Tennyson. Quar R 210:305-28 Ap '09

Fairchild, A. H. R.
"Break, break, break," and the "Dover Cliff" passage. Notes & Q 12th ser 7:426 N 27 '20

Fairchild, Hoxie Neale
The classic poets of English literature. XII. Alfred Lord Tennyson. Literary Digest International Book Review 3:488 Je '25

Faires, Rosabella Simonton
Philosophy of Tennyson's Idylls of the king. Masters essay, Univ. of North Carolina, 1909. 36ff

Fambri, Paulo
Maria Tudor sotto la penna dell' Hugo e del Tennyson. Nuova Antol 32:585-636 '82

Farrar, Frederick William
Lord Tennyson. *In* Men I have known. New York, Crowell [c1897] p1-41

Lord Tennyson as a religious teacher. R of Rs (NY) 6:570-2 D '92

Fashion in poetry. St P 1:702-3 Mr '68

Fausset, Hugh I'Anson
Alfred Tennyson in youth. Bookm (Lond) 79:168-9 D '30

Tennyson; a modern portrait. New York, Appleton, 1923. x,309p
(Rev by H. Warren in 19th Cent 94: 507-19 O '23; L. Binyon in Bookm (Lond) 64:23-4 Ap '23; G. R. Malloch in Algemeen Handelsblad Mr 24 '23; noted in T L S Mr 15 '23 p182; G. Thomas in Lond Q R 140:45-55 Jl '23)

Fehr, Bernhard
Alfred Tennyson. *In* Die englische literatur des 19. und 20. jahrhunderts. Berlin, Akademische verlagsgesellschaft [1925] p196-205

Felton, C. C.
Tennyson's poems. Christian Examiner 33:237-44 N '42

Fenn, Alice Maude
The borderlands of Surrey. Cent 24: 491 Ag '82

Ferrero, M.
Studio su "In Memoriam." Torino, Lattes, 1923. 6p

A few words about Tennyson. American Whig Review 12:176-81 Ag '50

Ficker, Georg
Bemerkungen zu sprache und wortschatz in Tennysons "Idylls of the King." Leipzig, Hinrichssche buchhandlung, 1904. 46p

Fields, Annie (Adams)
Tennyson. *In* Authors and friends. Boston, Houghton, Mifflin, 1896. p335-47)
(Rev in Nation (NY) 64:168-9 Mr 4 '97)

Tennyson. Harper M 86:309-12 Ja '93

To the memory of Tennyson. Dial 17: 57 Ag 1 '94

Figland, Lola
Change in Gawain's character. Masters essay, Vanderbilt univ. 1932-1933. For abstract see Bulletin of Vanderbilt univ. [Abstract of theses] 33:42 Ag '33

Filon, Augustin
Le centenaire de Tennyson a Oxford. J Débats S 29 '09 p1

Henry Irving; les drames de Tennyson. R Deux Mondes Ag 15 '95 p869-97

Lord Tennyson. J Débats Mr 11 '92; R Deux Mondes 71:70-101 S 1 '85

Finlayson, Thomas Campbell
Tennyson's "In Memoriam." *In* Essays, addresses, and lyrical translations. London, Macmillan, 1893. p1-35

Fischer, Heinrich
Englische poeten der gegenwart. I. Alfred Tennyson. Archiv 15:24-40 '54

Fischer, T. A.
Leben und werke Alfred Lord Tennysons. Gotha, Perthes, 1899. iv,290p
(Rev by R. Ackermann in Bei Anglia 10:353-4 Ap '00; Lit 4:171-2 F 18 '99; Deutsche Rundschau 101:195 '99)

Tennysonstudien und anderes. Mit dem bildnis Tennysons. Leipzig, Wigand, 1905. vii,224p

Fischer, W.
Zur "neunten woge." Bei Anglia 38: 158-9 My '27

Fisher, Charles
Tennyson, the man. Gent M 285:265-74 S '98

Tennyson's relations to science. New Century Review 7:456-65 Je '00

Fitch, George Hamlin
Tennyson leads the Victorian writers. *In* Modern English books of power. New York, Grosset, 1912. p96-105

Fitzgerald, Eileen M.
Science in the poetry of Tennyson, Hardy and Meredith. Masters essay, Mt. Holyoke college, 1929. 107ff

Fitzhopkins
Tennysoniana. Notes & Q 4th ser 1: 577 Je 20 '68

Fitzhugh, Harriet Lloyd and Fitzhugh, Percy R.
Alfred Tennyson. *In* Concise biographical dictionary. New York, Grosset and Dunlap [c1935] p678-9

Fletcher, Katherine Ogden
The use of sound in Tennyson. Masters essay, Columbia univ. 1912

Fletcher, Robert Huntington
The metrical forms used by Victorian poets. J Engl & Germ Philol 7:87-91 '07

Tennyson and Browning; a manual for college classes and other students. Cedar Rapids, Ia. Torch Press, 1913. 258p bibl p44-6

Flournay, Francis Roseboro
The sources of the Idylls of the king. Masters essay, Columbia univ. 1913

Foote, G. W.
Atheism and suicide. A reply to Lord Tennyson. [London, Freethought publishing co. 1881] 8p

For and against Tennyson. T L S Ap 12 '23 p237-8

Ford, C. Lawrence
"In Memoriam," LIV. Notes & Q 9th ser 1:110 F 5 '98

Tennysoniana. Notes & Q 9th ser 2:461-2 D 10 '98

Tennyson's "The Ancient Sage." Notes & Q 9th ser 3:376 My 13 '99

"The Foresters" [on the stage] National Observer 10:531 O 7 '93

"The Foresters." [parody] Critic (NY) 20: 232 Ap 16 '92

Forgues, E. D.
Alfred Tennyson. R Deux Mondes 5th ser 18:417-37 My 1 '47; *same*. Originaux et beau esprits de l'angleterre contemporaine. Paris, Charpentier, 1860. vol II p309-44

Forman, Harry Buxton
Alfred Tennyson. *In* Our living poets. An essay in criticism. London, Tinsley, 1871. p27-69
(Rev in Quar R 135:1-40 Jl '73)

Forman, Harry Buxton—*Continued*
Midnight: lines on the death of Alfred, Lord Tennyson. *In* Literary anecdotes of the nineteenth century. . . ed. by Nicoll, W. R. and Thomas J. Wise. London, Hodder and Stoughton, 1895. vol I p29-32

Formentin, C. H.
Tennyson chez Stéphane Mallarmé. Echo de Paris O 8 '92

Formont, M.
Maud. *In* Du roman en vers et de l'épopée domestique, étude littéraire. Bar-sur-Aube, Lebois, 1885. 23p

Forshaw, Charles F.
Lord Tennyson on tobacco. Notes & Q 8th ser 2:326, 450 O 22, D 3 '92

Forster, Joseph
[Tennyson] *In* Great teachers. . . London, Redway, 1898

Foucar, W. K.
Tennyson: his point of view. Masters essay, Univ. of Toronto, 1902

Fowler, William J.
Whittier and Tennyson. Arena 7:1-11 D '92

Fox, Arthur W.
Six studies in Tennyson's "Idylls of the King." London, Sunday School Association, 1909. 90p

Fox, William Johnson
Living poets and their services to the cause of political freedom and human progress. No. III. Alfred Tennyson. *In* Lectures addressed chiefly to the working classes. London, 1845. vol I p248-65

Frank, Maude Morrison
Alfred Tennyson. *In* Great authors in their youth. New York, Holt, 1915. p173-208

Franklin, H. C. T.
Tennyson as a sea poet. Temple 125: 185-91 F '02

Freed, L. C.
Contribution of the Idylls of the king to certain objectives of education for citizenship. Masters essay, Univ. of Southern California, 1926. 80ff

Freeland, H. W.
Tennyson's "In Memoriam." *In* Lectures and miscellanies. London, Longmans, 1857. p194-200

Frend, Grace Gilchrist
Great Victorians: some recollections of Tennyson, George Eliot and the Rossettis. Bookm (Lond) 77:9-11 O '29

Friswell, James Hain
Mr. Alfred Tennyson. *In* Modern men of letters honestly criticised. London, Hodder and Stoughton, 1870. p145-56
Tennyson and the "Plain Dealer." Notes & Q 4th ser 7:301 Ap 8 '71

Friswell, Laura Hain
see Myall, (Mrs) Laura Hain Friswell

Frodsham, George H.
A bishop's pleasaunce. London, Smith, Elder, 1915

Fruit, John Phelps
Browning and Tennyson. Mod Lang N 5:276-83 My '90

Fuchs, R.
[Tennyson] Leipziger Zeitung. Wissenschaftliche Beilage '88 p154, 163

[Fulford, W.]
Alfred Tennyson. Oxford and Cambridge Magazine 1:7-18, 73-81, 136-45 Ja, F, Mr '56

Fullerton, John
Alfred Tennyson: his life and writings. Broadway (Lond) 2d ser 3:507-14 Ja '70

The **funeral.** Spec 69:516-17 O 15 '92

Furnivall, F. J.
Mr. Hutton and Tennyson's "King Arthur." Notes & Q 4th ser 11:3-4 Ja 4 '73
Tennyson's Arthurian poem. Notes & Q 4th ser 10:348-9 N 2 '72

Füting, Adolf
Tennyson's jugenddrama "The devil and the lady." Marburg, Hamel, 1932. 85p Diss. Marburg

Fyson, George E.
Tennyson's "Poet's song." Spec 108: 271 F 17 '12

Gabrielli, Annibale
[Review of "Poemi drammatici di Alfredo Tennyson," translated by Emilio Girardini. Rome, 1919] Nuova Antol 285:85-91 My 1 '19

Gage, Minot G.
Tennyson: the man. Unitar 32:535-41 D '89

Galton, Arthur
"Lord Tennyson." *In* Urbana scripta. . . London, Stock, 1885. p36-58

Gannett, William Channing
The Idylls of the King: a Tennyson study. Poet Lore 13:588-90 '02
Tennyson's "In Memoriam": suggestions for study. Poet Lore 13:284-6 '02

Gannon, Nicholas J.
An essay on the characteristic errors of our most distinguished living poets. Dublin, 1853. 49p

Gardiner, Robert F.
"Locksley Hall": a prophecy. Notes & Q 7th ser 3:512 Je 25 '87

Garnett, Richard
. . . Alfred, Lord Tennyson; poem. Illustrated London News 101:474 O 15 '92

Gartzmann, Pauline
The historical background of Tennyson's drama "Becket." Masters essay, Stanford univ. 1916. 96ff

Gatch, Louise
Tristram, Launcelot, and the Holy Grail, as treated by Tennyson, Arnold, Morris, and Swinburne. Masters essay, Univ. of California, 1911. 130ff

Gatchell, Marie Ellen
The philosophy of Tennyson as developed in "In Memoriam" and "The Idylls of the King." Masters essay, George Washington univ. 1918. 60ff

Gates, Lewis Edwards
Nature in Tennyson's poetry. *In* Studies and appreciations. New York, Macmillan, 1900. p77-91

Romantic elements in Lord Tennyson's poetry. Harv Mo 15:45-60 N '92

Tennyson's relation to modern life. *In* Studies and appreciations. New York, Macmillan, 1900. p60-76; *also in* Critic (NY) 36:530-7 Je '00

Gatty, Alfred
The Idylls of the King: an allegory. Notes & Q 4th ser 11:30-1 Ja 11 '73

A key to Tennyson's "In Memoriam." London, Bogue, 1882. xi,144p (Rev in Lit W 13:71-2 Mr 11 '82)

A key to Tennyson's "In Memoriam": being a lecture delivered at Sheffield and Liverpool. . . Sheffield, Clark and Greenup, 1879. ii,45p

A line in "Locksley Hall." Notes & Q 8th ser 2:387 N 12 '92

"Locksley Hall Sixty Years After." Notes & Q 7th ser 3:347 Ap 30 '87

The poetical character: illustrated from the works of Alfred Tennyson. . . London, Bell and Daldy, 1860. 29p

Tennyson and Goethe. Spec 55:1111 Ag 26 '82

Tennyson's "In Memoriam." Notes & Q 5th ser 8:387 N 17 '77; Notes & Q 7th ser 12:97 Ag 1 '91

Tennyson's "Sleeping Beauty." Notes & Q 6th ser 1:320-1 Ap 17 '80

"What keeps a spirit wholly true?" Notes & Q 4th ser 10:381 N 9 '72

Gatty, Margaret
Passage in Tennyson's "In Memoriam." Notes & Q 2d ser 1:161 F 23 '56

Tennyson: Elaine: Camelot. Notes & Q 3d ser 11:464-5 Je 8 '67

Gaultier, Bon [pseud]
see Aytoun, William Edmondstoune and Martin, Theodore

The **genius** of Tennyson. Spec 69:522-4 O 15 '92; *same.* Liv Age 195:505-10 N 19 '92; *same.* Ecl M 119:808-17 D '92

Genung, John Franklin
The idylls and the ages, a valuation of Tennyson's Idylls of the King, elucidated in part by comparisons between Tennyson and Browning. New York, Crowell, 1907. vi,80p

Tennyson's In Memoriam; its purpose and its structure. Boston, Houghton, Mifflin, 1884. vi,199p (Rev in Critic (NY) 4:75 F 16 '84; Atlan 53:853-4 Je '84; E. D. A. Morshead in Acad 25:452 Je 28 '84; G. P. Lathrop in Atlan 53:853-4 Je '84; Lit W 15:42-3 F 9 '84)

Gerhart, Robert Leighton
Tennyson. Reformed Quarterly Review 27:538-76 O '80

Giddings, Joseph Addison
Some influences of Shakespeare upon the plays of Alfred Lord Tennyson. Masters essay, Cornell univ. 1928. 76ff

Gilbert, Levi
Tennyson and immortality. *In* Sidelights on immortality. Chicago, Revell, 1903

Gilbert, William S.
A respectful operatic perversion of Tennyson's "Princess," in three acts, entitled Princess Ida; or, Castle Adamant. . . London, Chappel, 1884. 48p

Gilchrist, Herbert Harlakenden, ed.
Anne Gilchrist, her life and writings. London, Unwin, 1887. passim

Gilder, Richard Watson
The silence of Tennyson; poem. Critic (NY) 21:204 O 15 '92; *same.* Current Opinion 11:475 D '92; *same in* The poems of Richard Watson Gilder. Boston, Houghton Mifflin, 1908. p206-7

Gilfillan, George
Alfred Tennyson. Tait's Edinburgh Magazine 14:229-34 Ap '47; *same.* Ecl M 11:161-8 Je '47; *same in* Modern literature and literary men. New York, Appleton, 1857. 3d ed p192-207

Gill, W. K.
The ornithology of Tennyson. Spec 85:238 Ag 25 '00

Gillet, Louis
Pour Tennyson. Nouvelles Littéraires O 24 '31 p6

Gillis, Lois Isabel
Art in the great Victorian poets. Masters essay, Univ. of Oklahoma, 1921. 265ff

Gingell, W. H.
"Birds in the highhall-garden." Notes & Q 12th ser 7:248 S 25 '20

Gingerich, Solomon Francis
Wordsworth, Tennyson, and Browning. A study in human freedom. Diss. Univ. of Michigan, 1909. 263ff

Wordsworth, Tennyson, and Browning; a study in human freedom. Ann Arbor, Michigan, Wahr, 1911. 8-263p (Rev in Acad 82:424 Ap 6 '12)

Giordano-Orsini, G. N.
La poesia di Alfred Tennyson; saggio critico (Biblioteca di cultura moderna. no 161) Bari, Laterza, 1928. 134p (Rev by M. Praz in English Studies 11:155 Ag '29)

Giordano-Orsini, G. N.—*Continued*
Tennyson e i suoi critici. La Cultura 5:543-50 '25-'26

Gladden, Washington
Essay on Tennyson. Boston, Old South Association

Gladstone, William Ewart
British poetry of the nineteenth century. Speaker 1:34 Ja 11 '90

Gladstone on the new "Locksley Hall." New York, Brentano, 1887. 39p (Rev in Critic (NY) 10:74 F 12 '87)

"Locksley Hall" and the jubilee. 19th Cent 21:1-18 Ja '87; *same.* Liv Age 172:311-20 Ja 29 '87; *same.* Ecl M 108:317-28 Mr '87

Tennyson. *In* Gleanings of past years. New York, Scribner [1879] vol II p131-79; *same.* Quar R 106:454-85 O 59; *also published in part as* Gladstone on Tennyson. [Boston, Directors of the Old South work, 1908] 20p

A **glimpse** of Tennyson. Notes & Q 155:7 Jl 7 '28

Godwin, Edward William
Pastoral play of fair Rosamund. Adapted and arranged in three acts, for the open-air . . . from Becket . . . [Albany, Brate, 1895] 68p

Gomont, Henri Augustin
Poètes anglais au XIXe siècle. Tennyson. Metz, Rousseau-Pallez, nd 19p; *same.* Revue de l'Est Ja F '65

Goodale, Ralph Hinsdale
Pessimism in English poetry and fiction, 1847-1900. *In* Abstracts of theses. . . Humanistic series Volume VI. . . Univ. of Chicago, Chicago, 1927. p347-51

Goodrich, N. L.
Matthew Arnold's and Tennyson's exhibition of the thought of their age. Kent prize essay, Amherst college, 1901. 53ff Typed ms in Amherst college library

Gordon, George Angier
Crossing the bar, a lyric of life everlasting. Boston, Pilgrim press [c1909] 32p

Gordon, William Clark
The social ideals of Alfred Tennyson as related to his time. . . Chicago, Univ. of Chicago press, 1906. vii,257p bibl p251-2 Diss. Univ. of Chicago (Rev in Acad 71:391-2 O 20 '06; Spec 97:686 N 3 '06)

Gosse, (Sir) Edmund William
A first sight of Tennyson. *In* Selected essays. London, Heinemann [c1928] 1st ser p111-18; *same in* Portraits and sketches. London, Heinemann, 1912. p127-34

Life of Tennyson. No Am 165:513-26 N '97

Tennyson. New Review 7:513-32 N '92; *same.* Liv Age 195:707-13 D 17 '92

Tennyson—and after. *In* Questions at issue. London, Heinemann, 1893. p175-98

Tennyson at eighty. Critic (NY) 15: 105-7 Ag 31 '89

Tennyson's last poem. Lit 2:23 Ja 8 '98

Tennyson's manuscripts. T L S Je 12 '19 p325

Gostwick, Joseph
Tennyson. *In* English poets. Twelve essays. New York, Stroefer & Kirchner [1875]

Gower, (Lord) Ronald Sutherland
My reminiscences. London, Kegan, Paul, Trench, 1883. p176-7

Graham, Peter Anderson
Art and scenery (Lord Tennyson). *In* Nature in books; some studies in biography. London, Methuen, 1891. p44-65

Lord Tennyson's childhood. Art J 53: 13-18, 46-50 '91

Grant, Charles
Tennyson. *In* The last hundred years of English literature. Jena, 1866. p147-62

Granville-Barker, Harley Granville
Some Victorians afield. The poet as dramatist. Theatre Arts Mo 13:361-72 My '29

Tennyson, Swinburne, Meredith and the theatre. *In* The eighteen-seventies. Essays by fellows of the Royal society of literature. . . Cambridge, Univ. press, 1929. p161-91

Three Victorians and the theatre. Fortn 131:655-72 My '29

Grappe, Georges
Alfred Tennyson. L'Opinion Ag 7 '09

Graves, Alfred Perceval
Tennyson in Ireland; a reminiscence. *In* Irish literary and musical studies. London, Mathews, 1913. p1-11; *also in* Cornhill 76:594-602 N '97

Tennyson's rhymes. Spec 119:491 N 3 '17

Gray, W. Forbes
Alfred, Lord Tennyson. *In* The poets Laureate of England. . . New York, Dutton, 1915. p252-73

[Grebanier, Mrs. Frances (Vinciguerra)] Frances Winwar [pseud]
Poor splendid wings. Boston, Little, Brown, 1933. p121-3

Greenblatt, Milton
A history and comparative study of the Tristram story in English literature (as treated by Malory, Arnold, Tennyson and Swinburne). Masters essay, Columbia univ. 1931

Greene, Maude Elaine
Tennyson's poems to and about his friends. Masters essay, Columbia univ. 1920

Greenfield, Lieurena Cole
Tennyson's attitude toward the sea contrasted with Byron's. Masters essay, Stanford univ. 1914. 134ff

Grendon, Felix
Fitzgerald on Tennyson: or, Tennyson before and after 1842. Sewanee R 14: 161-70 Ap '06
The influence of Keats upon the early poetry of Tennyson. Sewanee R 15: 285-96 Jl '07

Greswell, William
Tennyson and our imperial heritage. London, Gower, Dodson [1892] 23p

Grierson, Herbert J. C.
The Tennysons. In C H E L vol XIII p25-50

Griggs, Edward Howard
The poetry and philosophy of Tennyson. [Handbook of six lectures] New York, Huebsch, 1906. 44p bibl p40-4

Grindon, Leopold Hartley
The Tennyson flora. In Report of the Manchester field-naturalist's society. Manchester, 1888. p44-73

Griswold, Hattie Tyng
Alfred Tennyson. In Home life of great authors. Chicago, McClurg, 1887. p197-206
Alfred Tennyson. In Personal sketches of recent authors. Chicago, McClurg, 1898. p11-31
The silent singer; poem. Dial 13:231 O 16 '92

Die grossen todten. Deutsche Rundschau 73:308-9 '92

Groth, Ernst
Lord Tennysons neueste lyrik. Die Grenzboten 50 pt 1:417-24 Ja-Mr '91

Grove, George
On a song in "The Princess." Shilling Magazine F '66 p181-4
"Tears, idle tears": a commentary. Macmil 15:67-72 N '66

Grünert, Louis
Tennysons drama "Becket": eine quellenuntersuchung. Weimar, Wagner, 1913. x,121p bibl p[vi]-x Thesis, Leipzig

Guiliano, A.
Essai sur Locksley Hall sixty years after. Commentaire et Comparaison '07

Gunsaulus, Frank Wakeley
Alfred Tennyson. In The higher ministries of recent English poetry. New York, Revell [c1907] p107-77

Gurteen, Stephen Humphreys Villiers
The Arthurian epic. A comparative study of the Cambrian, Breton, and Anglo-Norman versions of the story and Tennyson's Idylls of the king. . . New York, Putnam, 1895. viii,437p

Gutbier, Elisabeth
Psychologisch-ästhetische studien zu Tristandichtungen der neueren englischen literatur. Erlangen, Dóres, 1932. 98p Diss. Erlangen

Gwynn, Stephen Lucius
Tennyson; a critical study. (Victorian era ser) London, Blackie, 1899. [vii]-viii, 234p
(Rev in Ath 1:561-2 My 6 '99; Spec 83: 467-8 O 7 '99; Lit 4:354-6 Ap 8 '99; Literary World (Lond) ns 59:489 My 26 '99; D. O'Brien in Truth (Lond) 46:834 O 5 '99; Bookm (Lond) 16: 57 My '99)

Hacker, John G.
Tennyson's Ode to Vergil, with music. Baltimore, Privately printed, 1930. 6p

Haight, Elizabeth Hazelton
Tennyson's use of Homeric material. Poet Lore 12:541-51 '00

Haines, C. R.
Tennyson's rhymes. Spec 119:411, 599 O 20, N 24 '17

Hale, Edward E. Jr.
Tennyson's place in poetry. Dial 14:101-2 F 16 '93

Hales, John W.
Alfred Tennyson. In Folia litteraria, essays and notes on English literature. New York, Macmillan, 1893. p332-6
South grammar school. Gent M ns 49: 562-73 D '92

Hall, Basil
Tennyson and Kingsley. Notes & Q 9th ser 11:57 Ja 17 '03

Hallam, Arthur Henry
Arthur Henry Hallam an advocate of Alfred and Charles Tennyson. In Literary anecdotes of the nineteenth century, ed. by Nicoll, W. R. and Wise, T. J. London, Hodder and Stoughton, 1895. vol I p21-7
Extract from a review of Tennyson's poems. In Remains in verse and prose. . . Boston, Ticknor and Fields, 1863. p[424]-41
The poems of Arthur Henry Hallam, together with his essay on the lyrical poems of Alfred Tennyson. Ed. with an introduction by Richard Le Gallienne. London, Mathews & Lane, 1893. xxxviii,139p

Hallam's remains. Notes & Q 7th ser 10: 244-5 S 27 '90

Halperin, Maurice
The last tournament. In Le roman de Tristan et Iseult dans la littérature anglo-américaine au XIXe et au XXe siècles. Paris, Jouve, 1931. p31-9 Diss. Paris

[Halsey, F. W.]
The Laureate's career. Critic (NY) 21: 204-12 O 15 '92

Halsey, John J.
Tennyson as a creator. Dial 14:135-6 Mr 1 '93

Hamann, Albert
An essay on Tennyson's Idylls of the king. (Wissenschaftliche beilage zum programm der Luisenschule) Berlin, Gaertner, 1887. 26p

Hamann, Helmut
Alfred Lord Tennyson und die zeitgenössische kritik (1830-1860). ms Diss. Jena, 1920. vi,120p Summary in Phil. Fak. Jena, Verzeichnis der Diss. 1920

Hamerton, Philip Gilbert
Word painting and colour painting. *In* A painter's camp in the highlands and thoughts about art. London, 1862. vol II p252-69

Hamilton, Walter
Alfred, Lord Tennyson. *In* Parodies of the works of English and American authors. . . London, Reeves and Turner, 1884. vol I p3-62, 142-86
(Rev in Literary World (Lond) ns 41: 267 Mr 21 '90)

Alfred Tennyson. *In* The poets Laureate of England. London, Stock, 1878. p[263]-300

Parodies of the works of English and American authors. . . London, Reeves & Turner, 1885. vol II p136-41, 260-80

Handly, John Marks
The Idylls of the Southland. Cath World 74:593-606 F '02

Hankin, St. John
Tennyson. *In* Lost masterpieces, and other verses. London, Constable, 1904. p16-17

Hardie, Martin
The Moxon Tennyson: 1857. Book-Lover's Magazine 7:45-51 '07-'08

Hardman, (Sir) William
A mid-Victorian Pepys; the letters and memories of Sir William Hardman. . . annotated and ed. by S. M. Ellis. London, Palmer [c1923] p311-12

[Hardy's New Year poem] Acad 72:3 Ja 5 '07

Harford-Battersby, D.
The ornithology of Tennyson. Spec 85: 238 Ag 25 '00

Harrison, Frederic
The burial of Tennyson. *In* Memories and thoughts. . . New York, Macmillan, 1906. p20-7

Literary and municipal problems in England. Forum 14:644-8 Ja '93

The millenary of King Alfred. *In* Memories and thoughts. New York, Macmillan, 1906. p47-54

Studies in Tennyson. *In* Among my books. . . New York, Macmillan, 1912. p284-96

Tennyson. *In* Tennyson, Ruskin, Mill and other literary estimates. New York, Macmillan, 1900. p1-47
(Rev by W. P. Trent in Cur Lit 29: 529 N '00; Sat R 89:108-9 Ja 27 '00;

Lit 5:605-6 D 23 '99; Lit W 31:44 F 3 '00; Nation (NY) 70:483-4 Je 21 '00; Ath 1:103 Ja 27 '00; Bookm (NY) 11: 88-9 Mr '00)

Tennyson; a new estimate. No Am 176: 856-67 Je '03

Tennyson centenary. 19th Cent 66:226-33 Ag '09; *same.* Liv Age 262:643-8 S 11 '09

Haskell, H. B.
Tennyson as a religious teacher. Masters essay, Univ. of Maine, 1906. 25ff

Hatton, Joseph
Becket at the Lyceum. Art J 55:105-9 Ap '93

Tennyson and Longfellow. *In* Old lamps and new. London, Hutchinson [1890?] p176-98

Haultain, Arnold
From Tennyson to Kipling. Canadian Magazine 30:533-6 Ap '08

Haweis, Hugh Reginald
Tennyson. *In* Poets in the pulpit. London, Low, 1890. p33-115

Hawkins, Frederick
"Becket." Theatre (Lond) ns 5:53-61 F 2 '85

Hayes, J. W.
Tennyson and scientific theology. London, Stock, 1909. 62p

Hayne, William H.
Tennyson's early and late lyrics; poem. Critic (NY) 21:332 D 10 '92

Haynes, Merrit Way
Tennyson's conception of the perfectibility of man. Hull prize essay, Univ. of Rochester, 1905. 15ff

Hayward, Abraham
Byron and Tennyson. *In* Sketches of eminent statesmen and writers. London, Murray, 1880. vol II p305-59

Healy, John
Catholic aspects of Mr. Tennyson's poetry. Irish Monthly 6:429-39 '78

Hearn, Lafcadio
Idylls of the King. *In* Occidental gleanings. New York, Dodd, Mead, 1925. vol I p1-23

Studies in Tennyson (a fragment). *In* Appreciations of poetry. . . New York, Dodd, Mead, 1916. p30-6

Tennyson and the great poetry. *In* A history of English literature, in a series of lectures. Tokyo, Hokuseido press, 1927. vol II p637-46

Hearnshaw, Fossey John Cobb
Tennyson twenty-five years after. Liv Age 295:503-6 N 24 '17; *same.* Spec 119:352-3, 522 O 6, N 10 '17

Hecht, Felix
The influence of Keats upon the early poetry of Tennyson. Masters essay, Columbia univ. 1902

Hedley, Irene
Browning and Tennyson considered as artists in poetry. Masters essay, Queen's univ. 1927. 30ff

Hegeman, Sister Elaine
"In Memoriam": the greatest of English elegies. Masters essay, Univ. of Notre Dame, 1929. 66ff

Hegner, Anna
Die evolutionsidee bei Tennyson und Browning. Wertheim, Bechstein, 1931. 31p Diss. Freiburg

Hendrickson, Amanda Ecurrent
Tennyson's reaction to the new scientific knowledge. Masters essay, Univ. of North Dakota, 1933. 34ff

Hengelhaupt, Margrit
Die personifikation bei George Meredith. Hannover, Küster, 1931. p3-7 Diss. Freiburg

Henley, William Ernest
Tennyson. In Views and reviews. Essays in appreciation. London, Nutt, 1908. vol I p183-8

Heraud, Edith
Lecture on Tennyson as delivered by her at Unity Church; Barnsbury Hall; and before the Society for the Fine Arts. London, Simpkin, Marshall [1878] 23p

Herford, Oliver
Godiva. In Overheard in a garden. . . New York, Scribner [c1900] p96-7

Heywood, J. C.
An over-rated poet. In How they strike me, these authors. Philadelphia, Lippincott, 1877. p126-47

Higgs, William
An open letter in re the article entitled "A poetical heartbreak." New Englander 53:276-83 S '90; see ibid. Ag '90 p126-42

Hill, N. W.
Tennyson and Terence. Notes & Q 10th ser 12:346-7 O 30 '09

Hillis, Newell Dwight
Tennyson's Idylls of the King. In Great books as life teachers. Chicago, Revell, 1899. p151-77

Hilton, A. C.
Tennyson. Notes & Q 4th ser 11:238 Mr 22 '73

Himes, John A.
The religious faith of Wordsworth and Tennyson as shown in their poems. Lutheran Church Quarterly 3:253-67 Ap '73

Hinchman, Walter Swain and Gummere, Francis B.
Alfred Tennyson. In Lives of great English writers from Chaucer to Browning. Boston, Houghton, Mifflin, 1908. p507-23

Hinckley, Henry B.
Tennyson and Crabbe. Nation (NY) 66:47-8 Ja 20 '98

Hixson, Jerome Canady
Tennyson, romanticist and Romany. Meadville, Pa. The author, 1924. 35p

Hoare, Barnard George
Mr. Hardy and Tennyson. Acad 72:75, 100 Ja 19, 26 '07
"Tennyson or another." Acad 73:757 Ag 3 '07

Hobson, William A.
The religion of Tennyson. Calcutta Review ns 5:189-99 Ap '17

Hodell, Charles W.
Tennyson, the thinker. Meth R 91:539-50 Jl '09
The three Christmases in "In Memoriam." Poet Lore 11:451-5 '99

Hodgkins, Louise Manning
Alfred Tennyson. In A guide to the study of the nineteenth century authors. Boston, Heath, 1895. p58-65

Hodgson, Geraldine E.
The legacy of Tennyson. In Criticism at a venture. London, Macdonald [1919] p1-25

Hodgson, S. H.
The supernatural in English poetry. In Outcast essays and verse. London, Longmans, Green, 1881. p99-205

Hogben, John
Tennyson's allusions to Christ. Sun M ns 13:761-4 '84

Holling, T. E.
Tennyson's clerical characters. Queen's Q 24:280-6 Ja-Mr '17

Hollowell, J. Hirst
Mr. Tennyson's "Despair." Congregationalist 11:824-31 O '82

Holmes, Mabel Dodge
. . . The poet as philosopher; a study of three philosophical poems: Nosce teipsum; the Essay on man; In Memoriam. . . Philadelphia, 1921. 190p bibl p187-90 Thesis (Ph.D.) Univ. of Pennsylvania

Home of Alfred Tennyson. Hours at Home 5:116-18 Je '67

Hood, Thomas (the younger)
In memoriam technicam; poem. In A century of parody and imitation, ed. by Walter Jerrold and R. M. Leonard. London, Oxford univ. press, 1913. p324

Hooley, Mary E.
Tennyson's Princess; [the education of woman, and Mary Wollstonecraft's vindication of the rights of woman] Masters essay, Columbia univ. 1926

Hooper, Joseph
Tennyson as a plagiarist. Lit W 14:327-8 O 6 '83

Hope, Henry Gerald
Tennyson on Havelock, 1857. Notes & Q 9th ser 2:184 S 3 '98

Horne, Richard Henry
Alfred Tennyson. In A new spirit of the age. New York, Harper, 1844. p193-210

Horton, Robert Forman
Alfred Tennyson: a saintly life (Saintly lives ser) London, Dent, 1900. xii,323p (Rev in Sat R 90:830 D 29 '00; Lit W 32:52 Ap 1 '01; A. M. Stoddart in Bookm (Lond) 19:88-9 D '00)

Hoskyns-Abrahall, J.
Tennyson's inspiration from the Pyrenees. Acad 25:422 Je 14 '84; Critic (NY) ns 1:310-11 Je 28 '84; Acad 32: 408-9 D 17 '87

House of Alfred Tennyson near Haslemere. Every Sat 9:132 F 26 '70

Houston, Percy Hazen
Tennyson, the representative poet of his age. Masters essay, Williams college, 1904

Howe, Mark Antony de Wolfe
Tennyson at Farringford: a Victorian vista. Drawn from the unpublished papers of Mrs. James T. Fields. Cornhill ns 63:447-57 O '27

Victorian poets: a side light. Atlan 152:226-7 Ag '33

Howe, Merrill Levi
Dante Gabriel Rossetti's comments on Maud. Mod Lang N 49:290-3 My '34

Howells, William Dean
Tennyson. In My literary passions. New York, Harper [c1895] p113-23

Howitt, William
Alfred Tennyson. In Homes and haunts of the most eminent British poets. London, Bentley, 1847. vol II p452-70 (Rev in Fraser 35:210-27 F '47)

Hoyt, Arthur S.
In memoriam: the way of faith. In The spiritual message of modern English poetry. New York, Macmillan, 1924. p89-112

Tennyson: the man and the poet. In The spiritual message of modern English poetry. New York, Macmillan, 1924. p67-85

Hubbard, Elbert
Alfred Tennyson. In Little journeys to the homes of English authors. New York, Putnam, 1903. p75-100

Hübel, Rudolf
Studien zur Tennyson's "Becket." Berlin, Trenkel, 1914. 114p Diss. Giessen

Huckel, Oliver
Through England with Tennyson; a pilgrimage to places associated with the great Laureate. . . New York, Crowell [1913] xii,249p

Hudson, J.
Tennyson's birthday; poem. Westm 174:210-11 Ag '10

Humbert, Gerald Vernon
Scientific thought in Tennyson. Masters essay, Univ. of Nebraska, 1930. 104ff

Hunt, May
A study of the sea in the greater Victorian poets. Masters essay, Univ. of Wisconsin, 1898. 214ff

Hunt, Theodore Whitfield
Tennyson's "Idylls of the King" and Tennyson's "In Memoriam." Bibliotheca Sacra 55:444-58 Jl '98; 54:249-63 Ap '97; same in English literary miscellany. Oberlin, Ohio, Bibliotheca Sacra co. 1914. ser 1 p271-318

Hutchinson, J.
Mr. Tennyson as a botanist. St P 13: 443-52 O '73; same. Liv Age 119:372-7 N 8 '73

Hutton, Laurence
The miller's daughter. Book B ns 6: 435-6 D '89

Hutton, Richard Holt
Browning and Tennyson. In Brief literary criticisms, selected from the "Spectator" and ed. by his niece Elizabeth M. Roscoe. London, Macmillan, 1906

"Locksley Hall" in youth and age. In Criticisms on contemporary thought and thinkers, selected from the Spectator. London, Macmillan, 1894. vol II p204-12

Newman and Tennyson. In Brief literary criticisms, selected from the "Spectator" and ed. by his niece Elizabeth M. Roscoe. London, Macmillan, 1906

Tennyson. Macmil 27:143-67 D '72

Tennyson. In Literary essays. London, Macmillan, 1892. p361-436

Tennyson's poem on "Despair." In Criticisms on contemporary thought and thinkers, selected from the Spectator. London, Macmillan, 1894. vol II p197-203

Hutton, William Holden
Two unfamiliar plays [Tennyson's Harold and Shakespeare's Timon of Athens] Church Q R 111:314-27 Ja '31

Huxley, Thomas Henry
Westminster Abbey, Oct. 12, 1892; poem. Critic (NY) 21:288 N 26 '92; same. 19th Cent 32:831-2 N '92

"I held it truth with him who sings." Notes & Q 4th ser 11:105 F 1 '73

Illustrations of animal life in Tennyson's poems. Cornhill 63:145-51 F '91; same. Liv Age 188:694-8 Mr 14 '91

Illustrations of Tennyson. Notes & Q 1st ser 3:319-20 Ap 26 '51

An imperial ode by Tennyson. Critic (NY) ns 5:235 My 8 '86

"In Memoriam." Notes & Q 4th ser 11:388 My 10 '73

"In Memoriam" [analysis] People's and Howitt's Journal ns 4:185-6 '51

In Memoriam after fifty years. Edin R 203:297-318 Ap '06; same. Liv Age 249: 587-602 Je 9 '06

"In Memoriam" and the Bible. Leisure Hour 23:71-3 '74

In Tennyson's country. Literary World (Lond) ns 64:176 S 13 '01

Inge, William Ralph
The Victorian age. (The Rede lecture for 1922) Cambridge, University press, 1922. 54p

The Victorian age. *In* Outspoken essays. London, Longmans, Green, 1922. 2d ser p199-205

Ingleby, C. Mansfield
Passage in Tennyson. Notes & Q 1st ser 6:272 S 18 '52

Ingram, John K.
Tennyson's works. *In* Afternoon lectures on English literature. London, Bell and Daldy, 1867. vol IV p47-94

Innes, Arthur Donald
Tennyson in particular. *In* Seers and singers. . . London, Innes, 1893. p26-49
(Rev in Literary World (Lond) ns 48:315 O 27 '93; Speaker 8:443 O 21 '93)

Irving, Walter [pseud]
see Brody, George M.

Is Tennyson a plagiarist? Lit W 14:291 S 8 '83

Is Tennyson a spiritualist? Pall Mall Gazette D 20 '88

Is Tennyson's influence on the wane? Cur Lit 47:275-8 S '09

Jack, Albert E.
Dr. Rolfe's notes on Tennyson. Dial 25:449-50 D 16 '98

Jacobs, Joseph
Alfred Tennyson. *In* Literary studies. London, Nutt, 1895. 2d ed p155-71

Obituary. Alfred Tennyson. Acad 42:335-7 O 15 '92

Tennyson and "In Memoriam"; an appreciation and a study. London, Nutt, 1892. viii,108p
(Rev in Spec 70:551 Ap 29 '83; Literary World (Lond) ns 47:316 Ap 7 '93; Nation (NY) 56:66 Ja 26 '93; Critic (NY) 22:58 F 4 '93)

Jacottet, Henri
Poètes modernes de l'angleterre; Alfred Tennyson. Bibliothèque Universelle et Revue Suisse 37:449-72, 38:89-114 Mr, Ap '88

Jacquart, Rolland R.
One of those immortalized by Tennyson. American Hebrew 121:965, 1021 My 4 '28

James, A.
Tennyson et Gladstone. La Société Nouvelle '87

James, Charles Canniff
A Tennyson pilgrimage, and Tennyson, the imperialist. Toronto, 1910. 22p; *same.* Acta Victoriana D '09

James, Henry
Tennyson's drama; Queen Mary and Harold. *In* Views and reviews. Boston, Ball, 1908. p165-204

Japikse, Cornelia Geertrui Hendrika
The dramas of Alfred Lord Tennyson. London, Macmillan, 1926. 167p Diss. Amsterdam
(Rev by B. Matthews in Out 144:537-8 D 22 '26)

[Japp, Alexander Hay] H. A. Page [pseud]
Alfred Lord Tennyson. *In* Miles, A. H. Poets and the poetry of the nineteenth century. London, Routledge, 1905. vol IV p67-100 [title of vol IV: Frederick Tennyson to Arthur Hugh Clough]

Three great teachers of our own time: Carlyle, Tennyson, and Ruskin. London, Smith, Elder, 1865. p87-186

Jarratt, F.
Tennyson's "The Ancient Sage." Notes & Q 9th ser 3:376 My 13 '99

Jebb, R. C.
Alfred, Lord Tennyson. *In* Ward, T. H. The English poets. New York, Macmillan, 1907. vol IV p755-64

On Mr. Tennyson's "Lucretius." Every Sat 6:101-4 Jl 25 '68; *same.* Macmil 18:97-103 Je '68

Jellinghaus, Paul
Tennysons drama "Harold." Eine quellenuntersuchung. Borna-Leipzig, Noske, 1905. ix,83p Diss. Münster

Jenkins, A. K.
A study of the elements of mysticism in the poetry of Alfred Lord Tennyson. Masters essay, Univ. of Southern California, 1931. 127ff

Jenkinson, Arthur
Alfred, Lord Tennyson, poet Laureate; a brief study of his life and poetry. London, Nisbet, 1892. xii,127p

Jennings, Henry James
"King Arthur" at the Lyceum. Gent M ns 54:202-11 F '95

Lord Tennyson; a biographical sketch. London, Chatto and Windus, 1884. vii, 270p
(Rev by E. D. A. Morshead in Acad 26:336 N 22 '84; Sat R 58:822-3 D 27 '84)

Jennings, James George
A note on the use of metaphor in "In Memoriam." *In* An essay on metaphor in poetry. . . London, Blackie, 1915. p81-94

Jerome, Jerome Klapka
Sunset. Play in one act . . . founded . . . upon . . . Tennyson's . . . poem of "The sisters." (French's acting ed. of plays. vol. 130) London, French [18—?] 26p [Produced first in 1888]

Jerram, C. S.
Mr. Churton Collins on Tennyson. Spec 90:453 Mr 21 '03

Jessup, A.
Frederick Harrison as a critic of Tennyson. Dial 31:311 N 1 '01

Jiriczek, Otto Luitpold
Die neunte woge. [Notes on the ninth wave in the "Coming of Arthur" verse 376] Bei Anglia 37:115-21 Ap '26

Tennyson; eine kritische würdigung zur hundertsten wiederkehr seines geburtstages. Engl Stud 41:28-69 '09

Johnson, Reginald Brimley
Story lives of nineteenth-century authors. London, Gardner, Darton, 1925

Tennyson and his poetry. London, Harrap, 1913. 160p

Johnson, Rossiter
Tennyson, Poe and Admiral Farragut. Critic (NY) 21:224 O 22 '92

Johnston, Bertha M.
Identification of Biblical allusions in selected writings of Tennyson. Masters essay, Univ. of North Dakota, 1932. 59ff

Jones, (Sir) Henry
The immortality of the soul in the poems of Tennyson and Browning. Boston, American Unitarian association, 1907. 51p

Tennyson. In Essays on literature and education. . . ed. by H. J. W. Hetherington. London, Hodder and Stoughton, 1924. p46-80; same in Brit Acad Proc 4:131-45 '09; same. Hibbert J 8:264-82 Ja '10

Jones, Richard D.
The ethical element in literature. . . Illustrated by an interpretation of the "In Memoriam". . . Bloomington, Ill. Public School Pub. Co. [c1891] 134p

The growth of the "Idylls of the King." Philadelphia, Lippincott, 1895. 5-161p

Jonson, G. C. Ashton
Tennyson's "In Memoriam." Poetry Review 22:181-201 My-Je '31

Jordan, Carol L.
The use of color in Tennyson. Masters essay, Columbia univ. 1916

Judge, Alice Marguerite
The social views of Alfred Tennyson. Masters essay, Tulane univ. 1926. 41ff

Jusserand, Jules Jean
Tennyson. In Histoire abrégée de la littérature anglaise. Paris, Delagrave, 1895

Kalisch, Carl
Studier over Tennyson med et kort omrids af digterens liv. Gad, 1893. vii,273p

Karkaria, R. P.
Tennyson on the signature in criticism. Lit 8:571 Je 29 '01

Kassel, Charles
Alfred Tennyson: a Victorian romance. So Atlan Q 25:139-53 Ap '26

Kellner, Leon
Alfred (Lord) Tennyson. In Die englische literatur der neuesten zeit von Dickens bis Shaw. Leipzig, Tauchnitz, 1921. p150-70

Die englische literatur im zeitalter der königin Viktoria. Leipzig, Tauchnitz, 1909. p259-99

Tennyson. Die Nation 15:288-90 F 12 '98

Kellogg, D. B.
Why Tennyson is not more read. Critic (NY) 22:11 Ja 7 '93

Kempling, W. Bailey
An apocryphal Tennyson poem. T L S Ap 3 '30 p298

Kennedy, William Sloane
Tennyson and other debtors to Spenser's "Faerie Queene." Poet Lore 10:492-506 '98

Kenyon, James Benjamin
Tennyson in new aspects. In Loiterings in old fields: literary sketches. New York, Eaton & Mains [1901] p1-48; same. Meth R 80:434-53 My '98

Ker, William Paton
Tennyson; the Leslie Stephen lecture delivered in the Senate house, Cambridge, on 11th of November, 1909. . . Cambridge, University press, 1909. 31p; also in Collected essays of W. P. Ker. . . London, Macmillan, 1925. vol I p258-76
(Rev in T L S N 19 '25 p768; J. B. Priestly in Sat R 140:571-2 N 14 '25)

Kerlin, Robert Thomas
Theocritus in English literature. Lynchburg, Virginia, Bell, 1910. p113-18 Diss. Yale univ.

Kern, Alfred Allan
King Lear and Pelleas and Ettarre. Mod Lang N 37:153-7 Mr '22

Kernahan, Coulson
Tennyson and some others. In Wise men and a fool. New York, Brentano, 1901. p129-47

King, Lauren Alfred
The verse technique of Alfred, Lord Tennyson. Diss. Ohio State Univ. 1930. Abstract in Ohio State Univ. Graduate School Abstracts of Doctor's Diss. 3:137-46 '30

King, Willard Parks
The trend of Tennyson criticism from his death to the present time. Masters essay, Stanford univ. 1928. 68ff

King, William Henry
Lord Tennyson. In Bookland. [London] Philip [1921] p216-21

Kingsley, Charles
Tennyson. In Sir Walter Raleigh and his time, with other papers. Boston, Ticknor and Fields, 1859. p177-95

Tennyson. In Literary and general lectures and essays. London, Macmillan, 1888. p103-24; same. Fraser 42:245-55 S '50

Kingsley, Maud Elma
Examination questions for Idylls of the King. Educa 30:245-6 D '09

Examination questions for Tennyson's Princess. Educa 29:391-3 F '09

A study of "Idylls of the King." Educa 23:356-70 F '03

Kitton, F. G.
Tennyson at Aldsworth. Gent M ns 54: 53-9 Ja '95; *same.* Liv Age 204:434-8 F 16 '95

Knight, William
Memoir of John Nichol. Glasgow, MacLehose, 1896. passim

A reminiscence of Tennyson. Blackw 162:264-70 Ag '97

Tennyson. *In* Retrospects. London, Smith, Elder, 1904. 1st ser p46-68

Knowles, J. T.
Tennyson's Arthurian poem. Spec 43: 15-17 Ja 1 '70

Knowles, James
Apotheosis; poem. 19th Cent 32:843-4 N '92

Aspects of Tennyson. 19th Cent 33: 164-88 Ja '93; *same.* Liv Age 196:515-29 F 25 '93

Characteristics of Tennyson. Critic (NY) 22:67-8 F 4 '93

Knox, Leona
Tennyson's "Idylls of the King": a study in aesthetics. Masters essay, Univ. of Texas, 1930. 257ff

Knox, Ronald Arbuthnott
The authorship of "In Memoriam." *In* Essays in satire. New York, Dutton [c1930]

Koeppel, Emil
Tennyson. Allgemeine Zeitung. Beilage '97

Tennyson. Berlin, Hofmann, 1899. vii, 175p
(Rev by R. Ackermann in Bei Anglia 10:355-7 Ap '00)

Tennysoniana. Engl Stud 28:397-406 '00

König, Robert
Tennyson. Neue Christoterpe '94 p125-62

Zu Alfred Tennysons gedächtnis. Daheim 29:102-4 N 19 '92

Krahmer, J.
Tennyson als frauenrechtler. Deutschland Monatschrift für die Gesamte Kultur 4:359-67 D '06

Kuhns, Oscar
Browning and Tennyson. *In* Dante and the English poets from Chaucer to Tennyson. New York, Holt, 1904. p239-56
(Rev in International Studio 24:xx-xxi '05)

Kynaston, Herbert
"Crossing the bar." National Observer 9:187, 239, 265 Ja 7, 21, 28 '93

Lambert, Agnes
The real Thomas Becket. 19th Cent 33: 273-92 F '93; *same.* Liv Age 197:18-32 Ap 1 '93

Lamia [pseud]
see Austin, Alfred

Lamont, Alexander
Tennyson's touch with nature. Sun M 18:378-87 Je '89

Lang, Andrew
Alfred Tennyson. (Modern English writers ser) New York, Dodd, Mead, 1901. ix,229p
(Rev in Nation (NY) 73:443-4 D 5 '01; Ath 2:551-2 O 26 '01; Literary World (Lond) ns 64:542 D 27 '01; Speaker ns 5:256-7 N 30 '01)

"Gaily the troubador"; poem. *In* A century of parody and imitation, ed. by Walter Jerrold and R. M. Leonard. London, Oxford univ. press, 1913. p356-7

On the death of Lord Tennyson. *In* The poetical works. . . ed. by Mrs. Lang. London, Longmans, Green, 1923. vol III p31

Tennyson and his commentators. Liv Age 231:781-4 D 21 '01

Lang, Leonora Blanche
The gateway to Tennyson. Tales and extracts from the poet's work. London, Nelson [1911?] 281p

Laprade, Victor de
Les contemporains. Tennysson. *In* Le sentiment de la nature chez les modernes. Paris, Didier, 1870. 2d ed. p285-9

The last message. Speaker 6:553-4 N 5 '92

The late Alfred, Baron Tennyson, poet Laureate. Illustrated London News 101:483-90 O 15 '92; *same.* Neuphilologisches Centralblatt 7:8-11 '93

The late Lord Tennyson. Pall Mall Budget 40:1639 N 3 '92

The late Lord Tennyson on the future life. Spec 70:283-4 Mr 4 '93

Latimer, M. D.
Tennyson's indebtedness to Malory. Bachelors essay, Univ. of Utah, 1910. 40ff

Laughlin, Clara Elizabeth
The peace that came to Tennyson. Good Words 44:793-800 '03; *same in* Stories of authors' loves. Philadelphia, Lippincott, 1902. vol I p15-34

The laughter of the muses: a satire on the reigning poetry of 1869. Glasgow, 1869. [v]-vi,89p

The Laureate. National Observer 5:10-11 N 22 '90

Laureate and his school. Dublin Review ns 2:363-85 '64

The Laureate of Lincolnshire. Blackw 164: 670-5 N '98

The Laureate under the microscope. Chamb J 44:404-7 Je 29 '67

The Laureate's career. Critic (NY) 21:204-9 O 15 '92

The **Laureate's** funeral. Critic (NY) 21:
223-4 O 22 '92

The **Laureate's** motto. Notes & Q 4th
ser 5:103 Ja 22 '70

The **Laureate's** new poem [Lucretius]
Punch 54:205 My 9 '68; *same.* Liv Age
97:824 Je 27 '68

The **Laureateship.** Spec 69:517-18 O 15 '92

Lauvrière, Emile
La morbidité de Tennyson. Revue Germ
9:557-65 '13

Repetition and parallelism in Tennyson.
London, Frowde, 1910. xi,107p

Layard, George Somes
Tennyson and his pre-Raphaelite illustrators. A book about a book. London, Stock, 1894. viii,68p
(Rev in Sat R 77:370 Ap 7 '94;
Literary World (Lond) ns 49:275 Mr
23 '94; Nation (NY) 59:270 O 11 '94;
Studio 2:221-2 Mr '94; Critic (NY) 25:
347-8 N 24 '94)

Leading men—Tennyson. Liv Age 65:24
Ap 7 '60

Leavitt, Charlotte Mendell
Tennyson as a critic. Masters essay,
Columbia univ. 1909

**Lebona, Francesca di Silvestri Falconieri,
duca di**
Lord Tennyson. Rome, Roma letteraria,
1911. 40p

Lechlitner, Ruth
Modern poetic treatments of Arthurian
material. Masters essay, Univ. of Iowa,
1926

Ledene, Adeline E.
Tennyson's structural and varied use of
rhetorical imagery in the Idylls of the
king. Masters essay, Univ. of South
Dakota, 1928. 69ff

Lee, Ernest Dare
Tennyson and his era. *In* The papers of
an Oxford man. London, Ingpen &
Grant [1928] p161-5

Lee, George
Tennyson's religion. American Catholic
Quarterly Review 25:119-32 Ja '00

Lee, John
The passing of Arthur. Lit & Philos
Soc 52:39-56 '98

Leeper, Alex
"Otherwhere" omitted in Tennyson con-
cordance. Notes & Q 12th ser 9:248
S 24 '21

Lees, Frederic
Tennyson and the old annuals. Lit 6:87-
8, 155 Ja 27, F 17 '00

Le Gallienne, Richard
Poets and publishers. Speaker 8:550 N
18 '93

The romantic '90s. Garden City, N. Y.
Doubleday, Page, 1925. p52-5, 115-26

Tennyson. *In* Attitudes and avowals. . .
New York, Lane [c1910] p212-26

"Tennyson" at the farm. *In* English
poems. London, Lane, 1895. p102

Leonard, Mary Emmer
Tennyson, the singer. Masters essay,
Cornell univ. 1894. 202ff

Lester, George
Christmas with Lord Tennyson. Fire-
side Magazine D '90

Lord Tennyson and the Bible. London,
Howe [1891] 152p

The poets Laureate of England. Alfred,
Lord Tennyson. Methodist Recorder
Mr 21 '89

Leveloh, Paul
Tennyson und Spenser. Eine unter-
suchung von Spensers einfluss auf
Tennyson mit berücksichtigung von
Keats. Borna-Leipzig (Marburg)
Noske, 1909. 141p Diss. Marburg

Levey, Sivori
Guinevere and Arthur. Adapted from
Tennyson's "Idylls of the King."
(Pilgrimage plays, no 4) London,
Fountain publishing co. [nd] 3-27p

Sir Gareth's quest. Adapted from
Tennyson's "Idylls of the King." And
arranged for costume representation.
. . (Pilgrimage plays, no 3) London,
Fountain publishing co. [nd] 32p

Lewis, W. Aldersey
Clough and Tennyson. Acad 66:82, 205
Ja 16, F 20 '04

Tennyson's "Poet's song." Spec 108:
475-6 Mr 23 '12

Lieberman, Elias
Five nineteenth century poets as dramatists, Byron, Shelley, Keats, Browning, Tennyson. The reasons for their
failure. Masters essay, New York
univ. 1906. 19ff

Lier, W.
Enoch Arden. Mittelschule und Höhere
Mädchenschule 18:175-81 '04

Lillie, Lucy C.
Tennyson's home life. Ind 44:1510-11 O
27 '92

Lilly, William Samuel
The mission of Tennyson. *In* Studies in
religion and literature. London, Chapman and Hall, 1904. p31-52; *same.*
Fortn ns 61:239-50 F 1 '97

The **Lincoln** monument to Tennyson. Ath
2:145 Jl 29 '05

Lindsay, James
Tennyson. *In* Essays, literary and
philosophical. Edinburgh, Blackwood,
1896

Line from Tennyson. Notes & Q 3d ser
10:413-14 N 24 '66

Lines by Tennyson. Notes & Q 12th ser
8:7 Ja 1 '21

Linker, John
Byron, Browning and Tennyson as dramatists. Masters essay, New York
univ. 1910. 28ff

Lintner, Robert Casper
"Twilight and evening bell." [Council Grove, Kansas, c1920] 11-45p

Literary notes. Pall Mall Budget 40:1190 Ag 11 '92

Literary sacrilege. Literary World (Lond) ns 69:388 Ap 22 '04

The **literature** of house-moving. . . T. P.'s Weekly 5:329 Mr 17 '05

The **literature** of the last fifty years. Blackw 141:740-3 Je '87

Littell, Philip
Moral element in Tennyson's poetry. New Repub 4:77 Ag 21 '15

Tennyson. *In* Books and things. New York, Harcourt, Brace and Howe, 1919. p167-72

Little, Charles J.
Some words about Tennyson. Meth R 70:203-21 Mr '88

Littledale, Harold
Essays on Lord Tennyson's Idylls of the King. London, Macmillan, 1893. [v]-x,308p
(Rev in Sat R 75:248-9 Mr 4 '93; A. Waugh in Acad 43:413-14 My 13 '93; Critic (NY) 22:285 My 6 '93; Speaker 7:434 Ap 15 '93; Literary World (Lond) ns 47:192-3 Mr 3 '93; Nation (NY) 57:194 S 14 '93)

Livingston, Luther Samuel
The first books of some English authors. The Tennysons. Bookm (NY) 10:123-7 O '99

Loane, George Green
Echoes in Tennyson, and other essays. . . London, Stockwell [1928] 24p

Locke, Ruth Wood
Tennyson's patriotism as revealed in his life and works. Masters essay, Stanford univ. 1915. 100ff

Locker-Lampson, Frederick
Unfortunate Miss Bailey. *In* A century of parody and imitation, ed. by Walter Jerrold and R. M. Leonard. London, Oxford univ. press, 1913. p268-9

Lockhart, John Gibson
Tennyson. *In* Lockhart's literary criticism. With introduction and bibliography by M. Clive Hildyard. Oxford, Blackwell, 1931. p132-44

"Locksley Hall." Notes & Q 5th ser 4:91-2 Jl 31 '75; 5th ser 12:471 D 13 '79

"Locksley Hall" earlier and later. Leisure Hour 36:137-40 '87

"Locksley Hall" in youth and age. Spec 59:1706-7 D 18 '86

Lockwood, Frank C.
Tennyson's religious faith. Meth R 91:783-7 S '09

Lockyer, (Sir) Joseph Norman and Winifred L. Lockyer
Tennyson as a student and poet of nature. . . London, Macmillan, 1910. x, 220p
(Rev in Spec 106:94-5 Ja 21 '11; Ath 2:736 D 10 '10)

Lodge, (Sir) Oliver Joseph
Attitude of Tennyson towards science. *In* Modern problems. London, Methuen, 1912. p301-7

Loliée, Frédéric
Les disparus. Alfred Tennyson. Nouvelle Revue 79:175-81 N '92

Longfellow, Henry Wadsworth
Wapentake. To Alfred Tennyson; poem. Atlan 40:731 D '77

Lord Tennyson. Westm 138:589-96 D '92; Sat R 74:405-6 O 8 '92; Acad 53:34-6 Ja 8 '98; Calcutta Review 96:193-202 Ja '93; Speaker 6:429-31 O 8 '92; Speaker 2:69-70 Jl 19 '90; Literary World (Lond) ns 46:284-5 O 14 '92; Pall Mall Budget 40:1465-72, 1500 O 6 '92

Lord Tennyson and Sir Henry Parkes. Pall Mall Budget 40:1750 N 24 '92

Lord Tennyson's fancy. Spec 68:458-9 Ap 2 '92

Lord Tennyson's funeral. Liv Age 195:510-12 N 19 '92; Dial 13:236 O 16 '92

Lord Tennyson's masters. Bookworm 7:18 '93

Loudon, K. M.
King Arthur: Malory and Tennyson. *In* Two mystic poets and other essays. Oxford, Blackwell, 1922. p31-82

Lounsbury, Thomas Raynesford
The life and times of Tennyson: 1809-50. New Haven, Yale univ. press, 1915. xvi,661p
(Rev by B. Matthews in Yale R 5:631-3 Ap '16; New Repub 6:80-1 F 19 '16; Liv Age 291:187-90 O 21 '16; G. Saintsbury in Bookm (Lond) 50:130-3 Ag '16; C. S. Northup in Dial 60:423-4 Ap 27 '16; Ath 2:317-18 Jl '16)

The two Locksley Halls. Scrib M 6:250-6 Ag '89

Lowe, Ralph Fernald
Relation of Tennyson to movements of religious thought in England, 1830-1890. Masters essay, Wesleyan univ. 1908. 37ff

Lowell, Edward Jackson
Alfred, Lord Tennyson. [a Memorial] [Boston, 1893] p420-32

Lucas, Frank Laurence
Tennyson. *In* Eight Victorian poets. New York, Macmillan, 1930. p3-19
(Rev in T L S N 13 '30 p936)

Luce, Morton
The evolution of the Idylls of the King. Acad 53:640-1 Je 11 '98

Luce, Morton—_Continued_
A handbook to the works of Alfred,
Lord Tennyson. London, Bell, 1906.
vi,454p "Chronological table" p[439]-
44
(Rev in Sat R 81:128-30 F 1 '96; Lit
W 27:71 Mr 7 '96; Literary World
(Lond) ns 53:92 Ja 31 '96; Lond Q R
86:179-80 Ap '96)

Nature in Tennyson. I. Birds. Liv Age
287:156-61 O 16 '15; _same._ British Review 11:420-32 S '15

Nature in Tennyson. II. Trees. Liv
Age 287:604-11 D 4 '15; _same._ British
Review 12:102-17 O '15

New studies in Tennyson. . . London,
Baker [pref 1893] 2d ed 96p

Tennyson. London, Dent, 1901. viii,166p

Lucy, (Sir) Henry
Alfred Tennyson: personal notes. Nation (NY) 99:69-71 Jl 16 '14

Ludlow, J. M.
Mr. Tennyson and the Eyre Defence
Fund. Spec 39:1225-6 N 3 '66

Moral aspects of Mr. Tennyson's "Idylls
of the King." Macmil 1:63-72 N '59

Lux, Jacques
Le centenaire de Tennyson. Revue
Bleue 47:254-6 Ag 21 '09

Lyall, (Sir) Alfred Comyns
Tennyson. (English men of letters. new
ser) London, Macmillan, 1902. vi,200p
(Rev in Ath 2:513-14 O 18 '02; Nation
(NY) 75:366-7 N 6 '02; F. J. Mather,
Jr. in Forum 34:397-8 Ja '03; F.
Harrison _in_ Memories and thoughts.
New York, Macmillan, 1906. p31-46;
Acad 63:411-12 O 18 '02; Sat R 94:
iii-iv O 18 '02; Public Opinion (NY)
33:597 N 6 '02; Literary World (Lond)
ns 66:308-9 O 24 '02; T L S O 10
'02 p297; H. D. Davray in Mercure Fr
44:834-5 D '02)

Lyall, Margaret Agnes
The dramas of Alfred, Lord Tennyson.
Masters essay, Univ. of Manitoba,
1932. 109ff

Lyall, William
Tennyson. A criticism. Rose-Belford's
Canadian Monthly & National Review
1:477-89 O '78

Lyell and Tennyson. Liv Age 70:417-20
Ag 17 '61; _same._ Sat R 11:631-2 Je 22
'61

Lynd, Robert
Tennyson: a contemporary criticism. _In_
Art of letters. New York, Scribner,
1921. p134-8

Lynn, W. T.
[Moonless stars i.e. moonless Mars]
Notes & Q 10th ser 9:13 Ja 4 '08

Lyon, William Henry
Renan and Tennyson. _In_ Five prophets
of today. . . Boston, Smith, 1892. p21-
38

Lyttleton, Arthur Temple
Tennyson. _In_ Modern poets of faith,
doubt, and other essays. London,
Murray, 1904. p1-32

Mabbott, Thomas Ollive
The correspondence of John Tomlin.
Letters from Tennyson and Aubrey
De Vere. Notes & Q 164:293 Ap 29
'33

Mabie, Hamilton Wright
How to study Tennyson and Emerson.
Ladies' Home Journal 25:32 Mr '08

The influence of Tennyson in America;
its sources and extent. R of Rs (NY)
6:553-6 D '92

The life of Tennyson. Atlan 80:577-89 N
'97

Tennyson the artist. Christian Union
46:786-7 O 29 '92

Tennyson's earlier poems. Book B ns 5:
457-60 D '88

McAlpin, Edwin Augustus
Tennyson and immortality. _In_ Old and
new books as life teachers. New
York, Doubleday, Doran, 1928. p80-95

MacArthur, James
Discarded poems of Tennyson's. Christian Union 46:787-9 O 29 '92

McCabe, Joseph Martin
A biographical dictionary of modern
rationalists. London, Watts, 1920.
p787-9

McCabe, W. Gordon
Personal recollections of Alfred, Lord
Tennyson. Cent 63:722-37 Mr '02

McCallum, Mary
Tennyson and Browning: a comparison
of their respective aesthetic theories
and methods. Masters essay, Queen's
univ. 1929. 122ff

MacCallum, Mungo William
Tennyson's Idylls of the King and
Arthurian story from the sixteenth
century. Glasgow, Maclehose, 1894.
xiv,435p
(Rev in Edin R 181:485-513 Ap '95;
Nation (NY) 58:471 Je 21 '94; A.
Waugh in Acad 45:390-1 My 12 '94;
National Observer 11:323-4 F 10 '94;
Literary World (Lond) ns 49:165 F 23
'94; Spec 72:653-5 My 12 '94; Speaker
9:449-50 Ap 21 '94; S. L. Gwynn in
Bookm (Lond) 6:53-4 My '94; Critic
(NY) 24:297-8 My 5 '94)

McCarthy, Justin Huntly
The Foresters. Gent M 272:528-34 My
'92

Thomas Carlyle—Alfred Tennyson. _In_
Portraits of the sixties. New York,
Harper, 1903. p38-44

McCloskey, Mary Magdalene
Reflection of the times in Tennyson's
"In Memoriam." Masters essay,
Indiana univ. 1913

MacColl, D. S.
Millais's portrait of Tennyson. Burlington Magazine 13:127-8 Je '08

McCorkindale, T. B.
Some elements in the religious teaching of Tennyson. Queen's Q 21:449-55 Ap-Je '14

McCrie, George
Alfred Tennyson. *In* The religion of our literature. . . London, Hodder and Stoughton, 1875. p110-80

Macdonald, M.
Tennyson's Königsidyllen. Beilage zum Hamburg no 5 '04

McDonnell, A. C.
XIX.-century poetry. (Literary epoch ser) London, Black, 1897. p107-20

MacEwen, V.
Knights of the Holy Eucharist. [Thoughts on the spiritual teaching of Tennyson's The Holy Grail] London, Gardner, 1912. 76p

McFee, Inez Nellie (Canfield)
Story of the Idylls of the king; Tennyson's Idylls of the king in their original form, also the stories of these poems; illustrated by M. L. Kirk. New York, Stokes, 1932. 394p

McGiffert, Margaret C.
Tennyson's use of archaic forms. Dial 22:240-1 Ap 16 '97

McGill, Anna Blanche
Some famous literary clans. II.-The Tennysons. Book B ns 21:30-7 Ag '00

Mackail, John William
Tennyson. *In* Studies of English poets. London, Longmans, Green, 1926. p227-51
(Rev in T L S Mr 11 '26 p179; St. L. Strachey in Spec 136:1083 Je 26 '26; Nat-Ath 39:78 Ap 17 '26; F. Bickley in Bookm (Lond) 70:226 Jl '26)

Theocritus and Tennyson. *In* Lectures on Greek poetry. London, Longmans, Green, 1910. p220-6

Mackay, Charles
Locksley Hall. Notes & Q 5th ser 4: 297-8 O 9 '75

Mackay, Eric i. e. George Eric
Vox clamantis; a comparison, analytical and critical, between the "Columbus at Seville" of Joseph Ellis. . . and the "Columbus" of the poet Laureate. London, Stewart [1887] 32p

Mackaye, Percy
Tennyson; poem. *In* Poems and plays. . . New York, Macmillan, 1916. vol I p16-20

McKeehan, Irene Pettit
A neglected example of the "In Memoriam" stanza. Mod Lang N 41:531-2 D '26

Mackie, Alexander
Tennyson as botanist, entomologist, ornithologist, geologist. *In* Nature knowledge in modern poetry. London, Longmans, Green, 1906

Mackie, Gascoigne
Tennyson and Wordsworth. Spec 121: 517 N 9 '18

Maclise's illustrations to Tennyson's "Princess." Dublin University Magazine 55:314-20 Mr '60

McMechan, Archibald McKellar
Alfred Tennyson, artist. University Magazine 7:53-75 F '08; *same in* The life of a little college and other papers. Boston, Houghton, Mifflin, 1914. p85-120

Introduction. *In* Select poems of Alfred Tennyson. (Belles-lettres ser) Boston, Heath, 1908. p[xv]-lviii

McNicoll, Thomas
Alfred Tennyson. *In* Essays on English literature. London, Pickering, 1861. p248-76

Macphail, Alexander
Lucretius or Scott? Spec 106:144 Ja 28 '11

Macphail, W. M.
Tennyson's Idylls of the king. London, Hitchcock [1892] 36p

Macquoid, Thomas R.
Tennyson's funeral. Lit W 23:388 N 5 '92

McRae, M. H. I.
Nature in Wordsworth and Tennyson. Masters essay, Univ. of Toronto, 1905

McReynolds, Grace Eleanor
The medieval element in Tennyson. Masters essay, Cornell univ. 1919. 41ff

Macy, John
Tennyson, the perfect Laureate. Bookm (NY) 69:375-86 Je '29

Madan, Geoffrey
Tennyson and the letter S. T L S My 18 '33 p348

Maddyn, D. Owen
The politics of the Poet Laureate. Constitutional Press Je '59

Magnus, Laurie
English literature in the nineteenth century. . . New York, Putnam, 1909. p280-6, 224-42

Tennyson a hundred years after. Cornhill 3d ser 66:660-70 My '29
(Rev in Notes & Q 156:381 Je 1 '29)

Magnus, Philip M.
Poetry and society since Tennyson. Edin R 249:301-14 Ap '29

Magruder, Caleb Clark, Jr.
Tennyson's "In Memoriam." Masters essay, George Washington univ. 1899. 24ff

Magruder, Ernest Pendleton
A critical estimate of the poetry of Tennyson. Masters essay, George Washington univ. 1900. 54ff

Magruder, Julia
Lancelot, Guinevere and Arthur. No Am 180:375-80 Mr '05; [Reply by J. E. Robb in No Am 180:918-26 Je '05]

Mair, G. H.
English literature; modern. (Home university library of modern knowledge no 27) New York, Holt [c1911] p194-201

Major, John Campbell
A comparative study of the sources of Tennyson's Lancelot and Elaine, and Guinevere. Masters essay, Univ. of Nebraska, 1928. 146ff

Malan, Edward
Hallam's grave. Notes & Q 6th ser 8: 221-3 S 22 '83; 11:66 Ja 24 '85

Malcolm, E. H.
Tennyson's "Enoch Arden." Notes & Q 5th ser 5:526-7 Je 24 '76

Mallarmé, Stéphane
Tennyson vu d'ici. In Divagations. Paris, Charpentier, 1897; same. National Observer 8:611-12 O 29 '92; same. Revue Blanche D '92

Mallock, William Hurrell
Tennyson's Ballads and poems. In Criticism and the value of life. London, Bentley, 1884. p83-146

Two poet Laureates on life. Nat R 47: 955-70 Ag '06; same. Liv Age 251:3-14 O 6 '06

Maness, M. May
The influence of Cambridge University upon Tennyson. Masters essay, Columbia univ. 1934

Mann, Robert James
Tennyson's "Maud" vindicated: an explanatory essay. London, Jarrold [1856] 78p

Mansell, Kathryn
Vitalizing the Idylls of the King. Engl J (High School ed) 23:225-7 Mr '34

Manuel, J.
Queen Elizabeth and "Queen Mary." Notes & Q 5th ser 5:486 Je 17 '76

Marble, Annie Russell
Messages of the nineteenth century poets. Dial 30:97-8 F 16 '01

Victoria's poets-Laureate. Critic (NY) 38:233-6 Mr '01

"Mariana." Notes & Q 6th ser 1:382-3 My 8 '80

Marshall, Ed.
Hallam's remains. Notes & Q 7th ser 10:354 N 1 '90

Marshall, James
see Mather, Marshall

Martin, Edwin
Tennyson's friendships. McClure's Magazine 2:54-60 D '93

Martin, Lucille
The influence of Shelley on Tennyson. Masters essay, Columbia univ. 1926

Martin, Theodore
Tennyson and "Cymbeline"; poem. Blackw 152:767 N '92

see also Aytoun, William Edmondstoune and Martin, Theodore

Martin, Werner
Die quellen zu Tennysons erstem drama "Queen Mary." Halle a. S. Hohmann, 1912. 166p Diss. Halle-Wittenberg

Mason, C.
Lord Tennyson's birthday. Notes & Q 7th ser 11:317 Ap 18 '91

Massey, Gerald
Tennyson's Princess. Christian Socialist S-N '51

Masson, D.
In the footsteps of the poets. London, Isbister, 1893. p333-81

Masterman, Charles Frederick Gurney
Tennyson as a religious teacher. . . London, Methuen, 1900. xii,253p
(Rev in Lit 6:168 F 24 '00; Spec 84: 214 F 10 '00; Literary World (Lond) ns 61:243 Mr 16 '00)

Mather, Marshall i. e. James Marshall
Tennyson, the moodist. In Popular studies of nineteenth century poets. London, Warne, 1892. p125-52

Mathews, C. E.
The earlier and less-known poems of Alfred Tennyson, poet-Laureate. . . Birmingham, Herald press, 1883. 34p

Matthews, J.
Tennyson's witness to the higher hope. Spec 69:594-5 O 29 '92

Matthison, Arthur
Enoch Arden; a drama in five acts, founded on Alfred Tennyson's great poem. . . (French's standard drama. The acting edition. no 377) London, French [c1872] [3]-35p

Max Heinrich and Richard Strauss' "Enoch Arden." Music 20:396-402 N '01

Maynadier, [Gustavus] Howard
Tennyson. In The Arthur of the English poets. Boston, Houghton, Mifflin, 1907. p410-38

Mayor, J. E. B.
Locksley Hall. Notes & Q 1st ser 2: 195 Ag 24 '50

Mayor, Joseph B.
A crux in Tennyson. Spec 107:310-11, 414-15 Ag 26, S 16 '11

Modern blank verse. Tennyson and Browning. In Chapters on English metre. London, Clay, 1886. p184-96

Meakin, Budgett
Tennyson's "Timbuctoo." Ath 2:722-3 N 25 '99

The **meaning** of Mr. Tennyson's "King Arthur." Contemp 21:938-48 My '73; same. Ecl M ns 18:142-8 Ag '73

Mercer, Arthur
"In Memoriam" as a revelation of the religious philosophy of Tennyson. New Church Review 16:540-59 O '09

Merivale, Charles
Autobiography & letters of Charles Merivale, dean of Ely; ed. by Judith

Anne Merivale. . . Oxford, Printed for private circulation by H. Hart, 1898. 499p
(Rev in Literary World (Lond) ns 60: 519 D '99)

The metre of "In Memoriam." Notes & Q 4th ser 11:37-8 Ja 11 '73

The metre of Tennyson's "Charge of the Six Hundred." Notes & Q 4th ser 10:390 N 16 '72

The metres of Tennyson. Notes & Q 4th ser 11:104-5 F 1 '73

Meyer, Wilhelm
Tennysons jugendgedichte in deutscher übersetzung. Münster i. W. Theissing, 1914. 127p

Meyers, Alicia Catherine
Dramatic monologue in Tennyson and Browning. Masters essay, Tulane univ. 1929. 63ff

Meynell, (Mrs) Alice Christiana Thompson
Some thoughts of a reader of Tennyson. In Hearts of controversy. London, Burns and Oates [1917] p1-22

Tennyson. Dublin Review 146:62-71 Ja '10

Miller, Bessie Porter
Some aspects of womanhood in Chaucer, Shakespeare and Tennyson. In Thom, Wm. Taylor. Shakespeare and Chaucer examinations. Boston, 1888. p307-46

Miller, Joaquin
The passing of Tennyson; [poem] Critic (NY) 21:256 N 5 '92

Milner, Kate
Tennyson and Browning as interpreters of their age. Masters essay, Indiana univ. 1888

Milsand, Joseph
Idylls of the king. In Littérature anglaise et philosophie. Dijon, Lamarche, 1893. p39-71; same. R Deux Mondes Jl 15 '51 p345-66

Mims, Edwin
Mysticism in Tennyson. Meth R 83:62-71 Ja '01

Minckwitz, M. J.
"Princess." Allgemeine Zeitung. Beilage no 32:4-6 F 8 '01

Mr. Eric Mackay and "Vox Clamantis." A summary of incidents controverting assertions contained in two letters addressed to the editor of "The Birmingham daily gazette." London, Stewart, 1887. 14p

Mr. Tennyson. Temple 26:179-94 My '69

Mr. Tennyson as a youthful poet. Lit W 10:200 Je 2 '79

Mr. Tennyson's "Death of Lucretius." Spec 41:523-4 My 2 '68

Mr. Tennyson's drama on the stage. Spec 49:526-7 Ap 22 '76

Mr. Tennyson's "Holy Grail." Spec 46: 600-1 My 10 '73

Mr. Tennyson's new volume. Notes & Q 3d ser 6:186-7 S 3 '64

Mr. Tennyson's peerage. Sat R 56:751-2 D 15 '83

Mr. Tennyson's play [The Promise of May] Sat R 54:670-1 N 18 '82

Mr. Tennyson's poetry. No Brit 53:378-425 Ja '71

Mitchell, Ellen M.
The way of the soul. A comparative study of Tennyson and Dante. [Syracuse, 1902] [13]ff

Modern English poets [Tennyson] Quar R 126:332-40 Ap '69

Modern men. The Laureate. National Observer 5:10-11 N 22 '90

The modern poetry of doubt. Spec 43:166-7 F 5 '70; same. New Ecl 6:490-4 Ap '70

Moeton, P. J.
Tennyson's "The Palace of Art" en onze tachtiger letterkundige beweging. Bloesem en Wrucht 3:515-38 '14

Moffatt, James Strong
Tennyson, Spenser, and the renaissance. Masters essay, Univ. of North Carolina, 1917. 75ff

Moggridge, M. W.
Idyllic poetry. Macmil 38:108 Je '78

Moir, David M.
Tennyson. In Sketches of the poetical literature of the past half-century. Edinburgh, Blackwood, 1852. 2d ed p312-21

Möllmann, Adelheid
Alfred Tennysons künstlerische arbeit an seinen gedichten. (Universitas-Archiv Bd 37) Münster, Helios-verlag, 1930. vii,81p bibl p79-81 Diss. Münster

Montégut, Émile
Essais sur Alfred Tennyson. I. Des premiers poèmes aux Idylls du Roi. II. Enoch Arden et les poèmes populaires. In Écrivains modernes de l'angleterre. Paris, Hachette, 1889. 2d ser p261-349

[Moody and Yeats on Tennyson] Dial 56: 286 Ap 1 '14

Moore, Charles Leonard
The Asiatic and the Greek spirit in literature. Dial 57:185-7 S 16 '14

The passionate Victorians. Dial 60:524 Je 8 '16

Moore, John Murray
Tennyson as a national poet. Lit & Philos Soc 52:85-118 S '98

Tennyson as a poet of humanity. Lit & Philos Soc 53:81-105 '99

Tennyson's nature studies. Lit & Philos Soc 51:189-215 N '97

Moore, John Murray—*Continued*
Three aspects of the late Alfred Lord Tennyson. Manchester, Marsden, 1901. 152p
(Rev in Literary World (Lond) ns 64: 542-3 D 27 '01)

More, Paul Elmer
Tennyson. Nation (NY) 88:82-5 Ja 28 '09

Tennyson. *In* Shelburne essays. New York, Putnam, 1910. 7th ser p64-94; *also in* Berdan, J. M. (ed) Modern essays. New York, Macmillan, 1916. p204-28

More Tennysoniana. Pall Mall Budget 40: 1558-9 O 20 '92

Morgan, Mary Louis
Galahad in the poetry of Tennyson. *In* Galahad in English literature. Diss. Catholic univ. 1932. p126-42

A **morning** performance at the Lyceum. Mr. Tennyson's "Cup." St J 48:195-203 Mr '81

Morr, Margaret and Skemp, Kathryn
A Tennyson festival. Popular Educator 41:38-42 S '23

Morris, Lewis
Poem. Critic (NY) 21:209-10 O 15 '92

[**Morris'** and Tennyson's treatment of medievalism] Atlan 39:102-3 Ja '77

Morton, Edward Payson
The technique of English non-dramatic blank verse. Chicago, Donnelley, 1910. p124-5 Thesis, Univ. of Chicago

Moses, Adolph [Eliezer Asher]
Alfred Tennyson. *In* Yahvism and other discourses. Louisville, Kentucky, Louisville section of the Council of Jewish women, 1903. p261-8

Moulton, Louise Chandler
From over the sea; poem. Critic (NY) 21:289 N 26 '92

Tennyson; poem. Lit W 23:476 D 17 '92

Mount, C. B.
"Aylmer's Field." Notes & Q 8th ser 1:524 Je 25 '92

Tennyson's "Aylmer's Field." Notes & Q 7th ser 12:510 D 26 '91

Moxon, T. Allen
Tennyson's "In Memoriam": its message to the bereaved and sorrowful. (Books of consolation ser) London, Skeffington, 1917. 93p

Mühlefeld, K[arl]
Französische und englische gedichte in metrischer übertragung. Osterode am Harz, 1901. Realgymnasium. 21p

Mullany, Patrick Francis
Spiritual sense of In Memoriam. *In* Phases of thought and criticism. Boston, Houghton, Mifflin, 1892. p183-264

Müller, Erich Guenter
Tennyson. Erlebnis und dichtung. Diss. Marburg, 1925. v,324p

Munger, Theodore Thorton
Interplay of Christianity and literature. *In* Essays for the day. Boston, Houghton, Mifflin, 1904. p91-7

Munro, Emily Gardner
Tennyson's Gareth and Lynette compared with Malory's. ms in Brown Univ. Library. (1898 commencement oration) 10ff

Murray, J. Malton
Crossing the bar. T. P.'s Weekly 12:10 Jl 3 '08

Murray, Robert Fuller
The poet's hat; poem. *In* A century of parody and imitation, ed. by Walter Jerrold and R. M. Leonard. London, Oxford univ. press, 1913. p382

A Tennysonian fragment; poem. *In* A century of parody and imitation, ed. by Walter Jerrold and R. M. Leonard. London, Oxford univ. press, 1913. p383

Mustard, Wilfrid Pirt
Classical echoes in Tennyson. (Columbia University studies in English. vol 3) New York, Macmillan, 1904. xii-xvi, 164p
(Rev in Nation (NY) 79:529 D 29 '04; noted in Ath 1:110 Ja 28 '05)

Tennyson and Catullus. Nation (NY) 66:362-3 My 12 '98

Tennyson and Homer. Am J Philol 21:143-53 '00

Tennyson and Horace. Nation (NY) 66: 438-9 Je 9 '98

Tennyson and Virgil. Baltimore, Md. Lord Baltimore press [1899] 11p; *same.* Am J Philol 20:186-94 '99

My Tennyson. Liv Age 195:446-8 N 12 '92; *same.* Speaker 6:461-2 O 15 '92

Myall, (Mrs) Laura Hain Friswell
In the sixties and seventies. Boston, Turner, 1906
(Rev by P. F. Bicknell in Dial 40:188-90 Mr 16 '06)

Myers, Frederick William Henry
The height and the deep; poem. 19th Cent 32:833-4 N '92

Modern poets and the meaning of life. 19th Cent 33:93-111 Ja '93

Tennyson as prophet. 19th Cent 25:381-96 Mr '89; *same.* Liv Age 180:811-19 Mr 30 '89; *same.* Ecl M 112:531-41 Ap '89; *same in* Science and a future life. London, Macmillan, 1901. p27-65

Napier, George G.
The homes and haunts of Alfred, Lord Tennyson. Glasgow, MacLehose, 1892. xvi,204p
(Rev in R of Rs (Lond) 6:298 S '92)

Negri, Gaetano
Gladstone and Tennyson. Die Gesellschaft 2:762-71 '98

Tennyson e Gladstone. *In* Segni dei tempi. Profili e bozzetti letterari. Milano, Hoepli, 1893. p[55]-72

Nencioni, Enrico
In Memoriam [and] the Idylls of the King. Fanfulla della Domenica My & S '83

Lord Tennyson. Nuova Antol 125:613-31 '92

Lord Tennyson. *In* Saggi critici di letteratura inglese. Firenze, 1897. p269-300

Maud. Domenica Litteraria Mr 19 '82

New poem by Tennyson. Northern Farmer. New style. Every Sat 9:2 Ja 1 '70

Newman and Tennyson. Spec 77:74-5 Jl 18 '96

Newton, Lewis William
The portrayal of common life in modern English poetry with special reference to Tennyson. Masters essay, Univ. of Texas, 1907. 130ff

Nicoll, (Sir) William Robertson
Alfred Tennyson: his life and works. Edinburgh, Macniven, 1881

Nicoll, (Sir) William Robertson and Wise, Thomas James (eds)
The building of the Idylls. *In* Literary anecdotes of the nineteenth century. . . London, Hodder & Stoughton, 1896. vol II p217-72
(Rev in Literary World (Lond) ns 55: 242 Mr 12 '97)

Tennysoniana. *In* Literary anecdotes of the nineteenth century. . . London, Hodder and Stoughton, 1896. vol II p419-41

Nicolson, Harold George
Tennyson; aspects of his life, character and poetry. . . London, Constable, 1923. ix,308p
(Rev by H. Warren in 19th Cent 94: 507-19 O '23; noted in T L S Mr 15 '23 p182; G. Thomas in Lond Q R 140: 45-55 Jl '23; L. Binyon in Bookm (Lond) 64:23-4 Ap '23)

Nisbet, (Mrs) Charles Richard
Tennyson and Browning compared. . . Charlotte, N. C. The Author, 1928. 2d ed 40p

Nitchie, Elizabeth
Vergil and the English poets. . . [Tennyson and the Victorians] New York, Columbia univ. press, 1919. p224-33 Diss. Columbia univ.

Noel, Roden Berkeley Wriothesley
The death of Tennyson; poem. 19th Cent 32:835-6 N '92

The poetry of Tennyson. Contemp 47: 202-24 F '85; *same*. Liv Age 164:771-84 Mr 28 '85; *same*. Ecl M 104:459-73 Ap '85; *same in* Essays on poetry and poets. London, Kegan Paul, Trench, 1886. p223-55

A **note** on Tennyson. Bookm (Lond) 3: 44-5 N '92

[**Note** on a Tennyson "plagiarism"] Lit 8:328 Ap 27 '01

[**Note** on Tennyson's "Locksley Hall"] Critic (NY) 10:31 Ja 15 '87

Notes on Mr. Tennyson's "Queen Mary." Macmil 32:434-41 S '75

Novelties in poetry and criticism. Fraser ns 5:588-96 My '72

Noyes, Alfred
Tennyson. Edinburgh, Blackwood, 1932. 61p

Tennyson and some recent critics. *In* Some aspects of modern poetry. London, Hodder & Stoughton, 1924. p133-76

Nutt, Alfred
Studies on the legend of the Holy Grail. London, Nutt, 1888

Oakley, J. H. I.
Tennyson's "Charge of the Six Hundred." Notes & Q 4th ser 10:479 D 14 '72

Oates, John
The teaching of Tennyson. London, Stock [1894] x,260p
(Rev in Literary World (Lond) ns 52: 344 N 1 '95; Literary World (Lond) ns 59:250 Mr 17 '99)

O'Connor, T. P.
[Tennyson] T. P.'s Weekly 12:811 D 18 '08

Tennyson in Iceland. T. P.'s Weekly 23:545-6 My 1 '14

O'Connor, V. C. Scott
Tennyson and his friends at Freshwater. Cent 33:240-68 D '97

O'Connor, W. A.
Tennyson's Palace of art. *In* Essays on literature and ethics. Manchester, 1889. p25-56

O'Hagan, Thomas
A study of Tennyson's "Princess." *In* Essays; literary, critical and historical. Toronto, Briggs, 1909. p9-42

Tennyson's "In Memoriam." *In* Studies in poetry, critical, analytical, interpretative. Boston, Marlier, Callanan, 1900. p1-23

Oliphant, Margaret O. W.
Alfred Tennyson; poem. Spec 69:528 O 15 '92; *same*. Liv Age 195:450 N 19 '92

Alfred Tennyson, 1809-92. *In* The Victorian age of English literature. New York, Tait [c1892] vol I p203-18

Oliver, Egbert
Tennyson's ontology. Masters essay, Univ. of Washington, 1929. 46ff

Olivero, Federico
La leggenda di Ulisse nel Tennyson e in alcuni poeti irlandesi. *In* Studi sur poeti e prosatori inglesi. Torino, Bocca, 1925. p212-32

Sulla lirica di Alfred Tennyson. Bari, Laterza, 1915. 148p bibl p147-8

Omond, T. S.
"These lame hexameters." T L S Jl 29, Ag 26 '20 p488, 552

On the early poetry of Alfred Tennyson. Notes & Q 3d ser 9:111-13 F 10 '66

One of Tennyson's poems. Boston Review 1:436-45 S '61

The **ornithology** of Tennyson. Spec 85: 203-4 Ag 18 '00; *same*. Liv Age 226: 836-9 S 29 '00

Orr, Guss
The influence of the romantic poets on Tennyson. Masters essay, Louisiana State univ. 1933. 83ff

Orsini, G. N. Giordano
see Giordano-Orsini, G. N.

Ortensi, Ulisse
Letterati contemporanei: Alfred Tennyson. Emporium 11:360-73 My '00

Osborne, E. A.
Tennyson's "Holy Grail." T L S Ag 25 '32 p596

Osborne, W. F.
Tennyson's "Idylls of the king." Masters essay, Univ. of Toronto, 1901

Osgood, Lucian Austin
Spiritual mysticism in the poetry of Tennyson. Masters essay, Univ. of South Dakota, 1922. 193ff

Osmond, Percy Herbert
Tennyson. *In* The mystical poets of the English church. London, Society for Promoting Christian Knowledge, 1919. p305-10

Our debt to Tennyson. Spec 103:230-1 Ag 14 '09

Owen, Cecil
"Memmian naphtha-pits" in Tennyson: medicinal mummies. Notes & Q 11th ser 10:176-7 Ag 29 '14

Tennyson and Goldsmith: a parallel. Notes & Q 11th ser 12:140 Ag 21 '15

Owens, Oscar Lee
Alfred Tennyson poet-prophet of the nineteenth century. Masters essay, George Washington univ. 1908. 27ff

Page, H. A. [pseud]
see Japp, Alexander Hay

Paget, R. H.
Frederic Harrison as a critic of Tennyson. Dial 31:355 N 15 '01

Paget, Walter and Dicksee, Herbert
Tennyson pictures. London, Nister, 1890. 12p
[Contains criticisms of poems illustrated]

Pain, Barry
The poets at tea. II. Tennyson, who took it hot. *In* Playthings and parodies. New York, Cassell [c1892] p225

Palgrave, Francis Turner
In pace; poem. 19th Cent 32:837-9 N '92

The landscape of Alfred Lord Tennyson. *In* Landscape in poetry from Homer to Tennyson... London, Macmillan, 1897. p279-97

[Visit to Portugal with Tennyson] Under the Crown nos 1-2 '59

Pallen, Condé Bénoist
A meaning of the "Idylls of the King." Cath World 41:43-54 Ap '85

The meaning of the Idylls of the King; an essay in interpretation. New York, American book [1904] 115p

Pallis, Elisabeth Hude
Tennysons og Swinburnes Arthurdigte. Edda 15:44-74 '21

Palmer, George Herbert
Alfred Tennyson. *In* Formative types in English poetry. (The Earl lecture for 1917) Boston, Houghton, Mifflin, 1918. p223-69

Palmer, J. Foster
Tennysoniana. Notes & Q 11th ser 2: 394 N 12 '10

Palmer, J. Luttrell
Tennyson's "Dora." Notes & Q 12th ser 3:475 N '17

Pancoast, Henry Spackman
Tennyson and his time. Bookn 27:813-17 Jl '09

Parker, Orpha M.
The spirit of chivalry in the poems of Tennyson and William Morris. Masters essay, Univ. of Colorado, 1911. 92ff

Parkin, George R.
Tennyson. Canadian Magazine 10:167-72 D '97

Parnell, John
Death of Tennyson; poem. London, 1893. 1 leaf

Parrish, Anne Catherine
Aspects of love in Tennyson and Browning. Masters essay, Tulane univ. 1929. 71ff

Parsons, Eugene
Introduction. *In* The poetical works of Alfred Lord Tennyson. New York, Crowell [c1900] p iii-xv

A literary biography. Chautauquan 26: 641-4 Mr '98

Mistakes about Tennyson. Dial 13:270 N 1 '92

Tennyson. Examiner (NY) F '90

Tennyson's art and genius. Baptist Quarterly Review 11:29-47 Ja '89

Tennyson's life and poetry: and mistakes concerning Tennyson. [Chicago, Craig press, 1892] 32p
(Noted in Critic (NY) 20:351 Je 25 '92)

Tennyson's quotableness. Chautauquan 13:334-7 Je '91

Tennyson's women. Chautauquan 23: 621-6 Ag '96

Pascal, Felicien
La maison natale d'Alfred Tennyson. Ann Pol et Litt 87:255 S 5 '26

Passage in Tennyson. Notes & Q 4th ser 2:510 N 28 '68; 1st ser 3:10-11 Ja 4 '51

Paterson, Arthur
The homes of Tennyson. Painted by Helen Allingham, described by A. Paterson. London, Black, 1905. x,98p (Rev in Spec 96:648 Ap 28 '06)

Paul, Herbert Woodfield
The classical poems of Tennyson. *In* Men and letters. London, Lane, 1901. p1-26; *also in* 19th Cent 33:436-53 Mr '93; *same.* Liv Age 197:407-18 My 13 '93

Is literature dying? Contemp 91:472-3 Ap '07

Tennyson. New Review 7:513-32 N '92; *same.* Liv Age 195:713-18 D 17 '92

Payne, Frederic Taylor
Essays on Sir Philip Sidney and Alfred Tennyson. London, Hazell, 1879. 72p

Payne, Jamie Jackson
Tennyson's treatment of nature. Masters essay, Tulane univ. 1926. 43ff

Payne, William Morton
Alfred Tennyson. *In* The greater English poets of the nineteenth century. New York, Holt, 1907. p221-50
In Memoriam. *In* Little leaders. Chicago, McClurg, 1902

Peacock, Edward
"Aylmer's Field" and John's Brand. Notes & Q 6th ser 2:314 O 16 '80

Peacock, Florence
The Tennysons. Bookm (Lond) 3:49-50 N '92

Peake, Leslie Sillman
Tennyson and faith. Lond Q R 157:182-9 Ap '32

Tennyson and the search for immortality. Sat R 153:192, 216-17, 266 F 20, 27, Mr 12 '32

Pearce, Helen
The criticism of Tennyson's poetry: a summary with special emphasis upon Tennyson's response to criticism as a factor in the development of his reputation. Diss. Univ. of California, 1930. v,272ff

Pearce, Maresco
The "In Memoriam" stanza. Reader 1:531 My 30 '63

Pearson, Charles William
Character and work of Tennyson. *In* Literary and biographical essays. Boston, Sherman, French, 1908. p131-47

Peck, Harry Thurston
Human side of Tennyson. *In* What is good English and other essays. New York, Dodd, Mead, 1899. p169-94; *also in* Bookm (NY) 29:600-9 Ag '09
The lyrics of Tennyson. *In* Studies in several literatures. New York, Dodd, Mead, 1909. p67-78

Peiper, Raymond Aloysius
Tennyson's Becket and the Becket of history. Masters essay, Catholic univ. 1930

Perry, Henry Ten Eyek
The Tennyson tragedy. Southwest Review 12:97-112 Ja '27

Personal Tennyson. Bookm (NY) 34:588-90 F '12

Personalia. Critic (NY) 21:289 N 26 '92

Petermann, Herta
Tennysons kunsttheoretische urteile. Diss. Würzburg, 1921. 119p

Phases of sorrow in Tennyson. Victoria Magazine 20:422-38 Mr '73

Phelps, William Lyon
Lancelot and that forward hussy Elaine as seen by "Godey's." Scrib M 95:434-5 '34

Tennyson's silence. [Baltimore, 1914] 1p; *same.* Mod Lang N 29:126-7 Ap '14

Phillips, Charles
Catholic note in Tennyson. American Catholic Quarterly Review 41:559-71 O '16

Phillips, T. M.
Colour in George Meredith and other modern English poets. Papers of the Manchester Literary Club 44:193-5 '18
Nature in modern English poetry. Manch Q 37:268-9 O '18

Phillips, W.
Tennyson and Oliver Cromwell. Notes & Q 5th ser 11:338 Ap 26 '79

Picton, J. A.
Dante and Tennyson: parallel passages. Notes & Q 5th ser 1:142-3 F 21 '74
"In Memoriam." Notes & Q 6th ser 5:404-5 My 27 '82
"Locksley Hall." Notes & Q 5th ser 4:349-50 O 30 '75
Tennyson: "All the swine were sows." Notes & Q 4th ser 11:345-6 Ap 26 '73

Pierpoint, Robert
Tennyson and opium. Notes & Q 12th ser 5:36-7 F '19

Pilon, E.
Sites et personnages. Paris, Grasset, 1912; *same.* Echo de Paris Ag 6 '09

Pinchbeck, W. H.
Tennyson queries. Notes & Q 12th ser 8:337 Ap 23 '21

Platner, John Winthrop
Tennysoniana. Nation (NY) 73:245 S 26 '01

Plaut, Julius
Das poetische genus personifizierter substantiva bei Alfred Lord Tennyson. Heidelberg, Winter, 1913. x,128p Diss. Kiel

Poe, Edgar Allan
Marginalia. United States Magazine & Democratic Review ns 15:580 D '44

The **poems** of Alfred, Lord Tennyson. Munsey's Magazine 39:435-8 Je '08

The **poet** Laureate. Once a Week 26:343-8 Ap 13 '72; Art J 36:27-8 '74

The **poet** Laureate and the knights of the round table. Notes & Q 5th ser 12: 244, 371-2 S 27, N 8 '79

The **poet** Laureate as philosopher and peer. To-Day 1:135-47 F '84

Poet of vision. Out 92:831-3 Ag 7 '09

Poet who knew and believed. Out 100: 388-9 F 24 '12

A **poetical** heartbreak. New Englander 53: 126-42, 276-83 Ag, S '90

The **poetry** of Alfred Tennyson. Chambers's Edinburgh Journal ns 4:25-9 Jl 12 '45

The **poetry** of Tennyson. Quar R 176:1-39 Ja '93

Pollock, Walter Herries
The Laureateship. National Observer 13:233-4 Ja 12 '95

[Portraits] Leisure Hour 12:121 '63; Bookn 27:818 Jl '09; Harper M 68:20 D '83; Bookn 11:ff 60 N '92; Cosmopolitan 14:169-78 D '92; Acad 51:429 Ap 17 '97; Illustrated London News 101:473, 509 O 15, 22 '92; Mag Art 20:205 '97; Scrib M 6:242 Ag '89; Scholastic 25:7 S 22 '34; Cent ns 41:642 Mr '02; Critic (NY) 38:234 Mr '01; Bookm (Lond) 77:facing 9 O '29; Critic (NY) 49:230 S '06; Book B ns 15:435, 439 D '97; Bookm (NY) 7:108-9 Ap '98; Bookm (NY) 34:475 Ja '12; Vanity Fair 6:26 Jl 22 '71; Bookm (NY) 29:381 Je '09; Art J 36:ff 27 '74; R of Rs (NY) 5:38 Ja '92; Critic (NY) 21:207 O 15 '92; Bookm (Lond) 37:1, 2, 13, 15, 18-21, 23, 24, 27, 29-34, fac 36 O '09; Bookm (NY) 2:467 F '96; Bookm (NY) 6: 186 N '97; Bookm (NY) 15:555 Ag '02; Appleton J 7:353 Mr 30 '72; Engl Illus 17:489 Jl '97; Bookm (Lond) 79:169 D '30; Bookm (Lond) 23 supp:8 D '02; Daheim 29:102-4 N 19 '92; Illustrirte Zeitung 99:440 O 15 '92; Bookm (Lond) 19:fac 90 D '00; Bookm (Lond) 21:176 F '02; Pall Mall Budget 40:1190, 1465, 1468, 1472, 1517, 1524, 1559 Ag 11, O 6, 13, 20 '92

Postma, J.
Tennyson as seen by his parodists. . . New York, Stechert, 1926. 199p bibl p198-9
(Rev by R. B. McK[errow] in Rev E S 3:490 O '27)

Poteat, Mary
Tennyson and the historical drama. Masters essay, Columbia univ. 1927

Potts, R. A.
Tennysoniana: Cleopatra. Notes & Q 10th ser 9:194 Mr 7 '08

Potwin, L. S.
The prologue to "In Memoriam," and certain commentaries. Western Reserve University Bulletin 6:13-19 My '03

Powell, Thomas
Alfred Tennyson. *In* The living authors of England. New York, Appleton, 1849. p36-60

Powles, Allen H.
Tennyson's rhymes. Spec 119:446 O 27 '17

Price, Thomas R.
What after Lord Tennyson? Ind 44: 1542-3 N 3 '92

Price, Walter
Days with the English poets: Tennyson, Browning, Byron. London, Hodder & Stoughton, 1911

Price, Warwick James
Tennyson's friendships. Sewanee R 19: 228-34 Ap '11

Tennyson's love story. Bookn 27:823-5 Jl '09

Prideaux, W. F.
FitzGerald's song in Tennyson's "Memoir." Notes & Q 10th ser 2:285 O 8 '04

Lord Tennyson and Mr. Churton Collins. Notes & Q 8th ser 2:170-1 Ag 27 '92

Tennyson's house, Twickenham. Notes & Q 10th ser 2:324 O 22 '04

The **Princess.** A sketch explanatory of Lord Tennyson's poems. [London, W. Rider, pref 1885]

Priolo, Paolo
Illustrations of Alfred Tennyson's Idylls of the King. . . London, 1863

A **proposed** Tennyson memorial. Dial 16: 342 Je 1 '94

Punch's fancy portraits.—No. 76. Alfred the Great. Punch 82:142 Mr 25 '82

Purton, H. B.
Tennyson. Notes & Q 5th ser 2:335 O 24 '74

Pyre, James Francis Augustine
The formation of Tennyson's style. . . (Univ. of Wisconsin studies in language and literature 12) Madison, Wis. Univ. of Wisconsin, 1920. 252p
(Rev by R. LeGallienne in N Y Times O 9 '21 p9; T L S N 17 '21 p748; H. Straus in Nation (NY) 114:23 Ja 4 '22)

The **"Quarterly Review"** on Mr. Tennyson's "Maud." Macmil 1:114-15 D '59

Quayle, William Alfred
The greater English elegies. *In* The poet's poet and other essays. Cincinnati, Curts & Jennings, 1897. p124-38

Recovered yesterdays. *In* Recovered yesterdays in literature. New York, Abingdon press, 1916. p186-203

Tennyson's men. *In* Recovered yesterdays in literature. New York, Abingdon press, 1916. p88-144

"Queen Mary." Notes & Q 5th ser 4:232-3 S 18 '75; Unsere Zeit 2:632-6 '75

Queries on Tennyson. Notes & Q 1st ser
3:493 Je 21 '51

Quesnel, Léo
La poésie au XIXe siècle en angleterre.
Le Correspondant 110:802-10 Mr 10 '78

The **question** of the Laureateship. Bookm
(Lond) 3:52-5 N '92

Quiller-Couch, (Sir) Arthur
On a proposed birthday-book. Speaker
7:720-1 Je 24 '93

Tennyson in 1833. *In* The poet as citizen, and other papers. New York,
Macmillan, 1935. p161-73

Titania; by Lord T—n; poem. *In* Green
bays; verses and parodies. London,
Oxford univ. press, 1930. new ed
p[1]-2

Rader, William
The elegy of faith; a study of Tenny-
son's In Memoriam. New York,
Crowell, 1902. 56p

Radford, G. H.
King Arthur. *In* Shylock and others:
eight studies. London, Unwin, 1894.
p153-76

Ragey, Le R. P.
Tennyson. Paris, Delhomme et Briguet,
1899. 409p

Rainy day with Tennyson and our poets.
Dublin University Magazine 55:62-5 Ja
'60

Raleigh, Walter S.
The poet Laureate and the Queen's English. Notes & Q 5th ser 4:148 Ag 21
'75

Ramage, C. T.
The Duke of Wellington. Notes & Q
4th ser 11:342 Ap 26 '73

Ode on the Death of the Duke of Wellington. Notes & Q 4th ser 12:95 Ag
2 '73

Ramsdell, Grace Richard
Philosophical implications in Tennyson's
"In Memoriam." Masters essay, Bos-
ton univ. 1933

Ramsey, Julia Emma
A twentieth century estimate of Tennyson. Masters essay, Duke univ. 1935.
98ff

Rances, Maurice
Through English literature . . . with
brief literary sketches. . . Paris,
Hachette, 1907

Ratzka, K.
Tennyson's landbesitz Farringford.
Daheim no 50 '24

Rawnsley, Hardwicke Drummond
In Memoriam. Lady Tennyson; poem.
Acad 50:130 Ag 22 '96

The Laureate dead; poem. Acad 42:335
O 15 '92; *same.* Lit W 23:476 D 17 '92;
same. Liv Age 195:706 D 17 '92

Leaving Aldworth; poem. Blackw 152:
768 N '92

Lincolnshire scenery and character as
illustrated by Mr. Tennyson. Macmil
29:140-4 D '73; *same.* Every Sat 16:13-
15 Ja 3 '74

Memories of the Tennysons. Glasgow,
MacLehose, 1900. xvi,252p
(Rev in Nation (NY) 72:75-6 Ja 24
'01; Sat R 91:112-13 Ja 26 '01; Lit 7:
461 D 8 '00; Literary World (Lond)
ns 62:433 N 30 '00; Acad 59:439-40 N
10 '00)

Tennyson. *In* Valete: Tennyson and
other memorial poems. Glasgow,
MacLehose, 1893. p1-35
(Rev in Speaker 8:444 O 21 '93)

Tennyson a south country man? Spec
92:639 Ap 23 '04

To Lord Tennyson; on his eightieth
birthday, August 6th, 1889; poem.
Macmil 60:293 Ag '89

Virgil and Tennyson. Macmil 33:43-9 N
'75; *same.* Liv Age 127:756-62 D 18
'75

Rawnsley, Willingham Franklin
Personal recollections of Tennyson.
19th Cent 97:1-9, 190-6 Ja, F '25

Tennyson centenary. *In* Introduction to
the poets. London, Routledge, 1912.
p243-313

Tennyson, 1809-1909; a lecture. . . Amble-
side, Middleton, 1909. 50p

Raybould, W.
Notes on Tennyson's Coming and Pass-
ing of Arthur. (Normal tutorial ser)
London, Simpkin, Marshall, Hamilton,
Kent, 1907

Read, William A.
Some traces of Keats' influence upon the
language of Tennyson. Engl Stud 26:
326-7 '99

Reade, Willoughby
Notes on the Arthurian epic and the
Idylls of the King. Alexandria, Va.
Bell's Potomac press, 1908. 31p

Reardon, Timothy Henry
Alfred Tennyson, poet Laureate. *In*
Petrarch and other essays. San Francisco, Doxey, 1897. p43-96; *same.* Overland Monthly 2d ser 1:17-33 Ja '83

Recent criticism on Tennyson. Temple 13:
354-62 F '65

Redden, Meta Augusta
Nature in Tennyson. Masters essay,
Columbia univ. 1920

Redgrave, M.
Tennyson in 1929. Cambridge Review
O 18 '29 p30-1

Reed, Henry
Elegiac poetry. *In* Lectures on English
literature, from Chaucer to Tennyson.
Philadelphia, Lippincott, 1860. p323-36

Rees, R. Wilkins
"Crossing the bar." Acad 59:497 N 24
'00

Reid, Forrest
The Moxon Tennyson. *In* Illustrators of the sixties. London, Faber and Gwyer [1928] p36-43

Reid, John
Tennyson in relation to his age. Kent Prize, Amherst college, 1896. 44ff Typed Ms. in the Amherst college library

Reid, (Sir) Thomas Wemyss
The life, letters, and friendships of Richard Monckton Milnes. London, Cassell, 1890. 2 vols passim
(Rev in Literary World (Lond) ns 42: 467-9 D 5 '90)

Religious aspects of Mr. Tennyson's poetry. Dublin University Magazine 55:353-6 Mr '60; *same*. Ecl M 50:52-6 My '60

Rendall, Vernon
A Tennyson puzzle? Sat R 153:175 F 13 '32

Wild flowers in literature. London, Scholartis press, 1934

Reputations reconsidered. III. Lord Tennyson. Acad 53:34-6 Ja 8 '98

Reynolds, Helen M.
Tennyson in class. Educa 13:359-64 F '93

Reynolds, Llywarch
"Locksley Hall." Notes & Q 6th ser 1: 326 Ap 17 '80

Rhys, Ernest
Lyric poetry. London, Dent, 1913. p326-33

Rhys, John
Studies in the Arthurian legend. Oxford, Clarendon press, 1891

Rice, Jessie Folsom
... The influence of Frederick Dennison [sic] Maurice on Tennyson. . . [Chicago] 1913. ii, 35f Diss. Univ. of Chicago

Rice, William North
The poet of science. *In* The poet of science and other addresses. New York, Abingdon press [c1919] p11-45

Richardson, Charles Francis
Book of beginnings [Enoch Arden] Nation (NY) 91:520-1 D 1 '10

Richardson, D. L.
Criticism of the day and Tennyson. *In* Literary recreations. London, Thacker, 1852. p291-305

Richardson, Robert K.
The idea of progress in "Locksley Hall." Wisconsin Academy of science, arts and letters. Transactions 28:341-61 '33

Rickert, Edith
Tennyson: a generation after. Bookn 27:819-21 Jl '09

Riddle, Bernice Sims
The dramas of Tennyson. Masters essay, State univ. of Iowa, 1925. 137ff

Rideing, William H.
Tennyson in the Isle of Wight. No Am 165:701-10 D '97

Ridley, Edwin
Genius of Tennyson. Westm 172:511-14 N '09

Riggs, Sparta Elizabeth
A study of mediaevalism in Tennyson's "Idylls of the King." Masters essay, Univ. of Texas, 1934. 141ff

The **Right** Hon. Lord Tennyson, D. C. L., F. R. S. Tinsley's 43:580-4 O '89

Riley, James Whitcomb
Tennyson: England, Oct. 5, 1892; poem. Critic (NY) 21:211 O 15 '92

Ritchie, Anne Isabella Thackeray
Alfred Tennyson. Harper M 68:21-41 D '83

Alfred Tennyson. *In* Records of Tennyson, Ruskin, Browning. New York, Harper, 1892. p3-60
(Rev in Critic (NY) 21:337 D 17 '92; Dial 13:339-42 D 1 '92; Sat R 74:545-6 N 5 '92; National Observer 8:539-40 O 8 '92; Literary World (Lond) ns 46: 299-300 O 21 '92; Speaker 6:447-8 O 8 '92)

Reminiscences. *In* Cameron, J. M. Alfred, Lord Tennyson and his friends. . . London, Unwin, 1893. p9-16

Robb, Juliet Everts
Arthur, Guinevere and Lancelot—an open letter to Miss Julia Magruder. No Am 180:918-26 Je '05 [see ibid. p375-80 Mr '05]

Roberts, Robert
Recollections of Tennyson. Bookm (Lond) 3:46-9 N '92

Robertson, Frederick William
Analysis of Mr. Tennyson's "In Memoriam." London, Smith, Elder, 1862. x,45p

Lectures and addresses. London, Smith, Elder, 1858. p124-41

Robertson, John Mackinnon
The art of Tennyson. *In* Essays toward a critical method. London, Unwin, 1889. p233-82

Browning and Tennyson as teachers. . . London, 1903

De mortuis. Tennyson. *In* Criticisms. London, Bonner, 1903. vol II p209-19

Robinson, A. Mary F.
Alfred Tennyson. Unsere Zeit ns 15: 81-94 Ja 15 '79

Robinson, Edna Moore
Tennyson's use of the Bible. Baltimore, Johns Hopkins press, 1917. v-ix,110p
(Noted in Ath 1:310 Je '17)

Rodriguez, Francesco
Lord Tennyson. Alcuni suoi scritti minori. Nuova Antol 112:318-40 Jl 16 '90

Studi e saggi: Lord Tennyson; Henry W. Longfellow; William Cowper. Roma, Forzani, 1891

Rogers, Arthur
An apocryphal Tennyson poem. T L S
Ap 3 '30 p298

Rogers, John
Tennyson and Leigh Hunt. Acad 67:
166-7 S 3 '04

Rolfe, William James
Biographical sketch. *In* The poetic and
dramatic works of Alfred Lord Tennyson. (Cambridge ed.) Boston, Houghton, Mifflin [c1898] p xi-xvii

The Christmases of "In Memoriam."
Poet Lore 13:151-3 '01

The metre of "In Memoriam." Dial 23:
7 Jl 1 '97

Misquotation, Shakespearian and other.
Lit W 15:233-4 Jl 12 '84

More Tennyson trifles. Critic (NY) 6:
301-2 Je 27 '85

The new and the old "Locksley Hall."
Critic (NY) 10:19 Ja 8 '87

Notes on Tennyson's "In Memoriam."
Poet Lore 7:428-35 '95

An old poem of Tennyson's. Critic
(NY) 10:2 Ja 1 '87

A recent visit to Tennyson. Critic (NY)
21:285-6 N 26 '92

Tennyson's annotations to "In Memoriam." Critic (NY) 48:453-5 My
'06

Tennyson's revisions of his poems. Nation (NY) 88:460-1 My 6 '09

Variations in Tennyson. Dial 30:327-9
My 16 '01

Roman Catholic poets [with summary]
Temple 27:170-86, 28:33-48 S, D '69

Róna, Éva
"The princess"; Tennyson és a nökérdés.
. . Irta Róna Éva. Budapest, 1929.
79p Diss. Budapest

Roscoe, William Caldwell
Tennyson. *In* Poems and essays of W.
C. Roscoe, ed. by R. H. Hutton. London, Chapman and Hall, 1860. vol II
p1-37

Rossetti, Dante Gabriel
The brothers; poem. *In* A century of
parody and imitation, ed. by Walter
Jerrold and R. M. Leonard. London,
Oxford univ. press, 1913. p290-1

MacCracken; poem. *In* A century of
parody and imitation, ed. by Walter
Jerrold and R. M. Leonard. London,
Oxford univ. press, 1913. p290

Rossetti, William Michael
Some reminiscences. London, Brown
Langham, 1906. vol I p247-59
(Rev in Bookm (Lond) 31:156 D '06)

The **"Round Table"** Tennyson. Critic
(NY) 24:38 Ja 20 '94

Roy, Eulah Josephine
Tennyson as a dramatist. Masters essay,
Univ. of Nebraska, 1929. 120ff

Roz, Firmin
Un poète national de l'Angleterre. Alfred
Lord Tennyson. R Deux Mondes 52:
809-43 Ag '09

Tennyson. Paris, Bloud, 1911. 230p

Ruhrmann, Friedrich G.
Tennyson. *In* Studien zur geschichte
und charakteristik des refrains in der
englischen literatur. Heidelberg,
Winter, 1927. p98-109

Rupprecht, Johann Georg
Tennyson naturschilderungen. . . Leipzig-
Reudnitz, Schmidt, 1893. 74p Diss.
Leipzig

Ruskin on the ancient and the modern
poets. Fraser 53:648-59 Je '56

Russell, George William Erskine
A group of poets. . . *In* Portraits of the
seventies. New York, Scribner, 1916.
p285-6
(Rev in Bookm (NY) 44:237 N '16)

Russell, John
Tennyson and the Ettrick Shepherd.
Notes & Q 5th ser 12:384 N 15 '79

Saeger, Mina Merritt
Man and the infinite in Tennyson's
poetry. Masters essay, Univ. of South
Dakota, 1926. 23ff

Saintsbury, George Edward Bateman
English and French poetry. *In* The
later nineteenth century. Edinburgh,
Blackwood, 1907. p1-12

Tennyson. *In* Corrected impressions,
essays on Victorian writers. New
York, Dodd, 1895. p21-40

Tennyson. *In* A history of nineteenth
century literature. New York, Macmillan, 1910. p253-68

Tennyson and Browning. *In* A history
of English prosody from the twelfth
century to the present day. London,
Macmillan, 1910. vol III p183-217

Tennyson and Browning. *In* A short
history of English literature. New
York, Macmillan, 1907. p727-33

The **sale** of Lord Tennyson's birthplace.
Pall Mall Budget 40:1268 Ag 25 '92

Salmon, Arthur L.
With Coleridge and Tennyson at Cleve-
don. Ecl M 145:512-18 N '05; *same.*
Temple 132:153-62 Ag '05

Salt, Henry Stephens
Tennyson as a thinker. Time 23:1055-66
O '90; *same published*: London, Reeves,
1893. iv,49p

The Tennysonian philosophy. *In* Literary sketches. London, Swan, Sonnenschein, Lowrey, 1888. p39-58; *same.*
To-Day 1:135-47 F '84

Sandys, J. Edwin
Tennyson's "Gareth and Lynette." Notes
& Q 4th ser 11:44-5 Ja 11 '73

Sangster, Margaret E.
Tennyson; poem. Critic (NY) 21:256 N
5 '92

Sargeaunt, John
"These lame hexameters." T L S Jl 22, Ag 19 '20 p472, 536

Sarrazin, Gabriel
Alfred Tennyson. In La renaissance de la poésie anglaise 1798-1889. Paris, Perrin, 1889. p149-98

Savage, W. H.
Tennyson's religion. Arena 9:582-92 Ap '94

Scaife, Christopher Henry Oldham
Poetry of Alfred Tennyson; an essay in appreciation. London, Cobden-Sanderson, 1930. 96p
(Rev by E. Lewis in Lond Merc 23: 387-8 F '31; T L S O 9 '30 p803; T. E. Welby in W E R O 4 '30 p457-8)

Schäfer, Bernhard
Englische gedichte in metrischer übertragung. Lünen a. d. Lippe, 1908. Progymnasium

Scharf, Lewis
Alfred Tennyson. In Literary impressions. Ascherslehen, Schlegel, 1881. Diss. Leipzig. p25-36

Schelling, Felix Emmanuel
The Victorian lyrists. In The English lyric. Boston, Houghton, Mifflin, 1913. p193-202, 220-2

Scherer, Edmond
Alfred Tennyson. Le Temps Ja 11 '70
Wordsworth et la poésie moderne de l'Angleterre. In Études sur la littérature contemporaine. Paris, Levy, 1882. 7th ser

Schladebach, Kurt
Tennysons und Wildenbruchs Harold-dramen. Studien zur Vergleichenden Litteraturgeschichte 2:215-28 '02

Schmerler, Heinrich Emil
Tennyson as a dramatic poet. (XVI. Programm des städtischen realgymnasiums zu Borna. . . Programm no 523) In Chips from English literature. Borna, Noske, 1889. 1st part 22p

Schmidt, Rudolf
Et digt af Tennyson. [Enoch Arden] For Ide og Virkelighed 2:544-64 '71

Schneider, Fritz
Tennyson und Keats. Eine untersuchung des einflusses von Keats auf Tennyson (mit Berücks. von Shelley) Weimer, Wagern, 1916. viii,110p Diss. Münster

Schrumpf, G. A.
An unacknowledged poem of Tennyson. . . Notes & Q 4th ser 4:345 O 23 '69

Schuman, A. T.
A ballade of poets; poem. Dial 19:25 Jl 1 '95

Scott, J. Loughran
Memoir of Alfred Lord Tennyson. In The works of Alfred Lord Tennyson. (Aldworth ed) Philadelphia, McKay [c1901] vol I p xiii-lxiv

Scott, Mabel Lavinia
The lyrics in the "Idylls of the King." Masters essay, George Washington univ. 1914. 37ff

Scott, Nellie Mahaffay
Poetic treatment of the Arthurian legend since 1850. Masters essay, Univ. of Oklahoma, 1929. 214ff

Scott, Walter B. jr.
Tennyson and his age, 1850-1875. Doctor's essay, Princeton univ. 1934

Scribner, Anne Nyhan
Illustrations of Tennyson from Greek poetry. Masters essay, Univ. of Wisconsin, 1900. 90ff

Scudder, Vida Dutton
Tennyson and "In Memoriam." In The life of the spirit in the modern English poets. Boston, Houghton, Mifflin, 1899. p281-90

Seaman, (Sir) Owen
Ars postera. In The battle of the bays. New York, Lane, 1896. p58-60 [parody of "Lady Clara Vere de Vere"]

Seccombe, Thomas
The poets Laureate of England. Bookm (NY) 15:554 Ag '02
A word about Tennyson. Readers' Review 2:125 S '09

Sélincourt, Ernest de
English poetry since 1815. In English poets and the national ideal. London, Oxford univ. press, 1915. p99-105

Selkirk, J. P. [pseud]
see Brown, James Bucham

Sencourt, Robert
The mutiny in England—Ruskin and Tennyson. In India in English literature. London, Simpkin, Marshall, Hamilton, Kent [pref. 1923] p441-8

Shairp, John Campbell
Tennyson. In Aspects of poetry. Boston, Houghton, Mifflin, 1891

Shakespeare, Charles
Tennyson's "Despair." Modern Review 3:462-73 Jl '82

Shanks, Edward Buxton
The return of Tennyson. In Second essays on literature. London, Collins [c1927] p163-76

Sharp, Amy
Alfred Tennyson. In Victorian poets. London, Methuen, 1891. p1-39
(Rev in Speaker 4:206-7 Ag 15 '91)

Sharp, Elizabeth A.
Introduction. In English idyls: The princess: and other poems by Alfred Lord Tennyson (Canterbury poets) London, Scott [nd] p vii-xxviii

Sharp, Robert Farquharson
Tennyson. In Architects of English literature. New York, Dutton, 1900. p314-26

Shaw, William J.
Forward forever: a response to Lord Tennyson's "Locksley Hall sixty years after," "Heaven on earth," etc. New York, Fowler & Wells, 1888. 34p

Shaylor, Joseph
Lord Tennyson. *In* Some favorite books and their authors. London, Richards, 1901. p257-9

Sheed, Maisie (Ward)
Wilfrid Ward and Tennyson. Commonweal 21:87-8 N 16 '34; *see also* Earls, M.

Shelton, Celia Dexter
The mediaeval element in Tennyson's poetry. Masters essay, Univ. of Washington, 1908. 28ff

Shepard, William [pseud]
see Walsh, William Shepard

Shepherd, Henry Elliott
A commentary upon Tennyson's In Memoriam. . . New York, Neale publishing co. 1908. 135p

Some phases of Tennyson's In Memoriam. P M L A 6:41-51 '91

A study of Tennyson's English. Mod Lang N 5:193-206 Ap '90

Tennyson's "In Memoriam." Sewanee R 1:402-9 Ag '93

Shepherd, Richard Herne
The genesis of "In Memoriam." Walford's Antiquarian Magazine 11:407-12 '87

The genesis of Tennyson's "Maud." No Am 139:356-61 O '84

Sherman, Eva May
A comparative study of the treatment of the Arthurian legend by Alfred Tennyson and by Edwin Arlington Robinson. Masters essay, Boston univ. 1932

Shewan, A.
Repetition in Homer and Tennyson. Classical Weekly 16:153-8, 162-6 Ap 2, 9 '23

Shields, Charles W.
The Arctic monument named for Tennyson by Dr. Kane. Cent 34:483-92 Ag '98

Shindler, Robert
Tennyson, Arnold and Clough. *In* On certain aspects of recent English literature (Neuphilologische Vorträge und Abhandlung. II) Leipzig, Teubner, 1902. p17-28

Shipman, Mary Evelyn
The didactic element in the poetry of Tennyson. Diss. Boston univ. 1932

Shoemaker, W. L.
To the detractors of Tennyson. Lit W 14:194 Je 16 '83

To the poet Laureate of England; poem. Lit W 10:363 N 8 '79

Shorey, Paul
A word with Tennyson dissenters. Dial 14:102-3 F 16 '93

Shorter, Clement King
Tennyson. Glasgow, Mackenzie [1888] 3p [from National Encyclopedia]

Victorian literature. New York, Dodd, Mead, 1897. p10-13

Shorthouse, Joseph Henry
The "Morte d'Arthur" and the "Idylls of the King." *In* Literary remains of J. H. Shorthouse, ed. by his wife. London, Macmillan, 1905. vol II p107-22

Sidey, Thomas K.
Some unnoted Latinisms in Tennyson. Mod Lang N 35:245-6 Ap '20

Sidgwick, Arthur
Tennyson. London, Sidgwick & Jackson, 1909. 34p

Siebold, Erika von
Tennyson: synästhesien in der englischen dichtung der 19. jahrhunderts. Engl Stud 53:269-79 '19-'20

Silvestri-Falconieri, Francesco di
Lord Tennyson. Roma, Roma Letteraria, 1911. 40p

Simcox, George Augustus
In memoriam—Lord Tennyson; poem. Bookm (Lond) 3:43-4 N '92

Simpson, William
Tennyson's "Princess." Notes & Q 2d ser 12:129 Ag 17 '61

Singer, S. W.
The "bar" of Michael Angelo. Notes & Q 1st ser 2:166 Ag 10 '50

Sinnett, Alfred Percy
The occultism in Tennyson's poetry. 19th Cent 83:582-91 Mr '18

Tennyson, an occultist, as his writings prove. . . London, Theosophical Pub. House, 1920. 89p

Sir Tray: an Arthurian idyl [a parody of Tennyson] Blackw 113:120-4 Ja '73

Skeat, Walter William
"All the swine were sows." Notes & Q 4th ser 11:346 Ap 26 '73

Grig. Notes & Q 3d ser 10:516 D 29 '66

"Locksley Hall." Notes & Q 5th ser 12:471 D 13 '79

Skewes, Alice Ruth
A study of metaphor and simile in Tennyson's poetry. Masters essay, Univ. of California, 1924. 71ff

Slicer, Thomas Roberts
Tennyson, the interpreter of legend and life. *In* From poet to premier. London, Grolier society, 1909. p159-91

Sloan, Rollin Post
Didacticism in the art of Tennyson. Masters essay, Univ. of Texas, 1931. 223ff

Smalley, George W.
Tennyson. *In* Studies of men. New York, Harper, 1895. p66-85

Smedley, Menella B.
"The victim." Notes & Q 4th ser 2:307 S 26 '68

Smith, Arnold
Tennyson. *In* The main tendencies of Victorian poetry. . . London, Simpkin, Marshall, Hamilton, Kent, 1907. p59-104

Smith, Byron Caldwell
A young scholar's letters, being a memoir of Byron Caldwell Smith, ed. by D. O. Kellogg. London, Putnam, 1897. p48-52

Smith, C. Alphonso
The metre of "In Memoriam." Dial 22: 351-2 Je 16 '97

Smith, Elizabeth Mina
The "Idylls of the King": studies in plot-structure and characterization. Masters essay, Univ. of Texas, 1927. 153ff

Smith, Frellsen Fletcher
The dramas of Tennyson. Masters essay, Univ. of Texas, 1930. 193ff

Smith, George
On three contemporary poets. Bentley's Miscellany 64:61-9 Jl '68

Smith, H[enry] L[awson]
Tennyson; his relation to romanticism with special reference to his political views. Masters essay, McGill univ. 1926. 31ff

Smith, Jean Pauline
The aesthetic nature of Tennyson. New York, White, 1920. 62p bibl p61-2
The appeal of the senses in Tennyson. Masters essay, Stanford univ. 1919. 49ff

Smith, Jephson Huband
Notes and marginalia, illustrative of the public life and works of Alfred Tennyson, poet-Laureate. London, Blackwood [1873] xx,202p
(Rev in Ath 2:393-4 S 27 '73)

Smith, Martha Maud
Woman in Tennyson. Masters essay, Univ. of Texas, 1901. 112ff

Smith, N. R.
Tennyson's trilogy on "The Making of England." Masters essay, Univ. of Nebraska, 1914. 54ff

Smyser, William Emery
Romanticism in Tennyson and his pre-Raphaelite illustrators. No Am 192: 504-15 O '10
Tennyson. Cincinnati, Eaton & Mains, 1907. 207p

Sneath, Elias Hershey
The mind of Tennyson; his thoughts on God, freedom, and immortality. Westminster, Constable, 1900. x,193p
(Rev in Literary World (Lond) ns 62: 253-4 O 12 '00)

Snell, Frederick John
Alfred Tennyson. *In* Boys who became famous. London, Harrap, 1914. p132-42

Societies [British Academy celebration of Tennyson's centenary] Ath 2:561-2 N 6 '09

Some nineteenth century reviews. Acad 77:301 Jl 10 '09

Some poets of the Victorian era. V.-Tennyson. Acad 79:173-5, 198-200 Ag 20, 27 '10

Song-writers. Dublin University Magazine 61:601-3 My '63

Souvenir of Becket by Alfred, Lord Tennyson. First presented at the Lyceum Theatre 6th Feb. 1893 by Henry Irving. London, "Black and White," 1893. [5]p [12] plates

Span, Reginald B.
Tennyson as a mystic. Westm 180:43-9 Jl '13

Spangenberg, Alice
Tennyson's attitude toward science. Masters essay, Boston univ. 1925

Sparke, Archibald
Tennyson's "The Captain." Notes & Q 147:236 S 27 '24

Sparrow, John
Tennyson and Thomson's shorter poems. Lond Merc 21:428-9 Mr '30

Sparvel-Bayly, J. A.
Tennyson and Oliver Cromwell. Notes & Q 5th ser 11:58-9 Ja 18 '79

Spedding, James
Tennyson's poems. *In* Reviews and discussions. London, Paul, 1879. p277-99

Spence, R. M.
"In Memoriam." Notes & Q 5th ser 8: 514 D 29 '77
"In Memoriam," LIV. Notes & Q 9th ser 1:18, 292 Ja 1, Ap 9 '98
Tennyson's "The Ancient Sage." Notes & Q 9th ser 3:248 Ap 1 '99

Spence, Walter
Idylls of the King, a spiritual interpretation. New York, Cochrane, 1909. 113p

Spender, Harold
Real Tennyson. Liv Age 248:696-8 Mr 17 '06
Tennyson: a study in poetic workmanship. Fortn ns 62:778-83 N '97
"The **spiteful** letter." Notes & Q 9th ser 3:317 Ap 22 '99

Spurgeon, Caroline Frances Eleanor
Mysticism in English poetry. Quar R 207:453-5 O '07
Philosophical mystics. *In* Mysticism in English literature. Cambridge, Univ. press, 1913. p84-8

[Squire, (Sir) John Collings] Solomon Eagle [pseud]
If Lord Byron had written "The Passing of Arthur." *In* Tricks of the trade. New York, Putnam, 1917. p72-9
Mr. H. G. Wells and Lord Tennyson. *In* Books in general. New York, Knopf, 1920. 2d ser p238-43

Stanley, Hiram M.
A closing word on Tennyson. Dial 14: 136 Mr 1 '93
Tennyson's place in poetry. Dial 14:72 F 1 '93

Tennyson's rank as a poet. *In* Essays on literary art. London, Swan Sonnenschein, 1897. p13-24

Starnes, De Witt Talmadge
The influence of Carlyle upon Tennyson. Texas Review 6:316-36 Jl '21

Stead, William T.
Genius and theology of Tennyson. Our Day 11:19-36 Ja '93

Tennyson the man: a character sketch. R of Rs (NY) 6:557-70 D '92

Stedman, Edmund Clarence
Alfred Tennyson. Scribner's Monthly 8: 100-7, 160-70 My, Je '74

Alfred Tennyson. *In* Victorian poets. Boston, Houghton, Mifflin, 1896. p150-200
(Rev in International Review 3:248-9 Ap '76)

The nature and elements of poetry. Boston, Houghton, Mifflin, 1892. p68-70

Tennyson and Theocritus. *In* Victorian poets. Boston, Houghton, Mifflin, 1896. p201-33; *same.* Atlan 28:513-26 N '71

Stedman, Laura and Gould, George M.
Life and letters of Edmund Clarence Stedman. New York, Moffat, Yard, 1910. 2 vols passim

Steffen, Paul
Die alliteration bei Tennyson. Kiel, Fiencke, 1905. viii,83p Diss. Kiel

Steigler, G.
Qui remplacera Tennyson? Echo de Paris O 18 '92

Stenberg, Theodore T.
A word on the sources of "The Charge of the Light Brigade." Mod Lang N 38:248-50 Ap '23

Stephanove, Constantine Demeter
The great Victorian—Tennyson and his poetry. (Annuaire de l'Université de Sofia: Faculté historico-philologique. Tome XXI. 6)

Stephen, Leslie
Life of Tennyson. *In* Studies of a biographer. New York, Putnam, 1898. vol II p196-240

Stephenson, Nathaniel Wright
One aspect of the "Idylls of the King." Harv Mo 11:187-91 F '91

Sterne, Ernest Staveley
In memory of Alfred, Lord Tennyson, the English Theocritus. London, Sterne [1892?] 1p

Stevenson, Lionel
Alfred Tennyson. *In* Darwin among the poets. Chicago, Univ. of Chicago press [c1932] p55-116

Stevenson, Morley
Spiritual teaching of Tennyson's "In Memoriam"; six Lenten addresses. London, Gardner, Darton, 1904. 114p

Stewart, Allegra
A comparison of Lowell and Tennyson. Masters essay, Columbia univ. 1923

Stewart, George
Alfred Tennyson. Cosmopolitan 14:169-78 D '92

Essays from reviews. Quebec, 1893. vol II p9-41

Stirling, James Hutchinson
Alfred Tennyson. *In* Jerrold, Tennyson and Macaulay, with other critical essays. Edinburgh, Edmonston & Douglas, 1868. p51-111

Stirling, Maria E. A.
Tennyson and Browning: a defense of the ideal. Canadian Magazine 40:294-7 Ja '13

Stitt, E. F. R.
Love and duty in Tennyson and Browning. Poet Lore 4:271-4 '92

Stockley, William Frederick Paul
"Faith" of "In Memoriam." Cath World 120:801-9 Mr '25

In Memoriam. Queen's Q 18:259-72 Ap-Je '11

Stockwell, Nina
Notes on Tennyson's Passing of Arthur. (Normal tutorial ser) London, Simpkin, Marshall, Hamilton, Kent, 1904

Stoddard, Richard Henry
Alfred Tennyson. National Magazine 9: 408-15 N '56; Appleton J 7:353-6 Mr 30 '72

The poetry of Lord Tennyson. Ind 44: 1469-70 O 20 '92

A study of Tennyson. No Am 133:82-107 Jl '81

Stone, John Morris
A missing page from the "Idylls of the King." *In* Studies from court and cloister. . . London, Sands, 1905; *same.* Dublin Review 103:259-74 O '88

Stone, Samuel John
Home aspect of Mr. Tennyson's poems. Leisure Hour 25:54-6 '76

Stork, Charles Wharton
Heine and Tennyson: an essay in comparative criticism. *In* Haverford essays; studies in modern literature. Haverford, Pa. 1909. p153-82

Strachan, L. R. M.
"Memmian Naphtha-pits" in Tennyson. Notes & Q 11th ser 9:67 Ja 24 '14

Tennyson portraits by Watts. Notes & Q 153:356 N 12 '27

"Titmarsh" in an alleged poem by Tennyson. Notes & Q 9:487 Je 20 '14

Strachey, Edward
Talk at a country house. Atlan 72:607-17 N '93

Straede, [Karl]
Tennyson's "Lucretius." Erklärung des gedichtes. Verhältnis zu dem lateinischen lehrgedicht, "de rerum natura" des Lucretius. Schlawe, Moldenhauer, 1905

Strong, Augustus Hopkins
Tennyson. *In* The great poets and their
theology. Philadelphia, Griffith &
Rowland press [c1897] p449-524
(Rev in Citizen (Philadelphia) 4:156
Ag '98)

Studies in Alfred Tennyson. Belgravia 4:
217-23 D '67

A **study** of Tennyson. Every Sat 9:90 F
5 '70

A **study** of Tennyson's "Locksley Hall"
and "Sixty Years After." Poet Lore
5:34-9 '93

Suddard, S. J. Mary
Essais de littérature anglaise. London,
Cambridge univ. press, 1912

Sundstrom, Esther Victoria
Pronouns of address in the "Idylls of the
King." Masters essay, Stanford univ.
1914. 168ff

Sutherland, Allan
"Sunset and evening star." Delineator
66:1081-3 D '05

Swanwick, Anna
Lord Tennyson. *In* Poets the interpreters of their age. London, Bell,
1892. p380-7

Sweeney, Helen M.
Tennyson and Holmes: a parallel. Cath
World 60:521-34 Ja '95

Swift, William H.
Tennyson in the twentieth century.
Search Quarterly 3:341-3 Ap '33

Swinburne, Algernon Charles
Dethroning Tennyson. 19th Cent 23:
127-9 Ja '88

Disgust: a dramatic monologue. Fortn
36:715-17 D '81 [a parody of Tennyson's "Despair"]

[Tennyson] *In* Under the microscope.
London, White, 1872. p36-45 [A cri-
ticism of Tennyson's treatment of the
Arthurian legend]

Tennyson and Musset. Fortn 35:129-53
F 1 '81; *same.* Ecl M 96:600-16 My '81;
also in Miscellanies. London, Chatto
& Windus, 1886. p219-59

Tennyson or Darwin? *In* Studies in
prose and poetry. London, Chatto &
Windus, 1894. p141-5

Threnody; Alfred, Lord Tennyson,
October 6, 1892. 19th Cent 33:1-3 Ja
'93; *same.* Ecl M 120:249-50 F '93

Swinburniana. T. P.'s Weekly 2:890 D 11
'03

Symonds, John Addington
Recollections of Lord Tennyson. Cent
46:32-7 My '93

Tabb, John B.
Alfred Tennyson; poem. Ind 44:1509 O
27 '92; *same.* Critic (NY) 21:256 N 5
'92

To Lord Tennyson; poem. Acad 40:115
Ag 8 '91

Table talk. Literary World (Lond) ns 46:
285-6 O 14 '92

Taine, Hippolyte Adolphe
Tennyson. *In* History of English literature. New York, Colonial press [c1900]
rev ed vol III p410-38

Tennyson. I. Son talent. II. Son oeuvre.
III. Son public. J Débats Ap 3, 4, 6 '61

Tainsh, Edward Campbell
A study of the works of Alfred Tenny-
son, D.C.L., poet Laureate. London,
Chapman and Hall, 1868. 256p
(Rev by E. Dowden in Fortn 9:582-4
My '68; Westm 140:345 S '93; A.
Waugh in Acad 44:106 Ag 5 '93; Critic
(NY) 23:270 O 28 '93; Lond Q R 31:
134-6 O '68; Sat R 25:521-2 Ap 18 '68;
same. Liv Age 97:814-16 Je 27 '68;
Spec 41:588-9 My 16 '68; *same.* Liv
Age 97:804-7 Je 27 '68)

Talbot, Ethel
Tennyson, or another? Acad 73:654 Jl 6
'07

A **tale** by Tennyson. Critic (NY) 28:81 F
1 '96

A **talk** about The Princess. American
Whig Review 8:28-39 Jl '48

Tallcott, Rollo Anson
Tennyson's fluxuations of doubt and
faith from 1820-1850. Masters essay,
Syracuse univ. 1920. 26p

Taylor, Achilles
Sermonettes from Tennyson. Birmingham, Leicester and Leamington, 1892.
68p

Taylor, Bayard
At home and abroad. New York, Putnam, 1860. p445-6

"Eustace Green." *In* The echo club,
and other literary diversions. Boston,
Osgood, 1876. p87-92

Tennyson. International Review 4:397-
418 My '77; *same in* Critical essays and
literary notes. New York, Putnam,
1880. p1-36

Taylor, (Sir) Henry
Correspondence of Henry Taylor, ed. by
Edward Dowden. London, Longmans,
Green, 1888. passim

Taylor, John
Tennyson and W. R. Spenser. Notes &
Q 3d ser 9:531 Je 30 '66

Taylor, Tom
The Laureate's bust at Trinity. *In* A
century of parody and imitation, ed. by
Walter Jerrold and R. M. Leonard.
London, Oxford univ. press, 1913. p266-
7

Taylor, W. V.
New lights on Tennyson. Sun M 23:344-
8 '94

Teeling, Bartle
A visit to the Tennysons in 1839.
Blackw 155:605-21 My '94; *same.* Ecl
M 123:79-92 Jl '94; *same.* Liv Age 201:
536-49 Je '94

Temple, Joseph
Tennyson and Bright. Lit 3:141 Ag 13
'98

Tennyson, Alfred
Alfred, Lord Tennyson and William
Kirby, unpublished correspondence to
which are added some letters from
Hallam, Lord Tennyson. Ed. by L. A.
Pierce. Toronto, Ontario, Macmillan,
1929. 71p

Aylmer's field
(Rev by A. Renaud in Revue Contemporaine 84:265-84 Ja '66; Archiv 47:
321-2 '70)

Ballads and other poems. London,
Kegan Paul, 1880. vi,184p
(Rev in Lit W 11:463 D 18 '80; S.
Colvin in Macmil 43:738-48 Ja '81;
Edin R 154:486-515 O '81; W. H.
Mallock *in* Atheism and the value of
life. London, Bentley, 1884. p83-146;
C. Placci in La Rassegna Nazionale
Mr '81 p524-34; G. Saintsbury in Acad
18:397-8 D 4 '80; Spec 53:1624-6 D 18
'80; Sat R 50:708-9 D 4 '80; Dial 1:
191-2 Ja '81; E. Nencioni in Fanfulla
Della Domenica Ap 10 '81; Brit Q 73:
218-19 Ja '81; G. P. Lathrop in Atlan
47:425-7 Mr '81; Harper M 62:633 Mr
'81; Scribner's Monthly 21:639-41 F
'81; G. B. Smith in International Review 10:178-83 F '81; Congregationalist
10:53-60 Ja '81)

Becket. London, Macmillan, 1884. viii,
213p
(Rev by J. W. Mackail in Acad 26:
421-2 D 27 '84; Lit W 16:39 F 7 '85;
Sat R 58:757-8 D 13 '84; Ath 1:7-9
Ja 3 '85; Blackw 138:57-66 Jl '85; Ecl
M 105:418-25 S '85; Macmil 51:287-94
F '85; Lond Q R 65:243-7 Ja '86;
Critic (NY) 6:14 Ja 10 '85; Spec 57:
1699-1700 D 20 '84; Westm ns 67:
581-2 Ap '85; G. E. Woodberry in
Atlan 55:565-6 Ap '85; Speaker 7:157-
8 F 11 '93; R. H. Stoddard in Book
B ns 2:10 F '85; M. F. Egan in Cath
World 42:382-95 D '85)

The cup and the falcon. London, Macmillan, 1884. iv,146p
(Rev by E. D. A. Morshead in Acad
25:160-1 Mr 8 '84; Ath 1:319-21 Mr 8
'84; Appleton J 25:253-6 Mr '81; Spec
57:316-17 Mr 8 '84; G. P. Lathrop in
Atlan 54:117-18 Jl '84)

Daphne
(Rev in Sat R 72:312-13 S 12 '91)

The day dream
(Rev in Lit W 16:433-4 N 28 '85)

The death of Oenone, Akbar's dream,
and other poems. London, Macmillan,
1892. vi,111p
(Rev in Ath 2:695-7 N 19 '92; L.
Johnson in Acad 42:403-5 N 5 '92;
Sat R 74:536-7 N 5 '92; Poet Lore
4:640-3 '92; Church Q R 35:485-506
Ja '93; Gent M 273:641-2 D '92; Lit
W 23:401-2 N 19 '92; E. Teza in Regia

Accademia di scienze, lettere, ed
arti in Padova. Atti e memorie ns 24:
33-49 '07-'08; G. P. Lathrop in American Catholic Quarterly Review 18:101-
21 Ja '93; Ecl M 119:853-4 D '92;
Critic (NY) 21:245 N 5 '92; National
Observer 8:660-1 N 12 '92; Literary
World (Lond) ns 46:347-8 N 4 '92;
W. M. Payne in Dial 13:344-6 D 1 '92;
Ind 44:1598 N 10 '92; Pall Mall Budget
40:1642 N 3 '92)

Demeter and other poems. London,
Macmillan, 1889. iv,175p
(Rev in Blackw 147:137-40 Ja '90;
Lond Q R 74:86-95 Ap '90; Spec 63:
883-4 D 21 '89; Ath 2:883-5 D 28 '89;
H. B. Garrod in Acad 36:413-14 D 28
'89; C. Porter in Poet Lore 2:201-7 '90;
Church Q R 35:485-506 Ja '93; W. R.
Thayer in American (Philadelphia) 19:
273-5 Ja 18 '90; Lit W 21:19-20 Ja
18 '90; Critic (NY) 16:13 Ja 11 '90;
G. E. Woodberry in Atlan 65:421-3
Mr '90; Ind 42:188 F 6 '90; Scots
Observer 3:127-8 D 21 '89; W. M.
Payne in Dial 10:280-1 F '90; Deutsche
Rundschau 62:477 '90)

The devil and the lady, ed. by Charles
Tennyson, his grandson. New York,
Macmillan, 1930. v-xi,67p
(Rev by St. J. Adcock in Bookm
(Lond) 77:336-7 Mr '30)

The early poems of Alfred Lord Tennyson, ed. with a critical introduction,
commentaries and notes, together with
the various readings, a transcript of
the poems temporarily and finally suppressed and a bibliography, by J. C.
Collins. London, Methuen, 1900. xlvi,
317p
(Rev by A. E. Jack in Dial 30:192-3 Mr
16 '01; Lit W 6:420-1 Je 2 '00; J. C.
Collins in Critic (NY) 37:508-10 D
'00; Spec 84:895-6 Je 30 '00; Spec 86:
26-7 Ja 5 '01; Ath 1:747-8 Je 16 '00;
Sat R 90:174-5 Ag 11 '00; Literary
World (Lond) ns 61:580-1 Je 22 '00;
Speaker ns 2:359-60 Je 30 '00; Bookm
(Lond) 18:122 Jl '00)

Elaine
(Rev in Spec 40:18 Ja 5 '67)

Enoch Arden. London, Moxon, 1864.
iv,178p
(Rev in Reader 4:187-8 Ag 13 '64;
E. Montégut in R Deux Mondes Mr
15 '66 p423-42; A. Renaud in Revue
Contemporaine 49:265-84 '66; Quar R
119:58-80 Ja '66; St J 11:224-38 '64;
Chamb J 41:620-2 S 24 '64; Westm
82:186-94 O '64; Lond Q R 23:153-69
O '64; Blackw 96:555-72 N '64; Atlan
14:518-20 O '64; Ath 2:201-2 Ag 13 '64;
Spec 37:991-2 Ag 27 '64; National
Review ns 1:27-67 N '64; *same.*
Liv Age 84:3-24 Ja 7 '65; *same.* Ecl M
64:273-84, 415-27 Mr, Ap '65; G. W.
Curtis in Harper M 29:675-6 O
'64; No Brit 41:231-52 Je '64; *same.*
Liv Age 83:163-74 O 22 '64; *same.* Ecl

Tennyson, Alfred—*Continued*

M 63:319-21 N '64; Literary World (Lond) ns 44:216 S 18 '91; Atlan 14: 518-20 O '64; J. R. Lowell in No Am 99:626 O '64; E. M. Thomas in Book B ns 4:401-3 D '87; Archiv 47:321-2 '70; A. Vermorel in Nouvelle Revue de Paris S '64; Liv Age 82:579-87 S 24 '64; A. Hamann in Archiv 76:338 '86; Dublin University Magazine 64:386-96 O '64; Brit Q 40:463-90 O '64; *same.* (translated) Bibliothèque Universelle et Revue Suisse ns 22:540-62 '65; 23: 107-28 '65)

Fairy Lilian
(Rev in Lit W 19:413 N 24 '88)

The Foresters; Robin Hood and Maid Marian. London, Macmillan, 1892. viii,155p
(Rev in Church Q R 35:485-506 Ja '93; W. Watson in Acad 41:341-2 Ap 9 '92; Lit W 23:141 Ap 23 '92; Ath 1:491-3 Ap 16 '92; Critic (NY) 20:186-7 Mr 26 '92; Ind 44:592 Ap 28 '92; National Observer 7:540 Ap 9 '92; W. M. Payne in Dial 13:51 Je '92; Book B ns 9:174-5 My '92; Literary World (Lond) ns 45:331-2 Ap 8 '92; Sat R 73:391-2 Ap 2 '92)

Gareth and Lynette. . . London, Strahan, 1872. vi,136p
(Rev by W. H. Browne in So M 12: 106-13 Ja '73; Nation (NY) 15:301-2 N 7 '72; Chamb J 49:813-16 D 21 '72; Lond Q R 39:394-405 Ja '73; Victoria Magazine 20:308-13 F '73; G. A. Simcox in Acad 3:423-4 N 15 '72; Westm 99:153-4 Ja '73; Spec 45:1363-5 O 26 '72; Ath 2:521-4 O 26 '72; Sat R 34:568-9 N 2 '72; Fortn 18:757-8 D '72; Blackw 112:760-5 D '72; Atlan 30: 747-8 D '72; Scribner's Monthly 5:397-8 Ja '73)

Harold. A drama. London, King, 1877 [1876] x,161p
(Rev by J. Weiss in Radical Magazine 1:158-65 My '77; Lit W 7:133-4 F '77; Nation (NY) 24:43-4 Ja 18 '77; F. Birrell in Nation (Lond) 43:45 Ap 14 '28; R. Jennings in Spec 140:563-4 Ap 14 '28; A. G. Macdonell in Lond Merc 18:87-8 My '28; Edin R 145:383-415 Ap '77; J. A. Symonds in Acad 11: 1-2 Ja 6 '77; Brit Q 65:267-8 Ap '77; Spec 49:1610-12 D 23 '76; Ath 2:882-4 D 30 '76; Sat R 43:21-3 Ja 6 '77; Penn Monthly 8:321-5 Ap '77; Westm ns 51:587-8 Ap '77; W. D. Howells in Atlan 39:242-3 F '77; International Review 4:282-3 Ap '77; Harper M 54:769-70 Ap '77; Scribner's Monthly 13:718-19 Mr '77; J. H. Ward in No Am 124: 157-9 Ja '77)

The Holy Grail, and other poems. London, Strahan, 1870 [1869] vi,222p
(Rev in Victoria Magazine 14:376-83 F '70; H. Alford in Contemp 13:104-25 Ja '70; Brit Q 51:200-14 Ap '70; Liv Age 106:131-50 '70; Edin R 131:502-39 Ap

'70; Lond Q R 34:154-86 Ap '70; Dublin Review 66:418-29 Ap '70; Ecl M 74: 339-44 Mr '70; Nation (NY) 10:109-10 F 17 '70; Quar R 128:1-17 Ja '70; New Englander 29:351-7 Ap '70; Chamb J 47:137-40 F 26 '70; St J ns 4:785-814 Ap '70; H. Lawrenny in Acad 1:91-4 Ja 8 '70; Ath 2:809-10 D 18 '69; Spec 42:1530-3 D 25 '69; *same.* New Ecl 6: 236-44 F '70; W. D. Howells in Atlan 25:249-50 F '70; New Englander 29: 351-7 Ap '70)

Idylls of the King. London, Moxon, 1859. viii,261p
(Rev in New Quarterly Review 8:336-51 Jl '59; J. Milsand in Le Magasin de Librairie 12:321-50 '60; Irish Quarterly Review 9:834-59 O '59; Liv Age 106:131-50 '70; Edin R 131:502-39 Ap '70; Lond Q R 34:154-86 Ap '70; E. Montegut in R Deux Mondes N 15 '59 p472-96; Meliora 2:225-48 '60; H. Alford in Contemp 13:104-25 Ja '70; G. B. Bacon in New Englander 18:1-42 F '60; Quar R 106:454-85 O '59; Ecl M 48:247-55 O '59; Blackw 86:608-27 N '59; No Brit 31:148-74 Ag '59; Fraser 60:301-14 S '59; Nat R 9:368-94 O '59; Liv Age 63:579-93 D 3 '59; Chamb J 32:121-4 Ag 20 '59; De Bow's Review 28:679-89 Je '60; Lond Q R 13:62-80 O '59; Ecl M 49:28-37 Ja '60; Eclectic Review 110:287-94 S '59; Spec 46:177-8 F 8 '73; Sat R 8:75-6 Jl 16 '59; Dublin University Magazine 55:62-5 Ja '60; National Magazine (Lond) 6:169-74 '69; C. C. Everett in No Am 90:1-21 Ja '60; C. Patmore in Edin R 110:247-63 Jl '59; J. Nichol in Westm 72:503-26 O '59; Tait's Edinburgh Magazine ns 26:464-70 Ag '59; Spec 100:1030-1 Je 27 '08; C. C. Smith in No Am 89: 554-5 O '59; Lond Q R 85:76-95 O '95; National Review 9:368-94 O '59; *same.* Liv Age 63:579-93 D 3 '59; W. Lee in New Rugbeian S '59 p267-71; Constitutional Press S '59)

Illustrated edition of Tennyson
(Rev in Sat R 3:601-2 Je 27 '57)

In Memoriam. London, Moxon, 1850. viii,210p
(Rev in Liv Age 26:167-71 Jl 27 '50; No Brit 13:532-55 Ag '50; Prospective Review 6:306-31 '50; Eclectic Review 92:330-41 S '50; Brit Q 12:291-2 Ag '50; Brownson's Quarterly Review ns 4:540-1 O '50; American Whig Review 13:534-8 Je '51; Southern Literary Messenger 16:686-91 N '50; Quar R 158:162-83 Jl '84; Ecl M 21:209-19 O '50; Westm 54:85-103 O '50; New Englander 8:598-615 N '50; Spec 90: 414-15 Mr 14 '03; Liv Age 248:496-9 F 24 '06; Spec 96:21-2 Ja 6 '06; Milsand, J. Littérature anglaise et philosophie. Dijon, Lamarche, 1893. p13-38; *same.* Mercure Fr Jl 15 '51; Acad 63:656 D 13 '02; United States Magazine and Democratic Review ns 27:204-7 S '50; Edin R 102:498-519 O '55; Every Sat

9:76 Ja 29 '70; G. Massey in Hogg's Instructor 5:1-14 Jl '55; *same*. Ecl M 36:616-28 S '55; Meliora 2:225-48 '60; L. Étienne in Revue Contemporaine 6: 205-30 '53; New Englander 53:492-4 N '90; T L S D 22 '05 p453-4; International Weekly Miscellany 1:34-5 Jl 8 '50; Sat R 95:489-90 Ap 18 '03; Harper M 1:570 S '50; Ind 49:1623 D 9 '97; Archiv 16:324-8 '54; Liv Age 26: 167-71 Jl 27 '50; Christian Examiner 49:289-90 S '50; Deutsche Rundschau 101:195 '99; J. Milsand in R Deux Mondes 21 année 11:345-66 Jl '51; C. Kingsley in Fraser 42:245-55 S '50; Tait's Edinburgh Magazine ns 17:499-505 Ag '50; Literary World (Lond) ns 67:245 Mr 13 '03; National Observer 10:381-2 Ag 26 '93; Literary World (Lond) ns 63:522 My 31 '01; Dublin University Magazine 36:213-14 Ag '50; Sharpe's London Magazine 12:119-21 '50; Putnam's Magazine 6:382-92 O '55)

Lady Clare
(Rev in Lit W 15:441 D 13 '84)

The lady of Shalott
(Rev in Lit W 12:477-8 D 17 '81)

The last tournament. London, Strahan, 1871. 54p
(Rev in Cath World 15:241-54 My '72; W. H. Browne in So M 10:371-7 Mr '72; T. H. L. Leary in Gent M 232: 423-30 Ap '72; Nation (NY) 13:418-19 D 28 '71; Congregationalist 1:718-26 D '72; Sat R 32:754-5 D 9 '71; W. D. Howells in Atlan 29:236-7 F '72; Scribner's Monthly 3:508-9 F '72)

[Letter to the Tennyson Society of Philadelphia dated Sept. 9, 1869] Notes & Q 4th ser 4:378 O 30 '69

Letters to Frederick Tennyson, ed. by H. J. Schonfield. London, Hogarth, 1930. 146p
(Rev in T L S O 16 '30 p831)

Locksley Hall and other poems
(Rev in Congregational Review 1:97-105 F '87; Hogg's Instructor ns 6:273-5 '51)

Locksley Hall sixty years after. . . London, Macmillan, 1886. viii,201p
(Rev in Critic (NY) 10:74 F 12 '87; Sat R 62:842-3 D 25 '86; Spec 59:1750-1 D 25 '86; J. Royce in Harv Mo 3: 127-37 Ja '87; H. C. Beeching in Acad 31:1-2 Ja 1 '87; J. Royce *in* Studies of good and evil. New York, Appleton, 1898. p76-88; T. R. Bacon in New Englander 46:155-67 F '87; Blackw 141:129-31 Ja '87; Ath 1:31-3 Ja 1 '87; New Princeton Review 3:265-71 Mr '87; G. E. Woodberry in Atlan 59:705-7 My '87; W. M. Payne in Dial 7:246-8 F '87; Westm 128:131-2 Ap '87; Nation (NY) 44:298 Ap 7 '87; Lit W 18:25 Ja 22 '87; Church Review 49:283-9 Mr '87; To-Day 7:93-5 Mr '87)

The lover's tale. London, Kegan Paul, 1879. 95p
(Rev in Congregationalist 8:672-81 Ag '79; Fraser 100:110-16 Jl '79; Spec 52: 790-1 Je 21 '79; Ath 1:723-5 Je 7 '79; E. Gosse in Acad 15:489 Je 7 '79; Harper M 59:629-30 S '79; Scribner's Monthly 18:628 Ag '79; Brit Q 70:133-4 Jl '79; Nation (NY) 29:30-1 Jl 10 '79; Westm ns 56:266-7 Jl '79; W. D. Howells in Atlan 44:268-9 Ag '79; Rose-Belford's Canadian Monthly & National Review 3:221-3 Ag '79)

Lucretius. Cambridge, Mass. Printed for private circulation, 1868. 27p
(Rev in Nation (NY) 6:352-3 Ap 30 '68; Lond Q R 31:249-54 O '68)

Lyrical poems. Selected and annotated by F. T. Palgrave. London, Macmillan, 1885
(Rev in Spec 58:1319-20 O 3 '85; Lit W 16:239 Jl 11 '85; Critic (NY) 7:51-2 Ag 1 '85)

Maud. London, Moxon, 1855. viii,154p
(Rev by A. Dudley in R Deux Mondes F 15 '56 p821-46; L. Hendrickson in National Quarterly Review 5:76-82 Je '62; Spec 69:325-7 S 3 '92; A. Renaud in Revue Contemporaine 35:476-504 '63; Putnam's Magazine 6:382-92 O '55; Meliora 2:225-48 '60; New Quarterly Review 4:393-7 O '55; Edin R 102:498-519 O '55; Blackw 78:311-21 S '55; *same*. Liv Age 47:51-9 O 6 '55; Fraser 52:264-73 S '55; Westm 64:596-601 O '55; Eclectic Review 102:568-75 N '55; Liv Age 46:654-61 S 15 '55; Brit Q 22:467-98 O '55; Lond Q R 5: 213-29 Ja '56; Ath 2:893-5 Ag 4 '55; Bentley's Magazine 38:262-5 '55; E. E. Hale in No Am 81:544-6 O '55; National Review 1:377-410 O '55; Dublin University Magazine 46:332-40 S '55)

Morte d'Arthur
(Rev in Liv Age 106:131-50 '70; Edin R 131:502-39 Ap '70)

Northern farmer
(Rev by J. M. Ludlow in Macmil 10: 486-9 O '64; noted by D. Asher in Archiv 37:238 '65)

Ode on the death of the Duke of Wellington. London, Moxon, 1852. 16p
(Rev by L. Étienne in Revue Contemporaine 6:205-30 '53; Ath 2:1263 N 20 '52; *same*. Liv Age 36:62-3 Ja 8 '53; Liv Age 37:441-3 My 14 '53)

Poems. London, Moxon, 1832. 163p
[Known as 1833 ed. *Poems* were also issued in 1842, 1843, 1846, etc.]
(Rev in Tait's Edinburgh Magazine 9: 502-8 Ag '42; London Univ. Magazine D '42; Mrs. Kemble in United States Magazine & Democratic Review 14:62-77 Ja '44; New Quarterly Review 3: 207-9 Ja '44; A. Gabrielli in Nuova Antol 285:85-91 My 1 '19; Edin R 66: 108-10 O '37; Ath 1:770-2 D 1 1832; *in*

Tennyson, Alfred—*Continued*
Early English poets, ed. by J. L.
Haney. Philadelphia, Egerton press,
1904. p152-75; J. G. Lockhart in Quar
R 49:81-96 Ap 1833: J. Sterling in
Quar R 70:385-416 O '42; J. Spedding
in Edin R 77:373-91 Ap '43; Brit Q
72:141-50 O '80; *same.* Liv Age 147:
786-95 D 25 '80; J. S. Mill in London
Review 1:402-24 Jl 1835; Christian Re-
view 16:36-50 Ja '51; Potter's American
Monthly 16:111 F '81; Fraser 42:245-55
S '50; J. Sterling *in* Essays and tales.
London, Parker, 1848. vol I p422-62;
No Brit 9:43-72 My '48; No Brit 53:378-
425 Ja '71; *same.* Liv Age 109:195-220
Ap 22 '71; Brit Q 2:46-71 Ag '45; New
Englander 3:57-66 Ja '45; Westm ns 12:
590-2 O '57; Ecl M 6:205-17 O '45; Ecl
M 17:169-82 Je '49; Blackw 65:453-67 Ap
'49; J. S. Mill *in* Early essays. London,
Bell, 1897. p236-67; Westm 51:265-90
Jl '49; New Monthly Magazine and
Literary Journal 37:69-74 Ja 1833; G.
Massey in Hogg's Instructor 5:1-14 Jl
'55; *same.* Ecl M 36:616-28 S '55; Select
Journal 2:106-21 Jl 1833; Contemp 93:
sup 13-16 F '08; R. M. Milnes in Westm
38:371-90 O '42; Quar R 106:454-85 O
'59; Chamb J 4:25-8 Jl 12 '45; Edin R
172:301-16 O '90; Meliora 2:225-48 '60;
C. E. Havens in Pioneer 3:28-34 Ja '55;
Christian Remembrancer ns 4:42-58 Jl
'42; C. C. Felton in Christian Examiner
33:237-44 N '42; J. S. Dwight in Christian Examiner 23:305-27 Ja 1833;
Southern Literary Messenger 10:240-6
Ap '44; Southern Literary Messenger
19:649-58 N '53; L. Étienne in Revue
Contemporaine 6:205-30 '53; Examiner
My 28 '42 p340-1; Spec 56:355-7 Mr 17
'83; Putnam's Magazine 6:382-92 O '55)

Poems, chiefly lyrical. London, Wilson,
1830. 154p
(Rev *in* Haney, John Louis. Early
reviews of English poets. Philadelphia, Egerton press, 1904. p152-75;
Westm 14:210-24 Ja 1831; Blackw 31:
721-41 My 1832; E. Stevenson *in* Early
reviews of greater writers (1786-1832)
London, Scott [1890?] p303-25; J.
Wilson *in* Essays, critical and imaginative. Edinburgh, Blackwood, 1856.
vol II p109-52; *same.* Blackw 31:721-
41 My 1832; L. Hunt in Tatler F 24,
Mr 3 1831; A. H. Hallam in Englishman's Magazine Ag 1831; W. J. Fox in
Monthly Repository Ja 1833)

The poems of Alfred Tennyson, 1830-
1870, with an introduction by T. H.
Warren. London, Frowde, 1913
(Rev in Spec 110:316-17 F 22 '13)

Poetical works
(Rev in Cath World 15:241-54 My '72;
Lond Q R 34:151-86 Ap '70; Lit W
16:431 N 28 '85; T. Bayne in Notes &
Q 10th ser 7:197 Mr 9 '07; C. C.
Everett in No Am 90:1-21 Ja '60;

Harper M 40:610-11 Mr '70; G.
Sarrazin in Nouvelle Revue 55:812-38
D '88)

The Princess; a medley. London,
Moxon, 1847. iv,164p
(Rev in Ecl M 17:169-82 Je '49;
Blackw 65:453-67 Ap '49; G. Massey in
Ecl M 36:616-28 S '55; *same.* Hogg's
Instructor 5:1-14 Jl '55; No Brit 9:43-72
My '48; Quar R 82:427-53 Mr '48; Liv
Age 16:441-5 Mr 4 '48; Quar R 106:454-
85 O '59; Christian Remembrancer 17:
381-401 Ap '49; L. Étienne in Revue
Contemporaine 6:205-30 '53; Milsand,
J. *in* Littérature anglaise et philo-
sophie. Dijon, Lamarche, 1893. p13-
'38; *same.* Mercure Fr Jl 15 '51; Meliora
2:225-48 '60; J. Hadley in New England-
er 7:193-215 My '49; *same in* Hadley, J.
Essays, philological and critical. New
York, Holt & Williams, 1873. p296-
324; *in* Early review of English poets,
ed. by J. L. Haney. Philadelphia,
Egerton press, 1904. p176-86; Eclectic
Review ns 23:415-23 Ap '48; J. Milsand
in R Deux Mondes 21 année 11:345-66
Jl 15 '51; C. Kingsley in Fraser 42:245-
55 S '50; A. De Vere in Edin R 90:
388-409 O '49; Putnam's Magazine 6:
382-92 O '55; Nation (NY) 33:15-16
Jl 7 '81; Literary World (Lond) ns
63:157 F 15 '01; Harper M 68:156 D
'83; Liv Age 16:441-5 Mr 4 '48)

Queen Mary. A drama. London, King,
1875. viii,278p
(Rev in Brit Q 62:181-93 O '75; Quar
R 139:231-48 Jl '75; Ecl M 85:251 Ag
'75; Lit W 6:14-15 Je '75; Nation
(NY) 21:60-1 Jl 22 '75; H. James, Jr.
in Galaxy 20:393-402 S '75; J. O.
Hagan in Irish Monthly 4:572-87 '76;
Cath World 22:1-12 O '75; W. H.
Browne in So M 17:372-80 S '75;
Blackw 118:322-35 S '75; Macmil 32:
434-41 S '75; Edin R 145:383-415 Ap
'77; Christian Observer 74:761-4 O '75;
Southern Review ns 18:484-92 O '75;
A. Lang in Acad 7:649-50 Je 26 '75;
Ath 2:13-14 Jl 3 '75; Ath 1:845-8 Je 26
'75; Sat R 40:19-21 Jl 3 '75; Spec 48:
820-2 Je 26 '75; H. Adams in No Am
121:422-9 O '75; New Englander 34:
789-90 O '75; L. Boucher in R Deux
Mondes Ap 15 '76 p887-909; W. D.
Howells in Atlan 36:240-1 Ag '75;
Scribner's Monthly 10:644-5 S '75;
Harper M 51:598-9 S '75; International
Review 2:701-2 O '75; P. Fambri in
Nuova Antol 62:585-636 Ap 15 '82)

The return of Ulysses. A drama
(Rev by E. Teza in Regia Accademia
di scienze, lettere, ed arti in Padova.
Atti e memorie. ns 23:125-32 '06-'07;
H. W. Mabie in Out 92:741-5 Jl 24 '09)

Sea dreams
(Rev by A. Renaud in Revue Contemporaine 84:265-84 Ja '66)

Selections
(Rev in Ath 1:144 F 3 '00; Lit W 15: 371 N 1 '84)

Sonnet "Me mine own fate to lasting sorrow doometh." Notes & Q 8th ser 2:361 N 5 '92

The suppressed poems of Tennyson. Edited by J. C. Thomson
(Rev by J. V. Squire *in* Essays on poetry. London, Hodder and Stoughton [1923] p63-87; *same*. Lond Merc 2:443-55 Ag '20)

Timbuctoo: a poem which obtained the Chancellor's Medal at the Cambridge Commencement, 1829. Printed in "Prolusiones Academicae; 1829. Cantabrigiae: typis academicis excudit Joannes Smith." 13p
(Rev *in* Early reviews of English poets, ed. by J. L. Haney. Philadelphia, Egerton press, 1904. p151; L. Meissner in Archiv 29:347-50 '61; Ath 2:456 Jl 22 1829)

Tiresias and other poems. London, Macmillan, 1885. viii,204p
(Rev in Sat R 60:810-11 D 19 '85; Ath 2:831-4 D 26 '85; S. G. Green in Leisure Hour 35:99-101 '86; Spec 58: 1649-51 D 12 '85; Spec 58:1649-51 D 12 '85; T. H. Caine in Acad 28:403-5 D 19 '85; Critic (NY) ns 5:4-5 Ja 2 '86; Deutsche Rundschau 47:317 '86; G. E. Woodberry in Atlan 57:423-6 Mr '86; Dial 6:246-8 Ja '86; T. H. S. Escott in Fortn 45:270-2 F '86; Westm ns 69: 581-2 Ap '86; Edin R 163:466-98 Ap '86; Book B ns 3:27 F '86)

Two voices
(Rev by Mrs. C. R. Corson in New Englander 22:638-53 O '63)

Unpublished early poems. . . ed. by Charles Tennyson. London, Macmillan, 1931. v-xiv,84p [Appeared earlier in 19th Cent 109:367-80, 495-508, 625-36, 756-64 Mr-Je '31]
(1500 copies only)
(Rev in W E R 4:800-1 D 19 '31; H. I'A. Fausset in Bookm (Lond) 81:227 Ja '32; R. A. Scott-James in Sat R 153: 102-3 Ja 23 '32; T L S D 10 '31 p1001)

Vastness
(Rev in Spec 58:1466-7 N 7 '85)

The window: or, The songs of the wrens. Words written for music by A. Tennyson. The music by Arthur Sullivan. London, Strahan, 1871 [Dec. 1870] x,82p
(Rev in Spec 43:1586-7 D 31 '70; Ath 2:793-4 D 17 '70; H. R. Haweis in St P 7:473-87 F '71)

Works
(Rev in Acad 74:457-8 F 15 '08; Lit W 16:27 Ja 24 '85; Acad 85:744 D 13 '13; Liv Age 256:180-3 Ja 18 '08; Spec 68: 201-2 F 6 '92; E. Faguet in Quar R 210:305-28 Ap '09; Lond Q R 34:151-86 Ap '70; Church Q R 35:485-506 Ja

'93; Brit Q 62:181-93 O '75; J. C. Squire *in* Essays on poetry. London, Hodder and Stoughton [1923]; Sat R 65:637 My 26 '88; Sat R 105:109-10, 378 Ja 25, Mr 21 '08; Brit Q 55:139-40 Ja '72; Edin R 181:485-513 Ap '95; Spec 99:988-9 D 14 '07; Spec 111:760-1 N 8 '13; Cambridge Review 16:97 N 22 '94; Spec 100:749-50 My 9 '08; Spec 101:445-6 S 26 '08)

Tennyson, Alfred and Tennyson, Charles
Poems by two brothers. London, Simpkins, Marshall, 1827 [really issued in 1826] xii,228p
(Rev in Literary Chronicle & Weekly Review My 19 1827; National Observer 9:654-5 My 13 '93; noted in Critic (NY) 22:333-5 My 20 '93; Sat R 75: 516-17 My 13 '93)

Tennyson, Hallam
Alfred Lord Tennyson: a memoir. . . London, Macmillan, 1897. 2 vols xxii, 516p; vi,551p
(Rev by G. Valbert in R Deux Mondes D 1 '97 p671-82; J. E. Graham in Scottish Review 31:23-51 Ja '98; Spec 79:522-4, 556-8 O 16, 23 '97; R. Ackermann in Bei Anglia 10:323-8 Mr '00; E. Faguet in Quar R 210:305-28 Ap '09; H. Van Dyke in Book B ns 15: 433-41 D '97; Sat R 84:423-4 O 16 '97; Good Words 38:785-92 '97; S. Gwynn in Macmil 77:57-66 N '97; A. Lang in Longman's Magazine 31:27-39 N '97; J. C. Squire *in* Essays on poetry. London, Hodder and Stoughton [1923] p63-87; *same*. Lond Merc 2:443-55 Ag '20; Leslie Stephen *in* Studies of a biographer. New York, Putnam, 1898. vol II p196-240; Lit W 28:389-90 N 13 '97; H. W. Mabie in Atlan 80:577-89 N '97; H. W. Mabie in Out 57:577-83 N 6 '97; W. H. McKellar in Sewanee R 6:94-100 Ja '98; M. Dronsart in Correspondant 189:533-50, 959-80 '97; Liv Age 215:295-306 O 30 '97; Edin R 186:275-306 O '97; Church Q R 45:331-56 Ja '98; Quar R 186:492-528 O '97; Acad 52:275-6 O 9 '97; Critic (NY) 31:213-14 O 16 '97; Ath 2:481-4, 521-4 O 9, 16 '97; Overland Monthly ns 31:255-60 Mr '98; F. Thompson in New Review 17: 536-48 N '97; Lit 1:3-5, 34-6 O 23, 30 '97; Acad 52:275-7 O 9 '97; St. James Gazette O 6 '97; Book Reviews 5:115-18 N '97; Ath 2:481-4, 521-4 O 9, 16 '97; Lond Q R 89:205-31 Ja '98; W. Jerrold in Literary World (Lond) ns 56:275-7 O 15 '97; F. Roz in Bibliothèque Universelle et Revue Suisse 115 année 59:227-61 N '10; Nation (NY) 65:379-81 N 11 '97; P. Arnstein in Das Litterarische Echo 1: 522-3 Ja 15 '99; Dial 23:212-14 O 16 '97; Bookm (NY) 6:357-60 D '97; Blackw 162:615-29 N '97; Deutsche Rundschau 101:195 '99; Lady Blennerhassett in Deutsche Rundschau 98:257-90 '99; Bookm (Lond) 13:36-8 N '97)

Tennyson, Wordsworth and Browning. Ecl M 64:273-84, 415-27 Mr, Ap '65

Tennysonian philosophy. Time 8:53-9 Ja '83

Tennysonian trees. Gardeners' Magazine D 29 '88

Tennysoniana. Dial 13:265-7 N 1 '92; Sun M 22:50-3, 122-5, 201-5 '93; Notes & Q 5th ser 7:265 Ap 7 '77; 11th ser 2:341-2 O 29 '10; 3d ser 12:283 O 12 '67; 4th ser 7:431 My 20 '71; 6th ser 8:337 O 27 '83; Gent M ns 49:535-40 N '92; Acad 45:57-8, 81 Ja 20, 27 '94; Critic (NY) 21:237-40, 254-6, 280-1, 315-16, 332 O 29, N 5, 19, D 3, 10 '92; Pall Mall Budget 40:1608 O 27 '92; Ath 2:741-2 N 26 '92

Tennyson's "Amphion." Notes & Q 9th ser 3:484 Je 24 '99

Tennyson's anachronisms. Spec 119:411 O 20 '17

Tennyson's "Aylmer's Field" and John's Brand. Notes & Q 6th ser 2:253-4 S 25 '80

Tennyson's "Ballads and other poems." Notes & Q 6th ser 3:85 Ja 29 '81

Tennyson's baronetcy. Spec 38:65-6 Ja 21 '65

[Tennyson's "Becket"] Book B ns 2:5 F '85

Tennyson's birthplace for sale. Critic (NY) 29:149 S 5 '96

Tennysons bruder. Allgemeine Zeitung. Beilage 2:96 '92

Tennyson's country. Notes & Q 5th ser 8:166 S 1 '77

Tennyson's earlier poems. Bookworm 2:92-3 '88

Tennyson's earliest poems. Critic (NY) 22:333-5 My 20 '93

Tennyson's early poems. Notes & Q 3d ser 12:415 N 23 '67

Tennyson's "Enid." Notes & Q 2d ser 8:155-6 Ag 20 '59

Tennyson's "Flower in the crannied wall." Notes & Q 11th ser 3:358 My 6 '11

Tennyson's "In Memoriam." Notes & Q 1st ser 3:458 Je 7 '51; 7th ser 11:94 Ja 31 '91

Tennyson's literary career. Lit W 13:280 Ag 26 '82

Tennyson's lost vogue. Lit Digest 55:29 N 3 '17

Tennyson's "Lucretius." Tinsley's 2:611-16 Jl '68

Tennyson's "Maid Marian." Notes & Q 8th ser 2:6, 55 Jl 2, 16 '92

Tennyson's "Margaret." Notes & Q 11th ser 2:94-5, 138 Jl 30, Ag 13 '10

Tennyson's "May Queen." [parody] Notes & Q 12th ser 11:215 S 9 '22

Tennyson's natural history. Notes & Q 4th ser 12:55-6 Jl 19 '73

Tennyson's notes on his poems. T L S D 12 '07 p380

Tennyson's ode on the death of the Duke of Wellington. Notes & Q 4th ser 11:473 Je 7 '73

Tennyson's "Oriana." Liv Age 38:2 Jl 2 '53

Tennyson's peerage. Nation (NY) 37:506 D 20 '83

Tennyson's philosophy.—In Memoriam. Dublin University Magazine 57:183-92 F '61; same. Ecl M 52:505-14 Ap '61

Tennyson's poem, "Gareth and Lynette." Notes & Q 4th ser 10:524 D 28 '72

Tennyson's poems: translations. Notes & Q 7th ser 12:332 O 24 '91

[Tennyson's poetry] Harper M 80:807 Ap '90

Tennyson's quiet old age. Critic (NY) 20:121 F 20 '92

Tennyson's relation to social politics. Pall Mall Budget 40:1718 N 17 '92

Tennyson's revisions. Acad 72:398 Ap 20 '07

Tennyson's ruling passion. Spec 79:207-8 Ag 14 '97

Tennyson's spiritual service to his generation. Andover Review 12:291-6 S '89

Tennyson's suppressed poems. Acad 65:45, 93 Jl 11, 25 '03

Tennyson's theology. Spec 69:642-3 N 5 '92; same. Ecl M 56:853-5 D '92

Tennyson's two Northern Farmers. Every Sat 9:34 Ja 15 '70

Tennyson's undertones. Spec 62:165-6 F 2 '89

Tennyson's "Will": misprints. Notes & Q 5th ser 8:126 Ag 18 '77

Terry, F. C. Birbeck
"A dream of fair women." Notes & Q 8th ser 2:407 N 19 '92

Thackeray, Francis St. John
Dante and Tennyson. Temple 102:387-97 Jl '94; same. Ecl M 123:352-8 S '94; same. Liv Age 202:259-65 Ag 4 '94

Darwin and Tennyson. Spec 103:197-8 Ag 7 '09

Thayer, Mary Rebecca
Alfred Lord Tennyson. In The influence of Horace on the chief English poets of the nineteenth century. (Cornell studies in English, II) New Haven, Yale Univ. press, 1916. p94-101

Thayer, Stephen Henry
Alfred Tennyson. Andover Review 18:460-78 N '92

Thein, Adelaide E.
The social background of Tennyson's "Princess." Masters essay, Univ. of Iowa, 1926

Theuriet, A.
Alfred Tennyson. Le Journal O 17 '92

Thistlethwaite, George Parker
Über die sprache in Tennyson's Idylls of the King, in ihrem verhältniss zu Malory's Morte d'Arthur and [sic] Mabinogion. Bei Anglia 23:473-515 '01

Über die sprache in Tennyson's Idylls of the King, in ihrem verhältniss zur Bibel und zu Shakspere. Halle, Kaemmerer, 1896. 53p Diss. Halle

Thomas, Anna Elizabeth
The Arthurian cycle of romance as treated by Tennyson. Masters essay, Cornell univ. 1894. 102ff

Thomas, Edward
Tennyson. In A literary pilgrim in England. New York, Dodd, Mead, 1917. p254-62

Thomas, Percy E.
Tennyson's philosophy of life. Masters essay, Northwestern univ. 1901. 48ff

Thomas, Ralph
Tennyson concordances. Notes & Q 10th ser 11:261-2 Ap 3 '09

Thomas, Walter
Littérature anglaise. Paris, Larousse, 1909

Thomas, William
The metre of "In Memoriam." Notes & Q 4th ser 10:403 N 16 '72

Thompson, Alexander Hamilton
Tennyson and the Victorian poets. In A history of English literature. London, Murray, 1901. p757-66

Thompson, Francis
Academy portraits. XXIII.—Tennyson. Acad 51:428-9 Ap 17 '97

The life of Tennyson. New Review 17:536-48 N '97

The withheld poems of Tennyson. Acad 52:326-7 O 23 '97

Thompson, Harold George
Contemporary criticism of Tennyson's stage plays. Masters essay, Yale univ. 1914

Thomson, J. C.
Tennyson's suppressed poems. Harper M 108:70-4 D '03

Tennyson's suppressed poems, now for the first time collected, ed. and annotated by J. C. Thomson. New York, Harper, 1903. ix,202p

Thomson, O. R. Howard
Tennyson's "The passing of Arthur." Dial 43:367 D 1 '07

The **three** poems "In Memoriam." Quar R 158:162-83 Jl '84; same. Liv Age 162:549-61 Ag 30 '84

Three poets in one court suit. Book-Lover (NY) 5:694 Je '04

Three representative poets:—Mr. Tennyson, Mr. Swinburne, and Mr. Browning. Scottish Review 2:334-43 S '83

Through the year with Tennyson. . . Boston [nd]

Ticknor, Caroline
Two "laureates." In Glimpses of authors. Boston, Houghton, Mifflin, 1922. p322-7

The **"Times"** and the poets. Tait's Edinburgh Magazine ns 19:18-21 Ja '52

Tipple, Ezra Squier
Somersby. In Some famous country parishes. . . New York, Eaton & Mains [c1911] p164-99

"Titmarsh" in an alleged poem by Tennyson. Notes & Q 11th ser 10:16 Jl 4 '14

Todhunter, John
In Westminster Abbey, October 12, 1892; poem. Acad 42:361 O 22 '92; same. Ecl M 56:820-1 D '92

Tollemache, Lionel Arthur
Jowett and Tennyson. Spec 119:411 O 20 '17

Mr. Tennyson's social philosophy. Fortn 21:225-47 F 1 '74

Swinburne, the Laureateship, and Tennyson. Guardian 64:763 My 12 '09

Tolman, Albert H.
Tennyson and "The Quarterly Review." Dial 46:108 F 16 '09

Tombs, J. S. O.
Tennyson's "Poet's song." Spec 108:271 F 17 '12

Tours through literary England. Through the Tennyson country. Sat R 150:139-40 Ag 2 '30

Toynbee, Paget
To Tennyson; poem. Acad 34:321 N 17 '88

Traill, Henry Duff
Aspects of Tennyson. 19th Cent 32:952-66 D '92; same. Liv Age 196:415-25 F 11 '93

Aspects of Tennyson. As a humorist. 19th Cent 33:761-74 My '94

The literature of the Victorian era. Fortn 67:830-1 Je '97

[Tennyson] In The new Lucian: series of dialogues of the dead. London, Chapman, 1900

Traubel, Horace
With Walt Whitman in Camden. New York, Kennerley, 1914. 3 vols passim

The **trees** and flowers of Tennyson. Temple 103:358-66 N '94; same. Ecl M 123:783-8 D '94

Trench, Richard Chenevix
The sonnets of Charles and Alfred Tennyson. In The afternoon lectures on literature and art. London, Bell and Daldy, 1867. 4th ser p163

Trent, William Peterfield
Tennyson and Musset once more. In Authority of criticism. New York, Scribner, 1899. p269-91; same. Bookm (NY) 7:108-14 Ap '98

Trevvett, Florence
A child story from Tennyson's "Enoch Arden." Chicago, Scroll publishing and literary syndicate, 1900. 55p

Tributes in verse. Critic (NY) 21:256 N 5 '92

[Tributes to Tennyson] Critic (NY) 21: 288-90 N 26 '92

The true poet of imperialism. Macmil 80: 192-5 Jl '99

Truman, Joseph
Victoria's poets; poem. Spec 78:476 Ap 3 '97

Tuckerman, Henry Theodore
Tennyson. *In* Thoughts on the poets. New York, Francis, 1851. p273-80

Tuell, Anne Kimball
Mrs. Meynell and her literary generation. New York, Dutton [c1925]

Turnbull, Arthur
Life and writings of Alfred, Lord Tennyson. New York, Scribner, 1915. xi, 225p

Tussing, Clara
Manifestations of the Puritan spirit in the works of Alfred Tennyson. Masters essay, Univ. of North Dakota, 1923. 61ff

Two centenaries [Johnson and Tennyson] Spec 103:409-10 S 18 '09

Two lights on Tennyson. Bookm (NY) 36:598-600 F '13

Tyrrell, R. Y.
"In Memoriam" and "The door of humility." Acad 71:158-9 Ag 18 '06

Tzeutschler, Artur
Zu Tennyson's "Locksley Hall": the poem of Amriolkais. . . Archiv 120: 332-6 '08

Unconsidered Tennysonian trifles. Critic (NY) 5:268-9 D 6 '84

Unwelcome visitors. Critic (NY) 21:225 O 22 '92

Unwin, S. Philip
Shakespeare, Tennyson, and the Lord Chief Justice. Speaker 7:746 Jl 1 '93

Urban, Sylvanus [pseud]
Alfred Baron Tennyson, born August 5, 1809. Died October 6, 1892. Gent M 273:535-40 N '92

The Laureate and Mr. Swinburne. Gent M 268:431 Ap '90

Valdes, Edgar
The birds of Tennyson. Temple 110: 495-512 '97; *same.* Liv Age 213:807-17 Je 19 '97

Van den Noort, Judokus
Theology in Tennyson. Masters essay, Boston univ. 1923

Van Dyke, Henry
Alfred Tennyson (1809-1892). *In* Warner, C. D. ed. Library of the world's best literature. . . Memorial ed. New York, Hill [c1902] vol XXXVI p14581-7

The Bible in Tennyson. Cent 38:515-22 Ag '89

The fame of Tennyson. Ind 42:66-7 Ja 16 '90

A filial portrait of a great poet. Book B ns 15:433-41 D '97

In lucem transitus; poem. Critic (NY) 21:211 O 15 '92

Introduction. *In* Poems of Tennyson. . . New York, Scribner, 1920. p xix-cxx

An introduction to the poems of Tennyson. Boston, Ginn, 1903. vi,93p

Milton and Tennyson. Presbyterian Review 4:681-709 O '83

On the study of Tennyson. Cent 42:502-10 Ag '91

Outline of lectures on Wordsworth, Browning, and Tennyson. . . Princeton, Princeton press [1900] 14p

The poetry of Tennyson. New York, Scribner, 1889. xiii,296p [By 1907 this volume had reached its tenth edition and had increased in size to: xvi,[3]-437p, with bibl p351-87]
(Rev in Igdrasil 1:78 F '90; Nation (NY) 50:20 Ja 2 '90; Literary World (Lond) ns 41:316-17 Ap 4 '90; Lit W 21:20 Ja 18 '90; 24:22 Ja 28 '93; W. Watson in Acad 37:217-18 Mr 29 '90)

Preface. *In* In Memoriam, by Alfred Tennyson. New York, Fords, Howard, and Hulbert, 1897. p v-xxiii

Studies in Tennyson. . . New York, Scribner, 1920. xi,316p bibl p239-73 [Much of the material in this volume comes from the author's "The Poetry of Tennyson"]

Tennyson. Critic (NY) 21:203-4 O 15 '92

Tennyson's first flight. Scrib M 6:242-9 Ag '89

Vicissitudes of a palace. New Princeton Review 62:65-74 Jl '87

The voice of Tennyson. Cent 45:539-44 F '93

Van Holmhof, J. F.
Tennyson's Konigsidyllen. Dietsche Warande en Belfort 2:366-92, 488-511

Vann, William Harvey
A prototype of Tennyson's Arthur. Sewanee R 29:98-103 Ja-Mr '21

Venables, Edmund
Tennyson's Cambridge contemporaries. Notes & Q 8th ser 2:441-2 D 3 '92

Vere, Aubrey de
[3 poems to Tennyson] 19th Cent 32: 840-1 N '92

To Alfred Tennyson. Cent 46:37 My '93

Verrall, A. W.
Aristophanes on Tennyson. New Quarterly 2:81-9 Ja '09

Vettermann, Ella
Die Balen-dichtungen und ihre quellen. (Zeitschrift für romanische philologie. Beih. 60) Halle, Niemeyer, 1918. x,318p

The Victorian garden of song. Dial 19: 238-9 N 1 '95

Villard, Léonie
The influence of Keats on Tennyson and Rossetti. Saint-Étienne, Mulcey, 1914. 94p Thesis, Paris

Vince, C. A.
Tennyson and Bright. Lit 3:186 Ag 27 '98

Vining, R. H.
Tennyson's "In Memoriam"; an introduction and analysis. Masters essay. Boston univ. 1917

[The **voice** of Tennyson. Hitherto unpublished Tennyson poem] First line: O! where is he, the simple fool. Bookm (NY) 40:233 N '14

Wace, Walter E.
Alfred Tennyson, his life and works. Edinburgh, Macniven & Wallace, 1881. viii,203p

Wainewright, John B.
Ben Jonson and Tennyson. Notes & Q 9th ser 12:277-8 O 3 '03

Tennyson on tobacco. Notes & Q 12th ser 6:234 My 22 '20

Waldau, Otto
Alfred Tennyson. Illustrirte Zeitung 99:439-40 O 15 '92

Waldmueller, R. [pseud]
see Duboc, C. E.

Walford, E.
Early notice of Tennyson. Notes & Q 8th ser 1:185 Mr 5 '92

Walford, L. B.
London letter. Critic (NY) 21:251 N 5 '92

London letter [Irving's production of "Becket"] Critic (NY) 22:116 F 25 '93

Walker, Hugh
Age of Tennyson. London, Bell, 1897. x,303p
(Rev in Sat R 85:85-6 Ja 15 '98; Literary World (Lond) ns 56:444 D 3 '97; Bookm (Lond) 13:51 N '97)

The dramas. *In* The greater Victorian poets. London, Swan Sonnenschein, 1895. p174-85

Faith and doubt. *In* The greater Victorian poets. London, Swan Sonnenschein, 1895. p320-7

The greater Victorian poets. Tennyson, Browning, and Arnold. New York, Macmillan, 1895
(Rev in Literary World (Lond) ns 52:220 S 27 '95; Ath 1:80-1 Ja 18 '96)

The influence of science. *In* The greater Victorian poets. London, Swan Sonnenschein, 1895. p248-51

The new kings: Tennyson and Browning. *In* The literature of the Victorian era. Cambridge, Univ. press, 1921. p287-309

The poetry of nature. *In* The greater Victorian poets. London, Swan Sonnenschein, 1895. p201-12

The second period of Tennyson's work. *In* The greater Victorian poets. London, Swan Sonnenschein, 1895. p70-90

The social and political aspects of the poets. *In* The greater Victorian poets. London, Swan Sonnenschein, 1895. p260-70

Tennyson. *In* The literature of the Victorian era. Cambridge, Univ. press, 1921. p374-410

Tennyson and Browning: the closing period. *In* The greater Victorian poets. London, Swan Sonnenschein, 1895. p150-5

Tennyson: the first period of authorship. *In* The greater Victorian poets. London, Swan Sonnenschein, 1895. p16-34

Walker, Hugh and Walker, (Mrs) Hugh
Poetry. *In* Outlines of Victorian literature. Cambridge, Univ. press, 1919. p49-58

Walker, (Mrs) Janie Roxburgh
Alfred Tennyson. *In* Stories of the Victorian writers. New York, Macmillan, 1922. p33-42

Walker, Thomas
Mr. Tennyson's "Despair." A lecture on its religious significance. London, Stock, 1882. 32p

Walkley, A. B.
Maid Marian on the stage. Theatre (Lond) ns 19:227-31 My '92

Wallis, Alfred
A "Tennyson" forgery. Notes & Q 6th ser 9:143-4 F 23 '84

Walsh, Henry C.
Introduction. *In* Idylls of the king by Alfred Lord Tennyson. (Altemus' ed.) Philadelphia, Altemus [1889] p iii-ix

Walsh, W.
Idylls of the King. Gent M ns 50:500 '93

[Walsh, William Shepard] Shepard, William [pseud]
Alfred Tennyson. *In* Enchiridion of criticism. . . Philadelphia, Lippincott, 1885. p222-34

Alfred Tennyson. *In* Pen pictures of modern authors. New York, Putnam, 1882. p74-85

Walter Scott: Tennyson. Notes & Q 5th ser 9:225 Mr 23 '78

Walters, John Cuming
In King Arthur's capital. Igdrasil 2:49-55 N '90

In Tennyson land. . . London, Redway, 1890. viii,108p
(Rev in Notes & Q 7th ser 9:299-300 Ap 12 '90; Spec 64:571 Ap 19 '90; Literary World (Lond) ns 41:216-17 Mr 7 '90; Nation (NY) 50:265 Mr 27 '90; Book B ns 7:66-7 Mr '90; Igdrasil 1:163 Ap '90; Lit W 21:99 Mr 29 '90)

Links with Tennyson's youth. Acad 47: 238 Mr 16 '95

Tennyson and Lincolnshire. Scots Observer 3:410 Mr 1 '90

"Tennyson—poet, philosopher, and idealist." Acad 45:128 F 10 '94

Tennyson: poet, philosopher, idealist. Studies of the life, work, and teaching of the poet Laureate. London, Paul, Trench, Trübner, 1893. viii,370p
(Rev in Nation (NY) 58:139 F 22 '94; Critic (NY) 24:15-16 Ja 13 '94; A. Waugh in Acad 45:96-8 F 3 '94)

The war passages in "Maud." Sat R 1: 14-15 N 3 '55

Ward, Aline
Philosophical themes of Tennyson's Idylls of the King. Masters essay, George Washington univ. 1923. 78ff

Ward, George Liggitt
The dramatic works of Tennyson. Masters essay, George Washington univ. 1901. 61ff

Ward, Julius H.
A Tennysonian retrospect. Atlan 44: 356-61 S '79

Ward, Louisa E.
Memorials for my children and recollections of Lord Tennyson. London, nd

Ward, M.
Wilfrid Ward and Tennyson. Commonweal 21:87-8 N 16 '34

Ward, Maisie
see Sheed, Maisie (Ward)

Ward, Wilfrid
Talks with Tennyson. New Review 15: 76-95 Jl '96; same. Liv Age 210:323-35 Ag 8 '96; same. Ecl M 127:317-28 S '96
(Rev in Critic (NY) 29:46-7 Jl 18 '96)

Tennyson. In Problems and persons. London, Longmans, Green, 1903

Tennyson at Freshwater. In Men and matters. New York, Longmans, Green, 1914. p251-72

Tennyson's religious philosophy. Spec 79:681-3 N 13 '97

Tennyson's religious poetry. Liv Age 263:523-33 N 27 '09; same. Dublin Review 145:306-22 O '09

Ward, William Godman
Tennyson's debt to his environment. . . A study of Tennyson's England as an introduction to his poems. Boston, Roberts, 1898. [5]-100p

Warfield, Ethelbert D.
Tennyson as a spiritual teacher. Ind 44:1473-4 O 20 '92

Warren, Kate M.
. . . Tennyson. . . London, National Home-Reading Union [1920] 29p

Warren, (Sir) Thomas Herbert
The centenary of Tennyson, 1809-1909. . . Oxford, Clarendon press, 1909. [5]-32p

"In Memoriam" after fifty years. In Essays of poets and poetry ancient and modern. London, Murray, 1909. p290-325

In Memoriam: Alfred, Lord Tennyson; poem. Spec 69:528 O 15 '92; same. Critic (NY) 21:288-9 N 26 '92; same. Liv Age 195:450 N 19 '92

The real Tennyson. 19th Cent 94:507-19 O '23

Tennyson and Dante. Monthly Review 14:117-38 Ja '04; same in Essays of poets and poetry ancient and modern. New York, Dutton, 1909. p243-69

To Lord Tennyson; poem. Spec 66:593 Ap 25 '91

Virgil and Tennyson: a literary parallel. In Essays of poets and poetry ancient and modern. New York, Dutton, 1909. p172-216; same. Quar R 193:99-129 Ja '01
(Noted in Spec 86:197-8 F 9 '01)

Was purple Tennyson's favorite color? Critic (NY) 45:15-16 Jl '04

Was Tennyson either gnostic or agnostic? Spec 70:10-11 Ja 7 '93; same. Liv Age 196:561-4 F 25 '93

Waters, Doris Geraldine
The literary relations of Arthur Henry Hallam and Alfred Lord Tennyson. Masters essay, Univ. of Oklahoma, 1929. 105ff

Watkins, Watkin
The birds of Tennyson. London, Porter, 1903

Watson, Aaron
Tennyson. (People's books) London, Jack, 1912
(Rev in Ath 2:688 D 7 '12)

Watson, William
Lachrymae musarum; poem. Illustrated London News 101:474 O 15 '92

Orgy on Parnassus; lines written in my copy of Tennyson; poem. Fortn 89: 569-70 Ap 1 '08; same. Liv Age 257: 258 My 2 '08; same. Cur Lit 44:678 Je '08

To Lord Tennyson; poem. In The collected poems of William Watson. New York, Lane, 1899. p83; same. Critic (NY) 21:289 N 26 '92

Watts, Henry Edward
Alfred Tennyson: a lecture, delivered at the Town Hall, Prahan, October 10th, 1864. Melbourne, Mullen, 1864. 37p

Watts, Theodore
see Watts-Dunton, Theodore

Watts-Dunton, Theodore
Alfred, Lord Tennyson. In Old familiar faces. London, Jenkins, 1916. p120-76

Alfred Tennyson: a lecture. London, 1864

The eightieth birthday; poem. Ath 2: 191 Ag 10 '89

In Westminster Abbey; poem. 19th Cent 32:842 N '92

Watts-Dunton, Theodore—_Continued_
Lord Tennyson. Ath 2:482-3, 555-6 O 8, 22 '92

Lord Tennyson's last volume. Ath 2:665 N 12 '92

Lord Tennyson's new play. [The Foresters] Ath 2:461, 493-4 O 3, 10 '91; _same._ Critic (NY) 19:238-9 O 31 '91

Tennyson as a nature poet. 19th Cent 33:836-56 My '93; _same._ Liv Age 198:28-42 Jl 1 & 8 '93

Tennyson as a poet of evolution. 19th Cent 34:657-72 O '93; _same._ Liv Age 199:611-22 D 9 '93

To Tennyson on his eighty-second birthday; poem. Lit W 22:332 S 26 '91; _same._ Ath 2:255 Ag 22 '91

Waugh, Arthur
Alfred, Lord Tennyson. A study of his life and work. London, Heinemann, 1892. xii,328p
(Rev by R. Le Gallienne in Acad 42:427-9 N 12 '92; Sat R 74:473-4 O 22 '92; Spec 70:82-3 Ja 21 '93; Dial 14:53-4 Ja 16 '93; Sat R 81:257 Mr 7 '96; Lit W 27:70-1 Mr 7 '96; Lit W 24:22 Ja 28 '93; Critic (NY) 21:369-70 D 31 '92)

"Crossing the bar." [a comment] Acad 59:473 N 17 '00 [_see also_ Rees, R. W. in Acad 59:497 N 24 '00 for additional comment]

London letter. Critic (NY) 23:260-1 O 21 '93

The poetry of faith and aspiration. _In_ Reticence in literature, and other papers. London, Wilson [1915] p43-5

"Tennyson and the old annuals." Lit 6:113 F 3 '00

Tennysoniana. Acad 42:461 N 19 '92

Way, A. S.
Tennyson and Quintus Calaber. Journal of English Studies 1 no 2 S '12-Ja '13

Weatherhead, Leslie D.
A new projection of Christian thought born of the fear of death—Tennyson. _In_ The after-world of the poets. . . London, Epworth press [1929] p79-122

Tennyson. _In_ After death. London, Epworth press [1930]

Tennyson's after-world. Lond Q R 144:157-74 O '25

Webb, W. Trego
Tennyson's "Crossing the bar." Spec 70:160 F 4 '93

Wedgwood, Julia
Tennyson as the religious exponent of his age. Sun M 22:34-8 Ja '93

Wedmore, Frederick
The stage. Tennyson's "Becket." Acad 43:158-9 F 18 '93

The stage. Tennyson's play ["The Promise of May"] Acad 22:370-1 N 18 '82

Weigand, W.
Lord Tennyson's neueste lyrik. Vossische Zeitung. Sonntagsbeilage no 3 '89

Weighing Tennyson. Every Sat 7:699-701 My 29 '69

Weiss, August
Tennysons letzte worte. Allgemeine Zeitung. Beilage D 8 '92 p 1-2

Weld, Agnes Grace
Glimpses of Tennyson and of some of his relations and friends. . . London, Williams and Norgate, 1903. viii,154p

Talks with Tennyson. Contemp 63:394-7 Mr '93; _same._ Liv Age 197:306-8 Ap 29 '93

Tennyson. Contemp 72:689-96 N '97

Wells, John Edwin
Variations in the "Idylls of the king." Nation (NY) 88:557-8 Je 3 '09

Westercamp, F. W.
Tennyson als dramatiker. Gegenwart 55:71-5 F 4 '99

What is the Laureate about? Tinsley's 2:262-7 Mr '68

Whipple, Edwin, P.
Essays and reviews. New York, Appleton, 1848. vol I p322-30

White, Harold
The treatment of immortality by poets of the nineteenth century. Masters essay, McGill univ. 1925. 96ff

White, James W.
Tennyson on the philosophy of the future life. Baptist Quarterly Review 12:158-82 Ap '90

Whitman, Walt
A word about Tennyson. _In_ November boughs. Philadelphia, McKay, 1888. p65-7; _same._ Critic (NY) 10:1-2 Ja 1 '87; _same in_ Democratic vistas. London, Scott, 1888. p125-9; _same in_ Rivulets of prose. New York, Greenberg, 1928. p92-8

Who will be Poet Laureate? Atlan 70:855-6 D '92

Whymper, A.
One of Tennyson's rustic friends. Sun M 27:221-3 Ap '98

Wiggins, Inez Louise
The women of Browning and of Tennyson. Masters essay, Cornell univ. 1907. 135ff

Wilcock, A. B.
Tennyson's earlier poems. Bookworm 3:317 '90

Wilde, (Lady) T. H. S. (Jane Francesca Elgee)
Notes on men, women, and books. . . London, Ward & Downey, 1891. p286-326

Wildman, Banks John
. . . A comparison of Lucretius' "De natura rerum" and Tennyson's "Lucretius". . . Chicago, 1904. 29ff Diss. Univ. of Chicago

Wiley, Margaret Lee
The religious poems of Tennyson, with special reference to present day unrest. Masters essay, Univ. of Texas, 1924. 142ff

Wilkinson, William Cleaver
Tennyson as artist in lyric verse. *In* Some new literary valuations. New York, Funk & Wagnalls, 1909. p201-50

Willcock, J.
Tennyson and Crabbe. Notes & Q 11th ser 11:450 Je 12 '15

Willcocks, Mary Patricia
Tennyson. *In* Between the old world and the new. London, Allen and Unwin [1925] p141-54; *same.* Engl R 36:171-82 F '23

Williams, Sparks Henderson
Tennyson. Notes & Q 4th ser 9:301 Ap 13 '72

Williams, Stanley Thomas
Studies in Victorian literature. New York, Dutton [c1923] passim
Tennyson and the humble life. Masters essay, Yale univ. 1914

Williamson, Claude C. H.
Tennyson and his ideas. *In* Writers of three centuries, 1789-1914. London, Richards, 1920. p170-6

Wilson, Edmund
Pope and Tennyson. New Repub 44:96-7 S 16 '25

Wilson, Epiphanius
The dead singer; poem. Critic (NY) 21:256 N 5 '92

Wilson, Henry Schütz
" 'Tis sixty years since"; or, The two Locksley Halls. London, Kegan, Paul, Trench, Trübner, 1894. 45p

Wilson, Josie
Alliteration of Tennyson. Masters essay, Univ. of Kansas, 1902. 36ff

Wilson, Katharine
Tennyson and the common people. Masters essay, Univ. of Kansas, 1914. 18ff

Wilson, William
Tennyson's "new" song. Ath 1:763 Je 17 '82

Wingfield-Stratford, Esmé Cecil
Those earnest Victorians. New York, Morrow, 1930. 340p

Winn, Edith Lynwood
A vision of fair women; a dramatic paraphrase based upon Tennyson's "Dream of Fair Women." (Baker's novelty list) Boston, Baker, 1891. 15p

Winter, William
Tennyson. *In* Shadows of the stage. Edinburgh, 1893. 2d ser p359-67
Tennyson's "Foresters." *In* Shadows of the stage. Edinburgh, 1892. p269-85

Winterwood, Geoffrey
In the Laureate's footsteps. Good Words 33:670-8 '92

Winwar, Frances [pseud]
see Grebanier, Mrs. Frances (Vinciguerra)

Wise, Thomas James
An apocryphal Tennyson poem. T L S Mr 27 '30 p274

With apologies to Tennyson's "Sleeping beauty" [a cartoon] Punch 124:25 Ja 14 '03

The withheld poems of Tennyson. Acad 52:326-7 O 23 '97

Witucka, M. Albensia
Tennyson's idea of higher education of women as expressed in "The Princess." Masters essay, Catholic univ. 1926

Wolfe, Humbert
Tennyson. . . (Poets on the poets, no 3) London, Faber and Faber, 1930. 60p (Rev by E. Lewis in Lond Merc 23:388 F '31; T L S O 9 '30 p803; T. E. Welby in W E R 2:457-8 O 4 '30)

Wood, Homa
The religion of Tennyson as shown by his works. Masters essay, Univ. of Oklahoma, 1915

Woodberry, George Edward
Late Victorian verse: Browning, Swinburne, Tennyson. *In* Studies of a littérateur. New York, Harcourt, Brace, 1921. p37-60

Woodbury, A. K.
Alfred Tennyson. California Magazine 3:192

Woods, Margaret L.
Poets of the 'eighties. *In* The eighteen-eighties. . . Cambridge, Univ. press, 1930. p1-2

Workard, Job J. B.
Tennyson's "Enoch Arden": bigamy and desertion. Notes & Q 3d ser 6:298 O 8 '64

Wright, Herbert Gladstone
Tennyson and Wales. *In* English Association. Essays and studies. 14:71-103 '29

Wright, W. H. K.
Tennyson's "Ballads and other poems." Notes & Q 6th ser 3:217-18 Mr 12 '81

Wrightson, James Owens
Alfred Tennyson, the man and the poet. Masters essay, George Washington univ. 1909. 20ff

Wülker, Richard Paul
Die Arthursage in der englischen literatur. Leipzig, Edelmann [1895] p37-9 Diss. Leipzig
Dramatische litteratur im 19. jahrhundert. Alfred Tennyson. *In* Geschichte der englischen litteratur von den ältesten zeiten bis zur gegenwart. Leipzig, Bibliographisches Institut, 1896. p596-603

Wüllenweber, Walther
Tennysons königsidylle The coming of Arthur und ihre quellen. Archiv 83:1-66 '89
Über Tennysons königsidylle The coming of Arthur und ihre quellen. . . Marburg, 1889. 66p. Diss. Marburg

Wynn, W. H.
Tennyson's Idylls of the King, an appreciation. Lutheran Church Quarterly Review 34:529-55 O '04

Wyzewa, Teodor de
Lord Tennyson. Le Figaro O 9 '92 p1

Lord Tennyson. *In* Ecrivains étrangers. Paris, Perrin, 1896. p75-81

Yardley, E.
Charles Lamb and Lord Tennyson. Notes & Q 8th ser 2:356 O 29 '92

Yates, Edmund Hodgson
Mr. Tennyson at Haslemere. *In* Celebrities at home. London, Office of "The World," 1877. p21-9

Young, A. B.
T. L. Peacock's "Maid Marian" and Tennyson's "Foresters." Notes & Q 10th ser 8:341-2 N 2 '07

Young and Tennyson. Notes & Q 9th ser 1:501-2 Je 25 '98

Zimmern, Helen
Alfred Tennyson. Velhagen und Klasings Monatshefte 7:499-511 Ja '93

Zocco, Irene
[Idylls of the King] *In* Spigolando. Catania, Niccolo Giannotta, 1900

Zuylen van Nijevelt, S. Ivan
Tennyson's vertegenwoordiger van het "Victoria tijdperk." Stemmen des Tijds p350-74 O '20